Strategic Planning
for Public Relations

Strategic Planning for Public Relations

Fourth Edition

Ronald D. Smith, APR

Routledge
Taylor & Francis Group

NEW YORK AND LONDON

Please visit the companion website for this book at
www.routledge.com/cw/smith

First published 2013
by Routledge
711 Third Avenue, New York, NY 10017

Simultaneously published in the UK
by Routledge
2 Park Square, Milton Park, Abingdon, Oxon OX14 4RN

Routledge is an imprint of the Taylor & Francis Group, an informa business

Library of Congress Cataloging in Publication Data
Smith, Ronald D., 1948–
    Strategic planning for public relations / Ronald D. Smith.—
    4th ed.
    p. cm.
    1. Public relations. 2. Strategic planning. I. Title.
    HM1221.S77 2013
    659.2—dc23
    2012023104

ISBN: 978-0-415-50676-2 (pbk)
ISBN: 978-0-203-08124-2 (ebk)

Typeset in Times New Roman and Helveica Neue
by Florence Production Ltd, Stoodleigh, Devon, UK

Brief Contents

Preface   xvii

Introduction   1

Phase One **FORMATIVE RESEARCH**   **19**

Step 1 Analyzing the Situation   21

Step 2 Analyzing the Organization   41

Step 3 Analyzing the Publics   57

Phase Two **STRATEGY**   **93**

Step 4 Establishing Goals and Objectives   95

Step 5 Formulating Action and Response Strategies   113

Step 6 Developing the Message Strategy   172

Phase Three **TACTICS**   **225**

Step 7 Selecting Communication Tactics   227

Step 8 Implementing the Strategic Plan   304

Phase Four **EVALUATIVE RESEARCH**   **329**

Step 9 Evaluating the Strategic Plan   331

Appendixes   **359**

A   Applied Research   361
B   Ethical Standards   410
C   Sample Campaigns   421
D   Effective Media Engagement   443

Glossary   464
Citations and Recommended Readings   495
Index   506

Contents

Preface   xvii

    New to This Fourth Edition   xvii
    Note to Students   xvii
    Note to Public Relations Practitioners   xviii
    Note to Instructors   xviii
    Who Uses This Book?   xix
    Acknowledgments   xx
    Personal Dedication   xx
    An Invitation   xxi

About the Author   xxii

Cases and Examples   xxiii

Introduction   1

    Organizational Process   2
    Strategic Communication   5
    Integrated Communication   6
    Advertising   12
    Strategic Public Relations   13
        Phase 1: Formative Research   *15*
        Phase 2: Strategy   *16*
        Phase 3: Tactics   *16*
        Phase 4: Evaluative Research   *17*
    Effective Creativity   17

Phase One **FORMATIVE RESEARCH**   19

STEP 1 **Analyzing the Situation**   21

    Public Relations Situation   21
        Obstacles into Opportunities   *22*
        Finding Consensus   *24*
    Issues Management   25
        Background of Issues Management   *26*
    Risk Management   27
    Crisis Management   30

Unpredicted, but Predictable   32

Public Relations and Ethics   36

What's Next?   37

Planning Example 1: Analyzing the Situation   38

Checklist 1: The Public Relations Situation   38

STEP 2   **Analyzing the Organization**   **41**

Internal Environment   43
    Performance   43
    Niche   44
    Structure   44
    Ethical Base   45
    Internal Impediments   45

Public Perception   45
    Visibility   45
    Reputation   45

External Environment   47
    Supporters   47
    Competitors   47
    Opponents   48

External Impediments   49

What's Next?   49

Planning Example 2: Analyzing the Organization   49

Checklist 2A: Internal Environment   51

Checklist 2B: Public Perception   53

Checklist 2C: External Environment   54

STEP 3   **Analyzing the Publics**   **57**

Public   57
    Public, Market, Audience and Stakeholder   57
    Characteristics of Publics   60
    Categories of Publics   61

Intercessory Public and Opinion Leader   65

Key Public   67

Planning Example 3A: Identifying Publics   69

Checklist 3A: Publics   72

Analyzing Key Publics   74
    Stages of Development   74
    Key Characteristics   76

Stereotype   78

Cultural Context   84
    Saving Face   84

Rethinking Your Publics 86
Benefit Statement 87
What's Next? 87
Planning Example 3B: Analyzing Key Publics 88
Checklist 3B: Key Publics 89

Phase Two STRATEGY   93

STEP 4 **Establishing Goals and Objectives**   95

Positioning 95
    Positioning Ethics *97*
Goal 97
Objective 100
    Elements of Objectives *101*
    Hierarchy of Objectives *104*
    Developing Objectives *106*
    Writing Objectives *107*
What's Next? 109
Planning Example 4: Establishing Goals and Objectives 110
Checklist 4: Goals and Objectives 111

STEP 5 **Formulating Action and Response Strategies**   113

Proactive Strategy 1: Action 113
    Organizational Performance *114*
    Audience Engagement *115*
    Special Event *117*
    Alliance and Coalition *120*
    Sponsorship *121*
    Strategic Philanthropy *123*
    Activism *128*
Proactive Strategy 2: Communication 130
    Publicity *130*
    Generating News *133*
    Newsworthy Information *137*
    Transparent Communication *140*
    Media Theory and Public Relations *142*
Reactive Public Relations Strategies 144
Reactive Strategy 1: Pre-emptive Action 145
    Prebuttal *145*
Reactive Strategy 2: Offensive Response 147
    Attack *147*
    Embarrassment *148*
    Shock *148*
    Threat *150*

Reactive Strategy 3: Defensive Response   150
  Denial   150
  Excuse   151
  Justification   151
  Reversal   152
Reactive Strategy 4: Diversionary Response   153
  Concession   153
  Ingratiation   154
  Disassociation   154
  Relabeling   155
Reactive Strategy 5: Vocal Commiseration   156
  Concern   156
  Condolence   156
  Regret   156
  Apology   157
Reactive Strategy 6: Rectifying Behavior   162
  Investigation   162
  Corrective Action   162
  Restitution   162
  Repentance   162
Reactive Strategy 7: Deliberate Inaction   164
  Strategic Silence   164
  Strategic Ambiguity   165
  Strategic Inaction   165
Weighing Options   166
What's Next?   168
Planning Example 5: Formulating Action and Response Strategies   168
Checklist 5: Action and Response Strategies   169

STEP 6 **Developing the Message Strategy**   **172**

Communication Process   172
  Information: Flow of Communication   173
  Persuasion: Attempts to Influence   173
  Dialogue: Quest for Understanding   173
Rhetorical Tradition   176
Ethos: Selecting Message Sources   178
  Credibility: Power to Inspire Belief   178
  Charisma: Power of Personal Charm   181
  Control: Power of Command   182
Organizational Spokespeople   183
  Celebrity Spokespersons   183
  Company Spokespeople   187
  Spokespeople and Ethics   188
Planning Example 6A: Selecting Message Sources   189

Checklist 6A: Message Sources   190

Logos: Appealing to Reason   191

    Verbal Evidence   192

    Visual Supporting Evidence   193

    Errors of Logic   193

    Statistics   194

Pathos: Appealing to Sentiment   196

    Positive Emotional Appeals   196

    Negative Emotional Appeals   199

Planning Example 6B: Determining Message Appeals   201

Checklist 6B: Message Appeals   202

Verbal Communication   204

    Message Structure   204

    Message Content   206

Nonverbal Communication   212

    Visual Communication   214

Planning Example 6C: Verbal and Nonverbal Communication   217

Checklist 6C: Verbal and Nonverbal Communication   218

Branding the Strategic Message   219

    Language of Branding   220

    Lessons about Branding   221

What's Next?   223

Phase Three TACTICS   225

STEP 7 **Selecting Communication Tactics**   227

Conventional Communication Tactics   227

Strategic Communication Tactics   229

Interpersonal Communication Techniques   230

    Strategy for Interpersonal Communication   231

    Personal Involvement   233

    Information Exchange   234

    Special Events   235

    Planning Special Events   241

Planning Example 7A: Selecting Interpersonal Communication Tactics   242

Checklist 7A: Interpersonal Communication Tactics   243

Organizational Media Tactics   245

    Strategy for Organizational Media   245

    Publications   245

    Direct Mail   250

    Electronic Media   251

    Digital Media   253

    Social Media   255

Planning Example 7B: Selecting Organizational Media Tactics   261

Checklist 7B: Organizational Media Tactics   262

News Media Tactics   264

    Strategy for News Media   264

    Newspaper   266

    Magazine   270

    Radio   271

    Television   272

    Media Information Needs   274

    Direct Information Subsidy   276

    Indirect Information Subsidy   281

    Opinion Subsidy   282

    Interactive Media Engagement   283

Planning Example 7C: Selecting News Media Tactics   287

Checklist 7C: News Media Tactics   288

Advertising and Promotional Media Tactics   289

    Strategy for Advertising and Promotional Media   289

    Print Advertising   291

    Electronic Media Advertising   292

    Out-of-Home Advertising   298

    Promotional Items   300

What's Next?   301

Planning Example 7D: Selecting Advertising and Promotional Tactics   301

Checklist 7D: Advertising and Promotional Tactics   302

STEP 8   Implementing the Strategic Plan   **304**

Packaging Communication Tactics   304

    Thinking Creatively   305

    Putting the Program Together   306

Planning Example 8A: Packaging the Communication Tactics   308

Checklist 8A: Packaging Communication Tactics   309

Campaign Plan Book   310

    Example: Tactics for Open House   311

Campaign Schedule   312

    Frequency of Tactics   312

    Timeline of Tasks   314

Campaign Budget   315

    Budget Items   316

    Approaches to Budgeting   318

    Budget Management   321

    Full-Cost Budgeting   324

    How Much Success Is Necessary?   325

What's Next?   326

Planning Example 8B: Implementing the Strategic Plan   326

Checklist 8B: Implementing the Strategic Plan   328

Phase Four EVALUATIVE RESEARCH   329

STEP 9 **Evaluating the Strategic Plan**   **331**

What to Evaluate   331
  Design Questions   332
  Evaluation Criteria   332
When to Evaluate   335
  Implementation Report   335
  Progress Report   335
  Final Report   336
  Research Design   336
How to Evaluate   339
  Judgmental Assessment   339
  Communication Outputs   340
  Awareness Objectives   343
  Acceptance Objectives   346
  Action Objectives   348
Data Analysis and Reports   350
Ultimate Evaluation: Value-Added Public Relations   352
  Public Relations Metrics   353
  Game Changer for Public Relations Evaluation   354
What's Next?   355
Planning Example 9: Evaluating the Strategic Plan   356
Checklist 9: Evaluation Plan   357

APPENDIXES   359

APPENDIX A **Applied Research**   **361**

Academic Research and Applied Research   361
  Research Topics   362
  Do-It-Yourself Research   363
Research Ethics   363
  Ethical Treatment of People   363
Sampling   366
  Nonprobability Sampling   367
  Probability Sampling   369
  Sampling Error and Size   371
Secondary Research   372
Types of Secondary Information   373
Interview   377
  Interview Questions   377
  Listening During an Interview   379

Focus Group   379
   Focus Group Process   380
   Conducting a Focus Group   382
Case Study   385
   Conducting a Case Study   387
Survey Research   389
   Response Rate   389
   Survey Administration   390
   Questionnaire   393
   Types of Responses   397
Content Analysis   401
   Using Content Analysis   402
   Pro and Con   403
   Doing Content Analysis   403

APPENDIX B   **Ethical Standards**   **410**

Public Relations Society of America (PRSA)   410
   Member Code of Ethics   410
   PRSA Member Statement of Professional Values   411
   PRSA Code Provisions   411
   PRSA Member Code of Ethics Pledge   415
Canadian Public Relations Society   415
   Declaration of Principles   415
International Public Relations Association   416
   IPRA Code of Conduct   416
American Marketing Association   418
   Statement of Ethics   418
   Ethical Norms   418
   Ethical Values   419

APPENDIX C   **Sample Campaigns**   **421**

Text4Baby: Going Mobile with Pregnancy Education   423
DeVry University: Getting an Education on Reputation Building   426
Connecting Army and America   430
Coca-Cola's Expedition 206: 365 Days, 206 Countries, 1 Mission   434
Philips Norelco: Deforest Yourself, Reforest the World   439

APPENDIX D   **Effective Media Engagement**   **443**

Reputation and Media Relations   444
   Reputation and Performance   445
   Reputation as a Strategic Tool   445
   Reputation Management   445
   Reputation and News Media   445

Reputation as a Participant Activity   446
Headlines and Bottom Lines   446
Media Relations   447
Media Relations . . . from the Media Side   447
Media Relations . . . from the Organization Side   447
Media Relations . . . from Both Sides   448
Reputational Bumps and Bruises   448
Twelve Principles of Effective Media Relations   448
Points for Consideration   449
Credibility   450
Interview Setting   450
If You Are Asked for an Interview   451
Dress for Interview Success   451
Interview Posture   452
Interview Planning   452
Preparing for the Interview   453
Be-Attitudes for Interview Success   454
Interview Attitude   454
Communicating during the Interview   455
Problem Interviews   455
After the Interview   456
Crisis Communication   457
Types of Crises   457
Six Principles for Crisis Communication   459
Crisis Strategy   460
Crisis Messaging   461
Preparing for Crisis   462
Flow of Information during a Crisis   462

Glossary   464
Citations and Recommended Readings   495
Index   506

Preface

Strategic Planning for Public Relations offers college and university students a new way to deepen their understanding of public relations and other kinds of strategic communication.

It is intended for people serious about entering a profession that is rapidly changing—a profession that is shedding a past that often involved merely performing tasks managed by others and taking on a newer, more mature role in the management of organizations based on research-driven strategic planning, ethical principles and programmatic evaluation.

This book provides an in-depth approach to public relations planning, more comprehensive than can be found anywhere else. It is built on a step-by-step unfolding of the planning process most often used in public relations, with explanations, examples and exercises that combine to guide students toward a contemporary understanding of the profession. It is written in a reader-friendly style designed to appeal both to students and practitioners.

The approach used in *Strategic Planning for Public Relations* is rooted in my belief and observation that students learn best through a threefold pattern of being exposed to an idea, seeing it in use and then applying it themselves. This is the rhythm of this book—its cadence, if you will. This is the design that takes a complex problem-solving and decision-making process and turns it into a series of easy-to-follow steps. These nine steps provide enough flexibility to make the process applicable to all kinds of situations and to organizations with different missions, diverse sizes, varying resources and differing skill levels among the staff.

New to This Fourth Edition

Textbooks are kept current by regular updating of information, addition of new material and publication as new editions.

The fourth edition of *Strategic Planning for Public Relations* follows the same format as previous editions. It updates many real-world examples with several new cases and current events in the practice of public relations.

It also highlights the results of many new research studies on opinions and practices within the discipline. Additionally, this edition adds overviews of several award-winning public relations campaigns.

On the request of instructors using previous editions, I have added a feature from the first two editions but dropped from the third, providing a systematic way for prioritizing publics.

Note to Students

If you are using this book in a public relations class, it is because your instructor finds it valuable for you.

Thank you for allowing me to share my ideas and insights into a profession that I have found to be both challenging and rewarding. I wish you much success as you proceed toward a career that I hope you, too, will discover to be exhilarating.

I stumbled into public relations somewhat by accident, at least not by my own conscious design. I began my career as a newspaper reporter, and later as an editor, with some side trips into television writing and producing, freelance magazine writing and newsletter editing. I then made the transition into public relations—at first building on a familiar base of media relations, publicity and newsletters, and only later navigating into issues management, crisis response, integrated communication and a host of related areas.

Along the way I incorporated the new technological developments (particularly e-mail, the Internet and social media) and now wonder how we once managed without these tools.

Frankly, I wish there had been a book like this to guide me toward doing the work of public relations, especially the research and planning parts. So I'm pleased to be able to share with you some of the insights I've picked up along the way.

With this book and the practical exercises that go with it, you are proceeding along the road to professional success. I wish you the best of luck. You should be aware that this book is intended for group development and class activities. While you certainly can use it alone, you will find that it comes more fully alive as a text to guide group projects. Even if you are not a student in a traditional classroom, try to use this book in the context of your own project task force or professional work team.

Note to Public Relations Practitioners

I am proud to note that the Public Relations Society of America has found *Strategic Planning for Public Relations* to be relevant for practitioners. PRSA selected the book for its short list of endorsed readings for candidates of the APR professional accrediting exam.

I've heard from many public relations practitioners who have used this book and are looking forward to this new edition. Some find it useful in their day-to-day work, particularly those who are working in public relations without benefit of an educational background in the discipline. I myself entered the professional with a background in journalism, so I understand the pros and cons of learning public relations on the job. I'm pleased that this book has been helpful to many of my professional colleagues.

The book also has spurred others who have written to me with issues and comments from their vantage as leaders within the field of public relations. It has been particularly rewarding to hear not only from the PRSA and various U.S. chapters, but also from our Canadian counterpart, the Canadian Public Relations Society, as well as public relations groups around the world, including the Azerbaijan Public Relations Association and practitioners, students and teachers in Russia, Romania, the United Kingdom, Turkey, Japan, Hong Kong, India and many other countries.

Note to Instructors

Thank you for choosing this textbook for your students. Thanks especially for the opportunity to share with them some of my thoughts and observations on an exciting profession. I trust that you will find the information contained in this book to be well within the framework of contemporary professional practice and academic principles.

Strategic Planning for Public Relations grew out of my observation that students seem to learn best when they understand concepts, have patterns to follow and adapt, and have the opportunity to work both individually and in groups on tasks that gradually unfold to reveal the bigger picture. This is my intention with this book—to provide a structure, yet to give you much flexibility in leading your students through the planning process.

I also can share with you that your colleagues have found this book useful in introductory courses as well as in courses focusing on campaign and case studies. Personally, I use the book for an intensive introductory course, supplemented with some online information on history and other foundational elements such as my website—http://faculty.buffalostate.edu/smithrd—which you are free to use if you find it helpful. We also use the book in our senior-level campaign course as the basis for students developing their own campaign proposals. Additionally, the book serves as a basis for the campaigns that are developed by our graduate students.

Who Uses This Book?

I am pleased by the international acceptance of this book since it was first published in 2002 and subsequently updated in 2005 and 2009.

As the author, I am humbled by the confidence that so many educators have placed in this book, and I am quite aware of my responsibility to their students to provide the best teaching resource that I can. To date, at least 180 colleges and universities in the US and Canada, Europe and the Middle East, have adopted this text for public relations classes at both the graduate and undergraduate levels. These courses include principles or foundations of public relations, advanced practice, campaigns, strategy, planning, research, advocacy, public relations administration/management, case studies, corporate communications, integrated communication and issues/problems in public relations. Nearly half of schools associated with the Accrediting Council on Education in Journalism and Mass Communications use this text.

More than 1,212 academic libraries in North America, Asia, Africa, Australia, Latin America, the Middle East, and both Western and Eastern Europe have acquired it for their collections.

I also am pleased with the acceptance of this book by my professional colleagues. The Public Relations Society of America includes this book on a short list of texts recommended for people preparing for the Universal Accreditation Exam. It has been similarly endorsed by the Canadian Public Relations Society, the Public Relations Council of India and several other national groups affiliated with the International Public Relations Association.

The book is listed by the professional resource centers of several PRSA chapters and by practitioner groups such as the Kargozar Public Relations agency in Iran. It is a recommended reading by Six Sigma Strategy Training of Sussex, England. It also has been recommended by several bloggers in the US and around the world who specialize in public relations and marketing communication.

Likewise, many of my fellow educators have shown confidence in this book by citing it in their own writing.

Strategic Planning for Public Relations has been cited in several recent books, including *Handbook of Communication and Corporate Social Responsibility* (Bartlett, May and Bronn, 2011), *Corporate Reputation* (Burke, Cooper and Martin, 2011), *Strategies and Communications for Innovation* (Hulsmann and Pfefferman, 2011), *PR-Evaluation* (Siewert, 2011), *Cases in Public Relations Management* (Swann, 2010), *Public Relations Writing: Form & Style* (Newsom & Haynes, 2008) *Strategic Sport Communication* (Pedersen, Miloch and Laucella, 2007), *Evaluating Public Relations* (Watson and Noble, 2007), *Function of Media and Function of Public Relations at International Crisis Situations* (Gorpe and Celik, 2007) and *The Future of Excellence in Public Relations and Communication Management* (Grunig, Grunig and Toth, 2007).

It also has been referenced in numerous academic and professional publications, including *Public Relations Journal, Romanian Journal of Marketing, Journal of Relationship Marketing, Journal of Vacation Marketing, Communication Theory, International Journal of Strategic Communication, Strategies and Communications for Innovations, Journal of Hospitality and Leisure Marketing, Public Relations Review, Journal of Business Ethics, Baltic Journal of Management, PRism Online PR Journal, Journal of Advertising, Engineering Economics* and *Public Relations Tactics.*

In all, Google Scholar lists 150 citations for *Strategic Planning for Public Relations.*

Acknowledgments

John Donne was right that no one is an island. Neither does an author write alone, but instead reflects in some way the insight of others in the field who write, teach and engage in the practice.

Strategic Planning for Public Relations enjoys the input of many people. As the author of this textbook, I'll take personal responsibility for any errors or omissions, but I'm confident these are fewer because of the advice and assistance of many knowledgeable people who helped along the way.

Collectively, my students have been major contributors to this book. It is in the classroom that I have tested and refined the ideas contained herein. My students have prodded me to articulate my ideas and to bolster them with plenty of real-world examples.

My academic colleagues at Buffalo State emphasize practical, applied communication, and I have benefited from ongoing professional conversations with them. My professional colleagues within the Public Relations Society of America consistently have helped me with their insight and constructive criticism.

The publishing team at Routledge/Taylor & Francis is superb. Linda Bathgate and her staff have guided me through the conceptual development of this edition, steering it to its final form.

Personal Dedication

Like the entirety of my life, *Strategic Planning for Public Relations* is dedicated to my family. Though they don't realize it, my three sons have been an inspiration as I worked on this book.

As he progressed through his teaching job near Kobe, Japan, through his doctoral studies at the University of Osaka, and now with his gardening/import business near Niagara Falls, my son Josh has challenged me to explain public relations every time I suggest that he consider the insights of the discipline on his own work. My son Aaron graduated with a degree in public relations and after starting his own business in the field joined the Army, continuing to develop his excellent writing skills and his keen strategic sense. My youngest son Matt is applying public relations principles in his work in horticulture and his avocation of music.

My greatest appreciation goes to my wife, Dawn Minier Smith. During the evolution of each edition of this and my other books—indeed, during my entire teaching career—Dawn has been my sounding board (no small feat, since I talk a lot). A teacher herself, Dawn has lent her ear as I tested ideas, tried out new ways to present lessons, and attempted to make sense of theories, cases and observations. Since she doesn't see any domestic value in a wife fawning over her husband, Dawn's constructive criticism has been always trustworthy and thus most valuable. I always take her suggestions seriously. Sometimes I've even had the good sense to follow them.

An Invitation

This book is the result of much dialogue with others, particularly feedback from my students. But reader reaction inevitably is useful. I invite all readers—students, teachers and practitioners—to share your thoughts with me. Give me comments and suggestions for future editions. Share your success stories and your frustrations with this book. I also invite you to use my website, where I have included an expanding number of pages and links related to public relations and other aspects of strategic communication.

—Ron Smith
smithrd@buffalostate.edu
http://faculty.buffalostate.edu/smithrd

Additionally, I invite you to take advantage of the excellent online resources that my publisher has created for instructors and students using this book. You can access this at www.routledge/cw/smith.

About the Author

Ronald D. Smith, APR, is a professor of public communication at Buffalo State, the largest college within the State University of New York and the only public institution in New York State accredited by the Accrediting Council on Education in Journalism and Mass Communications.

He has taught public relations planning, writing, research, and related courses to undergraduate and graduate students. For eight years, he served as chair of the 800-student Communication Department at Buffalo State, during which time his department gained ACEJMC accreditation. He currently is associate dean of the School of Arts and Humanities.

As time permits, he also is active as a consultant in public relations and strategic communication, assisting businesses and nonprofit organizations with planning, research, communication management and media training.

In this book, Smith draws on considerable professional experience. In addition to 22 years as an educator, he worked for 10 years as a public relations director and eight years as a newspaper reporter and editor. He also was a Navy journalist in Vietnam working in public affairs on the aircraft carrier USS Ranger.

Smith holds a bachelor's degree in English education from Lock Haven (Pennsylvania) State College (now Lock Haven University) and a master's degree in public relations from Syracuse University. He has presented numerous workshops and seminars, and has published research on public relations and persuasive communication.

He is the author of *Becoming a Public Relations Writer* (4th edition, 2012) and coauthor, with W. Richard Whitaker and Janet E. Ramsey, of *MediaWriting* (4th edition, 2012), both published by Routledge/Taylor & Francis. He currently is writing the manuscript for *Public Relations: The Basics* for Routledge.

Smith also has written *Introduction to Language and Communication: A Primer on Human and Media Communication* (United Arab Emirates University, 2004) and the chapter "Campaign Design and Management" in *21st Century Communication: A Reference Handbook*, edited by William F. Eadie (Sage, 2009).

Smith is the founding director of the American Indian Policy and Media Initiative at Buffalo State. He has been solo or lead researcher in several studies dealing with media and Native Americans, and he is coeditor of *Shoot the Indian: Media, Misperception and Native Truth* (AIPMI, 2007).

Smith is an accredited member of the Public Relations Society of America and has served as president of the PRSA's Buffalo/Niagara chapter and as chair of PRSA's Northeast District. He received the chapter's first distinguished service medal in 2010 and was named Practitioner of the Year in 1998, in addition to numerous other awards and citations. He also has twice been nominated as PRSA Educator of the Year.

Cases and Examples

Following is an index of actual cases, persons, organizations and events cited in *Strategic Planning for Public Relations* as examples of various principles, strategies, tactics and techniques.

3Com, branding rights 210
The 40-Year-Old Virgin, taglines 221

ABC News, prebuttal strategy 146
Abercrombie & Fitch: celebrity endorsement 186; promotional catalogs 251
Absolut Vodka, sponsorship 123
Academi, relabeling strategy 155
Accrediting Council on Education in Journalism and Mass Communications 339
Adidas, celebrity endorsement 186
Advertising Council, donated media 294
AFL-CIO union, alliances 122
Aflac: Aflac duck "spokes-character" and mascot 184, 216; mission statement 42
AirTran, celebrity endorsement 186
Emperor Akihito, regret strategy 157
Akron (Ohio) General Medical Center, sponsored public affairs programming 296–297
"Al Pieda," pie throwing 130
Al Qaeda Yemen, relabeling strategy 155
Alien, taglines 221
Kirstie Alley, celebrity endorsement 183, 193
Gregg Allman, promotional interviews 252
Allstate, taglines 220
Almond Board of Australia, photo ops 119
Altoids, taglines 223
Alzheimer's Association, celebrity influence 118, 132
Amazon, vision statement 42

American Airlines, sponsorship 123
American Cancer Society, integrated communication 13
American Family Association, sponsorship 123
American Heart Association, branding 220
American Idol, product placement 285
American Indian College Fund, donor rights 240
American Indians: Columbus Day protests 238; mascot imagery 216; website use 255
American Negro College Fund, donated media 294
American Paralysis Association, celebrity influence 118
American Society for the Prevention of Cruelty to Animals, taglines 223
Americans for Prosperity, naming ethics 209
Americans for Technology Leadership, naming ethics 209
America's Got Talent, product integration 295
Amnesty International: activism 128; power words 207
AMResorts, guarantees 306
Angel Network, celebrity strategy 118
Maya Angelou, celebrity endorsement 294
Annenberg Norman Lear Center, celebrity endorsement 132
Jennifer Anniston, and Oxfam 260
Anti-Defamation League, branding 220

Christine Applegate, celebrity participation 120

The Apprentice, product integration 295

Arby's, situation analysis 24

Lance Armstrong, celebrity influence 118

Arnold the Pig, character 305

Arthur Andersen, crisis management 30

Asian Nation, stereotyping 81

Associated Press, social media 261

Association for Healthcare Philanthropy, donor rights 240

AT&T: celebrity endorsement 186; naming ethics 209; volunteerism 126

Audi, web-only commercials 296

Aunt Jemima, corporate symbol 216

Avis, taglines 223

Avon, vision statement 42

Michelle Bachmann, use of music 215

David Banner, celebrity influence 126

Drew Barrymore, celebrity influence 184

Batman, Got Milk? campaign 347

Glenn Beck, attack strategy 168

David Beckham, celebrity endorsement 186

Beef Industry Council, celebrity endorsement 186

Richard Belzer, celebrity influence 118

Ben & Jerry's, sponsorship 123

Pope Benedict XVI, symbolic action 129

Edward Bernays 9; power words strategy 207

Halle Berry, celebrity influence 118, 183

Best Buy, sponsorship 123

Betty Crocker, corporate symbol 216

Justin Bieber, Twitter use 255

Big Brother, product integration 295

Billy Blanks Tae Bo workout program, infomercials 298

Black Planet, social networking 259

Blackwater: crisis management 30; relabeling strategy 155

blogs: businesses' use of 256; Dublin Zoo 286; journalists' use of 260

Blogspot, and emergency information 256

Mayor Bloomberg, news generation 136

Blue Cross, naming ethics 209

Boeing Corporation, strategic philanthropy 124

Bono, celebrity influence 183

"Boot the Bell" campaign 122

Borden's Milk, Elsie the Cow, "spokes-character" 184

Bosque de Chapultepec, Mexico City, visitor participation strategy 116

Boston Tea Party, symbolism 129

Bowl for the Cure, strategic philanthropy 124

Bowlfex, infomercials 298

BP: as a case study 386; concern strategy 156; crisis management 32, 34–35

Bridgestone/Firestone: apology 161; as a case study 386

Brigham Young University, goals 99

British Airways, crisis management 32

Chris Brown, regret strategy 157

Kobe Bryant, celebrity endorsement 18, 1856

Brylcreem, celebrity endorsement 186

Budweiser: Clydesdales, "spokes-character" 184; service marks 221; sponsorship 123

Burberry, celebrity endorsement 186

Burger King: alliances against 122; PETA shock strategy 148; service mark 221; situation analysis 24

President George W. Bush: apology 160; blogs 258; celebrity religious endorsements 184; credibility 178–179; opinion leaders 66–67; strategic ambiguity 165; strategic silence 165; symbolic clothing 216; VNRs 280

"Buy America," guilt appeal 201

CafeMom, social networking 259

Caldor Department Stores, apology 161

California Prune Board, product name 208

Call of Duty: Modern Warfare 2, wikis 256

Camp Cool Foundation, sponsorship 126

Camp Fire USA, service mark 221

"Campaign for Real Beauty," Dove, opportunities 22, 24

Naomi Campbell, celebrity endorsement 188

Carnival, strategic philanthropy 124

Steve Carrel, celebrity participation 120

Casting Hall, publicity 133

Catholic Charities, service mark 221

Center for Medicine in the Public Interest, naming ethics 209

Centers for Disease Control and Prevention, celebrity endorsement 132

Jackie Chan, Got Milk? campaign 347

Chanel, celebrity endorsement 186

Charlie the Tuna, "spokes-character" 184

Chase, branding rights 210

Dick Cheney, celebrity influence 132

Cher, infomercials 298

Cherokee Nation, media theory 143

Chevy trucks, taglines 223

Chicago Bears, strategic philanthropy 124

Children's Charity of Southern California, viral philanthropy 260

Chilean mine rescue, crisis management 33, 140

China, sporting events 237

Chirundu, social networking 259

Chocolate World, audience involvement 233

Chrysler, relabeling strategy 155

Church of Scientology: attack strategy 147–148, 168; ethics 37, 209

Cingular Wireless, blogs 257

Cirque du Soleil, Got Milk? campaign 347

Citizen's Bank, branding rights 210

Citizens Commission for Human Rights, naming ethics 209

Citizens for a Free Kuwait, naming ethics 209

Roger Clemens, celebrity endorsement 186

President Bill Clinton: news generation 136; use of music 215

George Clooney, celebrity influence 183

Clothes off Our Back, viral philanthropy 260

CNN: audience size 265; as a news source 230; stem cell research, wording of polls 393

Coalition of Immokalee Workers, alliances 122

Coalition for Responsible Healthcare Reform, naming ethics 209

Coca-Cola: celebrity endorsement 186; Expedition 206 sample campaign 421, 434–438; opinion leaders 67; product placement 295

Stephen Colbert, celebrity influence 132

Coldplay, promotional interviews 252

Colombia, social unrest, and social media 256

Colonel Sanders "spokes-character" 184

Columbian Coffee, Juan Valdez "spokes-character" 184

Columbine High School shootings, crisis management 30, 59

Sean Combs, celebrity influence 118

Condé Nast, strategic philanthropy 124

Conference of Catholic Bishops, stem cell research polls 393

Continental Airlines, apology strategy 157

Anderson Cooper, reversal strategy 152–153

Coors, branding rights 210

Billy Corgan, celebrity influence 132

Don Cornelius, triggering event 117

Coronation Street, celebrity influence 132

Corporation for National and Community Service, volunteerism 127

Ann Coulter, pie throwing 130

Council for the Advancement and Support of Education, donor rights 240

Council for Resource Development, donor rights 240

Katie Couric, celebrity influence 132

Covenant House scandal, case study 386

Perrish Cox, concern strategy 145

Tom Cruise, attack strategy 168; celebrity influence 183

CSI, product placement 295

Cult Awareness Network, naming ethics 209

Kevin Curtis, celebrity strategy 118

Billy Ray Cyrus, celebrity participation 120

Daddy's House Social Programs, celebrity strategy 118

Dawn Detergent, news strategy 139–140

De Beers, taglines 223

Deepwater Horizon *see* BP

Del Monte Foods, Snausages publicity events 241, 305

Denny's restaurant, rectifying behavior strategy 163

Denver Broncos, concern strategy 145

Denver Zoo, sponsorship 122–123

DeVry University, sample campaign 421, 426–430

Thomas Dewey, opinion polls 366

Dexter, wikis 256

Leonardo DiCaprio, celebrity influence 184

Disaboom, social networking 259

Discover Financial, branding rights 210

Doctors Without Borders, viral philanthropy 260

Dodge, symbols 214

Cardinal Timothy Dolan, promotional interviews 252

Dove "Campaign for Real Beauty," opportunities 22, 24

Dow Chemical, mission statement 42

Dow Corning: attack strategy 147; case study 386; risk management 28

Dublin Zoo, public relations initiative 286

Duke University, risk management 29

Dunkin' Donuts, web-only commercials 296

DuPont, branding rights 210

Durex, web-only commercials 296

Dyngas Day, reversal strategy 152–153

Dale Earnhardt Jr., celebrity endorsement 185, 187

Edelman: Free Sylva Campaign, 9; naming ethics 209

Edelman Southwest, transparent communication 142

Zac Efron, celebrity participation 120

Egypt, revolution, and social media 256

David Eisenstadt, strategic philanthropy 124

Queen Elizabeth II, strategic silence 165

Keith Ellison, stereotyping 83

Elsie the Cow, "spokes-character" 184

Energizer Bunny, audience confusion 313

Enron: branding rights 210; crisis management 30

Entertainment Industry Foundation 120

Epilepsy Foundation, message exposure 345

ESPN: celebrity endorsement 186; taglines 221

Exxon: case study 386; concession strategy 153–154; mitigation strategy 152; product name 208; reputation 28, 34–35, 131

Facebook: businesses' use of 256; Dublin Zoo 286; and emergency information 256; "Find Brittany" campaign 8; journalists' use of 275, 281; measuring impact 351; nonprofits' use of 255, 261; number of users 259; politicians' use of 255, 260; Rock the Vote campaign 126; viral philanthropy 260

Douglas Fairbanks, celebrity influence 184

Farmers for Clean Air and Water, naming ethics 209

Fast Horse, Coca-Cola Expedition 206 sample campaign 421, 434–438

Fatah party, Palestine, public relations 85

Federal Communication Commission (FCC), robocalls 252

Federated Department Stores, relabeling strategy 155

FedEx: branding rights 210; integrated communications 9; strategic philanthropy 125

FEMA, social media 256

Fenway Realty, branding rights 210

"Find Brittany" campaign 8, 66
Firestone, as a case study 386
Colin Firth, celebrity influence 183–184
Fitness First for Women, acceptance
    objectives 105
Flickr 261; measuring impact 351;
    SeaWorld San Antonio 350
Florida Catholic Conference, alliances 122
Doug Flutie, celebrity strategy 118
football, branding rights 210
Ford: apology 161; as a case study 386;
    mission statement 42; product
    placement 295; web-only commercials
    296
Betty Ford, celebrity strategy 118
Vivica A. Fox, celebrity influence 118, 183
Fox News: audience size 265; as a news
    source 230
Michael J. Fox, celebrity strategy 118
Fox Television, attack strategy 168
Al Franken, attack strategy 168
"Free Silva" campaign 8
Freedom Works, naming ethics 209
Thomas Friedman, pie throwing 130
Bruce Friedrich, shock strategy 148, 149
Frosted Flakes: product integration 295;
    Tony the Tiger "spokes-character"
    184
Fusion, face-saving 86

Gap, branded clothing 300
Bill Gates, pie throwing 130
Gatorade, celebrity endorsement 193
Geico insurance's gecko, "spokes-
    character" and mascot 184, 216
General Electric, blogs 257
General Mills, strategic philanthropy 124
Mel Gibson, negative publicity 133
Gillette, celebrity endorsement 185, 186
Newt Gingrich, use of music 215
Ginsu knives, infomercials 298
Gitam 99
Rudy Giuliani: mitigation strategy 152;
    negative publicity 131, 133; prebuttal
    strategy 146
Giving Institute, donor rights 240

Global Climate Coalition, naming ethics
    209
Going to Bat against Breast Cancer,
    strategic philanthropy 124
Whoopi Goldberg, celebrity endorsement
    193
Golden Palace, branding rights 210
Golden Spike, symbolism 129
Goldman Sachs, crisis management 32
Gold'n Plump Poultry, opportunities 22
Good Health Radio Hour, sponsored
    public affairs programming 296–297
Cuba Gooding Jr., celebrity influence 118,
    183
Goodyear, integrated communication 12
Google: ethics 34; mission statement 42; as
    a news source 230
Jeff Gordan, celebrity endorsement 187
Al Gore, use of music 215
Ray Gosling, viral video 261
Got Milk? campaign 347
Nancy Grace, "Find Brittany" campaign 66
Kat Graham, celebrity influence 126
Tom Green, celebrity influence 118
Greening Earth Society, naming ethics 209
Greenpeace: opportunities 24; sponsorship
    121–122; taglines 220
Greyhound, strategic philanthropy 125
Ground Zero Mosque, news generation
    134–136
Gucci, celebrity endorsement 186

Haiti earthquake, sources of information
    230
Halliburton: concern strategy 156; crisis
    management 33
Hallmark cards, emotional appeal 196–197
Hamas party, Palestine, public relations 85
Scott Hamilton, celebrity influence 118
Warren G. Harding, celebrity influence
    184
Silva Harotonian, public interest 8
Mariska Hartingay, celebrity participation
    120
Tony Hawk, Got Milk? campaign 347
Isaac Hayes, celebrity influence 183

Tony Hayward: concern strategy 156; crisis management 34
Hurley Hayward, celebrity influence 184
Heinz, branding rights 210
Henry Ford Hospital, Detroit, social media 256
Herbie Husker, mascot 216
Hershey Food, Chocolate World audience involvement 233
Hershey, taglines 223
Jennifer Love Hewitt, celebrity influence 183
Hewlett-Packard: crisis management 32; integrated communications 9
Hill & Knowlton: naming ethics 209; Text4Baby sample campaign 421, 423–425
Hip Hop Coalition for Political Change, sponsorship 126
HOGWASH (Hogs Opposed to Government Waste and Silly Highways) 305
Holiday Inn, branding 221
Holland America, strategic philanthropy 124
Holocaust on Your Plate, shock strategy 149–150
Home Depot, branding rights 210
Houston Astros, branding rights 210
Whitney Houston, triggering event 117
HSBC, vision statement 42
Hunter's Hope Foundation, celebrity strategy 118

Don Imus, nonapology 159
Independent Sector, donor rights 240
Indianapolis Zoo, sponsorship 123
INS (U.S. Immigration and Naturalization Service), alliances 120
Intel Pentium, as a case study 386
International Association of Chiefs of Police, strategic philanthropy 125
International Association of Fire Fighters, prebuttal strategy 146
International Baby Food Action Network 153

International Day of Action, activism 128
Iran, social unrest, and social media 256
IRENA (International Renewable Energy Agency), organizational performance 115

Jack-in-the-Box, crisis management 158
Janet Jackson: disassociation strategy 154; power words 208; relabeling strategy 156
Clay Jackson, Maytag repairman mascot 184
LeBron James, celebrity endorsement 185, 187
Jenny Craig weight-loss program, celebrity endorsement 193
JetBlue, apology 158–159
Derek Jeter, celebrity influence 185
Pope John Paul II, symbolism 129
Johnson & Johnson: as a case study 386; corrective action 162; crisis management 30, 32–33, 158; opportunities 22; publicity 131; sample campaign 421, 423–425
Magic Johnson, celebrity endorsement 118, 186
Angelina Jolie, celebrity endorsement 183, 186
Al Jolson, celebrity influence 184
Nick Jonas, celebrity influence 132
Michael Jordan: celebrity endorsement 187, 193; sponsorship 59
Lewis Jordan, condolence strategy 156
Journey to Atlantis roller-coaster, social media 350
King Juan Carlos, King, triggering event 117
Junior Achievement, volunteerism 127
Juvenile Diabetes Foundation, stem cell research poll 393

Jane Kaczmarek, viral philanthropy 260
James Kallstrom, strong quotes 210
Kasky v. Nike case 10
Kay Jewelers, taglines 220
Toby Keith, celebrity influence 118, 183

Kellog: product integration 295; Tony the Tiger "spokes-character" 184

Jim Kelly, celebrity influence 118

Kennedy Center for the Performing Arts, strategic philanthropy 124

Kermit the Frog, Got Milk? campaign 347

John Kerry: naming ethics 209; reactive strategies 144

Phil Kessel, celebrity strategy 118

KFC: Colonel Sanders "spokes-character" 184; PETA shock strategy 149

Nicole Kidman, celebrity influence 118, 132, 183

Kimberly-Clark, sponsorship 121–122

Kiwi Airlines, product name 208

Kleenex, sponsorship 121–122

Ralph Klein, pie throwing 130

K'naan 215

Gladys Knight, celebrity strategy 118

Keira Knightley, viral philanthropy 260

Knitters Without Borders, viral philanthropy 260

Koch Industries, naming ethics 209

Kodak, integrated communication 12

Kraft Foods: celebrity endorsement 186; disassociation strategy 155; sponsorship 123

Krispy Kreme Doughnuts, integrated communication 12

Mike Krzyzewski, promotional interviews 252

Labroots, social networking 259

Lace for the Cure, strategic philanthropy 124

Osama bin Laden, social media 256

Lady Gaga: celebrity influence 184; Twitter use 255

Doug Lambourn, prebuttal strategy 146, 147

Alf Landon, opinion polls 366

The Last Temptation of Christ, negative publicity 133

Lee Jeans, alliances 120

Annie Leibovitz, Got Milk? campaign 347

Levi Strauss, stealth ads 295

Lexus, sponsorship 123

I. Lewis "Scooter" Libby, blogs 258

Liberian Women's Peace Movement, embarrassment strategy 148

Libya, revolution, and social media 256

Lifeline of Ohio 305

Rush Limbaugh: celebrity endorsement 184–185; nonapology 159

Lincoln automobiles, celebrity endorsement 186

LinkedIn: and emergency information 256; nonprofits' use of 255; number of users 259

Literary Digest, opinion polls 366

Livestrong, celebrity strategy 118

Lindsey Lohan: celebrity influence 132; viral video 261

Frank Lorenzo, apology 157

Sue Lowden, embarrassment strategy 148

Mike Lowell, celebrity influence 118

Lucky Charms, product integration 295

Lucky Strike 9

Lucy Lui, celebrity participation 120

Lunarstorm, social networking 259

M&Ms, branding 222

John McCain: news generation 136; reactive strategies 144; use of music 215

McDonald's: attack strategy 168; as a case study 386; integrated communication 9, 12; opportunities 24; PETA shock strategy 148; Ronald McDonald, mascot 216

John McEnroe, celebrity influence 184

McGruff the Crime Dog: donated media 294; "spokes-character" 184

Macy's Group, relabeling strategy 155

Major League Baseball, strategic philanthropy 124

Makah people, website use 255

Karl Malone, celebrity influence 184

Manning Selvage and Lee, naming ethics 209

Marilyn Manson, Got Milk? campaign 347

Marcal, sponsorship 122

March of Dimes: service mark 221;
   taglines 220
Marine Corps: symbols 214; taglines 223
Judith Martin, apology 157
Massey Energy, crisis management 32
Mastercard, message exposure 345
Matsushita Kotobuki Electronics
   Industries, relabeling strategy 155
Mattel, nonapology 159
Maxwell House, emotional appeal
   196–197
Maytag: branding 221; repairman mascot
   184
Mazda, celebrity endorsement 186
MCI, relabeling strategy 155
The Medium, product integration 295
Memoirs of a Geisha, product integration
   295
Dan Merino, celebrity influence 185
Shawn Merriman, celebrity strategy 126
Metabolife, prebuttal strategy 146
Metlife, sponsorship 123
Michelin, emotional appeal 196
Phil Mickelson, celebrity endorsement 187
Microsoft: blogs 257; naming ethics 209;
   value statement 42
MiGente, social networking 259
A Million Penguins, wikis 256
Milwaukee Zoo, sponsorship 123
Miss Manners: apology strategy 157;
   publics 74
Mitsubishi Electric, face-saving 86
Molsen, branding rights 210
Monster Cable, branding rights 210
Morehouse State College, taglines 223
Morris the Cat, "spokes-character" 184
Kate Moss, celebrity endorsement 186
Mothers Against Drunk Drivers (MADD),
   spectaculars 299
motorcycle riders, organ donors campaign
   305
Motorola: integrated communications 9;
   publicity 131
Alozo Mourning 118
MSL Group, DeVry University sample
   campaign 421, 426–430

MSN, as a news source 230
MSNBC, audience size 265
MTV: relabeling strategy 156; strategic
   philanthropy 126–127
Muppets, celebrity influence 132
The Muppet Show, wikis 256
Rupert Murdoch, pie throwing 129
Museum of Flight, strategic philanthropy
   124
Muxlim, social networking 259
MySpace: and emergency information 256;
   and PETA 260

National Association for the Advancement
   of Colored People, alliances 120
National Cancer Institute's Entertainment
   Education Program, celebrity
   endorsement 132
National Catholic Development
   Conference, donor rights 240
National Committee on Planned Giving,
   donor rights 240
National Council of Churches, alliances
   122
National Crime Prevention Council,
   donated media 294
National Denim Day, alliances 120
National Fluid Milk Promotion Board,
   advertising campaign 347
National Mentoring Center, branding 220
National Rifle Association, taglines 221
National Runaway Switchboard, strategic
   philanthropy 125
National Wetlands Coalition, naming
   ethics 209
Native Americans, mascots 216
NBC News, stem cell research poll 393
David Neeleman, apology 158–159
Nelly, Got Milk? campaign 347
Nestlé: as a case study 386; concession
   strategy 153; risk management 27
Network Ten, reactive strategies 167
New Balance, strategic philanthropy 124
New Boyz, celebrity strategy 126
New York City: social media 256;
   television advertising 294

New York Times 267; service mark 221
Nike: celebrity endorsement 186; and
    Generation Y 59; *Kasky v. Nike* case
    10; mission statement 42; service
    mark 221; sponsorship 123; symbols
    214; taglines 220, 223
Nirvana, promotional interviews 252
Nokia, taglines 220
Norelco, web-only commercials 296
Chuck Norris, infomercials 298
Nuns on the Bus, publicity events 241
Nutrisystem, celebrity endorsement 185

Oakley Sunglasses, news strategy 140
President Barack Obama: and Generation Y
    59; news generation 136; as a news
    source 230; prebuttal strategy 146,
    147; and social media 260; use of
    music 215; website use 255
Conan O'Brien, Got Milk? campaign
    347
Occupy movement, activism 128
Odwalla, crisis management 158
Oldsmobile, repositioning 96
Olympic Games: as a case study 386; as a
    promotional event 237; sponsorship
    121–122
Omega, celebrity endorsement 186
On Deck for the Cure, strategic
    philanthropy 124
Shaquille O'Neal, celebrity endorsement
    187
OneVoice, Philips Norelco sample
    campaign 421, 439–442
Operation Home Free, strategic
    philanthropy 125
Orbitz, sponsorship 123
organ donors campaign 305
Orville Redenbacher, product integration
    295
Sharon Osborne, celebrity influence 118

Palestinian Authority 85
Sarah Palin, news generation 136
Panasonic Shikoku Electronics, relabeling
    strategy 155

The Passion of the Christ, negative
    publicity 133
Patagonia Company, promotional catalogs
    251
Jo Paterno, disassociation strategy
    154–155
Ron Paul, social media fundraising 260
Pope Paul VI, symbolism 129
David Hyde Pearce, celebrity influence
    132
Pele, celebrity endorsement 184–185
Sean Penn, celebrity influence 183
Penn State University: as a case study
    386; disassociation strategy
    154–155
John Pepper, pie throwing 130
Pepsi: branding 222; as a case study 387;
    crisis management 22; in Egypt 67;
    excuse strategy 151; product
    placement 295; VNRs 279
Perrier, deliberate inaction 164
Katy Perry, Twitter use 255
Rick Perry, viral video 261
PETA (People for the Ethical Treatment
    of Animals): branding 220; celebrity
    endorsement 188; naming ethics 209;
    pie throwing 129; publicity stunts 119;
    shock strategy 148, 149–150; social
    media 260
Tom Petty 215
Pfizer, integrated communication 12
Michael Phelps, celebrity endorsement
    185, 196
Fred Phelps, pie-throwing 129–130
Philip Morris: naming ethics 209;
    relabeling strategy 155
Philips Norelco: sample campaign 421,
    439–442; sex appeal 199
Philly Phanatic, mascot 216
Phoenix Children's Hospital, service mark
    221
Physicians Committee for Responsible
    Medicine, naming ethics 209
Mary Pickford, celebrity influence 184
Pillsbury Doughboy "spokes-character"
    184

Pink for the Cure, strategic philanthropy 124

Brad Pitt, celebrity influence 183

Harvey Pitt, transparent communication 142

Valerie Plame, blogs 258

Points of Light Foundation, volunteerism 126–127

Harry Potter books, integrated communication 13

Paula Poundstone, verbal communication 205

Colin Powell, celebrity influence 132

Powerade, celebrity endorsement 185, 186

Princess, strategic philanthropy 124

Procter & Gamble: news strategy 139–140; pie throwing 130

Frank Purdue, company spokesperson 187

Dennis Quaid, celebrity influence 132

Quran, symbolism 216

Race for the Cure, strategic philanthropy 124

Radio Rocks the Vote, sponsorship 126

Rally for the Cure, strategic philanthropy 124

Dan Rather, blogs 258

Rawlings, celebrity endorsement 186

Razoo, nonprofits' use of 261

President Ronald Reagan: credibility 178; influence 118

Orville Redenbacher, company spokesperson 187

J. J. Redick, celebrity influence 183

Reebok, celebrity endorsement 186

Christopher Reeve, celebrity influence 118

Oscar de la Renta, pie throwing 129

Reuters, social media 261

Michael Richards, viral video 261

Rihanna: Got Milk? campaign 347; Twitter use 255

Julia Roberts, celebrity influence 132

Rock the Vote campaign, sponsorship 126

Rogaine Extra Strength, celebrity endorsement 184

Mitt Romney: honesty 180; news generation 136; and social media 260; use of music 215

Ronald McDonald, mascot 216

Franklin Roosevelt, opinion polls 366

Roper Poll, opinion polls 366

Rosetta Stone, infomercials 298

Asher Roth, celebrity strategy 126

J. K. Rowling, integrated communication 13

Marco Rubio, attack strategy 148

Ruder-Finn, ethics 37

Renato Ruggerio, pie throwing 130

Rural/Metro Ambulance Service, promotional vehicles 305

Lillian Russell, celebrity influence 184

St. Bonaventure University, crisis management 23

St. John fashions, celebrity endorsement 186

St. Jude's Children's Hospital, taglines 223

St. Louis Zoo, sponsorship 123

Salvation Army, taglines 223

Pete Sampras, Got Milk? campaign 347

San Diego Chicken, mascot 216

San Diego Children's Hospital, transparent communication 141

Sanex, branding rights 210

Saw II, taglines 221

Scary Movie 2, taglines 221

Arnold Schwarznegger, apology strategy 157

Martin Scorsese, negative publicity 133

Sears Auto Centers, as a case study 386

Seattle Mariners, strategic philanthropy 124

SeaWorld San Antonio, social media 350

Securities and Exchange Commission, transparent communication 142

Seneca Nations of Indians, taglines 221

Shakira, Twitter use 255

Shanghai World Expo 2010, as a promotional event 237

Gail Shea, pie throwing 129

Charlie Sheen, viral video 261
Cybill Shepherd, celebrity endorsement 186
Brooke Shields, celebrity endorsement 193
Sierra Club, service mark 221
Silver Anvil Award, PRSA 421–442
Jessica Simpson, celebrity participation 120
Simpsons, Got Milk? campaign 347
The Simpsons Movie, taglines 221
Sirius Radio: interviews 252; sponsorship 123
Sisters Hospital, community opposition 386
Jean Smart, celebrity influence 184
Brittany Smith, public interest 8
Jimmy Smits, celebrity influence 118, 183
Smokey Bear, mascot 216
Snausages, publicity events 241, 305
Snickers, sponsorship 123
Snocrates, mascot 241
Ian Somerhalder, celebrity influence 132
Suzanne Somers, infomercials 298
Somerville Road, Worcester, auto insurance promotion 306
Sony Ericcson, branding rights 210
Sony, product integration 295
Mike "The Situation" Sorrentino; celebrity endorsement 186
Southwest Airlines, evaluative research 355
Speedo, celebrity endorsement 185, 186
Starbucks: branding 221; integrated communication 12
Starkist, Charlie the Tuna "spokes-character" 184
Ringo Starr, promotional interviews 252
stem cell research, wording of polls 393
Oliver Stone, strong quotes 210
Barbra Streisand, attack strategy 167
Student-Farmer Alliance, alliances 122
Super Bowl, viral video 261
Survey Research Office, University of Hawaii, direct mail 390
Survivor 215

Swift Boat Veterans for Truth, naming ethics 209
Swiss government, ethics 37

Taco Bell, alliances 122
TCI (The Communications Group), strategic philanthropy 124
Tea Party: embarrassment strategy 148; news generation 135, 136
TeachStreet, social networking 259
Tempur, infomercials 298
tennis, branding rights 210
Texaco: corrective action 162; disassociation strategy 154
Text4Baby, Johnson & Johnson sample campaign 421, 423–425
Dave Thomas, company spokesperson 187
Three Mile Island nuclear accident: as a case study 386; crisis management 35
Justin Timberlake: disassociation strategy 154; power words 208
Timex, branding 221, 223
Tommy Hilfiger, branded clothing 300
Tony the Tiger "spokes-character" 184
Toyota: crisis management 32; reputation 99–100; social media 255
Toys 'R' Us, vision statement 42
Trailway Bus Lines, strategic philanthropy 125
Transocean: concern strategy 156; crisis management 33
Harry Truman, opinion polls 366
Donald Trump, triggering events 117
Tunisia, revolution, and social media 256
Turkish Airlines, celebrity endorsement 185
Christy Turlington, celebrity influence 118
Twitpay, nonprofits' use of 261
Twitter: businesses' use of 256; celebrities' use of 255; Dublin Zoo 286; and emergency information 256; journalists' use of 260; nonprofits' use of 255; number of users 259; politicians' use of 255
Tylenol *see* Johnson & Johnson

UAHC (Union of American Hebrew Congregations), audience participation 116

Unequal, celebrity endorsement 186

Unilever, Dove "Campaign for Real Beauty," opportunity 22, 24

United Cerebral Palsy, branding 222

United Negro College Fund, taglines 221, 223

United Parcel Service, promotional vehicles 305

United Way of America, as a case study 386

United Way of America, donor rights 240

University of Texas at Austin, service mark 221

Univision, attack strategy 148

Upper Deck, celebrity endorsement 186

Urban League, Alliances 120

U.S. Army recruiting, sample campaign 421, 430–433

U.S. Bowling Congress, strategic philanthropy 124

U.S. Department of Education, branding 220

U.S. Department of Transport, donated media 294

U.S. flag, symbolism 129, 214

U.S. Forest Service, taglines 221

U.S. government, power words 207

U.S. Navy: apology strategy 160; as a case study 386; social media 256; television advertising 294

U.S. Postal Service eagle, mascot 216

USA Today 267; stem cell research poll 393

Usher, Got Milk? campaign 347

Juan Valdez "spokes-character" 184

ValuJet, condolence strategy 156

The Vampire Diaries, wikis 256

Verizon: naming ethics 209; product integration 295

Viagra, celebrity endorsement 184–185

Michael Vick: apology 157–158; celebrity endorsement 186

Villanova University, branding rights 210

Vimeo, politicians' use of 260

Virginia Slims, branding rights 210

Virginia Tech shootings: crisis management 30; social media 275–276

Visa: celebrity endorsement 186; product integration 295

Volkswagen, concession strategy 153

Helen Vollmer, transparent communication 142

Volunteer Match, volunteerism 127

Volvo: branding 221; web-only commercials 296

Scott Waddle, apology 160

Wal-Mart: attack strategy 148; blogs 257; crisis management 33; integrated communication 12; naming ethics 209; sponsorship 123

Wales, Jimmy, Wikipedia 257

Walgreens, sponsorship 123

Wall Street Journal 267, 270, 274; stem cell research poll 393

Mike Wallace, celebrity influence 184

Tionne T-Boz Watkins, celebrity influence 118

Weber Shandwick, U.S. Army recruiting campaign 421, 430–433

Michelle Wei, celebrity endorsement 187

Wheaties, taglines 223

White House, social media 256

Jesse White, Maytag repairman mascot 184

Bradley Whitford, viral philanthropy 260

Wikipedia 256, 257

Montel Williams, celebrity influence 118

Amy Winehouse, triggering events 117

Oprah Winfrey, celebrity influence 118

Reece Witherspoon, celebrity influence 118, 183

Tiger Woods: celebrity endorsement 187; Tiger Woods Foundation 118

Working Families for Wal-Mart, naming ethics 209

World Cup Soccer Championship, message exposure 345
World Literacy Crusade, naming ethics 209
World Trade Centre September 11 attacks 30, 59
WorldCom: crisis management 30; relabeling strategy 155
Wrangler jeans, celebrity endorsement 185
Wrigley, branding rights 210
WSDI Fox-61, ethics 297
WWF (World Wildlife Fund), triggering events 117

Xe Services, relabeling strategy 155
Xerox, integrated communication 9
Xt3, social networking 259

Yahoo, as a news source 230
Yarn Harlot, viral philanthropy 260
Yellow Pages, branding 222
Yomiuri Shimbun 267
YouTube 261; and emergency information 256; measuring impact 351; nonprofits' use of 255; number of users 259; politicians' use of 260; SeaWorld San Antonio 350; stealth ads 295; viral philanthropy 260
Yum! Brands, boycotts 122
Yves Saint Laurent, celebrity endorsement 186

Gerrit Zalm, pie throwing 130

Introduction

Why write a book on strategic planning for public relations? Because effective and creative planning is at the heart of all public relations and related activity. And because the field is changing. No longer is it enough merely to know *how* to do things. Now the effective communicator needs to know *what* to do, and *why*, and *how to evaluate* the effectiveness of the chosen approach. The call is now for strategic communicators.

Let's look at two categories of public relations practitioners: technicians and managers.

COMMUNICATION TECHNICIAN

Public relations professionals used to be called upon mainly for tasks such as writing news releases, drafting speeches, producing videos, editing newsletters, organizing displays, and so on. These are roles of **communication technicians**, specialists in public relations and marketing communication who typically perform these tasks at the direction of others. Often these tasks are associated with entry-level jobs.

COMMUNICATION MANAGER

Beyond the work of a communication technician, the profession also demands competency in directing research, making decisions, planning projects and campaigns, and solving problems. This is the work of a **communication manager**. Two types of communication managers have complementary roles within organizations. Consider the work of both of these types of communication managers, tactical and strategic.

A **tactical manager** makes day-to-day decisions on many practical and specific issues. Should they send a news release or hold a news conference? Are they better off with a brochure or a webpage? Should they develop a mall exhibit, or would it be more effective to create a computer presentation? Do they need another advertisement, and if so, for which publication or station, and with what message using which strategy?

A **strategic manager**, on the other hand, is concerned with management, trends, issues, policies and corporate structure. What problems are likely to face the organization over the next several years and how might they be addressed? What is the crisis readiness of the organization? Should senior personnel be offered an advanced level of media training? What should the policies be for tweeting?

In the workplace, public relations practitioners often find themselves functioning in both the technician and the managerial roles, but the balance is shifting. Today's environment—and more important, tomorrow's—calls for greater skill on the management side of communication.

The manager's job of strategic communication planning calls for four particular skills:

1. understanding research and planning;
2. knowing how to make strategic choices;
3. making selections from an expanding inventory of tactical choices;
4. completing the process by evaluating program effectiveness.

A premise underlying this book is that public relations and marketing communication are becoming more strategic, more scientific. It is this strategic perspective that will differentiate the effective practitioner from the one who simply performs tasks and provides basic services.

Strategic Planning for Public Relations is about making such decisions—not by hunches or instinct, but by solid and informed reasoning that draws on the science of communication as well as its various art forms. This book tries to make the complex process of strategic communication easily understandable by taking you through the process step by step. You'll find nine steps, each presented with the following three basic elements:

- explanations that are clear and understandable, drawn from contemporary theory and current practice;
- examples that help you see the concept in action, drawn from both nonprofit and for-profit organizations;
- hands-on exercises in both short form and expanded versions that help you apply the process in your own situation.

Note also that key terms, printed in boldface, are collected into a glossary at the end of the book.

Experience shows that this hybrid format—part textbook, part workbook—can make it easier to learn about the planning process because it helps you think, see and do. *Strategic Planning for Public Relations* gives you a solid, proven process that works. It doesn't offer any secrets of the trade, because there really are no secrets. Effective managers in public relations and marketing communication use these kinds of processes every day, and that's not much of a secret. What this book does is make field-tested procedures available to you in an understandable way so you can apply them yourself.

Organizational Process

Through contemporary eyes, public relations is seen as a central and essential aspect of organizational management.

In their influential book *Managing Public Relations,* James Grunig and Todd Hunt (1984) identified four now-famous evolutionary models of public relations. The first two—exemplified by press agentry and public information—rely on one-way dissemination of information. The latter models—an asymmetrical approach associated with persuasion and advocacy;

a symmetrical model dealing with dialogue and relationship-building—feature two-way communication for both dissemination and research/feedback. A close look at this evolution shows a practice becoming a profession, and a useful skill becoming an essential element of organizational management and the process of nurturing relationships between organizations and their publics.

Since 1982, the Public Relations Society of America (PRSA—prsa.org) has used an official statement positioning public relations as a process within organizations that encompasses activities such as opinion tracking and analysis, relationship building, research, planning, objective setting and evaluation. For three decades, PRSA called this role a "management function," though a newer definition finds that term misleading because it connotes top-down control using one-way communication. Instead, PRSA's new definition focuses on "process," which implies a more open two-way model.

In *Excellence in Public Relations and Communication Management*, Grunig (1992) used the earlier definition by Grunig and Hunt (1984), defining public relations as "management of communication between an organization and its publics" (p. 6). Meanwhile, for the last 25 years or so, textbooks have identified public relations as a management function. For example, Scott Cutlip, Allen Center and Glen Broom's *Effective Public Relations* (2012) define public relations as "the management function that identifies, establishes and maintains mutually beneficial relationships between an organization and the various publics on whom its success or failure depends." All serious textbooks in the field have followed suit with an emphasis on public relations as an element of organizational management.

At the same time, scholarly research has helped pave the way for seating public relations at the management table. Stephen Bruning is a leading researcher in the role of a relationship-management approach to public relations. He has identified relationship management as "a paradigm for public relations scholarship and practice" (Ledingham and Bruning, 2001, p. xiii). The model is rooted in the relationship between organizational and public interests, and it builds in both theory and practice on a foundation that includes research and evaluation.

DEFINITION OF PUBLIC RELATIONS

The Public Relations Society of America notes that the formal practice of what is now called "public relations" dates to the early twentieth century. Since then, public relations has been understood in many different ways, with the definition evolving as the practice of public relations has changed. The early definitions emphasized press agentry and publicity, while newer definitions focus on engagement and relationship building.

In 2011, PRSA began an international and grassroots project to modernize the definition of public relations. Several definitions were put forward, and in 2012 PRSA members voted for this definition:

Public relations is a strategic communication process that builds mutually beneficial relationships between organizations and their publics.

Introduction

PRSA explains that this definition is simple and straightforward, emphasizing the key characteristics of public relations: that it is a process of communication, strategic in nature, with a focus on mutually beneficial relationships.

The new definition coexists with a lengthier statement on public relations adopted by the PRSA Assembly in 1982. Following is the text of that statement:

Public relations helps our complex, pluralistic society to reach decisions and function more effectively by contributing to mutual understanding among groups and institutions. It serves to bring private and public policies into harmony.

Public relations serves a wide variety of institutions in society such as businesses, trade unions, government agencies, voluntary associations, foundations, hospitals, schools, colleges and religious institutions. To achieve their goals, these institutions must develop effective relationships with many different audiences or publics such as employees, members, customers, local communities, shareholders and other institutions, and with society at large.

The managements of institutions need to understand the attitudes and values of their publics in order to achieve institutional goals. The goals themselves are shaped by the external environment. The public relations practitioner acts as a counselor to management and as a mediator, helping to translate private aims into reasonable, publicly acceptable policy and action.

As a management function, public relations encompasses the following:

- Anticipating, analyzing and interpreting public opinion, attitudes and issues that might impact, for good or ill, the operations and plans of the organization.
- Counseling management at all levels in the organization with regard to policy decisions, courses of action, and communication, taking into account their public ramifications and the organization's social or citizenship responsibilities.
- Researching, conducting and evaluating, on a continuing basis, programs of action and communication to achieve the informed public understanding necessary to the success of an organization's aims. These may include marketing, financial, fund raising, employee, community or government relations and other programs.
- Planning and implementing the organization's efforts to influence or change public policy.
- Setting objectives, planning, budgeting, recruiting and training staff, developing facilities— in short, managing the resources needed to perform all of the above.

Examples of the knowledge that may be required in the professional practice of public relations include communication arts, psychology, social psychology, sociology, political science, economics, and the principles of management and ethics. Technical knowledge and skills are required for opinion research, public-issues analysis, media relations, direct mail, institutional advertising, publications, film/video productions, special events, speeches and presentations.

In helping to define and implement policy, the public relations practitioner uses a variety of professional communication skills and plays an integrative role both within the organization and between the organization and the external environment.

Strategic Communication

Ask executives in business and nonprofit organizations what kind of employee they value, and they'll probably refer to someone who can effectively and creatively solve problems and exploit opportunities.

An effective practitioner understands a problem and manages it to its successful conclusion. How do we manage problems? Sometimes by making them go away. Sometimes just by helping them run their course with the least harm to the organization. Public relations practitioners face all kinds of problems: low visibility, lack of public understanding, opposition from critics and insufficient support from funding sources. Marketing communicators face similar problems: unfamiliarity of companies or products, apathy among consumers, and product recalls and other liabilities. Both may deal with indifference among workers and misunderstanding by regulators. Practitioners also deal with opportunities, such as promoting new products and services or enhancing already effective programs. In most organizations, it is this positive communication that accounts for most of the time practitioners spend on the job.

Meanwhile, forward-looking practitioners try to transform obstacles into opportunities for their organizations and clients.

Strategic communication is the name for such planned communication campaigns. Specifically, it is the intentional communication undertaken by a business or nonprofit organization, sometimes by a less-structured group. It has a purpose and a plan, in which alternatives are considered and decisions are justified. Invariably, strategic communication is based on research and is subject to eventual evaluation. It operates within a particular environment, which involves both the organization and groups of people who affect it in some way.

Strategic communication often is either informational or persuasive. Its common purpose is to build understanding and support for ideas and causes, services and products.

Where do we find examples of strategic communication? They're all around us. Public relations is the most common embodiment of strategic communication, so much so that this book uses the two terms interchangeably. Actually, however, strategic communication is the concept and public relations is its primary example. In earlier days, much public relations activity was haphazard and reactive. But a more contemporary approach to public relations is strategic, and most practitioners see themselves as strategic communicators.

However, not all strategic communicators practice public relations in a narrow sense. Marketing communication also embodies the concept of strategic communication. Still other examples are public health and social marketing campaigns, diplomacy and international relations, constituent relations, political campaigns, ecumenical or interreligious affairs, and many types of lobbying and negotiation.

International relations deals with relationships among governments, and diplomacy involves the management of these relationships. Some analysts would note a difference between diplomacy (which is discrete, formal and official) and public diplomacy (which involves direct and open communication among governments and foreign publics, with the latter being more akin to the practice of public relations.

Meanwhile, public relations itself is sometimes known by alternative names, often linked to subsidiary areas such as media relations or employee communication. Nevertheless, a research-based strategic planning process is necessary for effective management of all the various aspects of public relations—regardless of their names—including community relations, special events planning and promotion, political campaigns, nonprofit events, and fund-raising and development (Austin and Pinkleton, 2006). To that list we can add other elements of strategic public relations: issues management, crisis communication, risk management, public information, public affairs, consumer and customer relations, lobbying, investor relations, and so on. Additionally, there are some new players on the field: litigation public relations, risk communication and reputation management.

Regardless of the label, we look to public relations for leadership and insight in the practice of strategic communication, because most of the related fields and specialties have adopted the set of skills and approaches that public relations has developed over the last 75 years or so (Botan, 1997; Botan and Soto, 1998). Meanwhile, public relations is beginning to more consciously borrow some of the techniques and approaches developed by other fields, particularly marketing and its primary communication tool, **advertising**. At the same time, the emerging field of social media is offering new tools that can be used to support the public relations missions of all kinds of organizations.

OLD, YET NEW

The ancient and enduring wisdom that nothing is new under the sun applies even to contemporary communication.

Building credibility, maintaining trust, repairing misunderstandings and promoting ideas are part of the human impulse. Today's public relations practitioner deals with the same kind of problems that faced our predecessors last year, last decade, last century. Nothing is new but the timing, the tools and perhaps our insight into the problem-solving process.

Integrated Communication

Public relations and marketing are distinct yet overlapping fields. Each has its own focus and its own particular tools, and each discipline fulfills different purposes within an organization. Yet more and more, it is becoming evident that the coordination of public relations and marketing communication can increase an organization's efficiency and effectiveness.

Let's look first at the common distinctions between public relations and marketing communication and then at how they complement each other.

- **Public relations** is a management function that classically focuses on long-term patterns of interaction between an organization and all of its various publics, both supportive and nonsupportive. In contemporary understanding and application, public relations seeks to enhance these relationships, thus generating mutual understanding, goodwill and support.
- **Marketing communication** also is a management function. Whereas public relations often takes a long-range approach, marketing communication focuses more immediately on products and services that respond to the wants and needs of consumers. It seeks to foster an economic exchange between an organization and its consumers.

Additionally, since marketing relies heavily on advertising, it is significantly more expensive than public relations.

Both public relations and marketing communication deserve a seat at the management table. Both disciplines identify wants, interests, needs and expectations of key groups of people, and both structure ways to interact and communicate with them.

Both of these disciplines rely on research, and they are rooted in the organization's mission and directed toward its bottom line. Finally, public relations and marketing communication share a concern about both the short-term and long-term interests of the organization.

The lines between marketing and public relations have never been neat and clean. Laypersons and the media use the terms more or less interchangeably, and distinctions have been built more on stereotypes than on a reality.

Consider, for example, the stale notions that advertising is solely a marketing tool or that public relations is only about publicity. In truth, public relations traditionally has engaged in public service advertising, and it is a public relations perspective that drives image and advocacy advertising. Marketing, meanwhile, has used media relations, publicity and special events while launching new or modified products, and many marketing concepts and techniques have proven useful to public relations practitioners in nonprofit organizations attempting to recruit volunteers or participants, lobby regulators and raise funds.

Integrated communication is this blending of communication functions within an organization designed to make all aspects of communication work together toward common goals, increasing impact at minimal cost.

Some organizations combine the concepts and the tools of public relations and marketing communication, though not always smoothly.

Purists argue against diluting the disciplines, often fearing that integration will demote public relations to just another piece of the marketing mix or subsume public relations under the advertising tent. Others accept integration in principle but dread lopsided implementation, such as the "full-service" advertising agency that claims to offer integrated communication while allocating most of the client's budget to advertising.

Guaranteed to make public relations practitioners take notice are articles such as the one about the "Future of Public Relations" study by Countrywide Porter Novelli—one of the United Kingdom's top five public relations agencies. It reported that public relations is "no longer a peripheral activity when it comes to marketing communication" but rather "an integral part of the marketing ethos" and "one of the most important aspects of the marketing mix" (Gray, 1998). Such language can incite turf battles by portraying public relations as merely an element of marketing, yet this same study reported some positive trends. Among marketing and corporate affairs directors, 92 percent said public relations is integral to business objectives, and 58 percent said public relations is of equal importance with advertising.

The State of the PR Profession Opinion Survey by the PRSA and Bacon's Information (PRSA, 2006) reported that top organizational managers and CEOs overwhelmingly believe that public relations enhances an organization's reputation (4.51 on a 5-point scale) and only slightly less that it furthers financial success and sales (3.94) and market share (3.90).

In its 2011 State of the Society presentation, PRSA pointed to increased credibility for public relations, including a finding that 9 in 10 business leaders think executives need more training in reputation management and strategic communication (PRSA, 2011a). PRSA's Business Leaders Survey found that 97 percent of business leaders think CEOs should

PUBLIC RELATIONS IN THE PUBLIC INTEREST

Public relations is known as an ally of marketing and an organizational function focused on the corporate bottom line. Occasionally, however, the bottom line of some organizations is about more than selling products, raising money, winning votes, increasing membership or building a customer base.

Sometimes public relations is about things that matter in more personal and societal ways, such as finding an abducted child or freeing a political prisoner. Here are two cases that had just those results (from the archives of Silver Anvil awards of the Public Relations Society of America (prsa.org/awards/silveranvil)).

Find Brittany

In December 2010, Trina Smith was murdered in Roanoke County, Va., and her 12-year-old daughter Brittany was abducted. Police suspected the mother's boyfriend and issued an Amber Alert. Meanwhile, the Roanoke public information office managed a communication plan toward finding Brittany. Strategies included developing strong internal communication with law-enforcement agencies, engaging news media to make this a national story, ensuring that information was available daily to the media, and keeping the child's family informed.

Tactics included daily news conferences, a special website with up-to-date information, distribution of fliers and photos, news releases, YouTube videos, and Twitter and Facebook social media sites.

Four days after her abduction, Brittany was found safe in San Francisco. From a report on CNN, a woman recognized Brittany begging for food outside a supermarket. She alerted police, who rescued Brittany and arrested her kidnapper. A month later, Facebook announced plans for 51 dedicated Amber Alert pages (one for each state, and another for the National Center for Missing and Exploited Children).

Free Silva

In June 2008, Silva Harotonian was arrested in Iran for plotting a "soft revolution." An Iranian-American of Armenian ancestry, Silva worked for the International Research and Exchanges Board, a nonprofit organization providing education and training for grassroots social workers. Her work focused on public health professionals working with mother-and-child projects.

Seven months after her arrest, Silva was convicted of attempting to overthrow the government of Iran. She was sentenced to three years in prison. Within a week of sentencing, her employer hired Edelman public relations firm to help secure her release.

Edelman prepared an international public-awareness campaign that called for a delicate balance. Outside influence would be needed, but Iran would take a hard line if too much pressure became evident. Understanding Iran's suspicion toward Americans in particular, the campaign sought to engage people who might influence Iran's president and top religious leader. It tried to maintain a respectful tone toward Iran as it reached out to human rights organizations and to Armenians in the US and Europe. Ironically for a public relations agency, much of Edelman's strategy involved behind-the-scenes private activity.

The campaign developed an advocacy website to leverage international support, provided interviews with Silva's family, targeted international media, and arranged for French and Armenian governments to appeal for Silva's release. After 11 months of detention, Silva was released from prison. A condition of her release was elimination of the advocacy website, so successful had it been.

understand reputation management and 98 percent believe that senior managers should have a working knowledge of building and protecting a company's credibility (PRSA, 2011b).

Conflicting advice has come from the academic community. When the Association for Education in Journalism and Mass Communication suggested integrating public relations and advertising into a shared curriculum to reflect new practices in the field, the PRSA Educational Affairs Committee reacted quickly to oppose such a blending. In the past dozen years, many educators are taking a second look at integration and practitioners seem to be embracing the opportunities that such blending can bring.

Controversy exists even on naming rights. Some people call the blending "integrated marketing communication." Others dub it "integrated communication," "marketing public relations" or "total communication." Some bulky new terms being kicked around are "marketing-based public relations" and "integrated communications (advertising and public relations)."

The key is to respect the complementary roles of marketing and public relations while maximizing the potential of cooperation and coordination. Leaders in the area of integrated communication include CEOs who direct their marketing and public relations teams to collaborate in new-product campaigns, and university presidents who enjoin their media relations people to be attentive to recruiting and fundraising needs.

Their ranks also involve professors and other educators who blend public relations and marketing/advertising within a single academic program. The annual survey *Where Shall I Go to Study Advertising and Public Relations?* (Ross and Richards, 2008) identifies 128 free-standing public relations programs, 92 advertising programs and 45 combined advertising/public relations programs. Thus, the combined programs account for 26 percent of all undergraduate programs studying public relations.

Communication integration seems to be happening globally. The concept is gaining momentum not only in the US but also in the United Kingdom, New Zealand, Australia and India.

In North America, the integrated model has been adopted by corporations such as Xerox, Motorola, Hewlett-Packard and Federal Express. Such companies use integrated communication on three levels: externally with a focus on customers; internally for vertical communication between senior management and frontline workers; and internally with horizontal communication across departments and other boundaries.

Some folks say the concept of integrated communication is wrapped in the history of public relations itself. After all, public relations founding father Edward Bernays engineered the debutante march in New York City's Easter parade in 1929 to make smoking fashionable among women, enabling Lucky Strike to sell more cigarettes.

Thomas L. Harris is a leading proponent of integrated communication, which he calls an outside-in process that begins with an understanding of the consumer publics, particularly their wants, interests, needs and lifestyles. Harris (2000) points out that public relations is particularly effective in building brand equity, which is based on the organization's reputation. The practical benefit of reputation is seen in the 1992 Los Angeles riots, when none of the 30 McDonald's restaurants in the riot area were touched while more than 2,000 other buildings were destroyed. Harris argues that is because McDonald's had long been involved and visible in the community.

Each of the four models that Grunig and Hunt observed in the evolution of public relations—press agentry, public information, persuasion/advocacy and dialogue/relationship-building—is evident today, often used by the same organization. While the latter two models

Introduction

CASE IN POINT **Kasky v. Nike**

The integrated link between public relations and marketing is a fact of life, often assumed by people and forces outside the professions more readily than it may be recognized from within.

Outsiders often link public relations and marketing, or publicity and advertising. Laypersons may ask, for example, how much it costs to get a news release published, or they may talk about sending an ad to a newspaper when they actually mean a news release.

Here's an example that is more ominous. Some external entities are forcing an unwanted link between public relations and marketing.

This was the problem in play in the legal case of *Kasky v. Nike*. Consumer activist Marc Kasky sued Nike under false advertising provisions over its public defense against charges of using child sweatshop labor.

The chill was caused when the California Supreme Court upheld Kasky's claim that Nike had engaged in **commercial speech**, a legal term denoting advertising messages. But Nike had done no advertising. Rather, it had defended itself against the charges by communicating through traditional public relations venues: news releases, its website, speeches and letters to the editor.

The court based its ruling on the premise that a commercial speaker (the Nike corporation) was communicating with a commercial audience (customers) and therefore any such communication was commercial speech. Never mind that previous rulings by the federal Supreme Court had anchored the concept of commercial speech to an advertising format, explicit reference to a product, and economic motivation (*Bolger v. Youngs Drug Products Corp*, 1983), specifically "expression related solely to the economic interests of the speaker and its audience" (*Central Hudson Gas & Electric Co. v. Public Service Commission*, 1980).

Kasky v. Nike posed a legal question that remains unanswered. An out-of-court settlement in 2003 ended the five-year legal battle, but it didn't settle the legal question of where public relations ends and marketing begins.

that build from two-way communication generally find more favor among theorists, none of the approaches is necessarily "the best." Each model has its purpose, and each can be effective in achieving particular organizational objectives.

An interesting tug-of-war exists between the persuasion and relationship models. In subsequent research, Grunig (1992) himself notes that many organizations still primarily practice the persuasion model. With only anecdotal evidence, it seems safe to suggest that most of today's public relations agencies are hired to engage in persuasion on behalf of their clients, who believe their problems can be solved if only they can gain the support of their publics.

Persuasion isn't necessarily bad: the same principles and techniques that persuade people to buy this CD or that perfume can be deployed on behalf of responsible sexual behavior, nutritional literacy, volunteerism or other social virtues. Public relations students are exposed

ATTRIBUTES OF A STRATEGIC COMMUNICATION PROGRAM

An effective communication program includes the following attributes, which apply equally to corporations and nonprofit organizations, as well as to large and small endeavors.

Spurred both by regulation and customer demand, organizations must be *accountable* to their publics. Most publics are increasing their expectations for *quality performance* and *open communication.* Organizations are successful in the long run only to the extent that they have high performance, delivering quality products and services. All organizations operate in a *competitive environment.* Publics besought by rivals will remain loyal to those organizations that earn loyalty consistently and continuously.

Effective communication involves *cooperation* between public relations and marketing. Just as each knight was an equal participant at the round table in King Arthur's court, so too should both disciplines have effective and equal voices.

The consumer philosophy has taken hold of all aspects of society, and organizations must answer with a *customer-driven response,* focusing on benefits for their publics. People support organizations that serve their interests and needs.

Organizational communication adheres to high *ethical standards* of honesty, accuracy, decency, truth, public interest and mutual good. Growing numbers of organizations have developed clear credos or codes of ethics.

Mergers, downsizing and restructuring have led both businesses and nonprofits to seek ways to operate with *lean resources,* and the duplication that exists amid the isolation of marketing from public relations often is too great a price for organizations to pay.

Strategic communication is part of an organization's *management role* and *decision-making process*. It is rooted in the organization's mission as lived out through its bottom line. This bottom line goes beyond money earned or raised; it focuses on the organization's fundamental purpose or mission. Strategists plot courses, set objectives and measure results.

Many *media changes* are affecting the way organizations communicate. The "mass media" have fragmented to the point that none rules supreme any more. Lines have blurred between news and entertainment. Meanwhile, increasing advertising costs and tighter promotional budgets have led organizations to look at the more cost-effective communication and promotional tools from the public relations side of the house.

Strategic communication uses *multiple tools,* drawing from all communication-related disciplines to talk with various groups of people. New technologies make it easier to supplement general media with more personal and interactive targeted communication vehicles.

The strategy of choice in a competitive environment is *proactive, two-way communication*, in which organizations plan for and initiate relationships with the people important to their success. This approach emphasizes dialogue over monologue.

Organizations are successful to the extent they enjoy a strong *reputation,* which results from neither accident nor luck. Strategic planning can identify and evaluate an organization's visibility and reputation. No organization can afford to be a "best-kept secret" among a relatively small number of supporters.

All kinds of organizations are realizing more keenly the need for long-term, mutually beneficial *relationships* between the organization and its various publics and market segments. Public relations practitioners long have recognized this, and marketing more recently has been discussing the need for relationship marketing.

to this persuasion-based model through case studies and campaigns courses, through practicums and senior seminars, and especially through professional internships.

Perhaps we need to envision public relations anew, seeing it as serving the persuasive needs of client organizations as well as fostering more productive and beneficial relationships between organizations and their various publics. Public relations practitioners should be prepared to help organizations engage their publics in both word and deed.

This is the vision that guides *Strategic Planning for Public Relations*. The planning process this book presents can be used for persuasion or dialogue, because each is a strategic activity and each helps practitioners influence behavior and generate consensus. The planning process also can help organizations both overcome obstacles and capitalize on opportunities. Additionally, the process works equally well for businesses and nonprofits, whether they be large or local or international, grassroots or well organized, richly endowed or impoverished.

Advertising

From the perspective of integrated communication, advertising can be seen as a tool for both public relations and marketing. Broadly defined, **advertising** is persuasive communication through purchased media to promote a product, service or idea on behalf of an identified organization or sponsor. As organizations set out to create such a cooperative environment, the political task can be dicey, but the potential rewards are huge. Often it is enlightened, organizational leaders who see the big picture, recognizing the value of a coordinated and strategic approach to communication.

Some of the most successful corporations in North America integrate their communication, blending the traditional disciplines of publicity and advertising to creatively present a clear and consistent message to their various publics. Here are some examples.

- When McDonald's introduced its McLean sandwich, it used publicity and other public relations tactics to create awareness through the media, followed by advertising messages to reinforce the publicity and promotion.
- When Kodak introduced its digital camera to Australia, it did so without much advertising. Instead, it used public relations research that showed that consumers needed education and reassurance about what was then a new and expensive alternative to film-based cameras. So the campaign identified consumer journalists in established media. It gave cameras for journalists to review and held launches for new products. The result was that Kodak became number one in camera sales in Australia.
- It was publicity that enabled Goodyear to sell 150,000 new Aquatred tires before the first advertisements ran.
- Pfizer used publicity alone to sell $250 million worth of Viagra and gain a 90 percent market share before any consumer advertising began.
- In several cities, when Krispy Kreme Doughnuts announced plans to open a store in a new area, the publicity created such a huge expectation among prospective customers that extra police had to be hired for opening day to handle the traffic jams.
- Wal-Mart became the world's largest retailer with little advertising.
- Starbucks spent less than $10 million in advertising during its first 10 years.

- The Harry Potter book series soared to previously unheard of sales without any appreciable advertising, making British author J. K. Rowling literally richer than the queen of England.

The integrated approach also has been used by nonprofit organizations such as the American Cancer Society in its campaign for sun block, and has been adopted by more loosely organized social campaigns dealing with bicycle safety, teen smoking, animal rights, birth control, utility deregulation and AIDS research. One study suggested that nonprofit organizations are particularly open to the coordinated use of public relations and marketing communication techniques (Nemec, 1999).

As a practical matter, an integrated approach to strategic communication often begins with publicity, followed by advertising. Al Ries and Laura Ries note this in *The Fall of Advertising and the Rise of PR*:

> The purpose of advertising is not to build a brand, but to defend a brand once the brand has been built by other means, primarily public relations or third-party endorsements . . . Advertising cannot start a fire. It can only fan a fire after it has been started.
>
> (2002)

Ries and Ries also note some of the differences between public relations (or publicity) and advertising: advertising uses a "big bang," while public relations uses a slow buildup. Advertising is visual; public relations is verbal. Advertising reaches a mass audience; public relations reaches a targeted audience. Advertising favors new lines and extensions; public relations favors new brands. Advertising likes old names; public relations likes new names.

The writers also present both an opinion (public relations is more creative than advertising) and a fact (public relations is more credible).

Strategic Public Relations

Most textbooks dealing with public relations encourage a four-phase process. Some use the RACE acronym (research, action, communication, evaluation) articulated by John Marston (1963) in *The Nature of Public Relations*. In *Public Relations Cases,* Jerry Hendrix and Darrell Hayes (2009) use the acronym ROPE (research, objectives, programming, evaluation). In *Public Relations Campaign Strategies,* Robert Kendall (1997) offers the RAISE formula (research, adaptation, implementation strategy, evaluation). Kathleen Kelly (2001) posits ROPES (research, objectives, program, evaluation, stewardship). Sheila Crifasi (2000) has come up with ROSIE (research, objectives, strategy, implementation, evaluation).

Most public relations textbooks, however, including this one, simply refer to a four-stage process without constraining it to an acronym.

Marketing communication books also present a step-by-step process, but with little consistency about the number of steps involved. While acronyms can be useful mnemonic devices, they can be too confining. The four stages of communication planning are sometimes more complex than acronyms indicate, though in their crossover text on social marketing, Philip Kotler, Ned Roberto and Nancy Lee (2002) identify sight steps in four general stages that focus on analysis of the environment, identification of audiences and objectives, development of a strategic approach and development of the implementation plan.

EXHIBIT INTRO.1 Four phases of strategic planning

PHASE ONE

FORMATIVE RESEARCH

1. Analyzing the Situation
2. Analyzing the Organization
3. Analyzing the Publics

PHASE TWO

STRATEGY

4. Establishing Goals and Objectives
5. Formulating Action and Response Strategies
6. Developing the Message Strategy

PHASE THREE

TACTICS

7. Selecting Communication Tactics
8. Implementing the Strategic Plan

PHASE FOUR

EVALUATIVE RESEARCH

9. Evaluating the Strategic Plan

Strategic Planning for Public Relations offers a model that is meant to be both logical and easy to follow. The steps are grouped into four phases that are both descriptive and accurate, but their names don't lend themselves to an acronym. So without a great deal of fanfare, this model is called, simply, the Nine Steps of Strategic Public Relations.

The process of these steps is deliberate, and they must be taken in sequence. After identifying a problem, our tendency too often is to skip ahead to seeking solutions, leaping over research and analysis. This can result in unwarranted assumptions that later prove to be costly, counterproductive and embarrassing. Careful planning leads to programs that are proactive and preventive rather than to activities that are reactive and remedial. At the same time, the steps in this process are flexible enough to allow for constant monitoring, testing and adjusting as needed.

If you ask experienced communication managers you may find that they don't necessarily articulate their planning specifically along the lines of these nine steps. But talk with them about their work and you are likely to find that they go through a process pretty much like the one being presented here, whether they identify "steps" or not.

A few practitioners may admit (somewhat guiltily) that they don't do much planning. If they are being honest, they'll tell you they know they've been lucky so far with their hunches. Perhaps they don't do formal planning because they don't have the time or because the environment is so unstable that all they can do is react. Some practitioners may tell you their bosses and clients want action rather than planning (though such shortsighted bosses and clients often don't remain in business very long).

If you could observe how professionals work, however, you'd probably find that effective communication managers do plan, and plan well. The good ones have learned how to build the research and planning components into their work, imbedding it in their service to clients and bosses. Increasingly, public relations organizations are using their websites to set the stage for such a four-stage planning process.

JARGON OF STRATEGIC PUBLIC RELATIONS

Consider the following terms that distinguish among various types of public relations activities:

- A **project** is a single and usually short-lived public relations activity designed to meet an objective. Examples: a news release, a Facebook page or a few related tactics for an open house.
- A **program** is an ongoing public relations activity dealing with several objectives associated with a goal. Programs have a continuing commission within the organization and focus on its relationship with a particular public. Examples: an organization's program in community relations or employee relations, or its social media program involving coordinated tools and venues.
- A **campaign** is a systematic set of public relations activities, each with a specific and finite purpose, sustained over a length of time and dealing with objectives associated with a particular issue. Examples: a campaign to reduce accidents associated with drunk driving, or a campaign to improve employee morale and productivity.

Phase 1: Formative Research

During the first of the four phases, the focus is on the preliminary work of communication planning, which is the need to gather information and analyze the situation. In three steps, the planner draws on existing information available to the organization and, at the same time, creates a research program for gaining additional information needed to drive the decisions that will come later in the planning process.

STEP 1: ANALYZING THE SITUATION

Your analysis of the situation is the crucial beginning to the process. It is imperative that all involved—planner, clients, supervisors, key colleagues, and the ultimate decision makers—are in solid agreement about the nature of the opportunity or obstacle to be addressed in this program.

STEP 2: ANALYZING THE ORGANIZATION

This step involves a careful and candid look at three aspects of the organization: (1) its internal environment (mission, performance and resources); (2) its public perception (reputation); and (3) its external environment (competitors and opponents, as well as supporters).

STEP 3: ANALYZING THE PUBLICS

In this step you identify and analyze your key publics—the various groups of people who interact with your organization on the issue at hand. *Strategic Planning for Public Relations* provides an objective technique for setting priorities among the various publics, helping you select those most important on the particular issue being dealt with. This step includes an analysis of each public in terms of its wants, needs, and expectations about the issue; its relationship to the organization; its involvement in communication and with various media; and a variety of social, economic, political, cultural and technological trends that may affect it.

Phase 2: Strategy

The second phase of the planning process deals with the heart of planning: making decisions dealing with the expected impact of the communication, as well as the nature of the communication itself.

STEP 4: ESTABLISHING GOALS AND OBJECTIVES

Step 4 focuses on the ultimate position sought for the organization and for the product or service. This step helps you develop clear, specific and measurable objectives that identify the organization's hoped-for impact on the awareness, acceptance and action of each key public. A good deal of attention is given to objectives dealing with acceptance of the message, because this is the most crucial area for public relations and marketing communication strategists.

STEP 5: FORMULATING ACTION AND RESPONSE STRATEGIES

A range of possible actions is available to the organization, and in this step you consider what you might do in various situations. This section includes typologies of public relations initiatives and responses. No strategic campaign would include every possible option, but a well-planned campaign would consider each in light of its goals and objectives.

STEP 6: DEVELOPING THE MESSAGE STRATEGY

This step deals with the various decisions about the message, such as the person or entity who will present the message to the key publics, the content of the message, its tone and style, verbal and nonverbal cues, and related issues. Lessons from research about persuasive communication and dialogue will be applied for the ultimate purpose of designing a message that reflects the information gained through Step 3 focusing on key publics.

Phase 3: Tactics

During the third phase, various communication tools are considered and the visible elements of the communication plan are created.

STEP 7: SELECTING COMMUNICATION TACTICS

This inventory deals with the various communication options. Specifically, the planner considers four categories: (1) face-to-face communication and opportunities for personal involvement; (2) organizational media (sometimes called controlled media); (3) news media (uncontrolled media); and (4) advertising and promotional media (another form of controlled media). While all of these tools can be used by any organization, not every tool is appropriate for each issue.

STEP 8: IMPLEMENTING THE STRATEGIC PLAN

This step turns the raw ingredients identified in the previous step into a recipe for successful public relations and marketing communication. In Step 8, planners package the tactics identified in the menu review of the previous step into a cohesive communication program. Here planners also develop budgets and schedules, and otherwise prepare to implement the communication program.

Phase 4: Evaluative Research

The final phase of strategic planning deals with evaluation and assessment. It enables you to determine the degree to which the stated objectives have been met and thus to modify or continue the communication activities.

STEP 9: EVALUATING THE STRATEGIC PLAN

This is the final planning element, indicating specific methods for measuring the effectiveness of each recommended tactic in meeting the stated objectives.

Effective Creativity

Before we begin putting a plan together, a word about creativity. Most communications professionals are creative people. They are visual or verbal artists who bring imaginative ideas to the task at hand.

But mere novelty doesn't guarantee success. We all have seen people whose creative ideas seem to flop around without any sense of direction, artists who can't seem to apply their artistic concept.

For creativity to be effective, it must have relevance. Innovative ideas need to serve a purpose. Too many campaigns never get off the ground because they are built more on novelty than on effectiveness. Some are just too cute for words; others are downright bizarre. An inside joke in the advertising industry is that sometimes agencies win creative awards but lose the account, because their innovative advertising programs didn't sell the product or their imaginative approach didn't achieve the desired results for the client. Not a very funny joke, is it?

In the not-so-distant past, some practitioners worried that strategic planning might interfere with their creativity. That is changing. In a crowded field of competitors all courting the same audiences, communication professionals have turned to greater use of research as a complement to the creative approach. Practitioners who once flew by the seat of their pants have found that careful planning can raise an organization's messages above the commotion of everyday life.

One thing has become clear: it really is counterproductive to separate creative and research people, because each can help the other. They share the common purpose of helping their client or their organization solve a problem.

Research nurtures creative inspiration, helps develop ideas, keeps things on target and evaluates the effectiveness of the creative endeavors. Creativity can take the facts and data generated through research and imbue them with pizzazz to produce a Wow! factor that can make a public relations campaign soar.

Strategic Planning for Public Relations is built on two notions that can help make you creatively effective.

- A step-by-step system of planning is essential to learning how to develop an effective communication program.
- Effective creativity is more likely to result from careful and insightful planning than from a lightning bolt of inspiration.

This book is for people who appreciate road maps. A map doesn't tell you where you must go; rather, it helps you explore possibilities. You consider options, make choices, select alternatives and develop contingencies. In short, you plan. Then you implement the plan by getting behind the wheel and beginning the road trip.

So it is with *Strategic Planning for Public Relations.* This book won't tell you what has to be done to develop your communication program, but it will lead you through the various decision points and options. The resulting program will be as unique as each individual student or practitioner and as tailored as each organization needs it to be. It will be a comprehensive, well-thought-out program that is both deliberate and creative.

Every person can be both deliberate and creative, each to a greater or lesser degree. *Strategic Planning for Public Relations* tries to help you cultivate both qualities. It helps creative people become more organized in their planning, and it helps methodical people bring more creative energy to their work.

This book gives you a model—one to be considered, adapted to fit your particular circumstances and used to the extent that it helps you be both effective and creative in your communication planning. Use *Strategic Planning for Public Relations* to nurture your creativity and channel it to make your work more effective.

CREATIVITY AND STRUCTURE

Most people consider themselves at either side of a coin. Some are creative people. Some are analytical types. *Strategic Planning for Public Relations* is geared to both.

Are you easily creative? This book will help transform your artistry, insight and spontaneity into something more than mere novelty. It will lead you to consider every aspect of a strategic communication plan, helping you be creative within an effective framework.

Are you analytical and well organized? This book will enhance your innate sense of organization and structure, freeing your creativity to enhance your program effectiveness.

The reality is that we are seldom one or the other, creative or structured. Don't use the visual metaphor of a coin with two sides. Rather, think of a pole with two ends. Then focus not on the ends but on the continuum in between. Regardless of where you place yourself on this continuum, *Strategic Planning for Public Relations* can help you work through your strengths and at the same time shore up less dominate aspects of your work style.

PHASE ONE

FORMATIVE RESEARCH

The phrase "shooting in the dark" refers to trying to hit a target without being able to see it. In the context of strategic communication planning, it is shooting in the dark to design a program without the necessary research. In any context, it's not a good idea!

Research is the strategic planner's foundation of every effective campaign for public relations and marketing communication. Your communication tactics might be innovative, but they will probably be ineffective if you don't have adequate research. Without research, you will probably end up sending messages of little value to your organization and little interest to your publics (who most likely won't be listening anyway).

How common is research in public relations and marketing communication? Various studies show that formative research for planning campaigns and projects is the most common type of public relations research, with lesser use of research to monitor progress and measure outcomes. Even during crises, when reaction time is minimal, many practitioners make time to do research to get a quick read on public opinion.

Anecdotal evidence suggests that research is becoming even more common. Virtually all practitioners report that they are doing more research than ever before.

The first of the four phases of the strategic planning process deals specifically with gathering and analyzing **formative research**, which is the data on which you will build your communication program. Fran Matera and Ray Artigue (2000) identify two types of such research.

- **Strategic research** is the systematic gathering of information about issues and publics that affect organizations, particularly as the organization engages in the two-way models of public relations that were outlined in the introduction to this book.
- **Tactical research** is information obtained to guide the production and dissemination of messages.

Whereas tactical research helps public relations practitioners do their job effectively, strategic research more directly impacts on the organization's overall mission.

During this formative research phase, focused as it is on strategy, you will conduct a comprehensive **situation analysis** to gather the information needed to make wise decisions. To accomplish this, you will gather information in three key areas: (1) the situation you are facing; (2) your organization or client; and (3) your intended publics. More specifically, you will obtain background information on the issue, assess the organization's performance and reputation and catalogue its resources, and identify and analyze key publics.

Don't let the idea of research scare you. Research begins with informal and often simple methods of gathering relevant information. Often you can look to a three-prong research program for most public relations projects:

- **Casual research** collects what is already known. Think about the situation. "Pick the brains" of clients, colleagues and other helpful individuals. Interview other people with experience and expertise. Brainstorm alone or with other planners.
- **Secondary research** looks for existing information. Using this approach, you will investigate organizational files to learn what already exists on the issue. Search the library for information from books, periodicals and special reports. Check for similar material on the **Internet** (but be wary about the validity of what you find there). Review and analyze how other organizations handled similar situations.
- **Primary research** is the gathering of original information. If necessary, conduct your own research. Appendix A: Applied Research Techniques will help with the basic primary research techniques such as surveys, focus groups and content analysis. The appendix also discusses the ethics of research.

As you conduct formative research, keep one thing in mind: The information you obtain through research will help in planning, but research does not offset the need for common sense. Your professional judgment remains the strongest resource you bring to the planning process. Use research to inform your professional judgment, but make decisions on relevant information as well as on your own reliable experience and professional insight.

This section looks at the three areas in which you will conduct your research, starting with an analysis of the situation.

Analyzing
the Situation

The first step in any effective public relations plan or marketing communication program is to carefully and accurately identify the situation facing your organization. This seems simple enough. Common sense, right? But sense isn't all that common, and people sometimes have different ideas about what the public relations situation is.

Public Relations Situation

Put simply, a **situation** is a set of circumstances facing an organization. Without an early and clear statement of the situation to be addressed, you will not be able to conduct efficient research or define the goal of your communication program later in the planning process.

A situation for an automotive manufacturer might be the availability of side airbags (rather than just front airbags) in its new model-year cars. For a small nonprofit organization dealing with at-risk youths, a situation might be the misunderstanding and fear that some people have of these youths.

Note that situations are stated as nouns—*availability* of airbags, *fear* of youths. Later when we talk about organizational goals, we will add the verbs to indicate how we want to impact on these situations—*promoting* consumer acceptance of the airbags, *dispelling* the notion that all at-risk youths are dangerous. For now, simply identify the situation without commenting on it.

A situation is similar in meaning to a problem, if by "problem" you use the classic notion of a question needing to be addressed. Based on that definition, a public relations situation can be either a positive or negative:

- **Opportunity**. The public relations situation may be identified as an opening, something to be embraced. An opportunity offers a potential advantage to the organization or its publics (such as side airbags).
- **Obstacle**. On the other hand, the public relations situation may be a roadblock, something to be overcome. Obstacles limit the organization in realizing its mission (such as fear of at-risk youth).

Two planners may look differently at the same situation, depending on how they assess the situation and its potential impact on the organization. One may call it an obstacle, the other an opportunity. So it is important to make sure that everyone involved in planning a public relations activity should approach it from the same perspective.

Note that even in crisis situations, obstacles can be approached as opportunities, if the problem has not been self-inflicted. Organizations under attack may use the public attention generated by a crisis to explain their values and demonstrate their quality.

Obstacles into Opportunities

In what is still a classic example of good public relations, Pepsi faced an accusation in 1993 that medical syringes had been found in cans of the company's products. Pepsi fought back by issuing video news releases showing how its production process made it impossible to contaminate the product before it left the plant.

Another classic illustration of good professional practice comes from Johnson & Johnson. The company used satellite news conferences when it reintroduced Tylenol after several people were killed in 1983, when someone tampered with the over-the-counter medicine. In doing so, the company, which already enjoyed a good reputation, emerged from the crisis with even more consumer respect and confidence.

But there are more contemporary examples of taking what might at first appear to be an obstacle and turning it into an opportunity.

Gold'n Plump Poultry is the Midwest's largest chicken company. In 2006, sales had tanked because of consumer fears about industry-wide health risks (avian flu, salmonella, arsenic in feed) spurred by ongoing media reports. The company budgeted $150,000 and launched a six-month "Takin' Names Tour" community relations campaign to shore up its relationship with its consumer base.

An old farm truck traveled throughout towns and villages in Minnesota and Wisconsin, asking residents to sign their names on the vehicle. For every signature, the company donated four meals to rural food shelves to help families in danger of losing their small farms. It also distributed "I give a peep about local family farmers" T-shirts. As the campaign ended, the company had donated 190,000 meals, generated media attention throughout the region, reversed its sales decline and rebuilt brand loyalty. Seven out of ten consumers said Gold'n Plump was the chicken they would buy. Even vegans who don't eat chicken applauded the company's community commitment.

Unilever is another company that turned a problem into an opportunity. The problem was that traditional marketing of beauty products relied on idealized portrayals of women. The opportunity: to redefine the situation.

Unilever, which produces Dove beauty products, commissioned an international study on women's attitudes toward beauty. What resulted was an entirely new approach called the "Campaign for Real Beauty." Dove advertising featured images of ordinary women, not supermodels. The company launched a new product line, Dove Firming, with no television advertising and only limited print ads, but with primary implementation through public relations venues.

The campaign produced exposure through 62 national television programs and 200 local news programs, as well as feature coverage in major national print media and more than 700 local newspapers. More than a million visitors logged onto its website (campaignforrealbeauty. com) in the first year alone. The campaign did more than simply sell beauty products, it also

SCANDAL REVEALS THE WORST . . . AND BRINGS OUT THE BEST

When St. Bonaventure University, a small Franciscan school in upstate New York, was rocked by a basketball eligibility scandal in 2003, the flap drew the scrutiny of national media. The ensuing scandal toppled the coaching staff, athletic director, even the president, and figured in the suicide of a university trustee. NACC gave the school a three-year suspension.

The small public relations staff moved quickly to respond to the sweeping crisis, which in just one week triggered more than 200 media inquiries and hundreds of calls from outraged alumni.

"It's important to note that our Board of Trustees did the right thing. We simply communicated their actions," David Ferguson, then vice president of marketing and public relations, told reporters. "But it's also vital that the way we communicated reflected our core values of community and respect for all."

Enlisting the help of expert crisis communications counsel (Ric Wanetik and Chan Cochran of Columbus, Ohio), Ferguson led the team in executing an action plan with four key goals:

1. Repair the damage done to St. Bonaventure's image by the scandal.
2. Recruit a strong class of incoming freshmen.
3. Turn the adversity into a vehicle for learning and personal growth on the part of members of the campus community.
4. Have the university viewed as a values-driven institution whose response to scandal stands as an example of a "best practice" in dealing with problems.

Pledging to deal "forthrightly, transparently and uncompromisingly" with the scandal, which had erupted over spring break, the trustees first called together the entire campus. At a unity convocation they shared the facts, apologized, announced interim leadership and established a committee to work with a National Collegiate Athletic Association investigation.

The university sent letters to alumni, parents and prospective students. It quickly developed a special issue of the alumni magazine and established communications links with key alumni and supporters. Meanwhile, the new campus leaders met with media in cities with large student and alumni populations.

The result? The incoming freshman class was the largest in a decade and the university received kudos from commentators on several fronts. Perhaps the sweetest compliment of all came from veteran newsman Bob Schieffer in unsolicited comments during his address as commencement speaker, who noted:

I am proud to be part of a ceremony at an institution that faced a hard choice and did the right thing. I am proud to associate myself with you and St. Bonaventure. Here's the headline: your school is not going to be remembered because a sports recruiting scandal happened here. There have been recruiting scandals before and I am sorry to say, human nature being what it is, there will be recruiting scandals again. What St. Bonaventure will be remembered for is doing the right thing and doing it quickly and without excuses.

Phase One

STEP
1

sparked an international discussion about women and beauty, drawing praise for Unilever from psychologists, teachers, parents, media analysts and real women with curves.

The Dove campaign is an example of a communication strategy that caught the public interest. But no good deed is above reproach, and even social responsibility is not without a downside. Unilever took some criticism because the corporation uses overt female sexuality to market its AXE deodorants. Greenpeace, meanwhile, took advantage of the visibility surrounding the campaign to accuse Unilever of buying palm oil from companies that destroy rain forests.

Finding Consensus

Whether the issue is viewed as an opportunity, an obstacle or simply an unrealized potential, the communication team and the organization's or client's leadership must come to a common understanding of the issue before it can be adequately addressed.

Consider the following example of mixed signals: the executive director of a drug abuse-prevention agency wanted a public relations consultant to focus on communication between the agency and external publics such as the courts, police and probation personnel. The board of directors, on the other hand, wanted a plan for better communication among the board, staff and executive director. Significantly different expectations, to say the least! How do you think you might handle this?

In this case, the consultant asked both the director and the board to reach consensus about the central issue and to rethink what they wanted. They asked themselves what the real issues were and concluded that the focus should be on the agency's visibility and reputation with its external publics. Once this was clarified, the consultant developed a strategic plan and helped the agency implement it. The strategic planning checklist at the end of this chapter will help you clarify the issue at hand for your organization.

Ongoing communication with the research client is imperative. In their book *Applied Research Design,* Terry Hedrick, Leonard Bickman and Debra Rog (1993) recommend at least four research touch points:

1. an initial meeting with the client to develop a common understanding of the client's research needs, resources and expected uses;
2. a meeting to agree on the scope of the project, particularly its costs and other resources;
3. following an initial review of literature and other secondary sources, a meeting to refine the research questions and discuss potential approaches and limitations;
4. a meeting for agreement on the proposed study approach.

Your job in this first step of the strategic planning process is to carefully identify the issue at hand. Come to consensus about whether it is seen as an opportunity or an obstacle, and if the latter, how it might be turned into an opportunity.

It is important to take the broad view in this. Fast food chains such as McDonald's, Arby's and Burger King, for example, could have ignored growing national and international concerns about obesity, particularly their long-term effects on young people. Yet all three companies introduced new menu items that are more healthful and less calorie-laden.

Maybe it's a matter of seeing the writing on the wall. Maybe it's a conversion. Maybe not. These are the companies that gave us supersized meals in the first place, so perhaps the

ZEN OF PUBLIC RELATIONS

Sometimes a new paradigm—a different perspective—can enhance our understanding. And what could be further from the practicality of public relations than spirituality?

To better understand an important public relations concept, consider the principle of interconnectedness—the duality in which everything is related. What appears to be opposite is not separate; it is only the other end of the one pole, the other side of the same lake.

When we think of public relations issues, our tendency often is to identify them as either *obstacles* or *opportunities*. But such words mask an important relationship. The spirituality associated with Zen values harmony. A problem is not necessarily something negative but instead something lacking harmony, a point of yet-unrealized potential. An obstacle puts us at a crossroads, allowing us to go this way or that, with consequences based on the choice we make.

The ultimate public relations problem is a *crisis*. Yet even that word gives us philosophical pause. Interestingly, the Chinese term *wei ji* and the parallel Japanese word *kiki,* both of which translate as "crisis," are made up of two characters—one meaning "danger," the other meaning "opportunity." A crisis is a decision point where choices point to consequences.

The job of public relations, then, is to restore harmony, to re-establish equilibrium.

health talk is simply part of the ongoing profit lust. Regardless of motivation, it's clear that fast-food companies are changing their ways in the face of mounting public concern over the issue of obesity.

Similarly, tobacco companies responded to public concern on the issue of smoking, particularly health aspects of secondhand smoke, and health-care providers have reacted to issues such as the cost of medical prescriptions.

Issues Management

An **issue** is a situation that presents matters of concern to organizations, what Abe Bakhsheshy (2003) of the University of Utah defines as a trend, an event, a development or a matter in dispute that may affect an organization. Issues exist within a changing environment and often are the result of conflicting values (either different values held by the organization and one of its publics, or a different balance among similar values). In their book *Agenda Setting*, John Dearing and Everett Rogers define an issue as "a social problem, often conflictual, that has received media coverage" (1996, p. 4).

Bakhsheshy notes that early anticipation permits an organization to study the issue, to orient itself to deal with the issue, and to better identify and potentially involve itself with its publics. He asks several questions in analyzing issues: Which stakeholders are affected by the issue? Who has an interest? Who is in a position to exert influence? Who ought to care? Who started the ball rolling? Who is now involved?

Issues management is the process by which an organization tries to anticipate emerging issues and respond to them before they get out of hand. It is a process of monitoring and evaluating information. Like many other aspects of public relations, issues management involves potential change. For example, insurance companies, hospitals and health-maintenance organizations are all trying to predict trends within the health care industry and to have some kind of impact on the future.

As some organizations weigh their options during issues management, they use a **best practice** approach. This is a method of documenting and analyzing the behavior of an acknowledged leader in the field. This approach to organizational problem solving tries to identify a *benchmark*, a specific and measurable standard, against which an organization can compare its own products and services, with an eye toward improving these.

The best practice approach involves research into how other organizations have handled similar situations, identifying those that handle them well. It is a continuous and systematic process of measuring an organization and its products and services against the best practices of strong competitors and recognized industry leaders, in order to improve the organization's performance. Put more simply, benchmarking is the search for better ways of doing the things you do.

Peter Schwartz and Blair Gibb (1999) note three benefits of benchmarking: (1) organizational initiative that prevents internal inertia from taking over; (2) continual awareness of innovations coming from competitors; and (3) introduction of fresh air from outside the organization.

Despite its name, issues management does not focus on control; neither does it involve one-way communication nor manipulation of a public. Rather, it helps the organization interact with its publics. It may help an organization settle the issue early or divert it, or perhaps even prevent its emergence. More likely, however, the organization will have to adjust itself to the issue in some way, trying to maximize the benefits or at least minimize the negative impact. Public relations often drives this early-warning system within an organization.

Background of Issues Management

F. J. Aguilar (1967) explained **environmental scanning** as a process of seeking "information about events and relationships in a company's outside environment, the knowledge of which would assist top management in its task of charting the company's future course of action" (p. 1).

W. Howard Chase (1977) coined the term issues management, though the concept has been around since the days when Ivy Lee first did the work of what has become known as public relations. But Chase pushed the concept forward, away from a catch-as-catch-can approach and toward a more systematic technique, which he outlined in five steps (Jones and Chase, 1979). Raymond Ewing (1997) expanded this into a seven-step process.

Here is an even newer six-stage synthesis of the process of issues management:

1. Identify future issues that are likely to affect an organization. Develop an early warning scanning system that considers where the organization wants to go and looks at potential roadblocks and other outside economic, political, technological, social and other kinds of pressures on the organization. Look for forces that could help move the organization along its path.

2. Research and analyze each issue. Carefully gather as many facts as possible about these issues. Consult specialists who are particularly familiar with the issues.
3. Consider options in responding to each issue. Use creative problem-solving techniques to discover as many alternatives as possible to deal with the issue at hand. Establish your standards for success and the criteria that your organization should use to make choices among the various alternatives.
4. Develop an action plan. Select the most appropriate option, usually in terms of cost-effectiveness, practicality and organizational fit. Then develop a specific plan to address the issue.
5. Implement this plan, giving as much energy and as many resources as it warrants.
6. Evaluate the effectiveness of the response, both during its implementation when there is still time to make appropriate adjustments and when the program is completed.

Archie Boe (1979), then CEO of Allstate Insurance Companies, explained that

issues management and strategic planning are both born of the dynamic tradition in American business management that rejects the passive approach of hoping to know the future and merely adjusting to it, for an affirmative posture of *creating* the future and *fitting* the corporate enterprise into it

(p. 5; emphasis in the original)

After interviewing 248 public relations managers, Martha Lauzen (1997) found a link between two-way public relations and both the early detection and accurate diagnosis of issues: "The answer lies in the confluence of public relations and issues management as they become true boundary-spanning functions, acting as the eyes and ears of organizations, serving as parts of an early warning system" (p. 79).

For practitioners, the conclusion is that two-way public relations, which inherently involves issues management, leads to more effective outcomes and ultimately will move the practitioner into the *dominant coalition*, that grouping of managers and executives who together wield power and make decisions within organizations. The expectation is that senior public relations managers are part of their organization's dominant coalition.

Risk Management

Strategic communicators often give the name **risk management** to the process of identifying, controlling and minimizing the impact of uncertain events on an organization. The term is used in many disciplines—from politics to engineering, business to biology.

Public relations people sometimes need to force their organizations and clients to listen to criticism. Many public relations disasters are rooted in the myopic failure to learn from others' mistakes or in the shortsightedness to fail to address internal flaws.

One reason for this is what Michael Regester and Judy Larkin (2005) call "believing your own PR." The risk management specialist gives as an example Nestlé International, which, he says, saw itself as a nurturing company and thus failed to recognize the intensity of criticism over its marketing of infant formula, an international protest and boycott that lasted more than 35 years and cost the corporation much in bad publicity, lost customers, legal fees and a weakened reputation.

Phase One

STEP
1

Similarly, Dow Corning saw itself as a conscientious company and believed that science was on its side, so it aggressively countered criticism and public concern about the safety of its silicone breast implants. When class-action lawsuits were filed, the company failed to take quick action because it didn't think any was needed. It followed common (and bad) legal advice to say nothing sympathetic about women who claimed they were harmed by the company's project, prepping the case for legal courts while ignoring the court of public opinion, where reputations are made and broken.

The case yielded record settlements: $5.4 million to one woman, $7.3 to another, $27.9 million to three women, $7 million to another victim. Dow Corning ended up in bankruptcy for nine years. The Dow Corning fiasco has been called a textbook case of how to mismanage a crisis.

CASE IN POINT Exxon

Exxon was another company that refused to take the critics seriously, apparently having little interest in risk management. As a result, the company suffered in the long term for its mishandling of the Alaska oil spill caused by its freighter *Valdez* in 1989.

Showing the ramifications of continuing anti-Exxon sentiment, a jury in 2000 ordered the oil company (now called ExxonMobil) to pay $3.5 billion for defrauding Alabama on royalties involving oil wells in the Gulf of Mexico. That verdict was set aside, and in a new trial in November 2003, the jury awarded the state damages of $11.9 billion. Jurors said one reason for the high penalties was that the Alaska situation showed them that Exxon was a company that could not be trusted and deserved to be punished.

A state appeals court later reduced the award to $3.5 billion, and in late 2007 the Alabama Supreme Court split on partisan lines (Republicans for ExxonMobil, the lone Democrat siding with the state) to eliminate the punitive damages, assessing the company a mere $52 million—the amount it had failed to pay Alabama in the first place. In 2008, the state came back with another lawsuit seeking $143 million in interest. Meanwhile, the company went to court because it said the state charged it too much in tax.

The case clearly revived public distrust of the corporate giant and underscored the long-term consequences of public opinion turned sour against a company.

While ExxonMobil in 2011 posted profits of $41 billion, it also has been probed for its political contributions and faced other lawsuits on human rights violation in Venezuela and pollution at a Texas refinery. Meanwhile, critics also saw the whole Exxon–Alabama affair as another example of the stench of corruption in state politics, calling for ethics charges against the eight Republican justices who, according to media reports, had accepted a total of $5.5 million in political contributions from ExxonMobil over the previous five years. Legal cases being what they are, the situation could drag on for years, providing a continuing embarrassment to ExxonMobil.

In another case involving a gasoline leak, a Maryland jury in 2011 ordered ExxonMobil to pay more than $1.5 billion (more than two-thirds of that in punitive damages), on top of a previous $150 judgment for another case related to the same spill. Clearly the company's reputation makes it easy for juries to exact a price.

CASE IN POINT	**Duke University**

Risk management involves a careful assessment of the potential impact on both the organization and its publics. Often this means taking into consideration the emotional elements that may be in play. An example of this is the "perfect storm" effect of the 2006 rape case at Duke University at Durham, N.C., what a British newspaper called a "gourmet feast, a deluxe news-hook omelette."

Here are the ingredients in that dish, destined to catapult the case into a major public relations crisis:

- *Race*. A black woman accused three white members of a university lacrosse team of raping her at a team party.
- *Sex*. In addition to the rape charge itself, the woman was an exotic dancer and escort who had been hired by the team as a stripper. One of the arrested players had an earlier charge of shouting antigay epithets at a man.
- *Class and Privilege*. The woman was a single mother at a small primarily black school, also in Durham. The accused were prep school graduates from wealthy families from Long Island.
- *Credibility*. The ongoing investigation yielded much confusion and many inconsistencies, much of this because the accuser's story kept changing. Additionally a second stripper disputed the rape claim. Evidence showed that the victim appeared to be under the influence of alcohol or drugs when she arrived at the party and that she had had multiple sex partners earlier in the day.
- *Legal Reversals*. Midway through the investigation, the rape charges were dismissed, but kidnapping and sexual offense charges remained. Eventually the state attorney general dismissed all charges.
- *Politics*. The district attorney was running for re-election, and many observers claimed he exploited the media interest to win votes. He later was disbarred for improper actions in the case, the first such penalty in state history.
- *Police Collusion*. The police department violated its own investigation rules in favor of the district attorney and allowed improper photo identification.
- *Media Scrutiny*. The district attorney gave at least 70 media interviews. National print and television media converged on Durham. Even international media covered the case.
- *Cause Advocates*. The case also fed several single-issue advocates: a feminist who said her research shows that women never lie about rape; another who said the case exploits social prejudice against strippers; others allying themselves with the racial themes; still others who decried white victimization.
- *Premature Campus Reaction*. The university tried to balance the seriousness of the issue, compassion for the victim, cooperation with police, and support for its students. In retrospect, campus actions left it open to criticism from all sides. The college forced the coach's resignation, canceled the remainder of the team's season and announced the suspension of the following season (later lifted).

With the legal charges dismissed and the resulting lawsuits by the fired coach, the three accused players and the rest of the team back in practice, the situation settled down. School public relations people recalled that their first priority was to the North Carolina media with which they interacted frequently, the media "we will be dealing with when the rest go home," said one official.

Notably, the one winner may have been the campus bookstore. Sales of Duke lacrosse T-shirts tripled during the months of public scrutiny.

Crisis Management

The purpose of issues management, as previously noted, is to deal with issues before they get out of hand. When that happens, the issue becomes a crisis.

Crisis management is the name given to the process by which an organization deals with out-of-control issues. But "management" is a bit of a misnomer. It's more about *coping* with crises.

Consider this analogy: issues management is like steering a sailboat. You run with the wind when it happens to be blowing in the direction you want to go, and you tack to make some progress against the wind. Sometimes you stall when there is no wind. But always, you adapt to an ever-changing environment. In a crisis situation, the analogy is more like trying to ride out a storm. Often the best you can do is drop sail, hang on, and hope the vessel is strong enough to survive without too much damage. A bit of luck helps, too.

Issues management deals with preparation for dealing with potential events; risk management is about implied threats; and crisis management focuses on reactive response to actual occurrences.

An organization committed to the concept of strategic communication is probably engaged in an ongoing issues management program that identifies crises in their early stages. Less nimble organizations that always seem to be in reactive mode are the ones likely to be caught off guard by a crisis.

Reality sometimes slaps you in the face and forces you to think the unthinkable. It happened at Virginia Polytechnic Institute and State University (Virginia Tech) in Blacksburg, Virginia, and at Columbine High School in Littleton, Colorado; and it happened in New York City with the attack on the World Trade Center.

What happened in Chicago in 1983 remains an example of how companies can be unshakable in facing the unthinkable. Johnson & Johnson woke up in crisis when somebody laced its Tylenol medicine with poisonous cyanide. Seven Chicago-area residents died. That's an unthinkable tragedy for a pharmaceutical company. As the country worried about the safety of its medicines (not only Tylenol, but by extension, all packaged medicine), Johnson & Johnson quickly issued a nationwide warning. It pulled 31 million bottles of Tylenol from store shelves. It then reintroduced the medicine with a triple-seal tamper-resistant package that soon became an industry standard, and it offered customer incentives such as free replacements and discount coupons. The incident also led insurance companies to introduce malicious-product-tampering coverage to companies that cover the cost of a recall, interruption of business, and public relations/marketing costs associated with rehabilitating the product and its brand. Amid predictions that the Tylenol brand was doomed, the company saw a quick recovery of its 35 percent market share and in the process fostered an ongoing customer loyalty.

Today, more than 20 years later, the legacy of Johnson & Johnson is a case study in good crisis communication and solid public relations, a morality tale that shows the value of a corporate conscientiousness that places its customers first and keeps its promise of safety.

But considering the subsequent scandals associated with corporations such as Blackwater, Enron, WorldCom and Arthur Andersen, obviously some companies didn't get the point. Nevertheless, those that did take note learned the value of proactive management and quick communication in crisis situations. Those forward-looking companies realized that preparedness is the key to effective issues management, particularly in crisis situations. James Lukaszewski

STRATEGIC PRINCIPLES FOR CRISIS MANAGEMENT

The strategic approach to crisis management might be encompassed in the following six principles:

1. *Existing Relationships*. During a crisis, communicate with employees, volunteers, stockholders, donors, community leaders, customers, government and professional authorities and other constituent groups, as well as with colleagues. Minimally, the principle of existing relationships means keep everyone informed, because their continued support will be important in your rebuilding activities following the crisis.

2. *Media-as-Ally*. Crises invite scrutiny because they have a potential impact on a large number of people. The media-as-ally principle calls for treating the news media as allies that provide opportunities to communicate with key publics. If the media become intrusive and/or hostile, this often is because an organization has not been forthcoming in providing legitimate information to the media and its other publics. A good pre-existing program of media relations can minimize media hostility.

3. *Reputational Priorities*. Your top priority after safety issues is to your organization's reputation. Remembering this can help you focus on doing what's best for your customers, employees and other key publics. Set objectives that deal with maintaining (or if necessary, restoring) your credibility. Use the crisis as an opportunity to enhance your reputation for social responsibility with your various publics.

4. *Quick Response*. Be accessible to your publics as quickly as possible. A standard guideline for crises that capture the immediate attention of the news media is the one-hour rule. Within an hour of learning about a crisis, the organization should have its first message available to its publics, particularly the media (which generally is the most compelling public in the early stages of an active crisis). For less attention-getting crises, an organization might be able to prepare for five or six hours before going public.

5. *Full Disclosure*. Silence is not an acceptable response during a crisis. Without admitting fault and without speculating about facts not yet known, the organization should provide as much information as possible. The presumption should be that everything the organization knows should be made available. Any decision not to release certain information should be based on careful deliberation with specific justification for the silence. Use of misleading or false information is never an ethical option.

6. *One Voice*. The principle of one voice calls for a single, trained spokesperson to represent the organization. If multiple spokespersons are needed, each should be aware of what the others are saying, and all should work together from the same set of facts and the same coordinated message

Phase One

STEP
1

(1997) focuses on a six-step program of preparedness: (1) early and competent leadership; (2) a prioritized approach; (3) strategies to preserve and/or recover the organization's reputation; (4) implementation of effective plans; (5) preauthorization for the organization to act quickly on its own; and (6) a response based on openness, truthfulness and empathy.

Some experts have banded together as a kind of self-help group to guide each other in risk and crisis situations. One such coalition is the British-based Crisis Communications Network (CCN), a register of business and communication people with experience in managing crises that is associated with the Institute for Public Relations. The CCN focuses on both external and internal communications, and it offers strong encouragement for engaging in employee communication to prevent potentially hurtful rumors from developing in the first place. Speaking about the network, Morag Cuddeford-Jones (2002) lists several tips for issues management:

- Develop active dialogue with various stakeholders.
- Make sure an issue is worth trying to manage.
- Nurture expert contacts who can provide third-party research and endorsement when necessary.
- Form a coalition with organizations similar to yours.
- Create a risk-management plan and review it regularly, updating and modifying it as necessary.
- Include senior management on this team.

Unpredicted, but Predictable

One thing to remember about crises: they may be sudden and unpredicted, but they seldom are unpredictable. Crises are more like volcanoes that smolder for a while before they erupt. Warning signs abound, at least to the trained eye.

A study by the Institute for Crisis Management (crisisexperts.com) reported in 2011 that only 39 percent of companies' crises burst suddenly onto the scene, while 61 percent had been smoldering situations that eventually ignited. The biggest crisis categories were white-collar crime (20 percent), facility damage (11 percent), casualty accidents (10 percent) and workplace violence (9 percent). Tying at 8 percent were labor disputes and mismanagement (which was down significantly from the previous year at 16 percent).

All of these represent areas in which organizations should be paying attention to the quality of their performance and its impact on their reputation. Even though many crises are triggered by natural disasters such as floods, earthquakes, and so on, many of these are links with human and organizational error: incompetent or unprepared management, repairs or readiness steps that were undone, warning signs that were unheeded.

Overall, the institute reported that management caused 50 percent of all crises, with employees causing another 32 percent. Only 18 percent were caused by outside influences.

The petroleum industry topped the study's Top 10 list of most crisis-prone industries, followed by ship building and repair, automobile industry, banking, air transport, pharmaceutical companies, security brokers, computers, coal mining and software.

The Top 10 specific crisis-prone companies was BP (of the Gulf oil-spill mess), followed by Toyota, Massey Energy, Goldman Sachs, Hewlett Packard, British Airways, Johnson &

Johnson, Transocean (also of the Gulf oil leak), Wal-Mart and Halliburton (also associated with the oil leak).

The institute concludes that two-thirds of the crises never need to reach crisis stage and could be prevented by effective risk-management programs that involve an appropriate communication plan and that put a premium on organization reputation—two issues paramount in public relations.

CASE IN POINT   Chilean Mine Rescue

Here's an example of good crisis communication. In 2010, the world watched as 33 men were trapped in a copper–gold mine in Chile. Following a cave-in, the men were able to signal that all were alive a half-mile below the earth's surface. But the government estimated that it would take four months to rescue them.

Two days' worth of emergency food rations stretched to more than two weeks before a lifeline hold could be dropped to provide the miners with fresh air and more food. Chilean health officials put the trapped miners on an exercise regimen.

After 69 days, far sooner than anticipated, the rescue shaft was completed and the rescue itself went flawlessly as the world watched in real time.

The trapped foreman of the work crew was in radio contact with mine owners and government officials. Communication transparency was key: videos were sent to the surface, including a 40-minute video recorded on a mini-camera sent from the surface through the emergency shaft. One miner organized an exercise regimen to help them lose weight and girth so they could fit through the small rescue shaft being drilled. Another served as the group's spiritual leader, setting up a chapel, leading daily prayers and distributing rosaries sent by Pope Benedict to each miner. Another miner monitored the health of his trapped colleagues. Still another became the host of numerous video journals sent to the surface.

Shortly before the rescue, the miners were prepped for their encounter with reporters, helping them deal with the media attention that was inevitable when they were rescued. The director of the government rescue program, a former radio journalist, gave hour-long daily training to the miners as they neared the end of their entrapment:

- Be yourself, speak from your heart.
- Use journalists as a way to communicate a positive message to the general public.
- Help the journalists tell your story.
- Don't become unnerved by a barrage of questions; pick the ones you want to answer.

The outcome was positive.

Above ground, the talk with reporters was about the rescue effort, without many words spent on who should be blamed or why government regulations didn't protect the miners, and so on.

Phase One

STEP 1

Phase One

> ### CASE IN POINT   Deepwater Horizon
>
> The 2010 Deepwater Horizon oil spill in the Gulf of Mexico was called the worst environmental disaster in U.S. history. It also was a public relations debacle for British Petroleum, raising questions about the capabilities of international corporations in crisis management.
>
> The events are well known: a deep-sea explosion off the coast of Louisiana killed 11 oil-rig workers and led to the release of nearly 4.9 million barrels of oil, polluting an area of 3,900 square miles. The out-of-control spill, and efforts to cap the well, led the news for weeks. The economic impact was severe: $2.5 billion in damages to the fishing industry and $24 billion to tourism, with predictions of decades-long effects.
>
> BP, once considered the greenest oil company in America, was blamed for the disaster and criticized for the way it handled it. For weeks its CEO, Tony Hayward, was the face of BP at the beginning of the crisis. He had a reputation in Britain as being a knowledgeable, trusted and seasoned corporate leader. But the confusion surrounding the facts in the crisis wore on him. Then he took his eye off the ball and was photographed sailing in a yacht race at the height of the crisis, followed by an outburst about "wanting his life back." All of this became a major liability and Hayward resigned several weeks after the explosion.
>
> How did BP handle its crisis communications?
>
> Early news releases tried to blame others, including drillers it had hired, owners of the rig and government regulators. This violated one of the tenets of good crisis communication: accept responsibility for fixing the problem and don't get caught up in laying blame.
>
> Rather quickly, BP's public relations strategy backed away from shifting blame, turning its messaging toward the future—how the company would contain the spill and compensate the victims. Toward that end, BP set up a $20 billion fund to reimburse victims for their economic loss. It was a good move, though one later threatened by charges that BP mismanaged the fund.
>
> On the point of explaining how it would contain the spill, critics observed that BP lost public confidence by ceding to the media the task (and opportunity) of providing public education about deep-water drilling. It let others tell its story, never a good step. BP eventually created an educational component to its website, but the details were too technical and confusing for average visitors to the site.
>
> A year and a half after the spill, BP engaged in some heavy-duty image repair. It launched a series of advertisements. It reported evidence that the gulf ecology was not severely damaged and that the fishing industry was showing signs of economic recovery. In some highly visible special events, BP hired chefs Emeril Lagasse and John Besh to promote gulf seafood, and it gave away fish tacos and seafood jambalaya at Sugar Bowl parties in New Orleans.
>
> Some of BP's responses raised ethical questions. For example, the company paid Google $3.7 billion to place its sponsored links above relevant news stories and other sites for search terms such as "oil spill" and "leak." It donated $5 million to the Dauphin Island Sea Lap shortly before the organization reported that dolphin deaths in the gulf were caused by cold water, not the oil.
>
> What are the public relations lessons to be learned?
>
> Inevitably, the Deepwater Horizon spill drew parallels with the rupture of the Exxon *Valdez* 21 years earlier, which had reigned as the classic example of bad crisis communications. Both companies made public relations blunders in appearing to emphasize technology over people. Both seemed to minimize the environmental consequences, and the emotional reaction to oil-slicked birds and

oil-drenched shorelines. But BP was much quicker to begin paying compensation to fishermen and other victims. It also cooperated with government regulators more than Exxon did.

Another difference was a factual one: where the fault belonged. The *Valdez* spill was caused because the ship's captain was not at the helm, and the cleanup was delayed because the company had removed clean-up equipment from the area prior to the accident as part of a corporate strategy to de-emphasize the risk of such a spill. In a poorly thought-out strategy, Exxon's CEO suggested that everyone who drives a car was responsible for the *Valdez* spill. The gulf explosion, meanwhile, resulted from the failure of safety equipment on a rig owned and operated by another company.

Both companies were accused of minimizing the extent of the spill and the environmental consequences. But BP's fault was more that it tried to remain optimistic that things were moving faster toward containing the spill without extensive or long-term pollution. It low-balled estimates of how much oil was being discharged, though some of this was based on what BP itself knew at the time.

Neither company appears to have had a workable crisis communications plan to address a worst-case scenario. Not only were the disasters unanticipated, but the companies seemed not to know how to act once they occurred. This violates another cardinal rule of crisis management: imagine the worst thing that could happen, then prepare for it.

But there are some significant differences that lead to the conclusion that BP handled the situation better than Exxon did. BP's corporate leaders were seen as part of the potential solution, rather than as avoiding responsibility and ducking public exposure as was the case in the *Valdez* spill. Also, BP produced fewer contradictory statements.

The question remains: can BP rebuild its reputation after the spill and regain credibility as a green company? Good public relations emerges from good corporate performance. Not a game of deception and misdirection, public relations is a very clear reflection of the organization, less what it says and more what it does. Thus if BP values the environment and is willing and able to stand by promises to manage the environmental recovery, BP may once again be perceived as a green organization.

When the worst nuclear accident in U.S. history occurred at Three Mile Island three and a half decades ago, it not only affected the corporation that ran the nuclear plant, it also resulted in new laws and regulatory oversight of the entire nuclear industry, a moratorium on building new plants, new requirements for emergency response planning, new rules for training and for preventative measures, and new clean-up procedures.

The Deepwater Horizon explosion is likely to fuel significant public debate about the future of off-shore drilling and how it can be made safer. A major player in this debate will be public relations, not only by the oil industry but also by government, environmental concerns and political interests.

Public Relations and Ethics

Part of your research into the situation should involve an examination of ethical aspects, particularly the basis on which practitioners and their organizations or clients make ethical decisions. You might begin by considering three classic approaches to making such determinations: deontological ethics, teleological ethics and situational ethics.

DEONTOLOGICAL ETHICS

The approach to decision making rooted in a standard or moral code is called **deontological ethics**. In essence, the deontological approach says that certain actions are, in and of themselves, good; others, bad.

On the positive side, this is a humanitarian approach in which actions are judged on basic principles of human rights and dignity. On the negative side, it can give way to a fundamentalist application of rules without regard to consequence.

An example of deontological ethics is professional codes, such as the Public Relations Member Code of Ethics (*see* Appendix B: Ethical Standards), which proclaims the intrinsic and unquestioned value of honesty, integrity, fairness, accuracy, and so on.

TELEOLOGICAL ETHICS

On the other hand, **teleological ethics** is an approach focused more on the impact that actions have on people. It is more results-oriented. The teleological approach is rooted in the notion that good actions produce good results. Thus something is judged to be ethical because it generates good consequences.

Teleological ethics asks the question: What will produce the greater good for the most people? A positive aspect of this approach is that it requires practitioners to consider the consequences of their actions. A negative aspect is that it creates a scenario in which the greater good, always difficult to calculate, sometimes is allowed to reign without account for the harm inflicted on the minority.

An example of the teleological approach also is implied in the Public Relations Society of America code, which connects the need for ethical behavior and conduct with the public interest.

SITUATIONAL ETHICS

A third approach to ethical decision making is **situational ethics** (otherwise called **ethical relativism**), which suggests that actions are ethical to the extent they reflect particular social norms. The situational approach is considered on a case-by-case basis. While an advantage of this approach is respect for cultural diversity and conflicting values, it has the mirrored disadvantage both of dominance of mainstream culture as well as an inability to judge the basic rightness or wrongness of actions.

Communication strategists help themselves and their organizations when they anticipate how they will approach ethical decisions. Without advance thinking, the planner often is left either with no guidelines on determining whether something is ethical or simply with an unexamined personal feeling. Neither of those choices is particularly useful.

Don't presume that you have to decide ahead of time which of the classic approaches to use. In truth, most organizations—as most individuals—slip back and forth among the three styles of ethical decision making. The value of advance thinking is that you can recognize

ETHICS BY COMMITTEE

Hospitals have their ethics committees, so why not public relations agencies? One such panel is found at the international public relations firm of Ruder-Finn. The company's ethics committee brings together account executives with outside ethical experts such as rabbis, ministers, priests, theologians and philosophers. Their goal: to struggle with the ethical dimension of issues and then to advise management.

Ruder-Finn's chief ethics officer, Emmanuel Tchividjian, coordinates the committee. He says the ethics team has reviewed issues such as whether the agency should continue a lucrative account with a national tourism office after a military coup in that country. After the committee (including an ethics professor at a theological seminary) went to the country to investigate, Ruder-Finn resigned from the account because it did not want to assist a military dictatorship.

The agency also considered whether to accept a book-promotion account involving the Church of Scientology. That account was rejected because the firm did not want to be involved with what it considered a religious cult.

But Ruder-Finn did accept an account with the Swiss government over the issue of money and gold that the Nazis took from Jews during the Holocaust—a particularly sensitive issue for an agency where most of the managers and staff are Jewish. That account, notes Tchividjian, was accepted on the belief that much could be gained by open communication. The committee serves to remind employees that "the bottom line is not the most important thing," he explains. "We do have to make money, but there are values that have a higher priority" (Tchividjian, interview with the author).

Another ethical innovation by Ruder-Finn was borrowed from the legal profession. When the company is approached by a potential client with an issue that raises ethical concerns, the agency conducts discovery research at the client's expense, soliciting information from industry insiders and ethicists about the moral dimension of the issue. Based on the findings, Ruder-Finn may reject the client or, conversely, it may use the information to help frame the client's position on the sensitive issue.

Phase One

STEP
1

the different foundations for determining ethical actions and responses and you can consider each approach as you make your decisions.

David Finn of the Ruder-Finn public relations agency in New York City has observed that ethical decision making is not a choice between good and bad but a choice between two conflicting goods. The challenge is first to discern the difference and then to make an appropriate choice. In a column on ethics in *Reputation Management* magazine, Finn (1998) observes that "addressing ethical issues intelligently calls for a probing as well as an open mind."

What's Next?

This concludes Step 1 of the planning process for strategic communication. Now that you have a good foundation on the situation facing an organization, next it's time to look at the organization itself.

PLANNING EXAMPLE 1 **Analyzing the Situation**

UPSTATE COLLEGE   Because it has received permission to expand from a two-year to a four-year program, Upstate College wants to develop a strategic communication plan to deal with student enrollment and retention, financial contributions and community support.

In the wake of the highly publicized recall of a defective crib toy, Tiny Tykes Toys needs a strategic communication plan focusing on consumer confidence and the eventual expansion of its customer base.

☑ *Checklist 1* **The Public Relations Situation**

To participate in this exercise, use a class or group project assigned by your instructor, or select an organization that has both your personal interest and of which you have some firsthand knowledge. For example, you might select your current business, nonprofit organization or client; a volunteer project; or an enterprise in which you were once involved. If you are a student, you might select an issue related to the college or university you attend.

Start with the basic planning questions. Careful consideration of these may satisfy your informational needs. You also may find it useful to address the more complete set of expanded planning questions. Use this checklist to the extent that the items can help you get a better understanding of the situation facing your organization. If some of these questions don't seem to address your specific planning needs, skip over them.

Basic Questions

1. What is the situation facing the organization?
2. What is the background of the situation?
3. What is the significance or importance of the situation?

Expanded Questions

A. EXISTING INFORMATION

Answer the following questions based on what you know directly or what you can learn from your client or from colleagues within your organization.

Background on the Issue

1. Is this the first time your organization has dealt with this situation, or are you setting out to modify an existing communication program?
    –   If the latter, is this a minor modification or a major one?
2. What is the cause of this situation?
3. Is there any dispute that this is the cause?
4. What is the history of this situation?
5. What are the important facts related to this situation?
6. Does this situation involve the organization's relationship with another group?
    –   If yes, what group(s)?

Consequences of the Situation

1. How important is this situation to the organization's mission?
2. How consistent is this situation with the mission statement or vision statement?
3. How serious a response is warranted to this situation?
4. What is the likely duration of this situation: one time, limited/short term or ongoing/long term?
5. Who or what is affected by this situation?
6. What predictions or trends are associated with this situation? (These can be organizational, industry-related, community relations, nation-related, etc.)
7. What potential impact can this situation make on the organization's mission or bottom line?
8. Do you consider this situation to be an opportunity (positive) or an obstacle (negative) for your organization? Why? If you consider this an obstacle, how might you turn it into an opportunity?

Resolution of the Situation

1. Might information (quality or quantity) affect how this situation is resolved?
2. How can this situation be resolved to the mutual benefit of everyone involved?
3. What priority does this situation hold for the public relations/communications staff and for the organization's top management?
4. How strong is the organization's commitment to resolving this situation?

B. RESEARCH PROGRAM

If there are any significant gaps in the existing information, you may have to conduct research to learn more about the issue. This section will guide you through consideration of that option.

What is the basis for the existing information noted above: previous formal research, informal or anecdotal feedback, organizational experience, personal observation, presumption/supposition by planner(s) and/or something else?

1. How accurate is this existing information?
2. How appropriate is it to conduct additional research?
3. What information remains to be obtained?

4. If the existing information is not highly reliable, consider additional research, such as the following:
    –   interviews with key people within the organization;
    –   review of organizational literature/information;
    –   additional personal observation;
    –   interviews with external experts or opinion leaders;
    –   surveys with representative publics.
5. What research methods will you use to obtain the needed information?

C. RESEARCH FINDINGS

After you have conducted formal research, indicate here your findings as they shed light on the issue facing your organization, and write a brief summary of the issue facing your organization.

Phase One

STEP
1

CONSENSUS CHECK

Does agreement exist within your organization and your planning team about the observations and findings about the public relations situation?

☐   Yes. Proceed to Step 2, Analyzing the Organization.

☐   No. Consider the value and/or possibility of achieving consensus before proceeding.

Analyzing
the Organization

The basis of effective communication is self-awareness. Before a successful strategic communication plan can be created, strategists must have a thorough and factual understanding of their organization: its performance, its reputation and its structure. They must also seek to understand any factors that might limit the plan's success.

Analyzing the organization begins with a clear focus on what the organization is, does and aspires to be. In broad categories, all organizations are either businesses or nonprofits. But within each of these categories are some important distinctions. Businesses are for-profit commercial organizations of various types. They might be multinational corporations (also called transnational or global corporations), or businesses with national, regional or local bases. Within these fields are businesses that can be classified as green, women-owned, minority-owned, start-up, home-based or online.

Noncommercial enterprises, sometimes called social benefit organizations, fit roughly into groupings nonprofit organizations (schools, hospitals, museums, and so on) that provide services and social enrichment, government (agencies and military units) that often involve regulatory oversight, membership associations (unions, consumer-interest groups), and non-governmental organizations (NGOs) that focus their activities on advocacy and social change. Sometimes such groups are defined by their focus: environmental, charitable, religions, cultural, service, and so on. Like corporations, nonprofit groups may be community based, national or international.

Regardless of answer, it is important that any public relations plan raises the questions: What kind of organization are we? What kind of organization do people think we are? What kind of organization do we want to be?

Often the response to that question is found in the organization's *mission statement*, a brief strategic description of the purpose of a company or nonprofit organization, indicated its major publics, and thus guides its decisions and is reflected in its actions. The mission statement focuses on the organization's present circumstances.

A *vision statement*, meanwhile, looks to the future. It is a brief strategic description of what the organization aspires to become. A vision statement serves as a starting point for positioning, which is part of Step 4 of the strategic planning process.

Some organizations also articulate a *values statement*, which is a set of beliefs that drive the organization and provide a framework for its decisions. A values statement often has a significant ethical dimension.

The second step of the strategic planning process involves a **public relations audit**, an analysis of the strengths and weaknesses of your organization or client. Writing in *Public Relations Tactics*, Rebecca Hart (2006) of the strategic communications/research firm of Hart & Partners, advises that an audit should be performed prior to developing an important new campaign, before rolling out a new product or service or after management changes within

MISSION, VISION AND VALUES STATEMENTS

Examples of Mission Statements

Aflac: To combine aggressive strategic marketing with quality products and services at competitive prices to provide the best insurance value for consumers.

Dow Chemical: To constantly improve what is essential to human progress by mastering science and technology.

Ford: We are a global family with a proud heritage passionately committed to providing personal mobility for people around the world.

Google: Google's mission is to organize the world's information and make it universally accessible and useful.

Nike: To bring inspiration and innovation to every athlete* in the world. (*If you have a body, you are an athlete.)

Examples of Vision Statements

Amazon: Our vision is to be earth's most customer-centric company; to build a place where people can come to find and discover anything they might want to buy online.

Avon: To be the company that best understands and satisfies the product, service and self-fulfillment needs of women—globally.

HSBC: To be the world's local bank.

Toys 'R' Us: Our vision is to put joy in kids' hearts and a smile on parents' faces.

Examples of Value Statement

Microsoft: As a company, and as individuals, we value integrity, honesty, openness, personal excellence, constructive self-criticism, continual self-improvement and mutual respect. We are committed to our customers and partners, and have a passion for technology. We take on big challenges and pride ourselves on seeing them through. We hold ourselves accountable to our customers, shareholders, partners and employees by honoring our commitments, providing results and striving for the highest quality.

an organization. On the company website (hartandpartners.com), she further suggests that audits should be conducted every five to seven years, as well as following a crisis situation. Hart also notes the value of audits for individual public relations practitioners:

> First, you will gain a better understanding of how communications fits into your organization's big picture and how you can help the organization succeed. Senior managers will appreciate your numbers-oriented approach to communications and will be more likely to turn to you for advice on measuring results in the future. Finally, you'll have demonstrated strategic thinking, initiative and business-savvy through your interactions with upper management, which will give you increased credibility for future situations.
>
> (2006)

A traditional method drawn from marketing is called **SWOT analysis**, because it considers the organization's strengths, weaknesses, opportunities and threats. Typically, a SWOT analysis would look at each of these from two perspectives: internal and external. Such an analysis would consider both internal factors and external forces when focusing on strengths, for example, and not allow an illusion that the organization itself is strong but that all weaknesses come from outside. (Recall the findings of the Institute for Crisis Management, noted in the previous chapter, which found that 82 percent of corporate and organizational crises began on the inside, most of them because of mismanagement.)

What follows here is a more elaborate analysis focusing on three aspects of the organization: internal environment, public perception and external environment. Exhibit 2.1 shows the relationship among the various elements of a public relations audit.

Before moving on to the details of the analysis, it is important to point out that candor is the key to this step. To create an effective communication program, you must take an honest look at your organization, identifying its weaknesses and limitations as well as its strengths. If your organization is second best, admit it and proceed from that basis. Don't delude yourself by pretending that your organization is something that it's not. No successful public relations program has ever been built on fiction, and it does not serve your purposes to overlook flaws or shortcomings within your organization. However, temper your candor with tact. Brutal or indiscriminate honesty may turn off a client or a boss.

Internal Environment

Because public relations involves more than words, begin the audit by looking at the organization's performance and structure, and any internal impediments to success. Here is an overview of each.

Performance

The most important aspect of the internal environment is *performance*. This involves the quality of the goods and services provided by the organization as well as the viability of the causes and ideas it espouses. The audit looks at this quality both as it is now and as it was in the past. It also considers the level of satisfaction that the organizational leadership has with this quality. Review the discussion of benchmarking in Step 1, since one of the purposes of benchmarking is to help an organization improve its performance.

EXHIBIT 2.1 The Public Relations Audit

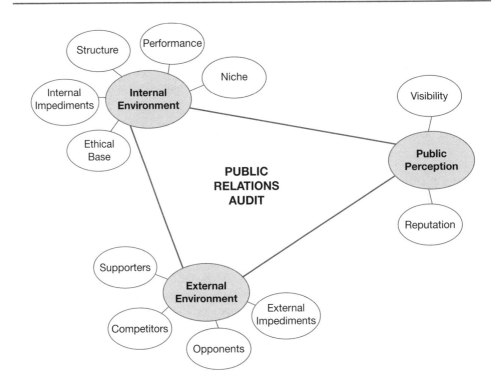

Niche

Within the topic of performance, the internal audit also looks at the organization's *niche*: its specialty, the function or role that makes the organization different from other organizations. The word **niche** originally referred to a wall recess or alcove for displaying a vase of flowers, a religious statue, a bust or some other accent piece. In the context of public relations and marketing, a niche retains some of that original notion. It is a viewing point, the nook or cubbyhole that an organization occupies in a position for all to see.

Structure

The audit also considers the **structure** of the public relations operation within the organization. Specifically, it reviews the purpose or mission of the organization as it relates to the situation at hand, as well as the role public relations plays within the organization's administration. One particularly important consideration is whether public relations sits at the management table as part of the organization's decision-making process or whether it merely receives orders after the decisions are made by others.

The audit also inventories organizational resources that can be marshaled for the communication program, such as personnel, equipment, time and budgets. No decisions or commitments are being made at this point as to what resources to use. During the audit stage, you merely are identifying the organization's available resources as they relate to the situation to be addressed.

Ethical Base

Public relations has been called the conscience of an organization, serving as its ethical base and moral grounding. In analyzing the internal environment of an organization, give thought to this ethical base. Consider whether the organization has a stated ethical ideal, and note if such an ideal is structural to the organization or personal to certain individuals. That is, is an ethical perspective based on how the organization sees itself, or is it merely the concern of an individual currently on the scene? If structural, the ethical base is likely to continue beyond the personal tenure of any individual manager or executive.

Internal Impediments

The final part of this internal audit is a look at **internal impediments**. Here you consider any impediments or obstacles within the organization that might limit the effectiveness of the public relations program. For example, many practitioners have expressed that their college education did not prepare them for the lack of organizational support, the need for continuing vigilance and the amount of political infighting that goes on within some organizations. Wounded egos, shortsighted executives, company favorites and other barriers must be considered as you develop the program.

The term *impediment* is chosen with care. An impediment is not an insurmountable barrier, such as a road blocked off for repaving. Rather, it is a hindrance, more like a slow-moving truck on a country road. You can allow the truck to set the pace and remain behind it, or you can carefully and safely pass the truck and continue on your way. Or you can find another road.

Public Perception

The second focus for a public relations audit is public perception. What people think about the organization is the key focus for the public relations audit. This perception is based on both visibility and reputation.

Visibility

The extent to which an organization is known is its **visibility**. More subtly, this includes whether people know about an organization, what they know about it and how accurate this information is. Public relations practitioners can do a great deal to affect the visibility of their organization or client.

Reputation

Based on an organization's visibility is its **reputation**, which deals with how people evaluate the information they have. It is the general, overall and long-term impression that people have of an organization. Reputation is based on both word and deed—that is, on the verbal, visual and behavioral messages, both planned and unplanned, that come from an organization.

Phase One

STEP 2

Reputation is part of the social capital of an organization, arguably its most important public relations asset. Though we speak of reputation as a single perception, it really may be inconsistent, varying from one public to another and from one time to another. Reputation generally lags behind an organization's conscious attempt to affect the way people perceive it. (For a fuller discussion of reputation, *see* the author's website: faculty.buffalostate.edu/smithrd/PR/reputation.htm.)

Generally, the stronger the organization's visibility and the more positive its reputation, the greater the ability it has to build on this positive base. On the other hand, low visibility suggests the need to create more awareness, and a poor reputation calls for efforts to rehabilitate the public perception of the organization, first by making sure the organization is offering quality performance, and then by trying to bring awareness into harmony with that performance.

Writing in *Communication World*, Pamela Klein (1999) notes that psychologically, a company with a solid reputation earns the benefit of the doubt in times of crisis. Supporting her claim, she points to an Ernst & Young study, *Measures That Matter*, which found that 40 percent of a company's market value is based on nonfinancial assets, including reputation. Klein also cites a Burson-Marsteller study, *Maximizing Corporate Reputations*, which reported that a CEO's reputation accounts for 40 percent of how a company is viewed by stakeholders and other publics.

SOURCES OF INFORMATION FOR A PUBLIC RELATIONS AUDIT

You can get information for a public relations audit from several different sources. Consider the following steps in gathering the information you will need:

1. See if past research has addressed some of the relevant issues and obtain that information.
2. Check the public information about your organization, such as your annual reports, past news releases and files of published stories about your organization.
3. Ask people close to your organization if they can provide some of the necessary information from their own experience. Talk with managers and long-time employees. Talk especially with your front-line staff, such as clerks and sales representatives, and with the key service providers, such as nurses in a hospital or teachers in a school. Ask all of these sources what customers and other people outside the organization are asking and saying.
4. Conduct your own research, beginning with free or low-cost technology for online polling. SurveyMonkey and Zoomerang are probably the best known, but dozens of companies offer similar products.
5. Check out your organization with an Internet search engine. In particular, see what bloggers may be saying about you and what others are posting on social media.

If additional information still is needed, conduct more formal research. Begin by broadening your resources for informal research. Eventually you may find that you require more formal research techniques. (See Appendix A: Applied Research for more information on secondary and primary research.)

A 2006 survey of health-care executives in collaboration with the Public Relations Society of America's Health Academy showed that 64 percent of CEOs rate reputation as critical or very important to their organization's success. Two-thirds (66 percent) say a positive shift in reputation can significantly or dramatically impact the bottom line, while 86 percent said a negative shift would hurt the organization. All self-reported that their corporations have good or excellent reputations. Aside from, perhaps, a bit of self-deception or wishful thinking about their own reputations, the CEOs clearly see the importance of a good reputation as a real business asset.

This chapter's strategic planning checklist on analyzing public perception contains an Image Index, a tool developed to help you determine the public perception of an organization. The index is a series of contrasting characteristics or attributes—fun or tedious, expensive or inexpensive, risky or safe—that can be applied to any organization. Obviously there is no right or wrong response to any of these characteristics, and the index does not lead to a numerical answer. Rather, it is meant to stimulate your insight. By considering your organization in relation to these terms, you may come to an inference or a conclusion that perhaps you did not have before. In the planning process, you can use the index twice, first based on what the organization thinks of itself and later based on what its publics think of it.

The related concepts of visibility and reputation play a significant role in crisis communication. Appendix D: Effective Media Engagement is rooted in the premise that, particularly in crisis situations when an organization's visibility is high, an important public relations objective should be to focus on reputation.

External Environment

The analysis of the organization concludes with an examination of its external environment. In particular, this analysis looks at supporters, competitors, opponents and other external impediments. Here is an overview of each.

Supporters

Every organization has a group of **supporters**, the people and groups who currently or at least potentially are likely to help the organization achieve its objectives. What groups share similar interests and values?

Competitors

Likewise, most organizations have **competitors**, people or groups who are doing the same thing as you in essentially the same arena. Research suggests that in a highly competitive environment, public relations activities often use messages and communication tactics to highlight differences with competitors, while lower levels of competition may lend themselves less to advocacy and more to relationship building. But an organization's environment also may be uneven; it may be competitive with one public while cooperative with another.

Additionally, the mere fact that an organization is doing essentially the same thing as yours does not make it an opponent. Proximity is important. For example, a candidate for mayor in Seattle may have several competitors, but the candidate for mayor in Baltimore is not one of them. Indeed, organizations doing similar things in different areas might better be considered as colleagues and, as such, valuable resources for sharing information and perhaps assistance.

Opponents

Another important aspect of the external analysis is to consider the nature of any rivalry that may exist. **Opponents** are people or groups who are against your organization, perhaps because of something it says or does, perhaps because of its very existence. They have the potential to damage your organization by limiting its ability to pursue its mission and achieve its goals.

Note that there can be a big difference between a competitor, who provides a similar product or service, and an opponent, who is fighting your organization. Consider a store selling fur coats: a competitor might be the other fur store across town, while an opponent might be an animal rights group. The other store just wants to sell its products, while the activists want to see you go out of business.

Even opponents come in different shapes and sizes, and planners have some important questions to ask about the nature of opposition. In some situations—political campaigns come to mind—opponents are competitors and opposing candidates, along with their political organizations and supporters, have a primary strategy of besting the opposition candidates.

Consider the various types of opponents and the potential impact of communication when you are analyzing this aspect of your external environment:

ADVOCATE

One type of opponent, an **advocate**, may oppose you because they support something else, and you appear to stand in the way of their goal. Their tactics are mainly vocal. Through public communication, you may be able to find common ground for discussion and perhaps even the creation of an alliance between your organization and the advocates.

DISSIDENT

Another type of opponent, a **dissident**, may oppose you primarily because of the position you hold or the actions you have undertaken. Their opposition is not irrational, and communication that addresses their interests and concerns might soften their opposition.

ANTI

A dissident on a global scale is called an **anti**. Antis are people or groups who seem to oppose everything. Often such opposition is generic toward any kind of change or toward any established institution, so public communication probably would have little impact on them unless it were able to show that the presumed change is only illusional. Realize that the antis are suspicious of your organization in the first place, so they probably won't trust your messages.

ACTIVIST

Similar to an advocate, an **activist** seeks change. But the activist has a range of tactics beyond discussion. For activists, opposition to your organization may be a by-product of their goal. Communication might reveal and promote a common basis for at least limited cooperation. Realize that activists, by definition, seek something specific and tangible, so talk alone won't move them.

MISSIONARY

A **missionary** is a self-righteous activist in support of a cause, often operating under the presumption of moral imperative. Communication would have only limited potential for moderating the opposition of missionaries, though it could help the organization avoid being an obvious target.

ZEALOT

One type of opponent is difficult to deal with. A **zealot** is a single-issue activist with a missionary fervor, so public communication is unlikely to coax zealots out of their opposition. These are the folks willing to engage in civil disobedience and risk jail to advance their cause.

FANATIC

Another type of opponent is dangerous. A **fanatic** is a zealot without the social stabilizers. These are the suicide bombers and terrorist snipers ready to go to any lengths in their opposition. Because of their willingness to undertake a no-holds-barred fight and to suffer personal injury, public communication can have little impact on them, though it may impact the less fanatical supporters in the cause.

External Impediments

Additionally, consider any **external impediments** such as social, political or economic factors outside an organization that might limit the effectiveness of a public relations program.

What's Next?

This concludes Step 2 of the planning process for strategic communication. You now should have information and insight into your organization's strengths and limitations, providing a strong foundation on which to build. Next you will focus attention on the various publics of the organization.

PLANNING EXAMPLE 2 **Analyzing the Organization**

Here is the analysis for Upstate College.

Internal Environment

Upstate College is a private liberal-arts college with 2,000 students, primarily commuters and residents from within a 100-mile radius. Most of the students had average grades in high school. They selected Upstate because of its reputation for small classes, reasonable tuition and practical programs. In the past, about half the graduates went into the workforce and half transferred to four-year colleges and universities. The college has a news bureau and marketing office with a one-person staff assisted by freelancers and alumni volunteers. The office has equipment for desktop publishing, and the college publishes a weekly student newspaper and a quarterly alumni newsletter and oversees a website. It has only a token advertising budget.

Public Perception

Upstate College sees its reputation as being beneficial, relatively inexpensive, practical and an essential ingredient in the educational mix of this part of the state.

External Environment

Higher education has been a relatively noncompetitive environment until recent years, when lower numbers of students, fewer funds and more alternatives for students have combined to create a climate that is somewhat competitive, though not unfriendly. Competition includes a private four-year college with very high entrance standards and even higher tuition, a large state university with entrance standards similar to Upstate's at about half the tuition, and a community college with only token costs, minimal entrance requirements and a background (and continuing reputation) as a trade school. Upstate City recently has lost several major employers and weakening family finances have begun to affect the ability of some Upstate College students to remain full-time students. Research reveals declining numbers of students in most area high schools, indicating a shrinking pool of traditional-age candidates for college. Additionally, general research reveals growing educational opportunities for web-based distance learning.

Here is the analysis for Tiny Tykes Toys.

Internal Environment

Tiny Tykes Toys manufactures toys for infants and toddlers. It recently voluntarily recalled one of its crib toys, a plush animal doll with a shiny nose. When babies chewed on the nose, it secreted an indelible green dye into their mouths and on their faces that lasted for several weeks. The dye was harmless, but the consumer lawsuits (minor) and resulting publicity (major and sensationalized) have caused a decrease in sales of other Tiny Tykes toys. The company has 130 union workers and 27 management staff. It also has a two-person public relations/marketing staff. Unrelated to the recall, but happening around the same time, a small but vocal group of employees began agitating for increased pay and shorter working hours.

Public Perception

The recall endangered the company's reputation for quality among stockholders, consumers, pediatricians and other interest groups. The defect has been eliminated in new versions of the toy. The company perceives its image as fun, low-tech, inexpensive, beneficial and safe.

External Environment

The business environment for children's toys is highly competitive, and it has become more so due to increasing international rivals and the expansion into the toy market of domestic companies once associated primarily with children's clothing. Tiny Tykes has several competitors, some of them nationally known companies with huge promotional budgets. Several of these companies have products of similar quality and cost to Tiny Tykes; they currently enjoy a more favorable reputation because of the recall. The overall business environment for toys is a growing and highly competitive market. The dissident employee faction has the potential for contributing to a wider consumer backlash against the company.

☑ *Checklist 2A* **Internal Environment**

Basic Questions

1. What is the quality of your organization's performance?
2. What communication resources, including budget, are available?
3. How supportive is the organization of public relations activity?

Expanded Questions

A. EXISTING INFORMATION

Answer the following questions based on what you know directly or what you can learn from your client or colleagues within your organization.

Performance

1. What service/product do you provide related to the issue identified in the Strategic Planning Exercise in Step 1?
2. What are the criteria for determining its quality?
3. What is its quality?
4. Within the last three years, has the quality improved, remained unchanged or deteriorated?
5. How satisfied is organizational leadership with this quality?
6. What benefit or advantage does the product/service offer?
7. What problems or disadvantages are associated with this product/service?
8. What is the niche or specialty that sets you apart from competitors?
9. How has the service/product changed within the last three years?
10. How is the service/product likely to change within the next two years?
11. Should changes be introduced to improve the service/product?
12. Are organizational leaders willing to make such changes?

Structure

1. What is the purpose/mission of your organization related to this issue?
2. How does this issue fit into the organizational vision?
3. Is this expressed in a strategic business plan for your organization?
4. What communication resources are available for potential public relations/marketing communication activity: personnel, equipment, time, money and/or something else?
5. Within the next three years, are these resources likely to increase, remain unchanged or decrease?
6. How strong is the public relations/communication staff's role in the organization's decision-making process?

Phase One

STEP
2

Internal Impediments

1. How supportive is the internal environment for public relations activities?
2. Are there any impediments or obstacles to success that come from within your organization:

<u>Among top management?</u>
- Are these impediments caused by policy/procedure?
- Are these impediments deliberate?

<u>Among public relations/marketing staff?</u>
- Are these impediments caused by policy/procedure?
- Are these impediments deliberate?

<u>Among other internal publics?</u>
- Are these impediments caused by policy/procedure?
- Are these impediments deliberate?

3. If you have identified impediments, how can you overcome them?

B. RESEARCH PROGRAM

If there are any significant gaps in the existing information, you may have to conduct research to learn more about the internal environment. This section will guide you through consideration of that option.

1. What is the basis for the existing information noted above: previous formal research, informal or anecdotal feedback, organizational experience, personal observation, presumption/supposition by planner(s) and/or something else?
2. How accurate is this existing information?
3. How appropriate would it be to conduct additional research?
4. What information remains to be obtained?
5. If the existing information is not highly reliable, consider additional research, such as the following:
   - interviews with key people within the organization;
   - review of organizational literature/information;
   - additional personal observation;
   - interviews with external experts or opinion leaders;
   - surveys with representative publics.
6. What research methods will you use to obtain the needed information?

C. RESEARCH FINDINGS

After you have conducted formal research, indicate your findings as they shed light on the internal environment of your organization and write a brief summary of the internal environment.

☑ Checklist 2B **Public Perception**

Basic Questions

1. How well known is your organization?
2. What is the reputation of your organization?
3. How do you want to affect this reputation?

Expanded Questions

A. EXISTING INFORMATION

Answer the following questions based on what you know directly or what you can learn from your client or colleagues within your organization.

Reputation

1. How visible is your service/product?
2. How widely used is your service/product?
3. How is the product/service generally perceived?
4. How is your organization generally perceived?
5. Is the public perception about your organization correct?
6. What communication already has been done about this situation?
7. Within the last three years, has your organization's reputation improved, remained unchanged or deteriorated?
8. How satisfied is organizational leadership with this reputation?

Image Index

Place an "X" at the appropriate location on the continuum of what this key public thinks of your organization's product(s) or service(s):

Contemporary	__	__	__	__	__	Traditional
Fun	__	__	__	__	__	Tedious
High-Tech	__	__	__	__	__	Low-Tech
Ordinary	__	__	__	__	__	Distinguished
Expensive	__	__	__	__	__	Inexpensive
Idealistic	__	__	__	__	__	Practical
Modest	__	__	__	__	__	Pretentious
Scarce	__	__	__	__	__	Abundant
Worthless	__	__	__	__	__	Beneficial
Efficient	__	__	__	__	__	Inefficient
Ordinary	__	__	__	__	__	Innovative
Essential	__	__	__	__	__	Luxury
Risky	__	__	__	__	__	Safe
High-Quality	__	__	__	__	__	Low-Quality

Phase One

STEP
2

B. RESEARCH PROGRAM

If there are any significant gaps in the existing information, you may have to conduct research to learn more about the public perception of your organization. This section will guide you through consideration of that option.

1. What is the basis for the existing information noted above: previous formal research, informal or anecdotal feedback, organizational experience, personal observation, presumption/supposition by planner(s) and/or something else?
2. How reliable is this existing information?
3. How appropriate would it be to conduct additional research?
4. If the existing information is not highly reliable, consider additional research, such as the following:
    *   interviews with key people within the organization;
    *   review of organizational literature/information;
    *   additional personal observation;
    *   interviews with external experts or opinion leaders;
    *   surveys with representative publics.

C. RESEARCH FINDINGS

After you have conducted formal research, indicate your findings as they shed light on the public perception of your organization and write a brief summary of the public perception.

 Checklist 2C **External Environment**

Basic Questions

1. What is the major competition for your organization?
2. What significant opposition exists?
3. Is anything happening in the environment that can limit the effectiveness of the public relations program?

Expanded Questions

A. EXISTING INFORMATION

Answer the following questions based on what you know directly or what you can learn from your client or colleagues within your organization.

Competition

1. How competitive is the external environment of your organization?
2. What other organizations compete on this issue?
3. What are their performance levels?

4. What are their reputations?
5. What are their resources?
6. What does the competition offer that you don't?
7. How has the competition changed within the last three years?
8. Within the next three years, is the competition likely to increase, remain unchanged or decrease?

Opposition

1. What groups exist with a mission to resist or hinder your organization?
2. How effective have these groups been in the past?
3. What is their reputation?
4. What are their resources?
5. How have these groups changed within the last three years?
6. How have their tactics changed?
7. Within the next three years, is the opposition likely to increase, remain unchanged or decrease?

External Impediments

1. Is the environment in which you are operating currently growing, stable, declining or unpredictable?
2. What changes, if any, are projected for this environment?
3. What impediments deal with customers?
4. What impediments deal with regulators?
5. What impediments have financial or economic origins?
6. What impediments have political origins?

What impediments originate in society at large?

B. RESEARCH PROGRAM

If there are any significant gaps in the existing information, you may have to conduct research to learn more about the external environment of your organization. This section will guide you through consideration of that option.

1. What is the basis for the existing information noted above: previous formal research, informal or anecdotal feedback, organizational experience, personal observation, presumption/supposition by planner(s) and/or something else?
2. How reliable is this existing information?
3. How appropriate would it be to conduct additional research?
4. What information remains to be obtained?
5. If the existing information is not highly reliable, consider additional research, such as the following:
   • review of organizational literature/information;
   • review of other published information (books, periodicals, etc.);
   • review of electronic information (Internet, CD-ROMs, etc.);
   • interviews with key people within the organization;

- interviews with external experts or opinion leaders;
- focus groups with representative publics;
- surveys with representative publics;
- content analysis of materials.

6. What research methods will you use to obtain the needed information?

C. RESEARCH FINDINGS

After you have conducted formal research, indicate your findings as they shed light on the external environment of your organization and write a brief summary of the external environment.

CONSENSUS CHECK

Does agreement exist within your organization and your planning team about the observations and findings about the public relations situation?

☐ Yes. Proceed to Step 3, Analyzing the Publics.

☐ No. Consider the value and/or possibility of achieving consensus before proceeding.

Analyzing
the Publics

T he planner's ability to identify and analyze publics is the cornerstone of an effective integrated communication campaign. Both elements of this step—identification and analysis—are equally important. First, the planner needs to address the right group of people, so as not to squander organizational resources or miss opportunities to interact with important publics. Second, the planner must carefully examine each public in order to develop a strategy to communicate effectively.

Public

What do we mean by the term *public*? One definition that still holds true is the classic definition given by social philosopher John Dewey in *The Public and Its Problems* (1927): A *public* is a group of people that shares a common interest vis-à-vis an organization, recognizes its significance and sets out to do something about it. Publics are homogeneous in that they are similar in their interests and characteristics. They usually are aware of the situation and their relationship with the organization. They think the issue is relevant, and they are at least potentially organized or energized to act on the issue.

Public, Market, Audience and Stakeholder

There are several different strategic groupings of people associated with an organization. The terms can be confusing, and sometimes they are used differently. Here's is an overview of these strategic groupings: publics, markets, audiences and stakeholders:

PUBLIC

Don't confuse publics with other labels for groups of people who may interact with your organization. A *public* is like your family. You don't pick them; they just are—like generous Cousin Ezekiel and crazy Aunt Bertie. Publics may be helpful or annoying, friendly or not, but an organization must deal with them regardless. Publics exist because of their interaction and interdependency with an organization or because both they and the organization face a common issue.

MARKET

A **market** (sometimes called a *market segment*) is more like your friends. You pick them; they pick you. Most people select friends on the basis of shared interests and common values. Markets are particular types of publics, and organizations develop marketing efforts among those publics with whom they intend to conduct business or generate support and participation. As segments of a particular population, markets include people with characteristics (age, income, lifestyle, and so on) that can help the organization achieve its bottom line. For public relations purposes, **bottom line** is a term that identifies an organization's mission or fundamental goal (selling cars, educating students, serving patients, and so on). It has less to do with finance and more with organizational success on the broader scale.

AUDIENCE

Don't confuse publics with **audiences**, which are merely people who pay attention to a particular medium of communication and receive messages through it. Both public relations and marketing will deal with audiences. An organization's relationship with an audience is usually brief, such as the length of time it takes to read an article or listen to a speech—much more temporary than its relationship with a public.

STAKEHOLDER

A final category is a **stakeholder**, which some people identify as different from a public. The concept is that a stakeholder relates to an organization through its potential impact on the organization's mission and objectives, whereas a public relates to an organization through its messages (Rawlins, 2006). Others take the position that publics are people who don't necessarily care about an organization, whereas stakeholders are people who are conscious of a mutual relationship with an organization (Sandman, 2003). In unveiling its new definition of public relations, PRSA explained its preference for the term "publics," which relates to the very public nature of the profession, whereas stakeholders are associated with publicly traded companies. Because the concept of stakeholders is variously defined and inconsistently used, this text generally will use the term "publics" in referring to groups of people who have a mutual relationship with an organization.

Let's consider the various ways of grouping people through the example of a presidential candidate. The audience includes people using a particular medium, such as those who hear a speech live or watch a television commercial. Some members of these audiences may be part of one of the candidate's wider publics, such as registered party members. Other registered members may not be found within a particular media audience, though they remain part of an important public for the candidate. Additionally, other members of the audiences may be members of a different public, such as voters registered with the opposing political party.

Usually audiences are not homogeneous but more often are **aggregates**, mere assortments of individuals with perhaps nothing in common other than their use of a particular communication medium. However, the more specialized the communication medium is, the more likely its audiences are to have in common both demographic characteristics (such as age and income) and psychographic characteristics (such as lifestyles and values). So the audiences of very specialized media may coincide with your public.

Audiences as such are relatively unimportant to your planning for strategic communication. Most organizations want to develop mutually beneficial relationships with their various publics, for example, a company that hopes to create satisfactory business relationships with

GENERATION Y AS A PUBLIC

The so-called Generation Y (teens and 20-somethings born roughly between 1980 and 2000) is of interest from both public relations and marketing perspectives. Consider the following facts and observations about Gen Y-ers. Linda P. Morton (2002b) has drawn some of this information from a variety of sources for her series on segmenting publics for *Public Relations Quarterly*.

Generation Y is the largest teen population in American history. At 60 or 65 million, this group is larger than the celebrated Generation X (about 50 million people born in the 1960s and 1970s). It is the largest cohort group since the 75 million baby boomers born in the 1940s and 1950s. Gen Y-ers' values and attitudes have been shaped by such formative public events as the 1999 shootings at Columbine High School in Littleton, Colorado; the contested 2000 election and extreme partisan politics ever since; the September 2001 terrorist attacks on the US and the resultant accusations of government secrecy, torture, and violation of human rights; the subsequent U.S. wars in Afghanistan and Iraq, as well as the international distrust associated with them; and topping off with the election of Barack Obama and extreme partisan political divisions.

More than one in three U.S. teens is not white, the largest percentage ever. Additionally, teens today have greater experience than previous generations with nontraditional family structures, which has fostered an appreciation for diversity, equality and tolerance. A concern for privacy and a distrust of both government and mass media also are characteristics of this generation.

Meanwhile, teens have more money to spend than in previous years. They are brand conscious but not necessarily brand loyal. Huge image campaigns mean little when brands simply go out of style. Teens don't like a hard sell, but they trust each other and respond to word-of-mouth endorsements—celebrity endorsements, not so much. For example, Nike may be losing its grip on Gen Y-ers, who don't find it particularly persuasive that a 50-year-old former athlete (basketball, was it?) named Michael Jordan endorses the brand.

Gen Y people don't read newspapers often. They do listen to a lot of radio, but only to a narrow range of stations; they are more likely to listen to individually tailored music sources such as an iPod. They watch TV and have access to an average of 62 channels.

They use the Internet a lot, but don't necessarily visit websites of even the organizations and brands that they like, and they don't necessarily purchase products or services associated with their favorite websites. And the high-speed action of the Internet also means that trends and fashions can change overnight.

Does this sound like anybody you know?

Phase One

STEP
3

its customers. Strategic communicators try to understand their publics and markets to identify the media through which to reach those publics.

Much overlap exists among publics, markets, audiences and stakeholders. While differences among these are important, sometimes it is their similarities that shed more light.

Characteristics of Publics

When you begin to identify publics, how do you know what to look for? Here are five important characteristics of a public: distinguishable, homogeneous, important, large enough and accessible.

DISTINGUISHABLE

A public is a recognizable grouping of individuals, though not necessarily a recognized organization or formal group. For example, a jewelry company might want to promote itself to "everyone who wants to buy expensive jewelry." But that isn't a public, because it does not identify a particular group of people. Rather, the jeweler might identify its public as "people with incomes above $50,000 who are marking life events such as birthdays, anniversaries, graduations, and so on."

HOMOGENEOUS

A public's members share common traits and features. They may not know each other, but they have enough in common for you to treat them as a group. For example, all college professors who teach criminal justice courses do not know each other and may not even agree on specific issues within the discipline. But their collective interest in and knowledge of criminal justice warrant their identification as a public by an organization such as the National Association of Chiefs of Police. Consumer publics labeled as market segments traditionally have been identified by common traits, such as baby boomers, ethnics, seniors, Generation X-ers, and so on.

IMPORTANT

Not every identifiable group and certainly not every isolated individual is important to your organization's success. Some can prudently be overlooked or deferred. Strategists for public relations and marketing communication are most interested in those publics that can significantly impact on an organization's bottom line and affect its progress toward achieving its mission.

LARGE ENOUGH

Make sure your public is large enough to warrant strategic attention and the possible use of public media. The question sometimes comes up: How big does a group of people need to be in order to consider it a public? That's hard to answer definitively.

Don't confuse publics with the actors or relevant participants in the situation. If you are dealing with only a few people, they generally don't constitute a public, and your programming tactics would probably be limited to personal communication tools. For example, a company with five employees wouldn't need an employee newsletter; any information that needed to be shared could be done face-to-face or through personalized written information. Or the family of a motorist hurt in an accident with a company truck wouldn't be a public; it more likely would be a relevant player in what might be a wider public relations situation of the company's record on highway safety.

But good public relations suggests the need to consciously develop message strategies for interacting with these groups. With the employee scenario above, let's say the small company wants to train these employees toward a new plan for enhancing customer satisfaction. Should the program be unveiled by the owner, or might that better come from the day-to-day manager? Or maybe from an expert from a local university or professional association? The next phase in this textbook offers information on messaging, credibility, and other strategic issues that might help you come to a decision on this point.

However, sometimes a small group will be treated as a public, and you may generate a sophisticated public relations effort toward such a small-but-important group. Your lobbying efforts may focus on only a handful of members of a senate committee, for example, but a public relations campaign might be directed toward them. Objectives might deal with increasing their awareness of potential benefits and ultimately securing their vote, or perhaps simply minimizing the opposition that some senators might mount. The campaign could include face-to-face lobbying meetings, engagement of their colleagues as potential intercessors, encouragement of constituent letters and background information for their staffs, as well as print and electronic backgrounders, fact sheets, PowerPoint presentations, and such. The effort might also involve the news media, such as with issue coverage in the senators' home district, orchestration of editorials and columns, placement of guests on talk radio/TV and generation of letters to the editor—all in an effort to create a supportive environment for the organization's position, making it easier for the senators to vote in the organization's interests.

ACCESSIBLE

A public is a group with which you are able to interact and communicate. For example, it is easy for a community college to reach potential students, because most are concentrated within a small geographic area, often in narrow demographics such as high school students or underemployed 20-somethings. It is more difficult for a university of world renown to reach potential students because they are thinly scattered throughout the world and have many and varied interests.

Categories of Publics

Good communication planning calls for the identification of an organization's various publics. As pointed out at the beginning of this section, there is no such thing as a general public. Rather, each public is linked with the organization in a unique relationship.

Over the years, sociologists studying organizations have developed the useful concept of **linkage**, which is the patterns of relationships that exist between an organization and its various publics (Grunig and Hunt, 1984). While various categories of linkages have been suggested, this book presents four useful categories of linkages: customers, producers, enablers and limiters. If you consider these linkages, you are likely to identify each relevant public for your program. Exhibit 3.1 shows the relationship among the various public relations linkages.

CUSTOMER

The most obvious type of public may be *customers*. These are the people who receive the products or services of an organization, such as current, potential or former consumers, as

EXHIBIT 3.1 Categories of Publics

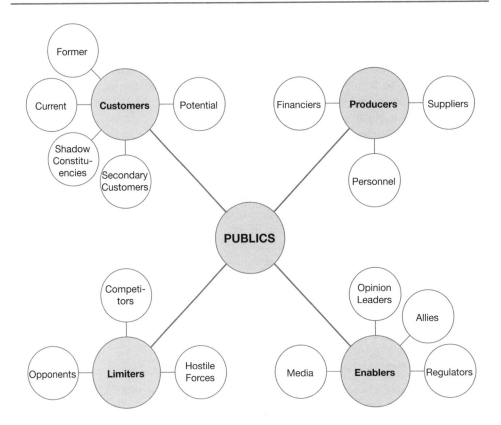

well as purchasers, clients, students, patients, fans, patrons, shoppers, parishioners, members, and so on. This category also includes **secondary customers**, who are the customers of your customers, such as the companies and graduate schools to which a college's graduating seniors apply. The category of customers also includes what has been called **shadow constituencies** (Mau and Dennis, 1994), people who may not have a direct link with the organization's products or services but who can affect the perception of an organization. For example, if hard times force a high-tech company known for its philanthropy to cut back on charitable contributions to the arts, members of the arts community (a shadow constituency) may vocally criticize the company, adding to its problems. Consider this example of a charity seeking to raise funds for research into amyotrophic lateral sclerosis (ALS), Lou Gehrig's Disease. Obvious stakeholders are the charity itself and people suffering from the fatal disease, but they are not likely to have the resources to support the organization financially. A better strategy might be to expand the concept of stakeholder to other groups: extended families of ALS patients who look on with frustration as their loved ones become paralyzed and die; medical people who treat ALS patients; and the insurance companies responsible for many of the costs associated with treatment.

PRODUCER

Those publics that provide input to the organization are called **producers**. These include personnel such as employees, volunteers and unions; producers of needed materials (such as vendors); and producers of the financial resources (such as investors, donors and stockholders).

ENABLER

Another type of public are **enablers**, groups that serve as regulators by setting the norms or standards for the organization (such as professional associations or governmental agencies), opinion leaders with influence over potential customers (such as stockbrokers and analysts) and groups that otherwise help make the organization successful (such as the media). Another type of enabler involves allies with which the organization may be able to nurture parallel interests to work on cooperative projects.

LIMITER

Those publics that in some way reduce or undermine the success of an organization (such as competitors, opponents and hostile forces) are known as **limiters**. The same activist groups that were cited above as potential enablers can become limiting publics when the organization is unable to walk in step with them. Likewise, an unfriendly newspaper or television station can become a limiting public.

The above four categories are not the only typology for identifying publics. Some practitioners distinguish between internal and external publics (often shorthand for producer and consumer publics). Another approach identifies primary, secondary and marginal publics, which seems to be rather a listing in order of importance to the task at hand. Another categorization looks at current versus future publics. Still another identifies proponents, opponents and uncommitted publics.

Some practitioners identify a category of special publics, groups usually outside the organization who are labeled according to age, race, ethnicity, gender, lifestyle or some other dominant demographic criterion. In the typology of publics presented in this book, we look at each public in its relationship to the organization (customers, producers, enablers and limiters). Thus, the concept of special publics has little practical value for a student or newcomer to the field of public relations and little to offer beyond the more comprehensive fourfold typology used here.

Additionally, some planners refer to primary publics as the key groups interacting with an organization, secondary publics as the intercessory groups who can influence the primary publics and tertiary publics as those special publics identified according to a relevant demographic.

Amid the confusing verbiage of different categorization styles, the aim remains the same: to identify all the possible publics interacting with an organization, and then to move on to analyzing their relationship(s) with the organization.

Having identified major categories of publics, the next step is to look at each of them in more detail. By more narrowly identifying our publics we can understand them better. For example, a university embarking on a recruiting campaign can't simply identify potential students as a public. That is too broad a category, because there are so many different kinds of potential students. Rather, it might classify its publics as high school students, junior college transfers, returning adult learners, employed people seeking retraining and professional

TYPOLOGY OF PUBLICS

Here are some examples of the common families of publics appropriate to various public relations or marketing communication situations. Let this list spark your creative thinking about identifying publics relevant to your organization.

Customer
Occasional/regular
Current/potential/former
Competitive/loyal
Age/ethnicity/spending potential/other variables
Members/casual customers
Geographic: local/regional/national/international
Online/in-person customers
Secondary customers
Shadow constituencies
Stakeholders
Voters/constituents

Producer
Employees/volunteers
Veteran/novice
Volunteers: leadership/grassroots
Line/staff
Management/nonmanagement
    Management: upper/middle
    Nonmanagement: supervisory/staff/
    maintenance/production/
    uniformed
Management/union
Families/retirees
Investors/shareholders
Donors: Consistent/occasional
Donors/foundations/grantors
Donors: Current/potential/former

Enabler
Community leaders:
    government/professional/business/union/
    educational/religious/ethnic
Community organizations:
    service/professional/religious/social/ethnic/
    cultural/political/environmental/activist

Industry association/regulatory agencies
Academic: faculty, alumni, trustees,
    administrators
Think tanks
Accreditation/licensing bodies and agencies
Professional experts/consultants/analysts
Government bodies:
    town/city/county/state/federal
    elective/appointive
    legislative/executive/judicial
    staff/advisory/committee/department
Diplomatic bodies: embassy/consulate
Military/civilian
Media: local/state/regional
    national/international
Specialized media:
    professional/financial/consumer/trade
    religious/ethnic/advocacy/academic
Media availability: general/limited/restricted
Print media: newspaper/magazine/newsletter
Newspapers: daily/nondaily
    online/in-print
Electronic media: television/radio/Internet
Television: broadcast/cable
Radio: AM/FM; commercial/public; satellite
Internet: newsgroups/websites/blogs
Opinion leaders

Limiter
Competitors
Opponents
Activists
Unfriendly media
Negative opinion leaders
Watchdog organizations

development, underserved minorities and perhaps even recreational learners. Each of these publics might have very different characteristics, and if the university is to be effective it must deal with each public individually.

We also want to eliminate from consideration groups that are not publics, having no present or impending relationship with an organization and thus no mutual consequences. For example, people getting married and planning a honeymoon would not be a public for a travel agency specializing in senior-citizen bus tours. The best advice in dealing with groups that are not publics is *don't*—don't waste time, don't spend money, don't try to communicate with people who have no reasonable or relevant relationship with your organization or no interest in your products or services.

Intercessory Public and Opinion Leader

In everyday situations, it is not uncommon to ask a friend to put in a good word with someone we want to impress. We do this to get dates, jobs and good deals on stereos. This practice is often called **networking**. But the more appropriate term is **intercession**, which basically means using an influential go-between. Accordingly, an intercessor is a person who presents your case to another, someone who uses her influence to intercede on your behalf to obtain a favor, mediate a dispute or to speak for you.

What's common in everyday life is also found in public relations activity. An organization often will address itself not only to its key publics but also to groups who already are in contact with that public. Such an **intercessory public** can serve as an influential bridge between an organization and its publics. In many planning situations, some of the publics listed as enablers can function as intercessory publics, because they already have the attention and respect of the ultimate public.

Take the news media, for example. In most public relations activities, the media are not the public you are finally trying to reach. Rather, they are a first point of contact, providing a means to reach another public, such as music lovers whom an opera company might identify as one of its key publics. In this case the media, particularly music critics, already have the attention of the music lovers, who presumably read and appreciate the reviews. So the public relations practitioner sets out to inform, interest and impress the critic.

As another example, consider an organization providing job training to high school dropouts in an inner-city area. The organization might find through research that coaches in community centers and ministers in urban churches can serve as intercessory publics. These people share the organization's interest in helping the young adults who left school early, and they often hold the confidence of the young people. The job-training agency could direct some attention toward coaches and ministers, increasing their knowledge of the program and the benefits it offers the community and the participants. With proper orchestration, coaches and ministers could become vocal supporters and even unofficial recruiters for the job-training program.

In addition to intercessory publics, we sometimes deal with intercessory individuals. Usually we call these people **opinion leaders**, men and women who have a particular influence over an organization's publics. Research provides some guidance into working with people who will carry an organization's messages to others. Paul Lazarsfeld's **two-step flow of communication theory** (Lazarsfeld, Berelson and Gaudet, 1944), and the multistep flow theory

Phase One

STEP
3

that evolved from it observe that the media influence opinion leaders, who in turn influence other people. Everett Rogers' **diffusion of innovations theory** (2003) notes that people who are quick to try new ideas or products are influential with latecomers to the innovation.

An opinion leader is an influential role model who has the respect and confidence of the public. Members of publics look to opinion leaders as they obtain information, form attitudes and opinions and determine action. Opinion leaders are particularly useful because they generate **word-of-mouth** support, perhaps the most effective type of communication precisely because opinion leaders are independent. That is, they do not speak under the auspices of the organization, nor do they directly benefit from it. Because of this independence they are often quite believable.

Consider these two types of opinion leaders:

- **Formal opinion leaders** have structured roles, such as elected or appointed officials or people who hold a recognized position of authority.
- **Informal opinion leaders** exert influence simply because they are informed, articulate and recognized leaders on a particular issue.

For both, their influence is based on existing relationships, real or perceived. Such relationships might involve family, neighborhoods, political parties or ethnicity, or they might be rooted in shared lifestyle, social or professional interests. Opinion leaders may be global or local.

For example, informal opinion leaders might include talk-show hosts or other media personalities; CNN commentator Nancy Grace played a key role in the media outreach of the "Find Brittany" campaign noted in the introductory chapter of this book. Such opinion leaders might also be local people, such as an opinionated clerk at the corner store or a well-read neighbor. Increasingly, bloggers fit this category. The common thread is that audiences heed and often seek out the advice of such information sources.

Some opinion leaders can be considered **vocal activists**, people who are linked to particular issues and who are known as advocates for their cause. While some activists can be dismissed as single-issue zealots, most are perceived as both independent and critical, and their support can add credibility to an organization's message. Opinion leaders may have some characteristics different from your publics.

A 2006 international study by researchers at Shih Tsin University in Taiwan looked at media habits of more than 2,000 people interested in issues of energy and technology (Mavis Tsai et al., 2006).

The study found that 68 percent of people obtained information about technology development from the Internet, 11 percent from magazines, 6 percent from television, 6 percent from newspapers, 2 percent from radio and the remaining 7 percent from other sources.

An earlier study by the Roper Organization found that people who are identified as opinion leaders prefer reading over television as a source of their information ("Opinion Leaders," 1992). They also initiate action on topics of interest by writing letters to the editor, attending public meetings and rallies, working with activist groups, and the like.

Opinion leaders not only draw attention to an issue, but also signal how others might respond or act. Matthew Nisbet of American University and John Kotcher of the National Academies in Washington, DC (2009) investigated the role of opinion leaders on climate change. They recounted George W. Bush's 2004 re-election campaign that sent an e-mail

> ## CASE IN POINT Coca-Cola in Egypt
>
> Opinion leaders can be especially important when practicing public relations in an international context.
>
> Pepsi has always been the soft-drink standard in Egypt and in most other Arab countries. To its cultural detriment, Coca-Cola has been linked with non-Arab Western interests and with American consumerism. An old saying in Egypt, laden with cultural implications, is that Pepsi is for Arabs and Coke is for Jews.
>
> A rumor circulated in 2000 that Coca-Cola was anti-Islam, "proof" of which was that when the Coke logo was viewed upside-down in a mirror, it read as "No Mohamed. No Mecca." Coke sales plummeted 20 percent. Protests erupted. Some areas banned Coke advertising and signage.
>
> Coca-Cola Egypt decided to move quickly, with a particular emphasis on the concept of opinion leader. The company requested a meeting with the grand mufti, the country's top religious leader, asking his advice. It also asked a panel of Islamic scholars to consider the matter. Both the grand mufti and the scholarly panel ruled that the rumor was unsubstantiated.
>
> In a public statement, the religious leader scolded those who disseminated the false rumor for risking the jobs of thousands of fellow Muslims employed by Coca-Cola; he also later said in interviews that he himself enjoyed a daily Coke.
>
> Besides relying on news coverage of the intervention, the company highly advertised the grand mufti's statement and gave copies to its drivers, distributors and sales people. Within weeks, sales returned to pre-crisis levels where Coke, though still a distant second in the cola wars, was playing in a more even cultural environment.

Phase One

STEP
3

questionnaire to 7 million volunteers and, based on responses, identified 2 million willing to write letters, talk with others, attend public meetings, call into radio talk shows, and otherwise promote the candidate. Each week, the campaign team sent e-mail talking points to these volunteer opinion leaders.

Their research points to a multi-prong outreach to opinion leaders: identification, recruiting and training; message coordination; and expansion of the role of online communication for digital opinion leaders; as well as the need for evaluation, transparency and ethical norms in future research on the role of opinion leaders and social media.

Key Public

Sometimes the task of selecting publics for a strategic communication program is an easy one. In many situations, the appropriate public is quite evident—a manufacturing plant seeking to increase productivity looks to its employees; a church wanting to increase contributions looks to its congregation; a politician seeking re-election targets voters in her district.

A major element of an effective communication campaign is the identification of appropriate specific publics, called **key publics** or **strategic publics**. (Note that this book uses the term "key publics" for those specific publics that the planner identifies as being most important to the public relations activity. Other books sometimes use the term "target public",

PRIORITIES WORKSHEET

Each public is not equally important, but how can strategic planners be objective in setting priorities among the various publics identified in Step 3?

Here is a worksheet that can be applied any time there is a need to set priorities among various options. Let's use it here to carefully rank publics—specifically to consider each public, evaluate it in relationship to the other publics and arrive rather dispassionately at a priority order among the publics that you have identified.

Based on choices you make in one-on-one comparisons among the identified publics, this worksheet will yield a score that reflects your priorities. Generally, you will select those publics with the highest score.

To illustrate how the priorities worksheet works, we'll use the publics identified in Planning Example 3A for the toy manufacturer.

1. Assign a letter for each public you want to compare. In this example, the lettering is from A to I. The worksheet can accommodate any number of publics. The order of listing these publics is of no consequence. List each public in the spaces marked A, B, C, . . . H along the right column and in spaces B, C, D, . . . I across the top row. Note that spaces A and I are not duplicated in the listings.

2. Compare each possible combination of items: AB, AC, AD, . . . BC, BD, BE, . . . through HI. In the corresponding block, mark the letter of the item you think is the more important of the two publics in the public relations situation to be addressed.

3. In each box, also mark a number indicating the intensity of your preference for the public you selected as being more important. Use 1 for a slightly stronger preference, 2 for a moderately stronger preference and 3 for a much stronger preference.

4. After all possible pairs are compared and your preference is marked on the worksheet, add the rating numbers for each letter. Enter this number as the prioritized score. If just one person is setting the priorities, enter that number as the prioritized score. If several people are working together to set the priority, enter the average of their individual scores. The resulting score provides a sense of the priority being given to each individual public identified for this project or campaign.

5. From this prioritized score, indicate the priority ranking. You may feel a need to adjust the ranking rather than merely base it on the scores provided through this worksheet. However, carefully consider how appropriate it would be to change the priority order if you have gone through the process of comparing each public against the others. If possible, trust the process to reflect your careful analysis of the relative importance of each public.

though this seems to suggest that the public is merely a bull's-eye for the organization's darts rather than part of a reciprocal relationship.)

Key publics are the people you want to engage in a communication process. Don't allow yourself to generalize here. The manufacturing plant may not need to address all of its employees. Some already are very productive; others are new and still learning their responsibilities, so an accent on productivity could hinder their progress. Instead, the company may focus on a particular work shift to increase productivity. Likewise, the church may raise funds primarily among its affluent parishioners and the politician may aim the re-election campaign particularly toward senior citizens who vote proportionately more often than younger residents.

If key publics are not readily obvious to your planning team, the examples and exercises that follow can help you identify them systematically and objectively. After you have identified your many publics, you will select those that are particularly important for the situation you are working on. These key publics often number from two to five, though this could increase considerably with complex issues.

Readers coming from a background in marketing should be forewarned: the tendency in marketing has been to identify objectives before selecting key publics. However, this book uses the publics-before-objectives order for three reasons: (1) the first two steps in the planning process have already helped you identify the focus for your planning; (2) publics exist in a relationship with an organization even prior to any objectives for impacting that relationship; and (3) objectives are relevant only when they link an organization's goals with a particular public.

Based on the issue you identified in Step 1: Analyzing the Situation, as well as the above information and insights about your various publics, select several publics that warrant particular attention. These become your key publics as you address this issue.

While all your publics may be important in various situations, not all warrant your attention as you deal with the situation at hand. For example, the college's recruiting program may not choose to involve its graduates and the toy company's competitors may not be a significant public in a campaign to regain consumer confidence.

This is the point in your planning process where you weed out the less important publics, concentrating instead on those few that have particular relevance and the most potential for the issue with which you are dealing.

Planning Example 3A Identifying Publics

Here is a listing of publics for Upstate College.

UPSTATE COLLEGE

- *Customers* include students and, in most cases, parents. Potential customers are academically average high school students or employed people seeking an education. Secondary customers include eventual employers and (with the program expansion) graduate schools.
- *Producers* include the faculty and administration, alumni and other donors, and banks and other financial aid programs.

Phase One

STEP 3

EXHIBIT 3.2 Worksheet

	I	H	G	F	E	D	C	B		
	A2	A3	G1	A2	A3	A2	C1	A2	A	Parents/Purchasers
	B2	B3	G1	B3	B3	B3	B1	x	B	Opinion Leaders
	C2	C3	G1	C2	C3	D1	x	x	C	Consumer Groups
	D2	D3	D1	D2	D1	x	x	x	D	Employees
	E1	E2	G1	E2	x	x	x	x	E	Stockholders
	F1	F3	G2	x	x	x	x	x	F	Am Toy Inst & Regulators
	G2	G3	x	x	x	x	x	x	G	Media
	I2	x	x	x	x	x	x	x	H	Competitors

Activist Groups, Competitors, Media, Am Toy Inst & Regulators, Stockholders, Employees, Consumer Groups, Opinion Leaders

Priority Publics

		Prioritized Score	Priority Ranking
A	Parents/Purchasers	14	**2**
B	Opinion Leaders	15	**1**
C	Consumer Groups	11	**Tie 3**
D	Employees	10	**5**
E	Stockholders	5	
F	Am Toy Inst & Regulators	4	
G	Media	11	**Tie 3**
H	Competitors	0	
I	Activist Groups	2	

- *Enablers* include the state education department and the media (both state and local). Opinion leaders include school counselors and other who offer career and educational advice.
- *Limiters* include other area colleges and universities as well as banks cutting back on student loans.

After due consideration, three key publics for this campaign are identified:

- high school students
- guidance counselors
- UC Alumni.

Here is a listing of publics for Tiny Tykes Toys.

TINY
TYKES
TOYS

- *Customers* include parents, grandparents and other purchasers of baby toys.
- *Producers* include employees (both union and management), stockholders and perhaps suppliers.
- *Enablers* include other members of the American Toy Institute and media (both financial media and family- and child-oriented media). This category also includes outside consumer groups that can exert some influence as well as consumer protection agencies that can regulate toy manufacturers). Opinion leaders include child-care professionals, pediatricians, early childhood educators and child psychologists.
- *Limiters* include other toy companies (especially importers of cheap toys), a consumer activist group threatening a boycott and a faction of disgruntled employees challenging the union and encouraging a walkout. Limiters might also include the same consumer groups, regulators and media also identified as enablers, depending on how the situation unfolds.

After due consideration, five key publics for this campaign are identified:

- opinion leaders
- parents and other purchasers
- consumer groups
- media
- employees.

Other publics not selected as being strategic on this issue include stockholders, who could be addressed in part through the media or in combination with employees; competitors, which do not need to be addressed specifically except through the media; the American Toy Institute and other regulators, who would be addressed directly rather than through public relations, though they also would have access to media coverage; and activist groups, who also would have access to media coverage.

Phase One

STEP
3

☑ *Checklist 3A* **Publics**

Basic Questions

1. Who are the major publics for your organization?
2. Who are the key publics for this situation?
3. Who are the intercessory publics or major opinion leaders?

Expanded Questions

A. EXISTING INFORMATION

Answer the following questions based on what you know directly or what you can learn from your client or colleagues within your organization.

Customers

1. Who are your primary customers?
2. Who are your secondary customers who use the products or services of your primary customers?
3. How have your customers changed within the last three years?
4. How are your customers likely to change within the next three years?

Producers

1. Who produces your service/product?
2. Who provides your organization with services and materials?
3. Who provides money?
4. How have your producers changed within the last three years?
5. How are your producers likely to change within the next three years?

Enablers

1. Who are opinion leaders among your customers?
2. Who are your colleagues?
3. Who are your regulators?
4. How have regulators helped you within the last three years?
5. With whom do you have contracts or agreements?
6. What media are available to you?
7. How have the media helped you in the last three years?
8. How have your enablers changed within the last three years?
9. How are your enablers likely to change within the next three years?

Limiters

1. Who are your competitors?
2. Who are your opponents?
3. What type of opponents are they: advocates, dissidents, activists or zealots?

4. Who can stop you or slow you down?
5. How have your limiters changed within the last three years?
6. How are your limiters likely to change within the next three years?
7. Who are intercessory publics and opinion leaders?
8. What publics are in a position of influence with your key publics?
9. How likely is it that they will speak for your organization's position?
10. Who are formal opinion leaders for this audience: elected government officials, appointed government officials or someone else?
11. How likely is it that they will speak for your organization's position?
12. Who are informal opinion leaders for this audience: family leaders, neighborhood leaders, occupational leaders, religious leaders, ethnic leaders and/or community leaders?
13. How likely is it that they will speak for your organization's position?
14. Who are vocal activists on this issue?
15. How close is their position on this issue vis-à-vis the organization's?
16. How likely is it that they will speak for your organization's position?

B. RESEARCH PROGRAM

If there are any significant gaps in the existing information, you may have to conduct research to learn more about your organization's various publics. This section will guide you through consideration of that option.

1. What is the basis for the existing information noted above: previous formal research, informal or anecdotal feedback, organizational experience, personal observation, presumption/supposition by planner(s) and/or something else?
2. How reliable is this existing information?
3. How appropriate would it be to conduct additional research?
4. What information remains to be obtained?
5. If the existing information is not highly reliable, consider additional research, such as the following:
   - review of organizational literature/information;
   - review of other published information (books, periodicals, etc.);
   - interviews with key people within the organization;
   - interviews with external experts or opinion leaders;
   - focus groups with representative publics;
   - surveys with representative publics.
6. What research methods will you use to obtain the needed information?

C. RESEARCH FINDINGS

After you have conducted formal research, indicate your findings as they shed light on the organization's publics.

Analyzing Key Publics

Here's a maxim that organizational communications can live by: Know your audience. The newspaper advice columnist Miss Manners demonstrates this effectively in some of her columns. Miss Manners is witty, if a bit stodgy, as she writes about protocol (which dinner fork to use), politeness (how to say thanks for a gift you don't like), relationships (how to introduce your lesbian lover to your father's former mistress) and other elements of etiquette (how to apologize for getting snockered at your best friend's wedding).

Clearly the know-your-audience counsel was unheeded by this letter writer—a 14-year-old girl whose mother wouldn't let her wear thong underwear and whose friends made fun of her because of it. Miss Manner's response: "Of all the advice columnists in the world, you chose Miss Manners as the most likely one to support the cause of thong underwear? And you wonder why your mother questions your judgment?" (Martin, 2008).

It is most important to understand the publics with which we seek to interact. Careful analysis of each key public is the cornerstone of the research phase. The more information and insight planners can bring to this step, the more effective the overall program.

The idea behind this step is to allow the planner to "get inside the mind" of the organization's key publics. Much of this information can be obtained through informal research such as interviews and brainstorming; some of it may require more formal research techniques such as focus groups and surveys. (*See* Appendix A: Applied Research for information on how to conduct these research methods.) Through formal and informal research, as well as good sense, the planner carefully examines each public.

One of the most important ways of analyzing a public is to consider the consequences it has on the organization and, conversely, the consequences the organization has on the public—actively or at least potentially. In a very real way, consequences create publics, and our public relations involvement with publics often is guided by an analysis of how real and obvious those consequences are.

In this section you will reconsider the general information uncovered in Step 2: Analyzing the Organization and apply it to each key public. You'll want to note the public's stage of development and its key characteristics. Each of these topics is discussed below.

Stages of Development

Publics are not fixed in concrete; rather, they are fluid and evolving. Grunig and Hunt (1984) have identified four stages of publics: nonpublics, latent publics, aware publics and active publics. To this list, this textbook adds a fifth type: apathetic publics. The relationship of each stage can be seen in Exhibit 3.3, where the solid arrow points to the changes that can be encouraged by effective public relations activity and the dotted arrow shows changes that may evolve with or without public relations input. Let's look at each type of public.

NONPUBLIC

A **nonpublic** is a group that does not share any issues with the organization and no real consequences exist to or from the organization. At this level and this time, this group simply is of no significance to the organization and vice versa. For example, a nonpublic for an animal adoption shelter would be people who live in apartments that don't allow pets. The logical public relations response for this public is observation, periodically monitoring the situation

EXHIBIT 3.3 Stages of Publics

to see if it changes; for example, if the restrictions are eased or if people move to a new building with different rules.

LATENT PUBLIC

A **latent public** (sometimes called an *inactive public*) shares an issue with the organization but does not yet recognize this situation or its potential. You might call it an embryonic public, because it has potential but as yet no self-awareness. Based on variables of knowledge and involvement as ways to identify various types of publics, a latent public has low levels of both—little information about a situation and little motivation regarding potential consequences. For the animal adoption shelter, senior citizens who might appreciate companionship would be a latent public. A latent public is unlikely to see information related to the situation. Thus an organization's public relations response is to plan communication to enhance its relationship with this public, perhaps by helping the shelter adapt itself to the interests of this group. For example, it may invite apartment dwellers to volunteer a couple of hours each week to interact with the animals awaiting adoption from the shelter, giving companionship and exercise to both the animals and the volunteers, creating knowledgeable people who might serve as opinion leaders for others who could adopt a pet and perhaps fostering future adoptions when the volunteers are in a pet-friendly environment.

APATHETIC PUBLIC

A public that faces an issue, knows it and simply doesn't care is an **apathetic public**. To this public, the issue is not significant enough to warrant its attention and/or the consequences are not perceived as being important. This can be frustrating for an organization, but properly identifying an apathetic public may help the organization reframe its message to overcome the apathy. An apathetic public for the animal adoption shelter might be people who don't particularly like pets. The public relations response to such a public is to monitor the situation carefully, for it could change quickly if the issue begins to capture the public imagination. Meanwhile, the organization also should develop plans to communicate with the apathetic public, trying to transform its apathy into interest. But realize that changing negative attitudes and opinions is a difficult task. Public relations is unlikely to be effective in transforming someone who doesn't like animals into a pet lover.

AWARE PUBLIC

An **aware public** recognizes that it shares an issue and perceives the consequences as being relevant, but it is not organized to discuss and act on the issue. An aware public for the animal adoption agency may be people who have learned that psychologists believe the companionship of pets improves the quality of life for senior citizens. The public relations response is to initiate proactive communication, providing information about the issue, stressing its significance to the public and presenting the organization's opinion or intended action. At this stage the organization can control the tone and themes of the message.

ACTIVE PUBLIC

In the final stage of its development, an **active public** has reached the fullness of what we identify as a public. It is discussing and acting on the shared issue. For the animal shelter, an active public might be the local chapter of a senior citizen organization that is actively encouraging senior citizens to adopt pets. In friendly circumstances such as the one described in this scenario, this can be an opportunity for building coalitions. In confrontational situations, on the other hand, an organization's response to an active public generally is reactive communication, responding to questions and often to accusations or even active opposition. In this reactive setting, the tone or message themes are no longer controlled by the organization but instead by the active public.

Sometimes, active publics split in their relationship to an organization and issues associated with it. A **single-issue public** may be active on all of the issues important to the organization, active only on some popular issues or active on single and often controversial issues. One animal rights group, for example, may confine its activism to local issues involving impounding of stray animals, neutering, credentialing of pet owners and other issues related to a particular shelter. Another group may be active on a wider range of issues, including testing of medicines and cosmetics on animals, fur and leather fashion, hunting and fishing, and vegetarianism.

Key Characteristics

After noting the stages of development, look at each public in reference to the following five key characteristics: the public relations situation, the organization, the public's communication behavior, its demographics and its personality.

- **Public Relations Situation**. Assess the public's wants, interests, needs and expectations related to the issue, as well as what it does not want or need. Consider relevant attitudes of the public. The hierarchy of needs (Maslow, 1987) outlined in this chapter can be useful aids in considering the interests and needs of publics.

MASLOW'S HIERARCHY OF NEEDS

Psychologist Abraham Maslow (1987) developed the **drive-motive** theory or the theory of **human motivation**, commonly known as the **hierarchy of needs**. This theory offers an understanding not only of what people need but also of what Maslow called **prepotency**, the ordered internal relationship among needs by which more basic needs must be addressed first. His theory is presented visually as a two-part pyramid of five levels, with the stronger needs at the base.

The base of the pyramid includes four levels of needs:

1. **Basic physiological needs** deal with oxygen, food and water, and sleep, as well as basic sexual urges.
2. **Safety needs** include shelter, employment, economic stability and other kinds of security.
3. **Love needs** focus on belonging, family, friends and group identity.
4. **Esteem needs** deal with respect and appreciation.

A final category rests at the top of the pyramid.

5. **Self-actualization needs** deal with achieving potential and with pursuing ideals such as spirituality and perfection, beauty and art, and peace and understanding.

Note that the self-actualization needs are in a category by themselves, separated from the others. Whereas a deficiency in any of the four levels in the base of the pyramid can create tension within a person, the fifth level adds to the person's freedom to explore and achieve his greatest ambitions.

Needs at each level of Maslow's pyramid are interrelated and can be fulfilled in different ways.

Recent research suggests that Maslow's categories of motivation are more important than their particular order. For example, while the sex urge is a basic psychological impulse, it is an urge that can be controlled and, at least temporarily, set aside. This is unlike the need for oxygen, food or sleep, which are required and ongoing.

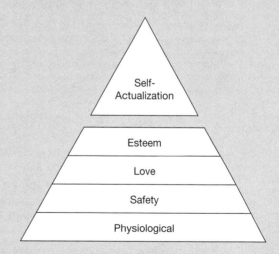

For some people, sex also can have application to a feeling of security. For others, it may be less associated with basic physiological needs and more with a sense of love and belonging, self-esteem, even spirituality.

Phase One

STEP
3

- *Organization.* Consider each key public's relationship with the organization—how your organization impacts on the public and vice versa. Also consider the visibility and reputation of your organization with this public.
- *Communication Behavior.* Study the public's communication habits, such as the media or communication channels it uses. Identify people who might be credible message sources for this public and who are its opinion leaders. Also indicate whether the public is seeking information on the issue. This assessment will have major impact later when you choose your communication tools, because information seekers are likely to initiate communication or make use of tactics that require their direct involvement.
- **Demographics**. Identify demographic traits such as age, income, gender, socio-economic status or other relevant information about this public.
- *Personality Preferences.* Consider the psychological and temperamental preferences of this key public. Appraise the relative merits of logical versus emotional appeals.

Knowing something about the personality of the key public and then tailoring messages to fit such psychological preferences can make communication more persuasive and more effective. During this step of the planning process, use the Personality Preferences checklist to look more closely at each of your key publics. Later in the process you will consider ways to craft messages that complement these preferences.

Like other aspects of this research phase, your answers to the questions posed in the planning checklist may be tentative and based on presumptions or common sense. However, insight from the organization's experience can prove useful as you begin to understand the communication preferences of your key publics. Eventually you may decide that formal research is needed; if so, consult Appendix A: Applied Research for some suggestions on various research techniques.

Stereotype

A **stereotype** is a short cut in describing groups of people. Stereotypes are based on common and repeated perceptions of who people are, how they act, and what they think and value. Stereotypes are what Walter Lippman (1922) called "pictures in our heads," and they are helpful precisely because they can whittle down the complexity of the real world.

Stereotyping has some value use for social interaction. We can identify threatening situations based on our ability to read other people. We are told to anticipate danger, drive defensively and otherwise use what we know (or presume) about others to our advantage. Parents tell their children not to associate with "a bad crowd" or "the wrong kind of people." Despite the obvious social concerns associated with profiling, law enforcement agencies know how to look at people's behaviors and conclude when they are acting suspiciously.

The problem with stereotyping is not that it is a generalization, though it is. The problem is rather that it is an overgeneralization. Good and appropriate stereotyping reflects judgments about people based on things about them over which they have some choice: their actions and behaviors, their choices in occupation, fashion, speech, grooming, and the like. It makes less sense to judge people based on aspects of over which they have little or no control: race, ethnicity, age, skin tone, religious or cultural background, language accent, and so on.

AMERICAN INDIANS: STEREOTYPE VS. REALITY

Of the many populations within American society, few are more assaulted by stereotypes than are Native Americans. Consider the following facts in light of the common stereotypes.

The 2010 U.S. Census reported 5.2 million American Indians, less than half of them of mixed ancestry. With nearly 2 percent of the total population, the collective Native population is the smallest minority group in America based on race. The largest Native nations are Cherokee, Navajo, Choctaw, Chippewa and Sioux.

The comprehensive designation of American Indians, Alaska Natives and Native Hawaiians sometimes is used. Half told the Census Bureau that they preferred the term "American Indian" and 38 percent preferred "Native American."

There are 565 federally recognized tribes in the US, plus another 250 or so seeking federal recognition. Each tribe is an autonomous and self-governing entity whose sovereignty is recognized by the federal government and whose lands are legally distinct from state lands that encircle them. Thus, in significant ways, tribal laws replace state law. Because tribes are autonomous, it is not appropriate to consider American Indians a single political entity. Official membership and citizenship eligibility varies by tribe.

Here are some facts that put stereotypes in a different light:

- *Growth*. The Native population is growing fast. While the total U.S. population grew less than 10 percent between 2000 and 2010, the American Indian/Alaska Native population increased by more than 39 percent.
- *Multiracial*. Many of these are multiracial people with some Native heritage. Additionally, 7 million Americans claim some Indian ancestry but are not officially counted within the Native population.
- *Language*. Native peoples of North America are richly diverse. About 200 languages are spoken by half a million people in the US and Canada, many with very different linguistic roots, often with sophisticated grammar. About 28 percent of the Indian population speak a language other than English at home.
- *Reservations*. Three-fourths of American Indians live outside traditional tribal areas. Only 22 percent of Indians live on 334 reservations.
- *Population Areas*. Native populations are concentrated in 10 states (led by Oklahoma, Arizona, California, Texas and New Mexico). Only three Eastern states (New York, North Carolina and Michigan) have sizable Native populations.
- *Age*. American Indians are younger than the general population. Their median age is 29, compared with 37 for the population as a whole.
- *Poverty*. Prosperity is increasing among American Indians. While 25 percent live below the poverty level, this is the same as most other ethnic and racial groups in America. Economically, Native Americans are second only to Asian Americans for income through minority-owned businesses. They also show an 84 percent growth in business ownership, particularly in service, construction and retail businesses.
- *Casinos*. Two-thirds of tribes do not run casinos. For those that do operate reservation-owned casinos, it is a $5 billion industry.

Phase One

STEP
3

- *Education*. School dropout rates are higher among Indians than any other population group. Nevertheless, 77 percent of adult Indians have a high school degree (compared with 86 percent of the total U.S. population). More than half of high school graduates attend college and 13 percent hold a bachelor's degree.
- *Mainstream*. Contemporary Indians are part of mainstream American life. They operate radio and television stations, run public relations agencies, sponsor colleges and work in every occupation. New York City and Los Angeles are the two biggest cities for Native-owned businesses.
- *Health*. Though life expectancy among Native Americans is 10 years less than the national average, health is steadily improving. Suicide rates are decreasing. Alcoholism remains high, and many deaths are accidental and alcohol related.
- *Taxation*. Indians pay federal income tax, state income tax except on income earned on reservations, sales tax on off-reservation purchases and off-reservation property tax. Federal and tribal laws, but not state laws, generally apply on reservations.
- *Governance*. Some tribes and nations are led not by chiefs but by presidents, governors or chairmen/chairwomen. Some are governed by councils.
- *Religion*. Many American Indians are members of mainstream Christian denominations, both Catholic and Protestant. Others participate in what is loosely called Native American religion, often a spiritual rooting in life rather than a formal religious structure. Additionally, many people combine Christianity with Native religious practices and beliefs.
- *Media*. Native Americans have national newspapers and radio programs. They are increasingly exercising a presence in public relations and the media. Most tribes have their own public relations department or functions, as do many Native-related organizations, such as the National Native American Law Students Association, the American Indian Science and Engineering Society, the (Canadian) Assembly of First Nations, and the (Catholic) Tekakwitha Conference.

Public relations strategists will be mindful of such diversity among the Native communities. In particular, communicators should be careful not to adopt icons and images of one Indian group and project it upon all.

Many Indians come from the Northeast and Southeast where buffalo never roamed. The stereotype of the Plains Indian with feathered headdresses and teepees simply does not apply to the Navajo and Apache of the Southwest, the Salish and Yakama of the Northwest, nor the Mohegan, Seminole or Haudenoshaunee (Iroquois) of the Eastern states. Additionally, not all Indians hold powwows. Some hold fiestas or festivals.

The Public Relations Society of America includes Native Americans in its Multicultural Affairs committee, and several Native-owned public relations agencies exist within the profession.

Treaty, taxation and casino-related issues are leading some Native Americans to get involved with government. Lobbying and the use of news media is increasing, as is activism in some areas. In New York, for example, the six nations of the Haudenoshaunee are fighting the state's sporadic attempts to collect sales taxes on tribal lands, which they see as a clear violation of federal treaties and law.

What's the value of all this information? It can serve as a reminder that stereotypes are inaccurate.

Are there differences between Native Americans and others? Certainly. Some are positive: close families, respect for the environment. Some are negative: higher school dropout rates, higher rates of alcoholism. But the stereotypes often perpetuated through movies, advertising and other forms of media are outdated at best, and often demeaning and hurtful—and thus of little value to an ethical and accurate strategic communicator.

Decisions about who is or is not part of a bad crowd may be made on the basis of the both types of stereotypes—ethnic background or family structure over which the person has little control, or grooming and fashion choices that the person has made.

Stereotype-based decisions also can be dead wrong. For years, stereotyping has led many people to associate drug use with inner-city youth rather than suburban youth, yet studies show that drug abuse, as well as underage drinking and drunk driving, is higher in the suburbs than in inner cities. The stereotype simply is wrong, and as public relations planners, we rely on such stereotypes to our own detriment.

Consider the following facts, which may challenge some of your own stereotypes about certain groups of people.

A 2003 poll by Zogby International found that 78 percent of teens associate Italian Americans with mobsters, gang members or restaurant workers. The U.S. Census Bureau reports that two-thirds of Italian Americans in the workforce are on professional jobs such as teachers, attorneys, executives and physicians.

Another poll found that 74 percent of adults think most Italian Americans are connected to organized crime, though the U.S. Justice Department reports less than .0025 percent of Italian Americans (that's one in 40,000) as being involved in organized crime. Nevertheless, the entertainment and advertising industries continue to draw heavily on the unreal mob-focused stereotype of America's fifth-largest ethnic group ("Italian American Stereotypes in U.S. Advertising," 2003).

Asian Americans are stereotypically thought of as well educated. The organization Asian Nation, drawing on Census Bureau data, reported in 2011 that 50 percent of Asian Americans over the age of 25 have a bachelor's degree, twice the rate for all Americans. That supports the stereotype.

On the other hand, a 2010 study by the University of California (Chang, 2010) reported that, while only 15 percent of the general American adult population lacks a high school education, the 45 percent of Hmongs and 40 percent of Laotians and Cambodians did not complete high school. Those facts go against the stereotype. Maybe the stereotype needs revision.

In analyzing publics, it is important to consider the level of diversity within them. Often, research and close observation reveals that a public is more diverse than it might appear from only a cursory glance. In particular, two groups within American society are subjected to all kinds of inaccurate stereotyping that masks a diversity that is much richer than may first appear. Consider the facts about Arab Americans and Native Americans in light of what you know to be the common stereotypes in the boxed insets.

Why are these issues important for us? Because public relations practitioners develop campaigns, craft speeches, prepare scripts, populate blogs, write newsletters, send Tweets,

Phase One

STEP
3

ARAB AMERICANS AND MUSLIMS

What little most Americans know about Arabs and Muslims they learn through the media, which—whether focused on news or entertainment—tends to continue negative and misleading stereotypes. Islamic and Arab publics are oversimplified by outsiders, but a good public relations strategist will work contacts within the Arab and Islamic communities to help understand the sometimes subtle differences.

First off, note the double focus of this section. The public generally confuses Arab (member of an ethnic group originating in the Middle East) and Muslim (member of a religious group known as Islam). The two are not the same. Most Arab Americans are not Muslims, and most Muslims are not Arab.

Arab Americans

Here are some relevant facts about Arab Americans:

- *Population*. Though statistics are a bit unreliable, most reports indicate that the US is home to about 3.5 million Arab Americans. Most are citizens born here.
- *Ancestry*. Nearly half of all Arab Americans (47 percent) trace their ancestry to Lebanon; most of their families came to the US a century ago. Other Arab Americans are from Arabia (14 percent), Syria (11 percent), and Egypt and Palestine (both 6 percent), with smaller numbers from Jordan, Morocco, the Sudan, Algeria, Libya, Yemen and other countries in the Middle East and northern Africa.
- *Growth*. Arab Americans are the fastest-growing minority in the US, with a 30 percent growth between 1990 and 2000 according to the federal census.
- *Politics*. Politically they are split fairly evenly between Democrats and Republicans.
- *Education*. About 85 percent of adult Arab-Americans have a high school degree. More than 40 percent have a bachelor's degree (compared to about 25 percent for Americans in general).
- *Economics*. Arab Americans generally have a higher household income than the U.S. average. They are more likely to run their own businesses.
- *Religion*. Two-thirds of Arab Americans are Christian. About 35 percent are Catholic, 18 percent Orthodox, and 10 percent Protestant. An estimated 25 percent are Muslim (according to a Zogby International Survey of 2002). Some Christian religious groups are historically rooted in the Arab community, such as the Catholic Maronites of Lebanon, the Coptic Orthodox Christians in Egypt and the Chaldean Catholics in Iraq.

American Muslims

Here are some related facts about Americans who are Muslims, adherents to the religion of Islam, making it the third-largest religious group in the US after Christianity and Judaism. The following data is drawn from the Census Bureau, the State Department and the Hartford Institute on Religious Practice.

- *Population*. Most reports indicate that the US is home to about 4 million Muslims, though some internal sources estimate twice that number. Most live in cities, with highest concentrations in California (where 20 percent of the American Muslim population resides), New York State (16 percent), Illinois (8 percent), and Indiana and New Jersey (4 percent each). The annual growth rate is about 6 percent, compared to less than 1 percent for the total U.S. population.

- *Immigrants*. Two-thirds of Muslims are immigrants or children of immigrants.
- *Ancestry*. In general, the Islamic community subdivides into four nearly equal segments: Southeast Asians; African Americans; Arabs; and other groups such as Turks, Kurds, Iranian/Persians, Berber/Moroccans, and so on. Muslim populations are growing six times faster than the general population, and Muslims have a younger population than the country overall.
- *Education*. Muslims lead national averages in education. About 67 percent of adults have at least a bachelor's degree (compared to 44 percent of the general population); 32 percent have a master's degree or doctorate (compared to 9 percent of the general population).
- *Income*. They also have higher incomes than the general population, and often are found in engineering, computing and medicine; they are under-represented in journalism and law, and are less likely than others to own their own businesses.
- *Islamic Centers*. There is religious diversity within Islamic America. About 2 million people are affiliated with more than 1,250 Islamic centers, mosques and other prayer locations. These are represented in every state, with the largest numbers in California, New York, Texas, Pennsylvania and Ohio. About 30 percent of mosque members are converts.
- *Mosque Membership*. The largest groups in mosque membership were South Asian Americans (33 percent), African Americans (30 percent) and Arab Americans (25 percent).
- *Intercultural Mosques*. Most U.S. mosques are intercultural, with members of various ethnic backgrounds. On average, membership is one-third South Asian, one-third African American and one-quarter Arab. In general, political and social divisions in the Middle East among Sunni, Shi'ite, Sufi and Wahabi Muslims and home-grown American sects such as the Nation of Islam have had only minimal effect on most American mosques.
- *Religious Schools*. Mosques operate about 200 day schools and 500 Sunday schools, and there are six schools of higher learning. But 97 percent of Islamic children acquire religious education in their homes.
- *Religious Practice*. Most Muslim religious practice is home-based. About 4 percent of American Muslims participate in weekly religious services, compared with 15 percent of American Jews and 40 percent of Christians.
- *Politics*. The first Muslim to be elected to the U.S. Congress is Keith Ellison, a Democratic congressman from Minnesota who was elected in 2007. In Texas that year, a Muslim running as a Republican was defeated for a congressional seat. In 2000, Muslim Americans voted overwhelmingly Republican; in 2008, 89 percent voted for Barack Obama. Muslims are becoming more politically active. Nearly 80 percent are registered to vote, and 85 percent of those registered say that they vote.

and in so many other ways research and write about people and issues that are affected by stereotyping. Our role is not to change the social structure of our environment but to be accurate with facts and fair to people.

Cultural Context

Publics do not exist in a vacuum. Understanding their cultural context is crucial in this research phase of the strategic planning process. Public relations practitioners who give a priority to learning the nuances of the culture in which the publics exist are likely to develop campaigns that can be successful.

This is particularly important in the international arena. What works for one culture may not be appropriate for another.

Even basic communication can be hampered in international contexts. Language itself can be a barrier to communication. This is particularly true in Africa. Nigeria, for example, has more than 390 dialects. South Africa has 11 different national languages.

Technological differences can add to the problem. Social media and mobile media so common in Western societies is not present in some parts of Africa to make them useful tools for public relations, though this is changing rapidly as many countries are experiencing sustained growth in cellular technology.

Outsiders do themselves and their public relations interests a disservice when they fail to understand the diversity that exists within a culture. In the US, for example, we should understand that there are major differences within the Hispanic community. Mistaking cultural perspectives among Puerto Ricans, Cuban Americans and other Hispanics from the Dominican Republic, say, can create embarrassment for organizations and counterproductive responses from publics. Likewise Mexican, Panamanian, Columbian and other Latin American cultures may share a common language base, but from a public relations perspective they may have more differences than similarities.

Situations get even more complicated when applied to other countries. Some nations such as Mexico, Canada, Australia and Japan have historic tensions between indigenous peoples and the dominant culture. Others experience significant differences, even hostility based on language (such as Canada), religion (Uganda and India), race (South Africa) or tribal background (Rwanda). Gender roles and socially acceptable relations among men and women also vary greatly, as do social attitudes toward people who are gay, aged, disabled or otherwise different from the social norm.

Saving Face

Sometimes we want to see people squirm, especially people who have opposed us in some way. Most especially if they have been arrogant about things. Public relations strategies sometimes can create conditions for a win–lose result, with the expectation that we win and they lose.

But there's another way to approach this, one that may fit well with the notion of cultural context. "Don't make your opponent look bad" isn't typical public relations advice. Yet in some cultures, face saving is important, and public relations in those cultures might well include developing strategies that allow opponents to save face in public, to resolve a situation while maintaining dignity and respect. Providing such an out can make it easier for an opponent to resolve the situation in your favor.

Face saving is particularly important in Eastern culture. The Chinese call it *mianzi*. It's *kao-o-tateru* in Japanese, *hifz ma'a wajh* in Arabic. Saving face is a universal concept, though taken much more seriously in Asia and the Middle East.

Asian business people seldom say "no" directly. A more polite euphemism for a negative decision is "Perhaps" or "The timing may not be right."

CASE IN POINT **Palestinian Public Relations**

Sometimes the cultural context affects public relations in a significant way. Consider, for example, the role of public relations within the Palestinian community, both in the contested geography of the Middle East (Israel, the West Bank and the Gaza Strip) and in the Palestinian diaspora (mostly in Jordan and neighboring states in the Middle East, but with large Palestinian communities in Chile, Brazil, Honduras, Canada, the US and various European countries).

A 2005 study by Ahmed Ibrahim Hammad of Aristotle University in Thessaloniki, Greece, looked at the Palestinian Authority. This administrative organization that governs the Palestinian Territories had five different government agencies dealing with the media, plus public relations departments in many other agencies. Hammad found that the public relations as practiced by the long-ruling Fatah party was focused on a one-way communication method, using the communication-technician model to project a favorable image of the Palestinian Authority.

Hammad and fellow communication researchers later assessed the broader role of public relations within Palestinian society, where they observed that public relations of international Palestinian activism is more sophisticated than internal commercial public relations. Because of the weak governmental structure and the lack of independent media in Palestine, "Palestinian public relations was seen as a political necessity," they said, ". . . for communicating internally among the Palestinians inside the territories and throughout the Palestinian diaspora as well as externally with foreign publics" (Zaharna, Hammad and Masri, 2009, p. 236).

Rather than media-focused campaigns, as might be found in many parts of the world, public relations in Palestine is more likely to center on interpersonal relationships. The research team noted that Palestine is a small territory with a close-knit social structure building around interconnected families. Mosques often are the center of social interaction. Taxi drivers are conveyers of news to many. Throughout society, the emphasis is less on disseminating information through the media but rather on circulating information among interwoven social structures.

The researchers looked at the 2006 election victory of the Hamas party, which took outsiders by surprise. They argued that the vote outcome would not have been such a surprise if observers had understood that Palestinian-style public relations is based in an interconnected social structure and focusing on relationship-building rather than public information. The media attention and support for the Fatah party that had long been in command had much less impact than Hamas' relationship-building approach within the Palestinian community.

Public relations practitioners who do business in South Korea, for example, note that companies are unlikely to directly criticize their competitors. They may help circulate negative information, but it's done behind the scenes. Direct criticism likely would cause them to be outcasts within their own profession or industry. Thus doing public relations in South Korea might involve developing strategies that allow opponents to save face in public.

Face saving is behind the practice in Japan of not asking questions at a news conference. Say what? In America and Europe, news conferences can erupt into a cacophony of competing questions shouted out by journalists. But in Japan, the presumption is that the corporate or governmental leader making a news announcement would be embarrassed if reporters had to ask follow-up questions, indicating that the spokesperson had not anticipated their information needs. So rather than embarrass the spokesperson by asking questions in public, a follow-up interview would be seen as less humiliating. It's just another example of the need for public relations practitioners to understand the cultural context in which they may find themselves.

A classic example shows the role of face saving in international business relationships. In the 1980s, Mitsubishi Electric was using a product that an American manufacturer, Fusion, claimed violated patent laws. Mitsubishi rejected the claim, and for 10 years Fusion mounted a negative publicity campaign in both the American and Japanese press. The public embarrassment failed to bring Mitsubishi to the bargaining table.

Eventually the two companies were able to resolve the differences in private, issuing a joint news release announcing an agreement that, in an important face-saving gesture, gave no details and no concession statements by either side.

Rethinking Your Publics

Occasionally, this part of the process may point out a problem in your earlier identification of key publics. If you find it difficult to identify traits common to your public, perhaps you have defined the public in terms that are too general.

Consider the plight of a group of planners—students in a university public relations class—developing a program to raise awareness, generate interest and obtain funds to help save the African elephant from human predators. The planners misidentified as one of their key publics "people with incomes above $50,000." As they analyzed their publics, the planners were having difficulty because they could not identify the mindset of this public, which was too broad and had no common traits other than income. That's because income wasn't really a public at all but rather a demographic description, and not a very comprehensive one at that.

So the planners redefined their public more specifically as "people with incomes above $50,000 who have a pre-existing interest in issues of conservation and endangered animals." With those criteria, the planning team then could develop a profile of its public: people who want to help animals, expect a workable plan for doing so, want an organization with a proven track record, have an altruistic spirit to make the world a better place and have the financial ability to contribute to this cause. This redefinition also helped the planners avoid wasting resources by trying to convert people to a cause in which they had no interest.

Sometimes an analysis of the publics will reveal that you simply need more information to take you beyond the insufficient common knowledge. For example, you may have identified African Americans as a key public for your campaign. Yet in your analysis you are likely to discover that, other than the physical characteristic of race itself, there may be few common elements within this public. For example, there are significant differences between American-born and foreign-born blacks; and in some cities, the foreign-born population is quite large—about a third in New York City and nearly half in Miami. Likewise, Southern blacks are culturally Southern, which may give them more in common with Southern whites than with Northern blacks.

Meanwhile, just as within Hispanic, Asian American and Native American communities, there is much diversity among black people. Significant cultural differences are to be found among blacks from Haiti, Senegal, Nigeria and Ethiopia (not to mention Newark, Baltimore, St. Louis and Anchorage, Alaska). A closer look will reveal a population divided by language as well. Additionally, one might suspect that the half-million black Mormons or the 200 million black Catholics worldwide might, at least on some issues, have more in common with their coreligionists than with members of their race with other religious perspectives.

Once you are satisfied that you have identified your publics appropriately, review the analysis of each and consider whether the information you have generated should lead you to make any changes in the lineup. For example, a public that earlier seemed to be key may now be shown to be too apathetic to justify your action at this time.

Remember: planning is a flexible process. The conclusion of Step 3 is one point along the way where you should rethink your plans so far, adjusting them based on the information becoming available to you through continuing research.

Benefit Statement

Conclude your analysis of the publics with a **benefit statement**, which is an articulation of the benefit or advantage your product or service can offer this public, or the way you can help satisfy its need or solve its problems. For example, the benefit a community foundation might offer its donors could be stated as follows: "The Equity Foundation offers donors the opportunity to pool their money with the donations of others, thereby compounding small donations into larger, more effective grants."

In more of a marketing vein, the benefit an online bookstore might offer college and university students could be written as this: "Cyber Booksellers can assure university students that it can provide class textbooks at discount prices with immediate delivery."

What's Next?

This concludes Step 3, in which you now have a good look at the key publics associated with the public relations situation that you have been addressing in this planning process.

Step 3 also closes out Formative Research, the first phase of the strategic planning process. Having completed steps associated with Phase One, you now should have some clear insights about your issue, the status of your organization as it relates to this issue, and your various publics and their relationship to your organization.

You are probably already beginning to get ideas about how to communicate with these publics. Jot down whatever may come to mind, but it's not yet the time to develop specific program tactics. That will come later.

The next phase of the planning process addresses strategic questions such as the outcomes you want to accomplish, the approach you will take, and the message you will use to communicate with your key publics.

Phase One

STEP
3

Planning Example 3B Analyzing Key Publics

UPSTATE COLLEGE

Upstate College alumni and other donors are a latent public on the issue of the college's program expansion. As circumstances change, it can be transformed into an active public.

Analysis of Key Characteristics

- *Issue*: The alumni/donor public will appreciate this program expansion; this public needs only basic information to instill appreciation.

- *Organization*: This key public provides continued support for the college, while the college provides this public with a sense of pride and value of the academic degree. This public has high knowledge of the college and thinks favorably about it. It can be called upon for action. It shares the college's self-image as a high-quality institution.

- *Communication*: This public occasionally participates in on-campus activities and has access to general news media as well as the college newsletter. The college has a mailing list of alumni and donors. This public is not actively seeking information because an announcement has not yet been made, but it could be expected to be attentive to information. Credible sources include famous alumni and respected donors.

- *Personality Preferences*: This is a diverse group, with some members having a preference for messages that are factual, logical and reality based, while others prefer messages focused on ideas, sentiment and vision.

- *Demographics*: Wide range. Higher than average in education. No particular significance in demographics other than geographic proximity to college.

Benefit Statement

Upstate College can provide information to alumni about the college's successes and strengths, giving alumni a sense of pride in their alma mater and an opportunity to help build on those strengths. (Note: Similar analyses would be made for each individual key public you have identified.)

Tiny Tykes Toy Company employees are an active public.

Analysis of Key Characteristics

- *Issue*: The employee public wants to see the company reputation improved and wants to see the employer regarded as a leader in the industry. Morale has been affected negatively by the recall: employee public does not want to feel bad about making an inferior infant product, needs information on quality and safety, and cautiously expects leadership from the company in improving quality and reputation.

- *Organization*: This employee public ultimately affects the quality and productivity of the company, knows the company intimately, and has organized for action through unions and through work teams. The company affects this public through continuing employment. Employees do not necessarily share management's self-image of being beneficial and safe.

- *Communication*: The employee public gets its information in an interpersonal setting with management and supervisors, can be reached through direct mailings and newsletters, and also receives information from local news media. This public is actively seeking info on this issue. Credible sources include management officials, veteran employees and union leaders.

- *Personality Preferences*: Rank-and-file employees are accustomed to receiving messages based on fact, certainty and logical analysis. Managers may be more disposed to messages that also deal with vision.

- *Demographics*: The employee public spans age groups but has in common lower-middle-class socioeconomic/educational background; there are many ethnic workers. Most members of this public do not personally use company products, but often in the past they have given the products as gifts to family and friends.

Benefit Statement

Tiny Tykes can provide information that will give employees renewed purpose and pride about the quality and safety of its products. (Note: Similar analyses would be made for each individual key public you have identified.)

Checklist 3B **Key Publics**

Basic Questions

1. What is the nature and type of each key public?
2. What are the major wants, interests, needs and expectations of each public?
3. What benefits can you offer this public?

Expanded Questions

A. EXISTING INFORMATION

Answer the following questions based on what you know directly or what you can learn from your client or colleagues within your organization.

1. Who is your key public?
2. Indicate the category below that best describes that key public at this time and consider the public relations response indicated.

Phase One

STEP
3

Category	Response
Latent public. Faces an obstacle or opportunity vis-à-vis the organization. Does not yet recognize this situation or its potential.	Monitor the situation, anticipating change toward awareness. Meanwhile, begin to plan a communication process to provide information about the issue, explain its significance to the public and present your organization's opinion or intended action.
Apathetic public. Recognizes an obstacle or opportunity vis-à-vis the organization. Does not perceive this issue as important or interesting.	Monitor the situation, looking for any change toward perceiving the relevance of the issue. Meanwhile, begin to plan a communication process to provide information about the issue, explain its significance to the public and present your organization's opinion or intended action.
Aware public. Recognizes an obstacle or opportunity vis-à-vis the organization. Not yet organized for action.	Initiate a communication process to present the issue, explain its significance to the public and present your organization's opinion or intended action.
Active public. Recognizes an obstacle or opportunity vis-à-vis the organization. Preparing to organize or already organized for action.	Because you did not communicate sooner, you must now engage in reactive communication, responding to questions and perhaps to criticism and accusations without being able to control the tone or themes of the messages.

Analysis of Key Characteristics

Issue

1. What does this key public know about this issue?
2. What does this public think about this issue?
3. What does this public want on this issue?
4. What does this public not want on this issue?
5. What does this public need on this issue?
6. What problem(s) does this public have related to this issue?
7. What does this public expect from the organization vis-à-vis this issue?
8. How free does this public see itself to act on this issue?

Organization (including product/service)

1. How does or how might the key public affect your organization?
2. How does or how might your organization affect this public?
3. What does this public know about your organization?
4. How accurate is this information (compared to information in Step 2)?
5. What does this public think about your organization?
6. How satisfied are you with this attitude?
7. What does this public expect from your organization?

8. How much loyalty does this public have for your organization?
9. How organized or ready for action on this issue is this public?
10. How influential does this public see itself as being within the organization?
11. How influential does the organization see this public as being?
12. Place an "X" at the appropriate location on the continuum of what this key public thinks of your organization's product(s) or service(s):

Contemporary	_ _ _ _ _	Traditional
Fun	_ _ _ _ _	Tedious
High-Tech	_ _ _ _ _	Low-Tech
Ordinary	_ _ _ _ _	Distinguished
Expensive	_ _ _ _ _	Inexpensive
Idealistic	_ _ _ _ _	Practical
Modest	_ _ _ _ _	Pretentious
Scarce	_ _ _ _ _	Abundant
Worthless	_ _ _ _ _	Beneficial
Efficient	_ _ _ _ _	Inefficient
Ordinary	_ _ _ _ _	Innovative
Essential	_ _ _ _ _	Luxury
Risky	_ _ _ _ _	Safe
High-Quality	_ _ _ _ _	Low-Quality

13. What are the similarities and the differences between your organization's self-image in the exercise from Step 2 and the image of it held by this public?

Communication

1. What media do this public use among each of the following: personal communication channels, organizational media, news media and advertising/promotional media?
2. Is this public actively seeking information on this issue?
3. How likely is this public to act on information it receives?
4. Who are credible sources and opinion leaders for this public?

Demographics/Psychographics

1. What is the average age of members of your key public?
2. Where is your key public located geographically?
3. What is the socioeconomic status of your key public?
4. What products or services does your key public commonly use?
5. What are the cultural/ethnic/religious traits of your key public?
6. What is the education level of your key public?
7. What lifestyle traits does your key public have?
8. Is this public likely to be persuaded more by facts, more by emotion or by a combination?
9. Is this public likely to be motivated more by appeals to the past (experience, success, track record) or by appeals to the future (motivation, inspiration, vision)?
10. Are there other relevant characteristics about your key public?

Phase One

STEP
3

Benefits

1. What benefit or advantage does your organization offer each public?
2. How does this benefit differ from the benefits available from other organizations?

B. RESEARCH PROGRAM

If there are any significant gaps in the existing information, you may have to conduct research to learn more about your organization's various publics. This section will guide you through consideration of that option.

1. What is the basis for existing information noted above—previous formal research, informal or anecdotal feedback, organizational experience, personal observation, presumption/supposition by planner(s) and/or something else?
2. How reliable is this existing information?
3. How appropriate would it be to conduct additional research?
4. What information remains to be obtained?
5. If the existing information is not highly reliable, consider additional research, such as the following:
   - review of organizational literature/information;
   - review of other published information (books, periodicals, etc.);
   - interviews with key people within the organization;
   - interviews with external experts or opinion leaders;
   - focus groups with representative publics;
   - surveys with representative publics.
6. What research methods will you use to obtain the needed information?

C. RESEARCH FINDINGS

After you have conducted formal research, indicate your findings as they shed light on the organization's publics. Also, write a benefit statement about how the organization can satisfy the wants and needs, address the interests and solve the problems of this particular key public.

CONSENSUS CHECK

Does agreement exist within your organization and your planning team about the selection and analysis of these key publics?

☐ Yes. Proceed to Step 4, Establishing Goals and Objectives.

☐ No. Consider the value and/or possibility of achieving consensus before proceeding.

PHASE TWO

STRATEGY

Strategy is the heart of planning for public relations, marketing communication and related areas. All the embodiments of strategic communication are rooted in the research already undertaken in the previous phase and growing toward the eventual choice of communication tactics. Just as rushing through the research phase would have jeopardized the foundation on which to build your public relations or marketing communication plan, so will failing to give adequate attention to strategy result in weak messages and pointless activity.

Simply stated, **strategy** is the organization's overall plan. It is the determination of how the organization decides what it wants to achieve and how it wants to achieve it. Strategy has a dual focus: the action of the organization (both proactive and responsive) and the content and presentation of its messages (theme, source, content and tone). Refer to strategy in the singular, because each program should have a single, unifying strategy.

Phase Two deals with mapping the course toward your overall destination, deciding both where to go and how to get there. By building on research from Phase One of the planning process, you will anchor your program in the mission or vision of the organization.

Specifically, this phase of the planning process leads you to a closer look at your organization: its vision of itself, as well as its hopes for the various publics important to it. These hopes will be fleshed out as goals, positioning statements and objectives. Then the strategy phase will focus your attention on two key aspects of your planning: what you will do, and what you will say about what you will do. The first of these delves into both action and response, following the premise that actions speak louder than words. First you focus on the things you do; then you turn your attention to how you communicate about those actions.

The entire strategic process is interrelated and interdependent: goals guide the development of objectives, which in turn help drive decisions about what persuasive strategies to use and what tactics to employ to address the problem or opportunity.

Admittedly, there are different approaches to strategic planning and various practitioners may use different terminology. For example, some planners set goals before they identify and analyze publics. This often is true when the planner comes from a marketing perspective, where the organization starts with its sales or promotional goals, then identifies potential customers who might be or become interested in the organization's products or services.

Public relations starts with publics. We generally build our strategic plans from an understanding of the ongoing relationship between our organization and its various publics. Then we look at how the organization's goals and objectives potentially impact on these publics.

Phase Two

Establishing Goals
and Objectives

This step is about looking inward and deciding what you want to achieve. To better understand this step, you need to understand the twin concepts of goals and objectives. It should be noted that public relations and marketing strategists generally make the distinction that goals are general and global while objectives are specific. However, some advertisers and other specialists rooted in business disciplines either reverse the meanings of the terms or use them interchangeably. In your actual practice, you may find people applying different definitions to these terms, so make sure you understand what the words mean and how colleagues use them. In *Strategic Planning for Public Relations*, we use the terms as they are outlined below.

Here are short definitions of key concepts used in this step. They will be fleshed out in the subsequent pages.

- A positioning statement is a general expression of how an organization wants its publics to distinguish it vis-à-vis its competition.
- A goal is a global indication of how an issue should be resolved.
- An objective is a statement of specific outcomes expected for a public, indicating a way to more precisely conceptualize the goal.

Positioning

As you set out to articulate the desired interaction you can have with your publics, first focus on positioning. Having previously identified the relevant public relations situation in Step 1, ask yourself these simple questions: What do we want people to think about us? What position do we seek with our publics?

A successful approach to strategic communication in a competitive environment is to position the organization according to its own particular niche.

Positioning is the process of managing how an organization distinguishes itself with a unique meaning in the mind of its publics—that is, how it wants to be seen and known by its publics, especially as distinct from its competitors. A **position statement** is the articulation of how an organization wants to be seen and known, especially vis-à-vis its competition.

The concept of distinctiveness is an important one for all organizations: large and small businesses, educational and charitable organizations, political and human service groups, hospitals, churches and sports teams.

In most settings, organizations are known more by their distinctiveness than by their similarities. For example, in the field of higher education, a dozen or more schools might be located in a particular metropolitan area. Each is likely to be identified by its unique characteristics: the large public university, the small church-affiliated college, the high-priced two-year private school, the community college with an open admissions policy, the midsized public institution that used to be a teachers' college, and so on. Problems can occur when the niche is not unique. For example, if your school is one of two small church-affiliated colleges in the area, you will emphasize what distinguishes it from the other, such as lower costs, a suburban campus, graduate degrees, evening/weekend programs or the particular denomination or religious community that sponsors the college.

Organizations have found that the concept of positioning is fluid, and some organizations have made successful attempts to reposition themselves to keep pace with a changing environment. Consider the "This is not your father's Oldsmobile" campaign, which tried to reposition Oldsmobile from a line of cars popular with middle-aged and senior drivers to one fashionable for a younger generation. The campaign had a lot going for it: a catchy slogan, upbeat music, a sporty new design for its new models. And it achieved high levels of awareness. Unfortunately, sales declined, and in terms of average age, the typical Olds owners became . . . well, older. So much for the value of awareness alone.

How does an organization position itself? First it conducts and analyzes research to determine just how the organization is perceived by various publics. It also considers the position held by its major competitors. The organization then identifies the position it would like to hold, seeking to capitalize on its uniqueness and to distinguish itself from its competition. Having done all this, the organization develops a strategy to modify its current position or perhaps simply to maintain the niche it already holds.

Make sure that your desired position is realistic. Who wouldn't want to be known as "the industry leader" or "the first name in (whatever)"? But there can be only one leader, one first

EXAMPLES OF POSITIONING STATEMENTS

Here are some examples of how various organizations might try to position themselves. Note how each statement highlights a desired attribute of the organization by implying a distinction from competitors:

- the leader that sets industry standards;
- the best value, reflecting low cost and high quality;
- the most economical;
- the most expensive and most prestigious;
- the hospital preferred by women;
- the family-friendly restaurant;
- the "green" brand.

name. A good strategic planner will be wary of pretense and of stretching beyond possibility. At best, it would be an exercise in futility. At worst, chasing an impossible dream wastes valuable organizational resources, invites ridicule and exposes the organization to risk.

Don't confuse the public relations concept of positioning with its use in marketing, where the term refers to the competitive approach for a persuasive message (that is, positioning according to features such as customer focus, competitive advantage, social responsibility, lifestyle or product attribute).

When we talk about positioning in public relations, we refer less to the presentation of the products or services and the messages about these, and more to perception—how we want our organization to be seen by our publics. As Al Ries and Jack Trout explain in *Positioning: The Battle for Your Mind*, "Positioning is not what you do to a product. Positioning is what you do to the mind of the prospect" (2001, p. 2).

Positioning Ethics

Carefully think through the ethical implications in creating a positioning statement for your organization.

Don't state your desired position merely to brag, particularly if the bragging is based on an inflated view of reality. Wanting to be the first, biggest, cleanest or fastest is not the same as actually being the first, fastest or whatever. Your publics will easily see through boasting and swaggering.

More important, don't use the positioning statement as a putdown for another organization. For example, a candidate for political office might seek to position herself as "a soccer mom who cares about her community." There could be a lot of potential to such an appeal. But it raises an ethical question if she were to aim at being seen as "a better parent than the other candidate." While that might be true, it's far better for individual voters to conclude this rather than for the candidate's political organization to explicitly state such a positioning theme.

Goal

With the positioning statement hinting of what we want people to think about us, we turn our attention to a more direct assertion of what we want to accomplish. This is called the **goal**. It is a short, simple statement rooted in the organization's mission or vision. Using everyday language, a goal acknowledges the issue and sketches out how the organization hopes to see it settled. A goal is stated in general terms and lacks measures; these will come later, as objectives.

In their classic book *Public Relations Management by Objectives*, Norman Nager and T. Harrell Allen (1984) use the analogy of transportation: Goals provide the direction while objectives pinpoint the destination.

Various explanations have been given for how to understand public relations objectives. This textbook presents a concept of three types of goals, an explanation that has been adopted by many public relations strategists, as well as by textbooks such as Patricia Swann's *Cases in Public Relations Management*. The concept presented here is that communication goals are of three types. These can be categorized as relating to a trinity of public relations situations that are part of the management function within every organization.

- **Reputation management goals** deal with the identity and perception of the organization.
- **Relationship management goals** focus on how the organization connects with its publics.
- **Task management goals** are concerned with getting certain things done.

The three types of goals together offer a way of laying out the various aims associated with public relations and integrated communication campaigns. It is unnecessary, even unlikely, that every campaign will have each type of goal. Planners mix and match these as they consider appropriate to their specific campaign.

Who sets an organization's communication goals? Generally, public relations managers do, usually as an implementation of the organization's strategic plans, which ideally the public relations people have had a hand in developing.

There are two sources for these overall organizational plans that give rise to goals. They may be global documents such as a strategic business plan. Or they may be embedded in implementation guidelines such as an annual strategic plan or a statement of priorities or directions.

Either way, public relations goals should map out a vision of success for achievements and consequences that are important to the organization as a whole. In doing so, strategic communication planners should note how the organization defines what it means to be successful and then develop goals that grow out of this understanding.

Phase Two

STEP 4

EXAMPLES OF PUBLIC RELATIONS GOALS

Here are several examples for each of the three different types of public relations goals.

Reputation Management Goals

- Improve the company's reputation within the industry.
- Enhance the hospital's prestige as the leading center for sports medicine.
- Reinforce the organization's image with potential donors or investors.
- Strengthen the agency's standing within the environmental movement.

Relationship Management Goals

- Promote better appreciation of the firm among potential clients.
- Enhance the relationship between the company and its customers.
- Maintain a favorable relationship amid social or organizational changes.

Task Management Goals

- Increase public support for organizational goals.
- Advance social change on a particular issue.
- Impact public behavior on matters associated with the organization's mission.
- Create a favorable climate for our client among regulatory agencies.
- Attract a sell-out crowd to a fundraising concert.

CASE IN POINT   BYU in Israel

Sometimes public relations goals are stated in negative terms: to reduce opposition or minimize hostility, perhaps even to prevent a situation from developing into a public issue. Such was the goal when Brigham Young University attempted to build a student center in Jerusalem. Initial opposition emerged from conservative Jewish organizations, fearful that the American-based Mormon university would use the proposed student center to try to convert Jews to its brand of Christianity.

Gitam, an Israeli public relations and advertising agency, signed on for a campaign aimed at reducing opposition. The agency focused on key publics such as conservative Jewish organizations, liberal secular groups and lawmakers who ultimately would decide the case. Research identified causes of public opposition and the potential basis for public support; it also identified opinion leaders on both sides of the issue.

Campaign messages focused on Israel's self-identity as a Jewish state that valued freedom for all religious organizations, on efforts to show Mormons as ordinary people doing ordinary things in Israel, and on portraying Mormons as threatened underdogs by publicizing curses and threats received by BYU's office in Jerusalem from hostile opponents. The campaign also sought to allay fears that Mormons would try to convert Jews. To this end, it featured a testimonial by the chief rabbi of Salt Lake City, home of the Mormon religion, pointing out that more Mormons converted to Judaism than Jews to Mormonism.

The result was permission for the student center, along with assurances that BYU would not enroll Jews and would require students and faculty to sign a non-proselytizing pledge.

CASE IN POINT   Toyota's Reputation

Toyota has shown the importance of reputation goals, which are particularly significant in crisis situations.

With auto recalls in 2009 and 2010, Toyota endured what was initially called the worst-handled auto recall in history, with predictions that the reputation of the Toyota brand would be damaged for years.

Faulty accelerators were linked to 19 deaths, and reports in both established and emerging social media whipped consumer anxiety to near-panic levels. The company that had built its reputation on quality and safety recalled 9 million vehicles worldwide to fix floor mats and faulty gas pedals that caused unintended acceleration.

Toyota's own confidence in its reputation may have caused the company to fumble its public relations in the early stage of the recall crisis. Perceiving a bigger transgression than faulty technology, some critics accused the company of corporate arrogance: withholding internal test reports; hiding the problem from unsuspecting customers; paying off lawsuits behind closed doors without remedying the problems.

The allegations sparked congressional hearings in Washington, though some accused the government of over-reaching, perhaps a political response to the simultaneous bailout of Toyota's U.S. competitors, General Motors and Chrysler. But there is no question that the incidents that surrounded the recalls increased customer fears and caused the company's stock prices to fall by

Phase Two

STEP
4

continued

15 percent. Kelley Blue Book lowered the resale value of the recalled Toyotas by 3.5 percent (about $300 for a Corolla).

Toyota supporters countered that the company acted as quickly as it could on the information. It took full-page ads in major U.S. Sunday newspapers alerting consumers of the recall, and it temporarily halted sales and shut down production until the problem could be corrected. American and Japanese officials gave television interviews and the company presented messages of reassurance.

Within a year, Toyota stock prices were even higher than before the recall and the Toyota reputation was once again an asset to the international corporation.

Toyota customers by-and-large stayed with the company, maintaining trust that the technical problems were correctable and negligible. Toyota continued as the No. 1 automaker in the world, with its Camry the best-selling car in America. Toyota held that position until it slipped to third place behind General Motors and Volkswagen, not because of the recall but after supply problems following the earthquake and tsunami in Japan.

Edmunds.com reported that, even after the recall, Toyota ranked 17 among the top 20 carmakers for customer complaints, with fewer complaints than American and most other imported automakers—another testimony to the importance of keeping reputation as a top goal of any organization.

A Rasmussen poll reported that 81 percent of Americans viewed Toyota favorably or very favorably. Another poll indicated that a quarter of Americans thought the government had criticized Toyota mainly to help General Motors after the bailout.

To an unknown extent, the manner of media coverage appeared to have made the crisis appear worse than it was. For example, most media reports failed to note other contributing factors in the accelerator-related accidents: reckless driving, texting or cell-phone use while driving, DUI. One driver was indicted for vehicular manslaughter and DUI for marijuana.

Analyses published in *Car and Driver* magazine said the risk of an unintended acceleration was 1 in 10,000 for the Toyota vehicles, compared with a more-frequent 1 in 8,000 for American-made cars.

Was there a silver lining to the recall? Perhaps. In the aftermath of the crisis, Toyota set a renewed priority on customer responsiveness.

Phase Two

STEP
4

Objective

A public relations **objective** is a statement consistent with an organization's positioning and emerging from the organization's goals.

An objective is a clear and measurable statement, written to point the way toward particular levels of awareness, acceptance or action. Objectives often are established by communication managers responding to broader organizational goals. Like goals, objectives deal with intended outcomes rather than procedures for reaching them.

A single goal may be the basis for several objectives. In fact, every goal should generate at least three objectives, focusing specifically on awareness, acceptance and action.

Management by objectives is the process by which effective and efficient organizations plan their activities. While the acronym **MBO** has somewhat gone out of favor, the approach remains useful. From this perspective, organizations don't merely do something because they can; rather, they act because managers have determined that doing this particular something will further the work of the organization in some strategic and measurable way.

For instance, a reactive and nonstrategic public relations or marketing communication department may decide that because the company has just purchased new publishing software, a scanner and a color printer, the department should prepare new promotional brochures and fliers. But a proactive and strategic department would first determine what needs to be done, say, to promote more understanding among potential customers. Then it might conclude that it should produce new brochures and buy the equipment with which to do so, or not. This is managing by objectives, not by whim.

As you can see by this example, objectives help direct the organization to act in ways that make sense.

Objectives also serve another purpose: They give the planner a reference point for evaluation. When you measure the effectiveness of your strategic communication program in Step 9, you will look back to your objectives and determine whether your messages and actions have had the effect you wanted. You will then scrutinize each objective to determine if you have been successful.

Elements of Objectives

An objective is a three-fold subset of a goal, an articulation of the various elements that are necessary to achieve the goal. Eleven specific elements can be identified for public relations objectives. These will become the elements of effective and practical objectives.

GOAL ROOTED

Objectives grow from the organization's goal statements, which themselves emerge from the mission or vision that the organization has defined for itself. Thus, objectives are responsive to a particular issue that the organization has recognized as important to its effectiveness. Public relations objectives often reflect organizational strategic plans and they may parallel financial projections, marketing ambitions, advertising or promotional expectations and objectives associated with other aspects of the organization.

PUBLIC FOCUSED

Objectives are linked firmly to a particular public. They are based on the wants, interests and needs of that public. Objectives for one public may be similar to those for another public, but each must be distinct.

IMPACT ORIENTED

Objectives are oriented toward the impact they can achieve. They define the effect you hope to make on your public, focusing not on the tools but on intended accomplishments. In writing objectives, avoid statements about writing and disseminating news releases, producing brochures, holding open houses and other activities that belong with an eventual tactical response to the objectives. Such nonobjective language is dangerous. It confuses activity with achievement, and it can lull you into a false belief that because you are doing something you are also accomplishing something.

Phase Two

STEP
4

RESEARCH BASED

Objectives are linked to the research that you gathered in Phase One of the planning process. Good objectives aren't just pulled out of the air; they are tied to research. For example, if research shows that 40 percent of your key public is familiar with your organization's products or services, your objective might be to increase that to 55 percent—not because 55 percent is a magic number, but because it represents a reasonable ambition based on the current situation, as revealed through research.

EXPLICIT

Objectives are specific and precise. There is no room for varying interpretations; everyone involved in the public relations activity must share a common understanding of where the objective is leading. Don't use ambiguous verbs such as "educate", "inform", "promote" or "encourage". Instead, use strong action verbs to state your objective specifically. For example, instead of saying you want "to enhance knowledge of recycling," say your objective is "to increase residents' understanding of the benefits of recycling."

MEASURABLE

Objectives are defined and quantifiable, with clear measures that state the degree of change being sought. These *key performance indicators* (KPIs) are known more commonly as *metrics*. Simply stated, metrics are performance indicators that can be quantified and compared to other data. Avoid adjectives such as "appropriate" or "reasonable." Instead, for example, state that you want "to effect a 20 percent increase in recycling of paper products." Metrics for public relations objectives can be milestones achieved, or they can be data showing how the performance compares with a benchmarked standard or with baseline performance.

TIME DEFINITE

Objectives are time definite. Objectives include a clear indication of a time frame—"by December 31," "within six months," "during the spring semester," and so on. Avoid ambiguous phrases such as "in the near future" or "as soon as possible." Some objectives may indicate a graduated or multistage approach to the time frame. For example, you might indicate that a certain effect is expected in two stages: a 50 percent increase within six months, a 75 percent increase after the first year.

SINGULAR

Objectives focus on one desired response from one public. Don't state in an objective that you want "to increase awareness and generate positive attitudes." You may be successful in the first effort but unsuccessful in the latter, making it difficult to evaluate your effectiveness. Most strategic communication programs will have multiple objectives, but each objective should be stated separately.

CHALLENGING

Objectives are challenging. They should stretch the organization a bit and inspire people to action. Don't aim at too safe a level of achievement or you might find that you haven't really achieved anything worthwhile. Instead, set your sights high.

ATTAINABLE

Though challenging, objectives need to be attainable and doable according to the organization's needs and resources, so don't set your sights too high. Seldom is it realistic to aim for 100 percent of anything, whether you are trying to expand your customer base or reduce opposition. Don't create a recipe for failure by setting objectives that are unattainable.

ACCEPTABLE

Objectives enjoy the understanding and support of the entire organizational team: public relations or communication staff, managers, right up to the CEO. The value of objectives is not that they are written but that they are used. They need the strength of consensus if they are to be useful to both your organization's planners and its decision makers.

EXAMPLES OF PUBLIC RELATIONS OBJECTIVES

Here are two examples of well-written objectives in each category.

Awareness Objectives

- To have an effect on the *awareness* of senior citizens in Lake County; specifically *to increase their understanding* of the advantages that Upstate Health Program offers senior patients (60 percent of senior residents within six months).
- To have an effect on the *awareness* of legislators from the Southern Tier; specifically to *increase their understanding* of the environmental impact that House Bill 311 will have on their constituents (all 15 Republican and seven Democratic members of the House Committee on Environmental Affairs within two months).

Acceptance Objectives

- To have an effect on the *acceptance* of senior citizens in Lake County; specifically to *increase their positive attitudes* toward membership in Upstate Health Program (30 percent within six months).
- To have an effect on the *acceptance* of legislators from the Southern Tier; specifically *to gain their interest* in the environmental issues addressed by House Bill 311 (10 of the 15 Republican members and six of the seven Democratic members of the House committee within two months).

Action Objectives

- To have an effect on the *action* of senior citizens in Lake County; specifically *to obtain an increase in their membership* in the Upstate Health Program (10 percent within six months, and an additional 10 percent within a year).
- To have an effect on the *action* of legislators from the Southern Tier; specifically for them *to vote in favor* of House Bill 311 (six of the 15 Republican members of the House and six of the seven Democratic members of the House committee when the bill comes to a vote next spring).

Phase Two

STEP
4

Hierarchy of Objectives

An ordered hierarchy exists among communication objectives, growing out of a logical progression through three stages of persuasion: awareness, acceptance and action.

- Awareness begins the process, increasing gradually. This aspect of persuasion is based on what we want people to know about our organization.
- Interest then builds in stages and attitudes bloom into an acceptable choice. This acceptance stage of the persuasion process deals with what we want our publics to think or feel about what they know.
- Verbal and physical actions are modified in steps. This culmination of the persuasion process focuses on how we want our publics to act, based on what they think or feel about what they know.

Note how this model parallels the AIDA pattern (attention, interest, desire and action), the hierarchy of effects associated with advertising since the 1920s (Lipstein, 1985). It also echoes the standard communication effects of cognitive, affective and conative changes (Ray, 1973). Similarly, Philip Kotler, Ned Roberto and Nancy Lee (2007) focused on objectives for social-marketing campaigns, identifying these as knowledge objectives (information or facts), belief objectives (values or attitudes) and behavior objectives (specific actions).

Whatever formula you use, remember: In your enthusiasm to resolve the issue, don't let your expectations get ahead of themselves. Develop a plan that will take your communication with each of your publics through each of the necessary steps. Make sure your message first will reach your target publics, who will then agree with this message and finally will act on it. Here's a closer look at the three levels of objectives:

Awareness objectives deal with information and knowledge.

- attention
- comprehension
- retention.

Acceptance objectives focus on how people react to information.

- interest
- attitude.

Action objectives address a hoped-for response to information and feelings.

- opinion
- behavior.

AWARENESS OBJECTIVE

The first level of objectives, **awareness objectives**, focuses on information, providing the **cognitive** (or thinking) **component** of the message. These objectives specify what information you want your publics first to be exposed to and then to know, understand and remember. Awareness objectives particularly deal with dissemination and message exposure, comprehension and retention.

When would you use awareness objectives? They are appropriate for transmitting purely functional information, for communicating on noncontroversial issues and for the early stages of any communication campaign. Awareness objectives also are particularly useful for publicity and public information models of public relations. In general, awareness objectives impact on what people know about an organization and its products, services and ideas.

ACCEPTANCE OBJECTIVE

The next level, **acceptance objectives**, deals with the **affective**, or feeling, **component** of the message—how people respond emotionally to information they have received. These objectives indicate the level of interest or the kind of attitude an organization hopes to generate among its publics. Acceptance objectives are useful in several situations: forming interests and attitudes where none existed before, reinforcing existing interests and attitudes, and changing existing positive or negative attitudes.

Acceptance objectives are particularly important amid controversy and in persuasive situations using the advocacy (or asymmetrical) model of public relations. They impact on *how* people feel about the organization and its products, services and ideas. Notice how the examples of acceptance objectives above differ from the earlier examples of awareness objectives.

Acceptance is the key to effective public relations, and its importance has been obvious since 1947 when one of the accepted "fathers" of public relations, Edward Bernays, wrote about "the engineering of consent." This implies more than merely disseminating information. It involves connecting with people's inner desires. We must take time to foster the public's acceptance of both our organization and its messages, through means that are both practical and ethical. For example, in a political campaign, news releases and debates may be useful tools for achieving awareness. But awareness doesn't guarantee acceptance, and through the release or the debate voters may actually learn that they disagree with the candidate on important issues. Thus, successful awareness efforts could actually hinder acceptance of your client—just one of life's little ironies.

Sometimes this affective element is the most direct way to realize a goal. Take, for example, Fitness First for Women. This women-owned, women-focused network of 13 gyms in the United Kingdom had a goal of increasing membership. Its objectives and subsequent strategy were focused on the emotional issue of how women feel about themselves and their bodies.

The campaign identified a theme of "sexy weight." This was described as an alternative to the often unrealistic and frequently unhealthy weight-loss target that some women set for themselves, usually based on what they thought would please their romantic partners (present or potential). Instead, the campaign set about to help women reimagine themselves, with an attitude that curves could be desirable. The specific task was to help women set an achievable weight goal at which they would feel more energized, their clothes would fit better and they would begin to feel good about themselves. Hence, their "sexy weight" (a term that became a registered trademark of the company).

The concept was researched through a nationwide survey. Psychologists were engaged both as advisers and as spokespersons. Eventually the campaign achieved measurable results, not only in attitude change associated with the presentation strategy, but also in actual numbers of new members for the fitness centers.

ACTION OBJECTIVE

The final level of objectives, **action objectives**, takes aim at expression and conduct, providing the **conative**, or behavioral, **component** of the message. These objectives offer two types of action: opinion (verbal action) and behavior (physical action). Action objectives may attempt to create new behaviors or change existing ones, positively or negatively. They should be focused on the organization's bottom line, such as customer buying, student enrollment, donor giving, fan attendance, and so on.

Action objectives can serve not only as persuasive objectives that encourage audiences to act according to the wishes of the organization but also as objectives for building consensus and enhancing the relationship between the organization and its publics.

Developing Objectives

Just as most issues will have more than one goal, so too will each goal have a full set of objectives—at least one in each of the above categories for each of the identified publics. Too often, efforts in public relations and marketing communication fail because they pursue the awareness objectives and then jump quickly to action, forgetting the important bridge step of generating acceptance.

Note how the action objectives shown in the example box differ from the earlier examples of awareness and acceptance objectives. As this hierarchy moves along the awareness–acceptance–action path from least important to most important objectives, the impact on the public will inevitably decrease. You might achieve an 80 percent awareness level among the public, for example, but perhaps only 40 percent will accept the message favorably, and only 15 percent or 20 percent may act on it.

Students often ask, "Where do you get the numbers from?" Good question. Here's an example that might shed some light, based on a real campaign being developed by a student group for a local Alzheimer's association. The goal was task-oriented: increasing volunteers for the local chapter. At first, the students were all over the place, setting unrealistic objectives. They were trying to create awareness in 40 percent of college students, acceptance in 20 percent and action in those same 20 percent. This meant that everyone who might want to volunteer actually would have done so. Unlikely. It also means that if the objectives were to be met, there would be 10,000 new volunteers, an impossible number for the chapter to deal with.

Here's how we talked things out in class. First we worked backwards, focusing on just how many volunteers the organization realistically could use. The number: about 200. Then we considered how many college and university students there were in the region: about 50,000. Then we discussed some realistic expectations. How many of those 50,000 could the campaign reach? The 40 percent (20,000) seemed realistic, given the fact that students are reachable through a relatively narrow channel of communication vehicles such as campus media, social networking, and perhaps direct mail with fraternities and sororities.

Then came the questions about acceptance and action. How many of those 20,000 students who hear about the organization would think it was a good idea? The planners estimated perhaps one in 10, or 2,000 students; that is, 4 percent of the original population. And how many of that 2,000 would be likely to volunteer? Perhaps another one in 10, or 200 student volunteers; 0.2 percent of the original total. Sounds like a small percentage, but that's just what the Alzheimer's association needed.

Adding some complexity to the process, the planners were aware that most of the current volunteers for the chapter were women and the organization needed some male volunteers. So a mix of 70 to 30 for women and men volunteers was factored in. Here are the resulting objectives:

- To create awareness of Alzheimer volunteer opportunities among college students, specifically 40 percent, or 20,000 of the 50,000 students in area colleges and universities within six months.
- To create acceptance among college students, specifically generating interest among 4 percent of the student population, or 2,000 students within six months (of these, 70 percent or 1,400 women; 30 percent or 600 men).
- To generate action among college specifically, specifically to achieve a 0.4 percent action rate with 200 new volunteers (70 percent or 140 women; 30 percent or 60 men).

Writing Objectives

In writing public relations objectives, keep your language simple and brief. Avoid jargon. Use everyday language and strong action verbs. As part of the planning for a strategic communication campaign, objectives are not meant to be presented publicly, so don't worry if they begin to sound repetitive and formulaic. The guidelines that follow can help you deal with each important element of a well-stated objective.

Phase Two

WRITING PUBLIC RELATIONS OBJECTIVES

Public	Objective for _____		
Category	To have an effect on	☐ Awareness	
		☐ Acceptance	
		☐ Action	
Direction	Specifically, to	☐ Create, Generate	
		☐ Increase, Maximize	
		☐ Maintain, Reinforce	
		☐ Decrease, Minimize	
Effect	(w/ awareness category)	☐ Attention or	☐ Comprehension
	(w/ acceptance category)	☐ Interest or	☐ Attitude
	(w/ action category)	☐ Opinion or	☐ Behavior
Focus	About _____		
Performance Measure	_____		
Time Period	_____		

PUBLIC

Indicate the public to whom the objective is addressed.

CATEGORY

Indicate simply the category of the objective: awareness, acceptance or action.

DIRECTION

Indicate the direction of movement you are seeking. Here are your choices: to *create* or *generate* something new that did not exist before; to *increase* or *maximize* a condition; to *maintain* effects or *reinforce* current conditions; or to *decrease* or *minimize* something. Notice that *elimination* is not an option because a public relations undertaking is seldom able to completely remove an unwanted effect; the best we can hope to do is minimize it. Another observation: public relations and other strategic communication programs too often don't pay enough attention to maintaining current support. While generating new support is important, don't overlook those who currently help you and agree with you.

SPECIFIC EFFECT

Indicate the specific effect that you will address. If you are writing an awareness objective, the specific effect should deal with receiving the message, remembering it and understanding it. If you are focusing on the acceptance level, deal with generating interest, reducing apathy or fostering attitudes (usually positive attitudes, such as support for wearing a helmet while bicycling; sometimes negative attitudes, such as a sentiment against drinking alcohol during pregnancy). For action objectives, focus on evoking a particular opinion or drawing out a desired action.

FOCUS

Indicate the focus of the specific effect you hope to achieve. Provide some detail about what you are seeking. However, don't move away from objectives by providing information about either strategy or tactics. That will come later in the planning process. Stick to articulating what impact you hope to make on your public. If you get into how to make the impact or what tools you will use to communicate, you've gone too far for this step.

PERFORMANCE MEASURE

Indicate the desired level of achievement in measurement terms. Raw numbers or percentages usually do this well. The number itself should reflect baseline research and/or desired outcomes. For example, a university library might calculate that 35 percent of students use the library facility in any two-week period. However, guidelines from the Association of College and Research Libraries might suggest that 50 percent is the desired usage pattern, including both in-person use and Internet connections. Therefore the campus library's public relations campaign might aim for a performance increase to 50 percent of the students. Stated other ways, the objective might specify a 30 percent increase over the present usage or an increase from the present 2,800 students to 4,000 out of a total student population of 8,000. Each variant aims for the same level of usage.

TIME PERIOD

Indicate the desired time frame, either within a single period or in multiple stages. Here again, you can be specific (a May 15 deadline) or relative (within six weeks, by the end of the fall semester).

POORLY WORDED OBJECTIVES

Here are three examples of poorly worded objectives. Note how each can be improved.

Poorly Worded Objective 1

- To interest more people in recycling as soon as possible.

Critique: No public is indicated, merely a vague reference to "people." "Interest" is a nonspecific term. Recycling is a very broad concept. The focus is on communication activity rather than impact in the public. Measurement is nonexistent. The time frame is imprecise.

Restatement: To have an effect on the *action* of Allen County residents; specifically *to generate telephone inquiries* to the CLEAN-UP help line (100 telephone calls during the first two months of the campaign; 400 telephone calls within six months).

Poorly Worded Objective 2

- To prepare a new brochure about recycling.

Critique: No public is indicated. The focus is on communication activity rather than impacting the public. Measurement and time frame are not included.

Restatement: To have an effect on the *awareness* of residents of the Oxford Apartments; specifically *to increase the understanding* of students about the benefits of recycling (45 percent during the fall semester).

Poorly Worded Objective 3

- To become more student focused.

Critique: This is a strategic choice more appropriate for the next step, but it doesn't indicate a desired outcome.

Restatement: To have an effect on the *acceptance* of students at St. Martin's College; specifically *to increase positive attitudes* toward the student-centeredness of the Career Counseling Center (50 percent increase within two years).

Phase Two

STEP
4

What's Next?

This concludes Step 4 in the strategic planning step. With this step behind you, you should have a clear indication of what you hope to achieve through your plan. This includes the positioning you hope to nurture, as well as the goals and associated measurable objectives that the plan aims to achieve.

PLANNING EXAMPLE 4 **Establishing Goals and Objectives**

Here is the first part of strategic planning for Upstate College.

UPSTATE COLLEGE

Position

Upstate College wants to be known for its quality education and for its accessibility in terms of both cost and admission standards.

Goals

1. Re-create the college's image into that of a four-year institution (reputational goal).
2. Recruit more students (task goal).
3. Generate new donor support (task goal).

Objectives

Re: Goal 2 for High School Students in a Three-County Area [selected examples]

2.1 To have an effect on *awareness* of high school students; specifically *to increase their knowledge* that Upstate College is expanding into a four-year college (75 percent of students during their junior year)

2.2 To have an effect on *acceptance*; specifically *to generate interest* in attending a growing institution (25 percent of high school students during their junior and senior years)

2.3 To have an effect on *action*; specifically *to obtain inquiries* from an average of 15 percent of high school students in the college's primary three-county area during their junior or senior years

2.4 To have an effect on *action*; specifically *to obtain applications* from an average of 5 percent of all high school graduates in the college's primary three-county area during their senior year.

[Note: You also will have objectives for each of your other key publics for every goal.]

Here is the first part of strategic planning for Tiny Tykes Toys.

Position

Tiny Tykes wants to be known as the company that cares about babies more than about its own profitability.

Goals

1. Regain customer confidence (reputational goal).
2. Recapture the company's previous sales rates (task goal).

Objectives
Re: Goals 1 and 2 for Parents [Selected examples]

- To have an effect on *awareness*; specifically *to create knowledge* among 75 percent of parent-customers about the redesign of the baby toy within six weeks.
- To have an effect on *awareness*; specifically *to create understanding* by 65 percent of the parents about the sacrifices and commitment that the company has made by recalling and redesigning the toys.
- To have an effect on *acceptance*; specifically *to regain trust* among 40 percent of these parents that the company has acted responsibly in redesigning the toy.
- To have an effect on *acceptance*; specifically *to create interest* among 30 percent of the parents in buying toys from the company within the next two years.
- To have an effect on *action*; specifically *to foster sales* to 25 percent of the parents from the company within the next two years.

[Note 1: You will have objectives for each of your other key publics for every goal.]

[Note 2: Each of these examples uses a different format for presenting the outline of goals and objectives. Use whatever style works best for your presentation.]

[Note 3: Numbering goals and objectives makes it easier to reference them within the planning team and when meeting with clients.]

 Checklist 4 **Goals and Objectives**

Basic Questions

1. What position do you seek?
2. What are the goals?
3. What are the specific objectives (awareness, acceptance and action for each public)?

Expanded Questions

A. POSITION

1. What is a key public for this product/service/concept?
2. What position do you seek for your product/service/concept for this public?
3. Is this desired position appropriate? If no, reconsider the position.
4. What is your current position?
5. What change do you need to make to achieve the desired position?
6. What is the competition?
7. What is its position?

[Note: Replicate the above position questions for each public.]

B. GOALS

1. What are the organization's reputation goals on this issue?
2. What are the organization's relationship goals on this issue?
3. What are the organization's task goals on this issue?
4. Do any of these goals contradict another goal? If yes, which goal(s) will you eliminate?
5. What is the relative priority among the viable goals?
6. Does the organization have resources (time, personnel, money, etc.) to achieve these goals? If no, can resources be obtained? From where?
7. Does the organization have willingness to work toward these goals? If no, how can willingness be generated?
8. Are there any ethical problems with these goals? If yes, how can you modify the goals to eliminate the problems?

C. OBJECTIVES

1. Write at least one awareness objective for each key public, such as "To have an effect on awareness; specifically . . ."
2. Write at least one acceptance objective for each key public, such as "To have an effect on acceptance; specifically . . ."
3. Write at least one action objective for each key public, such as "To have an effect on action; specifically . . ."
4. Answer the following questions for each individual objective:
   - Is this objective linked to the organization's mission or vision statement?
   - Is this objective responsive to the issue/problem/opportunity/goal?
   - Is this objective focused on a particular public?
   - Is this objective clearly measurable?
   - Does this objective indicate a time frame?
   - Is this objective challenging to the organization?
   - Is this objective realistically attainable?

CONSENSUS CHECK

Does agreement exist within your organization and your planning team about the recommended positioning, goals and objectives?

☐ Yes. Proceed to Step 5, Formulating Action and Response Strategies.

☐ No. Consider the value and/or possibility of achieving consensus before proceeding.

Formulating Action and Response Strategies

Effective public relations involves deeds as well as words, and strong programs can be built only on solid and consistent action. Ideally, actions and messages work hand in hand, complementing each other as the organization interacts with its publics. This step of the planning process will focus on your decisions about action strategies as you prepare to achieve your objectives.

Strategic communication planners have many options for what their organization can do and say on any particular issue. These actions can be either proactive or reactive.

PROACTIVE STRATEGY

Sometimes, an organization takes the initiative to engage its publics. Such a **proactive strategy** enables an organization to launch a communication program under the conditions and according to timelines that seem to best fit the organization's interests. There are two types of proactive strategies: action and communication.

Proactive strategies can be most effective because they are implemented according to the planning of the organization, rather than by a need to respond to outside pressure and expectations from publics.

Key proactive communication strategies include the generation of publicity, presentation of newsworthy information and development of a transparent communication process.

REACTIVE STRATEGY

Conversely, a **reactive strategy** responds to influences and opportunities from an organization's environment. Such **response strategies** include pre-emptive action, offensive and defensive responses, diversion, commiseration, rectifying behavior and strategic inaction.

Proactive Strategy 1: Action

The first category of proactive public relations strategies involves **action strategy** tangible deeds undertaken by the organization in an effort to achieve its objectives. Let's look at the

A TYPOLOGY OF PROACTIVE PUBLIC RELATIONS STRATEGIES

Proactive Strategy 1:
Action

Organizational performance

Audience engagement

Special events

Alliances and coalitions

Sponsorships

Strategic philanthropy

Activism

Proactive Strategy 2:
Communication

Publicity

Generating new newsworthy information

Transparent communication

seven categories: enhancement of organizational performance, audience participation, special events, development of alliances and coalitions, sponsorships, strategic philanthropy and sometimes activism.

Organizational Performance

The **performance** of the organization is what it does, as compared to what it says. This is the first and most important area to consider when weighing various strategic communication initiatives.

Ensure that the organization is working at its highest possible level of quality for its customers. One of the first questions in the formative research phase of this planning process (Step 2, Analyzing the Organization) was designed to identify the quality of the product or service associated with the issue being addressed. Public relations can't be expected to promote the good name of an organization that doesn't give good performance, and products or services should reflect a level of quality that meets the wants, interests, needs and expectations of key publics.

What do customers want? Quality products. Value. Customer service. Reasonable prices. They also expect the organizations they choose to patronize to be responsible members of society. For example, some companies have been unpleasantly surprised to find that customers won't buy products made by exploiting child laborers or cosmetics developed through animal testing. Consumers also may avoid firms with poor records on safety, pollution and discrimination. In his book *Building Your Company's Good Name*, Davis Young (1996) noted that a good reputation—an organization's most valuable asset—is built on performance rather than on mere words.

One of the principles of effective public relations is **adaptation**, the willingness and ability of the organization to make changes necessary to create harmony between itself and its key publics. Some organizations use strategic communication to convince their publics to conform to the offerings of the organization. This is the persuasive model of public relations. Another model of public relations aims to enhance the mutual relationship between the organization and its publics, which means that sometimes the organization will need to change.

If a university wants to promote registration for its summer program, for example, one of the first activities should be to research key publics (such as currently registered students, incoming freshmen and people who applied to the school and were accepted but who did not register), identifying the courses they want and the schedules they prefer. In other words, the school would create the summer program around its key publics' needs, rather than building it around the convenience of the faculty and administrators.

Similarly, if a dental office wants to attract a professional clientele, it might schedule office hours on weekends and evenings, perhaps on a couple of nights with appointments as late as 10 or 11 p.m. to accommodate busy executives.

The international campaign to select a world headquarters for the International Renewable Energy Agency shows the importance of performance and adaptation. IRENA required the agency's 130-plus members to agree on a location. Countries such as Denmark, Germany and Austria pushed their status as recognized leaders in renewable energy. But a public relations campaign on behalf of the United Arab Emirates helped shape a surprising outcome.

UAE is one of the world's leading producers of oil, and IRENA was focused on renewal energy. Fossil fuel was the enemy, or at least the energy source that IRENA hoped to relegate to the past. For years, though, UAE had been making a commitment to renewable energy. It was building the city of Masdar as the world's first carbon-neutral, zero-waste city with sustainable technology. Public relations showcased UAE's forward-looking energy policy and shored up its diplomatic role in the international community.

In 2009, IRENA voted to establish its international headquarters in Masdar, a recognition that UAE's performance on clean energy had matched its words.

Audience Engagement

Another important strategy initiative for the public relations planner is *audience engagement*. This involves using strong two-way communication tactics and engaging audiences and publics in your communication activities.

AUDIENCE INTEREST

One way to do this is to communicate about the audience's relevant interests rather than the needs of the message source or the sponsoring organization. The formal term for this is **salience** of the information—the degree to which information is perceived as being applicable or useful to the audience. Use examples and applications that address a key question of your public: What's in it for me?

In a fundraising letter for AIDS research, for example, tell your readers that they can help make a cure possible rather than merely citing the researchers' need for financial support. When possible, base your message on values shared by the organization and the public.

AUDIENCE PARTICIPATION

Audience participation can be built on activities that bring individual members of your publics into direct contact with the products and services of your organization. For example, police departments in many cities routinely use ride-along programs to give citizens a firsthand look at their communities from inside a patrol car. Cosmetic companies give free samples, health clubs give low-cost trial memberships and private schools have shadow programs for prospective students.

Several years ago the Union of American Hebrew Congregations (UAHC), the denominational leadership of Reform Judaism in the US, wanted to strengthen bonds with Reform Jews around the country. Invoking the principle of audience participation, UAHC invited its 800 member congregations to participate in a video project by sharing their success stories. More than 200 congregations responded and asked to be included in the documentary, gaining a sense of solidarity with the national association—virtually guaranteeing their use of the eventual video.

Audience participation was at the heart of a campaign to restore the Bosque de Chapultepec in Mexico City, the hemisphere's oldest urban park, where 15 million visitors a year had endangered the park's 686 hectares (1,700 acres). The public relations strategy centered on building a sense of public stewardship and a personal stake in the park among the city's residents and visitors, as well as creating strategic alliances with corporations.

Specifics of this approach included encouraging visitors to minimize and perhaps reverse pollution by using sanitary facilities. The plan also relied heavily on volunteers and donors.

Starting in 2004, the campaign developed several tactics including typical media relations activities such as news conferences and interviews. Tactics also included networking among environmentally involved groups, special events surrounded phased reopening after the park was closed for several months, and attention-getting activities such as concerts and cultural events by celebrities to attract local residents of various ages.

AUDIENCE FEEDBACK

Still another way to foster audience participation is by generating feedback. Create convenient ways your audience can respond to your message and engage in dialogue. Use techniques such as toll-free phone numbers, online surveys, question-and-answer sessions, interactive websites and similar tools.

A company may look to research in determining whether to establish a consumer complaints hotline as a form of feedback. A complaints department can gauge customer satisfaction, minimize the loss of customers and perhaps identify ways to prevent problems.

Several studies (Nyer, 2000; Kowalski and Erickson, 1997) suggest that soliciting complaints can actually help an organization reduce customer dissatisfaction. It seems that people feel better about the organization they complain against when they actually have an opportunity to voice those complaints. After venting, they also feel better about the product or service they had complained about, according to the studies.

TRIGGERING EVENT

You also can build into your program a **triggering event**. This is an activity that stimulates action among key publics. Examples of triggering events are speeches that conclude with an invitation for the audience to sign a petition, or an open house that ends with an opportunity to join.

Sometimes the triggering element is built into an event, such as election day as the triggering event for a political campaign. In themselves, awareness weeks don't cut it; they are too mundane. But good planning can create interesting activities that can draw attention to the sponsoring organization.

Experienced public relations practitioners realize that sometimes triggering events may be unplanned, so they are quick to take advantage of opportunities that present themselves. The election of the first openly gay Episcopalian bishop in 2005 served as a triggering event, both positive and negative, for issues such as gay rights and church unity.

Often the events themselves are tragic, but in their tragedy they focus attention on particular issues. Such is the case where the death of a celebrity can focus attention on the illness or lifestyle that caused the death: Whitney Huston and Amy Winehouse calling attention to drug and alcohol abuse, respectively, or Don Cornelius' suicide shedding light on depression.

Sometimes a triggering event brings unwanted notoriety. The Spanish public was outraged in 2012 when it learned that, while the country struggled with an economic crisis including 23 percent unemployment, King Juan Carlos had taken a lavish elephant hunt to Botswana. The public learned of the expensive safari only when the king broke his hip and had to be flown back to Madrid for surgery. The outrage prompted the first-ever public apology in his 23 years as monarch.

But Juan Carlos also was president of the Spanish branch of the World Wildlife Fund. For years his support of bullfighting had been a thorn in the side of pro-animal activists. But the international embarrassment of this ill-timed safari renewed attention on some of his earlier transgressions of environmental principles, including a previous elephant kill in Africa and bear hunts in Russia and Romania. WWF/Spain quickly removed Juan Carlos from the honorary leadership post.

This was not the first time that big-game hunting made the headlines. The incident came only a month after Donald Trump's two sons were photographed hunting elephants, leopards and other exotic animals in Zimbabwe.

Such incidents only serve to heighten international opposition to big-game hunting parties for the rich and/or famous, and focus renewed attention on the broader issue of human sport and threatened animal habitats in Africa and elsewhere.

Special Event

A **special event** is another useful way to generate audience participation. A special event is a **staged activity** (also called a **pseudo-event**), which is an activity that an organization develops or orchestrates to gain the attention and acceptance of key publics. Special events should be legitimate, meaning they are designed primarily as a means of engaging publics and encouraging their interaction with your organization, with the potential for media attention being secondary.

The polar opposite to this type of special event is the **publicity stunt**, which is merely a gimmick planned mainly to gain publicity, having little value beyond that.

Avoid self-serving publicity stunts, but don't dismiss the news value of legitimate special events. An appropriate event can attract the attention of reporters and generate interest among your publics.

A publicity stunt sometimes can provide a great *photo op* (short for photo opportunity) that can attract the attention of visual media and offer opportunities to extend the organization's message to newspapers and magazines, television and online video and photographic venues.

OPPORTUNITY BORN OF TRAGEDY

Suffering in silence may be a virtue, but suffering in public can make money. Public misfortune can make your cause hot.

When First Lady Betty Ford went public with her diagnosis and treatment for breast cancer in 1974, she broke a social taboo against discussing personal issues in the media. Her honesty and candor did more than put the disease on the public agenda; it also provided a lesson for public relations practitioners: Move quickly when injury or disease captures the nation's attention.

Often that attention surrounds celebrity. The National Parkinson Foundation found that public interest and donations grew when actor Michael J. Fox revealed that he suffered from Parkinson's disease. Fox created his own foundation, registered in both the US and his native Canada, which has raised $275 million for Parkinson's research.

With media interest comes money. Donations doubled for the American Paralysis Association after actor Christopher Reeve was paralyzed in a horse-riding accident; the association even changed its name to the Christopher Reeve Paralysis Association. And contributions to the Alzheimer's Association jumped after President Ronald Reagan was diagnosed with the disease.

Assisting the public relations efforts of some organizations, celebrities have helped turn the spotlight on illnesses and diseases afflicting themselves or their loved ones. Awareness of testicular cancer, for example, is the cause of comedian Tom Green, actor Richard Belzer, and athletes such as cyclist Lance Armstrong, hockey forward Phil Kessel, third baseman Mike Lowell, wide receiver Kevin Curtis and skater Scott Hamilton, themselves survivors of the disease. See checkyonutz.org to see how public relations students at Canisius College developed an awareness campaign for testicular cancer.

Model Christy Turlington became a spokesperson for her own disease, emphysema, and for the lung cancer that killed her father. Sharon Osborne dealt with her diagnosis of colorectal cancer during her reality TV show, earning praise for increasing public awareness about the disease.

Other celebrities giving publicity to various maladies include actor Jimmy Smits for colon cancer, country singer Toby Keith for childhood cancers, talk show host Montel Williams for multiple sclerosis, basketball star Alonzo Mourning for anemia, basketball star Magic Johnson for HIV/AIDS, R&B singer Tionne T-Boz Watkins for sickle cell disease and quarterback Doug Flutie for childhood autism. Diabetes awareness is the cause supported by soul singer Gladys Knight and actors Halle Barry and Cuba Gooding Jr. Breast cancer awareness has strong support from entertainers such as Reese Witherspoon, Nicole Kidman and Vivica A. Fox.

Like Michael J. Fox, some celebrities even have created their own foundations—Livestrong, the Lance Armstrong Foundation to fight cancer; Sean Combs' Daddy's House Social Programs for inner-city kids; the Whitney Houston Foundation for Children; Oprah Winfrey's Angel Network assisting Boys and Girls Clubs; the Tiger Woods Foundation for children; and Hunter's Hope Foundation founded by former Buffalo Bills quarterback Jim Kelly (named for his infant son, Hunter) to fight Krabbe's disease and to promote newborn screening for it.

ETHICS: PUBLICITY STUNT

In a campaign titled "Holocaust on Your Plate," People for the Ethical Treatment of Animals compared the slaughtering of chickens to the murder of Jews by Nazis in World War II. Not unexpectedly, PETA drew hostile criticism and a lot of media attention to its cause of animal rights. While attention does not necessarily result in support, the action did seem to further PETA's publicity agenda.

In developing public relations strategies, give thought to the ethical considerations that underlie publicity stunts.

- Does the action have any intrinsic value, or is it mainly for show?
- Will it be offensive? To whom?
- If it is offensive, does this matter to your organization?
- Does the publicity stunt trivialize an otherwise serious topic?

For example, the Almond Board of Australia has as its mission to promote the health benefits and good taste of almonds as a way to boost sales. In addition to the usual package of media interviews, the board developed a photo op in 2010 that played on visual imagery. The board asked an up-and-coming designer to create a dress hand-sewn with 3,000 almonds. It then had a model parade through a pedestrian mall in the central business district of Sydney, giving away tins of fresh almonds to passersby. Photos of the dress were uploaded to Flickr, and video of the stunt was placed on YouTube. The board achieved its objectives of generating coverage in print and online trade and consumer publications, achieving record sales in the following three months.

To distinguish a legitimate special event from a publicity stunt ask yourself: Even if the news media don't report this activity, will it still be worthwhile? If you can answer "yes" to this question, then it's probably a real special event.

Another important requirement for effective special events is that they should be creative, with a spark of originality that sets them apart from the ordinary and the routine. Brainstorming with your colleagues sometimes can suggest an approach that would be distinctive enough so that the special event can become, literally, "the talk of the town." There are many types of special events, which are outlined in the next section on tactics. For now, simply consider the wide range of possibilities:

- artistic programs, such as recitals and art shows;
- competitions, such as sporting events and essay contests;
- community events, such as parades, festivals and fairs;
- holiday celebrations for civic, cultural, ethnic, religious and other occasions;
- observances, such as anniversaries, birthdays, special days or months;
- progress-oriented activities, such as groundbreaking ceremonies, cornerstone placements and grand openings.

A later section on activism deals with special events of a more polemic or confrontational nature.

Phase Two

STEP
5

Alliance and Coalition

When two or more organizations join together in a common purpose, the combined energy offers a real opportunity for strategic communication initiatives.

- An **alliance** tends to be an informal, loosely structured and perhaps small working relationship among organizations.
- A **coalition** is a similar relationship that is a bit more formal and structured than an alliance.

Alliances and coalitions seek to forge relationships—often new ones—with groups that share similar values and concerns. Using this strength-in-numbers approach, organizations try to compound their influence toward meeting objectives and to enhance their ability to break through barriers while trying to relate to their publics.

Some alliances involve people (such as customers or celebrities) rather than organizations alone. When Lee Jeans joined with the Entertainment Industry Foundation (Hollywood's leading charitable organization) to promote National Denim Day, the company called on people to put on their favorite jeans and donate $5 for breast cancer research. Lee also invited the participation of celebrities: Zac Efron, Christine Applegate, Billy Ray Cyrus, Mariska Hargitay, Steve Carrel, Jessica Simpson, Lucy Liu and others. The annual Denim Day has raised more than $83 million in 15 years, making it one of the largest single-day fundraising events.

Sometimes organizations seek alliances with influential individuals, particularly with community leaders who are respected among the organization's publics. An organization trying to encourage African Americans to participate in a bone marrow screening, for instance, may look to respected minority leaders in the community or perhaps to influential organizations such as the National Association for the Advancement of Colored People or the Urban League, professional sports teams, black professional fraternities or sororities, or similar groups.

Organizations that recognize they have a poor reputation with their public sometimes seek alliances with organizations having a better standing with the public. For example, several years ago when the U.S. Immigration and Naturalization Service (INS) declared a legalization program for undocumented immigrants who met certain residency requirements, in several communities it turned to churches that had an existing credibility within the Hispanic community. The premise for this was the undocumented immigrants' distrust of the INS would be overcome by their greater trust in the churches. The third-party endorsement the churches were able to provide the INS helped many people become legal residents.

At times, coalition building can lead to some unlikely bedfellows. In some communities, for example, coalitions advocating sexual responsibility or access to prenatal and postnatal care bring together pro-life and pro-choice activists who otherwise would have little in common.

Alliances sometimes are made with internal publics, such as when a company convenes a task force of its employees to consider workplace concerns. Other alliances focus on external publics. For example, a health care system facing unprofitable duplication of services among several of its hospital sites might hold public hearings to discuss the problem and invite community input toward finding a solution, thus building an alliance with its publics.

ALLIANCES AND OPINION LEADERS

A particularly beneficial alliance can exist between an organization and opinion leaders. Having identified opinion leaders in Step 3, public relations planners can find themselves in a good place to develop a strategy for communicating with them.

One piece of advice from the field is to involve opinion leaders early. For example, 39 percent of pharmaceutical companies communicate with opinion leaders before they launch the public phase of their public relations tactics, according to a survey by Cutting Edge Information, a pharmaceutical research/planning firm in Durham, North Carolina.

Jason Richardson, president of Cutting Edge, explains the value of taking an early lead with opinion leaders: "One of the biggest mistakes pharmaceutical companies make is waiting to contact key opinion leaders—and not involving them enough. Opinion leader relationships are built on activities that begin years before a product reaches the market." Richardson also reports that too few companies allot adequate funds to communicate with opinion leaders, whom he calls "thought leaders."

A campaign to reduce AIDS and other sexually transmitted diseases consciously drew on Everett Rogers's diffusion of innovation theory by targeting bartenders as opinion leaders with influence through the social network of bars.

The campaign also identified as opinion leaders people who were popular and well-liked and who have frequent interaction with the key publics of the campaign. The campaign then enlisted the involvement of these opinion leaders, providing training on how to encourage behavioral changes to lower the risk of HIV infection. The campaign reported a 25–30 percent decrease in risky behaviors following the intervention of the opinion leaders.

Phase Two

STEP 5

Sponsorship

Another proactive step that organizations can take to gain visibility and respect among their key publics is through **sponsorship**. A sponsorship is a significant strategy for programs oriented toward community relations. It involves either providing a program directly, or providing financial, personnel or other resources the program requires.

Make sure there is a logical link between the activity being sponsored and the purpose or mission of your organization. For example, a science museum might sponsor a trip to view a space shuttle launch; a college might host a summer boot camp for high school journalists; a bookstore might support a literacy program.

Kleenex has engaged in such corporate sponsorship beginning with the 2004 Olympic Games. Its series of "Kleenex Moments" focused on human emotions in the various athletic events, which research showed were watched by couples. The campaign involved marketing, advertising, Internet and media relations. The media outreach alone generated more than 1,700 news stories with a total audience of nearly 135 million readers and viewers.

In an example of the no-good-deed-goes-unpunished maxim, the environmental organization Greenpeace used the publicity generated by Kleenex to criticize its parent company, Kimberly-Clark (K-C), the world's largest manufacturer of tissue products. At the time, the company was making 4 million tons of tissue products each year from old-growth forests

> **CASE IN POINT Student-Farmer Alliance**
>
> The nature of alliances is that they generate energy, cooperation and media attention around a single and often narrow issue.
>
> The Coalition of Immokalee Workers mounted a four-year boycott of Yum! Brands, the world's largest fast-food conglomerate (including Taco Bell, Pizza Hut and KFC, among others). The boycott was sponsored by the Student-Farmer Alliance, a nationwide network of youth, farmers, unions, clergy and workers. Focused as it was on improving conditions for migrant workers in Florida, the boycott was supported by groups including the National Council of Churches, Florida Catholic Conference and AFL-CIO union.
>
> The boycott ended after the company agreed to the alliance's demands: a penny a pound more for tomatoes picked by migrant workers from Haiti, Guatemala and Mexico working in Immokalee, improved working conditions and an end to harassment and threats against workers. The alliance had coordinated a nationwide "Boot the Bell" campaign that challenged Taco Bell establishments on high school and college campuses, organized a rolling nationwide hunger strike against Taco Bell and dispatched Taco Bell Truth Tours.
>
> The alliance and the public awareness it generated caused Notre Dame University to cancel Taco Bell's $75,000 sponsorship of its football program.
>
> After its Yum! victory, the alliance turned to Burger King. It sponsored a weeklong "Kingdoom Days of Action" with similar demands for a penny a pound more for tomato pickers and promising similar resistance if they didn't. The multibillion-dollar Burger King said the demand would cost $250,000 a year, and it threatened to buy tomatoes directly from Mexico instead of from Florida, where most winter tomatoes are grown for U.S. restaurants. Eventually, Burger King agreed to the alliance's demands and became a supporter of the coalition workers.

in Canada. Greenpeace leveraged the publicity associated with the 2006 Winter Olympics and gave Kleenex a "gold medal" for "a new world record for fastest forest destruction."

After a five-year global campaign against K-C, Greenpeace joined the corporation in a joint news conference in 2009 to announce a truce: The company pledged to no longer use trees from the ancient forests, to use more recycled paper and to strengthen its policy toward sustainable forest management, and Greenpeace would halt the boycott. Ironically, Greenpeace itself was criticized by Marcal, a company that manufactures paper goods from only 100 percent recycled products. Marcal accused Greenpeace of lowering its standards to get the K-C agreement.

It's also a good idea to establish levels or categories for potential sponsors so smaller businesses or individual funders will be able to participate, as well as larger and better-funded sponsors. An organization may seek a single program or "title" sponsor giving a major donation, as well as a dozen or more corporate patrons and individual sponsors giving lesser amounts.

Membership organizations, such as zoos, likewise have varying levels for individual sponsors. Beyond the levels of individual and family memberships, zoos often create categories for more involved donors. The Denver Zoo, for example, has a whole range of advanced levels for individual memberships: the Curator's Club ($275–$499), the Director's Circle

($500–$999), the President's Club ($1,000–$2,499), the Chairman's Circle ($2,500–$4,999), the Guardian Society ($5,000–$9,000) and the Conservation Society ($10,000 or higher). Some zoos use clever names: the Milwaukee Zoo has its Platypus Society, the St. Louis Zoo has a Safari Circle and a Wildlife Circle, and the Indianapolis Zoo has a Keeper's Circle.

Some sponsorships are based on existing marketing relationships. For example, Lexus sponsors polo championships because polo enthusiasts reflect the luxury car's customer base. So too with Budweiser's sponsorship of the Super Bowl and Snickers' arrangement as the official candy of Little League Baseball and U.S. Youth Soccer.

Other sponsorship programs are designed to appeal to new publics. These programs often have a clear marketing connection, paving the way for the company to obtain new customers.

Another type of sponsorship is the naming of buildings, stadiums, rooms and other locations. Corporations name buildings, and colleges ask donors to name art studios and science labs—all for a price, of course. More on this in the section on branding rights in the next step of this strategic planning process.

Sponsorships can stretch a company's promotion dollars much further than media advertising, at the same time creating more intensive relationships between the organization and its publics. For example, during the Gay Games IX in 2014, Cleveland expects to host 13,000 athletes (the 2010 games in Cologne attracted nearly 10,000 athletes from 70 nations).

The Cleveland organizers hope to woo many of the same sponsors that supported the Chicago games in 2006, the previous U.S. host. Those sponsors included Sirius Satellite Radio, Absolut Vodka, Walgreens, Orbitz, American Airlines, Best Buy, MetLife and Nike among 350 corporate backers.

Organizers, sponsors and consumers alike have noted the value of such sponsorships, and many participants and fans in past games reported that they went out of their way to buy from the sponsors. Advertisers and sponsors called it *niche marketing*, an approach to marketing and public relations intended to shore up its relationship with consumers.

Yet such sponsorships are not without risk. Both Kraft Foods and WalMart were heavily criticized by conservative consumers who were spurred on by the well-funded American Family Association, which charged the food corporation with promoting homosexuality.

Ben & Jerry's ignored possible criticism (but prepared for it) when research showed that key customers supported the company's commitment to social justice. In 2010 when same-sex marriage became legal in its home state of Vermont, Ben & Jerry's partnered with the Freedom to Marry organization to activate consumers to support marriage equality. The company mobilized a social-media campaign and renamed its iconic "Chubby Hubby" ice cream as "Hubby Hubby" in its Vermont stores. The campaign received nationwide media coverage (86 percent of it rated positive or neutral), increasing sales in the process.

Strategic Philanthropy

Successful sponsor organizations find ways to attract continuing visibility and reputational benefits. This is the notion of **strategic philanthropy**, in which businesses fund or otherwise support community relations gestures with an eye toward their employees and customers.

Strategic philanthropy is more than charity. It is part of the wider approach to corporate social responsibility in which organizations realize that their success depends in part on the goodwill of the community and their perception as being a contributing member of society.

Phase Two

STEP
5

Sometimes this philanthropy takes the form of financial support. Corporations may give money for scholarships, though increasingly they are asking what they get for their money. Recipients of corporate charity would be wise to find ways to publicly recognize their donors and other supporters, not only as a matter of common courtesy but also as a way to foster an ongoing mutually beneficial relationship between the corporate donor and the recipient organization.

The Boeing Corporation has an eye on its customers and other support bases as it uses strategic philanthropy to generate tangible benefits, create enduring value, reach target publics and build sustainable long-term relationships. Its corporate beneficiaries include the Kennedy Center for the Performing Arts and sponsorship of the national anthem at all home games of the Chicago Bears (Chicago being its corporate headquarters), as well as signage at the Seattle Mariners baseball field and support for its Museum of Flight near its operations in Seattle. The company, which posts its philanthropic criteria at its website (boeing.com), reported charitable giving of $160 million in 2010 from the corporation, its employees and its charitable trust.

David Eisenstadt, partner with TCI (The Communications Group) based in Toronto, points out that, in the past, some corporate giving was based on whim. The CEO's wife loved figure skating, so the company gave to a skating program. But such a gift didn't necessarily serve the corporate interest. Eisenstadt counsels that such philanthropy, part of a program of corporate social responsibility (CSR), should be a business decision, not an emotional one. "Our strategy is kind of back-to-basics," he told a reporter from *Strategy*, a Canadian marketing magazine. "If women are the people who make the buying decisions for our clients' services, then we would be looking at charitable organizations that have a strong female connect. The objective is that everybody should win" (Minogue, 2003).

Nonprofit organizations seeking corporate contributions should do their homework before seeking a corporate gift, first determining how to add public relations value for a potential donor. Before asking for funds, anticipate how you might acknowledge the gift, both immediately and in a continuing way. For example, tangible gifts might feature a sign or a plaque recognizing the donor, and other substantial gifts might result in using the corporate name for a program or facility. All gifts can be acknowledged in newsletters and at websites, and at events such as banquets and dedication ceremonies.

Increasingly, national causes are going local with a coordinated series of events, blending strategic philanthropy with alliances. One example of this is "Race for the Cure" (komen.org), which each year has more than a million runners in more than 100 local walks, races and marathons. Since its founding 30 years ago, the organization has raised nearly $2 billion for breast cancer awareness and research.

In addition to holding its own races throughout the country, the foundation works with affiliated activities such as "Bowl for the Cure," organized with the U.S. Bowling Congress, which raised $7 million over six years. General Mills donates about $2 million a year through its "Pink for the Cure" campaign from sales of pink-packaged cereal, soup, cookie mix and vegetables. "On Deck for the Cure" sponsored by Holland America, Princess, Carnival and several other cruise lines raised $1.7 million over four years through customer-focused events on board their ships. Major League Baseball has raised millions of dollars with its Mother's Day event, "Going to Bat against Breast Cancer," New Balance shoes has generated nearly $9 million with "Lace for the Cure," and Condé Naste publications' "Rally for the Cure" has raised $63 million.

PRINCIPLES OF STRATEGIC PHILANTHROPY

The guiding principle of strategic philanthropy is to get the biggest bang for the buck. This can be accomplished in three different ways.

Give More Bang for the Buck

This principle is one of basic economy: Provide something more valuable to others than it is costly to you. A dollar given that generates only a dollar's worth of benefit is not a good sponsorship investment. A more strategic sponsorship is a donation with more value to the recipient than cost to the giver.

For example, if a company that makes television sets wants to sponsor an educational program through the county library system, it could give $10,000 to the library for new books, earning a modest amount of visibility and appreciation. A better move, however, might be to donate $10,000 worth of television sets so that the library can expand its use of educational and cultural videos. This donation might have cost the company less than $4,000 to manufacture the TV sets, which would be a continuing reminder to library patrons of the company's donation to the community's quality of life.

Give What You Already Own

A parallel principle of sponsorship also is one of economy: Give something of value to others that you already own, and thus costs nothing to give away.

This is the premise behind Operation Home Free, begun by Trailways Bus Lines and continued when Greyhound bought that company. The program formed an alliance with the International Association of Chiefs of Police and the National Runaway Switchboard to help runaway youths. Over the years it provided free bus rides to about 10,000 runaways returning home.

The value? Tickets worth $120,000 in the first year alone.

The actual cost? Virtually nothing to Greyhound, since its buses already were running, usually with some empty seats.

The benefits? To runaways, a safe return home. To the police and runaway agencies, assistance in getting kids off the streets, into counseling and back home. To Greyhound, a boost in its reputation among employees, customers, police and other important publics.

A real win-win-win situation! The program has since been replicated by Greyhound Australia.

Maximize Your Investment

Another sponsorship principle is to make the most of what you donate, in terms of recognition. Consider giving several small gifts, each with the potential for significant publicity, instead of a single large one. While a large gift might yield one-time publicity, a series of well-timed and strategically placed smaller gifts might generate greater overall attention. Additionally, while anonymous giving may be good personally, corporate philanthropy generally needs the public spotlight. Give items or support projects that can be labeled with your organization's name, out there for all to see.

Some campaigns respond to data pointing toward the need for higher visibility in the public eye. This was the situation in 2007 when FedEx commissioned a national survey of 22,000 consumers and found that only 39 percent felt the company had a strong commitment to social responsibility. FedEx prized its social commitment and wanted to be recognized for it. The aftermath of Hurricane Katrina presented an opportunity for the transport giant, which created an event to transport 19 penguins back to the New Orleans aquarium from a temporary shelter in California where they had been taken after the hurricane. Drawing on its own prior experience in transporting pandas from China to Washington's National Zoo, FedEx realized that it should create a series of media moments for the "flight" of the flightless penguins.

The first media opportunity for the FedEx campaign was in Oakland, where police escorted the penguins to the airport for a bon voyage send-off. The next media moment came with the landing at the New Orleans airport, where the birds were greeted by a jazz band, a purple carpet for the matriarch penguin and another police escort. Finally, a large crowd, including 250 "influentials," was waiting at the aquarium as the penguins returned home.

FedEx counted 300 national and international media clips, many of them focused on the 200 local communities that the company had identified in its media plan. The event cost FedEx $36,000 in expenses, along with a $100,000 contribution to the new penguin habitat.

Some sponsorship activities focus more on issues rather than on events. An example of this is the Rock the Vote campaign (rockthevote.org), which encourages young adults to register to vote. Using donated radio and television spots, as well as its own online and social media, RTV has registered 5 million voters aged 18–29 since it began in national elections of 2000. The group cites research that 84 percent of young registered voters actually go to the polls during national elections.

The organization has built its success on alliances, including promotions cosponsored by malls, sporting events, and college campuses, as well as its interactive website and a toll-free 800 phone number promoted on television—particularly on MTV. It joined with Facebook to provide online registration for Facebook users. Working with LL Cool J's Camp Cool Foundation, RTV formed the Hip Hop Coalition for Political Change, extending its message into the inner city. It also formed Radio Rocks the Vote, a partnership with urban, alternative, and Top 40 stations. Such efforts attracted celebrities such as Kat Graham (*The Vampire Diaries*), Shawn Merriman (Buffalo Bills), and rappers Asher Roth, David Banner and the New Boyz.

Does all of this happen because MTV and the radio stations are civic-minded companies? They probably are. But there's also an element of self-service, as there is with every good sponsorship. The purpose behind Rock the Vote, founded in 1990 by recording industry folks concerned about free-speech issues, is to motivate a core of supporters who can use the political process to the advantage of the music industry.

Finally, some sponsorships have involved a strong component of volunteerism. AT&T provides its employees worldwide with paid time off for volunteer work in community activities. In 2010, AT&T employees contributed 8.2 million volunteer hours, worth more than $175 million. AT&T has been cited by Forbes magazine ranked as among the most generous corporate foundations. Altruism isn't the only motivation for community volunteer programs. AT&T believes the move gives it a better standing in the community and potentially higher profits.

The MTV Network, meanwhile, believes that its generous policy on employee volunteerism helps it attract and keep younger workers. The Points of Light Foundation (pointsoflight.org)

BENEFITS OF EMPLOYEE VOLUNTEER PROGRAMS

The Corporation for National and Community Service found that 26 percent of adult Americans (61 million people) volunteer 8.1 billion hours, worth $158 billion. It also found that 48 percent of companies include employee volunteerism as part of their overall business plan. The Bureau of Labor Statistics reports that most volunteer time goes to coaching, fundraising, tutoring, providing professional assistance and distributing food.

Both Junior Achievement (ja.org) and Volunteer Match (volunteermatch.org) pulled together these and several other studies on employee volunteer programs. Here are some of their findings in 2009 reports.

- *Corporate Benefits.* Employee volunteer programs offer bottom-line benefits to the company, according to survey respondents. Specifically volunteer programs address public relation goals (83 percent), meet marketing and communication objectives (64 percent), develop employee skills (60 percent), recruit/retain employees (58 percent), further corporate strategic goals (nearly 80 percent), attract better employees (almost 90 percent), keep valued employees (nearly 80 percent), contribute to the bottom line financially (64 percent) and boost productivity (reported by 60 percent of the executives, 75 percent by employees).

- *Employee Benefits.* Such programs offer specific employee benefits, including increasing competency by up to 17 percent, increasing job satisfaction (67 percent), improving leadership skills (75 percent) and improving morale (57 percent), all factors in increasing productivity.

- *Customer Benefits.* Employee volunteer programs also improve customer satisfaction, thus increasing company profits.

- *Community Benefits.* Finally, such volunteer programs offer indirect community benefits by helping create "healthier" communities and improving corporate public image (more than 90 percent each) and improving relations with the community and with local government (nearly 85 percent).

Phase Two

STEP
5

offers similar examples of corporate volunteerism: a law firm that gives an hour a week for each employee to tutor a child in the community; a manufacturer that allows up to 40 hours a year for volunteer work; a utility that bases 20 percent of its incentive pay on community involvement.

Such perceived value is not just anecdotal or wishful thinking. A health-care system, for example, tracked the productivity of its workers relative to its one and a half hours-a-week paid-time policy for volunteering. In the billing department, which processes checks, the company found that people who volunteer work faster, process more checks, are better organized, manage their time better and are more enthusiastic about their job. Other studies show that pro-volunteer policies increase employee morale, retention, productivity and team building, while providing training for employees.

Activism

Another initiative planners can use is **activism**, a confrontational strategy focused mainly on persuasive communication and the advocacy model of public relations. It's a strong strategy to be used only after careful consideration of the pros and cons. Activism offers many opportunities for organizations to present their messages and enhance their relationship with key publics, particularly their members and sympathizers.

Activism generally deals with causes or movements, such as social issues (crime, capital punishment or abortion, for example), environmental matters (pollution, suburban sprawl, nuclear waste), political concerns, and so on. A distinction might be made between advocates, who essentially are vocal proponents for causes, and activists, who are more inclined to act out their support for the cause. Look at the discussion on opponents in Step 3, Analyzing the Publics, for more background about advocates and other types of social activists.

Consider some of the tactics associated with the strategy of activism: strikes, pickets, sit-ins, petitions, boycotts, marches, vigils, rallies and outright civil disobedience.

Activists often make effective use of the news media because their tactics involve physical protests and thus are highly visible. The nonviolent international Occupy movement, against social and economic inequality, grew because it attracted the attention of both traditional and social media around the world. Sympathetic media coverage increased when video went viral showing police using pepper spray against peaceful Occupy Oakland protestors.

Effective activism often has an element of visual appeal. More than a publicity stunt, activist events involve newsworthy action done as much for the television viewers as for any other public. For example, when demonstrators have marched past the governor's mansion and capitol in various states to protest the death penalty, they often have dressed in mourning clothes and carried cardboard coffins and paper tombstones. News photographers and television crews undoubtedly appreciated their visual creativity.

Sometimes activism involves **civil disobedience**, a nonviolent and nonlegal—but generally visual—undertaking, often in support of social causes such as civil rights, environmentalism, Native American sovereignty and similar issues. Often such protests are loaded with symbolism.

This kind of activism often transforms itself into theater, particularly when protestors are courting TV coverage. The term **street theater** (alternatively called **guerrilla theater**) refers to social and political protests that take the form of dramatizations in public places. In 2007, members of a political activist/environmental group in Madison, Wisconsin, dressed as polar bears and staged a "die-in" at the local electric company to protest its coal-burning power plants, which the protestors said contribute to global warming and threaten polar bears and other species.

In 2008, Amnesty International coordinated an International Day of Action in 83 cities around the world, mostly near military bases or U.S. embassies. Protestors dressed in orange jumpsuits and black hoods, courting media attention as they protested the lack of due process for 275 prisoners held by the U.S. military at Guantanamo Bay, Cuba, for six years without charges or even access to lawyers. Some activities also took aim at allegations of torture of prisoners by the military.

The author's award for creative activist strategy goes to this well-orchestrated 1999 publicity stunt: Two dozen New York City community activists staged a sit-in on the marble floor of City Hall, singing "We Shall Overcome" accompanied by kazoos and wearing bee outfits and flowered hats. They were protesting the mayor's decision to auction off city-owned lots that neighborhood groups had turned into community gardens. Wait, there's more: Enter the New York Police Department in riot gear, and as the protestors went limp, the police had to carry them to a waiting police van. Now, that's entertainment!

Many protests are more serious. The Makah, a Native American tribe in Washington, is the only whaling tribe in the lower 48 states, the right to maintain its 2,000-year-old whaling tradition enshrined in federal treaty. After the tribal whaling commission declared its intention to return to its traditional ways and hold a whale hunt, its first in 70 years, a successful hunt was televised by American and international media, including the ceremonial butchering of the captured whale. Meanwhile the hunt attracted demonstrators including whaling protestors, animal-rights activists, and anti-Indian groups, all of them courting media attention.

Activists sometimes stretch ethical boundaries, entering an area that public relations practitioners should avoid. Pie throwing has become a tactic-of-choice for some activists, who found they could gain media attention and thus a platform for their messages by pulling their relatively benign stunts on famous people.

Targets of pieing-as-political-protest have included media executive Rupert Murdoch, pied in London during parliamentary hearings on phone hacking; Canadian oceans minister Gail Shea, pied by PETA to protest seal hunting; fashion designer Oscar de la Renta, pied because of his use of fur; Fred Phelps, pastor of the anti-gay Kansas church that pickets military

Phase Two

STEP 5

VALUE OF SYMBOLISM

Effective public relations activity should be more than mere words, and symbolic actions can be powerful tools that not only enhance the message but actually can become the message itself.

Consider some of the classic and more recent examples of symbolic action that support a public relations purpose.

Pope Benedict XVI not only used powerful words on his first visit to the US in 2008 regarding the sex abuse scandal in the Catholic Church ("I am ashamed") but he met privately with several abuse survivors. In another instance of symbolic action, his visit to a New York City synagogue high-lighted the similarities between the rabbi, a Holocaust survivor and the Pope himself, who as a German teenager had been drafted into Hitler's army and later deserted.

Because of their high visibility, popes have been particularly able to harness the power of symbolic action, such as the late Pope John Paul II's habit of kissing the ground on his international trips as a sign of respect for the land and its people, and Pope Paul VI's unexpected brotherly embrace of Greek Orthodox Patriarch Athenagoras I in Jerusalem after centuries of animosity between the Roman Catholic and Eastern Orthodox churches.

History also has many examples of powerful symbolic action: the Boston Tea Party; the driving of the Golden Spike that completed the transcontinental railroad; the raising of the U.S. flag over Iwo Jima.

Political and governmental leaders continue to engage in symbolic action because it often strikes a chord with voters. That's why you see political candidates serving sandwiches in soup kitchens and wearing hard hats at construction sites to show their concern for the poor and for working people, respectively.

funerals to protest homosexuality; Proctor & Gamble chairman John Pepper, over animal rights; Ralph Klein, premier of the Canadian province of Alberta, for opposing the Kyoto environmental accords; Dutch finance minister Gerrit Zalm, over the euro currency; Renato Ruggiero, director general of the World Trade Organization, over endangered sea turtles; and Microsoft chairman Bill Gates, just because.

Usually the only consequence of pie throwing is media coverage. But three San Francisco activists who protested the mayor's policies on the homeless by throwing tofu-cream and pumpkin pies in his face were sentenced to six months in prison. In Europe, several anti-Euro protestors who used lemon meringue as their weapon of choice received short jail terms. In Tucson, Arizona, two men calling themselves members of "Al Pieda" were arrested for assault and disorderly conduct after they pied conservative pundit Ann Coulter, but charges were reduced and fines suspended. No charges were filed against students at Brown University who pied New York Times columnist Thomas Friedman because they sought to dramatize their opposition to the university sponsoring him as part of 2008 Earth Day events.

If you are planning an activist strategy, keep a clear eye on all your publics. Certainly the news media are important. So too are the targets of your activism, whom you are attempting to persuade toward some kind of action or response. But perhaps most important is your internal public—generally volunteers, often with mixed motivations—who are being asked to give time and perhaps take risks on behalf of the cause. Activist strategy must provide for the "feeding" of these troops with continuing motivation, ongoing communication and, when possible, the attainment of milestone victories that can shore up their dedication.

Proactive Strategy 2: Communication

While the previous proactive strategies focus on the action of the organization, another cluster of strategies deals more with communication. **Communication strategy** is a category that includes publicity, newsworthy information and transparent communication.

Publicity

Most organizations intuitively understand the value of **publicity**, which is the attention given by the news media to an organization, person, event, product or idea. CEOs, program directors and other organizational leaders often put much faith in the premise that public attention is good. For this reason, they often press public relations specialists into holding news conferences, distributing news releases, and otherwise inviting the media to report on the activities and concerns of the organization.

What is the value of news reporting about your organization? Corporate executives sometimes believe there is a causal link between publicity and public support. It's not that easy, as we will see later in this section.

The underlying value of publicity is that it provides **third-party endorsement** for the organization's message. This refers to the extra credibility that comes with the endorsement of an outside and unbiased agent.

Particularly credible are media **gatekeepers**: reporters, editors, news directors, bloggers and others who control access to the media. Audiences assume that the news they obtain from television, radio and newspapers is more believable than information they obtain directly from the organization through advertising, websites, brochures and the like. That's because the information reported in the news media has passed the screen of the gatekeepers. Audiences know that not everything gets on the air or in the paper, so intuitively they recognize that the professional journalists have made some choices as to what information is worth presenting as news. A reporter or an editor considered what the organization had to say and decided it was accurate enough to pass along to the audience.

Some media are more believable than others and thus deserve particular attention from the public relations strategist. Specialized newspapers and magazines—in one category, those dealing with business, industry and the professions; in another, those focused on a specific ethnic, political, religious, cultural or lifestyle group—have particular credibility with their audiences. Likewise, certain commentators or talk show hosts carry enormous influence among their steady listeners and readers.

An interesting study by Kevin Barnhurst and Diana Mutz observes that newspaper journalism is moving away from simply reporting events to providing news analysis. They note that in 1960, 90 percent of front-page election stories were about events; 32 years later, 80 percent of front-page stories were interpretive. Meanwhile, in broadcast reporting, the length of candidate sound bites decreased during the same time period as election coverage became more centered on journalist commentators. "To qualify as news these days, an event also must fit into a larger body of interpretations and themes," the researchers report (1997, p. 51). The study hasn't been updated, but in today's media environment the trend seems to be evolving even more toward more-subjective reporting.

The lesson for practitioners, then, is to build your events and frame your messages around the larger issues that blip on the media agenda screen.

Sometimes you will find that newsworthy activities are occurring within your organization, and your role becomes that of an in-house journalist reporting on the existing news events. But more often your role will be that of public relations counselor and strategist. Public relations people regularly create or orchestrate newsworthy events within their organizations to carry an important message to the key publics.

There is a saying, "I don't care what they say about me, as long as they spell my name right." (For the record, it wasn't said by P.T. Barnum, despite that recurring miscitation.) That approach is simplistic and naive, because public relations professionals know that all publicity cannot be treated the same way. Positive publicity obviously helps an organization, but negative publicity can have a devastating impact.

When the media reported that the poison cyanide was discovered in Tylenol pain relief tablets, Johnson & Johnson stock dropped by $1 billion, 14 percent. Exxon stock dropped $3 billion after the *Exxon Valdez* oil spill. Motorola stock dropped $6 billion after reports linking cell phones and brain cancer. Those companies recovered financially, but some companies have gone bankrupt in the wake of negative publicity.

Sometimes, even negative publicity can help an organization. Traditionally, Boston was one of the first cities to book a play as it was leaving Broadway and beginning a nationwide tour. Because of Boston's conservative social sensitivities, it sometimes banned plays or books as being too offensive. Producers noted with interest that the very banning of plays in Boston often assured their success in attracting audiences elsewhere, and some theatrical companies deliberately tried to get banned from Boston.

Negative publicity often has had a positive effect on generating interest, particularly among potential audiences. Seldom is this more true than with religiously motivated protests. Rudy Giuliani unwittingly generated valuable publicity and increased audiences for museums when

FAMOUS NAMES MAKE NEWS

Public relations planners often try to involve celebrities who not only can attract media attention but who also might impact on key publics.

Because studies show that 88 percent of Americans get most of their health information from television, the National Cancer Institute's Entertainment Education Program works with Hollywood and with advocacy groups to promote TV storylines. It has tip sheets and other resources for writers and producers. NCI teamed with the Centers for Disease Control and Prevention and the Annenberg Norman Lear Center to recognize television's attention to health issues with the Sentinel for Health Awards.

Documented results of the cooperation between Hollywood and advocacy groups have been surprising, showing some celebrity-based activities to effect major public response.

TV journalist Katie Couric became a national spokesperson for awareness about colorectal cancer after her husband died from the disease. Couric underwent a colonoscopy live on national television. The result? Testing for the disease increased 22 percent nationwide and held steady for nine months. Media analysts dubbed this "The Couric Effect." Five years later, Couric broadcast her own mammogram to similarly influence women to undergo the potentially life-saving exam for breast cancer.

Similarly, publicity about celebrities and their illnesses also can cause others to pay closer attention to their own health. A study (Larson et al., 2005) showed that celebrity endorsements led to a 21 percent increase for mammograms, 31 percent for prostate exams, and 37 percent for colonoscopies. Health statisticians documented increased interest in diagnostic exams when Vice President Dick Cheney received a pacemaker for his heart condition in 2001 and when Secretary of State Colin Powell was treated for prostate cancer in 2003.

Other medical researchers pointed to a 2003 storyline in the British TV series *Coronation Street* about a woman's death from cervical cancer as the major cause of a 21 percent increase in testing for that disease.

Celebrities also are effective in focusing the attention of lawmakers on various social issues. The Alzheimer's Association said an appearance at a congressional caucus by its spokesperson, actor David Hyde Pierce, not only brought publicity for the cause but the increased participation of senators and representatives. Similarly, when film star Julia Roberts went to Congress to speak about a rare neurological disorder, Rhett syndrome, influential lawmakers paid attention.

Other celebrities have given congressional testimony on issues in which they are involved: actress and United Nations ambassador on domestic violence Nicole Kidman; Nick Jonas on the diabetes he suffers; Billy Corgan of The Smashing Pumpkins on music royalties; and Dennis Quaid on medical errors such as those that nearly killed his infant twins. With less-obvious credentials, Lindsay Lohan testified about jobs and Stephen Colbert spoke on immigration.

At first glance, some spokespersons seem unlikely. The Muppets have participated in congressional news conferences about public funding for television, but Elmo is the only non-human to address Congress, speaking in support of music education. Another spokesperson with dubious human credentials is Ian Somerhalder (*The Vampire Diaries*), who in 2011 used not only his fame but also his bona-fide credentials as an environmental philanthropist to speak on behalf of wildlife.

he publicly criticized them while he was major of New York City: an exhibit with a photo of Christ depicted as a naked black woman; a display with a portrait of the Virgin Mary covered with elephant dung. Movies such as Martin Scorsese's *The Last Temptation of Christ* and Mel Gibson's *The Passion of the Christ* gained attention and audiences as various religious groups lined up in protest. So maybe that old saying might make some sense after all.

To attract the interest of the news media, particularly of television reporters, the news and publicity events must have a strong visual element. Stand-up commentators or talking heads don't make it on most television news reports, other than on occasional local-access cable programs that few people watch. Audiences have become sophisticated, some might say spoiled. Regardless, they demand active, even entertaining, visual presentation of their news. Reporters do their best to comply with the expectations of their audiences. So unless you are able to present newsworthy information with a visual dimension, you are unlikely to find the news media receptive vehicles for your message.

The quest for a strong visual element to news is an opportunity for creative minds, as noted in the previous section on the strategy of activism. Even in nonconfrontational situations, events staged for their publicity value have their place—as long as they are vehicles for news and not simply hollow attention-getters. At one university, a student theater group called Casting Hall wanted to attract attention and new members, so its members went "fishing" in the student union on a very snowy January day. Students in waders carried fishing poles, casting and reeling in new members. It was a visual pun, appropriate for both the name and the theatrical nature of the organization. The gimmick drew attention, generated publicity, raised some interest and resulted in several new members.

Generating News

Alchemy doesn't work. It's not possible to turn lead into gold; neither is it possible to turn non-news into newsworthy information. Public relations practitioners shouldn't delude their bosses or clients, certainly not themselves, that facts without a news context are worth presenting to the media. Our credibility rests on the ability to determine what is news and what isn't.

But if a particular bit of information isn't newsworthy, we don't have to discard it. The media may not be able to use it right now, but there are two things we can do. One is to take the information directly to our publics, circumventing the media by using organization tools such as websites, a brochure, Facebook and other communication vehicles.

The second alternative is to generate newsworthy activity for an organization. We might creatively and strategically develop an approach that will become newsworthy. Here are 10 ways to generate news for an organization.

1. Give an award to draw attention to values and issues.
2. Hold a contest to involve others in your values and issues.
3. Select personnel to head a new program or begin a new project.
4. Comment on a local need or problem.
5. Conduct research and issue a report about a local need or problem.
6. Launch a campaign to accomplish something.
7. Give a speech to a significant audience and tell the media about it.

8. Involve a celebrity to visit and/or address your organization on a topic of concern to you.
9. Tie into an issue already high on the public or media agenda, or link your organization to the top news of the day.
10. Localize a general report.

For more on how to generate news, see Smith (2012).

CASE IN POINT   **Ground Zero Mosque**

For a few months in 2010, the news media were reporting, editorializing and providing a platform for voices on various sides of a rather simple issue: a plan by the Muslim-American community to build a cultural center in lower Manhattan, not far from the site of the World Trade Center terrorist attacks nearly a decade earlier.

It was a manufactured story, a contrived controversy that burst onto the media scene, ran its course, then (predictably) dropped out of sight. That in itself makes an interesting study in agenda setting and media manipulation. It's also a story full of lessons for public relations practitioners in dealing with an irrational bombardment of condemnation and disparagement.

The buzz was about, and largely against, what even mainstream media called the "Ground Zero mosque." But the media hype never seemed to jibe with the facts.

The proposed location isn't at the site of the World Trade Center attacks, which had become known as Ground Zero. It's two New York City blocks away, not even visible from the WTC site. The area includes porn shops, strip clubs and liquor stores, though these establishments didn't fuel the ire of opponents who claimed that the mosque would desecrate the "hallowed ground" of the terrorist attack that killed about 3,000 people—Christians, Jews, Hindus, Buddhists and nonbelievers as well as Muslims, all working together in the WTC towers. The neighborhood also was home to at least two mosques and, ironically, to several designated Islamic prayer spaces inside the WTC towers.

And the mosque wasn't even a mosque. Rather it was an Islamic community center with a prayer space on an upper floor as well as a performance hall, restaurant, fitness rooms, pools, child-care facilities, cooking school, bookstore and other activities that technically would be off-limits for a mosque.

How is it that such facts failed to suppress the rabid negative tone of criticism?

When the proposal was announced in 2009, it generated little controversy. What little attention it did receive when the *New York Times* and Fox News reported it, was positive. But for nearly half a year the story lay dormant.

Then right-wing bloggers and Rupert Murdoch's *New York Post* newspaper fanned anti-Islamic sentiment, with references to the proposed center as a "victory mosque for al-Qaida."

They called the imam a radical Islamist, though he was renowned for his work in interfaith outreach and tolerance, working with both the Bush and Obama administrations. *Time* magazine named him one of the 100 most influential people, calling him *continued*

a "global voice for interfaith dialogue [who] helped expose a virulent strain of American Islamophobia."

Extremists called for bombing the proposed site as well as destruction of Islamic holy sites in the Middle East. Some fundamentalist groups planned to publicly desecrate the Quran to protest the cultural center. The bloggers created a Stop Islamization of America group. The Republican Tea Party movement adopted it as a *cause du jour*, and ad campaigns by unidentified sponsors further vilified the project.

As the story emerged from the right-wing alternative media into the mainstream press, some parts of the story were sanitized for general consumption. Still, the tenor of the reporting was rooted in the historically dubious notion that America is a Christian nation and that the vision of religious pluralism and sectarian neutrality doesn't and shouldn't extend to Islam. The common theme was that the proposed center was, if not illegal, at least reprehensible and insensitive, something to be feared and defeated.

Several influential media voices trumpeted the notion that the cultural center would dishonor victims of the 9/11 attacks.

Where is the project now? Out of the limelight. After a five-month run, the controversy settled down. Those who fanned the anti-Muslim rhetoric moved on to other issues and politicians who latched onto the cause went back to throwing other stones at each other. Lawsuits against the project have been dismissed.

A year after the media controversy, the community center (renamed Park51) opened without incident in its temporary existing space, formerly a clothing warehouse. The project continues. It has been scaled back because of fundraising shortfalls, but the developer told reporters that he is moving at "a slower, more deliberate and more realistic approach." The board now includes the family of one of the 9/11 victims.

What are the lessons for public relations practitioners? There are several.

- *Fight for the naming rights*. The project began losing support when the term "Ground zero mosque" became legitimized through its use in the main-stream media. Since it was neither a mosque nor located at Ground Zero, the misnomer should have been correctable if the project developers had reacted sooner. But by the time they protested on the facts, the name had already stuck.

- *Counter false framing*. Don't allow the opposition to set the tone, especially in what may seem like a small issue. Originally the project was named Cordoba House. Developers said the name reflected the era of cooperation among Christians, Jews and Muslims in eighth to eleventh century Cordoba, Spain. Critics relabeled the title as a homage to the Muslim invasion of Christian lands. Project supporters did not effectively counter that propaganda.

- *Identify key publics*. Leaders of the project admitted to "public relations missteps." The lead developer said "the biggest mistake we made was not to

Phase Two

STEP
5

continued

include 9/11 families." Though some families spoke out in favor of the Islamic center, others opposed it, some of them vociferously. And because of their emotional link to the issue, the media gave them wide coverage.

- *Build a coalition of supporters*. The developers of the cultural center were largely left on their own. While some initial voices spoke on their behalf, there was no groundswell of support from mainline religious, cultural or political organizations. The project leaders later admitted that they failed to connect with community leaders and with activists.

- *Challenge the media to get it right*. The news media allowed the anti-Muslim critics to frame the message. Many media reports gave voice to the bigotry of the opponents without challenging the misinformation they presented. That's primarily a shortcoming of the reporters, but there were no public relations voices calling the media on this breach in journalistic standards.

- *Seek bipartisan support*. The project became politicized when the Tea Party movement adopted it, sparking Republican leaders (including Mitt Romney, John McCain, Sarah Palin and several primary candidates) to publicly oppose the cultural center. President Obama and New York City major Bloomberg spoke in favor of allowing the project to move forward, but their voices were drowned by a barrage of GOP-based critics.

- *Present a positive theme*. The planners originally had presented the project as a symbol of reconciliation, repairing the relationship between Muslims and other Americans. The imam's wife noted that many New York City Muslims were among the victims, as are "the silent majority of Muslims who suffer at the hands of extremists." But opponents counterpunched with another theme. They said the center, which some of them grudgingly admitted was legal, was nevertheless "insensitive" to 9/11 victims. Project developers gave no effective response to that criticism. President Clinton observed that the project may have had generated support if it had been dedicated to the Muslim victims of 9/11.

- *Listen*. The developer noted that, "We didn't understand that we had a responsibility to discuss our private project with family members that lost loved ones. Now," he said, "we're very committed to having them involved in our project. We're really listening."

- *Oppose false criticism quickly*. If there is one overriding lesson to be learned from the controversy surrounding the Park51 center, it is that organizations must confront criticism quickly and forcefully. The too-little-too-late public relations response from developers of the cultural center allowed opponents to gain and keep the upper hand.

Newsworthy information

Presenting newsworthy information is a must for any organization that hopes to use the news media to carry its message and capture the interest of its publics. For the communication strategist, news is one of the strongest proactive strategies because something truly newsworthy is almost guaranteed to gain the attention of the news media and, through them, the organization's other publics. Even if you are presenting a message through personal or organizational channels, keep in mind that your audiences will be more drawn to a newsworthy message.

What is news? **News** is information that offers the audience a new idea or the latest development. From a journalistic perspective—which is the perspective every public relations practitioner needs to respect and adopt—news is information that involves action, adventure, change, conflict, consequence, contest, controversy, drama, effect, fame, importance, interest, personality, prominence, proximity and dozens of other attributes often listed in journalism textbooks.

For our purposes, we will define news as significant information relevant to the local area, presented with balance and objectivity and in a timely manner. The value of news is magnified by two more elements: unusualness and fame. Let's simplify things with the acronym **SiLoBaTi + UnFa**. This convenient way to remember the main ingredients of news is made up of the first two letters of each of the elements: *si*gnificance, *lo*calness, *ba*lance and *ti*meliness, plus *un*usualness and *fa*me.

- *Significance*. First, news is information of importance and significance. It has meaning to many people, even those beyond the organization. It is information of consequence and magnitude.
- *Local*. News also deals with information relevant to the local area, as defined by the coverage area of the news medium featuring the information.
- *Balance*. News is information with objectivity and balance. While the public relations practitioner uses information to promote the organization or client, it should not be presented merely in a promotional manner. Rather, it should be presented with an air of detachment and neutrality.
- *Timely*. The final key ingredient in news is that it is current and timely, being connected with contemporary issues, especially those high on public and media agendas.

In addition to these four key elements, newsworthiness is magnified by two other factors.

- *Unusualness*. News interest is enhanced when the information deals with unusual situations. This is what writers call human interest, that hard-to-define quality involving rarity, novelty, uniqueness, milestones or slightly offbeat occurrences.
- *Fame*. News interest also is enhanced when the information involves fame. "Names make news" isn't idle chatter. Well-known or important people can add interest to a newsworthy situation. Sometimes their involvement can take an otherwise routine event and elevate it to the status of news.

For more about newsworthiness, see Smith (2012).

Phase Two

STEP
5

News judgment is relative. Public relations writers attempt to predict newsworthiness, but the decision to call something news is made only by the media gatekeepers, those people who control the flow of information in their various publications, newscasts or talk shows. Examples of media gatekeepers are editors, columnists, news directors, producers and webmasters.

As a public relations professional, part of your job is to analyze the relationship among three things to establish newsworthiness: (1) your organization's activities and messages; (2) the media agenda; and (3) the interests of a key public. The Venn diagram in Exhibit 5.1 shows this relationship through overlapping circles of interests.

- *Circle A* indicates information about the organization and issues important to it. This circle is of interest to the public relations practitioner.
- *Circle B* represents the interests of the news media. It is what the media consider to be newsworthy. This is what the media wish to report on because they consider it newsworthy and of potential interest to their audiences. Both determinations will vary with different media.
- *Circle C* signifies the interests of the organization's key public. Whether positive or negative it is something that coincides with their wants, interests and needs.

Each of these three components exist independent of the others. For example, the organization has much information that the media do not consider newsworthy, much of which also doesn't interest each public. But often the information in each circle may overlap, providing an environment for public relations to get into the action.

- *Area AB* depicts newsworthy information about the organization that the media might be interested in reporting. The media gatekeeper is focused on the people who read the newspaper or the blog, listen to the radio newscast or view the television broadcast. Your job, as a public relations person, is to find out where Circle A overlaps Circle B, then call this to the attention of the media gatekeeper.
- *Area AC* shows what we can call **direct news**. This is information that, though the news media may not care about it, nevertheless is of interest to the key public. Public relations writers dealing with such information may rework it to make it of more interest to the news media. Alternatively, they may take this information directly to the key public through organizational media, especially new technologies involving the Internet and social media.
- *Area BC* is of little interest to public relations writers, because it deals with news that doesn't involve the organization. The first inclination may simply be: Hands off. But practitioners might want to consider opportunities to insert their organizations into the news of the day.
- *Area ABC* represents **strategic news**, which is information involving your organization that is of interest not only to the news media but also to your key public. As news, it serves the interests of the media. Because it holds some benefit or consequence to your key public, it is likely to attract attention.

The ABC area represents information that is the primary focus of a media relations person. Often strategic public relations practitioners find that topics associated with all three groups

EXHIBIT 5.1 Model of Overlapping News Interests

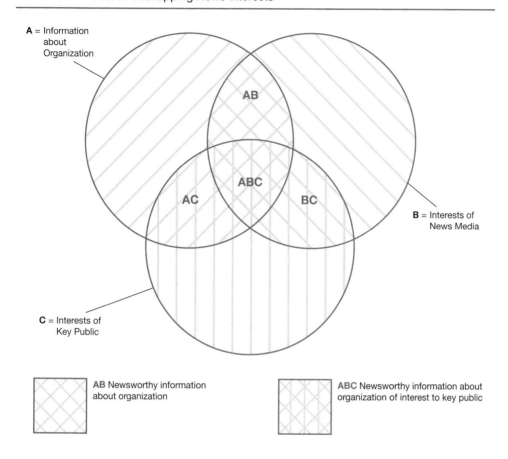

A = Information about Organization

AB

ABC

AC   **BC**

B = Interests of News Media

C = Interests of Key Public

AB Newsworthy information about organization

ABC Newsworthy information about organization of interest to key public

(media, publics and the organization) result in a **news peg**—that is, an item that the media is already reporting on that also touches, in some way, on the organization.

For example, if the media are reporting on a national story involving an international crisis in Asia, a local Asian-based cultural organization may contact the media and offer an informed local perspective on events half a world away. Or if a high-profile celebrity goes public with a diagnosis of depression, a mental-health clinic might move quickly to offer media interviews on how to identify and deal with the illness.

Here are two real-life examples of how organizations have attached themselves to a news peg.

DAWN DETERGENT

Dawn, a skin-friendly but high-powered cleaner, is used by International Bird Rescue Research Center as its cleaning agent of choice for oil-covered birds. The center persuaded the U.S. Fish and Wildlife Service to recommend Dawn for cleaning birds caught in oil slicks. After the Exxon oil spill in 1989, Proctor and Gamble gave IBRRC hundreds of cases of Dawn for the clean-up effort. The company also gave thousands of bottles to that group and to the Marine

Mammal Center for animal-rescue efforts in the Gulf oil spill of 2010. P&G also gives the detergent to many other less-publicized animal rescue projects around the world.

Proctor and Gamble received thousands of media mentions, so many that critics called it a PR stunt. But the company frames the donations as part of wider corporate commitment to wildlife, which includes a blog, Facebook and Twitter, corporate advertising and direct fundraising with consumers on wildlife issues.

OAKLEY SUNGLASSES

Oakley makes high-performance sunglasses with a high level of protection against ultraviolent rays. In Fall 2010, at the request of a Chilean insurance company, Oakley donated 35 pairs of its Radar-style glasses with special tints for the miners who had been trapped underground for 69 days. Oakley said the glasses would help the miners' eyes return to normal after so much time without sunlight. Each pair cost about $180. Front Row Analytics, a sponsorship evaluation company, used product-placement measures and estimated that the media exposure Oakley received when the miners emerged was worth $41 million.

Transparent Communication

A relatively new concept is an important idea in developing a proactive public relations communication strategy. Transparent communication is the term given to the notion that open and observable activity by an organization helps publics understand the organization and support its actions.

Transparent communication, which deals with the awareness objectives of increasing knowledge and understanding, simply means making your case. Many communication efforts have failed because the publics are aware of facts but not the reasons behind them.

Too often, organizations exhibit a "just trust us" mentality by announcing plans without providing reasons why those plans are necessary, and today's publics aren't inclined to trust blindly. For example, within a four-month period in one midsized city, community opposition was strong in four different situations—a proposed relocation of the zoo; an announcement by a health management organization to drop coverage for half the hospitals in the area; plans by a public radio station to suspend operations; and the decision of a bridge authority to turn away millions of federal dollars for a high-profile "signature" bridge in favor of a less architecturally impressive bridge. In each situation, the organization in question drew criticism because it had failed to provide plausible reasons for its plans. Publics had been left surprised, confused and only partly informed. Facts had been given, but there was no convincing rationale for the decisions and plans.

In an example of doing it right, the CIA's report of the crash of TWA flight 800 off Long Island, New York, not only detailed what the investigators found, but also included a thorough discussion of the investigation process that led to the conclusion. "Report goes beyond being 'open,'" wrote the late Pat Jackson in *PR Reporter*. "Open implies something else is closed, which raises questions. CIA's report is transparent—everything is laid on the line. Its thoroughness leaves no questions."

When organizations engage in transparent communication, they provide the kind of communication that identifies a problem, gets people interested, airs various options, and otherwise creates a climate of understanding and involvement before plans are announced that affect the publics. If financial pressures are pushing your organization to curtail services,

CASE IN POINT Children's Hospital

Balancing transparency and confidentiality were uppermost in the mind of leaders of San Diego's Children's Hospital in 2006, when two employees were arrested on child-abuse charges in unrelated cases. Police notified the hospital that they were investigating a respiratory therapist working with comatose children. A few days later, the man was arrested for abusing at least nine victims under his care at the hospital. Police discovered more than 100,000 child pornography images on his home computer.

The hospital's crisis plan went into effect. Letters in English and Spanish were sent to 176 families of his former patients. Another 30,000 letters were sent to people associated with the hospital, including employees, families of patients, donors and legislators. Hospital administrators met with the families of the therapist's patients. Adopting a posture of openness and transparency, the hospital gave media interviews, held a news conference and set up a special telephone inquiry line. The crisis plan called for speed and flexibility; it valued transparency of information while at the same time seeking patient confidentiality. Media and law enforcement generally agreed that the hospital was transparent in this approach to the public.

Then lightning struck twice. Within five and a half weeks, police notified the hospital that another employee was being investigated on similar charges. The hospital suspended the nurse, who a few days later was arrested for molesting a child at the hospital and for possessing child pornography at his home.

The hospital held a second news conference, with assurances that these were isolated cases. Eventually both men pleaded guilty, the first receiving a 45-year sentence, the second a 14-year prison term.

Later that year, the hospital presented its case study to colleagues attending the Boston convention of the National Association of Children's Hospitals and Related Institutions. It pointed to jarring statistics: An estimated 3–5 percent of males are sexually interested in prepubescent children and even a greater number in adolescents. Thus, a hospital with 1,000 male employees might expect 50 who are potential child abusers. More alarmingly, the presenters noted that organizations such as children's hospitals are magnets for people with perverse interests in children and may attract an even higher rate of potential abusers. Thus the need for a carefully prepared program to screen employees, minimize risk and respond responsibly when the crime occurs. The hospital director said that outcomes of the crisis included an awareness of the need for vigilance about sex abuse and an appreciation of the role of public relations in a crisis.

San Diego Children's Hospital offered several lessons to its colleagues: Have a crisis plan that balances transparency with patient privacy, involve the CEO visibly, frame the response agenda to emphasize quality improvement, communicate with all patients involved, expect leaks to the media, and visibly cooperate with law enforcement. As with other situations of crisis communication, the public relations potential in such circumstances allows the organization to show its true colors—undue concern for internal privacy, or transparent commitment to its many publics and its long-term reputation within the community.

Phase Two

STEP
5

let your publics know about the financial problems and the various options before announcing a service cutback. Nobody likes bad surprises, especially when it is clear that the organization has been hiding information from key publics.

Transparent communication is particularly relevant to the stereotypically secretive world of finance. When he was chairman of the federal Securities and Exchange Commission, Harvey Pitt identified one of the top SEC goals as "to ensure that our financial markets are transparent and fair to all investors." Helen Vollmer APR, president of Edelman Southwest, advises her clients that today's marketplace requires transparent communication between corporate leadership and stockholders. The company lists transparency second only to credibility as the most important ingredients of an IR program.

Media Theory and Public Relations

How powerful are the news media? Can they make us care about an issue or act on it in a certain way just because they report it? Or are they simply information sources used at the discretion of their audiences?

Insight into the issue begins with social psychology in general, as well as specific applications to media presentations and news audiences. In particular, three theories are useful in discussing the role of the news media: agenda-setting, priming and framing.

AGENDA-SETTING THEORY

Communication researchers and public relations practitioners believe there is a middle ground between powerful effects and minimal effects of the media. This is explained by the **agenda-setting theory** associated with Maxwell McCombs and Donald Shaw (1972). According to this theory, the news media are not powerful enough to force audiences to react in a certain way, but neither are they inconsequential. Rather, the media raise issues that both they and their audiences consider to be newsworthy. In simple terms, the news media tell us what to think about, but they don't tell us what to think.

Through the issues they choose to cover, called the **media agenda**, the news media can legitimize a story and raise it as a topic that the citizenry or media audiences are interested in, called the **public agenda**. Conversely, failure to report on issues marginalizes a topic as not being newsworthy. There is still a bit of a debate: does an issue move into the public interest because the media report it? Or, do the media report an issue because it already is a matter of public interest? Probably a bit of both.

For the public relations strategist, the important lesson from this theory is to link organizational information with the current news: what is the news of the day and how does my organization fit into it? Sometimes the link is obvious. During a high-profile trial in which child abuse is an issue, a child-services agency easily could become a resource to reporters about the nature and extent of child abuse in the local community.

At other times the public relations person must be creative in finding the connections: a hospital linking to news about genocide in Darfur because one of its doctors recently returned from a stint as a medical volunteer in that part of Sudan, or a university offering to host students from China who were displaced by an earthquake there.

PRIMING THEORY

Another theoretical concept is **priming**, which explains how the media set the stage to provide the context for public discourse on a topic. The observation is that the amount of time and space that media devote to an issue make an audience receptive and perhaps alert the audience to particular themes. Shanto Iyengar and Donald Kinder (1987) identified a priming process in which media attention to or avoidance of various issues creates a framework for relatively uninformed audiences, calling up past information and applying it to present situations. For example, voters may evaluate a political candidate according to themes resurrected from previous media reporting on topics such as taxation, abortion, gay rights and other topics selected by the media.

CASE IN POINT   Cherokee Citizenship

Consider three theories—agenda-setting, priming and framing—in light of news coverage of the 2007 citizenship vote by the Cherokee Nation.

In the vote, the tribal government sought to end a 100-year confusion caused when the federal government determined that after the Civil War certain ex-slaves (who came to be known as Freedmen) should be considered members of the tribe because they were living in the Indian territory of what is now Oklahoma. The Cherokees finally were voting on whether to restrict tribal citizenship to people—whether ethnically black, white or Indian—who actually have Cherokee blood lineage.

In terms of agenda setting, the Cherokee-Freedmen story failed to register in a major way on the national agenda. It received limited national and international coverage, often from media that had previously taken an editorial stand on the topic. But during the first two weeks of March 2007, other news was ranked higher on the media agenda: a scandal over conditions at Walter Reed Army Medical Center; the conviction of Lewis "Scooter" Libby for outing CIA agent Valerie Plame; scandals over politically inspired firing of federal attorneys; killer tornadoes in several states; continuing death in the Iraq War; and new attention on genocide in Darfur.

Priming influenced the Cherokee-Freedman story through prior ongoing media coverage of civil rights. Reports of the denial of voting rights in particular may have prepared audiences to see the story in that light. Likewise, the storytelling was impacted by the historical context unknown to journalists and audiences alike.

The relevant issue to the Cherokee-Freedmen story in the context of framing theory deals with the manner in which the media reports placed various elements. Such elements include the diversity of the mixed-race Cherokee community and the convoluted history involved. Other issues were racism, tribal sovereignty and federal government complicity in creating the problem in the first place, as well as nuances in the voting procedure and the precise language of the ballot question. Framing also entered into which news sources were quoted and which side received top billing.

For a full report of the media analysis on the citizenship vote by the author of this textbook, see "The Cherokee-Freedmen Story: What the Media Saw" at works.bepress.com/ronald_smith.

Phase Two

**STEP
5**

FRAMING THEORY

A related and perhaps more useful theory deals with **framing**. It focuses on the presentation of the story and organizes discourse about the topic. Framing explains how the media provide a perspective or frame of reference that influences public discourse on a topic. How do the news media frame a story? Is there an inherent "good guy" in the story? Whose side of the story gets top billing? Which version becomes the standard against which other points of view are measured?

Framing theory was developed by Erving Goffman (1974) and applied to communication studies by Dietram Scheufele (1999). Framing provides a rhetorical context for the text, involving the use of metaphor, storytelling, jargon, word choice and other narrative elements. For example, a report on repeat drunk driving might be framed in various ways: criminal recidivism, police incompetence, judicial lenience or the power of addiction. If agenda setting tells audiences what to think about, framing theory suggests that the media influence how the audience thinks about an issue.

Reactive Public Relations Strategies

When accusations or other criticisms have been made, or when an organization has been visited by difficulties, or worse, public relations strategists are thrown into a reactive mode. In responding to outside forces, organizations should develop objectives such as gaining public understanding, maintaining and restoring reputation, and rebuilding trust and support.

The field of crisis communication management is ripe with examples of response strategies that work.

The classical term for a communication response to negative situations is **apologia**, an explanation or formal defense that offers a compelling case for an organization's opinions, positions or actions. Don't confuse apologia with apology, which is an expression of fault and remorse. An apologia could include an apology, but it is much more. Through an apologia an organization explains its actions and positions with a clear eye toward convincing critics of its rightness.

Applying the concept of apologia to corporate crises, Keith Michael Hearit notes that an apologia offers an organization a strategic opportunity to manage its reputation in the wake of accusations of wrongdoing. Hearit suggests a threefold approach: persuasive accounts offering (1) an explanation, and if necessary a defense; (2) statements of regret; and (3) disassociation tactics to separate the organization from the problem (1994).

Another approach to public relations response strategy considers the **theory of accounts**, which refers to the use of communication to manage relationships in the wake of rebuke or criticism. Accounts can range from defensive to offensive. Some research (Cody and McLaughlin, 1985) has found that the harsher the criticism, the more a strong offensive account is warranted. That is a lesson not learned by several political candidates. John McCain in 2000 and John Kerry in 2004 both lost presidential campaigns in part because they failed to take seriously vicious political criticism that demeaned their military service as war heroes. Some political observers say McCain lost the 2008 election because he failed to take seriously the criticisms that he was out of touch with hard economic realities.

In *Accounts, Excuses, and Apologies*, William Benoit (1995) deals with accounts and apologia, drawing on research from sociology, social psychology and communication.

TYPOLOGY OF REACTIVE PUBLIC RELATIONS STRATEGIES

Reactive Strategy 1:
Pre-emptive Action
Prebuttal

Reactive Strategy 2:
Offensive Response
Attack
Embarrassment
Shock
Threat

Reactive Strategy 3:
Defensive Response
Denial
Excuse
Justification
Reversal

Reactive Strategy 4:
Diversionary Response
Concession
Ingratiation

Disassociation
Relabeling

Reactive Strategy 5:
Vocal Commiseration
Concern
Condolence
Regret
Apology

Reactive Strategy 6:
Rectifying Behavior
Investigation
Corrective Action
Restitution
Repentance

Reactive Strategy 7:
Deliberate Inaction
Strategic Silence
Strategic Ambiguity
Strategic Inaction

Phase Two

He presents a theory of **image restoration**, based on the presumption that, in the face of criticism, both people and organizations seek to maintain or rebuild a positive reputation.

Organizations can use a range of verbal and behavioral reactions in managing their response to opposition and their recovery from criticism. The following typology of public relations responses is based on a reflection of contemporary research and consulting practices, as well as the work of the above-mentioned researchers.

Reactive Strategy 1: Pre-emptive Action

One type of strategy involves a *pre-emptive strike*, which is taken before the opposition launches its first charge against the organization. Some organizational bureaucrats avoid such an approach in the naive hope that criticism won't emerge or bad news won't surface. The reality is that, if something bad has happened, word generally will get out.

Prebuttal

The strategy of an organization releasing bad news about itself is called a **prebuttal**. The term itself is a play on the word *rebuttal*. A prebuttal is a pre-emptive strike when bad news is inevitable. In today's era of viral messaging in a fast-paced sociopolitical environment, prebuttals are becoming commonplace attempts to deflate opposing arguments even before they are made.

It was a prebuttal when presidential candidate Rudy Giuliani criticized a video prior to its release, in which the International Association of Fire Fighters claimed that, contrary to Giuliani's self-promotion as a 9/11 hero, his actions on the day of the attacks actually caused the unnecessary death of many firemen.

It was a prebuttal in 2009 when congressional Republican leaders criticized President Obama's health-care bill even before the president presented it publicly; his Iraq policy in 2010; his jobs proposal in 2011.

The concept of prebuttal is based on the observation that the first one to tell the story sets the tone, against which all alternative versions must compete. It's a lesson you may have learned in elementary school, when your sister or brother beat you home with a story of how you got into trouble on the playground. Following that account, your own version may have been not only second place but somehow second best. The first telling of the story becomes normative, and other versions are considered in light of the first account.

The same thing holds true for organizations. When something bad is about to happen, organizations can do more than merely brace for the aftershock. *Carpe diem!* as the Romans said. *Seize the day!*

Consider this real-life situation: A hospital had to deal with a pending report that would list it as having one of the highest patient death rates in the state. Knowing that the report was only days away and that it was statistically accurate, the hospital held a news conference to announce the forthcoming report and to explain why the rate was high: this particular hospital accepted charity patients too poor to have regular health care, specialized in geriatrics and was the only hospital in the area treating AIDS patients at a time in the not-too-distant past when the disease meant certain death. These were important reasons explaining the high death rate. After getting the facts from the hospital, local reporters gave the announcement minimal coverage, and they virtually ignored the state report a few days later as old news.

When is a prebuttal warranted? When the public inevitably will hear the accusation or other bad news, and when the organization can offer strong evidence for its publics reasons to disregard the bad news or excuse the organization.

Attacking the news media is particularly risky, because they have the last word. But in 1999 Metabolife did so because it feared biased reporting from ABC News. The ABC program *20/20* had spent four months in research and interviews, and Metabolife worried about how its popular but controversial herbal diet pill would be portrayed.

Combining the strategies of prebuttal and attack, Metabolife posted a website with its own videotape of ABC's 70-minute interview with its CEO, along with a full transcript and additional medical information. The posting went up 10 days before the ABC program was scheduled to air. The company also purchased full-page ads in the *New York Times* and the *New York Post*, gained news coverage in the *Wall Street Journal* and ran radio commercials across the country to draw hits to the website—all prior to the story's broadcast. Metabolife also placed a short ad during the program, asking viewers to visit its website.

The website received 1.1 million hits a day, and the company later claimed that its pre-emptive action caused the 20/20 story to be fairer than it otherwise would have been. ABC denied Metabolife's interpretation, calling the company's action "a not-so-subtle form of intimidation" that it claimed had no effect on the report.

Many crisis communication experts suggest that an organizational interview or news conference should always include at least an audio recording, preferably a videotape, of the media encounter. Make sure the recording is obvious to the media. The presence of your own recording devices will serve notice that everything is on the record, minimizing the chance of being misquoted and providing proof if you are.

Prebuttals are frequently seen in the political arena. Congressman Doug Lamborn (R.–Colo.) quickly realized he had spoken with much insensitivity, many called it racism, when he called President Obama "a tar baby." He soon posted a note on his website with a presumptive element: Lamborn "today sent a personal letter to President Barack Obama apologizing for using a term some find insensitive . . . He regrets that he chose the phrase 'tar baby' rather than the word 'quagmire.' The Congressman is confident that the President will accept his heartfelt apology." Lamborn's pseudo-apology blamed people who were offended without accepting responsibility for having offended them; it then quickly kicked the ball to the other end of the field, setting up a scenario in which the president would look petty if he didn't accept Lamborn's quasi-contrition. Wisely, the White House ignored both the statement and the congressman's letter.

Reactive Strategy 2: Offensive Response

Public relations planners sometimes use *offensive response* strategies such as attack, embarrassment, shock, or threat in response to criticism. These are based on the premise that the organization is operating from a position of strength in the face of opposition. Here is an overview of each of these strategies.

Attack

An **attack** is an offensive response strategy of claiming that an accusation of wrongdoing is an attempt to impugn the organization's reputation by an accuser who is negligent or malicious. Often the objective behind this strategy is to encourage an opponent to retreat or at least to refrain from future criticism. Use this approach only when a strong case can be made that accusers have grossly overstated the organization's involvement in a problem. Let's look at two examples of the attack strategy—one that backfired, one that was successful.

In another classic public relations blunder from the late 1990s, Dow Corning used the attack strategy to its own misfortune in handling a series of class-action lawsuits over its silicone breast implants. Faced with reports filled with unfavorable scientific information, the company's first response was to attack the investigators. It unsuccessfully attempted a cover-up of the problem. It failed to demonstrate concern for women who said they were harmed. And it didn't address consumers who thought they had been deceived by the company.

Most of the strategy was driven by lawyers rather than by public relations counsel. The result was a $7.3 million judgment against the company and class-action lawsuits of more than $4 billion that put the corporation into Chapter 11 bankruptcy for nine years. All this despite the fact that no reputable scientific evidence showed that the implants caused disease or illness. In fact, the U.S. Institute of Medicine later found that silicone breast implants do not cause breast cancer.

On the other hand, some organizations have successfully attacked the attacker. The Church of Scientology proclaims that it's "not a turn-the-other-cheek religion." It has filed lawsuits against journalists, politicians, former church members and others who have criticized the organization, which has written guidelines on how to investigate and publicly attack its critics.

As the richest retailer in America, Wal-Mart receives its share of criticism. The company's policy is to fight back, portraying itself as a victim of unions, Democratic lawmakers, competitors and local zoning boards.

Many politicians often respond to criticism by attacking the media rather than defending themselves against accusations of wrongdoing. Often such counter-punches backfire. But sometimes they are successful. For example, Florida Sen. Marco Rubio fought back when Univision television reported that his brother-in-law had been arrested for his role in a cocaine and marijuana ring. But the incident happened 25 years earlier when the senator was a teenager. Lessons to be learned? Retaliatory attacks against a media messenger can be unsuccessful when the original attack appears personal, when the exposed wrongdoing is dated and relatively minor, when the media appear to be acting irresponsibly and when other media are willing to report fairly.

Embarrassment

A related offensive strategy deals with **embarrassment**, in which an organization tries to lessen an opponent's influence by using shame or humiliation.

An example of this strategy was the Liberian Women's Peace Movement, which held street demonstrations to embarrass the government into ending a violent civil war. In 2003, the women locked down a conference hall until a peace accord was signed. Soon after the UN charged Liberia's president with crimes against humanity. He resigned and was promptly exiled and replaced—by a woman.

The embarrassment tactic often plays a role in political communication. In her 2010 campaign to become a Nevada senator, Tea Party candidate Sue Lowden suggested that people barter for health care by paying doctors with chickens. Her opponents created a fake "Chickens for Checkups" website. The ridicule became so strong that the state of Nevada banned chicken costumes outside polling sites.

Shock

Sometimes, in an effort to make a point, embarrassment may take a turn toward alarm. In public relations and strategic communication, **shock** is the deliberate agitation of the mind or emotions, particularly through the use of surprise, disgust or some other strong and unexpected stimulus. As such, it seldom offers a long-term positive strategy for any organization unwilling to be seen as out of step with mainstream values of decency and fair play.

People for the Ethical Treatment of Animals has built a reputation for outrageous strategies in its animal-rights campaigns. PETA used shock strategy to force McDonald's to agree to more human practices in chicken coops and slaughterhouses under its control. The advocacy group distributed "Son of Ron Unhappy Meal" boxes with a plastic cow in blood-stained hay, a plastic butchered pig and a Ronald McDonald figure wearing a blood-spattered butcher's apron and wielding a meat cleaver. Parents complained that PETA was upsetting their children, though the group said more parents expressed disgust with how McDonald's treated animals.

After McDonald's conceded the fight, PETA turned its attention to how Burger King raised and killed chickens, quickly gaining the compliance of that company as well.

FAITH-BASED SHOCK STRATEGY

People for the Ethical Treatment of Animals has a strong and consistent anti-meat, pro-vegetarian, pro-animal rights message aimed at "total animal liberation." The organization has also taken up the challenge to convert religious observers of all faiths to its way of thinking, and it often uses a shock strategy that uses religious imagery designed to surprise and even outrage its audiences.

One PETA ad depicts the Holy Shroud of Turin, which many believe to be a remnant from biblical times with an image of Jesus' face, with the caption "Make a lasting impression. Go vegetarian." Another suggests that, despite recorded biblical evidence to the contrary, Jesus was a vegetarian—the "Prince of Peas." Still another provocatively proclaims to Christians that livestock, not Jesus, have died for their sins.

Announcing that it was "enlisting Jesus as its newest spokesperson," PETA used the icon of the Priests of the Sacred Heart, substituting an orange slice for a halo. When the Catholic religious order objected, PETA switched to an image of Jesus from the *South Park* TV series, also a copyright violation. Comedy Central found this unfunny, demanding that PETA stop using the cartoon.

Some ads focus on the Virgin Mary. One billboard depicted her breastfeeding the Infant Jesus with the caption "If it was good enough for Jesus . . . Dump Dairy." Reminiscent of medieval art, the ad didn't create much chatter. But Catholic groups demanded the removal of a subsequent billboard depicting the Virgin Mary cradling a chicken carcass à la Michelangelo's Pieta with the theologically perplexing caption "Go vegetarian. It's an Immaculate Conception."

PETA campaign director Bruce Friedrich wrote to the Pope asking him to tell Catholics to keep lamb off the traditional Easter menu in Italy. The Pope didn't respond, perhaps because previously during a papal visit to Chicago, PETA protestors dressed as a nun and a cow with a placard "Eating meat is a bad habit." Friedrich describes himself as a devout Catholic who believes that cruelty to animals is against his faith.

Activists in Jesus costumes have protested at barbecue restaurants in Texas, Alabama, Mississippi and other Southern states that take seriously both their religion and their barbecues. The group held a boisterous rally outside Southeast Christian Church in Louisville, Kentucky, where the president of KFC (formerly Kentucky Fried Chicken) was worshipping on Christmas Eve. During Holy Week, PETA placed a 10-foot cow dressed as the Pope with a crucified cow on his cross outside Catholic cathedrals in several Eastern cities. In New York, the cow-pope mobile was ticketed for an illegal turn on Fifth Avenue.

PETA spokespeople say such shock tactics are timed to generate the most publicity for their cause. For PETA, negative publicity is not considered . . . well, negative.

If nothing else, PETA is an equal-opportunity instrument of religious shock. Its "Holocaust on Your Plate" campaign said "six million people died in concentration camps, but six billion broiler chickens will die this year in slaughterhouses." As the exhibit toured 70 U.S. cities, three Canadian provinces and 15 foreign countries, the public outcry was what you'd expect: quick, loud and widespread. "Sometimes people need to be offended," PETA retorted.

Phase Two

STEP
5

In another Holocaust campaign, PETA displayed photos of dead Jews in Nazi concentration camps interspersed with photos of slaughtered pigs at a livestock farm. The caption: "The leather sofa and handbag are the moral equivalent of lampshades made from the skin of people killed in the death camps."

PETA has taken aim on kosher practice, asking Jews to abandon their ancient dietary laws. It placed billboards in Utah saying that Mormons misrepresent their scripture and urging them to heed PETA's call for vegetarianism. The group also has challenged Muslims' interpretation that the Quran permits meat eating.

To date, only the Hindus and the Buddhists seem to have escaped PETA's faith-based shock strategy.

Threat

Making a **threat** is another offensive strategy, involving the promise that harm will come to the accuser or the purveyor of bad news. The threatened harm may be in the form of a lawsuit for defamation, for example. Use public threats only if the information cannot be disputed in another way, and beware of the ethical concerns about misusing this strategy.

Reactive Strategy 3: Defensive Response

Another strategic communication response involves *defensive response* strategies such as denial, excuse or justification, all of which involve the organization reacting less aggressively to criticism.

Denial

Using the defensive strategy of **denial**, an organization tries not to accept blame, claiming that the reputed problem doesn't exist or didn't occur, or if it did, that it's not related to the organization. In the latter case, the claim generally is either one of **innocence** ("We didn't do it"), **mistaken identity** ("You have us confused with someone else") or **blame shifting** ("So-and-so did it").

A few years ago, a student at a public university was arrested for prostitution. She tried to justify her actions by claiming that she couldn't otherwise afford tuition because of a financial-aid error. The university was quick to say "That's absurd!" and shifted responsibility back to the student.

Be careful in shifting blame, however, because the strategy can backfire if the organization is ultimately responsible. An executive who claims that an employee's inappropriate action was against company policy must be prepared for scrutiny of both the company's official policy and its way of doing business. It is best to use the strategy of denial only when the case can be publicly supported and when it can be proven that neither the organization nor anyone in its policy-setting ranks was involved in the wrongdoing.

Phase Two

STEP
5

Excuse

A commonly used defensive strategy is **excuse**, in which an organization tries to minimize its responsibility for the harm or wrongdoing. Excuse can take several forms, including provocation, lack of control, accident, victimization and mere association.

The organization may claim **provocation**, essentially saying that it had no choice. Here's an example from one city. The police department had just eliminated its popular mounted patrol. Amid initial criticism, the police department excused this decision by explaining that the police union had insisted that seniority, not horse-riding ability, be the key factor in selecting officers for the patrol, thereby making the mounted patrol inefficient and even dangerous. Public criticism quickly shifted from the police department to the union.

A variation on the excuse theme is **lack of control**, in which the organization reports that its actions were forced upon it, such as the manager of a manufacturing plant who blames local employee layoffs on decisions made at national corporate offices.

Another excuse is **accident**, in which the organization suggests that factors beyond anyone's control led to a problem. An example of this is a mayor who excuses his city's slow progress in snow removal on unusually heavy snowfall during a two-week period.

A related but even stronger excuse is **victimization**, in which the organization shows that it was the target of criminals or a casualty of Mother Nature. Pepsi played this card successfully amid claims that syringes were found in diet drink cans in 1993—an excuse so thoroughly accepted that consumers barely cut back on their consumption, then rebounded to give the company one of its best quarters ever in terms of sales. Pepsi's handling of the syringe hoax has become a classic case of effective public relations.

This same victimization card has been played by many governors and mayors in excusing higher taxes and/or fewer services because they had to redirect resources toward rebuilding after natural disasters such as hurricanes, earthquakes, wildfires and floods.

A final type of excuse deals with mere **association**, in which the organization claims that it more or less inherited a problem. For example, a newly elected city administration might try to disassociate itself from a $2 million income shortfall by claiming that the financial loss was caused by careless planning by the previous administration. It's a tactic in political communication that's also been used in Washington and state capitals for years, not always successfully.

Justification

Another defensive strategy is **justification**, which admits the organization did the deed but did so for good reason. Like the excuse response, justification has several subcategories.

One type of justification is based on **good intention**, in which an organization attempts to soften the blow of bad results by claiming that it was trying to accomplish something positive. For example, a cab company may justify one of its drivers sideswiping a parked car by claiming the driver was trying to avoid hitting a pedestrian. This defense generally fails to cover what was a bad decision at the beginning. So if evidence were to show that the cab driver was speeding at the time of the accident, the good-intention justification wouldn't stand.

Another type of justification is **context**, in which the organization asks its publics to "look at it from our side." Robin Hood seen from the point of view of the sheriff of Nottingham

Phase Two

STEP
5

looks much different than from the perspective of the Nottingham peasants. Likewise, investors and environmentalists each may have different views of a company that violated technicalities of clean-air regulations. And the body politic often incredulously wonders how Democrats and Republicans can see the same facts and interpret them so differently.

Idealism is a type of justification based on an appeal to ethical, moral or spiritual values, such as leaders of a church protest against the death penalty who explain that their actions, though perhaps unpopular with some church members, are nevertheless in line with—even commanded by—their religious principles.

Here again, a card played doesn't guarantee a hand won. For years, Catholic bishops have been opposing the death penalty and most U.S. military entanglements; their Methodist and Episcopalian counterparts have been promoting same-sex equality—all without necessarily winning the hearts and minds of the folks in their pews.

A final type of justification involves **mitigation**. This admits to the problem but seeks to lessen blame because of impairment, illness, coercion, lack of training, and so on. However, if the mitigating factor is the responsibility of the organization, the attempt at justification probably will fail. Mitigation didn't offset the reported drunkenness of the *Valdez* captain that factored in the Alaskan oil spill. Nor did it satisfy critics blaming Mayor Giuliani for prior decisions that hampered 9/11 rescue and recovery efforts, and added to the death toll for police and firefighters.

Reversal

The phrase "turning the tables" comes from table games such as chess or backgammon. Turn the table around, and you play from the opponent's previous position. In public relations, this is an apt analogy for strategic *reversal*, in which the weakened party becomes the stronger one. It is a strategy in which an organization that finds itself under criticism gains the upper hand.

Often reversal can be accomplished with grace, even humor. That was the outcome when CNN commentator Anderson Cooper appeared to criticize the 2012 Dyngus Day celebration in Buffalo. "So stupid. Really so stupid," he said, later apologizing and trying to say that his remark was directed at himself for launching into a giggle fit befitting a 13-year-old girl, so much that he had to walk off camera to regain his composure.

Admittedly, Dyngus Day has some humorous elements. It's a Polish American custom on the day after Easter, celebrating romance and frivolity after the solemn spirit of Lent, a day with deep historic, religious, and ethnic roots. Young women, usually dressed in traditional Polish clothing, sprinkle men with water; the men tap women with pussy willow branches; and sometimes folks toss buckets of water at each other.

Polish-Americans often have been the brunt of jokes and demeaning stereotypes, so it was not surprising that they would take offense at the criticism, questioning Cooper's insensitivity in what they considered an ethnic slur. A Jewish senator said the TV host "shouldn't mock what he doesn't understand." Others flooded CNN with responses, including 500 comments, mostly negative, on Cooper's Facebook page. Some accused him of bigotry and drew parallels with ethnic criticism toward Kwanzaa or St. Patrick's Day.

Others saw humor in the entire incident and praised Cooper for apologizing on air the next day. With the apology, organizers of the annual event went for the reversal.

They accepted his apology and sent him some Polish sausage and pussy willows. They reprinted newspaper articles about the incident on their website (dyngusdaybuffalo.com). They also invited Cooper to Buffalo the following year to assume the title of Pussy Willow Prince and lead the world's largest Dyngus Day parade, something Cooper said he looked forward to.

Their website added: "Dziekuje [jen-KOO-yeh, thank you] Anderson Cooper for helping make Dyngus Day in Buffalo an international news story." The group reported 90,000 hits to its website in the two days following Cooper's initial story, and many more after his on-air apology.

Reactive Strategy 4: Diversionary Response

Several *diversionary response* strategies also are open to communication planners. They include concessions, ingratiation, disassociation and relabeling, all of which are attempts to shift the gaze of the publics from the problem associated with the organization.

Concession

Using the diversionary strategy of **concession**, an organization tries to rebuild its relationship with its publics by giving the public something it wants. The focus here should be on a concession that is mutually valued by both the organization and its public. For example, after objections to a car advertisement parodying Leonardo da Vinci's *The Last Supper* with the caption, "My friends, let us rejoice, because a new Golf is born," Volkswagen France and its advertising agency offered as a concession a major financial contribution to a religious charity whose work was supported by the protestors. The value of the donation by Volkswagen France was recognized by both the company and its offended public.

Public relations strategists should use concession only if the gift will be valued by adversaries and if the organization will remain committed to the concession. Amid criticism of its marketing of infant formula in lesser-developed nations during the 1980s, Nestlé established the International Council on Infant Food Industries and a code of ethics, attempting to offer its critics concession. But the strategy provided only a temporary diversion for critics, who quickly saw evidence that the company was not abiding by its own code of ethics. Subsequent opposition to Nestlé grew in the face of what critics viewed as insincerity and hypocrisy.

Thirty years later, the International Baby Food Action Network is still opposing the Swiss multinational. In 2011 the boycott was relaunched in the Asia-Pacific region. In 2012, the group's Baby Milk Action coalition sponsored a Nestlé-free week and urged supporters not to use Nestlé candy for Halloween. Meanwhile, the boycott coordinating committee claims success in 60 countries that have adopted stronger laws monitoring marketing practices, and many North American and European universities still ban the sale of Nestlé products on campus.

Instead of providing gifts to involved publics, some concessions are aimed at generating favorable publicity for an organization under fire. An example of this is found in *Crisis Response: Inside Stories in Managing Image Under Siege* (Gottschalk, 1993), in which crisis counselor James Lukaszewski revealed that he advised Exxon to charter aircraft to carry

Phase Two

**STEP
5**

volunteers from major U.S. cities to Alaska so they could help clean up some of the 11 million gallons of oil spilled in Prince William Sound. Exxon rejected the idea on grounds that the airlift would cost too much—a few hundred thousand dollars. The company eventually spent $2.2 billion in cleanup costs, another $1 billion to settle state and federal lawsuits, and $300 million in lost wages to Alaskan fishermen, plus millions in legal fees fighting lawsuits that ordered punitive damages as high as $11.9 billion, much of it linked to Exxon's poor reputation.

Certainly an environmental airlift would not have eliminated all of Exxon's expenses. But in hindsight, it seems fair to conclude that an airlift would have helped the company's reputation, which in turn could have eased its legal battles as well as its strained relations with stockholders, consumers, government agencies and the media. *Business Week* magazine later commented that "Exxon could have emerged from the case with a far better image if it had taken a more conciliatory approach . . . Instead, Exxon took a tough stand. And more than a decade later, the furious debates, and the bitterness, continue" ("Commentary: It's Time to Put the *Valdez* Behind Us," 1999). As noted in Step 1, the *Valdez* case also had negative residual effects, such as the continuing and costly legal disputes in Alabama and Maryland.

Ingratiation

Another diversionary strategy, one of questionable ethical standing, is **ingratiation**. Essentially, the organization attempts to manage the negative situation by charming its publics or "tossing a bone," giving something of relatively little significance to the organization in an attempt to turn the spotlight away from the accusations and criticisms.

Ingratiation differs from concessions in that the latter involves something of real value to the public, while ingratiation is more cosmetic. Examples of ingratiation are seen in the case of state lawmakers who vote against long-term tax reform for homeowners while offering a token and temporary tax reduction.

Disassociation

Another diversionary strategy is **disassociation**, which attempts to distance an organization from the wrongdoing associated with it. This can be effective when a mishap has occurred not because of organizational policy but because policy was not observed, especially when the organization has severed ties with the cause of the problem.

Texaco accomplished disassociation when its corporate chairman quickly and publicly apologized for racist statements made by several top executives, suspended two officials, ordered sensitivity training and established a corporate hotline for reporting violations of company antidiscrimination policies.

Think through the implications of disassociation. Justin Timberlake found that his success in distancing himself from Janet Jackson and the Super Bowl halftime controversy in 2004 also alienated many of his black fans.

Recall how quickly the trustees of Penn State University tried to disassociate their school from reports that an assistant football coach, since retired, had molested a 10-year-old boy in the locker room. The trustees said the school had not handled the charges appropriately after a graduate student reported what he had seen to head football coach Joe Paterno. The trustees immediately fired the revered coach, along with the president and other senior university officials.

From a public relations standpoint, the trustees clearly had to act decisively and quickly. But in a clumsy attempt to disassociate itself from the scandal by shifting blame to Paterno, the university alienated many supporters, including wealthy and previously generous donors.

Relabeling

Another diversionary strategy, **relabeling**, tries to distance the organization from criticism. It involves offering an agreeable name in replacement of a negative label that has been applied by others.

Some relabeling is innocuous. Prunes became dried plums and sales increased. Rapeseed sounded bad, so it became Canola oil.

Some relabeling is downright silly, like the unsuccessful attempt to rename French fries "freedom fries" because of anti-French sentiment after the US invaded Iraq. The same folks tried to give us "freedom toast," but they over-reached when they questioned the heredity and patriotism of French's mustard.

But some relabeling has more significant associations. The Al Qaeda organization in Yemen tried to become known as Ansar al Sharia because the original name has negative connotations. Some people say the deception associated with relabeling is exemplified by Chrysler. Charged with odometer fraud, the company said that corporate executives had merely driven new cars with disconnected odometers as part of a "quality test program." Chrysler was fined $7.6 million for selling the cars as new vehicles, even though some had been in accidents.

Much relabeling involves corporate names. For decades, Philip Morris was synonymous with tobacco, but when tobacco became a magnet for social criticism and lawsuits, Philip Morris Companies changed its name in 2003 to the Altria Group in an attempt to insulate the company from political pressure. The company also bought web domain names such as altriastinks.org and altriakills.com to prevent rogue sites from having easy dissemination of anti-Altria messages. The name change also allowed Altria subsidiaries such as Kraft Foods to disassociate themselves from the tainted tobacco label and, as one critic said, "to make itself invisible."

Similarly, trying to create a distance from its own record of fraud and bankruptcy, WorldCom in 2003 changed its name to MCI, the name of its more respected subsidiary. Charging that WorldCom had hijacked the name, critics called for a boycott, and the name change did not cause the company's reputation to improve.

Other examples of relabeling reflect a more positive rationale to capitalize on a particular consumer strength. Thus, in 2005, Matsushita Kotobuki Electronics Industries changed its name to that of its most recognized brand and became Panasonic Shikoku Electronics. In 2007, Federated Department Stores changed its name to the Macy's Group in a bow to the drawing power of its most famous brand. Blackwater, the private military company disgraced by its actions in Iraq, changed its name to Xe Services in 2009. Two years later it changed the name again, calling itself Academi, which its CEO said was intended to reflect a more boring image that wouldn't reflect the business' controversial mission as mercenary soldiers.

Phase Two

**STEP
5**

The strategy of relabeling can backfire if an organization's publics conclude that relabeling is deceptive or, worse, if it trivializes the problem. When MTV created a new phrase, "wardrobe malfunction," to explain Janet Jackson's exposed breast during the 2004 Super Bowl halftime show it produced, the FCC was unamused, fining CBS a record $550,000 for indecency. Relabeling is only a short step away from doublespeak, which is deliberately misleading language and a highly unethical practice. Don't go too far in your effort to put on the best face.

Reactive Strategy 5: Vocal Commiseration

Another family of strategies deals with *vocal commiseration*, in which the organization expresses empathy and understanding about the misfortune suffered by its publics. These include concern, condolence, regret and apology.

Concern

One type of vocal commiseration is **concern**, through which the organization expresses that it is not indifferent to a problem without admitting guilt. The Denver Broncos, for example, called "extremely serious and troubling" accounts that cornerback Perrish Cox sexually assaulted a woman and fathered her child. Cox was cut from the team in 2011 before his trial.

During the Deepwater Horizon oil leak in the Gulf of Mexico in 2010, many observers were willing to give the benefit of the doubt to BP, Transocean and Halliburton, in trying to repair the damage. Initially BP accepted responsibility and seemed to be fulfilling its promise to work hard to contain the spill and then clean it up. Public sentiment shifted when BP chief Tony Hayward minimized the disaster, then gushing thousands of barrels of oil a day into the sea, as "very, very modest," and when he subsequently complained, "There's no one who wants this over more than I do. I would like my life back."

Condolence

A more formal type of vocal commiseration is **condolence**, in which the organization expresses grief over someone's loss or misfortune, again without admitting guilt. A good example of this strategy is the response of ValuJet president Lewis Jordan to the crash of one of his airplanes in the Florida Everglades, killing 110 people—a crash later attributed to a shipper who had illegally mislabeled canisters of highly flammable oxygen. "It's Mother's Day weekend—we know that," Jordan said in a news conference the day after the crash. "Words in the English language, at least the ones I know, are inadequate to express the amount of grief and sadness we feel." The company, which later merged into AirTran, put action behind its words, sponsoring a memorial service for 46 victims whose remains could not be identified.

Regret

Another vocal strategy, **regret**, involves admitting sorrow and remorse for a situation, a wish that an event had not happened. Like compassion, regret does not necessarily imply fault; in fact, statements of regret may specifically not admit to any wrongdoing. This is an important perspective that public relations advisors bring in crisis situations. By expressing regret, public hostility can be tempered and the number and intensity of lawsuits may be contained.

Chris Brown expressed regret but stopped shy of apologizing, apparently on legal advice, in talking about an incident of domestic violence that hospitalized his girlfriend Rihanna in 2009. "Words cannot begin to express how sorry and saddened I am over what transpired," he said, promising to become a better person and complaining that the media had gotten it wrong.

Regret without apology sometimes is not enough. Japan's Emperor Akihito learned that lesson on a visit to England. The emperor spoke of his "deep sorrow and pain" over suffering during World War II. But former prisoners of war booed the emperor, and one protestor burned a Japanese flag in his presence. A spokesman for the veterans said, "The emperor's speech does not alter the position one jot as far as any expression of an apology to the POWs is concerned." The reluctance of the Japanese government to officially apologize for wartime military atrocities has strained its relations with a number of countries.

Regret sometimes extends to the actions of others. After Congress demanded a formal apology from Japan for sex slavery in occupied territories during World War II, Japan's prime minister said it was "regrettable." Not the wartime military action, but the American resolution. The prime minister said Japan had previously apologized and made amends, and did not plan to respond to the House resolution.

Congress also incurred the wrath of the Turkish government in 2007 when a House committee passed a similar nonbinding resolution labeling as "genocide" the Turkish massacre of Armenians during World War I. The irony is that Congress had yet to apologize to its own people for black slavery in the American South, or the forced relocation of Japanese Americans during World War II.

Apology

The vocal strategy focused most on the public's interests and least on the organization's is **apology**. Issuing an apology involves publicly accepting full responsibility and asking forgiveness. Use this strategy when the organization is clearly at fault and when long-term rebuilding of relationships is more important than short-term stalling or legal posturing.

Make sure the apology is straightforward, such as the statement by Frank Lorenzo, chairman of Continental Airlines, who said in a full-page newspaper ad, "We grew so fast that we made mistakes."

Communication strategists can take a lesson from etiquette columnist Judith Martin (1999), who advised in one of her Miss Manners columns that apologizing is a way to diffuse angry responses. A good apology should include an acknowledgment of having done something wrong, a sense of remorse, an attempt to repair the injustice (if possible), and a promise not to commit the offense again.

Also, make sure the apology is timely. When Arnold Schwarzenegger campaigned for governor in the 2003 California recall race, he wasted no time in defusing allegations of groping women and making lewd comments by acknowledging them in a general way, apologizing, and explaining them basically as the indiscretions of his youth. The strategy worked. Eight years later he admitted that he had fathered a child with his maid, prompting a divorce.

Michael Vick scored high points for his apology after pleading guilty to illegal dog fighting and being suspended as quarterback with the Atlanta Falcons (and later imprisoned). In a televised apology, Vick accepted personal responsibility, apologized to kids who look up to athletes as role models, and said he was ashamed of himself for having misled his teammates

Phase Two

STEP 5

CRISIS COUNSEL: PUBLIC RELATIONS VS. LEGAL

Odwalla, a producer of juice products, faced a crisis in 1996 when its apple juice was found to be contaminated with the bacteria E. coli. Several people became ill, and one child died.

Faced with media attention, Odwalla used classic public relations techniques associated with Johnson & Johnson's handling of the 1983 Tylenol cyanide poisoning crisis, which put the public safety and the common good above the individual interests of the company. Odwalla initiated a voluntary recall in eight Western states and a Canadian province. It sent representatives to meet with the family of the young victim, and it set up a webpage to update its customers.

Odwalla earned some praise for its response. A case study by Kathleen Martinelli and William Briggs (1998) noted that Odwalla relied on advice from both public relations and legal counselors, with strategists from each field taking a collaborative rather than an adversarial approach to the crisis.

They found that nearly 47 percent of the company's statements reflected traditional public relations responses: explaining its policy, investigating allegations, expressing concern for victims, taking steps to prevent a recurrence of the problem. Meanwhile, only 12 percent reflected the common legal response of denying guilt, minimizing responsibility and shifting blame to the plaintiffs. The remaining messages were mixed between legal and public relations approaches.

Kathy Fitzpatrick and Maureen Rubin (1995) have pointed out that such collaboration between public relations and legal counsel usually results in more favorable media coverage and thus a more positive public response, serving the organization's long-term interests if the situation ends up in court.

In the Odwalla case, sales actually increased after the recall, a response similar to Pepsi's following its smooth handling of the syringe hoax. Odwalla eventually was fined $1.5 million—a relatively mild sum, considering that juries have imposed much heavier fines in other cases that didn't involve a death. Continuing its public relations approach, the company responded to the fine with grace. "We hope the visibility of [the size of the fine] will raise awareness and send a message to consumers about food safety," said a company spokesman.

Compare Odwalla's experience with that of the 1993 Jack-in-the-Box fast food crisis, in which four people died from E. coli. The company's first response was from a legal standpoint: no comment, followed by attempts to shift blame to its supplier. Jack-in-the-Box eventually paid $58.5 million in fines.

by his initial statements of innocence. Later, after prison and bankruptcy, Vick regained some of his earlier product endorsements.

Corporations also benefit from quick action on the apology front. When it became public that JetBlue—a year earlier—had violated its own privacy policy by giving private passenger data to Pentagon researchers attempting to profile high-risk passengers following the 9/11 terrorist attacks, the company issued a quick apology. Public relations observers noted that the quick response shortened the news cycle, reduced speculation and allowed the story to become yesterday's news. JetBlue weathered the potential crisis well and remained popular and profitable.

When an ice storm grounded hundreds of JetBlue airplanes and stranded hundreds of thousands of travelers, JetBlue CEO David Neeleman again was quick to apologize: "We are sorry and embarrassed . . . Words cannot express how truly sorry we are for the anxiety, frustration, and inconvenience that you, your family, friends and colleagues experienced." No "if you were inconvenienced"; this was a flat out "I'm sorry" from the top guy, for a problem caused by Mother Nature. Other airlines had similar delays, but they didn't communicate with their passengers in such a forthright way.

As with the previously discussed concept of regret, nonapologies are worse than no apology.

A **nonapology** is an insincere or halfhearted apology, an expression that someone took offense rather than regret for having done something wrong in the first place. It blames the victim of the offense: "I'm sorry that you took offense" or "I regret your reaction to what I did." Or this from radio talker Rush Limbaugh: "I regret that you heard me say that."

Beware also similar false apologies that lament the effect but not the underlying transgression. Avoid pseudo-apologies such as those by any number of politicians who have felt compelled to apologize "for anything I may have done that offended you" or who add, "but it was only meant as a joke."

After using a double-barreled racist/sexist slur ("nappy-headed hos") against the Rutgers women's basketball team on live radio in 2007, "shock jock" Don Imus came under immediate fire. His apologies were seen as too little too late, also disingenuous (it was just a joke that "went way too far"). Imus lost his job with MSNBC-TV and NBC radio.

Sometimes an apology needs to be put into context so the public relations impact is not overlooked. That was the case as concern grew about the safety of Mattel toys made in China. A top Mattel official met with China's product-safety official to issue an apology to consumers. Mattel said it was sorry for the recall of millions of toys and that it would try to prevent future problems—at least, that's the version reported in Europe and North America. The Chinese version went more like this: "Mattel is sorry for having to recall Chinese-made toys due to the company's design flaws and for harming the reputation of Chinese manufacturing companies." It was, in fact, a design flaw that caused the recall of more than 17 million toys. Only 2 million of those were recalled because the Chinese firms used lead paint, which is prohibited in the US.

China had previously been stung with a series of recalls undermining confidence in its manufactured goods (pet food, toothpaste, packaged seafood, baby cribs). China needed the public apology, and it needed the explanation to be clear that the fault was with Mattel, who, critics agree, deserved the bigger blame because of corporate policies to cut costs and speed up production.

Like all strategies, apology must be considered in light of the particular public involved. Don't assume that how organizational managers or spokespersons want to frame an apology is the best way to do so. Consider culture and how the key public will respond to the apology. Naomi Sugimoto (1997) reported in a study, for example, that the Japanese are three times more likely than Americans are to ask for forgiveness as part of an apology, and the Japanese request is much more explicit ("Please forgive me") than is the typical American one ("I hope you will understand").

Apologies often are associated with relationship goals and with the symmetrical model of public relations that focuses on the long-term association of an organization with its publics. Michael J. Cody and Margaret L. McLaughlin (1990) point out that apologies are more likely to occur when it is important to save face.

Phase Two

STEP 5

CASE IN POINT **Navy Apology**

An apology can take on differing expectations depending on culture. In Japan, for example, a person who injures another is expected to personally apologize.

It was this cultural value that caused the CEO of Japan Airlines to visit the homes of 24 victims' families after the crash of one of his company's planes. This cultural norm also led the owner of Japan's largest milk company to visit each of his retail outlets to personally express his regrets after 13,000 people were poisoned by contaminated dairy products. Likewise, Prime Minister Naoto Kan apologized to farmers and business owners for the radiation leak from the Fukushima nuclear plant after an earthquake-induced tsunami.

Such a personal apology was expected following a sea tragedy off Hawaii in 2001, when a U.S. submarine surfaced quickly and collided with a small Japanese high school training boat. Five fishermen and four Japanese students were killed. The sub had been showing off for some civilian visitors; the visitors may actually have been at the controls when the accident occurred. Japanese media reported that the Navy ship did not try to assist survivors after the accident.

After the accident, the U.S. submarine captain issued a statement through his lawyer expressing "sincere regret." But that wasn't seen as a personal apology, and the Japanese rejected it as improper. President George W. Bush apologized on U.S. television, but the Japanese people remained unsatisfied. Likewise, public apologies from the secretaries of state and defense were dismissed, as was a personal apology by the U.S. commander of the Pacific fleet to the families of the victims. Even a personal apology by the U.S. ambassador to both the prime minister and the emperor were found insufficient.

Instead, the Japanese expected to hear directly and personally from the man who caused the accident, Commander Scott Waddle, who was captaining the submarine at the time of the accident.

Three weeks later, Waddle hand wrote nine letters and asked that they be delivered to the families of the victims. The Navy's second-ranking admiral went to a small town in Japan to meet with the fathers of two of the dead students. Bowing deeply in a gesture of profound humility, he personally apologized and promised a full investigation. That still wasn't the personal apology expected by the Japanese families.

Navy officials, apparently unfamiliar with the healing that a personal apology could bring, refused to allow Waddle to personally express his sorrow and contrition. But a month after the accident, Waddle—against his lawyers' advice—met with family members who had been brought to Hawaii to observe the Navy investigation. He bowed deeply and spoke with tears in his eyes about his remorse. And finally, the families understood his sincerity and accepted his apology.

Nearly two years later, newly resigned from the Navy, Waddle traveled to Ehime prefecture in Japan to apologize personally to the victim's families and to survivors of the accident.

Said the mother of one of the teenage boys who died in the accident: "I am first and foremost the family member of a victim, and Mr. Waddle is first and foremost a victimizer. But when I saw Mr. Waddle as a person who was crying and apologizing, I thought he was apologizing from the heart."

Such is the profound power of apology, done correctly.

The aftermath of the apology has brought a measure of reconciliation. Hawaii built a monument with an annual memorial service. Boys from Hawaii and Ehime play an annual memorial baseball tournament. The current relationship also includes a new sister-school program, mutual tree-planting ceremonies, and a summer internship in Ehime for University of Hawaii students.

Strategic apologies often are opposed by lawyers who fear they will be used against an organization in a lawsuit. This concern is legitimate, but it fails to consider the opportunities an apology makes possible. An apology can prevent lawsuits or at least limit damages sought by claimants or assessed by judges or juries. It also can be good business with stockholders. Fiona Lee, Christopher Peterson and Larissa Tiedens (2004) looked at annual stock prices for 14 companies over 21 years and concluded that stocks increased for companies that accepted responsibility for poor financial performances, compared with those that blamed external factors.

Immediate apologies have short-circuited what could have been serious repercussions, such as when the Caldor department store chain in Norwalk, Connecticut, quickly apologized after 11 million copies of an advertising circular placed in 85 newspapers had a picture of two smiling boys playing Scrabble on a board with the word RAPE spelled out. Instead of blaming its advertising agency, the company accepted responsibility and apologized. "Obviously, it's a mistake," a company told reporters. "It's not something that we would ever have done intentionally." It would be difficult to pursue legal or economic sanctions against a company that shows such integrity.

Conversely, lack of prompt apologies have been cited as the reason for lawsuits, such as a $400,000 claim against police in London, Ontario, by a man erroneously accused of drug trafficking. He explained that he sued the police mainly because they would not apologize.

Similarly, a Las Vegas man who sued a doctor for keeping him three hours in the waiting room said all he really wanted was an apology. After the trial, which ruled in the man's favor, the doctor retorted that the patient should be the one to apologize for dragging the doctor to court for two and a half days. Finally, six months after the waiting-room wait, the doctor wrote a letter of apology. He had to pay the patient $250 plus court costs and make a charitable contribution as well.

Ford and Bridgestone/Firestone faced massive lawsuits after their products were linked to 148 rollover deaths. In 2001, three Ford officials went to the bedside of a Texas woman who was paralyzed in one of the accidents. There they apologized, videotaping their action for broadcast on national television.

Defense attorneys often fear corporate apologies, but in personal-injury cases in particular, apologies can save the company money. Some attorneys point out that lawsuits often are brought by clients seeking an admission of corporate guilt, and a public apology can lessen the amount of money sought by an injured party or awarded by a sympathetic jury.

Easing the way for corporate apologies, Massachusetts passed a law that "statements, writings, or benevolent gestures expressing sympathy . . . relating to the pain, suffering or death of a person involved in an accident . . . shall be inadmissible as evidence of an admission of liability in a civil action." California, Texas, Florida and Washington followed with similar laws.

Additionally, 35 states have laws preventing expressions of condolence or apology by doctors to patients or their families as being admissible in court as evidence of wrongdoing. According to the Sorry Works Coalition (www.sorryworks.net), these "I'm sorry" laws are meant to promote communication between doctors and their patients and to assist doctors in lawsuits. Meanwhile, some states are considering medical apology laws that mitigate malpractice lawsuits when a doctor expresses regret over a patient's death or injury.

Phase Two

STEP
5

Reactive Strategy 6: Rectifying Behavior

A positive response to opposition and criticism involves *rectifying behavior* strategies, in which the organization does something to repair the damage done to its publics. These include investigation, corrective action, restitution and repentance.

Investigation

Using the rectifying behavior of **investigation**, the organization promises to examine the situation and then to act as the facts warrant. This is only a short-term strategy, a way of buying time. Eventually the organization will have to respond with more substance. Use the investigation strategy only when the facts are uncertain enough to warrant a delay in other strategic responses.

Corrective Action

A stronger rectifying behavior is **corrective action**, which involves taking steps to contain a problem, repair the damage and/or prevent its recurrence. This is a strategy that can serve the mutual interests of both the organization and its public. Take corrective action if the organization is in a position to fix a problem, especially if the organization was in some way unprepared or negligent.

This was the case with Texaco when, as noted previously, company executives made racist statements. Texaco responded aggressively with rectifying action that included sensitivity training and a procedure to weed out discrimination within the company.

Corrective action generally is expected when the organization has been at fault. But the response is even more powerful and positive when an organization willingly accepts responsibility for fixing a problem it did not cause. An example of this strategy is Johnson & Johnson's handling of the cyanide deaths associated with Tylenol. Though it was clear from the beginning that the company was not even negligently responsible for the product tampering, Johnson & Johnson nevertheless accepted the challenge to contain the damage and prevent any more. It recalled the product and then introduced a new triple-seal safety packaging that soon became the industry standard.

Restitution

Another rectifying behavior, **restitution**, serves the mutual interests of the organization and its publics. It involves making amends by compensating victims or restoring a situation to its earlier condition. Such a response may be forced upon an organization through the legal process, but some organizations have found it beneficial to offer restitution before it is required.

Repentance

The strongest type of rectifying behavior is **repentance**, which involves both a change of heart and a change in action. Repentance signals an organization's full atonement in the classic sense that it turns away from a former position and becomes an advocate for a new way of doing business. Many organizations, caught in a moral or legal embarrassment, promise repentance and a future of right doing, but few achieve such a turnaround.

DENNY'S DIVERSITY TURNABOUT

One example of an organization that seems to be repenting is the Denny's restaurant chain. Its story is one of transformation from a symbol of corporate racism to a model of workplace diversity.

Denny's faced accusations and lawsuits for racial discrimination at several of its restaurants during the 1990s. One of the most notorious cases involved 21 members of the Secret Service in 1994. While 15 white agents were served quickly, a waitress and manager delayed serving six black agents for nearly an hour, allowing their food to get cold.

The ensuing publicity highlighted a series of lawsuits for similar acts of discrimination at other Denny's restaurants: Asian American students at Syracuse University refused service and beaten by customers; Muslim customers in Montana served pork after asking for a vegetarian menu; Hispanic customers in San Jose refused service; a blind woman refused service because she was accompanied by a service dog; men of Middle Eastern descent kicked out of a restaurant in South Florida.

Denny's eventually paid $54 million in legal settlements. Denny's CDO (chief diversity officer) later looked back on that "historic low point" in the company's history as presenting "huge opportunities. We had no place to go but up."

Dramatically from a public relations perspective, the company seems to have embraced the concept of corporate repentance. It adopted an aggressive antidiscrimination policy that included hiring minority managers, training employees and firing those who discriminated. Denny's increased minority franchise ownership from 1 to 109 over a span of five years (currently 40 percent of all Denny's franchises, with 44 percent of its board of directors as minorities and/or women).

The company launched a $2 million antidiscrimination advertising series. It now purchases goods worth more than $100 million a year from minority vendors and gives proceeds from some sales to the King Center in Atlanta. It has worked with the Hispanic Association on Corporate Responsibility and the NAACP. It gave more than $1.5 million to civil rights groups and the United Negro College Fund as part of the settlement.

The result of this turnaround is that Denny's and its parent company ranked No. 1 in *Fortune* magazine's listing of best companies for minorities, two years running. It received similar awards from *Black Enterprise*, *Essence*, *Asian Enterprise* and *Hispanic Business* magazines.

So successful is its commitment to diversity, some white-nativist organizations now are calling for boycotts because Denny's has become too multicultural.

Denny's certainly isn't the only company with such problems, and with 1,600 franchises throughout the US incidents are bound to occur. But every time an allegation of discrimination is reported, the news media repeats the litany of past complaints against the company, while commentators and customers weigh the sincerity of Denny's protestations that it has repented of such sins and adopted new policies and training programs to prevent their repetition.

Phase Two

STEP
5

Often an organization will use several strategies. An apology, for example, may also involve investigation, justification, restitution, and concession. During the Tylenol crisis, Johnson & Johnson used the strategies of investigation, compassion, excuse, relabeling and corrective action.

Reactive Strategy 7: Deliberate Inaction

The final category of public relations responses involves deliberate inaction, the considered decision by an organization under siege to offer no substantive comment though perhaps to take some action (strategic silence), to respond vaguely and indistinctly (strategic ambiguity) or to say and do nothing and let the problem blow over (strategic inaction).

Strategic Silence

Occasionally the decision to remain nonresponsive—that is, **strategic silence**—is an appropriate public relations response, a strategy of patience and composure. By not responding to criticism an organization may be able to shorten the life span of a crisis situation.

Strategic silence can work when publics accept that an organization is remaining silent not out of guilt or embarrassment but because it is motivated by higher intentions such as compassion for victims, respect for privacy or other noble considerations or simply because it is working on the problem and refuses to get sidetracked into talking much about it.

When cancer-causing benzene was discovered in the bottled water produced by Perrier, the upscale European company pulled millions of bottles from store shelves. But the chairman refused to hold a news conference or give interviews. His silence, though frustrating for the media, prevented the company from appearing to be under siege. At the same time, Perrier moved publicly to correct the problem, fostering what was considered a successful survival of the crisis.

This concept of strategic silence sometimes is given the name **purdah** (an Arabic reference to the veil or protective screen used in the practice of social isolation of women in some Islamic and Hindu societies).

In some circumstances, the law requires organizations to maintain silence, at least on particulars. If so, this requirement should be explained by the organization as the reason for its silence. For example, the Family Educational Rights and Privacy Act (FERPA) prevents universities from providing details about students' academic records. Similarly, the Health Insurance Portability and Accountability Act (HIPPA) sets national standards to ensure the privacy of medical records and other personal health information.

When considering strategic silence, however, remember that the response is likely to be accepted only by those publics that already trust the integrity of the organization. Opponents will find plenty of ammunition in the lack of response.

Silence also risks allowing negative statements to stand unchallenged, which could hurt the organization in the long run. Additionally, a policy of strategic silence may be difficult to maintain if a strong opponent is able to insist on a public response. Remember that silence can imply indifference not only to an opponent but also to the issue itself. An issue might be of real interest to some of an organization's key publics. By dismissing it, the organization also risks slighting anyone who feels the issue is worthy of response.

Strategic silence is not the same as saying "No comment." Such a statement invariably is interpreted as an acknowledgment of guilt, implying that the organization not only did something wrong but did it so ineptly or so blatantly that it can't think of any explanation that would be accepted by its publics. Avoid "no comment" responses and related disdainful statements such as "we won't dignify that accusation with a reply."

If strategic silence is the chosen response, the organization or its defender nevertheless may need to make a public statement giving the reason it chooses not to address the issue further. That was the situation in late 2003 when President George W. Bush made a state visit to England, where he was hosted by Queen Elizabeth at Buckingham Palace. Bush brought with him five of his own personal chefs, news of which the miffed British monarch greeted with strategic silence. "Her Majesty greeted the news that President Bush was coming with his own chef with absolute silence," said a court source. "That's her general way of expressing disapproval. She's not thought to be thrilled about the visit, anyway, but when you consider that she has excellent cooks herself, you can see why this would be taken as a bit of an insult." Silence, and then the silence explained.

Strategic Ambiguity

Similar to the concept of strategic silence is **strategic ambiguity**, the refusal to be pinned down to a particular response. Often this involves the artful dodging of a question.

In an ideal world, ethical decisions would be simple and clear-cut. But the world isn't an ideal place, so be prepared to carefully discern among competing loyalties and differing values.

Politicians use strategic ambiguity frequently so they can avoid taking a public stand or tipping their hand about future potentials. U.S. diplomats, for example, have for decades been deliberately vague about what action might be taken if China moves to forcibly implement its claim that Taiwan is part of China and not an independent nation. Washington and Beijing exchange ambassadors. The State Department uses terms such as "acknowledging" rather than "recognizing" a single Chinese political entity, and diplomats "take note of" rather than "support" Beijing's claim to be the legitimate government of China. When President George W. Bush strayed from the standard U.S. party line and referred to Taiwan as a country, his aides corrected him without correcting him. They said he gave behind-the-scenes disclaimers that this was merely an informal designation and did not signal a shift in U.S. foreign policy.

Corporate leaders use the device to avoid negotiating in public and to maintain their options. Much of the literature of crisis communication suggests that companies can minimize fallout by avoiding quick responses to stakeholder demands.

Clearly there is an ethical dimension to the concept of strategic ambiguity. At what point does ambiguity become obfuscation? Under what circumstances, if any, is it ethical to answer a direct question with a deliberately evasive response? In the hierarchy of organizational objectives, does transparency trump ambiguity? How long can credibility be maintained when underlings have to explain away the language of the boss?

Strategic Inaction

A final category of the deliberate inaction strategy is **strategic inaction**, making no statement and taking no overt action. Instead, the organization simply waits it out and allows the situation to fade.

MAKING ETHICAL JUDGMENTS

In considering various proactive and reactive strategies, it's worth asking one of those sometimes uncomfortable ethical questions, the kind that doesn't have an easy answer, the kind that may give rise to more questions than answers.

"To whom is moral duty owed?" ask Clifford Christians and his fellow authors of *Media Ethics* (2011).

In response to this question, they suggest that communication strategists— journalists and editors, public relations practitioners and advertisers—clarify who will be influenced by our decisions and what obligations we have to them. Good advice. Here are five obligations or duties, along with some thoughts on relevant considerations:

- *Duty to Ourselves.* Be careful to distinguish between following your conscience and simply acting on your own careerist self-interest. One way to do this is to pause and reflect on the basis of your own moral values and on the consistency with which you apply them in your own decision making.
- *Duty to Our Clients.* Our clients, as well as our publics and audiences, deserve our best efforts, especially when they are paying the bills. But don't just blindly go where a client would send you without giving some thought to the client's motives and moral base and how these intersect with your own.
- *Duty to Our Companies or Bosses.* Strike a balance between company loyalty and stoogism. Stick to the recurring advice: Consider motivations and the impact that a company's policies and actions are likely to have.
- *Duty to Our Professional Colleagues.* Consider how your work is enhancing the prestige of your profession and the reputation of your fellow practitioners. Consider especially the commitments implied in the codes of ethics of the various professional organizations. (*See* Appendix B: Ethical Standards for the text of these codes.)
- *Duty to Society.* This is the ultimate ethical test: What does an action do for people? What does it do to them?

Strategic inaction may be a useful strategy if the stakes are not too high. But be forewarned: some problems do not fade away, especially those fanned by the opposition. By doing nothing, an organization risks allowing the problem to grow.

Weighing Options

Look back over the list of reactive public relations strategies. So many possibilities. How can an organization choose among all the options?

Research may play a role, as public relations practitioners consider some likely options and then put them to the test, perhaps by using focus groups, case studies and other forms of research. Experience also plays a role, as practitioners draw on their knowledge of what has worked (or not worked) for them in the past.

Consider the situation faced by Network Ten, one of the major networks in Australia known for some edgy programming. In 2012, the network commissioned a reality series called "The Shire," branded as Australia's version of the U.S. series "Jersey Shore" and the U.K. version "The Geordie Shore." Immediately the planned series captured popular attention.

A promo video was leaked, showing scenes about breast implants, domestic violence and wannabe porn stars. This created what some residents of Sutherland Shire saw as a negative impression of the Sydney-area community where the show was set. The mayor had what was described as "a heated meeting," telling the network executive that the Shire didn't want the series filmed there. The Shire council tried to ban producers from filming on area parks and beaches. A member of parliament planned to meet with the network bosses.

Network Ten faced several various options in reacting to the rogue (and by then, viral) video.

- *Strategic silence.* It simply could ignore the video, not draw more attention to it, and let the controversy die out.
- *Denial.* It could use a strategy of defensive response. The network's contention was that the promo video was nothing like its series. It might prove this by releasing an authorized video trailer of "The Shire," inviting audiences to see for themselves that the leaked version was a flawed comparison.
- *Reversal.* Network Ten could accept the leaked video as a compliment and light-heartedly play along with the interest it was generating.
- *Threat.* The network could use an offensive response strategy by threatening the bloggers with legal action if they did not take the video down.
- *Attack.* The network could actually make good on its threat and try to attack the messenger by forcing bloggers who posted the video to take it down.

Network Ten chose a combination of threat and attack. After threatening a blogger who had posted the video, the network filed a copyright claim. Not surprisingly, these steps created instant notoriety, drawing even more attention. The network eventually forced YouTube to temporarily remove the video—but not before it had attracted 30,000 viewers in the first two days. The video later returned to several different video-sharing sites, and the number of viewers jumped to six digits.

The strategy of offensive response—and the inept handling if the network really wished to minimize publicity—prompted media critics to suggest that Network Ten purposely "leaked" the video to draw attention to the planned series.

Regardless of its motivation, the strategy of attack was seen as an example of the **Streisand effect**, which refers to the unintended consequence of fueling publicity by trying to have something censored.

The Streisand effect is the backfiring of efforts to remove information, especially photos and videos disseminated over the Internet. The term stems from entertainer Barbra Streisand's 2003 attempt to ban photos of her home—just one of 12,000 photos of California coastal erosion—from being displayed at an environmental website. The entertainer's $50 million lawsuit, which was dismissed, created additional publicity. Before the lawsuit was filed, only six people had viewed the photo (two of them Streisand's attorneys). But publicity about the lawsuit drove half a million visitors to view the website photos, creating a boon for the environmental group.

Phase Two

STEP 5

Other celebrities have had similar experiences. Tom Cruise unsuccessfully attempted in 2008 to force YouTube to remove a video interview of him talking about his Church of Scientology, only to boost its popularity.

In 2009, Glenn Beck tried to shut down a satirical website raising the question of whether he had raped and murdered a girl, a question that parodied Beck's own interview style posing outrageous assertions to guests on his TV commentary. Beck lost the legal battle, but not before driving viewers to the social media sites posting the video and even attracting coverage by mainstream news media.

Corporations also have experienced the effect, such as when McDonald's sued two activists for passing out critical fliers at one London restaurant in 1990. Instead of having only a few hundred patrons exposed to the criticism, McDonald's launched a lawsuit that endured for 15 years, including a libel trial that lasted two and a half years, cost millions in legal fees and drew international media attention as the McLibel case, before it was finally settled in 2005. McDonald's lost.

When Fox Television sued Al Franken in 2003 claiming copyright infringement over the title of his book *Lies and the Lying Liars Who Tell Them: A Fair and Balanced Look at the Right*, the book shot to No. 1 on Amazon's best-seller list.

What's Next?

This concludes Step 5. You now should have a firm handle on the strategic direction of your planning. Specifically you have made some major decisions on using both proactive and reactive approaches to your key publics.

Next you will turn to the message itself—who should carry it and how it will draw on logical and/or emotional arguments.

PLANNING EXAMPLE 5 **Formulating Action and Response Strategies**

UPSTATE COLLEGE

Upstate College will develop the following strategies:

Proactive Strategy

1. Involve student public in celebrations and other special events focused on the academic expansion.
2. Enhance alliances with high schools based on new academic opportunities at the college.
3. Take advantage of the many newsworthy activities associated with the expansion.

Reactive Strategy

No responsive strategy is anticipated, because the expansion to a 4-year program is unlikely to generate opposition or criticism.

Tiny Tykes will develop the following strategies:

Proactive Strategy

1. Place a high priority on research and development as they relate to high-quality standards for toy products.
2. Form alliances with customers and consumer advocates focused on the safety of children's toys.
3. Initiate news activities focused on toy safety.
4. Engage in transparent communication to allow employees and consumer advocates to observe the company's efforts to produce safe and high-quality toys.

Reactive Strategy

1. Make a concession to customers and consumer advocates by sponsoring university research on the role of play in child psychological and educational development.
2. If necessary, reiterate statement of regret issued prior to the toy recall.
3. Display corporate repentance by publicly relaunching the product with a recommitment to quality and excellence.

[Note: Numbering strategies makes it easier to reference them within the planning team and when meeting with clients.]

✓ *Checklist 5* **Action and Response Strategies**

Basic Questions

1. What proactive strategies might you develop?
2. What reactive strategies might you develop?
3. How consistent are these strategies with past practices of your organization?

Expanded Questions

A. PROACTIVE STRATEGY

1. Is it appropriate to use any of the following approaches? If "yes," how?

Action
- organizational performance
- audience participation
- alliances
- sponsorships
- activism.

Phase Two

STEP
5

Communication
- publicity
- newsworthy information
- transparent communication.

2. Summarize the proactive strategy of your organization.

B. REACTIVE STRATEGY

1. Is it appropriate to use any of the following approaches? If "yes," how?

Pre-emptive Action

- prebuttal.

Offensive Response

- attack
- embarrassment
- shock
- threat.

Defensive Response

- denial
- excuse
- justification
- reversal.

Diversionary Response

- concession
- ingratiation
- disassociation
- relabeling.

Vocal Commiseration

- concern
- condolence
- regret
- apology.

Rectifying Behavior

- investigation
- corrective action
- restitution
- repentance.

Deliberate Inaction

- strategic silence
- strategic ambiguity
- strategic inaction.

2. Summarize the reactive strategy of your organization.

C. ACTION/RESPONSE CONSISTENCY

1. Is this action/response consistent with past verbal messages of this organization/spokesperson? If "no," explain the inconsistency.
2. Is the action/response consistent with past actions of this organization/spokesperson? If "no," explain the inconsistency.
3. Is the action/response consistent with the mission of this source? If "no," explain the inconsistency.
4. Is the action/response consistent with image of this source? If "no," explain the inconsistency.
5. Is the action/response ethical? If "no," develop a different response.

CONSENSUS CHECK

Does agreement exist within your organization and your planning team about the recommended strategies included within this step of the planning process?

☐ Yes. Proceed to Step 6, Developing the Message Strategy.

☐ No. Consider the value and/or possibility of achieving consensus before proceeding.

Phase Two

STEP
5

Developing the Message Strategy

Having identified your publics and established objectives for what you want to achieve, and having set into motion the way the organization is preparing to act to achieve those objectives, it is time to turn your attention to the best means of communication. Since strategic communication is carefully planned communication, this is an important step.

Remember what we said earlier about publics and audiences: Publics are groups of people in a relationship with your organization; audiences are people who receive messages. At this stage of the planning process, we begin treating publics as the audiences with whom we are communicating and we consider the various elements of effective communication. Who should present the message? What appeals should be made in the message? How should the message be structured? What words should be used? What symbols? How might we create a buzz?

Thousands of public relations and marketing messages bombard people each day. That's more than three different messages every minute of every waking hour—most of them trying to sell something or gain support in some way. Amid all this noise, how can your organization's message stand out? It's not easy, but effective communication can help your message rise above the clamor.

Communication Process

Several different approaches to communication are used in public relations and related fields. Three particular models are worth particular attention: information, persuasion and dialogue. These align loosely with the classic models of public relations outlined by James Grunig and Todd Hunt (*see* the Introduction to this book). The information model of communication plays out as press agentry and public information. The persuasion model is asymmetric, with a focus on advocacy and attempts to influence. The dialogue model of communication, meanwhile, is a symmetric approach rooted in relationships.

Let's look more closely at each of these communication processes.

Information: Flow of Communication

The **information model** of communication focuses on the content and channels of communication. It involves a message sent by a source to a receiver, with ideas encoded and interpreted through symbols (words or images) that are transmitted person to person or through some technical connection. Harold Lasswell (1948) offered a simple verbal formula of communication: "Who says what to whom with what effect." Today we add "how" and perhaps even "why" to this formula.

Exhibit 6.1 provides a visual model of information-based communication. This model is based on the frequently cited work of Claude Shannon and Warren Weaver (1949) and Norbert Wiener (1954), echoed later by David Berlo (1960) and Wilbur Schramm (1971).

Shannon and Weaver, scientists with Bell Telephone Laboratories, developed a visual model of what they called the **mathematical theory of communication**. Their approach was linear, with virtually tangible data encoded and transmitted through a channel to a receiver. In essence, theirs was a model for monologue, with the source person or organization talking at an audience, in simplified terms, the press agentry model of public relations. Wiener's **cybernetic model of communication** was more circular in design, involving feedback from the receiver to influence the sender. The model shown in Exhibit 6.1 is more focused on two-way communication, talking with an audience (similar to the public information model).

Persuasion: Attempts to Influence

Another process of communication, the **persuasion model**, consciously attempts to influence people, using ethical means that enhance a democratic society. Persuasion is an inherent part of social interaction, something people everywhere do. Don't confuse persuasion with deception; the latter relies on miscommunication. Neither is persuasive communication involved with coercion, which relies on force rather than on communication. Nor is it **propaganda**, which is a debasement of persuasive communication because it is associated with half-truths and hidden agendas.

Persuasion is particularly associated with advocacy, the asymmetric approach to strategic communication. An organization presents its point of view in an attempt to convince its publics to give their agreement and support.

The practice of persuasion is widespread and popular. In marketing, for example, most companies try to convince potential consumers to buy the company's products or services. In public relations, organizations try to convince publics to agree with this concept, support that candidate or follow those procedures. In public health and safety campaigns, agencies try to persuade young people to stop smoking, motorists to start wearing seat belts and middle-aged people to get more exercise. In international relations, governments try to convince counterparts in other countries to adopt democratic practices, and nongovernmental organizations try to influence governments to respect human rights or to eliminate gender-based, religious or racial discrimination. All of these are examples of persuasive communication.

Dialogue: Quest for Understanding

The **dialogue model** involves the deeply conscious interaction of two parties in communication. It involves a sincere and competent attempt at mutual understanding, paralleling the symmetrical model of public relations.

Phase Two

**STEP
6**

EXHIBIT 6.1 Information-Based Communication Model

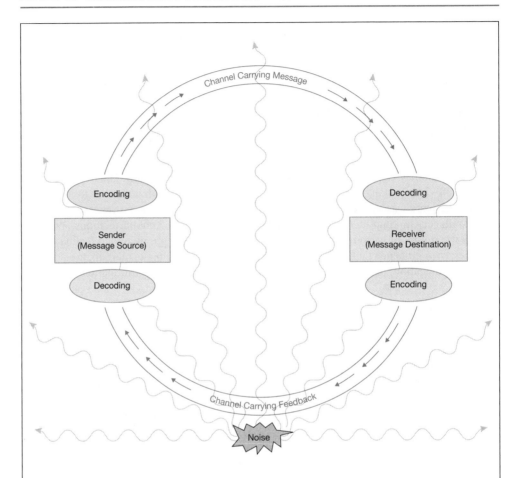

In this model of communication, a sender (which can be a person or an organization) encodes a message (using verbal and/or nonverbal symbols) that is carried through a particular channel (such as a speech, blog entry, phone call, photograph, brochure, etc.) to a receiver, who decodes (or interprets) the message. This is one-way communication, which would be the top half of this graphic visualization.

In a two-way communication situation, the receiver reacts and responds to the original message by encoding feedback that is sent back to the original sender. This might involve question or even applause from an audience, a blog comment, an ongoing phone conversation, and so on. This is depicted in the entire graphic.

A communication context potentially involves *noise*, which is any interference that limits the ability of the channel to carry a message faithfully from sender to receiver. Such interference can be in the encoding or decoding of the message or in the channels used to transmit the message.

RESEARCH BACKGROUND ON PERSUASION

Several theories dealing with persuasion are relevant to much public relations and marketing activity. Here are a few of the most common theories.

The **balance theory**, articulated by psychologist Fritz Heider (1958), is the oldest **consistency theory**, observing that unbalanced mental stances create tension and force an individual to restore balance. Theodore Newcomb (1953) extended this to groups, calling it the **symmetry theory**. Charles Osgood and Percy Tannenbaum's **congruity theory** (1955) added some measurement in attitude. The lesson of all these consistency theories for public relations practitioners is that attitude change can be stimulated by information that causes people to realize that two attitudes are in conflict and that the persuasiveness of the source is a major factor to accomplish this.

Social psychologist Leon Festinger's **cognitive dissonance theory** (1957) explained that the more people experience the psychological discomfort of having contradictory attitudes or beliefs, the more likely they will reduce the discomfort, usually by changing one of their attitudes or beliefs. An important element of this theory is the concept of *selective exposure*, which refers to seeking information that supports a currently held attitude while avoiding information that does not support it.

The **inoculation theory**, proposed by William McGuire and Demetrios Papageorgis (1961), suggests that unchallenged beliefs and attitudes can be swayed with persuasive information, while attitudes that have been tested are more resistant to change. This latter aspect is particularly useful to strategic communicators seeking to create resistance to potentially opposing arguments.

The **social judgment theory**, put forward by Muzafer Sherif and Carl Hovland (1961), observes that individuals accept or reject messages to the extent that they perceive the messages as corresponding to their internal anchors (attitudes and beliefs) and as being ego-involved (affecting the person's self-concept).

Phase Two

STEP
6

Dialogue is the kind of communication described by existentialist philosopher Martin Buber (1947). It is what Evelyn Sieberg called "confirming communication," which seeks to heal and strengthen relationships. "Confirmation," notes Sieberg, "like existential dialogue, is a mutual experience involving sharing at several levels—sharing of talking, sharing of self, sharing of respect, sharing of trust" (1976).

Dialogue involves four goals useful to public relations:

1. nurturing an information exchange between individuals or groups;
2. helping communication partners make responsible and mutually acceptable decisions;
3. reviving the original vitality of a relationship;
4. deepening a relationship that continues to unite communication partners ever more closely.

Dialogue also generates two management practices—consensus building and conflict resolution—that help parties consider issues in light of their mutual needs and arrive at solutions that enhance their relationships.

- **Consensus building** is a process of identifying and then preventing or overcoming barriers between people and/or organizations.
- **Conflict resolution** involves making peace and restoring harmony, often with communication as the primary tool.

Carl Botan (1997) has observed the relationship between dialogue and ethics. He notes that dialogic communication is characterized by a relationship in which both parties genuinely care about each other rather than merely seek to fulfill their own needs. This kind of relationship is embodied in the symmetrical model of public relations, in which organizations try to adapt and harmonize with their publics. It elevates publics to an equal footing with the organization itself, allowing either party in the interchange to take the initiative.

An example of dialogic communication would be an equal relationship between corporate management and either an external public such as an activist group or an internal public such as an employee union, in which either side could call meetings, propose agenda topics, conduct research, launch a communication program, and so on. Botan also noted that advances in communication technology have made it easier for organizations to engage with their publics in a two-way dialogue. Certainly advances in Internet-based technology are breaking down old hierarchical structures in communication.

In the practice of strategic communication, there is a role for each type of communication model: information, persuasion and dialogue. Information approaches to communication often focus on the message sender and receiver, while persuasive communication deals with the content of the message. Dialogue, in turn, emphasizes the relationship between the parties in the communication process. Each of these elements is important to public relations, which necessarily deals with the actors in the communication process, the messages shared between them, and the relationship they share.

Rhetorical Tradition

The use of communication to influence ideas and actions and to strengthen relationships is a basic element of human society. History has handed down to us some ancient examples of the art of effective communication. Much of it comes from the dawn of Western civilization in the lands encircling the Mediterranean Sea.

Two of the oldest-known pieces of literature, the *Iliad* and the *Odyssey*, both ascribed to the Greek poet Homer about 2,800 years ago, feature examples of effective persuasive speeches. Consider Odysseus's plea with the Cyclops about why the monster should not eat him, or Paris's entreaty for Helen to leave her husband and go off with him, or the acclaim given to Hector and Achilles for their speeches that stirred up their military troops.

Even earlier pieces of literature, though difficult to date precisely—the Pentateuch of the Hebrew Bible, the epic of Gilgamesh—have passages with strong persuasive rhetoric, such as Moses' persuasive skills before pharaoh or his verbal arguments with God. The Egyptian philosopher and court official Ptah-Hotep advised the pharaohs to link their message to the interests of their audience.

The effective use of persuasive communication was a particular interest in classical Greece, with its focus on participatory democracy. In the fifth century BCE, Corax of Syracuse wrote a handbook on **rhetoric**, the art of using words effectively in speaking and writing for the purpose of influencing, persuading or entertaining. Basically, rhetoric is persuasive

Phase Two

STEP
6

communication. Corax noted the relationship between certainty and probability: while physical evidence can prove something true and thus beyond argument, **verbal evidence** can show only greater or lesser probabilities that something is true.

Later, in Athens, Socrates and his student Plato criticized rhetoric as verbal maneuvering that could make right seem wrong and important appear unimportant. They called for a grounding in truth and taught some of the skills associated with ethical communication, such as logical organization of ideas. Plato outlined the differences between true and false rhetoric.

The first person known to have studied persuasive communication systematically was one of Plato's students, Aristotle, who became the court educator to Alexander the Great. Twenty-five centuries ago, in his treatise called *Rhetoric*, Aristotle identified three central elements that today remain the cornerstones of persuasive communication: ethos, logos and **pathos**. Following the don't-mess-with-success principle, *Strategic Planning for Public Relations* uses these elements as the framework for developing a strategic and effective public relations and marketing communication message. Each will be discussed in detail shortly.

From the Greek foundation, the study of communication passed over to classical Rome, where Marcus Tullius Cicero organized rhetoric into five principles (roughly, argumentation, organization, style, delivery and memorization). Marcus Fabius Quintillianus wrote on the education of communicators, advising that they were about more than simply persuasion; they also were in the business of informing, motivating and inspiring.

During the Middle Ages, the Saxon theologian Alcuin, teacher and advisor to the emperor Charlemagne, reinterpreted Roman rhetoric and applied it to practical areas such as public policy, legal and judicial proceedings, and the placement of blame or praise.

Rhetoric also influenced the field of religion, and vice versa. Augustine of Hippo, a professor of rhetoric at Milan who became a bishop in Roman Africa, was one of the most influential figures in persuasive communication with his study, teaching and personal examples dealing with preaching. Augustine was influential in developing the practice of **apologetics** (the systematic attempt to explain the reasonableness of religious faith and to refute opposing arguments) and **homiletics** (the study and application of effective communication for preaching).

After the fall of Western civilization, the teaching of Aristotle was virtually lost to European society. During the ninth century, Muslim scholars, Christian Arabs and Arabic-speaking Jews kept alive the study of Aristotle in the Middle East. The Crusades introduced Arab scholarship to the West, such as the "science of eloquence" associated with Abd al Jurjani. Through Arab scholars, the West also rediscovered Aristotle.

During the thirteenth century, the Italian philosopher-monk Thomas Aquinas applied Aristotelian principles of ethos, logos and pathos to the understanding and explanation of religious belief, and wrote on topics such as truth, knowledge and communication. He became known as the Christian Aristotle and is considered one of history's most influential theologians and philosophers.

During the Enlightenment period of the sixteenth century, Desiderius Erasmas of Rotterdam influenced a renewed interest in rhetoric with a more secular perspective. John Milton wrote a textbook on rhetoric.

More contemporary figures in the evolution of our understanding of communication include the English philosopher-friar Francis Bacon, credited with formulating the scientific method; philosopher Thomas Hobbes, who also wrote on rhetoric; American language theorist Kenneth Burke, who studied the nature and power of symbols in human interaction; language

Phase Two

STEP
6

critic Richard Weaver, who dealt with the cultural role of persuasion; Belgian philosopher Chaim Perelman, who analyzed how communicators can gain "the adherence of minds"; and Canadian theologian and philosopher Bernard Lonergan. Canadian theorist Marshall McLuhan wrote his doctoral theses at Cambridge University on the history of rhetorical thought; he became the most widely publicized scholar of rhetoric in the twentieth century.

Most of the study of rhetoric has been done from a Western perspective, though increasingly attention is being given to Asian traditions. From a Buddhist perspective, the characteristics of speech are said to be that it is true, real and useful. The Buddha's description of an effective preacher is a monk who abandons falsehood and is truthful, faithful and trustworthy. Confucius recognized that sincerity and respectfulness are important elements of effective speaking.

The African and Native American traditions emphasize storytelling, the graceful use of language, the development of consensus and even the communicative value of silence—all concepts with practical relevance for today's public relations practitioner.

Ethos: Selecting Message Sources

Ethos is communication effectiveness based on the character of the speaker and on the common ground shared by speakers and audiences.

Years of research by social scientists have produced a snapshot of an effective message source. This is a person or an organization perceived by an audience as being credible, having charisma, and exercising some kind of control—what we might call the "three Cs" of an effective communicator. These are presented visually in Exhibit 6.2. Individually, each of these perceptions is a powerful tool for the practitioner. In combination, they create a compelling factor in effective communication.

It is important to note that each of these elements is based on the audience's perception of the speaker. Aristotle observed that reputation precedes the speaker, setting the stage for the audience to accept or reject the speaker's message. Even before the speaker presents a message, the audience makes a judgment based on the speaker's prestige and prominence, as well as their presumption that they may or may not agree with the speaker. Precisely because reputation has such a direct and predictable impact on their ability to influence their publics, organizations pay much attention to what people know and think about them.

Let's look at the Three Cs in detail.

Credibility: Power to Inspire Belief

Credibility—the power to inspire belief—is tremendously important to persuasion. Though we might wish it were different, being a good speaker or writer is more effective than having good physical evidence. Sources perceived as being highly credible are believed on their own merits and whatever evidence they present has little added value. Even audiences that don't understand an issue often will accept a message when they think the source is believable.

Highly credible sources can appeal to fear and use intense or opinionated language that would be counterproductive coming from sources with lesser credibility. For example, it was his high credibility that allowed President Ronald Reagan to call the Soviet Union "an evil empire" and be effective in such extreme speech. When President George W. Bush revived the idea in reference to an "axis of evil" encompassing Iraq, Iran and North Korea, his

EXHIBIT 6.2 Three Cs of Effective Communication

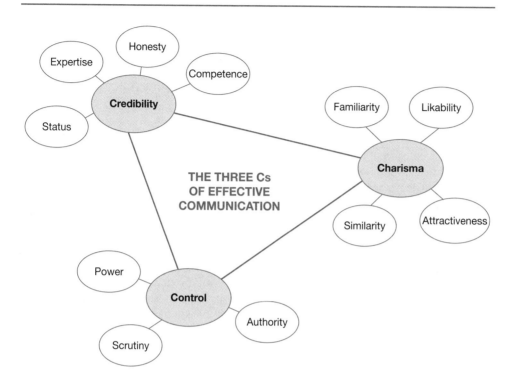

credibility was lower and the phrase was criticized, belittled and parodied as an "axis of weasels," "axis of feebles" and "asses of evil." As a result of such criticism, Bush didn't use the phrase again in a public speech.

As part of the process of strategic planning, you can enhance source credibility by reinforcing the characteristics of ethos. A credible source is one with expertise, status, competence and honesty.

Audiences need to see such qualities, whether real or imagined. Remember that perception is the key. The source's expertise and honesty must be apparent to the audience. Some campaigns have faltered because the audience didn't realize the source was an expert or because the source didn't appear trustworthy.

EXPERTISE

The most important factor in making a message source effective is **expertise**, which means that the source knows what he or she is talking about.

The perception of expertise can be intensified by using a message source who has experience, knowledge, intelligence, occupational or professional background, or the wisdom that comes with age. Of course, this must be relevant to the topic being addressed—a physician may be very credible on the issue of health but not particularly so on a political topic. Entertainers and athletes who make political pronouncements, for example, may find that they are ignored, even ridiculed, when they leap beyond their level of competence.

Expertise and status can be borrowed from recognized experts by quoting them, though the impact of this is weak.

STATUS

Related to expertise is **status**, but this rests more with the audience's deference to the social position or prestige of a message source. As with expertise, perceived status is enhanced by the use of message sources whom the audience sees as having prestige. Also similar to expertise, the status needs to be relevant to the topic for it to influence an audience.

COMPETENCE

Another related concept is **competence**, the ability to remain calm under pressure and to be clear and effective in presenting the message to others, especially those who may not share the same knowledge or loyalties.

Communication competence is a matter of perception. The audience perceives (or not) that the speaker is calm, clear and able to communicate well.

Perceived competence can be enhanced by two elements associated with effective presentations. One element is physical stature and stage presence. This includes being tall, sitting or standing erect, maintaining eye contact and having facial composure. The second element that enhances competence is vocal quality. This involves enunciating clearly, initiating communication, speaking with conviction and authority, exuding energy and enthusiasm, and avoiding language fillers such as *um* and *uh*. Two kinds of skill builders—coaching for public speaking and training for media interviews—can help a speaker strategically develop vocal emphasis, convincing gestures and other aspects of communication competence.

HONESTY

Finally, **honesty** means that the source is willing to provide full and accurate information, is operating without bias and thus is worthy of trust.

Like the other characteristics of credibility, audience perception of honesty can be enhanced to help a source appear more trustworthy by emphasizing the objectivity, integrity and neutrality with which the source approaches the subject. Message sources who advocate positions contrary to their personal interests or who take an unexpected position have a special credibility. For example, a physician who recommends herbal medicine will be particularly believable because the health care establishment traditionally has ignored, even scorned, the medicinal value of herbs. Honesty also is enhanced when the message source shows a consistency between past and present, and between words and deeds.

If you are presenting a position that differs from one taken by your organization in the past, signal the change and carefully explain not only the new posture but also the reason for the change. Try not to allow yourself to be labeled as inconsistent or as contradictory of past statements. In the current political and social climate, charges of flip-flopping on issues and changing positions are exploited by opponents as signs of weakness, lack of underlying values and political pandering. Recall the apparent inconsistency of presidential candidate Mitt Romney, whose record was both for and against abortion, gay rights, gun ownership, free trade with China and sundry other issues.

Certainly you may change your mind, but make sure you let your audience know the reason for such a change and see it as legitimate rather than merely pandering to the current whim.

CREDIBILITY AND NEWS SOURCES

A Yale University survey of 2,030 American adults—"American's Knowledge on Climate Change"—probed the relative credibility of different types of news sources on an environmental issue, specifically climate change. The researchers with the university's Project for Climate Change Communication (Leiserowitz, Smith and Marlon, 2010) identified several information sources and asked respondents to rate how much the trust or distrust of each as a source of information on climate change.

Here are the credibility levels (strongly or somewhat trust) reported in the survey:

78%	National Oceanographic and Atmospheric Administration
74%	National Science Foundation
72%	Scientists
72%	Science TV programs on PBS and Discovery
72%	Natural history and science museums
67%	Zoos and aquariums
64%	University professors
62%	School teachers
61%	Environmental Protection Agency
50%	TV weather forecasters
42%	Military leaders
35%	Mainstream news media

What's the lesson to be learned from this research? It deals with expertise. Recognized experts without apparent self-interest are the most credible message sources. The public may admire celebrities, but people are more likely to be persuaded by unbiased individuals and organizations that know what they are doing and saying.

Phase Two

STEP 6

Charisma: Power of Personal Charm

The magnetic appeal or personal charm that some message sources enjoy over an audience is called **charisma**, another important element of persuasion. Like credibility, charisma is a matter of perception, and it varies greatly from one person to another and from one public to another.

The so-called **halo effect** demonstrates that a source perceived as credible, charismatic and/or in control can rely on this reputation. Think of the many situations in which a politician—you supply the name, from either side of the aisle—can do no wrong in the eyes of his supporters but can do nothing right in the eyes of those who despise him. The same can be said about some athletes and entertainers who evoke passionate responses of either adoration or condemnation.

The halo effect is very useful for the communicator. But halos slip and stars fall, so be careful about where you shine your spotlight. Also, realize that while one person may have a halo effect on some members of an audience, the same person may have an opposite **horns**

effect on other members of the audience who dislike the messenger. Both halos and horns often evoke unreasonable passion.

Charisma has several specific characteristics: familiarity, likability, similarity and attractiveness.

FAMILIARITY

One important aspect of charisma is **familiarity**, the extent to which the audience already knows (or thinks it knows) the message source.

LIKABILITY

Charisma also involves **likability**, the extent to which the audience admires what it knows about the source or what it sees and hears when the source begins to communicate.

This generally means that the message source is neutral on divisive social and political issues and not associated with controversy or partisanship—unless the audience itself is partisan. The principle of likability may suggest that, for a general and mixed audience, you would avoid using a message source who is closely associated with a particular cultural, ethnic or religious group, because the audience may not like someone closely identified with alien characteristics.

SIMILARITY

Charisma also involves **similarity**, the extent to which the source resembles the audience (or the way in which audience members would like to see themselves). This may be a reflection of audience demographics in terms of age, gender, occupation, ethnicity, religion, culture, shared values or sociopolitical perspectives.

Thus the principle of similarity offers a parallel guideline to that of familiarity. You might consider using a message source closely associated with a particular cultural, ethnic, political or religious group when the audience also is associated with that group. Similarity is particularly important when a communicator is seeking long-term persuasion, less so for short-term objectives. It also is a major factor in enhancing dialogic communication.

ATTRACTIVENESS

Finally, charisma is affected by the **attractiveness** of the source, which involves the source's physical looks, demeanor, poise and presence. It also is impacted by both the clothing worn and the setting in which the source is presented. Note, however, that physical attractiveness and beauty are significantly less important than credibility and other aspects of charisma. Despite the Hollywood emphasis on sex appeal, beauty and hunkiness, average-looking people can be highly effective message sources. Indeed, speakers who are very good-looking, especially if they flaunt their looks, may have difficulty being perceived as much more than pretty faces and buff bodies.

Control: Power of Command

The third component of an effective message source is **control**, which is rooted in a message source's command over the audience and on the perceived willingness to exercise that control.

POWER

One of the most important aspects of control is **power**, the raw and recognized ability to dominate and to reward or punish. Guilt appeals (which we will discuss later) often are associated with powerful message sources.

AUTHORITY

Control also may be based on a message source's **authority**, which is the right to rule over or direct the actions of another. Authority implies that the audience more or less willingly has granted the right of control and thus will give obedience. Authority often involves a legal or social prerogative. It also can involve moral leverage, such as by summoning the audience to its stated values or calling it to its accepted duty. Both guilt appeals and virtue appeals (which we will discuss later) may be associated with authority figures.

SCRUTINY

Finally, the persuasive element of control suggests *scrutiny*, the ability to examine. Someone who is able to investigate you also is able to pronounce your blame, proclaim your innocence and perhaps grant forgiveness. As with the previous characteristics of an effective source, control must be perceived by the receiver. Keep in mind that perceptions change.

Organizational Spokespeople

The elements of credibility, charisma and control can be maximized as part of strategic planning, for example, by selecting an appropriate spokesperson who is likely to appeal to an organization's publics.

Celebrity Spokespersons

Celebrities often are used because they are charismatic and familiar. Entertainers and sports figures frequently are spokespersons for companies and nonprofit organizations as well as for social and political causes.

Celebrity endorsement doesn't automatically translate into money or votes, but it can garner media attention and public interest. It also encourages audiences to look at websites and to read brochures and letters they otherwise might ignore.

Celebrities are in great demand by charitable causes. Thus we find actors Nicole Kidman, Vivica A. Fox and Reese Witherspoon promoting breast cancer awareness; country singer Toby Keith creating attention for childhood cancers; Jimmy Smits for colon cancer; Halle Barry and Cuba Gooding Jr. for diabetes awareness; and J.J. Redick of the Orlando Magic basketball team for Torch Relay Children's Miracle Network on behalf of children's hospitals across the country.

Jennifer Love Hewitt has good things to say on behalf of the Veteran's Administration and various veterans groups, and Kirstie Alley, Tom Cruise and Isaac Hayes have pitched anti-drug messages.

Social causes also attract celebrities. Angelina Jolie is a goodwill ambassador for the U.N. High Commissioner for Refugees. She, Brad Pitt, George Clooney, Sean Penn and Bono are well known for espousing various humanitarian causes, many inspired by international crises. Meanwhile, actor Colin Firth promotes use of fair-trade products from developing countries; Drew Barrymore lobbies for child feeding programs as a goodwill ambassador for the U.N. World Food Program; and Leonardo DiCaprio works on various environmental causes.

Sometimes a local incident gains celebrity interest. After a 14-year-old boy in Buffalo, N.Y., committed suicide, Lady Gaga and her Born This Way Foundation sparked new awareness for the cause of anti-gay bullying.

After newsman Mike Wallace went public with his struggle against depression, the Colorado Behavioral Healthcare Council felt he would be just the famous face to use in its public service campaign on suicide and depression prevention. In 2006, organizers of the New York City Alzheimer's Association credited the presence of actor Jean Smart as emcee for a fundraising dinner for a $400,000 increase in donations from the previous year.

Meanwhile, politicians line up celebrity endorsements to translate fame into voter influence. Historians say the practice began in 1920 when Hollywood heavyweights Al Jolson, Lillian Russell, Douglas Fairbanks and Mary Pickford threw their fame behind presidential candidate Warren G. Harding. He won, and candidates have courted celebrity endorsement ever since.

Recent election cycles have continued the trend popularized by George W. Bush campaigns that drew heavily on celebrity religious endorsers. Republicans especially court such endorsements, which generally come from evangelical and nondenominational Christian clergy. Clergy are in the business of opinion leadership, but little research has been done to suggest whether endorsement by religious figures helps or hurts a candidate.

But as for general celebrity political endorsement, a 2010 study from North Carolina State University suggests that they are not particularly useful. Political science professor Michael Cobb found that celebrity endorsements don't help political candidates. Young voters actually may be turned off toward the candidate because of such endorsements.

Sometimes spokespersons actually are likable "spokes-characters," such as Morris the Cat for Nine Lives cat food, McGruff the Crime Dog or Geico insurance's gecko. Other spokes-characters have included the Budweiser Clydesdales, Elsie the Cow for Borden's Milk, and Charlie the Tuna for StarKist. *Advertising Week's* Walk of Fame on Madison Avenue in New York City honors advertising icons such as Juan Valdez (for Columbian Coffee), Colonel Sanders (for KFC), the Aflac duck, Tony the Tiger (for Kellogg's Frosted Flakes) and the Pillsbury Doughboy.

Occasionally an advertising mascot becomes a celebrity. Consider the lonely Maytag repairman. The mascot was created in 1967, and national auditions brought in Jesse White as the company face for 22 years. Another national search in 2007 brought Clay Jackson to the role. In addition to print and television commercials, Jackson shows up on TV talk shows, makes personal appearances around the country and sings the National Anthem at sporting events.

Public relations and marketing people selecting celebrity spokespersons generally look for a connection with their key publics. It's not accidental, for example, that Hurley Hayward is the spokesperson for Porsche. About 90 percent of Porsche's customers are men, and research showed that most of them are racing fans. Hayward, one of the world's best race-car drivers, is a multiple winner of the LeMans, Sebring and Daytona races.

Likewise, it makes sense for people such as tennis great John McEnroe and basketball player Karl Malone to be the pitchmen for Rogaine Extra Strength in an ongoing promotional campaign using sports figures who have had positive results with the hair-growth formula. Or Brazilian soccer legend Pele and conservative talk-radio host Rush Limbaugh doing ads

ETHICS AND CELEBRITY ENDORSEMENTS

There is an ethical consideration for nonprofit organizations over the use of celebrity endorsements.

Some charities simply cannot afford the price tag that comes with many celebrities—they don't necessarily donate their time. For some charities, fame is not worth the price. The American Diabetes Association, for example, chooses not to spend donated money on celebrity spokespersons. The ADA says it's not interested in redesigning its campaign to fit the publicity needs of celebrities and their agents.

Industry sources report that celebrity endorsers generally receive honorariums as high as $100,000. Not all celebrity spokespersons are paid. WebMD (webmd.com) reports that both the National Parkinson Foundation and the Alzheimer's Association, for example, indicate that their celebrity endorsers donate their time and even pick up their own travel expenses.

The Entertainment Industry Foundation, a clearinghouse for many entertainers who become involved with charity work, insists that the celebrity "ambassadors" work for free. Most of the expenses are picked up by sponsoring companies such as Revlon, People Magazine and Lee Jeans, but this is not so with pharmaceutical companies.

Pharmaceuticals sometimes offer to pick up the tab for celebrity endorsements of a medical charity. Such offers usually come with strings. Often the arrangement calls for the celebrity to endorse the company's product. Such an arrangement came to light when veteran actor Lauren Bacall, who generally avoided TV talk shows, started showing up on the circuit talking about friends with macular degeneration and the drug that treated it. The *Today Show* discovered that her appearance was paid for by the Norvatis drug company.

Lance Armstrong did a series of cancer-awareness ads sponsored by Bristol-Myers Squibb, the company that made the drugs that cured his testicular cancer. Meanwhile, Amgen company sponsors Rob Lowe to go on the talk-show circuit for its drug to treat a side effect of chemotherapy; Wyeth Laboratories paid Kathleen Turner to stump for its arthritis drug; and Roche Therapeutics hired Sally Field to promote Boniva.

Some observers question the criteria that some celebrities use in deciding whether to align themselves with charitable causes. Dr. Arthur Caplan, a medical ethicist at the University of Pennsylvania, has noted that some celebrities gravitate toward illnesses they perceive as "media-friendly—less stigmatizing and less embarrassing" and that "otherwise worthy diseases, some that impact far more people, go unrecognized simply because they have less sex appeal" (Bouchez, n.d., p. 2).

Phase Two

STEP
6

for the erectile-dysfunction drug Viagra. Meanwhile, Derek Jeter stumps for Gilette, Dan Marino for Nutrisystem, Lebron James for Powerade, Dale Earnhardt Jr. for Wrangler jeans and Michael Phelps for Speedo.

But it's hard to see how the logic of using celebrities connected with the product fits into the decision to have Kobe Bryant promote Turkish Airlines. He had never been to Turkey but said he's heard it a hot place to visit. He also got backlash from Armenian Americans angered over Turkey's historic refusal to acknowledge its role in the massacres against their grandparents 100 years ago that gave rise to the term "genocide."

CELEBRITY ENDORSERS GONE WILD

Both business and nonprofit organizations have found that they need to exercise discretion in identifying celebrity spokespersons. Fame might draw attention. But celebrities aren't yours alone, and endorsements can bring unwanted attention.

Some organizations have been humiliated by celebrity spokespersons and endorsements have fallen off, at least temporarily. *Sports Illustrated* reports that pitcher Roger Clemens earned $3.5 million in endorsements in 2007 from companies such as AT&T and promos for the ESPN sports network on TV. After a steroid scandal, endorsements fell.

Soccer great David Beckham lost endorsements when the British tabloid press reported that he had cheated on his wife. After the issue died down, he emerged with a $10 million contract with Gillette, followed by a $161 million lifetime deal with Adidas. Beckham later was courted by Nike.

L.A. Laker Kobe Bryant lost endorsements because of his 2003 sexual assault charge, but he came back as the second highest-paid pitchman in the National Basketball Association in 2008 with $16 million in endorsements.

After a British newspaper published a photo in 2009 of Michael Phelps smoking from a bong, the Olympic swimming champion salvaged millions in endorsement deals (Speedo, Omega, Mazda and Visa). He quickly apologized, attributing his transgression to youthful bad judgment and promising it wouldn't happen again. But advertising analysts warned that this, following a DUI arrest four years earlier, was Strike 2, Phelps' last chance to maintain his endorsement worth.

In 2007, AirTran, Powerade, Coca-Cola, Rawlings and Kraft Foods each dropped their advertising contracts with Atlanta Falcons quarterback Michael Vick after he pled guilty to illegal dog fighting. Nike dumped his $2 million annual contract, Reebok dropped his replica jersey, and Upper Deck pulled his trading card. When Vick emerged from jail, he was signed by the Philadelphia Eagles. He has spoken out against dog fighting and in 2011 picked up endorsements by Nike and by Unequal athletic gear.

Endorsement problems are not limited to celebrity athletes. After a British tabloid published photos of Kate Moss snorting cocaine, the model lost her contracts with Chanel and Burberry, but she kept contracts with Yves Saint Laurent and Gucci, which have edgier ads.

Similarly, St. John fashions dropped Angelina Jolie because it felt some customers were put off by her social activism. In 1991, Magic Johnson lost $9 million a year in endorsements when he went public with his HIV status; it wasn't until 2003 that he obtained another endorsement (for Lincoln automobiles).

Abercrombie & Fitch (A&F) pre-empted embarrassment by offering to pay Mike "The Situation" Sorrentino of *Jersey Shore* to stop wearing its clothing. A&F said in a news release that, by wearing its clothing, Sorrentino was damaging its reputation. The JS personality then sued A&F for $4 million for using his name in what MTV called "a clever PR stunt."

Some examples of wayward celebrity spokespersons fall into the "What were they thinking?" category. The Beef Industry Council dropped Cybill Shepherd after she told a national magazine that one of her beauty secrets is avoiding red meats. And when Brylcreem sales dropped 25 percent after its celebrity hairdo guy David Beckham shaved his head, Beckham lost his $7.9 million contract.

Researchers Alan Miciak and William Shanklin (1994) report that advertisers look for five characteristics in spokespersons: being trustworthy, readily recognizable, affordable, at little risk for negative publicity and appropriately matched to the audience.

Golf icon Tiger Woods once was among the highest-rated celebrities. A 2008 report indicated that he earned $105 million in endorsements, followed by fellow golfer Phil Mickelson, $63 million; basketball star LeBron James, $28 million; NASCAR winner Dale Earnhardt Jr., $25 million; golfer Michele Wei, $19.5 million; and a $15 million tie for NASCAR's Jeff Gordan and basketball's Shaquille O'Neal. In 2009, Tiger hit the billion-dollar mark for endorsements, with Michael Jordan a couple of years behind him. Then came that pesky scandal (car accident, extramarital affairs, call girls, public apology, messy divorce), and Tiger lost most of his endorsements.

Company Spokespeople

In identifying organizational spokespersons, don't confine yourself to a single individual if more than one would better serve your communication needs with various publics. Your organization must speak with a single voice, but effective communication may be accomplished with two or more speakers presenting coordinated and complementary messages. The important thing is to make sure that a single, consistent message is being presented in the name of your organization.

Also, give careful thought about who from your organization might be selected as a spokesperson for a particular issue. Some companies used the CEO-as-spokesperson approach, which has worked well with corporate founders while they lived: popcorn king Orville Redenbacher, Wendy's Dave Thomas, Frank Purdue of chicken fame. Redenbacher was authentic, Thomas was likable and Purdue—well, anybody who can successfully brag about dead chickens must have something going for himself.

But the CEO may not be the best person in every case. Here are three good reasons not to use the CEO as organizational spokesperson.

1. You don't want to overexpose the boss. Save her for the big issues.
2. The CEO may not know the level of detail necessary for a news conference or interview; perhaps a project planner, department manager or another hands-on person would be more knowledgeable and credible.
3. The CEO may not have the personality to exhibit in public or especially on camera the calm, credibility, charisma or other characteristics of an effective spokesperson.

Some organizations buffer the CEO by appointing another spokesperson for negative news, saving the CEO for the more positive public and media encounters. In a news conference, the CEO could be put on the spot and expected to indicate what the organization's activity or response might be. Another organizational spokesperson could more easily deflect such forecasts and avoid inappropriate speculation.

Don't presume that the public relations director should automatically become the spokesperson. Especially in confrontational or other crisis situations, the director may be busy behind the scenes advising on strategy and message delivery. Also, the media often don't recognize the public relations director as a high-ranking organizational official; instead they see her as a mere mouthpiece for the people they really wish to interview. In a 1999 study by

Phase Two

STEP
6

> # WHEN THE FUR FLIES
>
> People for the Ethical Treatment of Animals faced its own ethical problem when supermodel Naomi Campbell, a PETA volunteer who had pledged not to wear natural fur, was reported to be modeling in Europe wearing fur. After unsuccessful attempts to reach her, PETA took a public tack: With much fanfare, it fired Ms. Campbell as a spokesmodel.
>
> The firing was a strategic design, a twist to several of the news-making tips, such as involving a celebrity, tying in to a public issue and appointing personnel as a way to highlight an issue. Instead, PETA publicly "unappointed" a volunteer—not coincidentally, a wayward one who also happened to be a big celebrity.
>
> PETA spokesman Michael McGraw described the activist group's plan: Once it got the media's attention by firing Ms. Campbell, PETA would turn the focus back to the issue of the suffering caused to animals in the name of fashion. "We were able to turn something quite negative into something quite positive," said McGraw, "because what it allowed us to do was get the message out that the fur industry hurts animals and kills them and tortures them."

the Public Relations Society of America, public relations specialists ranked low in terms of credibility as corporate spokespersons. Most organizations use their public relations directors not as spokespersons but as preliminary media contacts, conduits for factual information that doesn't require attribution and sources for other media background information.

Spokespeople and Ethics

Celebrity or not, speakers should strive to identify with their audiences. One way is to emphasize similar backgrounds, especially when such common ground may not be evident to the audience. For example, a university professor before a group of entering freshmen may recall her first months in college or an affluent politician may explain to a group of inner-city residents his experience of growing up amid poverty, albeit of a rural variety.

Another way for speakers to emphasize similarity is to avoid language that separates them from their audience. A white speaker cannot use the phrase "you people" before a black audience without emphasizing his differentness and insulting his listeners.

Be careful about uncommon words that people may misunderstand. An aide to the mayor of Washington, DC, was fired (later rehired) because he used the term "niggardly" (meaning "stingy"). One listener mistook the reference for a racial slur. And the University of Wisconsin killed a proposed speech code after a student ignited a campus controversy because she was offended when a professor used the same term in a literature class. In both situations, the term "niggardly" was used correctly. But from a public relations perspective, it is best to avoid language that may not be properly understood, especially if they are not part of the shared experiences of both the speaker and the audience. After all, people who don't know any better may think "titillate," "jaculate," and "masticate" are nasty words.

Planning Example 6A Selecting Message Sources

In its current efforts to expand enrollment and retention, financial contributions and community support, Upstate will use the following three spokespeople:

UPSTATE COLLEGE

Dr. Alexandra Jolin, president of Upstate College

Dr. Jolin will be perceived by most audiences as highly credible because of her position. She is a dynamic speaker who projects an enthusiasm and friendliness that most people appreciate. In addition, she holds various leadership positions not only with the college but within the local community and within the state's higher education establishment.

Michael McMillan, chair of the Upstate College Board of Trustees, Upstate alumnus and prominent business leader in Upstate City

Mr. McMillan will be perceived as a credible source, especially by residents of Upstate City. He has received media training and is articulate and competent in media and other public presentations. He is in a position of leadership.

Inez SantaElana, president of the UC Student Government

Because of her leadership position with the student government, Ms. SantaElana will be perceived as a credible source, especially with current and potential students. She also is a regional celebrity among area high school students who has developed much poise and confidence as a result of her athletic achievements, including state records in speed skating.

In its campaign to increase consumer confidence, Tiny Tykes will use the following two spokespeople:

TINY
TYKES
TOYS

Michael Beaucheforte, senior vice president for consumer affairs

Mr. Beaucheforte will be perceived as credible because of his expertise within the company and because he was hired specifically to address consumer issues. He is a persuasive speaker, with a friendliness that exudes trust and disarms skeptics. (Note that company president Theodore Frankelberger should not be used as a spokesperson in media situations because he becomes very nervous when speaking in public; this nervousness is often perceived as insincerity and evasiveness.)

Mary Margaret O'Sullivan, Tiny Tykes Consumer Advisory Council member

Ms. O'Sullivan is a consumer whose child was stained by the defective toy. She now sits on the Consumer Advisory Council that helped relaunch the product. Because of her personal involvement, Ms. O'Sullivan will be perceived as a trustworthy and expert spokesperson. She is not an accomplished public speaker, but her uneasiness adds to her credibility and charisma.

Phase Two

☑ *Checklist 6A* **Message Sources**

Basic Questions

1. Identify several possible spokespersons who could present your message.
2. What is the level of credibility for each possible spokesperson?
3. What is the level of charisma for each?
4. What is the level of control for each?

Expanded Questions

Answer the following items for each possible message source. Then compare your responses to determine the sources best suited for this communication task. An effective message source will have mainly high and positive rankings in each item.

A. CREDIBILITY

1. How expert on this topic is the message source?
2. How well known are his/her credentials to the audience?
   If expertise is high, should the audience be reminded of this?
   If expertise is not known, can the audience be made informed of this?
3. Does the message source enunciate clearly?
4. Does the source speak with dynamism and authority?
5. Does the source speak calmly and reassuringly on this topic?
6. How trustworthy will the source be perceived as being?
7. Can the source speak truthfully and independently about the topic?
8. Does the source have any associations that compete with the organization?
9. Does the source have any associations that are inconsistent with the organization's image?
10. Is the source available to your organization?

B. CHARISMA

1. How similar is the source to the audience?
2. How familiar is the audience with the source?
3. How attractive is the source to the audience?
4. Can the source be presented in an attractive setting?

C. CONTROL

1. Does the source have any moral leverage with this audience?
2. Does the source have any power over this audience?
3. Does the source have the willingness to use this power?
4. Does the source have the ability to investigate this audience?
5. Does the source have the authority to reward or punish this audience?

Logos: Appealing to Reason

Having selected the spokesperson for the campaign or project, the strategic planning next focuses on the content of the message. What will be said, and how will the message be framed? Will you appeal to the intellect or to the emotions—or to both? What facts and arguments will you offer? What examples might you suggest?

Let's first consider messages based on logic; then later, messages on sentiment.

Communication effectiveness based on the rational appeal of the message was known to the ancient Greeks as **logos**. The conscious attempt to persuade by appealing to logos—logic and reason—is an obvious place to start planning your strategic message. Distill your message and resist the temptation to bombard your audience with every bit of information available to you. Clarify and simplify.

The ancient art of rhetoric is kept current with an expanding research base (see Benjamin, 1997; Infante, Rancer and Avtgis, 2009; Larson, 2000; Ross, 1994). Following is a summary of recommendations and conclusions from many different research studies into effective communication and persuasion.

The primary idea in a speech, editorial, advertisement, television program or any other communication vehicle is called a **proposition**, also known as a **claim**. Only one proposition should be presented at a time. More than one can confuse the audience and lessen the impact of the message. There are four kinds of propositions: factual, conjecture, value and policy.

- A **factual proposition** states that something exists, based on provable (usually physical) evidence. For example, environmental tests can offer proof of an increase in urban air pollution. Factual claims often link to communication objectives focused on awareness, which seek to increase attention or build greater understanding.
- A **conjecture proposition** states that something probably exists, based on reasoned conclusion drawn from physical evidence. It asks audiences to agree with the conclusion. An example of this is a conclusion for or against the continuation of affirmative action regulations, in which the conclusion flows logically from the facts as they are presented. Conjecture propositions often relate to communication objectives dealing with acceptance, fostering supportive attitudes.
- A **value proposition** identifies the virtue of something, such as the merits (or folly) of health care reform. Value claims also relate to objectives dealing with acceptance, which try to increase interest or build positive attitudes.
- A **policy proposition** identifies a course of action and encourages its adoption, such as advocacy for changing the legal drinking age or for beginning a school dress code. Policy claims often reflect objectives associated with opinion and action.

Whatever the type of proposition, it should be supported with strong arguments and clear proof. The value of such proof varies from person to person and from group to group. To some, an intelligent argument with understandable data and logical conclusions may prove a point; to others, only the strongest and most consistent of physical data may be considered as proof.

Occasionally, facts may be disputed by other facts, such as one study that contradicts another. The existence of such conflicting evidence likely will weaken the argument for the proposition.

Even more difficult to deal with is the phenomenon—some say a growing one—in which some people disbelieve facts, doubt science and dismiss evidence that runs counter to their bias and prejudices. Particularly uneducated or highly partisan people have adopted an anti-science stance that feeds their suspicion of science and education, resulting in an audience that essentially has made itself immune to facts and reasoning. Climate change is a current example of a topic that has some anti-science critics. There is little a public relations practitioner can do to create any convincing message when an audience will not permit itself to be open to evidence.

Similarly, some people may oppose a logical argument because they don't trust the data used to prove a point or the source of that data. Some critics, for example, are quick to disbelieve anything associated with government or with a particular political party. Again, public relations practitioners must concede that there is little they can do to dissuade such disbelief.

Verbal Evidence

About 2,500 years ago, Corax of Syracuse taught that disputes are settled easily when clear physical evidence shows inarguably the truth or falsity of a claim. That remains true today. Most of the time, however, we are not lucky enough to have such unchallenged hard evidence, so we have to rely on other arguments. This verbal evidence can take several different forms, including analogies, comparisons, examples, statistics and testimonials. Here's a brief look at each.

ANALOGY

As a type of persuasion technique, an **analogy** uses familiar situations and allusions to help an audience understand new ideas. Specifically, an analogy makes a comparison between two things that are essentially different but nevertheless strikingly alike in an important aspect. For example, cars double-parked on a congested city street can be analogous to the effect of cholesterol in clogging arteries. Analogies usually are presented as the grammatical forms of similes and metaphors.

COMPARISON

By highlighting the characteristics or values related to an issue, a **comparison** can liken it to something else the audience might understand. Positive comparisons are made to things the audience already acknowledges and admires, negative comparisons to things the audience holds in low esteem. Any such comparison should be easy to understand, showing how one issue, product or theme relates to another.

EXAMPLE

Another type of verbal evidence, an **example**, provides conclusions drawn from related instances. Such an illustration can be effective, particularly if the case is recent, reliable and relevant to the situation at hand. Be careful not to argue from far-fetched examples that are easy to dismiss as being not only irrelevant but also deceitful.

STATISTICS

The use of **statistics** can provide clear and hard-to-dispute facts in order to make the best case. For example, it is easy to argue the superiority of a particular automobile with statistics dealing with safety, cost, and other easily understood data. But be careful, because statistics can be misinterpreted and manipulated, and many people have learned through hard personal experience that comparative statistics are not always as neat and clean as they appear to be. More on this soon.

TESTIMONIAL AND ENDORSEMENT

Comment by witnesses or people who have used an organization's product or service is called a **testimonial**. Comment by people who espouse an idea an organization supports is called an **endorsement**. By these definitions, a testimonial is a type of endorsement.

Both testimonials and other types of endorsements can provide effective verbal evidence. Testimonials can take the form of letters or other statements of support from satisfied customers or engaged employees.

Similarly, endorsements and recommendations from celebrities can be persuasive, especially if the celebrity is known to have used the product (such as Michael Jordan and Gatorade), participated in the service or program (Kirstie Alley for the Jenny Craig weight-loss program) or espoused the idea being presented (Whoopi Goldberg for abortion rights, Brooke Shields for pro-life issues).

Visual Supporting Evidence

Strong visual presentation can enhance the effectiveness of these writing techniques. Use photographs, charts, graphs and diagrams as visual aids in presenting statistical and technical information. Also think about ways to include demonstrations and performances in your presentation. Consider, too, the role that computer-based presentations can make.

Errors of Logic

As you are preparing your rational message, avoid errors in logic. Some common errors result from unfounded presumptions.

For example, don't over-generalize the argument or leap to an **unwarranted conclusion**, which is a deduction that is not supported by evidence. Make sure your facts are indisputable and understood by your audience. Building on incorrect or uncertain data will create a case that is easy to refute.

Also, be careful not to make a **false assumption**, a conclusion that the audience may not accept. An example of a false assumption would be arguing that U.S. schools should adopt a Japanese school calendar on the untested presumption that the audience agrees that the intensity of Japanese education produces better graduates. A similar false assumption would be that the calendar and the associated number of days in school (average 180 in the US, and about 200 in Japan) is the reason for better-educated students.

Other errors in logic deal with ignoring the issue and instead attacking the person or reacting with an air of pity or disdain. Finally, remember that any appeal to authority or tradition will be effective only if the audience already respects and accepts that authority or tradition.

Phase Two

STEP 6

Statistics

The nineteenth-century British prime minister Benjamin Disraeli once wrote, "There are three kinds of lies: lies, damned lies and statistics." That captures the feeling of many people, who in the face of the supposed statistical evidence have learned that statistics aren't always to be trusted. Inaccurate data usually can be spotted. The problem lies less with the statistics and more in their interpretation. Often it's a matter of arriving at a common definition of terms.

Take the simple concept of "average." In general terms, **average** refers to the usual or ordinary instance. But in dealing with statistics, average can be a real sticking point for understanding, because it can mean different things. Consider the following information about 11 university students who share a dorm suite.

- Alan works in the dean's office and earns $10,000.
- Jere, Jamal and Monika work for the university police and earn $7,500 each.
- Maria and Tomiko work in the library and earn $5,000 each.
- Tim, Pat and Lori work in the department office and earn $4,000 each.
- Sylvia and Juan work with food service and earn $4,000 each.

What's their average salary? It could be $5,682 (if you calculate average as the **mean**, total wages divided by the number of wage earners). Or, the average is $5,000 (if you use the **median**, the middle number on the list; in this case, Tomiko). Or you can say the average is $4,000 (if you reference the **mode**, the most common number; that is, the number occurring most frequently). It all depends on how you define "average." All three of these definitions are legitimate. The point is, make sure you are clear in your terms and what they mean.

Often, the problem with statistics is how they are interpreted. Here's an example. Few things in society are more contested and controversial than the issue of abortion, and statistics seem only to muddy the waters. One side says most people support access to abortion services; the other side says most people oppose abortion. Both can't be right, can they? Well, yes, depending on how you interpret the nuance of the data. Consider the following survey results, all presumably accurate statistics.

- ABC/*Washington Post* Poll, 2011: 19 percent of Americans think abortion should be legal in all cases, 35 percent legal in most cases, 30 percent illegal in most cases and 15 percent illegal in all cases.
- Gallup Poll, 2011: 27 percent of Americans would have abortion legal in any circumstance, 5 percent sometimes legal, 22 percent always illegal. Additionally, 49 percent call themselves pro-choice, and 45 percent pro-life.
- Fox News Poll, 2007: 39 percent would have abortion legal in any circumstance, 50 percent illegal in all but life-threatening circumstances for the mother, and 10 percent are not sure. Meanwhile, a 2011 Fox poll reported that 50 percent of Americans consider themselves pro-life and 42 percent pro-choice.
- CBS News Poll, 2010: 36 percent say abortion should be generally available, 39 percent available under stricter limits and 23 percent not permitted.
- CNN Poll 2009: 49 percent pro-choice, 45 percent pro-life.

So what do such statistics say? One interpretation is that because 15–23 percent would ban abortion, the remaining 80 percent support abortion, right? Well, that's not quite what the data reveal. Another interpretation is that if 19–39 percent would allow abortions for any reason, the remaining 60–80 percent must be against abortion. Again, it's not quite that simple. Obviously, numbers can be found to support the bias of a writer, but perhaps the most fair interpretation is that the data show a lot of centrist opinions, not a clear-cut mandate on either side of this public policy discussion.

Here's another example of misleading statistics. Your campus provost's office tracks and reports on cases of plagiarism each year. The current report notes that 150 of the 200 incidents of plagiarism involved the Internet, 75 percent of the cases. This compares with 108 of 180 incidents during the previous year, 60 percent.

What can you say about this increase? You could report a 15-point rise in the percentage of Internet-assisted plagiarism cases. Or is it a 25 percent increase (the proportional difference from 60 to 75)? Or you might cite a 39 percent increase in the number of cases (180 compared to 150). All of the figures are mathematically accurate, but—obviously—they leave significantly different impressions.

The key to using statistics that do not mislead is to interpret them fairly and honestly, and to be clear about what the numbers really mean—in this example, whether you are comparing total plagiarism cases or the annual percentage change.

Sometimes the issue is about how accurately the statistics reflect the population under study. Accurate use of statistics involves what is included as well as what is left out—a matter

---

ACCURATE BUT IRRELEVANT FACTS

Statistics may be completely accurate, but if they are used in a false context or without logical reasoning, they can be meaningless. Irrelevant. Unethical.

Consider the following examples. In each, the fact is accurate. But each statement is irrelevant because it gives a false impression. The casual reader might be misled into presuming that the statement provides some insight. A more careful reader will be left wondering "So what?"

- There are about as many vegetarians in the US as there are Lutherans (about 12.5 million people, 4 percent of the population).
- Jews and gay people make up about the same proportion of voters (4 percent).
- The US prison population is the same as the number of German speakers in the US (2 million, 0.7 percent).
- There are as many French speakers in the US as Episcopalians (2.3 million, 0.8 percent).
- There are about as many atheists in the US as there are people who speak Tagalog. Also as many atheists as people whose families originated in Wales (1.1 million, 0.4 percent).

So what?

of context. Consider the scandal of sexual abuse among Catholic priests. "A casual observer relying on the mass media would form the overwhelming impression of a Church institution awash in perversion, conspiracy and criminality," notes Philip Jenkins (2003, p. 137). Early media reports relied on claims by activist and victims' groups, which counted as many as 10 percent of priests as pedophiles, about 5,000 of the 53,000 American priests living at that time.

More reliable statistics paint a different picture. Studies in some of the largest dioceses indicated that about 3 percent of priests had been accused, less than 2 percent with credible evidence. Many of the accusations involved adult women and men as well as adolescents—all, by definition, not pedophilia. A 2004 nationwide study found that 4 percent of priests had been accused during the previous 50 years.

Compare this to estimates by psychologists and law enforcement that 3–5 percent of the entire male population in North America is linked to child or adolescent sexual abuse. Meanwhile, clergy of other religious groups—Episcopalian, Presbyterian, Eastern Orthodox, Mormon, Southern Baptist, Hare Krishna and Orthodox Jews, among others—had been similarly accused of child sexual abuse. The Boy Scouts reported dismissing more than 5,000 scoutmasters for alleged sexual abuse—more than 3 percent of all Scout volunteers. An educational activist group reported that up to 5 percent of teachers sexually abuse their students, with more than a third of them keeping their jobs. In Step 5 we noted estimates of 5 percent or more of health workers who are sexually attracted to children, even higher among those working in children's hospitals.

So the clergy abuse situation seems no different statistically than the rest of the population, perhaps lower than in some professions. While this doesn't minimize the tragedy of sexual abuse, it serves to point out that statistics of doubtful reliability and/or out of context can mislead.

Pathos: Appealing to Sentiment

Human beings are not mere thinking machines. We see in Mr. Spock of the original *Star Trek* TV series examples of inappropriate responses that are so "logical" they are absurd. As humans, we rely heavily on our feelings, and effective communicators take this into consideration. An important part of the strategy of public relations and marketing communication is to link the message to an emotional appeal, either positive or negative.

Positive Emotional Appeals

Many persuasive appeals seek to generate responses based on a variety of positive emotions. Here is a brief look at positive appeals to love, virtue, humor and sex.

LOVE APPEAL

A **love appeal** can feature a variety of approaches: bittersweet poignancy, family togetherness, nostalgia, pity, compassion, sensitivity, sympathy or any of the many other sides of love. Pleasant images lead consumers not only to remember the persuasive message but also to be more likely to act on the message. For years, Michelin has built a successful advertising campaign around warm images of cute babies sitting in tires, and the verbal cue "so much is riding on your tires." Maxwell House coffee and Hallmark greeting cards also have been

APPEALING TO HEARTS AND MINDS

Research tells us that it is tremendously important to provide messages that appeal to both the mind and the heart. Three areas of study—two from psychology, one from physiology—shed some light on the question of how we can best frame messages to our audiences:

- *Psychological Type*. The concept of **psychological type** is based on the work of Carl Jung and the application of his theories by the mother–daughter team of Isabel Myers and Catharine Briggs (see Myers, 1987; Myers and Myers, 1980) and a host of their disciples. This approach observes that people have different natural preferences in how they gather information, make decisions and act on those decisions. Some people, labeled "thinkers" in Myers–Briggs terminology, tend to rely mainly on logic and data in making decisions. "Feelers," on the other hand, base their decisions more on sentiment and emotion. Seldom will your publics and audiences be so like-minded as to uniformly prefer one type of message appeal over the other. Thus, good strategy calls for the use of both types of messages.

    Note that this may not be a natural response for many practitioners, because many of the artistic or creative disciplines—writing, journalism, design, advertising—and public relations—tend to attract people who themselves are feelers rather than thinkers. The disciplines more associated with management, such as research and marketing, attract a higher-than-average percentage of thinkers. In either case, it is undependable to rely simply on your personal preferences.

- *Temperament*. The concept of **temperament** is an approach related to personality and natural disposition, associated with psychologist David Keirsey (1998). From him we learn of four specific temperaments—artisan, idealist, guardian and rationalist—with different innate preferences regarding organization and creativity.

- *Left Brain/Right Brain Differences*. The working of the human brain—and, in particular, the relationship between the two hemispheres of the brain—have been explored by Roger Sperry (1985) of the California Institute of Technology. He received a Nobel Prize in 1981 for his pioneering work in the field. Evidence suggests that the left side of the brain is responsible for logical and analytical thought, while the right side controls creativity and imagination. Like psychological type and temperament, hemispheric brain studies suggest that most individuals are stronger in one function and weaker in the other.

These three fields have many common bonds. That's not surprising for the first two, because Keirsey's research is a conscious reworking of the psychological insights of Myers and Briggs. Sperry took a different path that led him through physiology, but he arrived at surprisingly similar patterns.

By comparing and blending this research, evidence suggests that some people are innately more deliberate or logical, while others are more spontaneous and imaginative.

Phase Two

STEP
6

successful with this "warm and fuzzy" approach. Fundraising appeals frequently evoke images of compassion and sympathy.

VIRTUE APPEAL

An appeal based on something good, a **virtue appeal**, can evoke any of the various values that society or individuals hold in esteem. These are qualities that most people treasure. Consider how natural disasters such as earthquakes and floods inspire volunteerism, blood donations and financial contributions to relief agencies.

- Justice appeals deal with fairness, human or civil rights, and issues of right or wrong.
- Altruism appeals focus on generosity, charity, kindness and unselfishness.
- Loyalty appeals focus on patriotism and fidelity.
- Bravery appeals evoke images of boldness, endurance and courage.
- Piety appeals focus on religious faith, spirituality and prayer.
- Discretion appeals relate to restraint, moderation, wisdom and self-control.
- Improvement appeals focus on progress, social advancement and making the world a better place.
- Esteem appeals focus on self-respect, pride, vanity and self-worth.
- Social acceptance appeals focus on the importance of peer support—the everybody's-doing-it theme.

HUMOR APPEAL

A **humor appeal** can be powerful because comedy and amusement are strong human instincts. Humor is useful in reinforcing existing attitudes and behaviors, but it generally is not very effective in changing them. Humor can make the speaker more liked by the audience, but seldom does it make the speaker seem more credible. However, the use of humor can reduce the speaker's likability when audiences perceive the humor as excessive or inappropriate.

Humor gets old fast, so its use in public relations and advertising limits the effectiveness of the otherwise valuable practice of repeating messages. Finally, if audiences evaluate the message from an entertainment perspective, they can fail to take it as a serious persuasive message.

With these cautions in mind, here are some guidelines on using humor in persuasive communication.

1. The humor should complement a clear and consistent message about the organization or the product/service/concept. It should never be used as a substitute for an understandable message.
2. The humor should be relevant to the issue and appropriate for the organization. For instance, it is unlikely that a funeral home could effectively use humor in its brochures.
3. The humor should be tasteful. The *South Park* phenomenon aside, bathroom and bedroom humor generally are counterproductive for most audiences, as is disparaging humor directed against others, particularly groups of people. Self-deprecating humor can be effective in causing an audience to like a speaker.
4. The humor should be funny. This is difficult to achieve, because what is humorous to one person may be droll, too cute, ludicrous or simply unfunny to others. Make sure the humor does not insult people's intelligence by becoming absurd or pointless.

Also, given the choice, prefer the lighthearted and amusing touch over an attempt to present uproarious farce.

5. Humor is more effective with dull topics (which need sparking up) than with topics the audience already finds interesting. With interesting topics, humor can detract from the message.

SEX APPEAL

A **sex appeal** can range from nudity to double entendres to outright shock. These sexual messages can be effective in commanding attention, though audience demographics affect how that attention is received. But the very pulling power of sex appeals has a built-in problem. Tests show that audiences often remember the sexual content of an advertisement but fail to associate it with the brand being promoted or the sponsor presenting the message. Likewise, what one demographic group may find appropriate and positive, another may judge unnecessary and negative. For example, women respond to sex appeals less than men do, and younger people are more positively influenced by sex appeals than older audiences.

An even bigger problem with sex-appeal messages is that, for all their high ability to gain attention, they are notoriously weak in leading receivers toward desired action.

One consistent finding from persuasion research is that sex appeal should not be used simply for shock value. It is far more effective when the sexual theme has a legitimate association with the product (such as lingerie, perfume or condoms) or with the cause (such as birth control or responsible sexual behavior).

Sometimes humor and sex appeal comingle. When Phillips Norelco launched its Bodygroom "manscaping" shaver to young men, the promotion went edgy. The result was one of the most successful product launches in company history. It also helped mainstream a previously taboo subject—body grooming to enhance a man's self-esteem and sexual appeal. Strategy for the body groomer included power words and slogans such as "Shave Your Kiwis" when the product was previewed at the Sundance Film Festival; and "The Optical Inch" listener-interactive radio programming. Tactics included creation of a website called shaveeverywhere.com, loaded with innuendo; leveraging a partnership with Howard Stern; focusing an extensive media-relations program toward magazines popular with the key public; promoting a "Shave the Brave" manscaping-for-charity competition between firefighters in Chicago and New York.

Negative Emotional Appeals

Some messages invoke responses based on negative emotions—fear and guilt being the most common. A third type of negative appeal, to hatred, has no ethical use for public relations and thus is not worth considering here.

FEAR APPEAL

Fear is one of the strongest human emotions, and a **fear appeal** is intended to arouse anxiety or worry among receivers, such as advertising that focuses on the fear of body odor or political messages centered on the alleged disasters that await the public if the opposing candidate is elected.

Phase Two

STEP
6

Government, particularly in recent years, has stepped up its use of fear appeals to press for quick passage of security-based and financial-related legislation, often without time for thoughtful consideration of the potential impact. Electoral politics frequently uses fear appeals to scare voters away from opposing candidates or office holders. For all the talk that the electorate doesn't like negative ads or fear appeals, it's clear that they do, in fact, work.

The key to using fear appeals effectively is to accompany them with a quick fix featuring an easy, reasonable and immediate solution to the problem. Fear appeals to persuade audiences to obtain a one-time vaccination, for example, are more effective than those designed to persuade audiences to floss over a lifetime in the name of dental hygiene.

Beware of offering too much of a good thing. Moderate fear appeals can be effective, but too much fearful content can make people either avoid the message or take a defiant stance against it. Appeals that present harsh consequences may cause audiences to cope with their fear simply by refusing to consider the message or even by denying the underlying issue.

Another problem with fear appeals is that the balance point between effective and ineffective shifts according to varying demographic factors such as age, education and gender. Younger adults, for example, have higher resistance to fear appeal than do older adults. Some research suggests that fear appeals likewise have only a limited effect on audience members with high self-esteem who feel immune to impending doom.

Fear appeals may increase levels of awareness without delivering the desired action. For example, strong fear appeals used in a seat-belt campaign may make drivers aware of the consequences of not wearing seat belts—perhaps even fostering an intention of wearing them—without actually changing the likelihood that they will, indeed, buckle up.

Here is a way to make fear appeals more effective: Include in the message a strong how-to approach. For example, don't just deal with the dangers associated with poor nutrition, give several clear and simple examples of how to prepare or order more nutritional meals.

Source and significance also play a role in the effective use of fear appeals. For example, fear appeals are more effective when they come from highly credible sources who are dissimilar to the audience. Often this dissimilarity can be reinforced by symbols, such as clothing a doctor in a lab coat as she presents moderate fear-based information about disease prevention or using someone in a military uniform to speak about threats to national interests and preparation for war.

Fear appeals also can be effective when the issue is significant or important to the audience. In a study related to environmental threats—specifically, plutonium contamination from a nuclear weapons plant—Connie Roser and Margaret Thompson (1995) observed that fear appeals can motivate even latent publics to become active, especially to take action against the fear-producing organization.

Aaron Delwiche, a communication professor at Trinity University in San Antonio, Texas, supervises a propaganda website (propagandacritic.com) in which he identifies four elements of a successful fear appeal: (1) a threat; (2) a recommendation about how the audience should behave; (3) audience perception that the recommendation can effectively address the threat; and (4) perception that the audience can actually behave as recommended (Delwiche, n.d.).

GUILT APPEAL

Appeals to a personal sense of guilt or shame comprise another negative message strategy, one that is the flip side of the virtue appeal. A **guilt appeal** is a common persuasive technique, particularly in the area of marketing communication and fundraising.

Consider the "Buy American" theme. Only a fine line separates a positive appeal to patriotism and national pride from one that tries to make people feel guilty about buying goods produced in another country. With a positive approach, the message focuses on the common economic good, shared values among citizens and a healthy respect for the quality of American products. With a negative approach, however, the same appeal can elicit a sense of guilt for having bought foreign-made products. Since nobody wants to feel guilty, a typical reaction against guilt appeals is to justify our actions ("foreign cars are better made") and to lament the alternative ("American cars just don't last as long").

Like fear appeals, the use of guilt strategy can be effective in moderation. In a fundraising message, for example, a guilt message might try to make readers feel a bit uneasy or apologetic in their relative comfort amid so much misery elsewhere. But try to move guilt appeals away from the negative emotion and toward a positive sentiment such as compassion and justice.

If guilt appeals are to be effective, their messages must make people feel part of the solution. "Will you help? Or will you turn the page?" is the kind of modest guilt appeal that can be quite effective. Like the fear appeal, guilt appeals should feature solutions to the problem of conscience that they raise.

PLANNING EXAMPLE 6B **Determining Message Appeals**

Upstate College will combine rational and emotional message appeals in its message. UPSTATE COLLEGE

STEP 6

Rational Appeal

Upstate College will present two types of appeals:

- a factual proposition based on advantages to students, including current and future academic programs, accreditation, financial aid, and alumni and community commitments for internships and mentoring;
- a value proposition asserting that this expansion is in the best interests of students and this region of the state.

These messages will include statistics, personal endorsements and specific examples of hypothetical students in various academic and economic situations. They also will include visual elements such as photographs, charts and graphs.

Emotional Appeal

UC will present appeals to positive emotions, particularly the virtues of self-improvement and the realization of personal potential. For fundraising purposes, it will appeal to the virtue of altruism and sharing with students who need an assist in obtaining a college education.

Phase Two

Tiny Tykes will present both rational and emotional message appeals.

Rational Appeal

Tiny Tykes will present several rational propositions:

- a factual proposition based on information about the product redesign;
- a value proposition stating a renewed commitment to consumer safety;
- a policy proposition asserting the rightness of continuing to use Tiny Tykes products, which have a long history of being responsive to customer concerns.

These messages will include physical evidence from outside testing agencies about the safety of Tiny Tykes products, a comparison with similar products by competitors, and testimony by consumers and consumer advocacy groups.

Emotional Appeal

Tiny Tykes will present two types of emotional appeals:

- appeals to positive emotions, such as child development and family fun;
- appeals to negative emotions such as a mild level of fear appeal about using toys not tested and approved by independent agencies.

Regardless of the type of emotional appeal being made, consider the ethical ramifications. Ask yourself: Is this appeal ethical? Is it the right way to communicate about this issue? Is it fair? Will the organization gain respect by using this approach?

Phase Two *(side tab)*

STEP 6 *(side tab)*

 Checklist 6B **Message Appeals**

Basic Questions

1. What is the key message that forms the basis of this public relations or marketing communication program?
2. How does this message use a rational appeal?
3. How does this message use an emotional appeal?

Expanded Questions

1. Does your message include a rational appeal and/or an emotional appeal? (Note: Most persuasive messages provide both kinds of appeals.)

A. RATIONAL APPEAL

1. How does your message make a rational appeal?
2. Does the message feature a factual proposition, a value proposition or a policy proposition?

3.   Which of the following provide arguments for your claims: physical evidence, analogy, audience interest, comparison, context, examples, statistics, testimony and endorsements, and/or visual presentation?

B. EMOTIONAL APPEAL

1.   How does your message make an emotional appeal?
2.   Does the message feature an appeal to positive emotions or negative emotions?
3.   What is the emotion?

Love Appeal

- What kind of love?

Virtue Appeal

- What virtue?

Humor Appeal

- Will the use of humor make the source more persuasive?
- Is the humor relevant to the issue?
- Is the humor funny?
- Is the humor appropriate for the audience?
- Is the humor appropriate for the organization?
- Will the humor enhance the message?
- Will the humor help meet the objectives?

[Note: If you answer "yes" to these questions, the humorous message may be effective.]

Sex Appeal

- Will the use of sex appeal make the source more persuasive?
- Is the sex relevant to the issue?
- Is the sex appropriate for the audience?
- Is the sex appropriate for the organization?
- Will the sex help enhance the message?
- Will the sex help meet the objectives?

[Note: If you answer "yes" to these questions, the sexual message may be effective.]

Fear Appeal

- Will the use of fear appeal make the source more persuasive?
- Is the fear relevant to the issue?
- Is the fear appropriate for the audience?
- Is the fear appropriate for the organization?
- Does the message include a solution to overcome the fear?
- Will the fear enhance the message?
- Will the fear help meet the objectives?

[Note: If you answer "yes" to these questions, the fearful message may be effective.]

Guilt Appeal

- Will the use of guilt appeal make the source more persuasive?
- Is the guilt relevant to the issue?
- Is the guilt appropriate for the audience?
- Is the guilt appropriate for the organization?
- Does the message include a solution to overcome the guilt?
- Will the guilt enhance the message?
- Will the guilt help meet the objectives?

[Note: If you answer "yes" to these questions, the guilt appeal may be effective.]

Verbal Communication

Both kinds of appeals—logical and emotional—can be communicated either verbally or nonverbally. Let's look first at verbal and then at nonverbal communication as they apply to public relations, marketing and related disciplines.

Verbal communication occurs through written and spoken words. The right words—and the right use of those words—can effectively present your organization's message to its publics. Several verbal factors combine to create an effective message, among them structure, clarity, saliency, power words, product and program names, strong quotes, and both ethical and legal language. Here is a closer look at each of these.

Message Structure

The structure of the message has been the subject of much research. Several particular elements have been researched: giving one side or multiple sides of an argument, the order of presentation, and the value of drawing conclusions or making recommendations. Should you present only your point of view, or should you address the opposition's argument? The research suggests that it depends upon both the audience and the circumstances.

ONE-SIDED ARGUMENT

One-sided arguments present the organization's or speaker's point of view but not opposing views. This kind of argument is useful in reinforcing opinions, because one-sided arguments don't confuse the audience with alternatives. But one-sided arguments are less effective in changing opinions.

Four conditions warrant the use of one-sided arguments: (1) the audience is friendly and already agrees with your position; (2) its members have low educational or knowledge levels; (3) your position will be the only one presented; or (4) the objective is immediate opinion change. Presenting only one side of an argument can cause a temporary attitudinal change, but this probably will be eliminated if the audience later hears a convincing argument from the other side.

TWO-SIDED ARGUMENT

On the other hand, some arguments present both the pros and the cons of an issue, though not necessarily objectively. They usually criticize the opposition's position.

Two-sided arguments are necessary with better-educated audiences, with audiences that are undecided on an issue or initially opposed to the idea being presented, and with more knowledgeable audiences that are aware that another side of the issue exists or that are likely to be exposed to other sides in the future. Such two-sided arguments can improve your ability to persuade these audiences because you will be perceived as being more honest and more respectful of the audience's intelligence.

If you present each side of the argument, you have a better chance of achieving a greater attitude change that will remain high when the audience hears the opposing argument from another source.

ORDER OF PRESENTATION

The **order of presentation** refers to the way the argument unfolds. Should you present arguments in order of least to most important, or vice versa? It generally doesn't seem to matter, as long as you are consistent. In developing your persuasive message, you may have reason to choose one form over the other. For example, do you think your audience will be more attentive at the beginning of the message? If so, then use your strongest arguments there.

The final word is also very important, and plenty of research points out that the last point made is the one best remembered. This is especially true with less-sophisticated audiences, as well as for audiences that are less knowledgeable or less personally involved in the issue.

Comic Paula Poundstone said it well in a stand-up routine referring to a political campaign that dealt with the economy: "I don't know anything about the economy. I tend to agree with the last guy who spoke."

In two-sided arguments, sandwich the information. That is, first present your side—the first argument often is perceived as the strongest. Then present and refute the opposing arguments. Finally restate your position, because of the power of the last word.

DRAWING CONCLUSIONS

Presenting the evidence and then explicitly telling the audience how to interpret it—**drawing conclusions**—has been the subject of much research. Most of the findings suggest that making a recommendation or drawing a conclusion usually is more effective than leaving it to the audience to draw its own conclusion.

However, some evidence suggests that if audience members—especially educated ones—do draw their own conclusion, both the conclusion and the attitude on which it rests are more resistant to change than if the conclusion is presented by the source. Some studies have indicated that when the purpose of a message is to reduce criticism or opposition it may be better not to draw conclusions for the audience. However, can you risk not having the audience draw the "right" conclusion?

REITERATION

The final area to consider for effective message structure, **reiteration**, refers to internal repetition of the main ideas within a persuasive message. This is not the kind of redundancy that involves superfluous turns of phrase, such as "puppy dog," "totally destroyed" or "small village." Rather, reiteration means presenting the same message in different forms, with different words and different examples, each reinforcing the other.

For example, an effective fundraising e-mail will ask for a donation frequently throughout the letter, each time making the request with different words and phrases, and perhaps based

BARRIERS TO EFFECTIVE COMMUNICATION

Several factors can limit the effectiveness of communication. Each of these is a type of **noise** within the communication process. By knowing what they are, communication planners may be able to eliminate these noise types or at least minimize their impact. Here are some of the common barriers:

- **physical noise**, such as ineffective communication channels that do not transmit the message, or distracting sounds that interfere with the receiver's reception of the message;
- **psychological noise**, such as emotional distractions by the receiver;
- **semantic noise**, such as the use of a language in which the sender or receiver is not fluent, or jargon or other word choice that is not mutually understood by sender and receiver;
- **demographic noise**, such as differences between sender and receiver in terms of age, ethnicity, social status, and the like.

So many potential barriers to effective communication! It's a wonder people and organizations are able to communicate at all.

But the noise can be turned down and the barriers overcome. Senders who understand the potential communication pitfalls can find ways to avoid them; receivers can be particularly attentive to the message and engage in active listening to overcome communication noise.

on different types of appeals. Such internal repetition can make messages more memorable and, over time, more acceptable. Reiteration often means using synonyms—different words with similar meanings—as a way of restating the main point.

Another technique is to develop parallel structure within sentences and paragraphs to make your information easier to recognize and remember. For example, use a "B" list: "Be alert. Be prepared. Be resourceful." Alliteration, using words that have the same beginning sounds, is another memory enhancer.

Message Content

The content of the message contributes significantly to the effectiveness of the message strategy. Whether positive or negative, the importance of content cannot be overstressed.

CLARITY

A message first and foremost must be understood. **Clarity** is a quality of writing and speaking, a clearness of expression and thought that helps the audience easily understands your message.

To craft a message with clarity, use words precisely. Keep an eye on their exact and commonly understood meaning. Use simple language—"try" instead of "endeavor," "use" rather than "utilize," "say" instead of "articulate." Avoid jargon unless the language is shared by your listeners, readers or viewers. In all cases, use a vocabulary appropriate to your audience. Consider the differences in language fitting for teens, senior citizens or business executives.

Consider also the setting for your verbal message, such as the differences in language appropriate for boardrooms, locker rooms and dining rooms.

The **Fog Index** (also called the **Gunning Readability Formula**) is an easy-to-use tool that helps writers measure the level of reading difficulty for any piece of writing and then adjust the writing according to the skills of their audience. (Use a search engine to find an easy-to-use online Fog Index calculator. Some computer programs also can calculate grade-level **readability** measures.)

In addition to clear writing, communication strategists should ensure that their messages use correct and simple English, avoid redundancies, generally use an active voice, and observe other guidelines for good writing. Consult a good textbook on public relations writing to brush up on your writing skills.

SALIENCE

In advertising, planners focus on the **unique selling proposition** (USP), that special something that their product or service offers that is different from all the competition. The USP is a kind of niche statement that positions the product for the intended market segment.

We can use the concept of USP in public relations planning. We call it *salience*, the ability to stand out from the crowd. Specifically, salient information is that which speaks directly to the intended public by letting people know just how a product, service or idea will help them.

POWER WORDS

The use of strong language can play a significant role in communication effectiveness. **Power words**, also called **grabbers**, refer to terminology and definitions that are so influential that they often can determine public relations success for a movement or campaign.

Edward Bernays, the public relations pioneer who rooted the profession in social psychology, said he had achieved "semantic tyranny" with his name for the anniversary campaign to commemorate Thomas Edison's invention of the electric light. Light's Golden Jubilee was the title Bernays devised, linking three words that he believed guaranteed interest and support.

Bernays's advice to choose words carefully is particularly valid today, when media are overflowing with messages that compete for attention and interest. Descriptions such as "low-fat," "environment-friendly" and "Bible-believing," and labels such as "family values," "flip flopper," "job creators" and "tax-and-spend liberal" are terms that have been carefully orchestrated to present a particular emotional connotation.

Instead of referring to "political prisoners," Amnesty International uses the ennobling term "prisoners of conscience" while the U.S. government holds "detainees" in military prisons who, by that definition, are not entitled to legal protections of prisoners of war under international law.

Meanwhile, the gunmen who robbed, raped and mutilated villagers in Central America were called "freedom fighters" by their political supporters and "terrorists" by opponents. Southern border states deal with "illegal immigrants," the same people others call "undocumented workers." The latter term avoids the stigma of lawbreaking, which is precisely the issue for some people.

Sometimes the grabber is a full paragraph. Consider the following statement that could be used by any of the 560 or so American Indian nations to explain their historic relationship with their lands: "My people lived on this land when Moses was crossing the desert. We fished

Phase Two

STEP
6

these rivers when Cleopatra was queen. We hunted these mountains before Hannibal crossed the Alps. This land is as much a part of me as the color of my eyes."

Rhetorical warfare is associated with some of society's most divisive issues. For example, "pro-choice" activists generally disavow the label "pro-abortion" foisted upon them by the other side (which calls itself "pro-life," and which in turn is called "anti-choice" by opponents). One side speaks of a "fetus," the other side of an "unborn baby"—a differentiation in terminology on which hinges the entire controversy.

Sometimes the issue of power words becomes ethically compromised. The advocacy group Media Matters obtained a memo by a Fox News vice president telling his staff how to frame the debate around health care. "Please use the term 'government-run health insurance' or, when brevity is a concern, 'government option' whenever possible," read the memo. The advice was based on input from a Republican political consultant.

Consider the strategy of language, as well as your potential role in what U.S. News and World Report columnist John Leo calls "compassionate incoherence," a type of political correctness that jeopardizes understanding. (Check back to the previous chapter about "strategic ambiguity.") There was a strategy behind Justin Timberlake's statement dismissing Janet Jackson's nipple flash during the 2004 Super Bowl halftime show as merely a "wardrobe malfunction."

If rhetorical warfare is part of society's divisiveness, then rhetorical peacemaking can lead to more beneficial relationships when organizations and their publics engage in shared language, and the path of consensus building and conflict resolution is made smoother by sensitivity to the words used to communicate.

PRODUCT OR PROGRAM NAMES

What we call things can greatly affect how others perceive them.

A **product name** is a title, often developed through extensive research, strategically designed to associate a product with characteristics that are thought to be desirable in the mind of the key public. Product names receive much attention in commercial enterprises. The California Prune Board went to court for permission to market prunes under the name "dried plums" because consumers had a better response to the new term. Exxon changed the name of the tanker *Valdez* to *SeaRiver Mediterranean*, which was later sold and renamed *Dong Fang Ocean* and most recently *Oriental Nicety*.

We find luxury automobiles with names such as Imperial, Coupe de Ville, and Continental, while sport utility vehicles are named Explorer, Blazer and Pathfinder. If you aren't convinced of the power of names, try thinking up a promotional campaign for the all-wheel-drive Chevrolet Petunia, the luxury Ford Cockroach, the hybrid Toyota Slug or the sporty GM Aardvark. Perhaps one reason New Jersey-based Kiwi Airlines went bankrupt in 1996 was because it has the name of a bird that cannot fly.

A **program name** is the parallel of a product name for services of both nonprofit organizations and businesses. Nonprofit groups sometimes conduct less research and use less of a strategic approach for program naming than businesses give to than naming products. Organizations sometimes attempt to devise memorable acronyms, though these often end up being somewhat less effective than hoped. In the same locality, the acronym CASA might stand for Central American Scientific Association, Clean Air Strategic Alliance, Council on Alcoholism and Substance Abuse, Christian Associates in South America, Catholic Appeal for Saint Anthony, Center for the Advancement of Saudi Arabia, and Coalition to Annex South

NAMING ETHIC

Some program names can be misleading, and public relations professionals are careful not to be associated with such deception.

Front organizations are set up to appear to operate independently, when in fact they are controlled by another organization that wants to remain anonymous in the relationship. Serious ethical issues arise from names of front organizations or programs that fail to reflect their partisan or sectarian sponsors.

The Cult Awareness Network, World Literacy Crusade, and Citizens Commission for Human Rights have been exposed as front organizations for the Church of Scientology. The Physicians Committee for Responsible Medicine, which advocates vegetarianism, has been accused of being a front group for People for the Ethical Treatment of Animals. Americans for Technology Leadership, which advocates for limited government regulation, is said to be a front organization funded by Microsoft.

Because they are trying to hide their true nature, many front groups adopt misleading names. The oil company-funded Global Climate Coalition opposes climate controls. The National Wetlands Coalition funded by utilities and industrial companies actually opposes government efforts to protect wetlands. The Greening Earth Society was created by coal companies to present a message that coal burning is good for the environment. Farmers for Clean Air and Water was founded to lobby Congress to exempt large agricultural corporations from environmental regulations.

Meanwhile, a number of organizations have sprung up, purportedly over the issue of casino gaming, that adopt innocuous-sounding names dealing with equity and fairness but act on a consistent anti-American Indian agenda.

Related to front organizations are **Astroturf organizations**, which pretend to be grassroots efforts when they are in fact established and funded by corporations—hence the name suggesting artificial grass. The grassroots-sounding Coalition for Responsible Healthcare Reform was created by Blue Cross to fight the very thing that its name suggests. FreedomWorks and Americans for Prosperity are two related organizations with conservative agendas created and funded by individuals with strong Republican ties and by groups such as Koch Industries, Verizon, Philip Morris and AT&T.

Unfortunately for our profession, some Astroturf organizations have been created by public relations agencies to help their clients avoid the glare of publicity, a dubious approach for a profession that values honesty, openness and transparency. One of the most notorious of these was Citizens for a Free Kuwait, created by the Hill & Knowlton agency to promote the 1991 war in the Persian Gulf. Working Families for Wal-Mart is funded by—surprise!—Wal-Mart. It also is directed by the corporation's public relations agency, Edelman. Another agency, Manning Selvage and Lee, created the Center for Medicine in the Public Interest that furthers the interests of its many pharmaceutical clients.

During the 2004 presidential campaign, an organization was created called Swift Boat Veterans for Truth. Self-described as a nonpartisan group, it was found to be closely aligned with the Republican party. The group launched a smear campaign against Democratic candidate John Kerry, who had commanded a swift boat during the Vietnam War. During the war, Kerry received major military honors: three Purple Hearts, a Silver Star and a Bronze Star. Based on the group's widely publicized and soon discredited campaign against Kerry, a new political term "swift boating" arose to describe an unfair/unsubstantiated/untrue political assault that without evidence attacks a candidate's patriotism and credibility.

Phase Two

STEP
6

Alexandria. A title like CASA might look nice on the letterhead, but it doesn't communicate much about an organization.

BRANDING RIGHTS

The naming game can be a lucrative and mutually beneficial endeavor. Branding rights, the legal right to name a place or activity, has led corporations to spend big bucks to put their names on buildings and events. Sport venues and tournaments serve as the primary stage for branding rights.

After 21 years as the FedEx Orange Bowl, the annual football tournament is now the Discover Orange Bowl, named for its new corporate sponsor, Discover Financial. Once best known as the Virginia Slims Legends Tour for professional women's tennis, new sponsors renamed the event variously as the Chase, Sanex, Home Depot and Sony Ericcson Championships. In 2011, with no corporate sponsor, it was simply the WTA Tour.

Early branding examples for sports venues are the Boston baseball park named for Fenway Realty and the Chicago baseball field named for Wrigley chewing gum. Named sponsors often are local businesses, such as Molsen Amphitheatre in Toronto, Heinz Field in Pittsburgh and Coors Field in Denver.

San Francisco's historic Candlestick Park became a pawn in the corporate naming game when it became 3COM Park and later Monster Park. In 2004, voters decided to return to the historic Candlestick name permanently when Monster Cable's naming lease expired in 2008. But in 2009 voters once again decided to sell naming rights for the stadium.

In a non-sporting venue, Citizens Bank had naming rights for the Boston subway's State Street station. And when scientists auctioned off naming rights for a newly discovered species of monkey, the Golden Palace online casino paid $650,000 to name the GoldenPalace.com Monkey.

Even naming programs can become controversial. After John DuPont of the wealthy Philadelphia family was convicted of murdering an Olympic athlete and found to be mentally ill, Villanova University changed the name of its basketball arena, the DuPont Pavilion, to simply The Pavilion. And with the Enron crisis in 2002, the Houston Astros bought back the naming rights to Enron Field and rechristened it the following year as Minute Maid Field.

STRONG QUOTES

The statements that people make, *quotes*, are an important aspect of verbal communication. Such quotes should be memorable and meaty. Public relations writers should use strong quotes in their news releases, news conference statements and interviews, as well as on other occasions for interacting with the media.

Here is an example of a really pithy quote. In 1998 Oliver Stone directed a television special that promoted the theory that TWA Flight 800, which had exploded two years earlier, killing all 230 passengers and crew, was downed by a missile. FBI investigators had specifically ruled out that possibility. Consider the passion in this response by James Kallstrom, who headed the FBI investigation: "The real facts are glossed over by the likes of Mr. Stone and others who spend their life bottom-feeding in those small, dark crevices of doubt and hypocrisy." Wow! That is so much better than a dreary bureaucratic statement such as "The FBI stands by its original report" or "We disagree with Mr. Stone's missile theory." This is a quote with attitude. It both sings and stings.

ETHICAL LANGUAGE

Using ethical language is a must for every public relations practitioner. In considering the verbal formulation of your message, pay attention to the implication of language. Certainly you will want to use language with pizzazz. Power words can lead audiences to perceive an image instantly and to take on an immediate mood—"beautiful people," "cutting edge," "right wing," "workaholic." But be careful with the stereotypes on which power words are built and make sure that reality underlies these images.

Pretentious language involves words or phrases that imply more than is warranted. Avoid such language, because it can mislead readers. Examples of pretentious language are "experienced vehicles" for used cars or "follically impaired" for bald. Such words can have a backlash if they are perceived as either silly or too crafty. Sometimes pretentious language raises confusing questions. For example, if pets are "companion animals," then should pet owners be called "human associates of companion animals"?

Doublespeak is outright dishonest language meant to obscure the real meaning behind the words. Don't use such language. Besides being unethical, it invites the obvious criticism that the organization is trying to hide the facts. An example of doublespeak is military terms such as calling civilian wartime deaths "collateral damage" or genocide "ethnic cleansing." Likewise, references to employee layoffs as "downsizing," "rightsizing," "employee repositioning," "workforce readjustment" or "retirement for personal reasons." Bureaucratic reports have called drunkenness a "nonsober condition" and suicide on a train track "pedestrian involvement."

Unfortunately, many examples of doublespeak are associated with governmental agencies and officials who, through such language, betray an appalling lack of commitment to transparency and honest communication necessary in a democratic society. For example, the Secret Service in the second Bush administration had local police set up "free speech zones" to keep protesters far removed from the visiting president or vice president—and the television cameras. Business and other organizational leaders, too, have demonstrated far too much creativity in concocting language that clouds, rather than illuminates, and deceitful language that fails the transparency test.

The task for practitioners of strategic communication is to avoid dishonest language for themselves and to counsel their organizations and clients to avoid it as well. There are two reasons for this. One is the ethical consideration, because it's the right thing to do. The other is the practical benefit that honest and clear language provides the best means to communicate effectively and thus to generate understanding and continuing support.

LEGAL LANGUAGE

Strategic communicators also are familiar with laws affecting their choice of language, and they respect both the letter and the spirit of such laws.

Defamation is a legal condition to be avoided at all costs. Defamatory language meets a fivefold test: It (1) is false information; (2) is published or communicated to a third party; (3) identifies a person; and (4) holds that person up to public hatred, contempt or ridicule, while (5) involving some measure of negligence and/or malice on the part of the communicator. Defamation is classified either as *libel*, which is written or broadcast defamation, or **slander**, which is spoken defamation.

A related area of problematic language is information that intrudes on someone's **privacy**, which is the legal right to be left alone.

Phase Two

**STEP
6**

These language indiscretions generally can be avoided if you pay attention to ethical principles, such as those found in the professional conduct codes of such organizations as the Public Relations Society of America and the Canadian Public Relations Society. Such codes call upon practitioners to adhere to high standards of accuracy, honesty, fairness, truth and concern for the public interest. (*See* Appendix B: Ethical Standards.)

Nonverbal Communication

Nonverbal communication occurs through actions and cues other than words that carry meaning. Images and ambience create the most powerful and enduring aspects of communication.

When the words say "I'm happy to be here" but the facial expression shows boredom or disdain, we tend to believe our eyes. Likewise, corporate spokespersons who use facial or other body language associated with hedging and lying limit their effectiveness in gaining audience trust. Some of the 24-hour news and talk TV networks have begun hiring "body language experts" to dissect nonverbal cues of politicians and other newsmakers.

Nonverbal communication provides individuals and groups with many options for presenting or enhancing their messages. Here are some of the uses of nonverbal communication:

- to create impressions beyond the verbal element of communication;
- to repeat and reinforce what is said verbally;
- to manage and regulate the interaction among participants in the communication exchange;
- to express emotion beyond the verbal element;
- to convey relational messages of affection, power, dominance, respect, and so on;
- to promote honest communication by detecting deception or conveying suspicion;
- to provide group or social leadership by sending messages of power and persuasion.

Much communication occurs not through words but through visual messages. Nonverbal communication has several elements dealing with body language, eye contact, social space, touching, vocal cues and the use of time as an element of communication. Let's look briefly at each.

KINESICS

Kinesics deals with body language, sometimes called *affective displays*. It may deal with the body as a whole or with specific parts, particularly the face, hands and arms. Kinesics also deals with body posture and with eye and facial expressions such as arching the eyebrows or rolling the eyes.

Kinesics varies culturally, with significant differences in using hand movements, frowning, and so on. Smiling, for example, is universally associated with happiness. But in some cultures, smiling also is used to mask sadness, and giggling sometimes hides embarrassment.

Sign language is not part of kinesics, but this aspect of nonverbal communication does include emblems, which are physical gestures that support or reinforce what is said verbally. Some emblems are universal, such as the uplifted shoulders and upturned hands to indicate "I don't know." Other emblems are culture-bound. Consider the emblem of the encircled thumb and forefinger. That gesture can be interpreted as worthless in France, money in Japan, OK in the US, a curse in Arab cultures, and an obscenity in Germany, Brazil and Australia.

OCCULESICS

Occulesics is closely related to kinesics. It deals with eye behavior as an element of communication, such as a fixed gaze versus dynamic eye movement.

Eye contact is the subject of much interpretation by the observer, and much of it varies culturally. In the West, for example, direct eye contact (looking into the eyes of the other person) is common about 40 percent of the time while talking with someone and 70 percent while listening. In Japan, it is more common to look at the throat of the other person. In China and Indonesia, the practice is to lower the eyes because direct eye contact is considered bad manners, and in Hispanic culture direct eye contact is a form of challenge and disrespect. In Arab culture, it is common for both speakers and listeners to look directly into each other's eyes for long periods of time, indicating keen interest in the conversation.

PROXEMICS

The social use of space in a communication situation is called *proxemics*. One aspect of this is the closeness between people when they speak, and the significant rule that culture plays in this. Distance generally is described on a continuum from intimate space (zero–18 inches), personal space (18 inches–4 feet), social space (4–12 feet) and public space (beyond 12 feet).

Proxemics also deals with the effective use of space in social settings, such as businesses and homes, and the arrangement of space to encourage or inhibit communication.

HAPTICS

Touching as an element of communication is the subject of *haptics*. This include both the frequency and intensity of touching.

Like so many other aspects of nonverbal communication, haptics is very much a function of culture. Mediterranean, Middle Eastern and Latin American cultures use much social touching in conversation, including embraces and handholding. These are known as high-touch or high-contact cultures. Moderate-touch cultures are associated with North America and Northern Europe, where touching is used only occasionally, such as in handshakes and sporadic shoulder touching or back slapping. In low-contact cultures such as in Northern Asian cultures, meanwhile, social touching is rarely used at all.

VOCALICS

The category of *vocalics* or *paralanguage* deals with vocal cues such as accent, loudness, tempo, pitch, cadence, rate of speech, and nasality and tone. Vocalics includes several subcategories:

- Vocal characterizers include laughing, crying, yawning, and so on.
- Vocal qualifiers such as volume, pitch, rhythm and tempo also are associated with cultural distinctions. For example, speaking loudly indicates sincerity in Arab culture, whereas in North America it often is interpreted as aggressive.
- Vocal segregates are sounds such as "mmmm", "uh-huh", "oooo," and so on. These also differ greatly among various cultures.
- Vocal rate deals with the speed at which people talk, another factor that offers various interpretations.

Phase Two

STEP 6

CHRONEMICS

Chronemics deals with the use of time as an element of communication. It includes specifics such as punctuality, dominance or deference within a communication exchange, and the use of *monochronemics* (doing or talking about one thing at a time) versus *polychronemics* (doing or talking about several things at a time).

The impact of chronemics can vary with social settings, such as the likelihood among Americans of arriving early for business meetings but being "fashionably late" for social activities, while in Latin and Arab culture, business people often arrive at a time Westerns would consider "late," taking business meetings as occasions for hospitality and socializing. Meanwhile, the Sioux language doesn't even have a word for "late," reflecting a very relaxed attitude toward time.

Visual Communication

The visual dimension is another important part of nonverbal communication. Most communication relies not only on words but also on the images, symbols, setting, mood, music, clothing, and so on that carry messages. Here is an overview of some of the most common visual aspects of nonverbal communication.

SYMBOL

As visual representations of realities beyond themselves, **symbols** are among the most effective ways to communicate. Good symbols have a complex and rich psychological impact on people who see and use them. Baby harp seals and pink breast-cancer ribbons have generated widespread public acceptance for the causes associated with them; armbands associated with the Holocaust or classic news photos of 9/11 can evoke a powerful emotional response years after those events; and personal keepsakes from weddings, proms and special vacations summon up emotions over a lifetime.

Some of the most enduring symbols are rooted in religion (such as the crescent, cross, Star of David and Madonna figure) and country (for Americans the Capitol dome, the Statue of Liberty and especially the flag).

A nation's flag is more than a piece of cloth. To many people it is the symbol of family, country, patriotism, duty and honor, which many have been willing both to die for or kill for. As such, it has the power to inspire devotion and to invite disrespect, and much energy has been spent in nations around the world on the issue of the appropriate role the national flag plays in both patriotism and social protest.

In some countries, the national flag may symbolize less about reverence and patriotism and more about social cohesiveness and cultural exuberance.

Symbols also can become the source of controversy. When Marines posed with an American flag and twin lightning bolts reminiscent of the Nazi SS of World War II, the Corps quickly moved to apologize. Military officials said the Marines made a naive mistake, intending the symbols to stand for Sniper Scouts. The Corps used the incident as a teaching tool to explain to troops about the interpretation and acceptability of symbols.

LOGO

Corporate **logos** are special kinds of symbols that visually identify businesses, nonprofit organizations and other groups. Contemporary or traditional? Elegant or casual? Much attention goes into the development of a corporate logo, which needs to present the right image and send the proper message.

Consider the promotional value and enduring impact of the Nike "swoosh" or the Dodge star. For an organizational symbol to be effective, it must be both memorable and appropriate for the organization. It also must be unique to the organization, one reason that much legal energy is spent protecting registered trademarks.

MUSIC

Music has a special symbolic value. Songs such as "Auld Lang Syne," "God Bless America" and "Pomp and Circumstance" have special meanings related to New Year's Eve, patriotic holidays and graduation, respectively. The next time you go to the movies, pay attention to the power of the background music in setting the right mood for romance, happiness, impending doom, and so on.

Music also can stir negative passions. The singing of the national anthem at sporting events sometimes results in perceived disrespect by players or fans, or disapproval of the musical style or behavior of the singers themselves.

A controversy was sparked by the Ice Bowl on New Year's Day in 2008 with the Pittsburgh Penguins at the Buffalo Sabers, the highest-rated NHL game in 12 years. In Buffalo, because of its proximity to Ontario, it is standard to sing both the U.S. and Canadian anthems at all hockey games. Irish tenor/Sabres fan Ronan Tynan opened the game with "God Bless America" instead of the national anthem. Then the Sabre's regular anthem singer sang the Canadian national anthem. For days, critics complained about the appropriateness of the musical selections.

Passions were stirred in 1999 when Japan's parliament approved a law making the traditional "Kimigayo" the official national anthem. The vote over the imperial hymn, Japan's unofficial anthem since before World War II, revived bitter memories and renewed the controversy over nationalism and war guilt. Much of the debate centered on schools, particularly on how children should be educated about the war and on the role of national symbols such as the anthem and the flag in school ceremonies.

Consider also the role of music in presidential campaigns. The tradition goes back to the early days of the nation, but it has taken off in recent years as candidates issue official playlists of music associated with their campaigns. The list is lengthy. Barack Obama's 2012 playlist included 24 songs and artists. Here's a brief list of recent electoral music: Obama "Yes We Can" (will.i.am), Mitt Romney "Born Free" (Kidd Rock), John McCain "Take a Chance on Me" (ABBA), Al Gore "You Ain't Seen Nothin' Yet" (Bachman-Turner Overdrive) and Bill Clinton "Don't Stop Thinking about Tomorrow " (Fleetwood Mac").

But campaign music is not without controversy. Tom Petty sent a cease-and-desist letter to Michele Bachmann's campaign telling her not to use his song "American Girl." Survivor told Newt Gingrich to stop using "Eye of the Tiger." And K'naan told Romney to stay away from his song "Wavin' Flag."

LANGUAGE

In some contexts, language itself can be symbolic. Consider the cultural symbolism of Hebrew, Latin, Arabic, Hindi and other languages associated with religious traditions, as well as the recurring English-as-official-language controversy that appeals to populist feelings within American politics or the French versus English debate in Quebec. Consider also how some

Phase Two

STEP 6

of the "in" language used by groups of teenagers, for example, has a symbolism for its users that is neither appreciated nor understood—nor meant to be—by outsiders.

PHYSICAL ARTIFACT

Symbolic value is sometimes attached to physical artifacts, such as the gavel used by a presiding judge or the badge worn by a police officer. Over the years, cigarettes have been variously presented as symbols of independence, youth, rebellion, ruggedness and adventure. Automobiles are presented as symbolic mirrors of the people who drive them. And it was the symbolic power of the Pentagon and the World Trade Center as icons of America that led terrorists to target those buildings on 9/11.

When a Florida Christian preacher organized a Burn the Quran rally and when U.S. troops in Afghanistan burned the Quran, several people died in waves of anti-American protests in the Middle East and Central Asia. All this was because of the symbolic value of the Quran, ironically a value recognized by both the preacher and troops as well as the reacting protestors.

CLOTHING

A particular type of physical artifact, clothing, often takes on symbolic proportions. This is why much attention often is paid to military uniforms, academic attire, religious vestments, ethnic apparel or royal garb, where each design element often has a special meaning. When President George W. Bush wore a Navy flight suit on an aircraft carrier to proclaim the end of the war in Iraq, his choice of clothing got a strong reaction—both pro and con.

Small controversies sometimes arise over the symbolism of clothing, particularly for women, such as the appropriate dress for nurses, Catholic nuns or Muslim women. Attention is also given to less formal but nonetheless powerful symbols such as designer clothing or trendy brand-name eyeglasses. For persuasive purposes, a spokesperson might wear clothing related to a particular profession or occupation as a way of suggesting expertise.

PEOPLE

Even people can function as symbols—especially royalty such as a king or queen, religious figures such as the Dalai Lama or the Pope, and other important and well-known characters. As symbols, they stand as more than human beings; they represent the dignity and prestige of the office they hold. Media attention given to scandals involving princes, presidents and prime ministers, however, has weakened the symbolic value of such figures.

MASCOT

Another kind of symbol is the mascot. From Smokey Bear to the San Diego Chicken, from Philly Phanatic to Herbie Husker of the University of Nebraska Cornhuskers, mascots embody much of the spirit of an organization. Meanwhile, many companies and organizations also use promotional characters such as Ronald McDonald, the U.S. Postal Service eagle, the Aflac duck, and the Geico gecko.

The symbolic significance of such fictional personifications can change. Betty Crocker and Aunt Jemima have gotten younger and more professional looking each decade as their company's customers have changed. Sports teams are under increasing pressure to retire their Native American mascots, which many people find offensive and archaic.

COLOR

Colors also can be symbolic or emblematic—green for environmental issues, pink for breast cancer and for Owens-Corning fiberglass insulation, and so on.

The symbolic value of colors is socially defined. For example, the Western identification of black for funerals is not universally shared. In fact, in many part of the world, white is the appropriate color associated with death and funerals. This is something that communicators in international or multicultural settings need to consider.

SETTING

The setting or environment also has strong symbolic value, and much meaning can be created by putting a speaker in, say, a cemetery, laboratory or library.

PLANNING EXAMPLE 6C **Verbal and Nonverbal Communication**

Here is an outline of the verbal and nonverbal communication strategies for Upstate College.

UPSTATE COLLEGE

Phase Two

Verbal Communication

- One point of view will be presented: expansion is beneficial for students, the community and the college.
- A conclusion will be drawn: students should consider Upstate College.
- Message clarity will be enhanced by a Fog Index level of tenth grade.
- Messages will include power words such as "benefit to community" and "quality education."
- Messages will avoid any exaggeration.
- Messages will rely on facts and documentation rather than empty claims.

STEP
6

Nonverbal Communication

- The college logo will be featured in messages.
- Upbeat music popular with teens and young adults will be featured in messages.
- The college mascot, salamander "Upstate Eddie," will be featured.

Here is an outline of the verbal and nonverbal communication strategies for Tiny Tykes Toys.

TINY
TYKES
TOYS

Verbal Communication

- Opposing points of view will be included in messages: Tiny Tykes is committed to toy safety; the company had a problem in the past but has learned from mistakes and now is recommitted to toy safety.
- A conclusion will be drawn: the company now makes high-quality, safe toys and deserves consumer support.

- Message clarity will be enhanced by a Fog Index level of ninth grade.
- Messages will include power words such as "commitment to excellence" and "baby safe."
- Messages will avoid any exaggeration.
- Messages will rely on facts and documentation rather than empty claims.

Nonverbal Communication
- Messages will be enhanced by happy music.
- Corporate spokespersons will be shown wearing research and professional clothing, reinforcing the message of research and high standards.
- Clinical settings will be used for presentations by corporate spokespersons, reinforcing the message of research and high standards.

 Checklist 6C **Verbal and Nonverbal Communication**

Basic Questions

1. How does your message use verbal communication?
2. How does your message use nonverbal communication?
3. How can either be made stronger?

Expanded Questions

A. VERBAL COMMUNICATION

Message Structure

1. Does your message present only one point of view or more than one (opposing) point of view? If more than one point of view is presented, is your message sandwiched (stating your argument, noting the opposing argument, and finally restating your argument and refuting the opposing argument)?
2. Does your message present a conclusion?
3. Does your message reiterate its main idea?

Clarity
1. Will your publics find your message clear, simple and understandable?
2. What is the education level of your target public?
3. How does this compare with the Fog Index for your written message?

Power Words

1. Have you used powerful language in your message?
2. Does your product/program have a descriptive and memorable name?
3. Does your product/program have a descriptive and memorable slogan?

Ethical Language

1. Does your message use pretentious or exaggerated language?
2. Does your message use dishonest or misleading language?
3. Does your message use defamatory language?
4. How could any of these verbal elements be made stronger?

B. NONVERBAL COMMUNICATION

1. Does the presentation of your message include a symbol, a logo, music, symbolic language, symbolic physical artifacts, symbolic clothing, symbolic people, a mascot, symbolic use of color and/or a symbolic setting?
2. How could any of these nonverbal elements be made stronger?

CONSENSUS CHECK

Does agreement exist within your organization and your planning team about the recommended strategies included within this step of the planning process?

☐ Yes. Proceed to the next section, Branding the Strategic Message, and then on to Step 7, Selecting Communication Tactics.

☐ No. Consider the value and/or possibility of achieving consensus before proceeding.

Phase Two

STEP 6

Branding the Strategic Message

A concept drawn from marketing that should be part of strategic communication planning is **branding**, which is the creation of a clear and consistent message for an organization. If one traditional description of public relations is valid—that public relations is doing good and receiving credit for it—then it can be said that branding is seeing that truth well told.

A *brand* is the articulation of an organization's purpose, the way it is presented to customers, employees and other publics. The value of a brand is its ability to convey a message and associate the corporate name with a favorable concept in the mind of the consumer or other public.

Branding is rooted in an organization's strategic communication plan, shaping a messaging strategy to express its purpose and character so that audiences will understand it and differentiate it from other organizations.

The goal of branding is to foster understanding and goodwill, and to encourage participation and support. Strong brands come from what people say about you, not on what you say about yourself. That's one of the differences between public relations and advertising.

Corporations have used the concept of branding for years. Because it evolved in the corporate world, economic competition sometimes has taken the form of warfare. A car dealership has "the greatest deals in town," this toothpaste cleans "better than all the rest." There are good guys and bad; heroes and villains; us and them, the enemy.

It might be unseemly for a university to proclaim itself the best in the state, or for a hospital to slam the competition. But nonprofit organizations and other non-business entities can work with this competitive concept. The enemy probably won't be another organization, but it might easily be an intangible foe. Even wholesome organizations and uplifting causes have enemies to address. In fact, branding can fit particularly well with nonprofit organizations, for which the creation of an emotional perception is a natural goal of a communication campaign.

Thus the American Heart Association may declare war on obesity, the Anti-Defamation League can see religious bigotry as the enemy, and People for the Ethical Treatment of Animals might demonize some values of the fashion industry.

Consider some of the ideas presented by the National Mentoring Center and the U.S. Department of Education as part of a marketing panel for a program seeking male mentors for inner-city children.

- "We're looking for a few good MENtors."
- "Mentor one child. Change two lives."
- "See a man. Become a man."
- "Been there? Done that? Pass it on. Become a mentor."

Language of Branding

Previously in this step of the strategic planning process, we focused on verbal communication, particularly on developing the content of strategic messages. Particularly with an eye on branding, we can look to both verbal and nonverbal communication approaches toward creating an image for a business of nonprofit organization.

A **slogan** is the succinct catchphrase in a communication program. This sometimes is called a **verbal logo**. Along with an organization's graphic logo, the tagline presents a concise-yet-comprehensive message that identifies the organization and seeks to position it in the mind of consumers and other publics.

Often the term **tagline**, once associated mainly with marketing, is used in reference to slogans used for public relations and other promotional purposes. Serving more or less as a battle cry, a tagline can be quite effective, especially during the awareness phase of a strategic communication campaign.

Corporate advertising has created many notable taglines: Nokia "Connecting People," Nike "Just do it," Allstate "You're in good hands" and Kay Jewelers "Every kiss begins with Kay." Nonprofit organizations also have branded themselves with memorable taglines: Greenpeace "Take action for the climate" and March of Dimes "Saving babies, together." State tourism slogans such as "Find Yourself Here" for California, "Virginia is for Lovers" and "I ❤ New York" have been effective because they are both clear and open to having various interpretations.

Many effective taglines are associated with social movements or organizations. They serve the purpose of what anthropologists call **symbolic consensus**, a rallying cry for supporters. Consider these taglines of longstanding use associated with social causes: National Rifle Association "Guns don't kill people; people kill people," U.S. Forest Service "Only you can prevent wild fires" and United Negro College Fund "A mind is a terrible thing to waste."

The Seneca Nation of Indians developed a strong verbal logo amid an ongoing public controversy over state attempts to levy taxes on Indian lands. The Western New York-based tribe has a treaty with the federal government that business conducted in its territory is immune from state taxes. Using the slogan "Break a treaty, break the law," the campaign forced four successive New York governors to back away from plans to push for taxation.

The entertainment media use taglines aimed at potential audiences. Thus the film *Alien* promoted its sci-fi horror genre ("In space, no one can hear you scream"), the movie sequel *Saw II* drew on earlier success with the slogan "Oh yes, there will be blood," and *Scary Movie 2* appealed to a teen audience with the tagline "More sex! More blood! Less taste!" Humor was the theme for the tagline for *The Simpsons Movie* ("See our family. And feel better about yours") and *The 40-Year-Old Virgin* ("The longer you wait, the harder it gets").

ESPN achieved ratings increases for the sports network and several marketing awards after it opted for a serial tagline. Some of the print and TV spots were serious: "Without sports, how would we know what we're made of?" But most had a humorous twist: "Without sports, what would we do over the holidays?" "Without sports, would you know how to spell J-E-T-S?" "Without sports, weekends would be weekdays."

Closely related to a slogan or a tagline is a *service mark*, which is a word and phrase that marketing and public relations people develop to be closely associated with organizations. Essentially, these are taglines that have been registered, much as trademarks are. Corporate lawyers go to great lengths to protect them.

Examples of service marks are the Army's "Be all you can be," Budweiser's "This Bud's for you," and Nike's "Just do it." Burger King is the only restaurant that can legally claim to be the "Home of the Whopper" and the *New York Times* is the only paper that can claim to have "All the news that's fit to print."

Nonprofits also use such branding successfully. The University of Texas at Austin uses the tagline "What starts here changes the world." Homeboy Industries, which helps gang-involved youth, proclaims, "Nothing Stops a bullet like a job." The Sierra Club enjoins people to "Explore, enjoy and protect the planet." Catholic Charities focuses on "Providing help. Creating hope." Camp Fire USA touts "Today's kids. Tomorrow's leaders." Meanwhile "Only kids. Only Phoenix Children's Hospital" is a tagline for the only hospital in Arizona focused on children.

Lessons about Branding

Good branding is a twofer. It can help an organization (1) by defining and differentiating you in the minds of your publics (particularly customers) and (2) by providing a structure to convey a consistent message.

Consider some of the branding strategies associated with businesses. Volvo brands itself as the car for safety. Maytag presents a message of dependability. Starbucks takes premium coffee as a given and brands itself as for community-mindedness. Holiday Inn boasts about "Pleasing people the world over" and Timex highlights durability with its slogan "Takes a

BRAINSTORMING FOR BRANDING

How do people come up with ideas for branding messages? The process isn't magical; it doesn't require genius, and it isn't necessarily rooted in lightning-bolt inspiration. But there are ways to create creativity, or at least to create a process where creative ideas can ripen.

An easy-to-apply group creativity technique called **brainstorming** is a useful tool in this part of the strategic planning process. Brainstorming is associated with the effective creativity addressed in the introduction to this book.

The first step in brainstorming is **divergence**, in which the group surfaces a large number of ideas on how to solve a problem or answer a question. Here's how it can work. Assemble a small team of people to consider questions such as the following:

- What do we want people to remember about our organization? Pepsi wants you to make "The choice of a new generation."
- What do we want them to do? Example: The Yellow Pages people distilled this question into "Let your fingers do the walking."
- What feeling do we want to evoke, or what attitude do we want to bring to mind? Example: United Cerebral Palsy suggests "Life without limits for people with disabilities."
- What is our niche, or how are we different or unique? Example: M&Ms candies set themselves apart from other candy with "Melts in your mouth, not in your hands."

Do you have any artifacts associated with your organization? These might be personal items such as clothing and grooming, or cultural elements such as music, art and architecture. Disney draws on images of its theme parks with the slogan "The happiest place on earth."

Here are a few rules for effective brainstorming:

- Write down every idea.
- Don't edit yourself.
- Put criticism on hold, because nothing is too "far out" at this point.
- Work with your colleagues on the brainstorming team, tossing around ideas and building on each other's contributions.
- Get as many different ideas as possible on the table.
- Consider each one, and see how many variations you can come up with.

Next comes the **convergence** part of the brainstorming process. As you pare the list, select those few that are worth further consideration. With all of the ideas on the table, consider each one. It's best to have each member of the team rank each idea individually. Then compare results and hold on to those that seem most useful to the group.

At this point, you might want to get the input from others beyond the brainstorming team. Take the top three or four ideas to a wider group, perhaps a formal focus group.

licking and keeps on ticking." DeBeers' advertising line appeals to the sentiment of couples who see their relationship as permanent: "A diamond is forever."

Here are 15 suggestions about taglines:

1. Don't mistake a tagline for a proverb or a maxim, and don't think it's merely a mission statement, though that may suggest key phrases that can be developed into a branding message.
2. Make the tagline memorable. Cadence, rhythm and rhyme can enhance this.
3. Keep the tagline short and succinct. Some suggest that seven or eight words should be the maximum.
4. Look at the organizational goals and allow the tagline to energize them, as in the Salvation Army's "Doing the most good."
5. Use a branding tagline to highlight your unique situation and to distinguish you from competitors and colleagues alike, as in Altoids' "Curiously strong peppermints."
6. Focus on a benefit, as in the American Society for the Prevention of Cruelty to Animals' "We are their voice."
7. Focus on a potential, as in St. Jude's Children's Hospital's "Finding cures. Saving children."
8. Offer a challenge, as in "The few. The proud. The Marines" and "The Marines are looking for a few good men" (a slogan first used in a Navy recruiting ad in 1779).
9. Draw on a positive association with your product or service, as in Hershey Chocolates' website, "The sweetest site on the net."
10. Address the wants and needs of your audience, as in "Wheaties, the Breakfast of Champions."
11. Turn a disadvantage into an opportunity, as in No. 2 car rental company Avis's "We try harder."
12. Look for the inspiration, as in United Negro College Fund's "A mind is a terrible thing to waste."
13. Go with a pun. The public radio station at Morehouse State College, a historically black college in Atlanta, turned the tables with a health program called "A Waist Is a Terrible Thing to Mind."
14. Focus on a characteristics or quality, as in Chevy trucks' "Like a rock."
15. Focus on an attitude, as in Nike's "Just do it."

Note that, from a legal perspective, taglines are service marks, which enjoy protection similar to trademarks.

Phase Two

STEP 6

What's Next?

This is the end of Step 6, in which you have developed the message for your key publics.

This step also concludes Phase Two, the Strategy phase of the planning process for public relations and marketing communication. Having completed the three steps in this phase, which have built on those of the Formative Research phase, you now should have a clear sense of direction for your program.

Before going any further, present your planning thus far to the decision makers, such as your client or boss. Gain the buy-in from the key decision makers in your organization. They need to agree with the direction you suggest, with the objectives and with the resulting strategy recommendations. If there is not agreement, this is the time to rework the strategy before forging ahead.

In the next phase of planning, you will turn your attention to preparing and implementing specific communication tools to carry the strategic message you have just devised.

Phase Two

STEP
6

PHASE THREE

TACTICS

I f the strategy phase of the planning process provided the skeleton and muscles for your communication programming, then Phase Three is the flesh. This section deals specifically with **tactics**, which are the things we see. Tactics are the visible elements of a public relations or marketing communication plan.

In the introduction to *Strategic Planning for Public Relations*, you encountered the concept of **integrated communication**, the conscious blending of the instruments of both public relations and marketing communication. Integrated communication creates a comprehensive and cohesive program aimed at implementing the best possible mix of communication tools.

It is here in Phase Three that this integrated approach will become most visible, as you consider the various communication tools that can be used to achieve your objectives. The menu of tactics outlined in this phase features communication tools drawn from the full range of disciplines and specialties. For example, you consider interpersonal communication opportunities that involve speeches and special events, and organizational media such as newsletters, websites and Facebook entries. Also on the menu is a full plate of tactics involving the journalistic side of the news media, including applications in social media. Finally, you will consider tactics associated with advertising and promotion.

The activities in Phase Three will also lead you to select an effective mix of tactics, packaging your creative and strategic ideas into a comprehensive program. To accomplish this, you need to tap into your creative side. Your goal as you work through the two steps associated with Phase Three is to boost your plan well above the level of a mere laundry list of tactics. Instead, you attempt to create a compelling and resourceful action plan that can help your client organization achieve its goals and objectives.

You also will deal with the administrative details of budgeting and scheduling that are so important for the smooth implementation of your plan. This tactics phase calls for the twin skills of creativity and attention to detail. All aspects of implementation involve many components, and the person who can manage simultaneous tasks skillfully should find success in the field of strategic communication.

The need for micromanaging the various tasks might seem overwhelming at first. But by remaining focused on your plan, you will avoid unnecessary side trips that sap your time and drain your resources without advancing you toward your goal.

At the same time, effective tactics call for a measure of creativity and innovation— that certain spark that separates the ordinary from the unusual, replacing the commonplace with the memorable or exceptional.

Phase Three

STEP 7

Selecting Communication Tactics

A **communication tactic** is the visible element of a strategic plan. This is what people see and do: websites and news releases, tours and billboards, blogs and special events, and so much more. Tactics are also the elements of the plan that can carry a hefty price tag, so planning and coordination are particularly important.

The range of communication tactics is extensive, and it is continually growing because of technological advances. Step 7 offers you a convenient menu of the various tactics. These tactics should be considered in light of your goals and objectives, evaluated in relationship to each other, matched to the taste of the organization and the publics, and chosen with an eye toward time and budget constraints. At a restaurant, you wouldn't order every item on the menu; likewise, don't try every tactic you can think of. Instead, review this menu of public relations tactics carefully, then select a full plate of items appropriate to the situation you are addressing.

Before we review the menu, let's look at some of the conventional categories of communication tactics, along with a description of the distinctions this book uses.

Conventional Communication Tactics

Media and media tactics are often divided into categories based on distinguishing features. Here are several frequently used pairs that describe types of media. These are based on factors such as organizational control, organizational ties, audience size, audience type, audience interaction, media ownership and media production. Each categorization can be useful, but as we will see, these conventional communication categories have some limitations as well.

ORGANIZATIONAL CONTROL

One category of media is based on the organization's ability to control the content, timing, packaging and audience access of its messages.

Controlled media allow the organization to determine various attributes of the message— most notably its content, but also its timing, presentation, packaging, tone and distribution. Examples of controlled media are newsletters, brochures, corporate videos and websites.

Conversely, **uncontrolled media** are those in which someone unrelated to the organization, such as a media gatekeeper, determines those message attributes. Examples of uncontrolled media tactics include news conferences and interviews.

ORGANIZATIONAL TIE

Another category of media describes the relationship of the media to the organization, specifically whether these media are internal to the organization or external to it.

Internal media exist within the organization and thus parallel the previous definition of controlled media.

External media, which exist outside the organization, may be controlled (such as advertising media) or uncontrolled (such as news media). Specific examples include billboards, newspapers and television news broadcasts.

AUDIENCE SIZE

Still another category is defined by the size and breadth of the intended audience.

Mass media are those that are accessible to most people; thus they are media that enjoy vast audiences, such as television networks and the mainstream daily newspaper establishment.

On the other hand, **targeted media** have not only much narrower but also more homogeneous audiences. Examples of targeted media are special-interest publications (such as a magazine for people who live aboard sailboats), broadcast programs that appeal to a particular narrow audience (such as a program on retirement finances), and special-interest cable networks (such as the DIY Network or a religion channel).

AUDIENCE TYPE

Media also can be categorized by audience type, with differences between those media available to a wide audience and those that can be accessed primarily by a more narrow audience.

Popular media focus on information of interest to people in their personal lives, including fashion, grooming, relationships, hobbies and self-help, as well as news and current events. These are the publications found online or at the supermarket or bookstore. Examples of popular media include *Maxim*, *USA Today* and top-of-the-hour radio news broadcasts.

Trade media, on the other hand, generally are distributed via subscription and are read for professional or business purposes. They are a main focus for many public relations writers. Examples of trade media include *Auto Glass Journal* and *Wine Business Monthly*.

AUDIENCE INTERACTION

Some media can be described as one-way communication vehicles while others are two-way in nature.

One-way media allow an organization to send messages to an audience without the likelihood of significant feedback. Examples of one-way communication tactics are brochures, television commercials, speeches and news releases.

On the other hand, **interactive media** have two-way capabilities. They allow organizations to talk with their audiences. Examples of two-way communication tactics are blogs, question–answer sessions, teleconferences and in-person news conferences.

MEDIA OWNERSHIP

Another categorization defined by the audience, mainly in terms of availability and access, is public versus nonpublic media.

Public media generally are accessible to everybody. Examples of public media are local newspapers and both commercial and public radio and television stations.

Nonpublic media are more restricted in their coverage and their availability. They often choose to limit access and circulation to audiences drawn from specific occupations, professions or associations. Examples of nonpublic media are company newsletters, e-mail newsgroups, and magazines and other trade publications that circulate mainly to members of a particular industry or profession.

MEDIA PRODUCTION

A final categorization of media is based on the technical production methods of the medium.

Print media are those that involve the printed word, such as newsletters, newspapers and magazines.

Electronic media are based on newer technologies. Examples of electronic media include television (both broadcast and cable) as well as radio.

Digital media involve the newest and emerging technologies. These are the computer-based media such as e-mail, websites and mobile media.

Strategic Communication Tactics

Don't look for any single categorization style to suit every purpose. For one thing, there is a significant amount of overlap in the conventional category systems. For another, none of the classification systems is necessarily superior to the others.

Rather, use these various categories to analyze the pros and cons of each communication tool you might consider as you put together your tactical plan.

Strategic Planning for Public Relations looks at the various media and communication tactics in their complexity. In doing so, this book tries to avoid oversimplification, so you won't find media grouped according to any of the conventional categories described in the section above. This is not a rejection of the conventional approach but rather an attempt to go beyond the inherent limitations.

A better way to categorize communication media and tactics is to consider their distinctiveness as they relate to the organization using them. Thus, this book presents a menu of communication tactics in four categories.

- **Interpersonal communication** offers face-to-face opportunities for personal involvement and interaction.
- **Organizational media** are published or produced by the organization, which controls the message content as well as its timing, packaging, distribution and audience access.
- **News media** provide opportunities for the credible presentation of organizational messages to large audiences via journalistic organizations.
- **Advertising and promotional media** are controlled media, either internal or external to the organization, that also can offer access to large audiences.

Phase Three

STEP
7

Together, these four categories offer hundreds of different communication tactics. Each can be used by organizations to communicate with their publics, though not every tool is appropriate for each issue. Remember to be selective in choosing your communication tools.

These four categories of communication tactics complement each other. In Exhibit 7.1 (opposite), notice how they fit within a ying–yang pyramid pattern. This reflects the relationship between the size of the audience that each type of media can reach and the impact it can have on that audience. Interpersonal tactics may reach only a few people, but they have a stronger impact on their audiences than any other form of communication. The reverse is true of advertising and promotional media: They can reach people in great numbers, but with far less impact. Don't forget that impact often is the bottom line for a strategic communication program, whether it uses the persuasion or the dialogue model of communication.

With insight into the strengths and limitations of various kinds of media, communication planners try to create a tactical mix, using several types of communication activities to engage key publics in different ways that, when blended together, will effectively and efficiently achieve the organization's public relations or marketing objectives.

Technological advancements are offering ever more new tools for communicators. Blogs and social media are new additions to the communicator's toolbox. Satellite-based telecommunication tools make low-cost interactive conferencing a practical tactic, and land-based mobile media are expanding their scope and reach.

The interesting thing about new technology is that it isn't squeezing out the old. People still report getting information from all kinds of media. A Pew study in 2011 reported that 81 percent of Americans get news from television, 55 percent from newspapers, 15 percent from the **Internet** and 19 percent from radio.

A study by Barb Palser in *American Journalism Review* (Spring 2010) reported that audiences used both social media and traditional media to learn about the Haiti earthquake. She found that social media are good at getting messages out to the traditional media, and from there to widespread audiences.

Credibility is another point of comparison among various types of media and news sources. A 2011 study by the Pew Research Center for the People and the Press reported that 69 percent of respondents say they trust information from local news organizations, 59 percent from national news organizations, 51 percent from state government, 50 percent from the Obama administration, 44 percent from federal agencies, 41 percent from business corporations, 37 percent from congress and 29 percent from candidates running for office. Seventy-two percent said they get the same information from social media and traditional news media, but they use social media because they are more convenient. Internet users turn to Google as their first choice for news (21 percent), compared with 14 percent for Yahoo, 13 percent for CNN, 8 percent for local news sites, and 6 percent each for Fox News and MSNBC.

Interpersonal Communication Techniques

In the disciplines of public relations and marketing communication, both the academic experts who are proficient in concepts and theories, and the professional experts with applied training and practical experience agree on a crucial point: Interpersonal communication is the most persuasive and engaging of all the communication tactics.

Don't think this statement demeans other forms of communication. To the contrary, newspaper and television news reports can extend an organization's message to vast audiences.

EXHIBIT 7.1 Audience Reach vis-à-vis Persuasive Impact

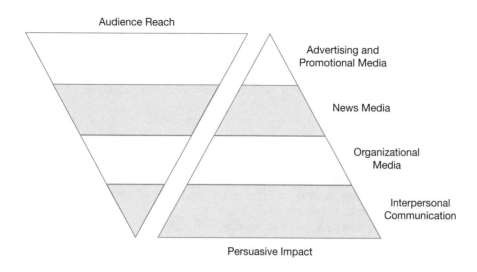

Direct mail can be a cost-effective way to reach great numbers of the key public. Advertising can present messages to large numbers of people with great precision.

In terms of influential communication, however, the effectiveness of other types of communication pales beside the vigor of direct, face-to-face, interpersonal communication.

Interpersonal communication channels can serve the needs of both businesses and nonprofit organizations. In your consideration of the various tools of communication, then, interpersonal methods should get your first attention. Let's consider the strategy of using interpersonal tactics and then we'll look at the various types of face-to-face communication that can be used for public relations purposes: personal involvement, information exchange and special events.

Strategy for Interpersonal Communication

Interpersonal communication tactics offer several strategic advantages to organizations. For one thing, they are controlled tactics through which the organization can oversee its message and the way that message is delivered. Remember, however, that audience response to the message can't be controlled.

For example, elected government officials can take their messages directly to their constituents through tactics such as town-hall meetings. But they cannot control how the audience may react to their message, the kind and intensity of questioning they may receive, even the hecklers and trash-talkers who may use the occasion to get their own message out in front of voters and news cameras.

Like all public relations tactics, interpersonal ones can be misused if they are applied too generally. But with careful planning, they can be tailored for specific publics, both internal and external.

Phase Three

STEP
7

INTERPERSONAL COMMUNICATION TACTICS

Personal Involvement

- organizational site involvement (plant tour, open house, test drive, trial membership, free class, shadow program, ride along, sneak preview, premiere performance);
- audience site involvement (door-to-door canvassing, in-home demonstration).

Information Exchange

- educational gathering (convention, council, convocation, synod, conclave, conference, seminar, symposium, colloquium, class, workshop, training session);
- product exhibition (trade show);
- meeting (annual stockholder meeting, lobbying exchange, public affairs meeting);
- demonstration (rally, march, picket, boycott);
- speech (oration, talk, guest lecture, address, keynote speech, sermon, homily, panel, debate, forum, town meeting, speaker's bureau).

Special Events

- civic event (fair, festival, carnival, circus, parade, flotilla);
- sporting event (tournament, marathon, triathlon, outdoor spectator event, track meet, field days, rodeo, games, match, meet);
- contest (science fair, spelling bee, beauty pageant, talent contest, dance-a-thon);
- holiday event;
- progress-oriented event (launching, procession, motorcade, ground-breaking ceremony, cornerstone ceremony, dedication, ribbon-cutting, tour, grand opening);
- historic commemoration (founders' days, anniversary, centennial, play, pageant, caravan);
- social event (luncheon, banquet, roast, awards dinner, recognition lunch, party, dance, fashion show, tea);
- artistic event (concert, concert tour, recital, play, film festival, art show, photo exhibit);
- fundraising event (antique show, auction, haunted house, pony ride, murder mystery dinner theater, fashion show, house or garden tour, tasting party);
- publicity event.

STEP
7

In terms of organizational resources, interpersonal tactics generally are relatively inexpensive. Costs associated with these tactics generally are only modest, though some types of special events can become quite expensive projects if the budget permits. Interpersonal tactics as a group claim more staff time to plan and implement than some of the other categories of tactics that we will consider.

Interpersonal tactics can work with either internal or external publics, but the organization should have some relationship with the publics for these tactics to be successful.

Interpersonal tactics have the potential to make a strong impact. They are particularly useful in achieving acceptance objectives, which is the most difficult category of objective to

Phase Three

reach. Through interpersonal tactics, the organization can communicate with its publics in ways that can have a major effect not only on what they know but especially on how they feel about that information. Thus interpersonal tactics are useful for both the persuasion and dialogue models of communication.

Similarly, interpersonal tactics generally involve **information-seeking publics**—people who have gone somewhat out of their way to interact with the organization. These people presumably are already interested in the issue, perhaps have some knowledge of the relevant facts and are at least open to (perhaps even leaning toward) the organization's message. They are the ones who attend town-hall meetings and speeches, who sign up for workshops and who participate in special events.

The downside? Interpersonal tactics reach only a small number of people, compared to tactics in other categories. So if numbers are important, these tactics won't be heavy producers.

Like all the categories of tactics presented in this book, interpersonal ones should never be considered in isolation from those in other categories. These are the first ones to consider precisely because they can make such an impact (and because we have to start somewhere). But they are not necessarily the first ones that will be used in your general order of tactics.

Let's look at three different types of interpersonal communication tactics: personal involvement, information exchange and special events.

Personal Involvement

Personal involvement is a powerful element of communication, whether for purposes of information, education, persuasion or dialogue. When the organization actively involves its publics and creates an environment rooted in two-way communication, the mutual interests of both the organization and its publics are likely to be addressed. This category of tactics includes organizational-site involvement and audience-site involvement.

ORGANIZATIONAL-SITE INVOLVEMENT

A growing number of audience-involvement activities are bringing members of the audience to the organization, as more and more organizations realize the importance of public interaction. "Keep out" signs are being replaced by welcome mats. Examples of this type of audience interaction include plant tours and open houses. For example, Hershey Foods sponsors Chocolate World, a free plant tour that feels like a theme park.

Such tactics offer for-profit and nonprofit organizations alike an opportunity to "show off" for the various publics of the organization: employees and volunteers, both current and prospective; current and would-be customers; investors, donors and other funding sources; community or governmental supporters.

Some interpersonal tactics involve hands-on activities. Auto dealers, for example, give test drives. Fitness clubs, dance studios and other activity centers offer trial memberships so potential members can experience the facility and its atmosphere. Educational activities such as martial-arts programs and cooking schools may offer a limited number of free classes to give potential recruits a sample of their offerings.

Private schools have shadow programs in which potential students are invited to spend a day accompanying a current student on the daily round of classes. Police, fire and emergency crews offer ride-alongs so local residents can see firsthand how various situations are handled.

Sneak previews and premiere performances of movies and plays also are effective in generating future audiences.

AUDIENCE-SITE INVOLVEMENT

Instead of inviting the public in, sometimes the organization goes to its publics, a real convenience for the audience. For example, door-to-door canvassing offers an opportunity for organizations with a political, social or religious cause to take their message or charitable solicitation directly to people who might be interested. Petition drives seek to get signatures of voters and other constituents. The downside of this, of course, is that people sometimes resent the knock on the door by an advocate with a message to share.

Meanwhile, some organizations offer in-home demonstrations to help potential customers to see how various products or services will work and personally evaluate their effectiveness. These demonstrations generally are scheduled ahead of time, usually at the initiative of the customer.

Information Exchange

Another significant category of interpersonal communication tactics, **information exchange**, centers on opportunities for organizations and their publics to meet face to face and thus to exchange information, ask questions and clarify understandings. This category includes educational gatherings, product exhibitions, meetings, demonstrations and speeches.

EDUCATIONAL GATHERING

Various types of meetings provide an opportunity for both commercial and nonprofit organizations to educate large numbers of information-seeking people.

Be aware that the following terms sometimes may be used somewhat interchangeably. But here is a definition of the difference among the various types of educational gatherings. Conventions are gatherings that generally involve the transaction of organizational business such as the election of officers; many conventions also have a component of education or professional development. Conferences are similar to conventions, though conferences transfer the focus away from organizational business and toward professional development and education. Councils are meetings with a policy-setting agenda. Convocations, synods and conclaves are formal conventions, often with a religious or academic purpose.

Seminars are educational meetings, often ones that bring together peers who discuss issues among themselves. Symposiums also are educational meetings in which specialists deliver short papers, whereas colloquiums are educational meetings in which specialists deliver formal addresses and then conduct a public discussion of the topic. Workshops and training sessions have a more practical, applied focus, often with an interactive presentation style.

PRODUCT EXHIBITION

Companies often seek opportunities to display their products to sales people and potential customers. The special feature of these trade shows is that they bring together information-seeking publics—often people who attend trade shows specifically to find out about new products—as well as companies and their competitors. Because competitors are displaying their wares at the same show, each company is challenged to provide a bigger and better presentation than others with a similar product line. For this reason, trade shows generally feature elaborate displays and state-of-the-art interactive technology, often with colorful and attention-getting entertainment and refreshments.

Trade shows often are held as part of conferences and conventions that bring together potential customers. Indeed, one of the reasons people attend conferences is to view the latest products associated with their industry or profession.

MEETING

Meetings provide an excellent opportunity for organizations to set up positive information interchanges with their publics. Some of these settings are formal occasions. For example, companies that issue stock are required to hold annual stockholder meetings.

While many such meetings are pretty dull, a growing number of companies are turning the required annual event into a sort of internal trade show with elaborate luncheons and colorful displays about the company's current and future products as well as its financial success. Some stockholder meetings feature top-notch entertainers.

Often meetings are businesslike occasions that involve only a limited number of participants. Lobbying exchanges and public affairs meetings, for example, may involve just one or two representatives of an organization and a few staff members to an elected official.

RALLY

Some activities focus on advocacy or opposition. Rallies and other types of public demonstrations can bring together hundreds—even thousands—of people in support of a particular cause, often with speakers. Similarly, marches are public processions, often for the purpose of making a political or social statement. Consider, for example, the numerous rallies for social or political causes that are staged in Washington, DC, and in state capitals and other major cities.

Parades, meanwhile, often demonstrate civic pride such as with a victorious sports team, or community appreciation as with parades for returning military troops.

Other public gatherings may be confrontational or negative in nature. Demonstrations, with an element of protest, are opportunities for information exchange, often through speakers as well as by the distribution of printed literature.

Pickets are demonstrations against a particular organization. Often they involve an element of disruption, such as encouraging or trying to prevent people from doing business with the organization. Usually they include vocal and visual messages criticizing the organization.

Boycotts, meanwhile, are public protests, sometimes accompanied by picketing, in which customers refrain from using the products or services of the organization being opposed. Boycotts often are accompanied by public education endeavors.

All of these types of rallies and demonstrations also tend to generate news coverage, which we discuss later. Additionally, they can galvanize existing support.

SPEECH

Speeches are public discourses in which the speaker controls the presentation and intends to impact the awareness, acceptance or action of an audience. As such, speeches are excellent vehicles for face-to-face communication, especially when question-and-answer sessions are part of the speech presentation.

Consider the different varieties of speeches. Orations are very formal and dignified presentations with a high and eloquent rhetorical style. Talks, on the other hand, are informal, off-the-cuff speeches, usually on a professional subject.

Lectures are carefully prepared speeches associated with classrooms and the presentation of academic information; guest lectures are often more practical educational presentations given by an expert in a particular area.

Addresses are formal speeches that require significant preparation, and keynote speeches are major addresses at conferences and other meetings. Two kinds of speeches are associated with the field of religion: sermons, which are moral exhortations, based on religious teaching, and homilies, which are explanations of the practical application of a scriptural passage.

In some speech-like situations, the speaker gives up much of the control of the communication. Consider, for example, panels in which a moderator guides the discussion of several speakers. Panels often involve a short, formal opening statement followed by questions offered by the moderator or by other panelists. Debates are formal, adversarial speaking occasions in which one side (an individual or a team) argues with an opponent using a set of formal rules. Forums and town meetings are speeches with questions and generally lively discussion, usually on topics of civic or public interest.

A concept related to speech is the **speaker's bureau**, which is a program within an organization to promote the availability of knowledgeable and trained employees or volunteers to give presentations. These presentations usually are free for organizations within the community on topics related to the organization's interests.

For example, a fuel-gas company may make speakers available to community associations, tenants groups and homeowners clubs, as well as to business and professional organizations that often have the ear of various opinion leaders. Topics for such a company might include energy saving, high-efficiency heating and cooling equipment, and energy tax matters.

Special Events

The most common category of interpersonal communication tactics is a *special event*, an activity created by an organization mainly to provide a venue to interact with members of its publics.

The list of special events is bounded only by the imagination of the planner. Some of the more common types of special events are civic events, sporting events, contests, holiday events, progress-oriented events, historic commemorations, social events, artistic events, fundraising events and general publicity events.

CIVIC EVENT

Public activities can bring a community together in celebration and fun. One popular civic activity is a fair, which features food and entertainment. Another is a festival, which often has games and sometimes is organized around a theme such as ethnic heritage, flowers or music. Carnivals with an atmosphere of public merriment and circuses with performing animals can also be important civic events.

Parades on land and flotillas on water are other forms of popular civic celebration, as are themed events such as those associated with community history.

SPORTING EVENT

Many special events are created around a sports theme.

Tournaments are often held for such activities as skiing, fishing and golf that have several levels of difficulty and thus can attract a wide range of participants. Marathons are races of all sorts. Triathlons that typically combine running, cycling and swimming are increasingly popular athletic events.

Also popular are outdoor spectator activities such as rodeos, lumberjack roundups and Highland games.

Some athletic activities, such as track meets and field days, provide opportunities to turn sporting events into larger community activities. Many sporting events are designed both for participant interaction and as spectator activities.

The Olympics are perhaps the best example of sporting events that impact both public relations and public diplomacy. China used the 2008 Olympics and the 2010 Shanghai World Expo to promote "the Chinese brand." These extravagant events were designed to capture the world's attention and create a positive environment for Chinese culture and commerce, and Nielsen Media Research reported that 4.7 billion television viewers watched some part of the games.

Along with a platform for positive messaging to potentially massive audiences, events such as the Olympics also provide a stage for protests. China drew international criticism for expelling 100 Christian missionaries as it prepared to put a good face on the Olympics. It received environmental complaints for its inability to reduce air pollution in Beijing, causing health concerns for the athletes. And the 85,000-mile relay with the Olympic torch provided many opportunities for pro-Tibet protestors to shine an international spotlight on one of the negative aspects of Chinese policy.

CONTEST

Competitive engagements offer another type of special event, allowing participants to display their knowledge, skills or other assets. By their nature, contests create winners, which leads to increased visibility because of the built-in news value.

Science fairs, spelling bees and other types of academically oriented contests are popular, as are those that mimic various television quiz shows or reality shows. These and similar events such as beauty pageants, talent contests and sing-offs can attract wide audiences of both participants and spectators.

Often grand openings and similar events feature purely fun contests—for pizza tossing, pie eating, dancing, and the like—in which every participant is a winner.

HOLIDAY EVENT

Some special events are based on popular and widespread observances. Many of these are civic celebrations, such as Memorial Day, Independence Day, Labor Day and Thanksgiving. Some holiday activities are rooted within a particular cultural group, such as the Kwanzaa and Juneteenth celebrations in the African American community, or Chinese New Year and the Moon Festival in Chinese and some other Asian cultures.

Some of the most popular holidays, such as Hanukkah, Christmas and Easter, have religious roots. Be careful not to give offense by trivializing an event that some of your publics consider sacred in nature.

Phase Three

STEP 7

Other events are hybrids of popular religion and cultural celebrations, such as St. Patrick's Day, observed by both the Irish and Irish-at-heart, or the pre-Lenten Mardi Gras and other Carnival festivities.

Holidays sometimes become occasions for social comment and action. For example, many American Indian protests around Columbus Day highlight the devastating effects—both intended and unintended—of European contact.

PROGRESS-ORIENTED EVENT

Several kinds of events celebrate the growth and development of an organization or community. Ships and boats traditionally are launched by smashing a champagne bottle on the ship's bow, or now by the more environmentally friendly pouring of champagne over the bow. Progress-oriented events often are marked by musical entertainment, fireworks and other celebratory activities.

When a school or religious congregation moves into a new building nearby, the transition often is marked by a procession from the old building to the new. For example, students might carry symbols such as textbooks, globes and other artifacts of school life to the new school site. Similarly, a motorcade might be arranged to inaugurate the opening of a new bridge.

A single project might lend itself to a series of progress-oriented special events. Consider, for example, the building of a new community center. You might schedule a groundbreaking ceremony for the turning of the first shovelful of dirt, a cornerstone ceremony when construction begins, and a dedication ceremony including a ribbon cutting to mark the completion of the center, and then follow these with tours and grand opening events.

HISTORIC COMMEMORATION

The history of an organization or community provides the background for another kind of special event. Towns observe founders' days; companies mark the anniversary of their incorporation. Sometimes historic events are observed by re-creating the sights and sounds of an earlier era, such as a centennial celebration that features costumes, buggies or antique cars, and music and food of the bygone era.

Some historic commemorations include plays, dramatic reenactments of historical events, and pageants or historical plays with a certain amount of music and pomp. Additionally, caravans re-enact historic travels.

SOCIAL EVENT

Social events comprise a major type of special event. Luncheons and dinners are events sponsored by all kinds of organizations. These social events involve entertainment activities. Receptions with beverages and hors d'oeuvres or snacks are a similar kind of event.

Among the various special types of ceremonial meals are tributes that honor people or organizations and banquets that offer more sumptuous menus and entertainment. Roasts use sarcastic humor to recognize a person's achievements and contributions.

Many social events are aimed at employees and volunteers, and their purpose is to thank or recognize members of an important public. The purpose of such awards dinners and recognition lunches is to enhance the camaraderie among people who work together, a potential boost to worker productivity. In other cases, luncheons and banquets often may have educational or fundraising objectives and involve a variety of publics. Other social events include fashion shows and teas.

Social events often occur at elegant or unusual locations, including cruise ships, museums and private mansions. Budget limitations can be offset by an extra dash of creativity, and many social events have been successful because they have had an interesting theme, such as an imitation Caribbean island getaway complete with appropriate music, food and dancing, or historical themes related to the Old West, medieval knights or the flapper era. Futuristic themes also can be popular.

Be attentive to ethical considerations of social events. A party with the theme of the antebellum South may evoke images of fancy dress balls and sumptuous banquets amid lavish architecture, but that era also was associated with slavery—hardly a fitting theme for a fundraiser or recognition event for most publics.

ARTISTIC EVENT

Another area of special events deals with art and culture. Consider events such as concerts or concert tours, recitals, plays, film festivals, arts shows, photo exhibits and related activities.

FUNDRAISING EVENT

Activities in which nonprofit organizations interact with their key publics, especially individual donors, for the purpose of generating support can be important public relations opportunities. Americans donated more than $291 billion to charitable organizations (Giving USA, 2011). About 73 percent of this was given by individuals, the remainder through bequests and by foundations (14 percent), bequests (8 percent) and corporations (5 percent).

Religious organizations received more than a third of the total (35 percent) followed by education (14 percent), grant-giving independent and community foundations (11 percent), human-service organizations (9 percent), public-society benefit organizations such as United Way (8 percent), health agencies (8 percent), the arts and cultural groups (5 percent), international affairs (5 percent), environment and animals (2 percent), and the remainder in miscellaneous categories.

In addition, national elections now raise vast sums in contributions—$5 billion in 2008, $6 billion or more in 2012. Such contributions mushroomed in the wake of the Supreme Court ruling allowing unlimited and anonymous corporate funds. Still, that's only about 2 percent of all charitable giving in the US.

The variety of fundraising events is limitless. Consider the following ideas: an antique show, an auction, a haunted house, pony rides, murder mystery dinner theater, fashion show, house or garden tour, or tasting party (see Amos, 1995; Williams, 1994). All of these require careful planning and an eye for detail.

The ethics of both public relations and fundraising require honest and forthright disclosure of organizational information to donors and to the media.

PUBLICITY EVENT

Some activities simply fall into a category of general publicity activities. They include the staged activities noted in Step 5. Such events are limited only by the creativity of the planners, tempered by the ethical restraint of needing to offer legitimate news while posturing for the media. Within such ethical bounds, there are many activities that could be developed to present the organization's message amid a creative and camera-friendly presentation that offers news to the media.

Phase Three

**STEP
7**

DONOR BILL OF RIGHTS

Philanthropy is based on voluntary action for the common good. It is a tradition of giving and sharing that is primary to the quality of life. To assure that philanthropy merits the respect and trust of the general public, and that donors and prospective donors can have full confidence in the not-for-profit organizations and causes they are asked to support, we declare that all donors have these rights:

1. To be informed of the organization's mission, of the way the organization intends to use donated resources and of its capacity to use donations effectively and for their intended purposes.
2. To be informed of the identity of those serving on the organization's governing board, and to expect the board to exercise prudent judgment in its stewardship responsibilities.
3. To have access to the organization's most recent financial statements.
4. To be assured that their gifts will be used for the purposes for which they were given.
5. To receive appropriate acknowledgment and recognition.
6. To be assured the information about their donations is handled with respect and with confidentiality to the extent provided by law.
7. To expect that all relationships with individuals representing organizations of interest to the donor will be professional in nature.
8. To be informed whether those seeking donations are volunteers, employees of the organization, or hired solicitors.
9. To have the opportunity for their names to be deleted from mailing lists that an organization may intend to share.
10. To feel free to ask questions when making a donation and to receive prompt, truthful and forthright answers.

This statement was developed cooperatively by the Giving Institute (aafrc.org), the Association of Fundraising Professionals (afpnet.org), the Association for Healthcare Philanthropy (ahp.org) and the Council for the Advancement and Support of Education (case.org).

It has been officially endorsed by numerous other organizations such as the Independent Sector (indepsec.org), National Catholic Development Conference (ncdc.org), National Committee on Planned Giving (ncpg.org), Council for Resource Development (crdnet.org), American Indian College Fund (collegefund.org) and United Way of America (unitedway.org), as well as hundreds of individual hospitals, colleges and nonprofit charitable, religious, educational, medical and human-service organizations in both the US and Canada.

Here's an example of a successful and ethical publicity event that promoted a dog-food brand and raised money for animal charities. Snausages is a brand of doggie treats made by Del Monte Foods. Its future was threatened by competitors who were outspending the company in advertising, enough to cause some retailers to threaten to pull the product off their shelves. Snausages turned to public relations to pull out of its slump.

The Iditarod is a well-known dogsled race, with teams of huskies pulling drivers more than 1,000 miles across Alaska. Snausages turned the tables and garnered national and local publicity, including ESPN, with a "man sled" race in 2010.

Teams of men pulled canine mushers (dogs that had previously pulled in the Iditarod). An Associated Press photo of the event was the most e-mailed photo on Yahoo News for three days running. The brand mascot, Snocrates, refereed the race, ensuring the Snausages connection in photos and video footage. Donations went to animal charities of all the human participants in the race, upping the publicity factor.

The event created a 30 percent increase to traffic at the Snausages website, and increased customer demand ensured that the Del Monte brand kept all of its shelf status and distribution levels.

Another type of special event can be used as part of an advocacy campaign to attract attention to an issue. This was the strategy for the Nuns on the Bus information tour during the 2012 US presidential campaign. The strategy involved plenty of visual appeal. A group of Catholic nuns traveled through eight states in a brightly painted bus. With backdrops of homeless shelters and soup kitchens along the way, as well as legislative offices, the nuns focused international media attention and much local awareness as they lobbied legislators and otherwise provided a platform to speak out on social justice in opposition to budget-cutting proposals in congress that they said would unduly hurt the poor.

Planning Special Events

The various types of **special events** and most of the other tactics noted in this section require a tremendous amount of careful planning.

Attention to detail is a must during the preparation stages. Organizations sometimes handle these details internally; other times, they hire events-management companies to help plan and execute the activities. Either way, consider some of the following practical questions that can arise around a special event:

- Is the event of legitimate interest to the identified key publics? If the intention is to attract media attention, is there a significant news element to warrant inviting journalists to report the event?
- Is the date appropriate for everyone? Does it conflict with holidays (particularly cultural or religious holidays that may not be familiar to the planners)? Does it conflict with other major happenings, such as sporting or social activities—not only local events but larger events such as the Kentucky Derby, the Super Bowl, an important soccer game, or the opening of the fishing season? Any such competition can limit attendance at your event.
- What is the appropriate length of an event? If it is too long, participants will become bored or restless and may leave early. If it is too short, they may decide it's not worth attending in the first place.

- Is the theme appropriate? Will it offend anyone, or will anyone feel excluded because of it?
- Is the site appropriate and accessible? Is climate a factor? If it is an outdoor event, is there an indoor location to serve as a backup in the event of bad weather? Does the location of a conference or meeting offer too many diversions that might tempt participants away from the conference itself?
- Are speakers and entertainers appropriate to the participants of the special event or meeting?
- Is planning assistance available through a convention center or visitors' bureau in the host city of the meeting? If so, the agency may be able to simplify local contacts.

All special events call for careful planning, staffing and financing, and they need creative promotion. Use the planning process presented throughout this book to identify and analyze key publics, establish objectives, and develop a strategy for the special event or other type of interpersonal communication tactic. Also make sure to evaluate its effectiveness, showing in measurable terms how well the activity achieved its objectives.

PLANNING EXAMPLE 7A **Selecting Interpersonal Communication Tactics**

Upstate College will develop interpersonal communication tactics to publicize its expanded program:

Interpersonal Tactic 1: Open house for recruiting

- Key publics, hands-on, low cost, audience feedback

Interpersonal Tactic 2: Rededication ceremony

- Low cost, news value, reaffirming existing support

Interpersonal Tactic 3: Existing event

- Little additional cost, news value, power of ritualization

Interpersonal Tactic 4: Musical events

- Key student publics, moderate cost, serving acceptance objectives

Interpersonal Tactic 5: Festival

- Key student publics, high visibility, moderate cost

Interpersonal Tactic 6: Banquet

- Key publics (community leaders, donors), high cost, high impact

Tiny Tykes will develop the following interpersonal communication tactics for an employee-oriented public relations program:

Interpersonal Tactic 1: Customer satisfaction workshops

- Key external publics, high impact

Interpersonal Tactic 2: Work-group meeting

- Key internal public, interaction and feedback

Interpersonal Tactic 3: Product safety and quality session

- Key publics, direct benefit to employees and training management, indirect benefits to customers

Interpersonal Tactic 4: Motivational speech by CEO about safety and quality

- Key employee public, low cost, moderate impact

Interpersonal Tactic 5: Samples of reintroduced products

- Maintain credibility with employees (and family/friends of employees) as customers, moderate cost

---

 Checklist 7A **Interpersonal Communication Tactics**

Basic Questions

1. What interpersonal communication tactics will you use?
2. How will these tactics help the organization achieve its objectives?
3. What resources will these tactics require?

Expanded Questions

A. SELECTION OF TACTICS

From the following categories of interpersonal tactics, identify several that you would consider using:

Personal Involvement

- organizational-site involvement (plant tour, open house, test drive, trial membership, free class, sample, shadow program, ride-along, premiere);
- audience-site involvement;
- door-to-door canvassing, in-home demonstration, petition drive.

Phase Three

STEP
7

Information Exchange

- educational gathering (convention, council, convocation, synod, conclave, conference, seminar, symposium, colloquium, workshop, training session);
- product exhibition;
- trade show;
- meeting (annual stockholder meeting, lobbying exchange, public affairs meeting);
- demonstration (rally, march, demonstration, picket, boycott);
- speech (question-and-answer session, oration, talk, lecture, guest lecture, address, keynote, sermon, homily, panel, debate, speaker's bureau, forum, town meeting).

Special event

- civic event (fair, festival, carnival, circus, parade, theme event);
- sporting event (tournament, marathon, triathlon, outdoor spectator event, meet, field day);
- contest (science fair, spelling bee, beauty pageant, talent contest);
- holiday event (civic, cultural, religious);
- progress-oriented event (procession, motorcade, grand opening, groundbreaking, cornerstone, dedication, ribbon cutting);
- historic event (founders' day, anniversary, centennial, play, pageant, caravan);
- social event (luncheon, dinner, reception, tribute, banquet, roast, awards, recognition, fashion show, tea);
- artistic event (concert, concert tour, recital, play, film festival, art show, photo exhibit);
- fundraising event.

B. STRATEGIC IMPLICATIONS

For each item identified, answer the following questions:

1. Will this tactic help the organization to interact with the appropriate public?
2. What level of impact will this tactic make on the key public?
3. Will this tactic advance the organization toward its awareness objectives?
4. Will this tactic advance the organization toward its acceptance objectives?
5. Will this tactic advance the organization toward its action objectives?
6. What is the main advantage to this tactic?
7. What advantages does this tactic offer that other tactics do not?
8. Are there any disadvantages to this tactic? If so, what are they?

C. IMPLEMENTATION ITEMS

For each item identified, answer the following questions:

1. How much will it cost to implement this tactic? Is the cost justified? Is the cost practical, based on the organization's resources?
2. How much staff time will it take to implement this tactic? Is the time practical, based on the organization's resources?
3. What level of skill, equipment and expertise is needed to implement this tactic? Is the needed level available within the organization? Is it available from outside sources?

Phase Three

STEP
7

Organizational Media Tactics

A host of communication vehicles are managed by each organization and are used at its discretion. These media generally are controlled, internal, nonpublic media that we can look at in four categories: general publications, direct mail, miscellaneous print media and audiovisual/digital media. Let's consider the overall strategy and then look at each category of organizational media.

Strategy for Organizational Media

When should you select organizational media tactics? When your publics are too widespread or too large to interact with on a more personal level, but when you yet want to keep control of the content of your organization's message as well as its timing and distribution.

Conversely, when would you not use organizational media? When the audience is too small to warrant it, or so scattered that dissemination would be next to impossible. Or when you need the higher credibility that might be associated with other news tactics or the greater visibility that might be possible through advertising.

One of the benefits of organizational media tactics is that they provide a middle ground between high-impact, small-audience interpersonal tactics and lower-impact, large-audience news and advertising tactics. Organizational media can reasonably be addressed to both internal and external publics that fall in the midsized range. Because tactics in this category can be tailored to specific publics, they are more likely than news or advertising tactics to achieve success with acceptance and action objectives.

Another significant benefit of organizational media is that they are likely to be used by **information-seeking publics**, those who are actively searching for information on a particular topic. These are the people who will access a website, read a brochure or watch a video.

Organizational media can be expensive to use, but because they can be targeted to specific publics and individuals, they usually are cost-effective. For example, the tactic of direct mail can involve high postage costs. But the impact of direct mail—if done properly—is higher than most other media, and thus the results should be greater.

Remember that organizational media are only one set of tools for public relations and marketing communication. Consider them carefully, but always with the intention of combining them with other kinds of communication tactics.

Publications

General publications include a variety of materials published and printed by an organization. Their distribution generally is handled by the organization as well. This category includes serial publications, stand-alone publications, reprints, progress reports, user kits and research reports.

SERIAL PUBLICATION

Most organizations make heavy use of serial publications, which may be issued weekly, monthly or quarterly. The most common serial publication is a **newsletter**, an organizational publication that combines the informative approach of newspapers and magazines with the relationship-building features of mail. It's hard to tell just how many organizational newsletters

Phase Three

STEP
7

ORGANIZATIONAL MEDIA TACTICS

General Publications

- serial publication (newsletter, bulletin)
- stand-alone publication (brochure, flier, booklet, folder, pamphlet, tract, circular, fact sheet, FAQ)
- progress report (annual report, quarterly report)
- user kit
- research report
- miscellaneous print media.

Direct Mail

- memo
- letter (appeal letter, marketing letter)
- postcard
- invitation
- catalog (retail, full-line, specialty, business-to-business).

Electronic Media

- audio media (telephone, dial-a-message, recorded information, voicemail, toll-free line, demo tape, demo CD, podcast)
- video media (nonbroadcast video, videoconference, teleconference, videotape, slide show)
- digital media (presentations software, e-mail, **listserv**, Internet, newsgroup, websites, web home page, web-based television, web-based radio, touch-sensitive computer, cell phone)
- electronic publishing.

Social Media

- Wiki
- blog
- social networking.

Phase Three

STEP 7

exist. Guesses range from 150,000 to more than a million. But some figures are available. For example, more than 50,000 in-house corporate newsletters in the US have a combined readership of about 500 million. *Newsletters in Print* lists more than 12,000 newsletters in the US and Canada that are national or regional in their outlook and are available to the public; many of these are available in online versions as well. Additionally, there are untold numbers of private publications and house organs, which are newsletters published by companies and organizations, with distribution to members, employees and other groups of readers.

Whatever the total, an estimated two-thirds of newsletters are internal publications directed toward employees, volunteers, alumni, members, customers, patients, and so on.

The remaining third are external publications, a category that includes advocacy newsletters aimed at persuading readers, such as that published by a waste management company as part of a campaign to minimize opposition among local residents, and special-interest newsletters dealing with a particular industry profession, or pursuit (such as financial investments, stamp collecting or white-water canoeing), or with a particular group of people (such as economists, breast-cancer survivors or former nuns). Another type of external newsletter is the subscription newsletter, which is often a high-cost publication providing insider information on a particular profession or industry; two such newsletters popular with public relations and marketing practitioners are *Media Relations Report* (ragan.com) and *Communication Briefings* (communicationbriefings.com).

Many public relations and marketing communication campaigns publish one or more newsletters as a convenient way to communicate with an organization's publics. If you plan to use the tactic of newsletters, having an appropriate mailing list is a must. When writing newsletters, follow the principles of newsworthiness and audience self-interest. Make sure the articles provide information of interest to the readers, and not just data that the organization wishes to present to the readers.

A **bulletin**, meanwhile, is a different kind of serial publication. Confusingly, some people use the two terms—newsletters and bulletins—interchangeably, though it is helpful to practitioners to distinguish between the two types of serial publications.

Typographically, bulletins often feature only headlines and short body text, with little or no graphic content. They generally include official organizational information and are most often circulated to internal audiences. Some examples of bulletins are listings of jobs or internships, notices of contracts or requests for proposals (called RFPs), or timely announcements by organizations such as churches or schools.

STAND-ALONE PUBLICATION

Another commonly used tactic in public relations is the stand-alone publication, which differs from a newsletter or bulletin in that it usually is issued only once rather than periodically (though stand-alone publications may occasionally be updated). This category of publications includes brochures, fliers and fact sheets.

A **brochure** is a common stand-alone organizational publication, dealing with a particular topic or issue. Organizational brochures often focus on recruiting, product/service lines, membership services, organizational history or some other aspect of a particular organization. Advocacy brochures attempt to educate or generate support on a particular issue important to the sponsoring organization. Additionally, some brochures are action-oriented publications with a definite sales pitch, though these are more likely to be associated with marketing efforts than with public relations activities.

A **flier** is similar to a brochure in that it is a stand-alone piece. Whereas a brochure is meant to be read in panels, a flier is meant to be read as a single unit.

Note that brochure and flier are commonly accepted terms for stand-alone organizational publications, but other names also may be used. Some names deal with the size of the publication. In addition to fliers, other terms for single-sheet publications include leaflets or folders. Alternative terms for brochures are pamphlets or booklets. Other name distinctions grow out of the purpose of the publication. Persuasive brochures called tracts deal with political or religious topics, and marketing-oriented stand-alone publications are often called circulars.

Phase Three

STEP
7

A **fact sheet** that presents information in bullet form is another common stand-alone piece, as is an **FAQ**, a presentation of frequently asked questions about a particular issue or organization.

REPRINT

Copies of published articles about an organization or an issue significant to it can be useful in meeting public relations objectives. Reprints are articles previously published in newspapers, magazines or newsletters. By issuing a reprint, the organization is able to extend the reach and impact of the original publication, particularly by giving it to the organization's publics, who may not have had access to the original article.

Fair-use provisions in copyright law allow an organization to circulate a limited number of copies of a published article for educational, research or news purposes. Note that in 1991 a federal court ruled in the case of *Basic Books Inc. v. Kinko's Graphics Corp.* that it is illegal to photocopy published materials even for educational purposes except for brief passages. Informally, a passage of about 300 consecutive words is considered the maximum length that can be used without permission. This is not fixed and may be less for smaller works.

Make sure to obtain permission from the original publisher before disseminating a reprinted article or photograph to a wide group for promotional purposes. This may involve a fee, and the permission granted is generally for one-time use only.

A similar tactic is to reprint speeches, especially formal presentations such as keynote addresses or testimony before state, provincial or federal legislative bodies. These often are shared with key publics, such as boards of directors, major donors or stockholders, community and civic leaders, and other opinion leaders.

Related to reprints is the distribution of news releases to internal audiences. News releases will be discussed more in the section News Media Tactics later in this chapter. While releases are meant primarily for distribution to journalists, some public relations practitioners also selectively send them to key internal publics, such as senior executives, major donors and stockholders.

PROGRESS REPORT

Several different types of progress reports focus on the continuing development of an organization, particularly its activity within a recent period of time.

The **annual report** is a special kind of progress report. Annual reports are required by the federal Securities and Exchange Commission (SEC) for American companies that issue stock. These can be simple statements with required information, such as the identification of corporate officials, the salaries and benefits of the top executives, financial statements and the auditor's certification of accuracy. Often, however, they feature much more. Many annual reports are glossy, magazine-like publications designed not only to provide required information but also to affirm investors' loyalty to the company, attract new investors, and enhance the company's reputation with financial analysts and the financial media.

Some companies also produce **quarterly reports**, though these are not required by the SEC. Quarterly reports usually are not as elaborate as annual reports.

Though nonprofit organizations and private (non-stock issuing) companies are not required to issue annual reports, many do so. These often provide financial and organizational information of interest to donors and other supporters. Businesses often find that annual and quarterly reports are convenient vehicles for attracting new customers by demonstrating the work they have previously done.

USER KIT

Another common print tactic, generically called a **user kit** or **consumer kit**, is associated with the people who use a product or service. These kits or manuals often include background and how-to information as well as implementation ideas. For example, teacher kits provide a variety of information and materials that can be used in the classroom. These often include sample lesson plans, suggestions for activities, posters, student handouts and even test items. To produce these, the public relations person will often team up with teachers so the information is most useful to the intended public.

RESEARCH REPORT

Sometimes, when organizations conduct or sponsor formal research on an issue related to their interests, they consider the information to be proprietary—that is, private and confidential. After all, they paid for the research and they may not want to share it with competitors.

Other times, however, they may choose to share the research findings. Many organizations are engaged in medical, social or educational research, and their mission is to create knowledge and share it with others.

In issuing a research report, organizations have an ethical requirement to be clear as to their involvement in the research study. The report should include background information, a description of the research methods and how any samples were drawn, presentation and analysis of the research findings, and a discussion of the significance of the findings. Some reports also include recommendations based on the findings. The report may be distributed like other organizational media—to organizational managers, employees, stockholders or donors, regulators, and others.

The report also may be shared with the news media. It is never a good idea to conduct research simply so it can be used for publicity. That would be more like a publicity stunt, and it raises ethical questions about the appropriate use of research and thus about the organization's professionalism. But if the organization believes that a legitimate research report contains some newsworthy information, it may decide to publicize its findings. Often this involves providing reporters with the research report as well as a news release.

In the release, emphasize the validity and objectivity of the study while acknowledging the organization's involvement. Don't use the organization's name too many times in the release.

MISCELLANEOUS PRINT MEDIA

A whole range of other tactics offer several opportunities for the public relations planner. Consider the following tactics.

Posters are visual materials, often approximately three by five feet in size, that can be displayed prominently. Companies often use window displays to give visibility to their products or services; nonprofit organizations sometimes use commercial storefront space made available to them, often when there is a temporary vacancy in a store in a mall or on a downtown street.

Employees and customers alike can benefit from well-maintained bulletin boards, and suggestion boxes are excellent opportunities for organizations to solicit feedback and input

Phase Three

STEP
7

from their publics. Other traditional tactics that still have value are pay stuffers or bill inserts, which are messages placed within pay envelopes or bills, respectively. Door hangers that advocate a cause or promote a product or service also can be useful.

Business cards remain another effective tactic for organizations to keep their names before potential customers and associates.

Some miscellaneous tactics involve recognition programs. For example, certificates are used to acknowledge achievement or participation. Formal proclamations are issued by governmental and sometimes by organizational leaders to draw public attention to a particular cause or theme.

Direct Mail

Direct mail is a category of organizational print media that, though perhaps general in nature, can be addressed to individual recipients. Direct mail pieces can include memos, letters, postcards, invitations and catalogs.

LETTER

In the category of direct mail, the most common vehicle is the business letter, which generally is a form letter addressed to individuals. Often these will carry the actual name of the reader, such as "Dear Mary Jones" or "Dear Ms. Jones." Sometimes for very large mailings the letters will be addressed more generically, such as "Dear Friend of the Environment" or "Dear Fellow Stamp Collector."

Appeal letters are direct-mail pieces sent to potential donors by nonprofit organizations engaged in fund-raising campaigns. Marketing letters are direct-mail pieces sent by businesses for advertising purposes.

With both types of these direct-mail letters, response rates generally are very low, often less than 1 percent. But the response rate increases considerably when the letters are sent to people who in the past have made contributions or have done business with the sending organization. The best advice regarding direct mail, as with every other form of public relations or marketing communication, is to target the mail to each public and address the reader's self-interest.

Direct-mail packages generally contain more than a marketing or appeal letter. They often also include a brochure about the company or organization, a response device such as a donor card or order form, and a return device such as a payment envelope, usually with return-postage paid.

MEMO

A memorandum or **memo** is a brief written message addressed to an individual or to a group of people. Memos generally are internal messages; when issued externally, they usually are directed to persons known to the sender.

Memos begin with a format that clearly identifies the sender, recipient, date and subject. In writing style, memos are informal, crisp and usually action-oriented. Memos can be a good public relations vehicle for communicating with colleagues, media gatekeepers or members of key publics, such as when you attach a memo to a reprint you are sending to a major benefactor or stockholder.

POSTCARD

Similar to letters, postcards generally are addressed to individuals, usually by name. Postcards, which include brief messages, are not placed in envelopes, and thus their content should never be of a personal or confidential nature.

Postcards often are used as announcements or reminders, and they often complement messages presented through news or advertising media. In some cases, postcards may replace other such tactics, especially when it is possible to obtain a mailing list of members of the key public. Organizations sometimes use postcards to drive traffic to their websites.

INVITATION

Organizations that sponsor events, whether public or private, often send formal, personalized invitations to prospective participants.

CATALOG

Catalogs are books or brochures aimed at consumer publics, generally with an inventory of items available for purchase, though nonprofit organizations can use the catalog approach to list available services or programs.

Several types of catalogs can be developed. Retail catalogs, with merchandise available in the sponsors' stores, seek to generate in-store consumer traffic. Full-line catalogs feature the entire range of items in a department store. Specialty or boutique catalogs feature products of very narrow consumer interest, such as a catalog of weaving supplies. Business-to-business catalogs contain information on products of specific interest to businesses.

In recent years, some companies have developed catalogs along the lines of lifestyle-oriented magazines, turning a traditional marketing tool into a public relations vehicle. For example, the Patagonia Company (patagonia.com) enhances its clothing catalog with pictures by award-winning outdoor photographers, commentaries on the environment and field reports about outdoor activities around the world.

Abercrombie & Fitch (abercrombie.com) sparked calls for a boycott of the clothing store over what critics called racy photos and soft porn in its catalog. The company defended its quarterly publication as being not only a sales tool but also a magazine aimed at the college market.

Electronic Media

Technology has added new choices to the menu of tactics that can be used for public relations and marketing communication. Most of these electronic technologies in some way enhance the audio and/or visual aspects of communication. Specifically, this category includes audio media and video media, as well as electronic publishing.

AUDIO MEDIA

An expanding inventory of audio media is available to public relations planners. Telephone media involve new opportunities for information on demand, such as dial-a-message tactics that allow people to obtain information on topics such as weather or sports scores or to access self-help information and advice on a variety of categories. Dial-a-message services also offer prayers, jokes, and so on.

Phase Three

STEP
7

Technology makes it possible to disseminate recorded messages to thousands of phone users. Such automated calls can be used for telemarketing and for public education campaigns and other public service programs. They are most commonly associated with political candidates and partisan groups around election time. In that context, such **robocalls** (so named because the call comes from robots, automated telephone calls) are particularly controversial.

The benefits? They are inexpensive and fast—as many as a million calls within a half hour. The disadvantages? First, there is little evidence to suggest such calls are effective. Second, they evoke a negative response, from mild annoyance to anger. Studies show that the more such calls are made during a political campaign, the less effective they are. Only 31 percent listen to robocalls, according to a 2010 report by the Pew Research Center for the People and the Press (people-press.org). This compares to 73 percent of people who listen to phone calls from a person. But the high hang-up rate for robocalls is offset by the reach to wide numbers of people.

The Federal Communication Commission prohibits telemarketers from using robocalls to cell phones, but political groups and some other charitable nonprofit organizations are exempt from that exclusion. Additionally, the FCC allows informational calls such as a school district might make to parents to announce a delay in school opening. Thus such calls can play a role in an organization's public relations program and for emergency public announcements.

Telephone media also can involve the use of recorded information or persuasive messages to help people wile away the time spent waiting on a telephone. Some organizations add a public relations dimension to their voicemail, such as a community college or car dealership whose president has recorded a brief welcome message as part of the routing of all incoming phone calls.

Organizations make frequent use of toll-free lines that give customers and other publics free telephone access to the organization; similar 900 lines, in which callers are charged for the phone call, can generate income for organizations. Some organizations also have found that demo tapes or demo CDs can be useful audio tools.

A **podcast** (a portmanteau for *iPod* and *broadcast*) essentially is an Internet-based audio feed that allow users to listen to postings. They have many public relations uses. Consider the following: a destination guide by a hotel or travel agency; reviews by a restaurant or wine store; orientation information by a university; interview or speech by a political candidate; financial advice by an investment company; author interview by a publishing company; or actor interviews by a movie studio.

Many universities podcast guest lectures or interviews with faculty experts. Police departments, museums, churches and advocacy groups use podcasts to present their messages to interested audiences. Many public relations agencies now include podcasts and other social media among the professional services they offer.

Sirius radio added a new dimension to audio tactics with its Town Hall series of interviews. The satellite radio network arranged exclusive interviews with high-profile guests, including entertainers such as Ringo Starr and Gregg Allman, musical groups Nirvana and Coldplay, and newsworthy individuals including Cardinal Timothy Dolan of the New York City Catholic archdiocese and Duke University basketball coach Mike Krzyzewski. The studio interviews involve a host and moderator; in a unique twist, they also include several Sirius subscribers selected on the basis of pre-submitted questions for the interview guest.

VIDEO MEDIA

Various types of video media offer opportunities in nonbroadcast video that use television technology to produce programs that are then disseminated through organizational rather than public channels. For example, organizations may use **nonbroadcast video** in conjunction with a stockholders' meeting, fundraising event, open house or some other type of interpersonal tactic. Businesses use nonbroadcast video (also called **corporate video** and **internal video**) for training, employee information, product information for customers, annual meetings and internal marketing.

A particular use of nonbroadcast video is as direct-mail video to promote products or causes. *Advertising Age* reported the effectiveness of direct-mail video (Kim, 1995). In one case, 94 percent of people viewed the video they received from a gubernatorial candidate in New Jersey. In another study, a direct-mail video that inaugurated a campaign to encourage landowners in the Connecticut River Tidelands region to develop long-term conservation plans was evaluated as being both educational and persuasive, with increases in six key indicators of environmental behavior (Tyson and Snyder, 1999).

Nonbroadcast video sometimes occurs live—as in **videoconferences**, also called **teleconferences**. Videoconferences use television technology to produce live informational or educational programs for remote audiences. These events are made interactive through the use of satellite or fiber-optic video transmission, sometimes with long-distance telephone connections to link the remote sites to the originating studio.

Some organizations use DVDs as vehicles for presenting information to donors and stockholders as well as potential customers. Such video also can be useful for employee training. Increasingly, organizations are turning to the Internet to post their nonbroadcast video products. This **web video** or **streaming video** is a common feature on multipurpose cell phones that provide not only voice transmission but also text messaging, Internet access and a range of video options.

Presentation software such as Microsoft PowerPoint, Apple Keynote, Flash, Prezi, SlideRocket and Google Docs provide a platform for informational or educational presentations. New technology enhances this tactic by making possible interactive multiple-slide presentations.

ELECTRONIC PUBLISHING

Another category of electronic media involves electronic publishing. Public relations departments can publish brochures and position papers, newsletters, even books and magazines, using their own in-house computers and printers rather than having to rely on outside printing companies.

Digital Media

This brings us to the growing field of computer-based **digital media**, which provides even newer strategic communication opportunities.

E-MAIL

A mushrooming group of these tactics is associated with e-mail. The benefits of instantaneous communication unbounded by distance are obvious to public relations and marketing practitioners. Organizations use e-mail as the platform for preparing and disseminating

Phase Three

STEP
7

newsletters, fundraising appeals, news releases, and for notifying journalists, donors and other key publics of new information posted as organizational blogs or websites.

ONLINE PUBLICATION

Just about any tactic identified previously in this section on organization media can be packaged and disseminated not only in printed form but also digitally. Brochures, annual reports, FAQs, consumer kits and catalogs can serve an organization well when they are available online.

Some organizations, for example, have replaced printed newsletters entirely with online versions. One benefit of online newsletters is that they can be archived so readers can peruse past issues. Another benefit is that online newsletters can be evolutionary, with new daily or weekly postings as newsworthy information becomes available. Public relations practitioners often herald newsletters or updates with e-mail alerts to potential readers. But be aware that inbox congestion is a growing concern; it's best to direct online newsletters only to those readers who have signed up to receive them.

Good practice, however, calls for modifying online publications to take advantage of the many opportunities for linking documents and allowing users to browse in an information-on-demand environment. The alternative to this is called **shovelware**, a poorly thought-out technique of merely dumping a printed publication into an online format without modifying it to maximize the potential of the online milieu.

Technology also is translating many elements of audio and video media into digital. Video is usually recorded digitally rather than onto videocassettes, and editing is now done digitally. Video footage is stored and transmitted using computer technology.

MOBILE DEVICE

Smart phones are another form of digital media increasingly being used for public relations and marketing purposes. These offer more than telephone service. They are cameras and camcorders. They link wirelessly with computers. They are used for texting, Internet browsing, music playback, games, radio reception, recording, video calling, and downloading for audio and video streaming. They also have calendars, clocks and calculators among a rapidly expanding list of features and applications.

Meanwhile, other mobile devices, particularly electronic tablets, extend the portability of digital media. These wireless mobile computers have remote or on-screen virtual keyboards or digital pens to digitize handwriting. They also have thousands of apps with many positive implications for public relations: banking services, voting, ticket purchases, order-tracking, maps and scanner readers. Some apps write news releases or pitch letters from information you submit.

Electronic publishing also has digital benefits to public relations practitioners. Some hardware and/or software can translate printed books into electronic formats. Some can actually translate from one language to another, or convert text into audio books.

WEBSITE

The Internet has made it possible for every organization and individual to have a **website**, a series of interconnected web pages, usually prepared and maintained as a collection of information by a person, group or organization. Corporations and colleges, social advocates and political groups, cultural and arts organizations all use websites to communicate with people who are actively seeking their information.

The implication for public relations is enormous. For example, as the Makah people were planning to revive a dormant practice of hunting whales in the Pacific Northwest, the American Indian tribe used a website (makah.org) to provide a detailed question-and-answer page about its controversial plan. Animal rights protestors retaliated with a counterfeit rogue site (makah.com) that mocked the tribal site. (The tribe has since obtained rights to the dot-com site.)

When he was campaigning to be elected president, Barack Obama established a website specifically to counter personal and political rumors and viral attacks. Websites also give organizations access to online tactics associated with news media and promotional/advertising media. These will be discussed in subsequent sections of this chapter.

Additionally, touch-sensitive computers make it possible to apply an information-on-demand approach to several situations in which customers can use the computer to interact with the organization, both gaining and giving information.

Internet users distinguish between **Web 1.0**, which essentially was a one-way posting of commercial or promotional information by an organization, and **Web 2.0**, which involves using the Internet for interactivity, collaboration and communication. Web 2.0 allows users to share postings and generate content for the website. Blogs, wikis, mashups and other examples of social media are outgrowths of Web 2.0.

Social Media

The still-emerging phenomenon of social media provides various types of interactive media in which the audience is an active participant in the development and presentation of the messages.

Some politicians have as many Facebook friends and Twitter followers as athletes and rock stars. Even the Pope uses Twitter to preach Lenten retreats, turning to his Facebook and YouTube accounts when his message is longer than 140 characters.

But the number of the Pope's Twitter followers pales in comparison to the top tweeters. A report in 2012 showed Lady Gaga leading the pack with 20 million Twitter followers, with close follow-ups by Justin Bieber, Katy Perry, Shakira and Rihanna. With 13 million followers, Barack Obama was the most popular non-celebrity tweeter. A 2011 study reported that every U.S. cabinet agency tweets, as well as 84 percent of state governors, 40 percent of global religious leaders, 99 percent of American's top 200 nonprofit organizations, 87 percent of Billboard's top 100 musicians.

Corporations likewise use social media. The Socialware company reported in 2011 that 79 percent of Fortune 500 firms use Twitter, YouTube, Facebook or blogs to communicate with customers and other stakeholders. When it had to recall 2.3 million cars in 2010 because of faulty accelerator pedals, Toyota used social media to answer questions from customers.

Nonprofit organizations also make extensive use of social media. In 2010, the Nonprofit Social Networking Report found that 86 percent of nonprofit organizations use Facebook. The following year, a report by the University of Massachusetts upped that to 97 percent for all types of social media, concluding that nonprofits use Facebook, Twitter, LinkedIn and YouTube even more than businesses do. Among the nonprofits, international groups lead the way, followed by environmental groups, with arts and cultural organizations coming in a close third.

A 2011 study by the University of Massachusetts Dartmouth found that 7 of the 10 fastest-growing private companies increased using social media—70 percent increase for Facebook, 59 percent for Twitter and 50 percent for customer blogs. Henry Ford Hospital in Detroit, for example, tweeted live from an operating room about the progress of a kidney surgery. This was a good marketing tactic as well as a public relations activity that educated people about the treatment of kidney disease.

Meanwhile, 77 percent of all Fortune Global 500 companies had a Twitter account in 2011, according to the Realtime Report on business and social media. Additionally, 61 percent had a Facebook page, 57 percent used YouTube, and 36 percent had a corporate blog.

The military and the government also use Facebook, Twitter, blogs and other social media. The Navy used a social media mix in 2011 to commemorate the anniversary of the attack on Pearl Harbor. The White House used social media to debunk myths about healthcare reform and to orchestrate a worldwide audience to announce the killing of Osama bin Laden. FEMA gives disaster guidance on Twitter.

Social media can come in handy during emergencies. Both FEMA and New York City used Twitter to present urgent information during Hurricane Irene. Philadelphia set up a network involving Facebook, LinkedIn, MySpace, Twitter, Blogspot and YouTube to release emergency information. Smaller communities such as Evanston, Ill., and Moorhead, Minn., use Facebook, Twitter and blogs to communicate information on natural disasters and public health advisories.

Anybody paying attention to world affairs knows that the grass-roots revolutions in Egypt and Tunisia in 2011 were successful in large part because of social media. The previous year's uprising in Iran also was fueled by social media, as were groups advocating for social or political change in Colombia and Libya.

How does all this use of social media help public relations? Obviously, it enhances our toolbox with a powerful and wide-reaching new family of media. For another, it enhances credibility. A 2007 Nielsen Report found that only 55 percent of Americans trust advertising, but 78 percent trust recommendations on social media by other consumers.

WIKI

As a collaborative community website, a **wiki** allows any user to edit the content of the website by adding material, modifying it, even deleting it if they wish. One of the most-used wikis is Wikipedia. Some companies and organizations use wikis as an active substitute for the more static Intranet that users cannot edit.

Some wikis draw on popular culture, such as a wiki about television series such as *Dexter* (dexter.wikia.com) and *The Vampire Diaries* (www.vampirediaries.wikia.com). There's also a Muppet Wiki for *The Muppet Show* (muppet.wikia.com) and for *Call of Duty: Modern Warfare 2* video game (callofduty.wikia.com).

For six weeks in 2007, more than 1,500 anonymous writers around the world participated in writing an online novel, *A Million Penguins*, but critics said the resulting wikinovel was a confusing and unstructured verification of the too-many-cooks-in-the-kitchen adage.

One problem with wikis is online vandalism in which users add false information, thus calling into question the credibility of all wiki information and fueling the criticism that wikis by nature favor consensus over credentials. Many college professors, for example, ban material from Wikipedia from being cited in academic research papers.

What are the implications for public relations practitioners? For one thing, don't be surprised to see information about your company or organization at a wiki site. Realize, however, that the rules of engagement on public relations use of social media are still evolving. Wikipedia, for example, allows anyone except public relations people to edit postings. Company policy specifically bans public relations practitioners from modifying entries on behalf of their organizations or clients. Instead, founder Jimmy Wales has said that public relations practitioners may merely post comments in the discussion section of the entry. Regardless of any such internal controls, the PRSA Code of Ethics (see Appendix B: Ethical Standards) calls for public relations practitioners to disclose any financial or other connections to subjects they write about.

A 2008 study published in **Public Relations Review** reported that 18 percent of public relations practitioners use wikis. It also found that 41 percent use blogs and 24 percent use social networking sites (the next two items in this inventory of social media vehicles).

BLOG

Another type of social media is the **blog** (a portmanteau for *web log*). This is an open-to-all website maintained usually by an individual. Blogs feature postings of commentary, news, photos and graphics, and links to other blogs or sites. Users are invited to react with additional questions, comments and responses. Blogs generally focus on a particular topic, and the topics run the gamut: politics, travel, ethics, business, religion, environment, education, lifestyle, art, sports, and the like.

Blogs also commonly feature external links with social media used by the author or organization, such as a company Facebook site or an organization's YouTube page.

Adaptations of blogs include art blogs or photoblogs with their unique and obvious emphasis. Some specialty blogs even have their own names: **vlog** (a blog that contain primarily videos), **MP3 blog** (music) and *moblog* (written on mobile device such as a cell phone).

Like blogs themselves, bloggers are a diverse group. Blogging is done by singers and athletes, senators and CEOs. Newspapers and television news stations have their own blogs in which reporters interact with audience members, and audience members with each other.

Blogs also are merging with more traditional forms of news media. Some bloggers consider themselves journalists, and some have broken stories that later are taken up by mainstream newspapers and television. In other situations, journalists publish their own blogs to provide additional commentary and insight into the stories they are reporting.

Blogs also are gaining influence in the political arena. Political blogs such as the *Daily Kos*, *Politico*, *Huffington Post*, *Drudge Report* and *Salon* are hugely influential in American politics. Sometimes, blogs beat the mainstream media in reporting news.

Bloggers also create third-party endorsement, those independent and influential voices that have the ear of an organization's publics. Because of their independence, they also have potential high credibility. That's why Wal-Mart enlisted bloggers in its campaign to counter media-reported criticism of its efforts to open new stores against rising consumer opposition. That's also why companies such as Cingular Wireless, Microsoft and General Electric have met with bloggers before going public with new products.

The rules about blogging vis-à-vis public relations are still emerging. Blog readers expect to find only firsthand accounts posted online, and most bloggers resent blatant public relations use of their medium.

Phase Three

STEP
7

Standard public relations practice involves providing advice and assistance on getting the message out. A political or business executive may hire a ghostwriter to help with an op-ed piece or magazine article, and consultants often draft speeches and public statements. But many people feel that **ghost blogging** in someone else's name crosses the ethical line. The key seems to be the extent to which the blog is presented as being personal rather than corporate, and the amount to involvement that the named author of the blog has in the piece. The ultimate test is whether readers feel betrayed if they find out that someone ghosted the blog.

In a similar situation, some bloggers have lost credibility for themselves by willingly publishing verbatim "plants" from government or corporate sources without identifying them as handouts.

Blogs generally are search-engine friendly, and with now more than 57 million blogs (and the number doubling every five or six months) it's not surprising that many organizations

BLOGGER RELATIONS

Steve Rubel of Edelman Public Relations recommends that public relations practitioners should focus on how they can help bloggers rather than how bloggers can help the practitioners' clients or organizations. Practitioners are accepting social media, but not necessarily embracing it, he comments.

In a Marketing Voices podcast posted at www.podtech.net, Rubel advocates a strategy of blending both traditional media and bloggers in an effort to extend the reach and impact of an organization's message.

The NewPR/Wiki website (thenewpr.com/wiki/pmwiki.php) lists corporate and organizational blogs, as well as tips on developing **blogger relations** (a new form of public relations focused on the key public of bloggers). The site includes information pieces such as "Top Ten Things You Can Do to Get Blogged" and "7 Habits of Highly Effective Blog PR."

Many bloggers see themselves involved in **participatory journalism**, a phenomenon also known as **citizen journalism** or **grassroots journalism**.

The principle at work here is that such bloggers self-identify as playing an active role in gathering, reporting and commenting on news. A few news bloggers have a growing credibility with mainstream news media, in part because, as mavericks who are not constrained by some of the corporate or ethical boundaries of professional journalists, they have occasionally broken important news stories. But some bloggers are seen merely as digital hacks unrestrained by ethical or other journalistic standards.

The 2011 State of the News Media report by the Project for Excellence in Journalism, which is affiliated with the Columbia University Graduate School of Journalism, found that only a few bloggers report original news research. Most blogs play the role of an alert system, repeating news from more standard journalistic sources.

Nevertheless, bloggers are making their presence felt. It was bloggers who fueled the debunking of military documents that newscaster Dan Rather and CBS News used in questioning President George W. Bush's military service. In 2007, the Associated Press partnered with the Media Bloggers Association to carry blog-generated news reports in its coverage of I. Lewis "Scooter" Libby's trial for outing CIA agent Valerie Plame for political purposes on behalf of the White House.

are eyeing the use of blogs to promote their products, services and causes. Some organizations even have people assigned to the post of **blogger relations**.

Many people in public relations and marketing communications make it part of their daily research to monitor blogs dealing with topics of interest to their organizations or clients. Blogs can provide a look at the competition and an insight into the interests of customers, donors, fans and other publics. As an advance glimpse into what could grow into widespread public opinion, they also provide an early warning system into potential problems with your own organization.

How should you pitch a story to bloggers? Alice Marshall of Presto Vivace Communications in Fairfax, Virginia, reminds people attending her workshops that, unlike reporters who work for editors, bloggers work for themselves (or, figuratively, for their audiences). She offers the following tips to pitching to bloggers ("Rules of Engagement," 2005).

1. Remember that it's a conversation, not a confrontation. Reader feedback is a highly prized premium.
2. Introduce yourself to lower-profile bloggers, the people who have links with the top bloggers in your field. A posting there often may attract attention up the line.
3. Be familiar with the blog, and make sure that your topic is appropriate to the audience.
4. Be up front about who you are, and don't hide behind a false identity. Let readers know that you are a public relations person with a vested interest in the conversation.
5. Remember that bloggers are much more likely than journalists to pounce on poorly written or overly pushy news releases, and they may use their blog to rant against you and your organization or client.
6. Try to be known within your organization for your work in blog relations.

SOCIAL NETWORKING

In general, **social networking** refers to an online service aimed at building and reflecting a relationship among people who share common interests. About 47 percent of American adults use at least one social network.

Posted information, responses, photos and videos are common elements of social network sites such as Facebook (with more than 800 million registered users), Twitter (175 million) and LinkedIn (120 million). It also includes sites for sharing photos and video, such as Flickr (32 million) and YouTube (which does not require users to be registered in order to watch videos).

Some social networking sites are specialized for particular audiences: ethnic-oriented sites such as BlackPlanet for African Americans and MiGente for the Hispanic community; religion-focused sites such as Muxlim for young Muslims and Xt3 for young Catholics; and nationally oriented sites such as LunarStorm for Swedish teens and Chirundu, which bills itself as "the place for homesick Africans." Other sites are focused around particular interests such as CafeMom for mothers and Disaboom for people with disabilities, or around occupations, such as Labroots for scientists and TeachStreet for teachers.

With such widespread presence, it's not surprising that corporations and organizations are finding social media useful. Politicians in particular have made social media a staple of their communication programs.

Barack Obama announced his 2012 re-election campaign with a digital video e-mailed to 13 million online supporters. Mitt Romney tweeted the start of his campaign. Candidates attack each other not only in traditional television ads and during televised debates, but also through tweets and video posted at Vimeo and YouTube.

Politicians, as well as their supporters and opponents, use Twitter, Facebook and other social media to announce, comment, criticize, berate and otherwise communicate on every political topic imaginable. They try to turn their virtual friends into real, live voters. They also use social media to raise money, as Congressman Ron Paul did successfully when his online "money bomb" raised $2.75 million in two days, an impressive sum that nevertheless paled in comparison with the $10 million that Obama raised online in one 24-hour blitz.

The strategy of political candidates is not simply to use social media to issue pronouncements but rather to engage supporters, encourage them to share Facebook and tweets with others, register their "likes," and to re-tweet and re-blog their messages.

VIRAL PHILANTHROPY

The global relief agency Oxfam had no advertising budget for its program to raise $35 million to address the famine in East Africa. So Oxfam turned to YouTube and Facebook. The agency parlayed the donation of a dress worn to the Academy Awards by Jennifer Anniston into a 9-day eBay auction that raised $50,000 — enough to immunize 50,000 children in Africa.

More important for Oxfam's long-term visibility with a new and younger audience, the auction attracted 2,500 online observers for the final bidding.

The Oxfam project is one example of nonprofit organizations using social media to raise awareness of a social issue and to raise funds to address the problem. It's called **viral philanthropy**, an emerging aspect of fundraising in which many people are asked to give a little bit to the cause and encourage their friends to do likewise.

With little or no advertising budget, viral philanthropy turns its attention to social media such as bloggers and social networking media such as MySpace and Facebook, which have embraced the concept of charitable giving among participants. Facebook Causes, for example, claims to have raised money for about 20,000 different charities. MySpace's Impact has similar claims of success in online philanthropy among young people.

The Anniston gift to Oxfam was part of a campaign by the Clothes Off Our Back celebrity auction program founded by husband-and-wife actors Bradley Whitford and Jane Kaczmarek. The foundation has raised more than $4 million in 10 years. Meanwhile, Keira Knightley gave the gown she wore in the movie *Atonement*. That dress was auctioned on eBay for the benefit of the Children's Charity of Southern California. From an opening bid of $1,000, bidding reached $46,000.

Other organizations have turned to social networking media to support humanitarian causes. Following the Asian tsunami in 2004, the Yarn Harlot, a blog about knitting, asked readers to give $1 each to Doctors Without Borders, an international medical aid agency. The project, called Knitters Without Borders, raised more than $435,000 in two years and continues to receive donations for the medical charity.

Meanwhile, People for the Ethical Treatment of Animals created a MySpace profile and recruited 120,000 new supporters interested in animal rights.

Nonprofit organizations also use social media to increase membership and to raise funds. Facebook Causes, a site for Facebook members to promote or even create a cause, claims to have raised more than $40 million for everything from educating girls in Africa and fighting anti-Semitism to opposing bullying and supporting arts in public schools. Other social networking sites for similar philanthropy include Razoo and Twitpay.

YouTube began as a video sharing website, and Flickr as a photograph sharing site. Public relations practitioners have found use for both. Companies post job openings and marketing materials, news clips and product how-tos. Some postings using video news clips and clips from films have raised copyright concerns on the part of mainstream news and entertainment media.

The Associate Press and Reuters news agencies are posting videos to YouTube, and other businesses and organizations are using the various video media to strategically present their messages to younger audiences.

A study by the Pew Research Center for the People and the Press reported in 2011 that 65 percent of Americans who use the Internet are on social networking sites, with the greatest growth among people 50–64 (32 percent of boomers, compared with 20 percent the previous year).

Meanwhile, the growing availability of user-generated *viral video* is playing an increasing role in strategic communication efforts. The term refers to the widespread dissemination and popularity of a video clip, generally circulated via e-mail or text messaging and posted on Internet blogs or other websites.

Some viral videos were originally caught on cell phones: a Texas judge beating his disabled daughter, Ryan Gosling's street fight, Michael Richard's racist rant. Others are news clips that take on a life of their own: police in California using pepper spray on already subdued student protestors and Mitt Romney's famous 47 percent remark.

Viral video has played a notable role in marketing of bands and movies. Super Bowl ads often get similar attention, as do celebrity shenanigans involving people such as Charlie Sheen and Lindsey Lohan.

PLANNING EXAMPLE 7B **Selecting Organizational Media Tactics**

Upstate College will develop the following tactics using organizational media to publicize its expanded program:

- virtual college tour—key publics, high visual impact;
- online transfer brochure—key publics, high impact, low cost;
- letter to former applicants—targeted, low cost;
- poster—moderate cost, high visual impact;
- video—targeting key publics, high cost;
- home page at upstatecoll.edu—information-seeking publics, low cost, for potential transfer students, interactive.

UPSTATE COLLEGE

STEP
7

Phase Three

Tiny Tykes will develop the following tactics using organizational media for an employee-oriented public relations program:

- newsletter articles in employee publication about safety, quality and customer satisfaction—key public, low cost;
- memo about product reintroduction—key public, low cost;
- employee bulletin with updates on customer response to product reintroduction (pro and con)—key public, low cost;
- brochures about safety, quality and customer satisfaction—moderate cost;
- letter to families of employees thanking them for supporting employees and company during difficult reintroduction period—key public, low cost;
- suggestion box soliciting employee input about safety and quality, with feedback via employee—key public, low cost;
- newsletter—low cost, interactive.

☑ *Checklist 7B* **Organizational Media Tactics**

Basic Questions

1. What organizational media tactics will you use?
2. How will these tactics help the organization achieve its objectives?
3. What resources will these tactics require?

Expanded Questions

A. SELECTION OF TACTICS

From the following categories of organizational media tactics, identify several that you would consider using:

Publications
- serial publications (newsletter, house organ, bulletin)
- stand-alone publications (brochure, leaflet, folder, pamphlet, booklet, tract, circular)
- reprints (internal news release)
- progress reports (annual report, quarterly report)
- user kits, teacher kits
- research reports
- miscellaneous print media.

Direct Mail
- memos
- letters (appeal letter, marketing letter, postcard, invitation, catalog)

- postcards
- invitations
- catalogs.

Electronic Media

- audio (telephone, dial-a-message, recorded information, demo tape, demo CD, podcast)
- video (nonbroadcast video, corporate video, internal video, video conference, teleconference, slide show)
- electronic publishing.

Digital Media

- e-mail
- listservs
- website
- cell phone.

Social Media

- wiki
- blog
- social networking.

B. STRATEGIC IMPLICATIONS

For each item identified, answer the following questions:
1. Will this tactic help the organization to interact with the appropriate public?
2. What level of impact will this tactic make on the key public?
3. Will this tactic advance the organization toward its awareness objectives?
4. Will this tactic advance the organization toward its acceptance objectives?
5. Will this tactic advance the organization toward its action objectives?
6. What is the main advantage to this tactic?
7. What advantages does this tactic offer that other tactics do not?
8. Are there any disadvantages with this tactic? If so, what are they?

C. IMPLEMENTATION ITEMS

For each item identified, answer the following questions:

1. How much will it cost to implement this tactic? Is the cost justified? Is the cost practical, based on the organization's resources?
2. How much staff time will it take to implement this tactic? Is the time practical, based on the organization's resources?
3. What skill level, equipment and expertise are needed to implement this tactic? Is the needed level available within the organization? Is it available from outside sources?

Phase Three

STEP
7

News Media Tactics

The **news media** are communication vehicles that exist primarily to present newsworthy information to various audiences. There is much diversity among news media. Consider the possibilities:

- print media, such as newspapers and magazines (both in traditional print style and/or in digital format);
- broadcast media, including radio and television;
- interactive news tactics, including interviews and conferences.

Though all of these media are focused on news, each provides a somewhat different opportunity for public relations and marketing communication.

Strategy for News Media

The news media offer public relations and marketing practitioners several benefits not usually associated with tactics in the other categories.

First, the news media generally reach large audiences—certainly larger than most audiences associated with interpersonal communication tactics, and usually larger than those for organizational media. News media audiences may encompass most residents of a particular community, most members of a certain profession, or most people who are seriously interested in a given topic. Thus, news media tactics can further an organization's pursuit of awareness objectives.

Second, the publicity that can be generated through these media is free. Unlike the built-in cost of organizational media and the high fees associated with advertising, no price tag is associated with publicity. Obviously the organization will have overhead costs, such as staff or agency/contractor time in researching and writing materials such as news releases, as well as the cost associated with printing and distributing such releases or producing electronic versions. But these are internal administrative costs and incidental expenses.

The news media are considered uncontrolled media, creating the environment for the third, and perhaps most important, benefit they offer: They can add credibility to an organization's message. They have the power of what's called **third-party endorsement**, meaning that someone outside the organization preparing the message—in this case, a reporter, editor or news director—is attesting to the significance and validity of the information being presented.

Unlike a newsletter, website or advertisement in which the organization can say pretty much anything it likes, the news media demand a certain level of accuracy and neutrality. Reporters can evaluate the accuracy of information presented and check the claims being made before the story is presented to readers, listeners or viewers. This added credibility can go a long way toward achieving the acceptance objectives of the organization.

Traditionally, this concept of third-party endorsement has given the news media high marks as credible disseminators of messages. However, some generational shifts are taking place that may mean significant changes in the future. A study by the Pew Research Center for the People and the Press in 2008 found that 59 percent of Americans younger than 30 get their news online. This ties with television, which also is the preferred news source for 59 percent of younger Americans and 70 percent of all. Newspapers are the main news source for only 29 percent of younger Americans and 35 percent of all.

STATE OF THE NEWS MEDIA

The Project for Excellence in Journalism is a nonpartisan project associated with the Pew Research Center, which has published several extensive audits on the state of the health and status of American news media, including its annual State of the News Media Report, which can be found at the project's website (stateofthenewsmedia.com). The 2011 report indicated findings for U.S. media such as these:

- *Daily newspapers in print.* Most of the largest newspapers lost circulation, but the loss was less than in previous years, and many newspapers report a growing audience. Overall, 37 percent of adults read newspapers on a regular basis, compared with 43 percent in 2006.
- *Daily newspapers online.* Online readership is growing. More than half of adult newspaper readers say they have increased their use of online newspapers.
- *Weekly newspapers.* Audiences also dropped for alternative weeklies to about 7.5 million.
- *Newsweeklies.* Circulation was flat, but niche publications found growing audiences; newsweeklies moved more toward digital outlets.
- *Internet news.* An integrated audience using both print and online news sources grew, with 34 percent of adults (68 million) using the Internet daily for news; 37 percent of adults (57 million) said they at least occasionally read blogs.
- *TV network news.* The audience is dropping about 1 million a year, but still 58 percent of adults say they watch TV news regularly. The credibility of network news fell from 31 percent to 22 percent over a 10-year period.
- *Cable news.* Audiences for cable news fell significantly. In measures of the number of different viewers each month, the major networks draw similar-sized audiences: 42 million CNN viewers, 41 million for Fox and 37 million for MSNBC.
- *Alternative cable news.* Program sources increased, but with limited audience access. For example, most North Americans could view Al Jazeera only over the Internet. Comedy Central's satirical *Daily Show with Jon Stewart* and *The Colbert Report* increased to 1.6 million and 1.2 million viewers, respectively.
- *Local TV news.* After years of decline, audiences for local television news held steady, and most stations added newscasts in new time slots. Increasing numbers of local news stations are providing information via smart phones and electronic tablets and pads.
- *Radio news.* Nine out of 10 adults (actually, 92 percent) listen to AM or FM radio each week, and audiences for radio news and talk remained steady.
- *Alternative audio.* New program sources proliferated, with podcasts, cell phone news and PDA news, but audiences were slow to adopt them. More than half of adults (52 percent) access online radio.
- *Ethnic media.* Audiences grew as the number of non-English speaking households increased, led by 1.9 million readers of Spanish-language daily newspapers and more than 11 million readers for Spanish weeklies. The audience is nearly 22 million weekly listeners for the 1,323 Spanish radio stations and 12 million weekly viewers of Spanish television. African American media mirrored general media, with decreasing audiences for newspapers and increasing online use.

Phase Three

STEP 7

There often is talk that the news media are dying. Not true. But they are changing. Young people in particular are accessing the news media in ways that are different from their parents. The Knight Foundation surveyed high school students in 2011. The study showed that, in a typical day, 77 percent of teens get their news from television, 54 percent by reading an article online, 48 percent by watching news video online and 42 percent by reading an article in a newspaper. Meanwhile, 56 percent say they use social networks for news and information each day, 33 percent use the Internet and 31 percent use mobile media.

Yet 88 percent of the high schoolers said newspapers are generally truthful, compared with 78 percent of television news and 58 percent of websites. Least truthful of all are social media at only 34 percent.

A Harris Poll the same year reported a low trust level for all media. Specifically, the poll found that 44 percent of adults tend to trust radio news (the rest tend not to trust or are unsure); 41 percent Internet news sources, 36 percent television and 30 percent the press. Among Republicans, trust in television and print news is well below the norm.

Another aspect of the strategy of communicating through the news media involves providing journalists with information in formats that they can use. Review Step 5 and make sure that you are offering real news.

Package news from your organization or client in a manner that journalists prefer. That means, for example, using Associated Press style guidelines for writing news releases and fact sheets. The Dallas chapter of the International Association of Business Communicators in 2006 reported the results of an online survey indicating that 88 percent of public relations communicators feel it is important to use AP style.

Another strategic concern is to understand how audiences use the news media and then to write accordingly. The news media carry the organization's message to people who are not actively seeking it. Readers and viewers intend to catch up on the day's events when they sit down in the evening with the newspaper or when they log on to an Internet news source, but they aren't especially looking for information about a particular organization. They more or less stumble over it and, if it seems to suit their interests and needs, they will read the information and perhaps act on it.

The lesson for public relations: Provide enough background and context so that audiences learning about your organization for the first time will have enough information to act on if they are so inclined.

Newspaper

Newspapers are publications that boast of up-to-date printed information—reports of what happened the previous day or even earlier on the same day of their distribution. They may be published daily or nondaily (usually weekly, some with more or less frequency).

A helpful tool for public relations practitioners is a **media directory**, which is a book or online resource providing information on media outlets. This includes names of editors, publication information, advertising rates and other helpful information. Media directories list more than 12,000 newspapers in the U.S. and Canada—1,556 daily newspapers with a total circulation of nearly 75 million. Advertising revenue for the 1,476 U.S. newspapers is nearly $50 billion a year.

Additionally, the U.S. and Canada count an estimated 900 Sunday papers, 700 bi- or tri-weekly, 8,000 weekly and 1,100 less often than weekly.

Circulation for some daily newspapers is high. In the US, the *Wall Street Journal*, *USA Today* and the *New York Times* are the three largest newspapers, circulating more than 1.7 million, 1.6 million and 1.1 million copies respectively. Internationally, the *Yomiuri Shimbun* in Tokyo circulates more than 14 million copies daily to a total reading audience of 26 million. The world's five largest newspapers are published in Japan, with the largest U.S. newspaper in twenty-third place.

At the other end of the spectrum, two-thirds of daily newspapers in North America circulate in towns and cities of fewer than 50,000 residents, *Editor & Publisher International Year Book* (2008). Many weekly newspapers circulate only a few hundred to a few thousand copies.

The number of newspapers has been declining in recent decades as the cost of publishing, corporate mergers and the pressures of competition have forced financially weaker publications out of business. Simultaneously, the newspaper audience is declining: audiences are getting older, and younger information consumers are more likely to get their news online or from radio or television than from newspapers. Nevertheless, most opinion leaders—business people, educators, politicians, clergy and others in positions of influence—are staunch newspaper readers, and many "average citizens" make newspaper reading a part of their daily information-gathering habit.

The Newspaper Association of America's audience profile (naa.org/Trends-and-Numbers.asp) reports the following profile of U.S. newspaper readers for 2011 for both print and online versions of daily newspapers: 48 percent male readers, 52 percent female; 71 percent age 35 or older, 32 percent age 55 or older; 89 percent white; 63 percent married; 51 percent income of $50,000 or more; 26 percent college graduate. This profile could affect the future practice of public relations, with low newspaper readership among growing demographic groups within the population, particularly youth and minorities.

Here is a look at several categories of newspapers.

GENERAL-INTEREST NEWSPAPER

A **general-interest newspaper** represents the most common types of newspapers, appealing to the diverse interests of a wide spectrum of readers. Most of these are local newspapers published for the residents of a particular town, city or metropolitan area.

General-interest newspapers cover topics such as current events, including crimes, accidents, births and deaths; political and business news; sports and entertainment reports and reviews; information about the arts and leisure pursuits such as cooking and gardening; announcements of upcoming meetings and activities; and specialized information relating to issues such as education and health. Most local newspapers also include opinion sections with editorials and letters from readers.

General-interest newspapers can be further divided into three major subcategories: national newspapers such as *USA Today,* city or metropolitan newspapers such as the *Atlanta Constitution*, and community newspapers such as the weekly *Idaho Enterprise* in rural Malad City, Idaho.

Phase Three

STEP
7

NEWS MEDIA TACTICS

Direct News Material

- news fact sheet
- event listing
- interview notes
- news release (announcement, response, hometowner, news brief)
- feature release (biography, history, backgrounder, question-and-answer piece, service article)
- actuality
- audio news release
- video B-roll
- video news release
- social media release
- media kit.

Indirect News Material

- media advisor
- story idea memo
- query letter.

Opinion Material

- position statement (position paper, white paper, position paragraph, contingency statement)
- letter to the editor
- guest editorial.

Interactive News Opportunities

- news interview
- news conference
- studio interview
- satellite media tour
- editorial conference.

For detailed instruction on writing for these various formats, see Smith (2012). Now in its 4th edition, *Becoming a Public Relations Writer* has been adopted by 138 colleges and universities and has been acquired by 557 academic universities throughout the world.

TRADE NEWSPAPER

Another type of publication, a **trade newspaper**, focuses on a particular industry or profession. Unlike organizational newspapers that are published by a particular company or nonprofit organization, trade newspapers are usually published by professional organizations or trade associations that serve the needs of several different companies and nonprofit groups linked to a particular industry or profession.

Some trade newspapers are independently published, such as *Overdrive,* a biweekly newspaper for truckers. Others are published by industry associations for people working in that field, such as *Carolina Cattle Connection,* the official newspaper for members of both the North Carolina and South Carolina Cattlemen's Associations.

SPECIAL-INTEREST NEWSPAPER

Special-interest newspapers are devoted to markets such as the arts, business, sports, entertainment or other specific sectors. Though the topic for each publication is narrow, information in such newspapers is intended for a wide audience. *The Hockey News* and *Indian Country Today* are examples of special-interest newspapers.

SPECIAL-AUDIENCE NEWSPAPER

A **special-audience newspaper** is similar to a special-interest newspaper, but written for particular audiences, such as gay and lesbian readers, the military, African Americans, and Jewish or Hispanic readers.

Media directories such as *Editor & Publisher International Year Book* and the *Gale Directory of Publications and Broadcast Media* report special-audience newspapers published for more than 40 ethnic, religious, national, cultural or other such groups. Information in these newspapers is often diverse, though the appeal is clearly linked to a specific audience. Often such newspapers are printed in languages other than English.

ORGANIZATIONAL NEWSPAPER

An **organizational newspaper**, also called a **house organ**, is published by a political, ethnic, religious, educational and other type of group. Information in them generally deals with those organizations and their members. *Public Relations Tactics*, published for members of the Public Relations Society of America, is an example of an organizational newspaper.

LEAD TIME

The amount of time it takes reporters and other media professionals to gather and present their news is called **lead time**. This varies with both the type of medium and the kind of presentation that will be given.

The best way to know the lead time required by various media is to ask. Contact the city editor of a newspaper, the news director or assignment editor of a radio or television station, or the acquisitions editor or news editor of a magazine. Or ask an individual reporter or columnist.

Here is an outline of typical lead times needed for various news media tactics:

Daily newspapers. Give about a week's notice for routine information, a day or several hours for important news, and less than an hour for major on-deadline news. Information for special sections such as travel, food and social events may have a longer lead time. News releases can be submitted at any time but Sunday and Monday often find less competition for space because weekends traditionally are slow news days, are lightly staffed by most newspapers and have more pages because of increased advertising.

Nondaily newspapers. Plan to provide information three publication dates before the relevant date of the information. For example, allow three weeks for a weekly newspaper, or a week and a half for a twice-weekly newspaper.

Magazines. Most monthly magazines require at least a two-month lead time for information to be published. Weekly news magazines have a much shorter lead time but seldom take information from public relations sources.

Radio. Give about a week's notice for routine information and for upcoming events that reporters might cover, with important news being handled up to news time. Breaking news may be covered live. Other live coverage may be planned with a lead time of a week or longer. Talk shows and other programs with guests may require several weeks to schedule.

Television. Provide up to a week's notice for routine information and for events that reporters might cover, with important news being handled up to news time. Breaking news may be covered live. Talk shows and programs with guests may require several weeks to schedule.

Phase Three

STEP
7

As a category, this sometimes overlaps special interest and special audience papers. For example, the *Navajo Times* is the official newspaper of the Navajo Nation that is primarily read—not surprisingly—by Navajos (special audience) and by others who are particularly interested in Native Americans in general or the Navajo people in particular (special interest).

Magazine

A **magazine** is a publication with less frequency and less immediacy than a newspaper. Prepublication time may be several days, even several weeks, from when a story is written until the time that magazine is distributed to readers. Some magazines are local or regional and thus focused on a particular geographic area, but most are of more general interest and their content is more feature-based than most newspapers.

Like newspapers, magazines based in the US and Canada are published in many different languages—about 50 in all. These include the three most common languages in North America—English, French and Spanish—as well as several Native American or Native Canadian languages, and also less-common languages such as Welsh, Urdu, Latin and Icelandic.

Writer's Market, a comprehensive listing of magazines published in North America, lists thousands of **popular magazines** (also called **consumer magazines**), the kind found on newsstands and through subscription services. These are published in several different categories: general circulation, college, health, foreign language, ethnic, music, men's interest, women's interest, sports, and so on.

Additionally, there are an untold number of house organs produced within a particular company or organization. These usually focus on organizational issues and are intended for employees, volunteers, stockholders, donors and other interested audiences. Examples of house organs are *Women Police,* a quarterly magazine published by the International Association of Women Police, and *Handball,* the official magazine of the U.S. Handball Association.

Sometimes the categories can overlap. Some magazines are published for special audiences, such as *Essence* for black women, *Seventeen* for teenage girls and *Sisters Today* for nuns. Meanwhile, trade magazines are published by and/or for particular businesses, professions and industries. Some of these are published by organizations, such as the *Canadian Guernsey Journal* published by the Canadian Guernsey Association. Others are independently published, such as *Sheep!* a magazine for sheep farmers.

Especially in the trade press, distinctions often blur among newspapers, magazines and newsletters, both printed and online versions. That is because the distinguishing features related to physical format are offset by a similar content and readership.

Consider the financial media, for example. It includes daily business-oriented newspapers such as the *Wall Street Journal,* weekly newspapers such as the *Business Journal of Central New York*, regional magazines such as *Colorado Business*, the business sections of most metropolitan daily newspapers, business magazines such as *Barron's* and *Business Week*, consumer magazines such as *Money* and *Fortune,* financial newsletters such as the *Kiplinger Report*, company newsletters published by brokerage firms and investment companies, and financial columnists such as Jane Bryant Quinn.

The actual number of magazines is impossible to calculate accurately, but it is vast. In just the area of religion, for example, The American Society of Magazine Editors lists

784 magazines focused on religion, many of them associated with a particular denomination, diocese or religious order. *Religious Periodicals of the United States: Academic and Scholarly Journals* has estimated that there are more than 2,500 religious magazines.

A new addition to the publishing field is the *e-zine*, an e-mail-based magazine. The trend toward e-zines began in the mid-1990s, when magazine publishers began placing editorial content, stories and photographs at their magazine websites. Now thousands of e-zines are published online.

Many online magazines also feature interactive opportunities for readers, much of this involving catalog sections of the magazines in which readers can order products from a variety of companies. Examples are *Stylehog.com* about fashion on a budget, *WeirdMusic.net* about creative indie music and *The Dive Site.co.za* for scuba divers.

Radio

Radio provides opportunities in the traditional terrestrial or over-the-air radio as well as satellite and Internet radio alternatives.

Whether in traditional or new configurations, radio is found virtually everywhere. Audiences are large, with 19 out of 20 people listening to radio at some time during a typical week. Combination news, talk and information stations have the most listeners, followed by stations with a country-music format, according to Arbitron ratings. One of the benefits of radio is its mobility—a positive quality in that it can travel with people, but also a negative one from a public relations standpoint because people listen passively to radio while doing other things (such as driving, working and reading).

Indeed, many people who turn on radios can hardly be called listeners. They use radio mainly to overcome silence, without really listening to it. Because of this, research shows that audience recall of radio commercials is less than that for television commercials. However, the relatively low cost of radio advertising allows for heavier repetition than many organizations generally can afford via television. On the other hand, radio generally attracts individuals alone (unlike television, which often is watched by people in groups). So when radio audiences do really listen, they focus on what is being said.

Because radio formats are specific, audiences tend to be very different from one station to another. National Public Radio, for example, is popular with people who are identified as opinion leaders in many different environments. Classic rock stations, meanwhile, find that two-thirds of their listeners are between the ages of 18 and 34; they are particularly strong with young men under age 25. News and talk stations draw an audience heavy with men and women 35–54, with the total audience better educated than Americans in general. Studies also report that stations focused on contemporary music attract women under 30 and teenagers. And country music stations, long a staple in radio broadcasting, are losing audiences, particularly in urban areas where ethnic populations prefer different styles of music. Thus it is important to know your key publics before making decisions about particular stations.

What are the strategic implications of all this? Let's say you are operating a restaurant or a retail store. If you want to attract younger customers, pipe classic rock or progressive rock over the sound system. On the other hand, if you want more senior citizens, use easy listening or nostalgic music. Country music listeners tend to be women aged 25–54, with lower incomes than women in the Top 40 audience.

Phase Three

STEP
7

This kind of demographic information has implications for public relations strategists, for example, in the kind of music-related events they might sponsor or possible topics for articles in a newsletter or website for consumer or employee publics.

Here is an overview of three types of radio services: terrestrial, online and satellite.

TERRESTRIAL RADIO

The category of **terrestrial radio** includes both the AM and FM formats, with signals sent via transmitters. Generally AM is more oriented toward news, sports or talk, whereas FM often includes more all-music formats. The stations may be commercial or public.

Experts count about 44,000 radio stations worldwide. The US and Canada together have about 14,500 radio stations; about 5,100 are AM stations and 9,400 are FM stations. Most of these are commercial stations but about 1,260 are public, plus about 2,500 educational stations.

Many radio news opportunities exist at the local level, others through about 115 national networks. These include large networks such as ABC Radio or the UPI Radio Network, and smaller, specialized networks such as the Beethoven Satellite Network of classical music; Tobacco Radio Network with agricultural information; and Kidwaves Radio Network with children's programming.

ONLINE RADIO

The new forms of radio are making inroads in the audiences. **Online radio** (sometimes called **Internet radio** or **streaming radio**) carries web-based stations as well as radio-like collections of music in categories tailored to the individual listener's interests such as Pandora and Google Music.

Internet radio is a meaningful competitor to traditional AM and FM stations. EMarketer estimated in 2011 that 38 percent of adult Americans listen to online radio, predicting 67 percent by 2015. It also calculated that online radio generates $800 million in annual revenue.

SATELLITE RADIO

Another category, satellite radio (sometimes called **subscription radio** or **digital radio**), offers clear digital signals to audience members who subscribe to the service. The signal is transmitted via satellite, so it covers thousands of miles, compared to the limited listening area of terrestrial stations. Satellite radio has advantages of being free from U.S. Federal Communications Commission content restrictions and of being relatively devoid of commercials. It is growing, while struggling for a wider audience.

Satellite radio generally is a subscription-based service that, unlike terrestrial radio, is nonlocal. The largest satellite radio company in North America is Sirius XM, which operates Sirius as a commercial-free system and XM with commercials. The company uses geosynchronous satellites to obtain a footprint that covers most of Canada, the US, and the northern third of Mexico.

Television

Like radio, television may be commercial or public, with opportunities to reach audiences through both local stations and national or regional networks. Other television opportunities include cable programming, both through national networks and local production facilities.

Nearly 2,300 television stations operate throughout the US and Canada. These stations generally broadcast news and sports, as well as entertainment programming. Some of this programming is locally produced, but most stations draw most of their programming from an affiliated network, which is a content producer and distributor of television programming. In the US, the largest commercial networks are ABC, NBC, CBS and Fox, with PBS as the public network. Each of these reaches about 97 percent of U.S. households. In Canada, CBC and CTV are nationwide English-language television networks, and Radio-Canada is the French-language public TV network.

More than 80 television networks operate in North America, including many specialized networks such as Inuit Television of Canada, Newfoundland Television, Univision, and Telemundo Spanish-language networks, home-focused networks such as DIY and HGTV, several state-based PBS affiliates such as the Pennsylvania Public Television Network, four major home-shopping networks and nearly 30 religious networks.

When public relations is able to gain the attention of television reporters, organizations find themselves facing potentially vast audiences. Obviously, however, not every public relations activity is newsworthy, nor should it be. To help you determine what is or is not newsworthy, review the definition of news and the characteristics of newsworthiness in Phase Two, Strategy.

Several types of television services are common: terrestrial, digital, cable and satellite. Here is a look at each.

TERRESTRIAL TELEVISION

The most common types of broadcast television is **terrestrial television**, also called **over-the-air television**; it can be defined by what it is not. It does not transmit via cable or satellite, but rather by radio waves sent to and from antennas. Most local television stations provide an over-the-air signal, which can be accessed for free with a home antenna or rabbit ears.

DIGITAL TELEVISION

Since 2009 in the US and 2011 in Canada, all television stations are required to offer a digital signal, which generally is stronger than over-the-air television. Digital television also offers many more channels.

CABLE TELEVISION

About 59 percent of U.S. households receive **cable television**, which is a system of providing TV programming via coaxial or fiber-optic cables. Comcast and Time Warner are the largest cable TV providers in the U.S. More than 325 cable television networks are in business, including CNBC, Discovery Channel, MTV and Nickelodeon. Major categories include arts, entertainment, foreign, Hispanic programming, children's programming, sports, shopping, religion, music and pay-per-view. Cable TV audiences tend to be middle-class, suburban residents with higher-than-average income who purchase cable programming through subscriptions and as pay-per-view options.

SATELLITE TELEVISION

Satellite television allows customers to view TV signals on television sets or on computers. Some programming is free, though most satellite television is subscription-based. Programming generally includes a range of networks similar to cable television.

Phase Three

STEP
7

Media Information Needs

The relationship between a public relations practitioner and a journalist is symbiotic; that is, it is a relationship in which each side needs the other and benefits from the other.

- Public relations people need journalists and information programmers who can provide a vehicle to present the organization's messages.
- Reporters need public relations practitioners to help them identify newsworthy stories and report on them.

Most newspapers are private commercial enterprises. About 73 percent of their income derives from advertising and the rest from circulation; news and commentary are the products these companies are selling. As businesses protected by the First Amendment of the U.S. Constitution, American newspapers are not required to publish any particular material, including news releases and other information originating from public relations practitioners. Not even government agencies can command news coverage.

Television and radio stations generally are private businesses as well. While they must meet certain government regulations (because they have, in effect, a franchise to operate on

PUBLIC RELATIONS HELPS WRITE THE NEWS

The news media owe a lot to public relations. Estimates vary on how much information carried in the news media comes from public relations practitioners, but it's evident that most editors and reporters get a lot of their information from public relations sources.

A press secretary to a former New York City mayor estimated that public relations generates 50 percent of stories in that city's newspapers (Wilcox and Cameron, 2009). That's consistent with a classic 1981 study in *Columbia Journalism Review*, which counted 45 percent of the 188 news stories in one edition of the *Wall Street Journal* as originating with public relations practitioners. Another academic journal reported that 78 percent of journalists use news releases, at least to spark story ideas, more than half of the time (Curtain, 1999). In that survey, many journalists said their publications and stations have strict guidelines for using public relations materials, such as using only those from nonprofit organizations promoting social causes but not from businesses seeking economic gain.

The term for such assistance is **information subsidy**—information from public relations sources that increasingly short-staffed editors use to help underwrite the costs of gathering news. Newsrooms have been turning more frequently to low-cost public relations information subsidies. That can be good for public relations practitioners.

But there is a downside to the trend. If the media lower their journalistic standards to the point that they lose credibility with their audiences, public relations people will find less value in news media coverage. Thus, despite easier entrée to the news columns and broadcasts, media coverage would be worth less.

Something to think about.

a particular channel frequency), they nevertheless have much discretion over what news to cover. An exception to this private ownership, of course, is the system of public radio and television networks.

Editors and news directors usually are receptive to public relations information when they believe it will satisfy the interests of their readers. The term **information subsidy** describes news and or editorial material provided to journalists by public relations.

An estimated one-half to two-thirds of the information in daily newspapers originates from public relations practitioners, either through vehicles initiated by practitioners, such as news releases, news conferences and media alerts, or because practitioners have responded to journalists with interviews or background information.

The rate for radio and television news broadcasts is slightly lower, because these media proportionally give more coverage to accidents, crime and other breaking news. As rising corporate costs lead to news-gathering teams becoming smaller at many publications and broadcast stations, news-oriented public relations practitioners can be of increasing assistance to the remaining reporters, and thus more effective in service to their organizations.

The most common way for public relations practitioners to provide news people with information is to give it to them in writing. A 2012 survey by TEKGroup International found that 95 percent of working journalists prefer to receive news and story ideas via e-mail, and 60 percent want to get news from public relations practitioners on their wireless devices. Additionally, 43 percent prefer to receive news via Twitter.

A Survey of Media in the Wired World reported in 2011 that 75 percent of journalists use Facebook as a tool for reporting; 70 percent use blogs, 69 percent use Twitter and 69 percent use mobile technology to gather reportable information. It found that, overall, 95 percent of journalists believe that social media are a reliable tool for sourcing stories. Additionally, 96 percent of journalists say they sometimes quote bloggers and 39 percent maintain their own blog. The survey was conducted by Middleberg Communications and the Society for New Communications Research (middlebergcommunications.com).

Additionally, many organizations service reporters through online newsrooms where reporters can download news releases, fact sheets, interview notes, photos and many other resources for their reporting.

What's a public relations person to do with such information? For starters, use it to develop a media-friendly website and online newsroom. Make the information easy for journalists to find, generally as a well-placed link from the organization's home page. Include the kind of information a journalist might need: basic facts, history, downloadable photos, stats, and so on. Include an easy-to-navigate link to a public relations staff person. Invite reporters to sign up for customized e-mails that will alert them to topics of interest. Make sure you keep the site updated frequently, perhaps daily.

A 2008 study looked at information subsidies during the coverage of the Virginia Tech shootings the previous year. Shelley Wigley and Maria Fontenot found that, in today's high-tech media environment, early crisis reports may use eye-witness accounts, often accessed through cell-phone video, texting, blogs, Facebook and tweets. They called this new type of crisis media non-official technology sources. They found that reporters used unofficial sources (students, experts, community organizations, and so on) three-to-one over official sources (such as websites and interviews with university officials and police). In the Virginia Tech coverage, technology sources provided information subsidies to the traditional print and broadcast media in the early reporting of the crisis, followed by more official sources as coverage continued. Perhaps this says something about the availability of public relations sources, or the information they have, early in a crisis.

Let's look at some of the ways in which public relations practitioners can provide the news media with newsworthy information and thus disseminate their messages to the vast media audiences. There are four general ways to present information through the news media: direct information subsidy, indirect information subsidy, opinion subsidy and interactive news opportunities.

Direct Information Subsidy

One of the most frequently used categories of news media tactics is **direct information subsidy**—information that is presented to the media more or less ready for use. These tactics include news fact sheets, event listings, interview notes, news releases, feature releases, actualities, audio news releases, video B-rolls, video news releases, e-mail releases, social media releases, media kits and online newsrooms. Here's a brief overview of each.

NEWS FACT SHEET

A brief, generally one-page, outline of information about a newsworthy event or activity is called a **news fact sheet**. These often are presented as bulleted items. The format makes it easy for reporters in both print and electronic media to use the information as they write their own stories. Fact sheets also can be used by people other than reporters, such as speechwriters, tour guides, employees and customers.

Fact sheets are easy to prepare. Simply gather the relevant information and present it along the traditional journalistic lines of who, what, when, where, why and how. It also may be useful to add sections on background, history, significance and benefits. Additionally, it may be appropriate to include a brief direct quote.

EVENT LISTING

Another information format for print media is the **event listing**, also called a **community calendar**. These are simple notices that most newspapers and many magazines print about upcoming activities such as benefits, meetings, entertainment events, public lectures, and the like. Many publications also offer online postings of community events.

INTERVIEW NOTES

Another useful tactic is **interview notes**, which are verbatim transcripts presented in a question-and-answer format, based on an interview that a public relations writer has done with an organizational news source. For example, a university news bureau might interview a geology professor about breakthrough work involving earthquake prediction, then provide the transcript of that interview for science writers. Interview notes usually begin with a brief narrative paragraph to set the stage. They often include a biographical sketch of the person being interviewed.

Interview notes allow reporters to build their stories as they see fit. Even if they decide to do their own interviews, the interview notes can save them time and give them information to build on.

NEWS RELEASE

Most organizations find that the **news release** is a mainstay of media relations. A news release is a news story written by public relations practitioners and given to media gatekeepers for use in their news publications, programs and online information sites.

Submit news releases to newspaper city editors or to editors or beat reporters of special interest such as sports, business or entertainment sections. Special-interest magazines also may use news releases, especially for brief items. For broadcast media, submit news releases to news directors or assignment editors. Also, consider taking the time to rewrite standard (print-oriented) releases when you intend to send them to radio or television stations.

In the past, news releases were distributed through the mail or were hand delivered, either by the public relations practitioners or by a courier. Some practitioners still try to maintain face-to-face interaction with reporters by delivering their releases. The Survey of Media in the Wired World—noted in the previous section of this chapter—reported that emerging media are supplementing but not supplanting older forms of media. For example, 53 percent of journalists prefer receiving e-mail news releases and 34 percent prefer to interview news contacts over the phone.

Increasingly, organizations are disseminating news releases via e-mail to individual journalists, or they are posting releases on websites where reporters can retrieve the information.

TRUSTED NEWS SOURCES

A report for the Public Relations Society of America by Harris Interactive (2005) focused in part on the trust level for various information sources by a cross-section of American civil society: adult consumers, corporate executives and bipartisan congressional staffers. The study found that National Public Radio (NPR) and TV's Public Broadcasting Service (PBS) are the most trusted news sources, and advertising the least trusted.

Here's a synopsis of the findings. The three numbers indicate the positive percentage of adult consumers, corporate executives and congressional staffers, respectively.

- Belief that most of the news is accurate and unbiased (43, 38, 33 percent).
- Reliance on independent news sources such as Internet chat rooms, blogs or other alternative media (42, 21, 30).
- Trust levels regarding news via NPR or PBS (61, 75, 70).
- Trust levels regarding news in national newspapers (56, 78, 78).
- Trust levels regarding television and radio network news (53, 59, 62).
- Trust levels regarding advocacy organizations such as the National Rifle Association, the American Association of Retired Persons, and the American Civil Liberties Union (44, 18, 39).
- Trust levels regarding public relations sources (37, 29, 29).
- Trust levels regarding celebrity spokespersons (30, 8, 13).
- Trust levels regarding advertising sources (25, 24, 20).
- Public relations people presenting misleading information (85, 67, 85).
- Public relations people raising public awareness on important issues (71, 84, 84).

Phase Three

STEP
7

Some practitioners notify reporters via an e-mail distribution list when they post news releases on their websites.

News releases also may be disseminated through commercial public relations wire services like PR Newswire.

If you are considering preparing a news release, note that there are several different kinds. An **announcement release**, for example, often is subcategorized as dealing with events, personnel, progress, bad news, programs or products. A **response release** deals with new or updated information, comments, public interest tie-ins and speeches. A **hometowner release** is sent to newspapers serving the permanent residential areas of employees, students, members of the military, and so on.

Whereas a news release involves a page or more of information, a **news brief** is likely to be only a two- or three-paragraph story that provides the basic information of the summary lead as well as a clear indication of the benefit. Some public relations writers try to write each news release so the first couple of paragraphs can be pulled out to serve as a news brief. Written this way, the news-brief portion also can serve as part of an online menu of articles, linking to the longer version for readers seeking more in-depth information.

Note that the news media are not obligated to use news releases. In fact, most releases are rejected, usually because they are either more self-promoting than news reporting or because they are weak in local interest.

FEATURE RELEASE

In addition to releases that present solid news, other releases focus on some kind of background on the news. Known as a **feature release**, this public relations tactic has several categories: biographies, histories, backgrounders, question-and-answer pieces and service articles.

A **biography** provides the personal background on newsmakers and other people significant to an organization. This can be written in chronological style or as personality profiles.

A **history**, meanwhile, provides a similar focus on the organization itself, usually providing a chronological narrative or an outline of the development of the organization since its founding. Histories generally deal not only with milestones but also with issues facing the organization. Both histories and biographies are written so they can be updated easily when new developments warrant.

A narrative article providing objective information on an issue is called a **backgrounder**. Such pieces usually deal with the cause of the problem or issue, a chronological history of how the issue has progressed, its current status and perhaps clear projections of its direction and likely future. Backgrounders also provide information on the significance or impact of the issue. The key element for a backgrounder is that it should remain neutral—objective and free of opinion or unsupported speculation; indeed, all sides in an issue should be able to agree on the facts within a well-written backgrounder.

Other categories of feature articles are labeled according to the writing format used in the release. Some releases are presented as a **question-and-answer piece** (also called a *Q&A*). Others are written in the step-by-step format of a **service article or how-to piece**, which provides readers with an instructional approach to solving a problem.

ACTUALITY

When public relations writers want to quote someone in a news release going to print journalists, they include a sentence or phrase in quotation marks. When they want to provide radio reports with similar quoted material, they use an **actuality** (sometimes called a **sound bite**), because radio stations need to present quoted information in the voice of the news source. An actuality is a recording—usually digitized and accessible by computer. It involves a couple of highlight quotes from a speech or statement by an organizational spokesperson.

AUDIO NEWS RELEASE

Whereas an actuality is an audio sound bite, an **audio news release** (ANR) is an edited story package that public relations writers offer to radio journalists. ANRs are news stories complete with announcer and sound bite. Most U.S. radio stations use audio news releases in some ways, particularly if the ANR has a local angle. The ANRs that get on the air are most commonly 60-second spots plugged into the morning drive-time reports. Nonprofit organizations, corporations and government agencies produce audio news releases. For example, the U.S. Department of Labor posts ANRs with other materials at its media website (www. dol.gov/dol/media).

VIDEO B-ROLL

Quoted statements and other visual information can be made available to television stations through a **video B-roll**, which is a tape providing a series of unedited video shots and sound bites related to the news story. A written news release or other background material often accompany B-rolls to give television reporters an idea of what the story is all about. B-rolls are becoming increasingly popular with television stations.

VIDEO NEWS RELEASE

A packaged video bite edited into a complete story package is the **video news release** (VNR). This is given to television journalists by public relations people. VNRs usually run 30 to 90 seconds long with narration, interviews and background video, even names titled at the bottom of the screen. B-rolls are sometimes used with VNRs to provide for easier editing of newsworthy material.

VNRs generally are one of two types. A timely release focuses on a current news event. An evergreen release, often taking a human-interest approach, has a longer potential time frame for use.

Television stations use about 5,000 VNRs each year. Nielsen Media Research has reported that three out of four television stations use VNRs weekly, and WestGlen Communications reported that 85 percent of television stations in the U.S. use outside-produced video for some newscasts. Morning and early evening are the two news slots when VNRs and B-rolls are most likely to be used.

Many VNRs are not used, however, because television news directors judge them to be lacking in local news value or some other important criterion. Another reason some VNRs are rejected is that they are overly commercial, lacking what the reporters consider strong news judgment. Still, when they are used, the impact can be huge. Pepsi-Cola reached an estimated 365 million viewers with four VNRs in 1993, when a hoax was perpetrated that claimed syringes had been found in cans of Pepsi products.

Because of the production costs involved, most video news releases are developed by organizations with widespread publics rather than for single-market use. VNRs and B-rolls may be distributed nationally or regionally. National distribution can cost from $25,000 to more than $100,000. Local or regional distribution, especially of B-rolls, can involve only a

Phase Three

STEP
7

nominal expense for an organization that has its own video production setup or the assistance of a video production studio.

VNRs have sparked some controversy. The watchdog group Center for Media and Democracy, which is critical of many public relations practices, campaigns against VNRs as "fake news." The second Bush administration used tax money to produce and distribute VNRs promoting its version of a Medicare reform bill, sparking congressional criticism and an investigation by the Federal Communications Commission and the Government Accountability Office. The GAO ruled that the VNRs were illegal forms of "covert propaganda," but the Justice Department told federal agencies to ignore the ruling, and the administration continued to produce VNRs at taxpayers' expense.

Both the Public Relations Society of America and the Radio Television Digital News Association have ethical guidelines calling for TV stations to indicate the source of VNR material used in newscasts. A 2005 study by Harris Interactive found that 71 percent of adult consumers believe that TV news sources should be required to indicate the sources of stories generated by companies, government or other outside organizations.

E-MAIL RELEASE

News releases sent via e-mail differ a bit from the conventional printed release. An **e-mail release** presents news within the text of an e-mail rather than as an attachment. It generally is shorter than a printed release, often only five or six paragraphs. The subject line serves as the headline, making it easy to archive such releases. Often the text of an e-mail release resembles a fact sheet, with subheads and bullets to highlight information for reporters and other recipients.

SOCIAL MEDIA RELEASE

A new communication tactic is the **social media release** (SMR), a type of news release intended for blogs, websites and other online uses. It is the result of new technology and changing information patterns.

The SMR includes many elements not found in a standard news release: liberal use of subheads as well as headlines to help move the reader along; summary statement as in a news brief; and bulleted facts (similar to those in the news fact sheet previously noted).

Social media releases also include many kinds of links and feeds: links to photos, MP3 files, podcasts and other audio clips; graphics; logos; various types of video; downloads of related information and background materials; links to other coverage of the topic; links to additional commentary and quotes from organizational news sources; and links to additional background information, finances, history, and products or services of the organization, as well as a link to a traditional news release. The social news release also generally includes a time-date stamp to indicate when the information was last updated.

MEDIA KIT

Most of the above-described direct news materials can be gathered together in a **media kit**, sometimes called a *press packet*. These are presented to the journalists who attend news conferences and often are delivered to invited reporters who fail to attend. Media kits generally include one or more news releases along with fact sheets, feature releases, photos and other graphics.

ONLINE NEWSROOM

Online newsrooms have become a staple of media relations, a trend that is only becoming stronger. In researching stories, 98 percent of working journalists said they visit online newsrooms, 26 percent of them every day. That's from a comprehensive study by TEKGroup International, an Internet software company that develops social media online newsrooms. Its 2012 Online Newsroom Survey reported that 92 percent of journalists visit corporate blogs in researching a news story and 26 percent visit a company's Facebook page often.

Here are some other findings of the report about what journalists think about online newsrooms:

- 98 percent say organizations should have an online newsroom;
- 98 percent think such newsrooms should give them access to news releases;
- 98 percent want searchable archives of those releases;
- 82 percent say it's important to access investor relations information;
- 94 percent look for breaking news;
- 94 percent want photographs in both high and low resolution;
- 61 percent seek audio files;
- 75 percent want to find video files.

The full report is available at tekgroup.com.

ONLINE NEWSROOM

An online newsroom is a comprehensive set of pages within a website that provides a home for most of the items listed above. An online newsroom generally includes print and social media releases, fact sheets, a photo gallery, executive bios and organizational histories, audio and video material, and virtual tours. Many also post videos of speeches and interviews, videos of their own news conferences, and reprints or links of media coverage and videos of their own news conferences.

Indirect Information Subsidy

In addition to the direct materials noted earlier, public relations practitioners also can use **indirect information subsidy** to communicate with reporters, editors and news directors. These are messages that are not meant to be published but are intended to interest or inform media gatekeepers. Consider the following in your tactical program: media advisories, story idea memos and query letters.

MEDIA ADVISORY

A brief note given to media gatekeepers is called a **media advisory** or **media alert**. These memos inform the gatekeepers of upcoming news opportunities. For example, a public relations practitioner might use a media advisory to announce a news conference, to invite photographers to a newsworthy event or to inform editors and news directors about a newsworthy activity involving the organization to which they are invited.

Media advisories differ from news releases in that the advisory is not meant to be published but rather is intended as useful information for a journalist. Realize, however, that information in a media advisory is not off the record, and enterprising journalists may use the memo to craft a news report preempting the announced news conference or special event. Therefore, be careful not to provide too much information in an advisory.

STORY IDEA MEMO

Another useful news-oriented tactic is the **story idea memo** or **tip sheet**. These are informal idea memos submitted to the gatekeepers of newspapers, magazines, and electronic and digital news media. The intention is to spark a reporter's interest in developing a feature article. The public relations practitioners suggest available interview subjects or topics for articles that can be developed by the publication's own writers.

QUERY LETTER

A letter written to editors or broadcasters proposing a story and inquiring about their interest in it is called a **query letter**. These are commonly used by freelance writers more than by public relations practitioners, and they often are directed to magazines or feature supplements to Sunday newspapers. However, some practitioners find it useful to query magazines and then prepare feature articles if an editor expresses interest. Additionally, some practitioners work with freelance writers who prepare stories on assignment for magazines.

Opinion Subsidy

Another category of tactics rooted in the news media involves several opportunities for using newspapers, magazines, and radio and television stations to present an organization's opinion rather than simply the factual information that is the focus of most of the preceding news tactics. Both in proactive situations in which the organization wishes to advocate for a particular position, or when it reactively seeks to explain or defend its position, an organization often realizes several benefits by producing this opinion material.

Consider the following vehicles through which organizations can present their formal opinions about various issues: position statements, letters to the editor and guest editorials.

POSITION STATEMENT

Going a step beyond backgrounders (which were discussed earlier, in the section Direct Information Subisdy), a **position statement** adds an organization's official and considered opinion on an issue.

Position statements can be used in a variety of ways. They are materials for journalists preparing news stories or editorials. They also serve as the basis for editorials in organizational publications, source material for speeches and organizational letters, and documents to be provided directly to employees, donors or stockholders, supporters, legislators and other influential publics. Position statements often are published as stand-alone organizational publications.

Position statements can vary in their depth and intensity. A position paper, sometimes called a **white paper**, may be a detailed and lengthy discussion of a major issue of long-term significance. A **position paragraph** is a much shorter statement, often providing an organization's comments on a local or short-lived issue.

A **contingency statement** or **standby statement** is a prepared comment written so an organization may express its voice in various potential situations. For example, a company nearing the resolution of a lawsuit may prepare several contingency statements to cover the possible outcomes: winning the case, losing it, being convicted of lesser charges, having the charge dismissed, and so on. Obviously, contingency statements should be kept in strict confidence until one of them is needed.

LETTER TO THE EDITOR

Opinion letters written to newspapers and magazines offer many opportunities for public relations practitioners to communicate through the news media even when the gatekeepers have overlooked the organization.

Public relations practitioners use letters to the editor as publicity vehicles to announce things that don't make it into the news columns. They also use letters to advocate a cause that likewise hasn't caught the attention of journalists. Occasionally letters can be used to correct errors, though most organizations find it better to ignore all but the most serious factual misstatements in published reports.

GUEST EDITORIAL

Some commentaries can go beyond the length and impact of letters to the editor. A **guest editorial** generally is placed opposite the editorial page of a newspaper, hence its alternative name, **op-ed piece**.

A guest editorial is a grander version of a letter to the editor. It is a signed essay that, because of its length and placement, has higher prestige and credibility than a letter. Usually it's necessary to contact the publication before submitting an essay to be considered as a guest editorial.

In many cases, guest editorials are written by public relations people but carry the signature of an organizational executive, thereby giving the piece additional credibility because of a high-ranking message source.

Interactive Media Engagement

A final category of news activities is interactive news opportunities, those communication opportunities in which public relations practitioners and journalists interact with each other. These include news interviews, news conferences, studio interviews, satellite media tours and editorial conferences.

NEWS INTERVIEW

Sessions in which journalists ask questions and public relations practitioners or organizational spokespersons respond are a mainstay of the interaction between an organization and the news media.

A **news interview** usually is a one-on-one question-and-answer session. Public relations practitioners prepare for interviews by anticipating questions reporters may ask and gathering relevant information to answer the questions. They also help organizational spokespersons frame appropriate responses to reporters' questions. Often this coaching includes mock interviews prior to the actual encounter between the spokesperson and the reporters.

Phase Three

STEP
7

Most interviews are face-to-face encounters. Sometimes, however, when a reporter is seeking mainly factual information, especially from a news source the reporter has worked with in the past, the interview may take place over the telephone or via e-mail. See Appendix D, Effective Media Engagement, for tips on good interviewing.

NEWS CONFERENCE

Essentially a group interview, a **news conference** is a contrived media happening in which an organizational spokesperson makes a newsworthy statement. Generally this is followed by a question-and-answer session with reporters.

Journalists do not particularly like news conferences because the format puts them in the awkward position of doing their news gathering—always a highly competitive endeavor—in the presence of their competitors.

Only a few circumstances justify holding a news conference:

1. To announce news or give a response of major importance (in the eyes of the media, not simply the hopes of the organization), such as a new product or policy initiative, response to an attack, update in a crisis situation or comment on a breaking news story.
2. To serve the media's interests when a prominent spokesperson or news maker is available for only a short period of time, such as the whirlwind visit or sandwiched-in interview of a celebrity, official, candidate or some other newsworthy person.
3. To avoid accusations of playing favorites among reporters, such as by disseminating information to one medium ahead of another.

As an alternative to a news conference, consider making the announcement through a news release, or invite reporters to a coordinated series of interviews with an organizational spokesperson. Another option is to invite reporters to a participatory activity, such as a media preview of the opening of a new roller coaster by an amusement park.

If you do judge it appropriate to invite reporters to a news conference, consider the following guidelines:

- Invite all media that may be interested, even those you don't like. Notify the wire services, which in turn may announce the news conference as part of their advisories to member media.
- In a major market with a variety of media outlets, schedule the news conference mid- to late morning, if possible. Because normal business is slow on weekends, also consider Sunday or early Monday news conferences. In a smaller market with few print reporters and television reporters from stations miles away, you'll have to accommodate the schedule of the reporters. In either case, ask key reporters about convenient times and conflicting news events.
- Hold the news conference in a meeting room rather than in an office. Or if possible, hold the conference at an appropriate on-site location relevant to the information. For example, if you are announcing a new public housing project, hold the news conference at the building site.

Most news conferences are open to all reporters. Generally the word goes out, often posted on media events listings, and interested news media will send reporters. Increasingly, however, invitation-only news conferences are being held, often open only to journalists credentialed by a government or corporate press overseer. As an attempt to control the media or show favorites, these invitation-only events can damage an organization's overall media-relations program.

Remember that journalists seek various outcomes from news conferences. Television reporters need visuals, so try to overcome the talking heads with some creative graphics or locations. Newspaper reporters need facts and a lot of them; media kits and online newsrooms can provide many supplemental materials for them. Bloggers and other alternative journalists may be interested in only a narrow area; some organizations have scheduled separate news conferences for them.

MEDIA RELATIONS PRACTICES

A national survey of more than 2,000 journalists reported some interesting findings. The Journalist Survey on Media Relations Practices conducted by Bulldog Reporter and TEKgroup International (2010) sought to establish benchmarks for journalists who use the Internet to research and report on the news. Here are some of the findings:

- *Internet research*. On the biggest change in journalistic practices, nearly 79 percent of journalists identified their ability to use the Internet to conduct their research 24 hours a day; 68 percent identified access to media contact info online; 46 percent access to electronic press kits online; 43 percent identified the ability to search corporate news archives online.
- *Corporate websites*. More than 85 percent of journalists visit a corporate website at least once a month; more than half do so at least weekly.
- *Obscured information*. Reporters complain that corporate websites often obscure contact information for media relations representatives of the organization.
- *Blogs*. Nearly 70 percent say they follow at least one blog regularly; more than 28 percent say they visit a social media site at least weekly as part of their reporting.
- *Audio and video feeds*. Nearly half of reporters say they use audio or video material from corporate websites at least occasionally; 51 percent said they never seek such information.
- *Understanding the media*. Half of reporters say public relations people don't understand the media.
- *Phone calls*. More than 48 percent say phone calls from public relations people are a waste of time.
- *Quick response*. More than 54 percent of journalists disagreed with the notion that public relations people do not respond quickly enough.
- *Truthfulness*. More than 52 percent disagreed with the notion that public relations practitioners do not tell the truth.
- *Preferences*. Nearly 78 percent said they prefer to receive news releases via e-mail; less than 2 percent sought releases via postal mail.

Phase Three

STEP
7

CASE IN POINT Dublin Zoo

Facing a decline in visitors amid a national economic recession that led to a decrease in government funding, Dublin Zoo faced an uncertain future. Taking a step toward enhancing its own survival, Ireland's largest zoo embarked on a public relations plan in 2010. The goal was to attract more visitors at full-price admissions.

The campaign relied heavily on a strategy of media relations, as the zoo solicited (and gained) media support from many sectors.

To that purpose, the campaign provided media training for key zookeepers and became more proactive in reaching out to journalists. It developed a series of media-friendly events, such as a mock "zoo election" to select the zoo's most popular inhabitants. (The winner was an orangutan named Sibu.)

The zoo provided media access leading to coverage of the birth of several new arrivals: a hippo, giraffe, elephant, rhinoceros, bongo, gorilla and a pair of pandas. It also created special events such as Orangutan Awareness Week with a strong television presence to present a message of conservation and endangered animals.

On the responsive side of media relations, the campaign used the news media effectively in several high-profile animal incidents, including the high-profile theft of a penguin that was returned unharmed. It produced a behind-the-scenes TV series called "The Zoo" that attracted about 300,000 viewers.

Moving beyond established news media, the campaign created new social media opportunities. It developed an interactive website and promoted the zoo among 15,000 Facebook fans and 2,200 Twitter followers. The zoo also organized a "blogger's walk" with exclusive early-morning access for 20 of Ireland's leading bloggers and photobloggers.

The result of the campaign was the highest profile among established news media profile the zoo ever had, along with a social media presence with more than 15,000 supporters.

The bottom line? Dublin Zoo recorded the highest paid attendance—963,053—in its 180-year history. The benefits continued, with the zoo attracting more than a million visitors the following year and raising enough money to open a new Gorilla Rainforest.

The campaign received a top award from the Public Relations Consultants Association of Ireland, Public Relations Institute of Ireland, the Chartered Institute of Public Relations in Northern Ireland and the All Ireland Marketing Awards.

STUDIO INTERVIEW

Another tactic is the **studio interview**, which is a hybrid between the regular interview and the news conference. Like regular interviews, studio interviews involve a reporter/questioner and generally a single interviewee. Sometimes they are set up as a questioner moderating an interview panel. Like a news conference, they often are televised, so everything is presented in "real time" with all the spontaneity of a live interview (even if it is taped for later broadcast).

The growth in popularity of talk radio and, increasingly, talk television offer opportunities to public relations and marketing people promoting new ideas, products, books, and the like. At-home interviews generally include feature or personality profiles for celebrities and other newsmakers. They can be useful in helping to humanize organizational leaders.

SATELLITE MEDIA TOUR

A related development in interviewing style is the **satellite media tour** (SMT), a kind of in-studio interview or news conference with a widely dispersed audience.

The unique feature of the SMT is that a news source is interviewed by reporters who are in different locations, connected via a special television signal or computer link transmitted through satellite technology from the interviewee's location to many reporters throughout the nation, even around the world. Usually these are individual one-on-one interviews, packaged in segments of five minutes or less. SMTs have a role both in political campaigning and in crisis communications.

EDITORIAL CONFERENCE

Public relations representatives sometimes meet in an **editorial conference**, a meeting with editors and editorial boards of newspapers to present them with background information on important issues. Generally such conferences are arranged on the invitation of the editors, though public relations people often try to solicit such invitations. Such conferences may generate news reports, feature stories and editorial comment on the issue.

PLANNING EXAMPLE 7C **Selecting News Media Tactics**

Upstate College will develop the following news media tactics to publicize its expanded program:

UPSTATE COLLEGE

- *news release*—low cost, accessible, target to potential students, parents, donors and community leaders;
- *fact sheet for media*—low cost, directed toward media publics;
- *fact sheet for students*—low cost, directed toward potential students;
- *media alert*—low cost;
- *social media release*—low cost, information-on-demand for key publics;
- *photo and caption of preparation for ceremony*—low cost, interests community about expanded program;
- *letter to the editor*—low cost, aimed at key publics (parents, donors, community leaders);
- *editorial conference*—low cost, interactive with media, potential to generate support for recruitment and fundraising;
- *news interview with reporters*—low cost, high visibility.

Phase Three

STEP
7

Tiny Tykes will develop the following news media tactics to publicize its dedication to consumer safety and demonstrate its improved crib toy:

- *letters to the editor*—low cost, directed toward key publics;
- *story idea memo to reporters*—low cost, possibly high visibility;
- *news release*—low cost, accessible, aimed at key publics;
- *video news release*—high cost, possibly high visibility;
- *social media release*—low cost, targeted for parents.

 Checklist 7C **News Media Tactics**

Basic Questions

1. What news media tactics will you use?
2. How will these tactics help the organization achieve its objectives?
3. What resources will these tactics require?

Expanded Questions

A. SELECTION OF TACTICS

From the following categories of news media tactics, identify several that you would consider using:

Direct News Material

- news fact sheet
- event listing
- interview notes
- news release
- feature release
- actuality
- audio news release.

- video B-roll
- video news release
- e-mail release
- social media release
- media kit
- online newsroom.

Indirect News Material

- media advisory
- story idea memo
- query letter.

Opinion Material

- position statement
- letter to the editor
- guest editorial/op-ed piece.

Interactive News Opportunity

- news interview
- news conference
- studio interview

- satellite media tour
- editorial conference.

B. STRATEGIC IMPLICATIONS

For each item identified, answer the following questions:

1. Will this tactic help the organization to interact with the appropriate public?
2. What level of impact will this tactic make on the key public?
3. Will this tactic advance the organization toward its awareness objectives?
4. Will this tactic advance the organization toward its acceptance objectives?
5. Will this tactic advance the organization toward its action objectives?
6. What is the main advantage to this tactic?
7. What advantages does this tactic offer that other tactics do not?
8. Are there any disadvantages to this tactic?

C. IMPLEMENTATION ITEMS

For each item identified, answer the following questions:

1. How much will it cost to implement this tactic? Is the cost justified? Is the cost practical, based on the organization's resources?
2. How much staff time will it take to implement this tactic? Is the time practical, based on the organization's resources?
3. What skill level, equipment and expertise are needed to implement this tactic? Is the needed level available within the organization? Is it available from outside sources?

Advertising and Promotional Media Tactics

The final category of communication tactics involves media associated with advertising and promotion. The list in this category includes four major sections: print advertising media, electronic advertising media, out-of-home advertising media and promotional items.

Strategy for Advertising and Promotional Media

Most advertising is used for marketing purposes, to sell a particular product or service, or to position a particular brand in the minds of its customers. As noted earlier, the tools and techniques of advertising can serve the public relations goals of an organization as well.

Advertising can combine the strengths of two other important categories of tactics: organizational media and news media. Like organizational media, advertising is a form of controlled media that provides another opportunity for the organization to oversee all the details of its messages: content, tone, presentation style and timing. Advertising also can reach vast audiences, a characteristic shared with the news media.

Phase Three

**STEP
7**

At the same time, advertising has the combined weaknesses of these tactics. Like organizational media, advertising lacks the credibility of third-party endorsement found in the news media. Like the news media, advertising tends not to be able to address itself to information-seeking publics but instead can simply be available when people stumble upon the message, such as while they are reading a magazine or watching television.

Advertising is more of a public medium than a personal one, and it is used most often with external publics, mainly because many forms of interpersonal and organizational medium are better suited for internal publics.

A major negative for advertising is the cost. It is the most expensive of all the categories of communication tactics discussed so far. A midsized daily newspaper, for example, might charge $185 **per column inch** (pci) for an ad, meaning that one full-page ad (pci cost times

ADVERTISING AND PROMOTIONAL TACTICS

Print Advertising Media
- magazine advertising (center spread, advertisorial, breakout ad)
- newspaper advertising (display ad, classified ad)
- directory advertising
- house advertising.

Electronic Media Advertising
- television commercial (network placement, spot, infomercial)
- cable TV advertising (cable crawl)
- radio commercial (network radio, spot)
- digital media advertising (interstitial ad, superstitial ad, virtual ad).

Out-of-Home Advertising
- outdoor poster (billboard, paint, rotary paint, digital billboard, spectacular, extra, wallscape)
- arena poster
- signage
- out-of-home video
- transit advertising (bus sign, car card, station poster, diorama, shelter poster, mobile billboard)
- aerial advertising (blimp, airplane tow, skywriting)
- inflatable.

Promotional Items
- clothing
- costume
- office accessory
- home accessory.

157 column inches) would cost more than $29,000. National magazines may charge $150,000 per page. One 30-second spot on the local TV evening news might cost $5,000 in a midsized market. Compare this with the cost of other tactics, and it is easy to see why advertising often is used as a tactic of last resort.

At one time, advertising was thought of only as a mass medium, but increasingly it is able to target its audiences. This is so largely because advertising can piggyback on more and better targeted media, both print and electronic.

Print Advertising

Because it can reach both local and more widespread audiences, and because it is less expensive than broadcasting alternatives, print advertising is used by many organizations. There are various opportunities available in the category of print advertising: magazine advertising, newspaper advertising, directory advertising and house ads.

MAGAZINE ADVERTISING

Ads in magazines tend to focus on national brands rather than local retail outlets and individual products, because of the diverse and widespread readership of most magazines and because of the high advertising cost.

Magazine advertising generally is sold on the basis of full or partial pages. Most advertising is placed as **run of book** (ROB), which means the ad can be placed anywhere within the magazine. Trade magazines sometimes place ads with an eye toward the articles that are on the same or facing pages.

Special placements usually entail extra costs, with the highest costs going to advertising on the inside or outside covers. There are extra charges for a **bleed ad**, which eliminates the white border and carries the advertising image to the edge of the page, and for a **center spread**, which features two facing pages. Some magazines also can feature an **advertising insert** such as a coupon or postcard. Occasionally magazines will publish an advertising section, sometimes called an **advertisorial**, a series of consecutive pages dealing with a single theme or product/service line.

Increasingly, advertisers can place a **breakout ad** in national publications for distribution to particular groups of readers. Breakout ads run only in specific geographic editions, those copies of a magazine that are distributed within a particular region, perhaps a metropolitan area or a single state.

Some magazines also offer demographic editions aimed at subscribers with particular interests or backgrounds. For example, *Sports Illustrated* has special advertising packages for editions that are distributed to golf enthusiasts, homeowners, residents of particular regions and residents of high-income zip code areas. *Time* magazine has an advertising package that can be directed to high-income and/or managerial subscribers.

Information on advertising rates is published in most media directories. A particularly comprehensive information source is the Standard Rate & Data Service (srds.com).

NEWSPAPER ADVERTISING

Newspaper ads offer several different opportunities for promoting goods, services and ideas. The two different kinds of newspaper advertising are display ads and classified ads.

Phase Three

STEP
7

A **display ad** is a common newspaper advertisement located anywhere throughout the newspaper. Display ads generally feature illustrations, headlines and copy blocks. Most are marketing-oriented ads placed by local retailers selling various products and promoting sales.

Some display ads, however, are placed for public relations purposes, such as to promote events, support political candidates, or present position statements on public issues. For example, a hospital that has come under public scrutiny because of accusations of sexual or racial discrimination may choose to address those charges in a full-page newspaper ad where it can control the entire message—its content, packaging and timing. Likewise, a health maintenance organization that feels reporters have not adequately explained its new coverage policy may use a full-page ad; the HMO may use such an ad even if it likes what reporters have written, simply as a way to increase awareness of its new policy.

Most newspaper advertising is purchased to run anywhere within the newspaper, called **run of press** (ROP), as compared to special placement on a particular page as in a specific section.

A **classified ad** is a brief, all-text message. In most newspapers, the three largest categories of classified ads deal with employment, real estate and automotive sales, but they also are used to find roommates, sell used vacuum cleaners, find homes for puppies and promote social causes. Classified ads may be used for some public relations purposes, such as to invite participants to job-training programs, college courses and similar activities.

DIRECTORY ADVERTISING

Directory advertising uses the *Yellow Pages* and professional directories to place business promotional announcements. Some directories are focused on particular industries or professionals, such as the *Public Relations Tactics Green Book* published by the Public Relations Society of America with listings of service providers, and the PRSA *Blue Book* listing organizational members. Others are more geographic, such as directories published by telephone companies and by independent publishers who may target a particular area. Increasingly, directories are putting both their information listings and their advertising online.

HOUSE ADVERTISING

Some organizations place **house ads** or program advertising, honorary or congratulatory announcements in the organization's name that are placed in programs and publications associated with special events or in publications such as school yearbooks and member directories. Opportunities for this type of advertising include a variety of programs for sporting events, banquets, anniversaries, graduations and other occasions. This kind of advertising may involve full-page or partial-page display ads similar to those used in newspapers and directories, or they may be business-card ads.

Electronic Media Advertising

Advertising on radio, television and related media is a high-cost promotional expense that also can generate vast audiences. Consider the following possibilities: television commercials, cable television advertising, radio commercials and computer media.

TELEVISION COMMERCIAL

Commercial and public relations advertising messages are placed on television in one of two ways. **Network placement** puts the advertisement on all of the stations affiliated with the network. For some of the largest of the 115 television networks in North America, that could mean hundreds of different local stations. Alternatively, organizations can use **spot advertising** to place messages on individual local stations.

Most television commercials are 30 seconds long, though stations are opening up shorter slots for 10-, 15- and 20-second advertisements. Less-competitive time slots sometimes carry 60-second advertisements. In addition to the regular commercial, most stations provide times of 30 minutes or more for an **infomercial**, a program-length advertisements that often is packaged as an interview, talk show, game show or educational program, sometimes masking its true identity as paid advertisements. Certainly there is nothing wrong with combining

DAYPARTS

The broadcast day is divided into what the industry calls **dayparts**, which are blocks of time based on different audience patterns. Here are the common designations for dayparts for both television and radio.

Television Dayparts

Here are the standard time periods within a typical broadcast day for television stations. Times reflect Eastern Standard Time; there may be some variations with network programs in other time zones.

- Early morning—6 a.m. to 9 a.m.
- Daytime—9 a.m. to 4:30 p.m.
- Early fringe—4:30 p.m. to 7 p.m.
- Prime access—7 p.m. to 8 p.m.
- Prime time—8 p.m. to 11 p.m.
- Late news time—11 p.m. to 11:30 p.m.
- Late night—11:30 p.m. to 1 a.m.
- Overnight—1 a.m. to 6 a.m.
- Weekend morning—8 a.m. to 1 p.m.
- Weekend afternoon—1 p.m. to 7 p.m.

Radio Dayparts

Here are the standard time periods within a typical broadcast day for radio stations. Times are for Eastern Standard Time; there may be some variations with network programs in other time zones.

- Morning drive time—6 a.m. to 10 a.m.
- Midday or daytime—10 a.m. to 3 p.m.
- Afternoon drive time—3 p.m. to 7 p.m.
- Evening—7 p.m. to midnight
- Late night—midnight to 6 a.m.

Phase Three

STEP
7

promotion and entertainment, but an organization raises serious ethical questions if it hides behind artificial news or entertainment programs when in reality it is presenting a sales pitch.

When placing television advertising, consider the specific time of day the ad will run. Television programming is broken into **dayparts**, time periods that reflect different viewing patterns and thus have different costs associated with buying advertising and different opportunities for the public relations or marketing communications practitioner.

Local advertising tends to focus on specific stores or venues for purchasing products (for example, the Uptown Chevrolet dealership on North Main Street). National television advertising is associated with marketing of companies (the Chevrolet brand) or specific company products (the Chevy Equinox crossover SUV).

Television advertising also provides some public relations opportunities. One such opportunity is associated with campaigns aimed at building awareness, acceptance and supportive action toward an organization or an industry group (such as the Got Milk? campaign for the National Fluid Milk Processor Promotion Board). Additionally, public service advertising takes on even more public relations functions when it becomes an advocate, such as television spots encouraging the use of seat belts or the early detection of breast cancer, or discouraging drug abuse.

Nonprofit organizations sometimes find that limited budgets require them to be creative, but this also can produce some very effective campaigns. Additionally, many spots for nonprofit organizations are based on contributed services through the Advertising Council, a cooperative venture of the American Association of Advertising Agencies, the Association of National Advertisers and various media.

The Ad Council estimates that its annual campaigns are worth $2 billion of donated media. It has produced many memorable campaigns, such as a series for the United Negro College Fund showcasing poet Maya Angelou, the McGruff the Crime Dog "Take a Bite Out of Crime" series for the National Crime Prevention Council, and the "Friends Don't Let Friends Drive Drunk" campaign for the U.S. Department of Transportation.

Because of the appeal of many nonprofit causes, some high-profile organizations are able to attract top talent. For example, when the U.S. Navy fell 7,000 recruits short of its goal several years ago, it turned to the BBDO advertising agency, which hired director Spike Lee to produce a series of recruiting commercials. Lee used a documentary style that focused on Navy SEALS, travel opportunities, sailors in a rock band and related high-interest topics. The Navy ended the following years with more recruits than expected, while the Air Force, Army and Marines fell short of their recruitment goals, despite an increase in marketing budgets for all branches of the armed forces.

Similarly, after New York City budgeted $10 million for an advertising campaign to help recruit minority candidates for its police department and to enhance the overall reputation of the department, Arnell Group Brand Consulting volunteered to develop the campaign, freeing the budget for the purchase of newspaper ads, TV commercials, and subway and bus posters.

Another type of entertainment advertisement is the **stealth ad**, also called **product placement**. PQ Media, which tracks product placement on television, estimates that in 2005 the major networks featured 100,000 product placements valued at nearly $2.2 billion, with a growth trend to $7 billion in 2012. That's why you see fellow judges on *American Idol* with their ever-visible Coke cups. *CSI* characters drink Pepsi and drive Fords because those companies paid to make it so.

Some stealth ads are placed directly online. Levi Strauss paid only a fraction of what it would have cost to advertise on national television to produce a web video of guys backflipping in jeans. It became one of YouTube's most-viewed videos, 14 million viewers in the first few months, and received coverage by mainstream media.

Closely related is **product integration**, also called **branded entertainment** or **embedded market**, in which a commercial product is woven into the storyline of films, television shows, songs, videogames, music videos, even comic books. Sony, Verizon, Visa and other advertisers, for example, paid $1 million an episode to be the featured company in *The Apprentice*. Soap operas have been doing this for decades (the very name comes from both sponsorship by soap companies and product integration into the storyline).

The James Bond *Skyfall* film had $45 million in product placement by Virgin Atlantic, Sony, Coke, Tom Ford and others—one-third of the film's production cost. Heineken spend $75 million to promote the film as part of the deal.

Recently product integration has become commonplace in prime-time television as well. Lucky Charms and Frosted Flakes figure in *Big Brother* episodes, and contestants on *America's Got Talent* eat Orville Redenbacher's popcorn in the lounge. The film producers of *Memoirs of a Geisha* paid for a triple plug to be mentioned positively within the storyline of TV's *The Medium*.

Stealth advertising is even making inroads into news reporting. Jim Upshaw, journalism professor at the University of Oregon, reported a study that found that 90 percent of 294 monitored newscasts had at least one example of stealth advertising in each newscast. The average was 2.5 instances. The study also reveals some disturbing trends in the public relations–journalism relationships, including a bank executive in Washington, DC, who meets regularly with television producers to plan news coverage for his bank, and a San Francisco news producer who has established a "product integration fee."

CABLE TELEVISION ADVERTISING

Cable networks offer much the same opportunities for advertising as do broadcast networks and local television stations. Additionally, cable television also offers the opportunity to feature **cable crawls**, messages that scroll out across the bottom of the TV screen, often on channels focused on weather, news or television program listings.

In many areas, advertising contacts with cable companies are handled not by the individual cable system but by a cable broker that places advertising on a variety of cable systems.

RADIO COMMERCIAL

In placing commercials with radio stations, consider the audience you are aiming for and the time of day the spot will run. Media buyers and radio sales people can provide information on several aspects of a radio audience that you can use in comparing stations to make the proper placement choices.

Radio advertising spots generally run for 10, 30 or 60 seconds. Like television advertising placement, radio placement can be made through **network radio**, which includes about 115 national or regional networks providing advertising to perhaps several hundred network-affiliated stations, or as **spot radio**, which means placement on individual local radio stations. Radio commercials can be designated for a specific daypart, or they can be given to the station for use at any time, called **run of station** (ROS) placement.

Phase Three

STEP
7

DIGITAL MEDIA AD

The newest communication channel for electronic advertising is in the rapidly expanding field of computer-based **digital media**. Internet websites offer a growing number of advertising and promotional opportunities.

For example, companies such as Volvo, Norelco and Ford have created **web-only commercials**, video advertisements that are used only on the Internet. In 2006, Foster's beer dropped all television advertising in favor of web dissemination. Not only are such promotional strategies less expensive than television-based ads, but they also can appeal to younger audiences with an edgier message or presentation than might not be appropriate for broadcast television. Dunkin' Donuts, Audi and Durex condoms have developed web-only ads targeted toward a younger demographic.

Much creativity goes into Internet promotion. For example, some beer sites on the Internet don't simply advertise beer, they have games, music downloads and contests so the sites can reinforce one of the perceived benefits of the beverage: fun and excitement. Likewise, websites for investment companies feature interactive financial and retirement planning. Provide the asked-for data about your income, lifestyle, work plans and financial obligations, and the program will tell you how much money to invest for the eventual savings you desire.

Several new forms of computer-based advertising have potential for public relations messages. Some websites feature **pop-ups** or **interstitial ads** that insinuate themselves onto the screen as a person is using the Internet. At other times while the user is waiting for a linked connection to load, pages called **superstitial ads** can appear to fill in the time.

Meanwhile, in a blend of computer and television technology, some companies are using **virtual ads** such as product billboards that appear in the background during a televised sporting event—except that the signs don't really exist on the field; they are digitally inserted for the TV audience. Thus they can be used in sequence to promote more than one sponsor during the program, or they can be tailored for viewers in different geographic areas.

Electronic catalogs are not merely electronic versions of printed catalogs. Instead they are interactive versions designed to engage the customers. For example, an online clothing catalog or a similar site for a furniture store can let users select among a range of styles, fabrics and colors, and then see the result of this custom design.

LONG-FORM TELEVISION AND RADIO

An emerging area of advertising focuses on **long-form television and radio**, generally defined as anything longer than two minutes (as compared to the traditional 30-second advertising spots).

One form is **sponsored news** or *sponsored public affairs programming*, in which organizations use their expertise to present objective and credible information to their publics. Strategically, this fits into their overall mix of media tactics, generally in support of information-based objectives.

One such example is *The Good Health Radio Hour*, a weekly 60-minute medical discussion program sponsored by Akron (Ohio) General Medical Center on local AM radio. Production costs are low and are handled through the hospital's public relations staff working with an outside production company. Guests are booked from the hospital staff and other local experts. The program ranks 7 out of 20 in its Saturday time slot. The sponsored radio program costs only one-third of what the hospital would spend on magazine advertising to pursue similar objectives. (For a full report, see James Armstrong's article in *Public Relations Tactics*, October 2007.)

The prospect of long-form sponsored programs raises ethical concerns. One is that the sponsor of such programming be clearly identified. Another cause for anxiety is in the potential for further muddling the already blurred line between news and advertising. For decades, nonprofit concerns such as schools, hospitals, religious groups and environmental organizations have provided television and radio programming in the format of news or public affairs. But when corporations get into the act, it raises some new fears.

PUSHING THE ENVELOPE A BIT TOO FAR

Imagine that you are a public relations director for a company or nonprofit organization, and you receive the following offer via fax and a follow-up phone call from a local television station:

> We plan to produce a series of news segments highlighting prominent businesses in the area, and we want you to be part of this series. Specifically we will produce three news segments in one week about your organization, along with several promotional spots. Remember that our newscast is the most credible programming for the image of your company. This will cost you $15,000.

That's the offer made a few years ago by WDSI Fox-61 television in Chattanooga, Tennessee. The offer surprised and shocked several area public relations practitioners, who criticized the TV station for "putting a price on its newscast." One called it "grossly unethical." Another said his organization wanted "to earn any good publicity we receive."

The TV station quickly backed away from its controversial offer, saying it had been considered but should not have been made. The offer was attributed to the naive but nevertheless good intentions of the advertising department.

Let's consider the ethical questions raised by this scenario.

- Is it ever appropriate for a television news team to offer (or appear to be offering) favorable news coverage for a price?
- Is it ever appropriate for a public relations or marketing communication practitioner to accept such an offer?
- Is this offer substantively different from the practice of some television stations in which advertising sales people try to solicit ads from companies that, independent of the advertising department, are being featured in news stories?
- Is it substantively different from the common practice among newspapers of publishing topical advertising sections or progress editions in which stories and photos from the advertisers are prominently featured?
- Is it substantively different from the common practice within the trade press of linking advertisements with news or feature stories?

Phase Three

STEP
7

Long-form advertising sometimes is presented as an **infomercial**, a portmanteau of information and commercial. The term is properly reserved for advertisements that frequently push a product toward the audience. Infomercials usually are full of demonstrations and testimonials. They also often employ direct-response marketing techniques, such as inviting viewers or listeners to call 800 numbers, log into websites, or similarly interact with the company making the pitch for the product (which often is "not available in stores").

Anybody with insomnia or late-night viewing habits is likely to be familiar with infomercials for products such as the Bowflex home gym, TempurPedic mattress, Rosetta Stone language system, Billy Blanks Tae Bo workout program, Ginsu knives, and other assorted products "not available in stores." Some feature currently washed-up entertainers, such as Cher pitching hair-care products, Chuck Norris for home gyms, and Suzanne Somers for thigh and ab tighteners.

Out-of-Home Advertising

Out-of-home advertising focuses on several different opportunities to take a persuasive message to a public that is on the move, making it possible to reach people subtly. Sometimes the advertising itself can become an attractive diversion. For example, people waiting for a bus, riding on the subway, or sitting in the stands at a sporting event often pay attention to outside advertising.

This kind of advertising offers several advantages over print and electronic advertising. For example, outdoor ads have 24–7 visibility to a wide variety of people. They also offer repeat exposure to the advertising message. On the downside, out-of-home advertisements are expensive, and they are limited to short, simple messages.

Categories of out-of-home advertising include outdoor posters, arena posters, signage, out-of-home videos, transit advertising, aerial advertising and inflatables.

OUTDOOR POSTER

In the realm of advertising media, **poster** is a generic name for several different kinds of outdoor stationary ad venues: billboards, paints and spectaculars.

A **billboard** is a huge sign placed along highways or on the side of a building, where it most often is intended to be seen by motorists. Sheets of paper or vinyl are glued onto the billboards, usually for one-month periods. Many billboards are lighted so they can be easily seen day or night. Advertisers have found ways to enhance the basic posters, often with the help of computer-produced images. Some advertisers add **snipes** to their billboards, strips pasted over part of an existing billboard so its message can be updated without the poster being completely changed.

A *painted bulletin* or **paint** is another type of outdoor sign. These are larger than posters, usually 14 × 48 feet, and because they actually are painted signs they generally are more permanent than billboard posters. Most paints are sold on an annual basis. Permanent paints are displayed in a single location, most often along highways, where they advertise motels, restaurants and tourist attractions. A **rotary paint** can be physically moved from one location to another.

Increasingly, public relations and marketing clients are turning to the **digital billboard** for both advertising and public service purposes. Images on digital billboards can change every few seconds, creating both visual appeal and opportunities for shared, part-time costs. Some states and communities are banning or heavily regulating digital billboards because of traffic safety concerns, such as motorists who glance too long at the changing and often distracting digital images. On the other hand, some communities use digital billboards to promote security by focusing on missing children and assisting police in searching for witnesses or suspected criminals.

A **spectacular** is another type of outdoor poster involving some kind of extra elements, creatively called **extras**, to the basic flat rectangular surface of the poster. For example, some such billboards feature three-dimensional elements, such as one for an auto dealer with blinking "headlights" or another for a golf course featuring a giant 3-D golf ball. On one spectacular, Mothers Against Drunk Drivers (MADD) hung the actual wreck of a car in which a family had been killed. Extras also may be sections added on a poster to alter its basic rectangular shape. Some spectaculars use computers to add a continuously changing message to billboards, such as a state lottery billboard with the amount of the current week's payout.

Another outdoor venue is the **wall mural** or *wallscape*, the painted exterior of a building leased for advertising purposes.

ARENA POSTER

Billboard-like advertisements placed on walls and fences of arenas such as sports stadiums and ballparks are called **arena posters**. Smaller posters are located inside arenas, often hanging in front of the various levels of seating. Some of these posters are computer generated, allowing for message crawls. In many sports venues, computer-generated posters are rotated every few minutes to provide a sequence of showing during a single public event.

SIGNAGE

Visible and appropriate signs can be important aspects in an organization's promotional program. **Signage** includes a variety of stationary outdoor signs, including signs enhanced by a variety of lighting techniques.

Some organizations try to make sure that their exterior signage is consistent with their architectural design. A Southwestern university with adobe-style buildings, for example, might want its signage to blend into that theme, as would a northeastern campus with Adirondack-style architecture or a campus with a classic neo-Greek design.

While most signage is considered permanent, some is meant to be temporary. Special signage is needed only a few days for a campus open house, yet attention to this tactic can go beyond the topical stick-in-the-ground signs such as those used to promote houses for sale or to solicit votes for the county sheriff. Temporary doesn't mean disposable, and some organizations invest in temporary signage that can be reused each year or for different events.

Another type of temporary signage is sidewalk chalk, which is often used in urban areas to promote events or to solicit support for political or social causes. Regular sidewalk chalk washes away with the first rain, but spray-on chalk lasts about three months, making it a more efficient medium for some signage. Specially formulated turf paints used on athletic fields also can be useful in decorative landscaping for civic, cultural and commercial buildings.

OUT-OF-HOME VIDEO

The category of **out-of-home video** is one of the newest additions to the inventory of advertising and promotional vehicles. Out-of-home video includes the giant video screens on which some sports arenas and concert halls present poster-like or full-video images. Another example of this tactic is the **video wall** that features an ever-moving series of computer-generated images.

Advertisements in movie theaters that precede the showing of feature films also fall into the category of out-of-home videos. Because of the variety in films, such advertising can be targeted to specific audience demographics.

TRANSIT ADVERTISING

Mobile ads placed on and inside of public commuter vehicles such as buses and trains are known collectively as **transit advertising**. The term also includes stationary ads located on bus shelters and at locations such as subway stations and airport terminals.

Bus signs are available in several common sizes for different areas of busses: streetside, curbside, front or back. Each can target different audiences. **Car cards** are signs placed above the windows inside buses and trains. **Station posters** or **dioramas** often are small vertical panels located in subway, train and bus stations, as well as in airport terminals. **Shelter posters** are located in bus shelters.

An advantage to transit advertising is that it can be very specific, focusing on local organizations and addressed to people who live in a particular neighborhood. In large cities, for example, shelter and subway signs may be in a language other than English that is used by a majority of the residents, or they may feature highly specific ethnic images or cultural symbols.

The category of transit advertising also includes **mobile billboards**, the painted sides of tractor-trailers or delivery trucks that increasingly are being rented out as advertising venues.

AERIAL ADVERTISING

Aerial advertising includes various vehicles: blimps with signs or computer-generated scroll messages; airplane tows featuring planes pulling banners over beaches and ballparks; and skywriting airplanes that trail smoke and write messages in the sky. These techniques can be particularly effective if a large number of your target audience is assembled in a single location, such as a resort restaurant might use above a popular beach.

INFLATABLE

Air-filled objects called **inflatables** are sometimes used as attention-getters. Inflatables range from giant outdoor balloons with a corporate logo to air-filled promotional items such as an ice-cream cone for the grand opening of a dairy bar. Some rooftop inflatables are 20 feet high or larger.

Promotional Items

Many organizations augment their advertising program with promotional items, giveaways for customers that the organization hopes will be a continuing reminder of its cause, product or service.

Branded clothing includes designer labels such as Tommy Hilfiger or the Gap, which, because they are trendy, are particularly sought out by young people. Not all advertisers, however, are lucky enough to find that their logo is a popular status symbol. On the contrary, it is usually the advertiser that pays to place the logo on T-shirts, athletic and leisure clothing, and other garments. Uniforms for sports teams and individual athletes often carry the name and logo of the corporate sponsor. Companies increasingly are applying their name, with strong visual reminders, to everything from sports cars and golf tournaments to sports arenas and hospital waiting rooms.

Costumes are another type of promotional clothing, such as the flamboyant chicken suits that might be worn by promoters for the opening of a new fried-chicken restaurant.

Some organizations place promotional logos or messages on office accessories such as calendars, pens and notepads. Others promote themselves through home accessories such as coffee mugs, refrigerator magnets, bottle openers, matches, napkins and related goods.

Direct-mail gimmicks are another type of promotional item. Small or miniaturized samples of company products, for example, can be mailed to potential clients. Symbolic items also can be quite effective.

Be careful, however, about what you send through the mail. When one California law firm wanted to let potential clients know that it had the ammunition to fight their legal battles, it mailed out hundreds of fake hand grenades. The come-ons looked so real that some recipients evacuated buildings and called the bomb squads and postal inspectors.

In another what-were-they-thinking case, a dot-com company wanted to warn prospects not to be unprepared for computer viruses. Its message strategy: Don't shoot yourself in the foot. So the company mailed out empty bullet shells on a postcard without a return address—just to build suspense—asking, "Who's been shooting [your] readers?" Again, the police and FBI were called in.

What's Next?

This concludes the inventory of tactics that are available to public relations and marketing communication practitioners.

The next step will deal with developing these tactics into a cohesive and comprehensive package that can effectively and efficiently generate the outcomes identified in the previous Strategy phase.

PLANNING EXAMPLE 7D **Selecting Advertising and Promotional Tactics**

Upstate College will develop the following advertising and promotional tactics to publicize its expanded program:

UPSTATE COLLEGE

Phase Three

STEP 7

- *display ad in local newspaper*—moderate to high cost, focus on key publics;
- *display ad in campus newspapers at other colleges*—low cost, highlight directed toward transfer students;
- *cable TV crawl*—low cost, low impact;
- *radio commercial*—moderate to high cost, directed toward potential students;
- *promotional T-shirt*—moderate cost.

(Note: No television advertising will be used because of the expense involved.)

Tiny Tykes will develop the following tactics for an employee-oriented public relations program:

- *T-shirts with safety logo*—low cost;
- *display ads in trade magazine* featuring employees with theme of customer safety—moderate cost, directed toward industry leaders;
- *display ads in consumer magazines* featuring employees with theme of customer safety—high cost, directed toward parents;
- *sponsorship of public television series* about raising infants and toddlers—moderate to high cost, directed toward parents.

 Checklist 7D **Advertising and Promotional Tactics**

Basic Questions

1. What advertising media and promotional tactics will you use?
2. How will these tactics help the organization achieve its objectives?
3. What resources will these tactics require?

Expanded Questions

A. SELECTION OF TACTICS

From the following categories of advertising and promotional tactics, identify several that you would consider using:

Print Advertising Media

- magazine advertising, advertisorial
- newspaper advertising: display, classified, personal classified
- directory advertising
- house ads
- program advertising.

Electronic Advertising Media

- television: commercial, spot, infomercial
- radio: commercial, network radio, spot radio
- cable television: advertising, cable crawl
- computer media: e-zine, electronic catalog.

Out-of-Home Advertising

- outdoor poster: billboard, paint, spectacular, wall mural
- arena poster

- signage
- out-of-home video, video wall
- transit advertising: bus sign, car card, station poster, diorama, shelter poster, mobile billboard
- aerial advertising: blimp, airplane tows, skywriting, inflatable.

Promotional Items

- clothing, costume, office accessory, home accessory.

B. STRATEGIC IMPLICATIONS

For each item identified, answer the following questions:

1. Will this tactic help the organization to interact with the appropriate public?
2. What level of impact will this tactic make on the key public?
3. Will this tactic advance the organization toward its awareness objectives?
4. Will this tactic advance the organization toward its acceptance objectives?
5. Will this tactic advance the organization toward its action objectives?
6. What is the main advantage to this tactic?
7. What advantages does this tactic offer that other tactics do not?
8. Are there any disadvantages to this tactic?

C. IMPLEMENTATION ITEMS

For each item identified, answer the following questions:

1. How much will it cost to implement this tactic? Is the cost justified? Is the cost practical, based on the organization's resources?
2. How much staff time will it take to implement this tactic? Is the time practical, based on the organization's resources?
3. What skill level, equipment and expertise are needed to implement this tactic? Is the needed skill level available within the organization? Is it available from outside sources?

Phase Three

STEP
7

Implementing
the Strategic Plan

Now that you have put together a full plate of ways to present your message, turn your attention to implementing these tactics. In this step, you will consider two aspects of implementation: turning your inventory of tactics into a logical and cohesive program, and then dealing with the specifics of scheduling and budgeting.

Packaging Communication Tactics

The various communication tactics have been likened to items on a menu, so let's take the analogy a step further. Menu items can be grouped into categories: appetizers, salads, main courses, desserts, beverages, and the like. When you order a meal, you'll probably cover the whole range of menu categories.

Additionally, when you review the restaurant menu, you often make your selections based on a particular culinary focus—Japanese, Tex-Mex, Southern, Italian, and so on. You don't order every item, and you don't order haphazardly.

It's unlikely you would start with tuna sashimi as an appetizer, add a dollop of cole slaw on a bed of lettuce, feature jalapeño chili relleno as main course, add sides of grits and ravioli, and end with a flaming cherries jubilee for dessert—served with ouzo and Pepsi Max. Rather, you'd probably develop a culinary theme. You would creatively package your choices to concoct a special dining experience appropriate to the occasion and suitable to your resources, needs, and interests.

The same is true with strategic planning for communication. In Step 7, you considered items in each of the menu categories. You discarded some possibilities and sketched out ways to do others.

Now you need to package them into an effective set of tactics to help you achieve your objectives. This should be much more than a "to do" list. Consider how various tactics can be woven together. Group some around the themes associated with your strategic planning from Steps 5 and 6.

Remember: You don't need to be tied into a chronological implementation scheme just because you selected interpersonal items before those in the other categories. Let the natural relationship among tactics determine how they fit into your plan.

Consider what you learned in Phase Two, Strategy. For example, the diffusion of innovations theory tells us that information presented through the news media can pave the way for personal interaction between opinion leaders and the ultimate public. Also, think about the example of some companies mentioned in the Introduction of this book. There is precedence for implementing a publicity program before an advertising schedule, thus allowing for a smaller advertising budget with higher-than-usual results.

Thinking Creatively

What's the best way to present your plan? You decide. Look for the simplest and most logical way to present the tactics that grow out of your planning. Later on we'll look at some suggestions to help you get started. First let's consider the importance of creative thinking. As you decide how to package your tactics, try to leap ahead of the crowd with an innovative approach to the problem or opportunity you are dealing with.

For example, if you have a new organizational logo to unveil, consider making it a real unveiling. How about a ceremonial removal of a sequined cloth covering the logo? Or maybe you could have the logo painted large on the outside of the company's building, temporarily draped. One nonprofit organization introduced a new logo by involving five local political and media celebrities who each gave a short testimonial about the organization and then, one by one, placed together cut-out pieces of a giant jigsaw puzzle to create the new logo.

Consider another scenario. Your organization has an announcement to make—usually a routine matter. But you want to have it stand out. One corporation engineered an interactive announcement in two cities at different ends of New York State, with a teleconference hook-up. The president of the corporation was in one city, a congressman who actively supported the organization in the other. The two together announced a significant multimillion-dollar project that the corporation was developing. Just in case the technology failed, the public relations planner had prepared a script and a videotape that could be used at each location.

An Indiana group used a symbolic protest as part of its announcement strategy. Hogs Opposed to Government Waste and Silly Highways (HOGWASH) sent Arnold the Pig to deliver a ham to the governor's press secretary, announcing its opposition to the extension of a highway in southern Indiana. The protesters said the road project was an example of pork-barrel politics, so it was only fitting for Arnold to be their spokespig.

Some organizations have specially designed vehicles used for promotion and other public relations objectives. For example, Rural/Metro Ambulance Service has a three-foot high talking, winking, lighted ambulance called Amby that paramedics take into classrooms during safety presentations. United Parcel Service has a miniature delivery truck that it uses in athletic arenas to deliver a coin for the ceremonial coin toss, such as at the start of football games. Notice that each of these vehicles relates to the primary mission of the organization.

Some award-winning campaigns have found their success through creativity, such as the "man sled" race by Snausages (for details, see Step 7, Interpersonal Communication Tactics, Special Events, p. 235).

"Organ donor" is a negative reference to motorcycle riders. But the nonprofit Lifeline of Ohio creatively embraced the term as a double entendre, changing it from an insult to a positive. The campaign registered 3,000 new organ donors among motorcyclists in Central and Southeastern Ohio, with thousands more expected over the four-year cycle for renewing riders' licenses.

Phase Three

STEP 8

Likewise, AMResorts and its public relations agency got creative to combat health worries. The company's Mexican resort hotels were only half-full in 2009 because of fears of H1N1 swine flu. The company issued a "flu-free guarantee," promising that any guest who contracted swine flu at one of its resorts would get free return visits over each of the next three years. Bookings shot up 140 percent. Several other resort chains imitated the guarantee, and the Mexican government praised AMResorts for helping get Mexico's economy back to recovery.

Another example comes from a public relations agency in England trying to raise brand awareness of an auto-insurance company. Goals included driving traffic to its website, increasing visibility and generating requests for insurance quotes.

Company statistics on insurance claims were researched to identify the most accident-prone street in the United Kingdom: Somerville Road in Worcester. Then eight people worked 12 hours to bubble wrap the entire street. Nearly 1,800 square yards (1,500 square meters) of bubble wrap covered cars and trucks, houses, bicycles, dog houses, swing sets, trees and shrubs, even garden gnomes. The light-hearted publicity event carried a serious message about the dangers of winter driving, raising it well above the level of a mere publicity stunt devoid of news value. Rather, it was a means of attracting media attention to a serious issue of public safety.

The public relations team contacted established news media, including major national newspapers, as well as emerging social media by posting photos on Twitter, Flickr and Facebook. The combined buzz attracted more than 125 million viewers to blogs and articles, and the story was picked up by international news media in Australia and the US. The company's website saw a 20 percent increase in visitors on the first day of the publicity event, which passed its objective of generating an additional 4,000 requests for insurance quotes.

In a final burst of publicity, the bubble wrap was donated to Oxfam, the international food-aid program, that used it to package aid to earthquake victims in Haiti.

Putting the Program Together

When the time comes to begin putting your public relations or marketing communication program together, first review the information gathered during the research phase of the program (Steps 1, 2 and 3). Reconsider the issue and review pertinent information about the organization, its environment and perceptions about it. Next examine the various publics and your analysis of them.

Following this review, consider several different ways to package the tactics you have chosen. No particular format is best for every issue, so let common sense be your guide. Consider the most distinctive element of your program. Your purpose is to select the format that most readily allows you to present your analysis and recommendations to your colleagues, boss or client.

Among the various ways of packaging your tactics is by tactical media category, public, goal, objective and department. Look at each of these with an open mind. Perhaps you'll be able to devise a more effective way to package the tactical recommendations in your program.

PACKAGING BY MEDIA CATEGORY

Using this approach, you move from the research phase to an overview of the goals, objectives and strategy associated with Steps 4, 5 and 6. Next, list each tactic according to the outline of media categories provided in the Step 7 inventory. That is, list each tactic in order of interpersonal communication, organizational media, news media and advertising media. With each tactic, indicate the relevant publics and objectives.

This presentation by media type can guide you to draw tactics from each category, though the presentation can appear a bit disjointed because it may overlook a more logical grouping of tactics. Nevertheless, it may be a good starting point, at least an effective preliminary checklist before using one of the following presentation formats. The presentation by tactics is followed by evaluation methods (Step 9), which will come a bit later in this book.

PACKAGING BY PUBLIC

The research phase moves to an outline of each key public and, for each, an overview of the relevant goals and objectives (Step 4). Then the strategy phase focuses on interacting and communicating with each public (Steps 5 and 6). This approach to packaging should include tactics associated with each strategy (Step 7) and evaluation methods (Step 9).

Use this format if the internal cohesion of your plan centers on the differences among several publics. For example, if you are planning a program that identifies three categories of publics—customers, employees and community—you may decide that you can present your analysis and ideas best by focusing separately on each public.

PACKAGING BY GOAL

Using this approach, the plan begins with the common research phase and provides an overview of goals associated with the issue. It then identifies a series of initiatives based on each goal and focuses the rest of the plan serially on each initiative.

In your presentation of each initiative, identify relevant research and background information, key publics (Step 3), objectives (Step 4), strategy with key messages (Steps 5 and 6) tactics (Step 7), and evaluation methods (Step 9).

Use this format when goals are sufficiently distinct to allow you to treat each one independently. For example, a public relations and marketing communication program for a university might identify several goal-based initiatives. These might include enhancing the university's reputation among students in high school and community colleges; increasing support from the business and civic community; recruiting more students to professional development programs; and enhancing knowledge and pride among students, faculty, staff and alumni. Campaign tactics could be associated with each of the four goals, a kind of sub-campaign for each component.

PACKAGING BY OBJECTIVE

Presentation by objective begins, like the previous approach, with the common research phase of Steps 1, 2 and 3. It then provides an overview of the goals and objectives from Step 4. Then it selects each objective as the focus for the remainder of the presentation, identifying key publics (Step 3), strategy with key messages (Steps 5 and 6), tactics (Step 7) and evaluation methods (Step 9) for each objective.

Use this approach when the objectives rather than the goals or publics are the most significant distinction within the plan. For example, a plan that has only a single goal might be presented according to the objectives associated with awareness, acceptance and action.

PACKAGING BY DEPARTMENT

Similar to presentation by goals or objectives, presentation by department acknowledges that the distinctive segments of the strategic communication plan parallel existing organizational structures, such as departments, divisions and programs within the organization.

Use this approach when the structure of the client's organization coincides with program areas in your strategic plan.

PLANNING EXAMPLE 8A **Packaging the Communication Tactics**

The following initiative is packaged according to one of the four task goals identified in Planning Example 4: Establishing Goals and Objectives.

Initiative on Transfer Students

(Transcribe research, goal, key public, objectives and strategy information.)

- *Interpersonal Communication Tactics*: Upstate College will sponsor the "Celebration! UC" *weekend* (Friday evening, Saturday afternoon and evening, and Sunday afternoon), celebrating the expansion of UC to a four-year institution. Entertainment during this event will include a *picnic* with two *bands*, a formal *banquet* and strolling *entertainers*. The event will include a *rededication ceremony* with public officials, leaders of neighboring colleges and universities, and UC students, faculty and alumni; a *fall festival* for current students and alumni; and *an open house* for prospective transfer students

- *Organizational Media Tactics*: Support materials for the festival will include a revision of the college *viewbook*, a new transfer *brochure* and a *poster*, as well as production of a *video*. A special page will be added to the UC *website* home page. Students who applied to UC within the last two years and were accepted but did not attend will be sent a letter inviting them to the festival events, along with a *fact sheet* about Upstate College.

- *News Media Tactics*: More generally, the festival will be promoted with media fact sheets and *news releases*, a *photo* with caption and a *cable TV crawl*. Students attending the event will be given an Upstate College *T-shirt* designed by UC art students. A *media advisory* will be sent to the news media, inviting them to cover the event, and *news interviews* will be offered with the UC president, provost and student government president. Additionally, the media relations office will seek out an *editorial conference* with the local newspaper to elicit editorial support for the expansion. Failing that, a *letter to the editor* will be sent by a UC official noting the benefits of the program expansion for the community.

- *Advertising and Promotional Media Tactics*: The festival also will be promoted with a *newspaper advertisement* in campus newspapers at other colleges and with radio *commercials*. Additionally, a *display ad* in the local newspaper will be aimed at parents as well as community leaders, alumni and donors.

(Note that each of the other goals would be developed in a similar manner.)

Phase Three

STEP 8

The following initiative is packaged according to the four key publics identified in Planning Example 3A: Identifying Publics.

Public Relations Program for Tiny Tykes Employees

(Transcribe research, goal, objectives and strategy information.)

- *Internal Tactics*: The internal component of a training program for employees will include *workshops* on customer satisfaction as well as a *training session* on product safety and quality; *brochures* and *e-mail notices* about safety and quality issues will be available. Several *work-group meetings* will be held, at least one involving a *motivational speech* by the CEO. Similar motivational themes will be presented in *newsletter articles* and in the online employee *bulletin*.
- *External Tactics*: The program will have an external component to provide employee support. Elements of this component will *include letters to families* of employees, *letters to the editors* of local newspapers about employee dedication to customer safety, and print *advertisements* in trade magazines and in the local newspaper. A *news release* will announce the new safety and quality initiatives, and a *story idea memo* will be given to reporters about employee dedication to customer safety.

(Note that each of the other publics would be developed in a similar manner.)

 Checklist 8A **Packaging Communication Tactics**

Basic Questions

1. What specific initiatives or sections make up this plan?
2. What tactics are associated with this plan?
3. What public and objective does each tactic serve?

Expanded Questions

A. SELECTING THE APPROACH

1. From the following categories, indicate which one offers the greatest likelihood of a package of program tactics that is cohesive and logical: by public, by goal, by objective, by department or by tactic.
2. List specific initiatives or sections in your plan.

B. STRATEGIC IMPLICATIONS

1. Will this approach help the organization to interact with the appropriate public?
2. What is the main advantage to this approach?
3. What advantages does this approach offer that other approaches do not?
4. Are there any disadvantages to this approach?

Phase Three

STEP
8

Campaign Plan Book

The **campaign plan book**—or, more simply, the book—is the formal written presentation of your research findings and program recommendations for strategy, tactics and evaluation. This report should be concise in writing, professional in style and confident in tone. Here are some of the elements the plan book should include:

- *Title Page.* List a program name as well as the names of the client organization, consultant or team members, and date.
- *Executive Summary.* Prepare a one- or two-page synopsis of the plan written as an overview for busy executives and for readers who are not directly involved in the program.
- *Table of Contents.* Outline the major segments of the program.
- *Statement of Principles* (optional). Lay out the planner's approach to strategic communication campaigns (particularly whether it is rooted in public relations, marketing communication or integrated communication). Also included are definitions of key concepts used in the book.
- *Situation Analysis.* Outline your research and synthesis of the issue (Step 1), organization (Step 2) and publics (Step 3). Some program plans present the research data and summaries on paper of a different color from the rest of the report.
- *Strategic Approach.* Present your strategic recommendations such as spokesperson, theme, key message, etc.
- *Tactical Program.* Present your tactical recommendations in whatever format you think works best (such as by public, by goal, by objective, by program or by tactic) to show your plans and to address the issue.
- *Schedule.* Outline the time and calendar considerations for implementing the various tactics.
- *Budget.* Outline resources needed for the program. Include in this figure the cost of personnel time, money and equipment, as well as any income to be generated.
- *Evaluation Plan.* Provide information on the methods to be used to measure the program's effectiveness.
- *Consultant Credentials & Resources* (optional). Indicate the resources the consultant or agency can offer. This element of the plan is especially useful in competitive situations in which more than one consultant or agency prepares program recommendations. A complete strategic campaign is located in Appendix C, Sample Campaigns.

Sometimes you may decide not to use a particular tactic, perhaps passing up even a particular category of communication tactics. For example, an employee relations project may not lend itself to involving the news media, or an investor relations project may not include advertising. It is appropriate to note the absence of a tactic and the reason behind your choice for not using it.

When you choose not to use what might seem to be an obvious tactic, it is particularly important to offer your reasoning in your plan. Especially if you are developing a proposal on competitive-bid basis, let the potential client know why you recommend against using what others might suggest.

Regardless of the way you package your tactics, it is important to show the internal logic within your planning program. Make it clear to your client or boss how the various elements work together for a common purpose.

A good way to show this internal harmony is to note for each tactic the specific public, goal and objective to which it is linked. In this way, planners can make sure that each public is adequately served by the various tactics. Likewise, planners can be certain that each goal and objective is played out through a variety of tactics.

Example: Tactics for Open House

Consider the following example outlining one tactic, an open house as part of a campaign proposal for a new graduate program at a university in a mid-sized city. This tactic shows the internal linkage between a single tactic, previously identified publics, already determined objectives and strategy, administrative details such as budgeting, and subsequent evaluation methods.

- *Public*: Professional architects (specifically, approximately 145 practicing architects within a three-county area).

- *Objective*: To increase the understanding of professional architects about the new program (50 percent of the professional community prior to beginning the academic program).

- *Strategy*: Attract attention of the professional community and create a core of opinion leaders; give specific attention to leading architects, particularly those who have received recognition from the Midstate Association of Professional Architects.

- *Tactical Elements*:
  1. Promotional materials including news release, e-mail invitations, Facebook note and outreach to appropriate blogs ($100).
  2. Information materials including an eight-minute video ($15,000 value; $1,000 cost in-house by broadcasting students).
  3. Information packet for visitors, with parallel information at website ($200).
  4. Logistical support including reserved space, parking arrangements, snacks and beverages ($100).

- *Budget*: $14,500 value. Actual cost $1,500.

- *Evaluation Methods*: Attendance figures; follow-up minisurvey conducted as part of a telephone thank-you for attending.

- *Oversight*: Assistant Director of Community Relations

In a complete proposal, each tactic would receive similar treatment. Even individual tactics might have multiple components. For example, the open house noted earlier might have additional publics, perhaps donors or potential students. Each of these would require its own statement of objectives and strategies, though the budget and evaluation methods may remain constant.

Phase Three

STEP
8

Campaign Schedule

You already addressed one aspect of scheduling when you built into your objectives in Step 4 an indication of when you planned to achieve each. This provided the deadline upon which you will measure your effectiveness in reaching the objectives.

Now that Step 7 has generated an outline of tactics, you can establish specific time requirements. This involves two considerations: (1) the pattern and frequency of your communication tactics and (2) the actual timeline of tasks to be accomplished as the tactics are implemented.

Frequency of Tactics

As noted in Step 6, the average person is exposed to thousands of public relations and marketing messages each day, yet most fall on deaf ears. Clearly, mere exposure to a message is insufficient to move someone to action. However, the frequency of exposure is an important factor in whether the message takes root in a person's consciousness.

Repetition increases awareness and leads to greater acceptance. Research has been done both on **message frequency** (the number and pattern of messages presented to a particular public in a given period of time) and on **message reach** (the number of different people who are exposed to a single message).

Most of this research has been focused either on advertising or on the learning process. However, it is possible to generalize a bit about applications for public relations. It is known, for example, that one exposure to a message has little or no effect unless the audience is unusually attentive. Three exposures are needed to make an impact.

This concept has enjoyed general support within the advertising trade since it was articulated by ad manager and theoretician Herbert Krugman (1972). Subsequent researchers have noted that studies in laboratory settings confirmed Krugman's three-exposure formula. However, in natural settings in which consumers are distracted by competing messages, three presentations of the message may not be enough to generate three mindful exposures to the intended audience.

What do we learn from such research? Here are a few of the important lessons and observations for the public relations manager.

MULTIPLE PRESENTATIONS

Don't rely on just one presentation of your message to key publics. Don't think that even three exposures guarantee success. Find ways to repeat and reinforce your message, especially through various media. This will not only increase retention among your key publics but also add to the credibility of the message because it will have the third-party endorsement of several different media gatekeepers.

REPETITION OVER TIME

Another lesson gleaned from research is the value of repetition over a period of time. Most audiences remember a message they have seen daily for several days more than one presented several times in a single day. Too-frequent presentation of the message seems unnecessarily redundant and can lead to wear-out—which, by the way, comes faster with a humorous message than with a neutral or serious one.

AUDIENCE CONFUSION

A message presented may not be a message heard, and there is no specific number for how many repetitions are best. Sometimes, even your best efforts won't gain complete success, especially with audiences who are not particularly interested in the issue. This is an unavoidable result of the information overload that all audiences encounter every day. They are aware of a message, but not particularly mindful of its content.

For example, for several years one of the most consistent television advertising campaigns featured a pink rabbit beating the drum for a battery company. Yet 40 percent of viewers in a national survey identified the wrong company as the sponsor of the ad, despite the company's best effort to promote the Energizer Bunny.

KEY PUBLIC

Bruce Vanden Bergh and Helen Katz (1999) point out that most organizations with limited budgets must find a balance between reach and frequency. A basic guideline for advertising seems to hold true for other aspects of marketing communication and public relations: Focus on key publics. Rather than trying to reach a greater number of people, try instead to reach a targeted number of strategically important people more frequently.

PATTERNS OF MESSAGE REPETITION

An insight drawn from advertising is that the pattern of communication can be of crucial importance for public relations and marketing communications. If you know that a one-time message is not likely to be effective, the questions are about when and how you should plan for repetition of the message.

Consider four concepts: continuity, flighting, pulsing and massing.

- **Continuity** is an approach to scheduling that presents a message at a consistent level throughout a particular period of time. Use this approach if you need to maintain a consistent presence over a given period of time. But realize that it is expensive to use a continuous approach with enough intensity to generate an effective reach and frequency.
- **Flighting** (also called **bursting**) refers to the presentation of messages in waves, with periods of intense communication interspersed with dark periods of communication inactivity. A variety of media can be used during the peak communication periods. This approach is useful when organizational activity falls into predictable and discrete periods.
- **Pulsing** is a combination of the two approaches, with a continuous base augmented by intermittent bursts of communication activity.
- **Massing** is the bunching of various presentations of a message into a short period of time.

These techniques are associated with advertising and most commonly involve different ways of timing a single advertising message. However, the concept of timing can be used to plan and schedule various complimentary public relations and marketing communication tactics. These could involve not only advertising messages but also meetings and special events, posters and brochures, blogs and e-mail, postings on the online newsroom, and so on.

Phase Three

STEP
8

Timeline of Tasks

At this point in your planning, you know three things about your tactics: (1) which ones you want to use; (2) how you will package them; and (3) how often to run them. Now turn your attention to carefully considering each significant task needed for these tactics. One of the easiest ways to schedule tasks is to work backward from the final tactic date. For example, if you want a brochure to be received in the readers' homes by May 15, work backward to develop the following hypothetical schedule:

May 12	Deliver to the post office.
May 11	Attach address labels.
May 10	Receive from printer.
May 5	Deliver to printer.
April 29	Finalize copy and design, and obtain approvals.
April 21	Complete draft, including copy, artwork and layout.
April 14	Begin writing, develop artwork.
April 8	Assign writer and designer.
April 6	Obtain approval for objectives, determine budget.
April 2	Begin planning for brochure.

Total time required: **45 days**.

This plan is your **timeline** or implementation schedule. Timelines are essential when you are dealing with a variety of tactics and managing different programs at the same time. Having a written plan makes it easier to train others and delegate responsibilities. Similarly, having a written timeline makes it easier to keep work records that may be needed for billing purposes.

A good way to manage the scheduling process is to chart out each of the tasks you have identified. You could use a large calendar or a timetable narrative with sections for time periods and bulleted task items to be accomplished during each time period.

However, flow charts are particularly helpful in tracking public relations tactics because they provide a visual representation of the tasks to be completed. Two commonly used types of flow charts at the Gantt chart and the PERT chart.

GANTT CHART

One frequently used type of flow chart is the **Gantt chart**. This was developed by engineer Henry Gantt during World War I to track shipbuilding projects. The Gantt chart lists each tactic and the various associated tasks, then indicates the time needed for each task. Times can be indicated in days, weeks or months, depending on the type of project.

The advantage of the Gantt chart is that it provides a map of the work that needs to be done. These charts can be kept on computer, written on paper charts or displayed as wall charts. Several free templates for Gantt charts are available for download from online sites that can be found with a search engine. Some software or online sites allow for interactive Gantt charts so multiple users can work on comprehensive projects.

Exhibit 8.1 shows a Gantt chart for an activity for which implementation is just beginning. X indicates planned tasks. When these tasks are completed, replace the Xs with solid dashes.

EXHIBIT 8.1 Gantt Chart for Brochure

	April		May	
	2 4 6 8 10 12 14 16 18 20 22 24 26 28 30		2 4 6 8 10 12 14	

Brochure
Planning (myself)   xxxxxxx
Objectives (supervisor)   x
Assign writer (myself)   x
Writing (freelancer)   xxxxxxxxx
Complete draft (freelancer)   x
Final copy (myself)   xxxxxx
To printer (myself)   x
From printer (printer)   x
Labels (staff)   x
To Post Office (staff)   x
Deliver (Post Office)   xxx

Because the Gantt chart shows every task associated with the various tactics, planners can spread out activity according to a convenient schedule. For example, under normal conditions preparation of a brochure may take about six weeks. But the Gantt chart may show that several other important and time-consuming activities will be taking place within the same six-week period. Thus you may need to begin work on the brochure earlier.

PERT CHART

Another commonly used flow chart is the **PERT chart**, a process first developed for the Polaris missile system in the 1950s. PERT (Program Evaluation and Review Technique) charts generally include dates and assignment to particular individuals, though they lack the calendaring aspect of the Gantt chart. This chart, shown in Exhibit 8.2, lists tasks within circles or boxes, with arrows indicating how one task flows into another.

An effective implementation schedule of public relations tactics generally includes more than dates. Include the name of the person or group responsible for the task. In addition to the deadline date, some charts indicate the latest date by which the tactic can be implemented and still remain useful.

Campaign Budget

The development of resources needed to achieve objectives, **budget**, is a topic that has been "on the table" since the beginning of this planning process.

In Step 1, you considered the importance of the issue and its potential impact on the bottom line of the organization. In Step 2, you analyzed the organization itself, with some consideration going to the level of resources available to address various aspects of public relations and marketing communications. These resources included personnel, equipment, time and budgeted money.

Phase Three

STEP
8

EXHIBIT 8.2 PERT Chart

Throughout the strategic development in Steps 4, 5 and 6, you were advised to be realistic in setting forth on a course of action appropriate to the organization. One measure of propriety is based on the organization's resources. At every turn in a planning process, you must be practical. Consider budget constraints and limitations—no organization is free of these—so your recommendations will be realistic, practical and doable.

Budget Items

Remember that budgeting is about more than money. It deals with all the needed resources to implement a tactic. Thus budgets for public relations and marketing communications should consider five categories of items to be budgeted: personnel, material, media costs, equipment and facilities, and administrative costs.

PERSONNEL

Personnel items in a budget include the number of people and the amount of time needed to achieve the results expected of the tactic. This may include both organizational personnel and outside people, such as consultants, agency staff, subcontracted specialists and freelance workers. Personnel costs may be associated with research, analysis, planning, writing, editing, design, photography, events management, and the like.

Personnel costs can be expressed either in terms of time (hours or days) needed to complete the task or in labor dollars. In some billing situations, public relations agencies present personnel items in the form of billable hours. Some agencies have a general and average hourly rate. Others make distinctions among strategic planning, research, account management, and administrative and support activities.

Remember to account for the time of salaried public relations staff within an organization. Increasingly, many corporations and nonprofit organizations have structured their public relations department to serve as in-house agencies. These often charge back the cost of their public relations activities on behalf of other departments, at least on paper. This chargeback allows the organization to more accurately see the role of public relations in its various programs and projects.

MATERIAL

Material items in a budget include the "things" associated with the tactics: paper for brochures, banners for an open house, media kits for a news conference, software for an online newsroom, uniforms for the company-sponsored softball team, and so on. Additionally, material items may be associated with research activities, such as the cost of questionnaires or materials for focus groups. This category also includes the time associated with activities such as developing websites and overseeing MySpace sites.

Each of these tasks and items carries a price tag, and it is very important to know exactly the cost of each recommended tactic. If you simply guess or work from old figures, you may find that you cannot implement the tactic for the amount that has been budgeted. By budgeting for each item separately, you are able to make adjustments if, for example, you need to decrease the overall budget or channel more money toward a particular tactic.

MEDIA COST

Money generally is needed for outside communication activities, particularly the purchase of time and space associated with advertising tactics. Budgets often identify commissionable media, which is advertising in newspapers and magazines, or commercials on radio and television.

When working with an advertising agency, you may find that a commission or agency fee of about 15 percent has been added as a surcharge to the cost of the final art, production charges for audio and video, and talent or model fees, as well as the cost of buying advertising time or space. Public relations agencies sometimes bill all out-of-pocket expenses (perhaps with the exception of travel expenses) at cost plus 15 percent. In the face of growing competition among agencies, however, commissions increasingly are being replaced with flat fees.

FEE STRUCTURES FOR PUBLIC RELATIONS AGENCIES

Several different approaches to billing are common with public relations consultants and agencies, as well as with the growing number of public relations departments that are being reorganized using the in-house agency model.

- **Hourly** or **per diem** **rates plus expenses** are based on the actual amount of time spent on a project, plus the amount of money spent on materials, production costs and media purchases. Some agencies lower the hourly rate as the actual number of hours increases. Examples of hourly rates are $45 an hour for copyediting, $150 an hour for research analysis, or $200 an hour for account supervision.
- **Project fees** or **fixed fees** are flat charges for projects, such as $250 for a news release or $1,000 for preparing a brochure for printing.
- **Retainer fees** are fixed monthly base charges paid in advance for a predetermined level of agency availability. The benefit to the agency is that a minimum income is guaranteed. The client benefit is that the retaining charge is calculated lower than regular hourly rates and gives the client access to a guaranteed minimum amount of public relations services.
- **Performance fees** are a new and somewhat controversial way of obtaining compensation from a client. Under this system, the agency bills based on its success in achieving stated objectives, such as placement of news releases, generation of telephone calls or web hits, and so on. This is controversial because public relations practitioners deserve to be paid for their work, which cannot always be guaranteed to have the desired effect. For example, a practitioner can research, write and distribute a news release, but he or she cannot guarantee that the new media will print it. If the client is charged only for releases that actually are published, the agency must be prepared to absorb the cost of work done on behalf of the client that does not generate the hoped-for use.

Phase Three

STEP 8

EQUIPMENT AND FACILITIES

This category includes the capital cost of equipment that must be purchased to implement a tactic. Examples of this would include computers, scanners, printers or software needed to publish a newsletter or support a blog. Also included here are the capital costs of obtaining a needed facility, such as modifying a storage area into an in-house television studio.

Note that items in this category generally are one-time expenditures. Thus the cost might be calculated separately from the project for which the resources are purchased, under the notion that they may be used for other projects in the future. However, a forward-looking budget process would amortize such expenses over the expected life of the equipment or facility and would be prepared for the time when replacements will be needed.

ADMINISTRATIVE ITEMS

A budget also should include the cost of telephone charges, delivery costs, photocopying and other office activities, as well as travel costs associated with the project. Some organizations assess a surcharge, often 15 percent, to offset the cost of overhead expenses such as rent, maintenance, utilities, taxes, and so on. Items such as software licenses and maintenance contracts also are included in this category.

Approaches to Budgeting

A recurring problem with budgeting is that public relations sometimes is seen not as strategic management but rather as the mere production and distribution of messages. Public relations may be thought to deal with hard-to-measure intangibles such as goodwill or visibility.

Because of this mindset, public relations budgets sometimes are set according to a formula based on last year's budget, or worse, as an arbitrary percentage of the wider administration or marketing program of an organization.

If you have followed the guidelines in *Strategic Planning for Public Relations*, you should find that you can overcome these difficulties. You have learned to conduct public relations and marketing communication as a management activity, and you have learned to work with precise objectives that bring an element of measurement to concepts such as goodwill and support.

Still, the question often comes up: How much should an organization spend on public relations and marketing communications?

People asking this are often looking for a simple, accepted formula. But there is no simple answer to that question, because so much depends on variables: the nature of the issue being addressed, the objectives sought, the tactics employed, and so on.

Some nonprofit organizations can operate impressive and successful campaigns for only a few hundred dollars. On the other hand, some corporations may spend literally millions on public relations and marketing communications tactics. For example, some major motion pictures, which easily run into the hundreds of millions of dollars to produce, may spend even more on promotions, most of that for paid advertising. National political campaigns raise millions of dollars for advertising and other promotional activities.

Every organization and every issue is different. Each requires careful attention and insightful management.

Establishing an appropriate budget can be a difficult task. Often you will find that a client simply has no notion what the appropriate budget should be. Every organization wants to prevent unnecessary spending, but most also are willing to spend the necessary amount to get the job done.

Let's consider some of the many different ways to approach budgeting: competitive parity, same-as-before, percentage-of-sales, unit-of-sales, all-you-can-afford, cost-benefit analysis, what-if-not-funded, stage-of-life-cycle, zero-based and objectives-based methods.

COMPETITIVE PARITY

The **competitive parity** approach bases an organization's budget for various activities on the level of similar activity by major competitors. For example, University A may base its budget for recruiting new students on the apparent budget of University B, its biggest competitor.

A drawback of this approach is that University A will have to guess what University B is spending, and much of that may not be apparent. Additionally, the two universities may have significantly different situations, such as the amount of informal recruiting being done by alumni, the reputation of the two institutions, and their financial resources.

SAME-AS-BEFORE BUDGETING

A budget developed on the **same-as-before** approach looks at how much the organization spent on a similar recent project and allows the same budget for this project. But such an approach presumes that two projects are sufficiently similar that one can serve as a benchmark for the other. It also presumes that the first project was successful and deserves to be imitated.

A related approach is *same-as-before-but-more* budgeting, which adds an inflationary increase to a same-as-before budget.

PERCENTAGE-OF-SALES BUDGETING

The **percentage-of-sales** approach to budgeting is drawn from the field of marketing, where some companies base their advertising budget on the previous year's profits. This approach may give a generous marketing budget following a good year but only a meager budget after a lean year—perhaps just the opposite of what is needed to overcome a sales slump.

In the university recruiting scenario above, the budget for public relations might be based on the amount of money obtained through tuition fees. For example, 2 percent of each tuition payment may be earmarked for the recruiting public relations program. However, because much public relations activity is difficult to quantify on a short-term basis, the percentage-of-sales method generally is a weak approach in this field.

UNIT-OF-SALES BUDGETING

Similar to percentage-of-sales budgeting, the **unit-of-sales** approach is based not on dollars but on prior outcomes.

In the university recruiting situation, the budget might be pegged to the number of people who register as full-time students. For example, for every student recruited, the university might earmark $100 for the public relations program. This approach has a similar drawback to the percentage-of-sales approach in that it pegs future budgets on past prosperity rather than current needs.

ALL-YOU-CAN-AFFORD BUDGETING

The **all-you-can-afford** approach to budgeting works better in good times than in bad. It provides for public relations funding when the organization's financial condition is sound, but limits funding during lean times. While this is not a good approach, in reality it is the way too many organizations approach public relations, as an optional luxury that can be dispensed with when money is tight. Actually, the hard times are when even more public relations activity may be needed.

COST-BENEFIT ANALYSIS

A budget based on the **cost-benefit analysis** approach identifies the cost of implementing a tactic, then compares this cost to the estimated value of the expected results. Ideally, the cost will be significantly less than the probable benefit.

For example, the cost of holding an open house for a day-care center for seniors with Alzheimer's disease might be $1,500, while the benefit of this tactic, if the projected registration goal is met, might be $10,000 from new donors to the program. Based on this formula, the open house would be considered a tactic worthy of being implemented.

WHAT-IF-NOT-FUNDED ANALYSIS

The consequence of inaction and the effect on the organization's mission is the concept underlying the **what-if-not-funded budget**. This approach forces a planner to consider expected outcomes. It is tied to objectives that previously have been accepted by the organization.

For example, the what-if-not-funded scenario for the tactic of producing a video would have you indicate the expenses necessary to achieve the objective without the video. This might mean more workshops involving additional time from the CEO, or perhaps more brochures with fewer benefits than with the video. Implicitly or explicitly, the recommended tactic is compared with the alternatives. Some organizations pair the WINF scenario with a cost-benefit analysis to keep the advantages in view while comparing alternatives.

STAGE-OF LIFE-CYCLE BUDGETING

The **stage-of-life-cycle** approach to budgeting looks closely at the phase of development of the issue, knowing that start-up programs generally require more financial resources than maintenance programs.

Consider, for example, the needs of a university communication department in transition. Let's say the university is well known for its "academic" approach to communication, with a focus on research, theory and critical analysis. Let's further presume that the university decides to extend itself into more applied communication areas such as public relations, advertising and electronic journalism. Because of the change in emphasis, the financial resources needed to recruit students for the new program will be greater than what is simply needed to maintain applications to the current program focus.

ZERO-BASED BUDGETING

A technique known as **zero-based budgeting** is rooted in current needs rather than past expenditures. It is commonly used with ongoing organizational budgets, such as those associated with annual community relations or investor relations programs. However, the zero-based approach can work with one-time campaigns as well.

In this approach, various tactics are ranked according to their importance. The cumulative cost of each tactic is then calculated. The cut-off line of the predetermined budget indicates in effect when the client has run out of money and therefore must reject the remaining tactics.

This is not really an effective method for public relations planning, because it allows a financial formula and a calculator to determine what tactics will be implemented. It can, however, serve as a useful first look at tactical planning, but this initial ranking needs to be re-evaluated with a cost-benefit analysis and a what-if-not-funded approach.

OBJECTIVE-BASED BUDGETING

A more enlightened approach is *objective-based budgeting*. By focusing on objectives, this approach deals with already identified needs and goals. It aligns with decisions already made by the organization or client.

The underlying premise of objective-based budgeting is that the organization will provide the resources necessary to achieve its objectives, which already have been approved by organizational decision makers. The consensus check that concludes Step 4 is perhaps the most important part of this approach to budgeting. It is at that point that agreement is reached on what must be accomplished. The tactics simply provide ways to achieve what already has been adopted as the objective.

Usually, this means that the organization will assign the needed resources to carry out tactics that are integral to reaching the set objectives. Occasionally, however, it means that the organization will scale back objectives to limit some of the tactics originally recommended.

Either way, objective-based budgeting puts the responsibility on the organization or client to establish objectives that it will support with appropriate tactics.

Even with the objective-based approach to budgeting, financial reality and common sense must rule. The wise strategic planner will develop tactics that are within the reach of the organization. The ability to create effective programs suitable to almost any budget is one of the real advantages of an integrated approach to public relations and marketing communication.

Budget Management

In Step 8, you are developing the actual budget for your public relations program. The best way to do this is to list each of the tactics you recommended in Step 7, then indicate the various costs associated with each tactic.

For example, if you have recommended the creation of a brochure, indicate the various costs associated with this tactic. Include one-time costs such as copywriting, artwork and design. Include costs based on the number of brochures needed, such as paper, printing, folding and mailing. Add in the value of personnel time, such as hourly figures based on annual salaries of organizational employees or the hourly fees for outside consultants, agency personnel or freelance workers. Then total these various costs to obtain a full cost for the brochure tactic. Exhibit 8.3 shows how this budget item might look as a fixed amount (that is, for a specified number of brochures produced).

By breaking down each of the various costs associated with the tactic, you are able to more precisely predict the total cost associated with the program. Additionally, this breakdown allows you to adjust the total budget more easily. Say, for example, that all of your recommended tactics add up to $12,500, but your overall budget is supposed to be only $11,000. You need to shave $1,500 from your recommendations.

One way would be to find a tactic that costs $1,500 and eliminate it, but this probably would leave a hole in your plan. After all, the tactic was recommended to achieve a particular objective.

EXHIBIT 8.3 Sample Fixed Budget for Brochure

$125	for administrative cost for public relations director (in house) • 7 hours @ $17.85/hour, based on annual salary of $37,000
$1,500	for creative costs • $800 copywriting (8 hours @ $100/hour) • $500 artwork (4 hours @ $150/hour) • $200 design (4 hours @ $50/hour)
$775	for production costs @ 2,500 copies • $125 paper • $600 printing (two-color @ $0.24) • $50 folding
$500	for distribution cost
$2,900	TOTAL

However, by knowing the cost of each aspect of every tactic, you can make minor revisions in several areas. Perhaps you could use spot color rather than four-color printing and save a few hundred dollars on the brochure, or perhaps mail fewer brochures and find an alternative distribution method that would cost less. By modifying enough tactics without eliminating any of them, you can keep your original plan intact and still meet the budget.

How closely should you stick with the overall budget that your boss or client originally indicated? That probably depends on the boss or client, and how you read the budget projection. If you think the budget was meant merely as a guideline, then going a bit over probably won't hurt. If you know the boss to be the type of manager who routinely cuts a percentage of every budget request, then you may be tempted to pad your budget request a bit, knowing that it will be cut back to the point where you really want it to be. But if you sense that the budget figure was firm, you should make sure your recommendations fall within the projected budget.

When a budget doesn't seem to stretch quite far enough for your ideas, one solution is to offer the client a range of costs—low-end and high-end tactics, perhaps with a preferred or optimal level of funding. Take another look at the brochure budget. The $2,900 total cost is based on printing with spot color as an accent. But the final cost actually could range from a low of $2,275 by printing in one color only and not using the mail for distribution, to a high of $3,500 for four-color printing and mail distribution. Exhibit 8.4 presents such a variable budget.

EXHIBIT 8.4 Sample Variable Budget for Brochure

$125	for administrative cost for public relations director (in house)
	• 7 hours @ $17.85/hour, based on annual salary of $37,000)
$1,500	for creative costs
	• $800 copywriting (8 hours @ $100/hour)
	• $500 artwork (4 hours @ $150/hour)
	• $200 design (4 hours @ $50/hour)
$550–$1,375	for production costs @2,500 copies
	• $125 paper
	• $275–$1,200 printing (one-color @ $0.15; two-color @ $0.24, four-color @ $0.48)
	• $50 folding
$100–$500	for distribution cost
	• $100 non-mail/bulk-mail distribution
	• $0–$500 mail distribution
$2,275–$3,500	TOTAL

Still another way to stretch a budget is to provide a basic set of recommendations that fits within the projected budget, then offer an add-on list of optional tactics that the client may wish to fund because of the added expected benefit.

Budgets also have a way of inching upward. Perhaps a supplier charges a bit more than when you first called for an estimate. Or some of your expense items were based on a similar project six months ago, but those items now have increased in price. Most organizations are aware that budget creep can occur, and agencies or consultants often build into their contracts provisions for such changes. A common technique is to assure the client that, for any increase of more than 10 percent, the cost overrun will be submitted for the client's prior approval.

Once the budget has been approved, it should be used as a tool to help manage the implementation of the project. The budget can offer guidance in scheduling tasks, monitoring their progress and assessing their results.

The budget should be treated as part of a living document. The strategic plan is not set in stone once it is approved. Rather, it must have the flexibility to respond to a changing environment and differing organizational needs.

Phase Three

STEP
8

Full-Cost Budgeting

In presenting the budget to your boss or client, include the full cost of all the tactics in the program (**full-cost budget**). Some tactics may not have a specific price tag, but if they are of value to the organization they should be noted, along with equivalent costs if the tactics were to be purchased.

Note the value of donated or contributed services. In particular, include the value of volunteer time as you calculate the full cost of the budget items. For example, a human service agency might get help from a college public relations class in developing a brochure for new clients. The students may not charge for their services, but the project budget should include a dollar estimate of what those services would cost if the agency had to hire professionals such as a freelance copywriter or a design firm.

Communication plans usually don't include many income items, but don't overlook implicit revenues. Corporate sponsorship may have a specific dollar value, which should be presented in the budget as an offset to expenses. It also is appropriate to include projected revenues if you have built a fundraising tactic into your program recommendations.

Likewise, it may be appropriate to include both the actual expense and real value of that expense item. For example, the full value of discounted consulting fees or free airtime for a

EXHIBIT 8.5 Sample Full-Cost Budget

$0 cost	for administrative cost for public relations director; *actual value $125 for administrative costs* (in house; 7 hours; $17.85/hour, based on annual salary of $37,000)
$600	for creative cost; *actual value $1,500* • $0 photography donated; actual value $500 (4 hours @ $150/hour) • $400 copywriting discounted; *actual value $800* (8 hours @ 50/hour; discounted from $100/hour) • $200 design (4 hours @ $50/hour)
$775	for production costs @ 2,500 copies • $125 paper • $600 printing (two-color @ $0.24) • $50 folding
$500 for distribution cost	
$1,875	TOTAL *$2,900 actual value*

public service advertisement can be listed to show the difference between the total value and the actual cost to the organization. A word of caution: Don't be tempted to set a dollar value on publicity by calculating how much the same space would cost for advertising. This is discussed in more detail in Step 9; for now let's just agree that publicity should not be confused with advertising.

By including all of this information, you are presenting a full view of the real value of the campaign, even though the organization's actual cost may be considerably less.

Exhibit 8.5 presents an example of a hypothetical budget for a brochure project for a nonprofit organization, a community dance troupe. Let's say that a friend of the artistic director for the troupe is a professional photographer whose daughter dances with the troupe. He is volunteering to take photos for the brochure and an accompanying website. Let's also say that a woman with a decade of public relations experience is relocating to this community and wants to network and become known as she sets up a freelance business. She has done similar work with artistic groups in other cities is offering to cut her copywriting fees by 50 percent as she introduces herself to this community. Exhibit 8.5 shows how the budget for this project might look.

How Much Success Is Necessary?

It sometimes is important to ask the question: How much success is necessary? Or put another way: What level of achievement is needed simply to cover the cost of the program?

Calculate the **break-even point** (BEP) in three steps:

1. Identify the total project cost (c).
2. Determine the outcome value (v), the dollar value for each unit of the desired outcome, especially those associated with the action objectives.
3. Divide the total project cost by the value of the desired outcome.

Thus the formula is:

$$BEP = c/v \text{ (cost divided by value).}$$

Let's say a private college will spend $160,000 of its recruiting budget this year to develop brochures and booklets, produce and distribute an informational video, and place paid radio commercials and billboards. Let's add $100,000 in salaries associated with this particular project. Add another $20,000 for expenses such as postage, travel and phone calls. That's $280,000 for c, the total project cost.

Now let's presume that tuition at this private college is $35,000. Apply the formula: cost $280,000 ($c$) divided by outcome value $35,000 ($v$) equals 8 (BEP). That's the break-even point. Eight additional students must be recruited through these brochures, videos and commercials before the communication program has paid for itself. (Note that this is an oversimplified example that doesn't take into account that the real cost of education is borne not only by tuition but also by donations, endowments and state aid.)

Another useful budgetary calculation is the **per-capita cost**, the cost associated with the number of people needed to cover the cost. Calculate the per-capita cost (PCC) by dividing

Phase Three

STEP
8

the total project cost (c) by the number of people (p) who perform the desired outcome. The formula is:

$$PCC = v/p.$$

Returning to the college scenario, divide the cost by the number of new recruits (let's say that's 1,800). Apply the formula: $280,000 divided by 1,800, which equals $156. This is how much the college is spending to recruit each new student through these new tactics of the brochures, videos and commercials. In percentage terms, this is about 0.0056% of tuition income, or less than half a penny for every dollar of the $35,000 tuition.

Break-even points and per-capita costs also can be calculated for other public relations objectives, as long as the objectives themselves have been stated in precise and measurable terms.

What's Next?

By completing this step, you have brought your campaign to the point of implementation. Practically, you can say you have completed your strategic planning.

But there is one more element, which is the evaluation that will take place after the plan has been implemented. Even though you won't do the evaluation until later, you plan for it now. That's the focus of Step 9.

PLANNING EXAMPLE 8B **Implementing the Strategic Plan**

The following schedule shows one of several events within the four initiatives of the plan to publicize Upstate College's expanding program. It shows the event and its component tactics, along with a cost, an assigned manager, and a start date for each tactic (as the number of weeks prior to the event).

Event: Rededication Ceremony

Tactic 1: Print and mail 1,000 invitations

Cost: $800   Manager: Publications Office   Begin Work: 12 weeks prior

Tactic 2: Print 500 programs

Cost: $0   Manager: Publications Office   Begin Work: 10 weeks prior

Tactic 3: Keynote speaker honorarium

Cost: $1,000   Manager: President's Office   Begin Work: 12 weeks prior

Tactic 4: Musicians

Cost: $800   Manager: Music Dept. Chair   Begin Work: 6 weeks prior

Tactic 5: Academic processional/ritual

Cost: $200   Manager: Provost   Begin Work: 6 weeks prior

Tactic 6: Video about UC expansion

Cost: $4,000   Manager: Video Task Force   Begin work: 20 weeks prior

Tactic 7: Viewing equipment

Cost $300   Manager: Facilities Office   Begin work: 4 weeks prior

Tactic 8: Plaque engraving

Cost: $400   Manager: Facilities Office   Begin work: 4 weeks prior

––––––––––––––––

The following schedule shows one of the several events outlined for the employee publics of the strategic communication plan focusing on consumer confidence.

Tactic: Newsletter articles in employee publication about safety, quality and customer satisfaction.

Implementation Schedule: With publication slated for the first Wednesday of each month, relevant articles will be written for each publication date, according to the following schedule:

Safety Issues

- *January*: Industry-wide safety standards and government safety regulations;
- *April*: Product safety record of Tiny Tykes Toys for the last 15 years;
- *July*: External—marketing consequences of product safety;
- *October*: Internal—employee consequences of product safety.

Quality Issues

- *February*: Industry-wide quality issues in the toy industry;
- *May*: Quality comparison between Tiny Tykes Toys and major competitors;
- *August*: Quality-control and quality-goal programs at Tiny Tykes Toys;
- *November*: Involvement of employees in quality issues at Tiny Tykes Toys.

Customer Satisfaction Issues

- *March*: Industry-wide importance of customer satisfaction to company's bottom line;
- *June*: Importance of customer satisfaction to Tiny Tykes Toys' reputation;
- *September*: Empowering employees to achieve customer satisfaction;
- *December*: Employee training/motivation for customer satisfaction.

Staffing: The communication director in the public relations office will notify appropriate interviewees two months prior to publication date. A communication specialist will arrange interviews three to four weeks prior to publication and will give completed article to the communication director two weeks prior to publication date.

Budget: There is no significant operating cost to research or write articles. Staff time is already provided, but approximately five hours will be allocated for each article for preparation, research, interviewing and writing.

Phase Three

STEP
8

☑ *Checklist 8B* **Implementing the Strategic Plan**

Basic Questions

1. What is the schedule for this project?
2. What is the budget for this project?
3. Who is responsible for this project?

Expanded Questions

A. SCHEDULING

1. What is the message repetition?
2. What is the message frequency?
3. What is the scheduling pattern (optional): continuous, flighting, pulsing or massing?
4. What is the timeline for each tactic?
5. Who is the assigned manager for each tactic?

B. BUDGET

1. Identify the following budget line items:
   - personnel
   - materials
   - media costs
   - equipment and facilities
   - miscellaneous expenses.
2. What is the full-cost budget?
3. What administrative cost items are associated with this tactic?
4. What is the break-even point?
5. What is the per-capita cost?

CONSENSUS CHECK

Does agreement exist within your organization and your planning team about the selection and analysis of these key publics?

☐ Yes. Proceed to Step 9, Evaluating the Strategic Plan.

☐ No. Consider the value and/or possibility of achieving consensus before proceeding.

PHASE FOUR

EVALUATIVE RESEARCH

The strategic planning that began with research in Phase One comes full circle in this final phase of the process. Here you turn once again to research techniques, preparing to evaluate the effectiveness of your tactics in achieving your objectives.

Perform well in this phase and you may be able to soar above the competition, because public relations practitioners too often are weak in evaluative research. And they're the first to concede this fault. Professional workshops and conference presentations in evaluation and measurement always seem to draw large audiences.

Professionals and educators in the disciplines associated with strategic communication talk a lot about research. But interest doesn't guarantee implementation.

PRSA expects its Silver Anvil entries to specify how campaigns are evaluated. Implementation of program evaluation is becoming more common, but it is far from universal in practice. Even marketing executives—who are generally more comfortable with quantifiable evaluation criteria than are public relations executives—often put more attention on "doing marketing" than on proving that it works.

Surveys of public relations practitioners in all kinds of settings—agencies, corporations, and nonprofit organizations—indicate that, while they may talk a lot about doing evaluative research, often their actions don't quite match their words.

Most practitioners, certainly most upper-level public relations managers and supervisors, say they recognize the importance of evaluative research. Yet in the same surveys and interviews, they admit that here are many times when they fail to act on that recognition, when they choose—for whatever reason—not to incorporate evaluation into the campaign design.

Much talk. Why not more action? Here are a half dozen reasons (excuses, really) for the dearth of research in public relations programming.

1. It sometimes is difficult to know just what to evaluate and how to do so. Research is a specialty many practitioners have not mastered, perhaps not even studied.
2. Public relations measures may not be as precise as those used in areas such as finance, operations and safety.

3. Another difficulty in measuring public relations is that everything is in motion, clouding the possibility of an accurate count. It's like going into a tropical fish store and trying to count the number of neons in a tank.
4. Similarly, public relations campaigns and projects do not exist in a vacuum. Other forces are working on key publics at the same time an organization is mounting its public relations activities. It is difficult to isolate the influence of public relations.
5. Some public relations measures are negatives—to what extent something bad did *not* happen, or how many negative opinions were minimized.
6. Research takes time, money and creative energy, three things public relations practitioners guard as precious commodities to be used in only the most important situations.

After all the explanations and excuses, it comes down to this: Evaluation is infrequent because public relations practitioners—or their bosses or clients—simply don't recognize its value and aren't willing to pay for it.

As you will discover in this final section of *Strategic Planning for Public Relations*, good evaluative research does not have to be costly or time consuming. Nor is it beyond the means of an adequately prepared practitioner.

Properly built into the overall strategic plan, evaluative research can increase the effectiveness of public relations and marketing communication. Additionally, it can save time and money in future endeavors. These advantages should appeal to bosses and clients everywhere.

Finally, proper evaluation can enhance the prestige and role of public relations within an organization. That's an even bigger advantage—one that every practitioner surely can recognize.

Note that it is not the intention of this textbook to indict public relations professionals for not putting enough emphasis on evaluation. Rather, the purpose of this admittedly negative introduction to the final step is to lay the groundwork for students who wish to prepare themselves to be a step above their future competitors in the job market.

Employers value colleagues who know the importance of evaluation and who have the skills to do it cost effectively. Employers hire such people entering the job market. Thus the logic here is that students who want to get hired should take advantage of this opportunity to learn about an aspect of public relations planning that employers both recognize as important and admit that they need help with.

Evaluating
the Strategic Plan

Program evaluation is the systematic measurement of the outcomes of a project, program or campaign based on the extent to which stated objectives are achieved. As part of the strategic planning process, establishing appropriate and practical evaluation methods wraps up all the previous plans, ideas and recommendations.

In this section, we will look at various aspects of evaluative research: what, when, and—most important—how to evaluate.

What to Evaluate

You've heard the phrase "starting off on the right foot." In precision marching, the first step is the most important, because it sets up the pattern for the rest of the cadence. The same is true in putting together an effective research program. Starting on the right foot means setting out to answer the appropriate questions.

Katie Delahaye Paine, an authority on evaluation research, notes that "the future of public relations lies in the development of relationships, and the future of measurement lies in the accurate analysis of those relationships" (2011, p 217).

The key to creating any program evaluation is to establish appropriate criteria for judging what is effective. This research plan considers several issues: the criteria that should be used to gauge success, timing of the evaluation and specific ways to measure each of the levels of objectives (awareness, acceptance and action). It may prescribe the various evaluation tools, and it also should indicate how the evaluation would be used.

Note that this planning happens before any tactics are implemented. Although the design of evaluative research focuses on the results of the program, it is developed as part of the initial planning. It points to how evaluation will be conducted at the appropriate times.

Phase Four

Design Questions

As you design an effective program for evaluation research, ask yourself the following questions:

- On what criteria should the program be judged?
- What information is needed to make the assessment?
- What standards of accuracy and reliability are needed for this assessment?

Next, focus some attention on the source of the information needed:

- Who has this information?
- How can this information be obtained from them?

Finally, consider how the information will be used:

- Who will receive the final evaluation and what will be done with the information?
- How willing and able are decision makers to receive less-than-fully-positive evaluations?
- Besides decision makers, who else would have an interest in the evaluation?

Remember that research design is always a trade-off between the perfect and the practical. Strategic planners must make choices about the importance of the program, the accuracy and reliability of the information to be received, and the needed resources (time, personnel, financial, and so on).

Evaluation Criteria

Before you develop specific evaluation techniques, consider first the criteria on which you will judge something to be effective. These criteria are called *metrics*, the standards of measurement to assess the outcome of a program or project. Each metric needs to be appropriate for the objective it is measuring. In essence, a metric is the yardstick against which an objective is measured.

What metrics should you use? The appropriate standards vary with the objectives and the tactics, but here are a few general guidelines. Evaluation criteria should be (1) useful to the organization by being clearly linked with the established objectives; (2) realistic, feasible and appropriate as to cost, time and other resources; (3) ethical and socially responsible; (4) credible because it is supported by accurate data; and (5) presented in a timely manner.

Consider various criteria that might be evaluated in a public relations campaign. The best structure for this is to draw on the earlier-stated objectives. Here are some categories of appropriate evaluation metrics for each of the three types of objectives:

- *To evaluate awareness objectives*:
  - Metric: media coverage and calculation of media impressions;
  - Metric: post-campaign awareness survey.

- *To evaluate acceptance objectives*:

  - Metric: tabulation of requests for information;
  - Metric: post-campaign attitude/opinion survey;
  - Metric: tabulation of letters, e-mails and phone calls expressing interest or support;
  - Metric: post-event audience evaluation.

- *To evaluate action objectives*:

  - Metric: measures of results (ticket sales, attendance, memberships, donations and so on);
  - Metric: measures of improvement;
  - Metric: organizational or environmental change.

Additionally, be prepared to identify and evaluate unplanned results of a campaign. Sometimes a campaign generates reaction beyond what was anticipated. This reaction may be positive or negative in the eyes of the organization, but it is worth considering unplanned results and unintended consequences, if for no other reason than they might be built into subsequent similar campaigns.

Here is an example of how one organization established criteria to judge the effectiveness of its website:

- ability to navigate easily throughout the site (a measure of awareness objectives);
- breadth of content (awareness objectives);
- ability to convey key messages (awareness objectives);
- stats tracking the number of web visitors (awareness objectives);
- number and tenor of questions and comments by site visitors (acceptance objectives);
- number of visitor names that are captured for organizational response or follow-up (action objectives);
- number of web visitors who take online surveys or respond to online offers (awareness or action objectives).

Notice that measures of message production and exposure are not included as significant. For example, what matters is not so much the number of hits but rather the number and content of comments by visitors to the site and the number of retrievable names so the organization can engage the visitor in two-way communication. With appropriate evaluation metrics in mind, the public relations strategist can turn to the task of developing evaluation measures that can rate the website on those criteria.

Notice, too, that all of the criteria should be developed before any implementation of the website, because the particular criteria you identify as necessary will determine some of what you do in putting the website together.

It is interesting to note that public relations practitioners generally value positive media stories more highly than CEOs value such publicity. It's not hard to understand this disparity. Public relations people operate in a world in which awareness generated through media is an intrinsic value. CEOs live in a show-me world where the value of results needs

Phase Four

TWELVE REMINDERS ABOUT EVALUATIVE RESEARCH

Here are a dozen suggestions for an effective evaluative research program. Most of these tips are based on common-sense principles that you probably already know. But reminders are meant to be remembered, so review these tips as you prepare your evaluation program.

1. *Don't wait for the program's completion before you evaluate*. Evaluation begins with the planning process, before you actually "do" anything. Effective planning means you determine in advance what you will evaluate and how you will measure.

2. *Guesses aren't good enough*. Evaluation must rely on facts, not estimates. Hunches and gut feelings can point the way, but hard facts are needed to accurately assess impact.

3. *Friends may be telling you what they think you want to hear*. Get beyond the limitations of information volunteered by people who already look kindly on your organization. Be cautious of relying too heavily on information solicited from friends and other supporters in situations that don't encourage candor.

4. *Employees have a stake in the program's success*. Realize that they may be seeing what they want to see, for the programs they evaluate affect their own job security and economic future, as well as their day-to-day social relationships on the job.

5. *Samples must reflect the population*. Formal evaluative research draws on a sample that represents the publics addressed in the public relations activity. This kind of research is likely to generate information that is accurate.

6. *Hard work and cost aren't measures of effectiveness*. Be careful not to equate activity with achievement. Your campaign may have claimed many resources in time, energy and budgets, but these are not the measure of program effectiveness.

7. *Creativity is not a gauge of effectiveness*. "Everybody thinks it's a neat idea" may indicate innovation and a professional award may attest to your ingenuity. But neither is the mark of a successful program.

8. *Dissemination doesn't equal communication*. A mainstay principle of public relations is that distribution of a message does not guarantee that real communication is achieved. Every piece of unopened junk mail, every commercial zapped or TiVo'd, and every half-time show missed by spectators heading for the rest room is an example of failed communication.

9. *Knowledge doesn't always lead to acceptance*. Well-informed publics are supportive ones, says the common wisdom. Not necessarily. Knowledge is important on the road to support, but this road has an off-ramp as well. Sometimes the more people know about an organization or the issues it faces, the less supportive they may be.

10. *Behavior is the ultimate measure*. Awareness and acceptance objectives are important, and many public relations activities seek to increase knowledge, generate favorable attitudes or foster supportive opinions. But knowledge that doesn't lead to action is pretty weak, and attitudes or opinions that don't have an outcome in behavior are like books sitting unread on the shelf. Missed opportunities. Unrealized potential.

11. *Evaluation doesn't have to be expensive or time-consuming*. Like other aspects of strategic planning, evaluation research is linked to the organization's resources. Proper evaluation requires insight and creative thinking, not necessarily a lot of time or money.

12. *Evaluative research enables action*. It allows organizations to modify programs, analyze and justify the current program, or make decisions about similar future programs.

to be documented. But the question is worth asking: Just what should we be measuring? Or more pointedly: Why should we continue to focus on awareness when our bosses and clients want to see how we influenced action?

Ken Gofton (1999) has noted the difference between advertising and public relations measurement. He observes that advertising often focuses evaluative research on audience exposure. Public relations evaluation, on the other hand, goes beyond exposure metrics toward techniques such as profiling audiences, tracking attitude change and assessing impact in terms of behavioral outcomes.

Walter Lindenmann, the guru of public relations research, observed that CEOs and organizational executives are increasingly more demanding of public relations practitioners. They expect practitioners to justify their existence, be accountable for their programs and document their contributions to the bottom line.

A study of evaluation research for the Institute for Public Relations (Lindenmann, 2006) suggests that any credible evaluation program requires four major components: setting measurable goals and objectives, measuring outputs, measuring out-takes and outcomes, and measuring institutional outcomes.

When to Evaluate

There are three stages in the process of program evaluation related to timing: implementation reports, progress reports and final evaluation. Each is different; each is important.

Implementation Report

The first potential point for evaluation is in tracking the implementation of each tactic, making sure that it is proceeding according to plan. This **implementation report** documents how the program tactics were carried out. In it, include a schedule of progress to date toward implementing each tactic, as well as any work remaining. Identify any gaps, defects or potential delays that could hurt the plan. Note any difficulties encountered and how they were (or might be) resolved. Discuss the efficiency with which the tactics were set in motion.

Additionally, note the name of the person or group responsible for each tactic, as well as other personnel resources such as staff, freelancers, consultants, and so on. It might also be useful to include budgetary information, such as how much money has been spent or committed thus far.

Progress Report

It is important to monitor progress at various key points as the tactics are being implemented. **Progress reports** are preliminary evaluations on which planners can make strategic modifications as they further implement the program. Such midcourse corrections can keep the project functioning at peak efficiency. In this way, the plan is used as a written guideline rather than a rigid rulebook.

Consider this analogy of an interactive computer travel map for a cross-country road trip. This mapping program receives hourly weather updates and daily progress reports on highway construction projects. It also monitors traffic jams around congested urban areas and newspaper reports of tourism-related events. Before you leave on the road trip, you map out a tentative

Phase Four

plan, indicating your goal (travelling cross country) and your objectives (stopping at various points of interest along the way to the destination). A rigid use of your plan would be to follow the map with no deviation—after all, you've planned this trip for a long time and you shouldn't be distracted by unscheduled changes. However, a more effective use of the map would allow the computerized mapping program to alert you to an interesting community festival only a few miles off the scheduled route or to travel delays resulting from snow build-up on a mountain pass.

The mapping program demonstrates the value of feedback: You can use information gathered during the course of the project to update strategy, modify objectives and adjust tactics. This type of in-process evaluation is important for both public relations and marketing communication programs. After a pilot project and following each significant phase within a program, evaluate whether the program is unfolding as it was planned to do. Ask questions: Are the messages being disseminated as expected? Are they being understood? Are people responding as expected? If the answers turn out to be "no," there is still time to make adjustments before the rest of the program is implemented.

This kind of evaluation allows a public relations plan to be a living document that enhances the atmosphere of open communication. It allows the planning organization to be impacted by its environment and by its publics.

Final Report

Final reports, sometimes called **summative reports**, review the whole of the program. They measure impact and outcome for the various tactics. The final evaluation gauges how well the tactics achieved what they set out to achieve—namely, the various objectives.

Research Design

The question of when to evaluate leads to a related aspect of **research design**: how to structure the evaluation in relation to the measurement standards. There are several possibilities, the most common being after-only studies and various approaches to before-and-after models.

AFTER-ONLY STUDY

The simplest research design is the **after-only study**, which is common in public relations precisely because of its simplicity. Implement a tactic, measure its impact, and presume that the tactic caused the impact. This approach can be appropriate for action objectives that measure audience response, such as attendance, contributions, purchase and other easily measured reactions. For example, a political candidate running for office may need no preliminary baseline. She simply would be interested in the numbers of votes received in the election.

However, the after-only approach is not appropriate for every situation. Its weakness is its very simplicity, because this design presumes a cause-and-effect relationship that may not be accurate. The after-only approach does not prove that the tactic caused the observed level of awareness or acceptance, only that the result occurred after the tactic. Perhaps the levels were there all along but simply not noticed.

BEFORE-AND-AFTER STUDY

Another format for evaluation research is the **before-and-after study**, also called a **pretest/post-test study**. This model involves an observation before any public relations programming is implemented. The initial observation provides a benchmark or baseline for comparing studies that will be conducted later.

For example, if the candidate noted above wanted to gauge the effectiveness of a new campaign message, she would need to measure her support before the message was presented and measure it again following the presentation. The difference would indicate the change—positive or negative—created by the new campaign message. In another example, a public transit system might compare ridership figures before and after a promotional campaign. Note that a before-and-after study is integrated into both the formative research and evaluative research phases of the planning process.

The simplest before-and-after study involves three stages: (1) observe and measure a public; (2) expose the public to a public relations tactic; and (3) measure the public again. Any change in the public's awareness, acceptance or action can likely be attributed to the tactic.

Remember, however, that public relations activities generally don't take place in a vacuum or in a pure environment. Be aware of extraneous factors. Not every change in your key public may appropriately be linked, cause-and-effect fashion, to your programming. One of the challenges for evaluative research is to sort out the effective public relations tactics from unrelated outside forces.

CONTROLLED BEFORE-AND-AFTER STUDY

A more sophisticated type of evaluative research takes into account those unrelated outside forces. A **controlled before-and-after study** involves two sample groups drawn from the same key public. One sample is the group to receive the message; the other is a control group that does not receive the message.

This process has four elements: (1) observe and measure each group; (2) expose one group to a tactic, but do not expose the control group; (3) measure each group again; and (4) compare the results of each group.

The control group is likely to have remained unchanged, while any change noted in the exposed group presumably can be linked to exposure to the public relations tactic—the key difference between the two groups. For example, the transit system noted above might also compare before-and-after ridership figures with those of a transit system in a similar city in another state (the control group), where riders were not exposed to the promotional campaign.

Remember that research design is always a trade-off. Strategic planners must make choices that consider the importance of the program, the accuracy and reliability of the information to be received, and the needed resources (time, personnel, financial and the like). They also should look at the whole picture, focusing not on each tactic in isolation but on how the various tactics together have achieved their objectives.

Also be aware of extraneous factors that can mask your evaluation efforts. Not every change in a public's awareness, acceptance or action may be caused by your public relations programming. Try to account for other activities and influences that the publics have been exposed to.

Let's return to the example of the transit system. If, a few days after the ridership campaign begins, an international political crisis sends oil prices up 30 percent, you probably would notice a lot more riders on the trains and buses. But you shouldn't attribute this to your public relations campaign. It's more likely that motorists are reacting to the higher cost of gasoline at the pumps, and your research report must note this.

Phase Four

CYBERNETICS AND PUBLIC RELATIONS

Norbert Wiener's cybernetic model of communication (1954) was noted in Step 6, Developing the Message Strategy.

Cybernetics deals with the feedback mechanisms of goal-seeking systems, in which goals are established, action and **output** is monitored, and feedback mechanisms implement corrective action to keep the system on the target of its goal. Furnace thermostats, heat-seeking missiles and cruise-control devices on cars are examples of cybernetics.

In public relations and marketing communication, examples of cybernetics include crisis planning and issues management that feature a radar-like early warning system of monitoring the environment in which the organization operates. An example is the kind of in-process evaluative research being presented in this book.

Cybernetics in public relations operates most effectively in an open-systems approach. In this approach, public relations functions as the liaison between the organization and its publics, with responsibilities to each and to the mutual benefits of both.

Two-way communication between the organization and the environment keeps the organization moving toward its goal, with this approach continuously adjusted through the feedback provided by the publics.

A benefit of most evaluative research is that it is a form of **unobtrusive research**—the subjects in the study do not know they are being observed, at least not until after the fact, when their awareness of being observed can't affect what they have already done.

An exception to this is the before-and-after study. When conducting a before-and-after study, be aware of the **Hawthorne effect**, also called the **placebo effect**.

In the 1930s, researchers at Hawthorne Works, an electric power company near Chicago, were trying to find out how the intensity of lighting affected factory workers. The researchers increased the lighting, and productivity increased, then slowly settled back to the earlier level. Then they decreased the lighting and productivity increased again. At first, the researchers believed the changes were the result of teamwork among the employees. Similar studies manipulated other aspects of the work environment: pay incentives, shorter hours, longer hours, more breaks, fewer breaks. In each case, productivity increased for a short time.

In 1955, Henry Landsberger reanalyzed the older studies. He concluded that the boost in productivity was not caused at all by the amount of lighting but simply because the subjects knew they were being observed and knew that the company was concerned about worker productivity. Landsberger coined the term "Hawthorne effect," which since has been broadened to explain any impact, usually short-term, through which employees are made to feel important or are aware that they are being observed.

How to Evaluate

A question was posed at the beginning of Step 9: What information is needed in order to evaluate a program's effectiveness? Answer this question wisely, and you'll have a strong final phase to your strategic planning. Answer blindly, and you could end up measuring the wrong thing. Consider five levels of evaluation: judgmental assessments, evaluation of communication outputs, awareness, acceptance and action.

Judgmental Assessment

An evaluation made on hunches and experience is called a **judgmental assessment**. This type of informal feedback, sometimes called **seat-of-the-pants evaluation**, is not uncommon in public relations and marketing communication. It is the kind of research that everybody seems to do sometimes, because it comes naturally.

Judgmental assessment relies on personal and subjective observations such as the following: "The boss liked it," "The client asked us to continue the project," "Everybody said this was a success," "The customers seem happy" and "Hey, we won an award for this project."

This approach is based on personal observation, which can be both a strength and a limitation. Some judgmental evaluations, though informal, can be helpful to an organization. For example, assessment by outside experts, perhaps public relations colleagues in another organization, might offer an excellent analysis of the program.

So too with judgmental assessments based on a formal review of an organization's program by a panel of outside experts. An example is the review teams fielded by the Accrediting Council on Education in Journalism and Mass Communications that assess various aspects of a college or university communication program seeking professional accreditation. Another example is an evaluation based on a program that received an award through a competition sponsored by a professional organization, such as the Silver Anvil sponsored by the Public Relations Society of America or the Gold Quill Award of the International Association of Business Communicators.

Additionally, senior practitioners often draw on their experience to make informal judgments about program effectiveness.

Such informal research has its limitations, however. For one thing, informal assessments often are made by program managers, who are never disinterested and seldom impartial. For another, their personal observations are often imprecise and arbitrary, sometimes downright fickle. Granted, the anecdotes on which this feedback is based can provide much insight into the success or failure of a program, but because informal research and gut feelings don't involve representative samples and standard measures they can't confirm the effectiveness of public relations activity.

Another problem with judgmental assessment is that it often gives undue emphasis to apparent creativity and to the expenditure of energy and resources. Throughout this entire planning process you have put in a great deal of effort and energy. In doing so, you have articulated a strategy and produced a range of tactics. These, of course, are important, but they are not what you should be measuring. Rather, the evaluation phase should focus on your objectives at each of their three levels: awareness, acceptance and action. Just like objectives, evaluation research should deal with the impact your program has made on your various publics.

METHODS OF EVALUATIVE RESEARCH

Like formative research, evaluative research involves techniques that can be either quantitative or qualitative.

- **Quantitative research** methods used frequently for evaluation include surveys, content analyses, cost-effectiveness studies, readership studies, head counts and tracking of feedback, as well as direct observation and monitoring of specific results.
- **Qualitative research** techniques commonly used for evaluation include interviews, focus groups and case studies.

Don't let the availability of so many different research methods hide the fact that direct observation of outcomes can be the simplest way to evaluate the effectiveness of public relations programs. For more information on research techniques, see Appendix A, Applied Research.

Judgmental assessment also can lull you into taking for granted what you should be analyzing. Consider tax-free shopping weeks. Increasingly, state lawmakers are periodically waiving sales tax to encourage spending and help consumers save money. One popular time is the back-to-school shopping time in late August. It's oh-so-obvious that consumers win; they save money when buying clothing and school supplies. Politicians benefit from the gratitude of their constituents. And merchants like it because buyers flock into their stores. On the surface, tax-free shopping weeks are both popular and successful.

Yet is popularity a valid standard? Some stores that used to discount merchandise 15 or 20 percent no longer have sales because they know the consumers will flock in to save— what? 8.5 percent (the average sales tax across the country)? Meanwhile, states lose important tax revenues, threatening services or leading to increases in other kinds of taxes and fees to make up the difference. So customer satisfaction, if it is based on whim rather than fact, isn't a useful measure.

The lesson is this: Effective evaluation requires careful analysis. Don't rely only on the obvious—because what obviously seems true sometimes isn't. Let's look at a complementary approach to evaluation, this one based on the results of communication tactics.

Communication Outputs

Measuring communication products and their distribution is the focus of **outputs evaluation**, a method that concentrates on the development and presentation of a message. As an evaluation method it is not particularly effective.

Outputs may be necessary tasks to do, but they really are not effective measurement tools. Yet current researchers report that many practitioners still rely primarily on output measures (Rice and Atkin, 2002; Xavier et al., 2005). Various methods of measuring **communication outputs** include message production, message dissemination, message cost, publicity value and advertising equivalency. Let's look at each.

Phase Four

STEP
9

MESSAGE PRODUCTION

Several techniques of evaluation research deal simply with whether the message is produced. For example, count the number of news releases written, brochures printed or pages formatted for a website. Or note the creation of special message vehicles, such as a company float for the Fourth of July parade. Measurement of **message production** quantifies the work output of a public relations office, but not much more. While it may be useful for a measure of individual job performance, don't be deluded into thinking that it is a measure of program effectiveness.

MESSAGE DISTRIBUTION

Another approach to awareness evaluation focuses not merely on the production of messages but also on their **distribution**. In this category, the evaluator focuses on media contacts and asks how many news releases were mailed, faxed, tweeted, posted on the blog or uploaded to the website. Measuring message dissemination tells what an organization did to spread the message, but it doesn't measure the message's effectiveness or its impact.

MESSAGE COST

Another type of measurement deals with **message cost**. This approach analyzes how much money an organization spends to present its message. For paid media, such as brochures or advertisements, the organization simply divides the cost of the communication vehicle by the number of times the message has been reproduced. For example, if it costs $150 to produce 2,500 copies of a flier, then each piece costs 6 cents.

When dealing with electronic media, the common standard is **cost per thousand**, identified as **CPM** (from the Latin word *mille,* meaning "thousand"). For example, if a radio station with 75,000 listeners during a particular time period charges $150 for a 30-second commercial, it would cost $2 for each thousand listeners—a mere one-fifth of a penny per listener. Cost per thousand is an effective way to compare costs among various media, even print vehicles. Consider the following:

- A national magazine with a regional edition circulating 17,000 copies charges $9,000 for a full-page color ad; CPM = $529 (nearly 53 cents per each local subscriber).
- A city newspaper with a circulation of 338,000 charges $22,000 for a full-page ad; CPM = $65 (about $6\frac{1}{2}$ cents per reader).
- A local radio station with an estimated 10,000 listeners charges $35 for a 30-second commercial; CPM = $3.50.
- A transit system of bus and light rail service in a metropolitan area charges $290 for each transit poster, with 40 needed to saturate coverage in what is called "100 showing" (100 percent of the audience, 3 million people likely to see the poster within a 30-day period). The cost for 40 posters is $11,600; CPM = $3.87.
- A cable advertising service charges $150 for a 30-second commercial on a cable network providing 25 channels to 520,000 subscriber households (average per-channel subscriber base of 20,800); CPM = $7.21 (less than a penny per subscriber).

When comparing media costs, however, remember that the elements you are comparing may not be similar. The impact of various media and the amount of repeat presentation for messages to have an impact must be considered, as well as how closely a particular media audience coincides with an organization's key public.

Phase Four

Consider this example of a newspaper ad and a direct-mail letter. A 50,000-circulation newspaper charges $5,500 for a half-page ad; CPM = $110. A printer charges $600 for 10,000 copies of a direct-mail letter; CPM = $60. Additionally, it will cost $1,900 to distribute the letters; now the CPM cost to the organization is $250 for the direct-mail letter.

Purely based on production and distribution costs, the newspaper ad is a better deal. But most newspaper readers skip over the ads because they are not particularly interested in the topic. Chances are you don't need to communicate with 50,000 newspaper readers because most of them are not even in the key public you identified in your planning. Meanwhile, people who receive letters are often more likely to read them, especially if the organization did a good job identifying its public and designed the letter to be of obvious interest to the readers. So the $2,500 letter could well be the more cost-effective way to communicate with members of the key publics. It costs less and, more important, results in more effective message delivery. On the other hand, if your public is widespread and difficult to reach individually, then the newspaper cost would be the better way to communicate with them.

PUBLICITY VALUE

The measurement committee of the Canadian Public Relations Society has developed a point system now used by most Canadian public relations agencies. Called **media relations rating points** (MRP), it is a standard for evaluating and reporting editorial media coverage for public relations initiatives. MRP is intended to help both practitioners and clients understand the relative value of various public relations tactics.

The principle is simple: The practice of public relations is enhanced by having a consistent and systematic way to calculate the relative value of various communication tactics.

While the principle is simple, the process of MRP is sophisticated. Using proprietary software, MRP yields a percentage point based on a calculation that includes the total number of articles or reports, reach or total impressions, budget and tone. It also takes into account company/brand and product mentions, quotes by spokespersons, use of photos, call-to-action, key messages and the length of the broadcast/print/online report.

ADVERTISING VALUE EQUIVALENCY

A common but highly inappropriate evaluation technique is related to the message cost. **Advertising value equivalency** (called AVE for short) means trying to place a dollar value on publicity. The technique treats a nonadvertising item as if it were an ad. Specifically, AVE tries to measure the supposed value of news coverage, equating the amount of publication space or broadcast time to the cost of purchasing that same amount as advertising.

For example, a news report about your organization is published in a local newspaper, involving a space totaling 21 column inches including headline, story and photo. How can you evaluate this report? Using the advertising equivalency method, you would look up the advertising cost for a 21-inch ad in that newspaper. At $165 per column inch, for example, that story would have cost $3,465 if it were an advertisement. So the publicity is said to be worth exactly $3,465.

That's a neat way to put a dollar figure on a news story, costing it out as if it were an ad. But that "as if" causes a big problem. A news story isn't an advertisement, so the dollar figure is meaningless. Why? Audiences know the difference between news and advertising, and they treat the two information vehicles differently. Generally news stories are far more credible than are advertisements. So how much extra should you add for credibility?

On the other hand, many news stories don't necessarily have only positive information about an organization. Maybe you should you deduct some amount because the news report wasn't glowingly positive. But wait. People read news stories more than they do ads. Perhaps you should add value because of higher audience attention. Then again, what's the value of no coverage when the organization's public relations practitioners have been trying to keep a story out of the papers?

Back and forth it goes, and in the end any dollar value you give to the news story is simply a fiction, and bad fiction at that. It is worse than worthless because it gives a false impression that a meaningful assessment has been made.

Despite the obvious misconception that underlies advertising equivalency, it's a myth that doesn't want to go away. Some public relations or marketing agencies even have devised formulas to impress their clients, taking AVE to the next absurd level. They apply a **multiplier**, calculating that if A represents the cost of advertising time or space in the media, as publicity it must be worth A x B. For example, they calculate the value of publicity as being four times the cost of advertising. Or ten times. They can calculate it however they want. It's still just an arbitrary weighting scheme that is all smoke and mirrors.

The Institute for Public Relations points to two major shortcomings with AVE:

- Editorial matter is not "free advertising."
- Dollar cost does not equal dollar value.

Why has AVE survived in the practice?

For one thing, it's simple, it looks good and it appeals to a client or boss without savvy. But the overwhelming argument to shove AVE off the research palette is that it's a work of fiction. Advertising is not public relations, and thus any attempt to give a dollar value to public relations tactics as if they were advertising simply doesn't make sense. Advertising value equivalency simply isn't equivalent.

The Institute for Public Relations says "AVEs, random use of multipliers, and other silly metrics and practices diminish the integrity of the profession . . ." and adds that AVEs are "rejected as a concept to value public relations."

Organizations have an obvious desire to track their return on their investment, so it's not unreasonable to look for a way to do this. The following sections outline several more valid alternatives that do have a place in the public relations game plan.

Awareness Objectives

The methods associated with outputs evaluation focus on documenting communication activity. Perhaps that's a worthwhile exercise, but it doesn't give a solid basis for measuring effectiveness. Rather, it is more important to demonstrate the value that communication tactics offer an organization, specifically their effectiveness in achieving awareness, attitude and action objectives that already have been established.

The first level of public relations objectives—awareness—provides an important category of evaluation research.

Awareness evaluation focuses on the content of the message. It considers how many people were exposed to the message, how easy the message is to understand, and how much of the message is remembered. Some of the common measures for awareness evaluation include message exposure, message content, readability measures and message recall.

OUTPUTS, OUT-TAKES AND OUTCOMES

Public relations evaluation includes some related concepts: output, out-take and outcome. It is important to make a clear distinction among these terms.

James Bissland (1990) identifies a communication output as the work done in a public relations activity. He likens this work to the who-says-what-in-which-channel part of Harold Lasswell's classic verbal formula for communication. Walter K. Lindenmann (2006) has described outputs as short-term, immediate results of a public relations program.

Outputs are the "things" produced by public relations practitioners: news releases, tweets, blog posts, special events, and so on. They often involve numbers: How many speaking engagements? How often is a company official quoted? How many people attend a special event? How many web pages are viewed? How many placements appear in the media?

Being things that people see and hear, outcomes are relatively easy to measure. Often this is done by observing audience participation or by measuring program results.

An **out-take** is the thing that publics take away, such as their understanding of a news report or their initial emotional response to a speech. Out-takes might be considered short-term results. Often they are measured through benchmarking and monitoring of the social environment.

A **communication outcome** is far more important. Bissland calls outcomes "terminal goals," but often they are more like what this book calls objectives because they are measurable and time-specific. Examples of outcomes are the number of new recruits, the amount of money raised or the passage of desired legislation.

Writing for the Institute for Public Relations Research, Lindenmann focused on the communication process. Outcomes "measure whether target audience groups actually received the messages directed at them, paid attention to them, understood the messages, and retained the messages in any shape or form. They also measure whether the communications materials and messages which were disseminated have resulted in any opinion, attitude and/or behavior change on the part of those targeted audiences to whom the messages were directed" (Lindenmann, 2006, p. 14).

Measuring outcomes often calls for more sophisticated research techniques.

What do we learn from this glossary of evaluation terms? Measure outputs if you wish. They can provide useful assessment of what has been done and how you have used your resources. But don't stop there. Measure out-takes every time you engage your publics. Even more importantly, measure program outcomes, specifically as they relate to your objectives.

MESSAGE EXPOSURE

Measurement of **message exposure**, which focuses on the number of people in key publics who were exposed to the message, is a bit more sophisticated than the previous evaluation methodologies. That's because these objectives-based measures look more closely at communication tactics, evaluating not only distribution but also audience attention.

For example, the evaluator may use metrics for media exposure that ask how many hits were registered at a website or the actual number of people in the audience who heard a speech or saw a performance. Instead of counting the number of news releases distributed, the evaluator would ask how many newspaper stories or broadcast reports resulted from the release or, more important, how many people actually read those newspaper stories, heard the broadcast reports or read the online posting of the news release.

This can be a difficult number to obtain. Some public relations offices track this on their own. Others may hire a **clipping service**, a company that tracks publications and/or broadcasts on a regional, national or even international basis. A variety of services and software exists to track traffic at an organization's website, which might include a media room where reporters can download releases and other visitors can read releases. The software can measure not only the number of visitors but where they came from, how long they stay at the site, what pages they visit, what they download, and so on.

Some measures of message exposure count actual audiences, such as the number of people who attend an open house or some other public relations event. Unfortunately, some other measures deal with inferred or potential audiences, weakening the value of this measure by linking it to mere estimates.

Some concepts associated with message exposure are drawn from advertising. Audiences could have been exposed to the message presented in various media, from interpersonal settings, to viewers of a television newscast, to motorists who pass by a billboard. Sometimes these calculations can be quite impressive, even seductive. Consider, for example, the 1.1 billion impressions counted by MasterCard for its sponsorship of the World Cup Soccer Championship through public relations tactics such as news conferences, news releases, interviews and bylined columns. Or the Epilepsy Foundation, which recorded 140 million impressions through a public service radio advertisement and a news release.

The Interactive Advertising Bureau has some guidelines on how to measure advertising impressions among new and emerging media.

Remember, however, that **media impressions** and other counts of message exposure may simply estimate audience size. Even if the count is an actual one, such measures indicate only how many people saw or heard the message. They don't measure the extent to which the audience overlaps with key publics. And they don't indicate whether the audiences understood it, accepted it or acted on it in any way.

MESSAGE CONTENT

An important type of evaluation focuses on the content of the message. Was it positive or did it provide erroneous data? Unwarranted conclusions? Outdated information? It is far more important to analyze the content of a message than merely to count the number of newspaper clippings. Appendix A, Applied Research, provides specific information on how to conduct a content analysis. For now, don't forget to include this method of research prominently in your evaluation program.

READABILITY MEASURES

Another way to evaluate awareness deals with comprehension—how easy a message is to understand. One of the first steps in developing a public relations plan is to identify and analyze the publics to be addressed. Part of that analysis involves an assessment of their reading level, usually translated into the level of education achieved by members of the public.

For example, most newspapers are written at about a ninth-grade reading level so everybody with that level of education or more—the majority of readers—should be able to understand the articles, columns and editorials. They may not necessarily agree with them or even be interested in them, but they are able to understand the writing. If you are preparing a news release or guest editorial for such a publication, plan on writing for readers with a ninth-grade reading ability. On the other hand, if you are writing a fundraising letter aimed at health care professionals, it would be safe to presume that all your readers will have completed some level of higher education. Whatever you estimate to be the appropriate reading level, test your writing against that estimate.

Robert Gunning's **Fog Index**, which measures reading ease or difficulty, is one of the easiest readability measures to use; review the directions in the discussion of verbal communication in Phase Two, Strategy. Some other commonly used readability instruments include Rudolf Flesch's Readability Score, which is more complicated than the Fog Index but which measures human interest; the associated Flesch-Kincaid readability grade level; Edward Fry's readability graph, which relies on a chart to calculate reading ease; the Dale-Chall formula, based on sentence length and the number of infrequently used words; the Cloze Procedure, which measures comprehension of spoken and visual messages; and Irving Fang's Easy Listening Formula, which provides a comparable way to calculate the comprehension of broadcast copy.

Many computer word-processing programs feature one or more of these readership aids in the program's tools section. For example, Microsoft Word counts 17.2 words per sentence in this chapter and calculates a 12.3 grade-level readability score, based on the Flesch-Kincaid score.

MESSAGE RECALL

Message recall involves techniques drawn from advertising research, where day-after recall studies are commonplace. Using this method, participants in interviews, surveys or focus groups are exposed to a news story, television program or the like. Then they are interviewed to determine what they remember from the message. A staple of research drawn from advertising is the Starch Readership Reports (starchresearch.com/services.html). These indicate three levels of reader study: "noted" readers who remember having previously seen an advertisement; "associated" readers who can link the advertisement with a particular brand or advertiser; and "read most" readers who are able to describe most of the written material in the ad.

Consider this awareness objective: to increase clients' understanding of changes in insurance policy coverage. Possible evaluation metrics include noting exposure patterns, doing content analysis to gauge how consistent the messages are with the facts, and asking a focus group to discuss message recall.

Here's another awareness objective: to increase awareness of a new consumer product being manufactured by a client. Three ways to evaluate this might include tracking dissemination of messages and noting the size of the potential audience, analyzing the message content with attention to its accuracy and the use of the client's telephone number and/or website address, and surveying customers in the company data base regarding message recall.

Acceptance Objectives

A major shortcoming of all the message-based evaluation techniques noted earlier is that they do not address the consequence of the public relations tactics. Instead, they simply gauge the existence of the tactics. At best, message-based evaluation techniques can deal with the level of awareness surrounding a public relations message.

WHAT SHOULD BE MEASURED?

Knowing what to measure often is the key to effective evaluation research. The answer for what metrics to use generally can be found in the objectives. But sometimes the objectives themselves are in conflict, with one of them measuring positively and another barely moving the dial.

That was the case with the Got Milk? campaign by the National Fluid Milk Processor Promotion Board, which presumably sought—as a range of objectives—awareness, acceptance and action.

The advertising series, which began in 1993, features celebrity photographer Annie Leibovitz's popular photos of celebrities with milk mustaches. Visibility is high, and everybody seems to be familiar with the campaign and the ads. The Promotion Board claims a 90 percent awareness rate.

Acceptance also runs high. The Promotion Board's research shows that attitudes toward milk have improved. The ads themselves have become collector items and have earned praise from creative designers. They found appeal with a diverse audience largely because of their use of many different celebrities and characters: Batman, David Beckham, Jackie Chan, Cirque du Soleil, Tony Hawk, Kermit the Frog, Marilyn Manson, Nelly, Conan O'Brien, Rihanna, Pete Sampras, Usher, Bart and Lisa Simpson—the list goes on and on.

There's just one problem: It costs $110 million a year, and there's no evidence that the campaign has increased milk consumption beyond California, where it was modestly successful the first couple of years. The U.S. Department of Agriculture's inspector general reported that milk usage was up 0.85 percent one year, down 0.42 percent the next.

Overall milk sales have, in fact, dropped. Oops! Milk usage continues on an overall downward spiral, as Americans consume only about half the amount of milk recommended by the government's dietary guidelines.

So the question is posed: How effective is a campaign that generates high awareness, measurable acceptance and even improved attitudes but doesn't effect action?

However, a more effective area of evaluation is based on levels of acceptance and action. Objectives in Phase Two, Strategy, note the desired impact on interest and attitudes (acceptance) and on opinion and behavior (action). Take steps now to evaluate how well each of those objectives has been achieved.

Two common approaches to measuring acceptance objectives are audience feedback and benchmark studies.

AUDIENCE FEEDBACK

Some evaluation measures count and analyze the voluntary reaction of the audience, such as the number of hits on a webpage, the number of telephone calls and letters, or the number of requests for additional information. Such **audience feedback**, an acceptance evaluation based on the voluntary reaction of an audience, can be an effective measure of the level of the audience's information and interest.

BENCHMARK STUDY

Another type of research is a **benchmark study** (also called **baseline study**), which provides a basis for comparing program outcomes against a standard. Actually, benchmark studies can

Phase Four

STEP
9

REAL-WORLD RESEARCH PRACTICES

Broadcast Mainland, a British public relations agency, reported on its 2010 study of how senior in-house public relations and marketing professionals evaluate their communication activities. Here are some highlights:

51%	do not measure broadcast coverage;
50%	measure social media coverage based on gut reaction;
50%	not satisfied with tools they use to measure social media;
40%	expected to demonstrate value of public relations to senior executives;
48%	use advertising equivalency to demonstrate such value;
34%	realize that advertising equivalency is misleading.

Interestingly, this study shows a greater reliance on advertising equivalency when compared with an earlier study by Ketchum Public Relations (Corder, Deasy and Thompson, 1999). Here are some highlights from that study:

61%	increase in sales volume;
59%	number of news releases, direct mail and other tactics distributed;
53%	number of impressions generated;
45%	content analysis of key messages in reported stories;
37%	advertising equivalency;
33%	opinion change based on before-and-after surveys.

be based on any of several different standards: the starting levels of interest or positive attitudes, outcomes of similar programs by other organizations, outcomes of the same program during a previous year or cycle, outcomes of industry or professional models, or the hypothetical outcomes of an "ideal" program.

Consider this acceptance objective: to enhance favorable employee attitudes toward a client's company. Here are four possible evaluation metrics: (1) Compare retention figures from before and after the tactic was implemented; (2) record oral and written comments given to the human resource department of the company; (3) solicit anecdotal input from managers and supervisors; and (4) survey employees about their attitudes and try to learn what they have been telling family and friends about working for the company.

Here's another acceptance objective: to increase employee affirmation of the company's need to change employee benefits. Possible evaluation techniques include recording immediate anecdotal feedback after the announcement is made, conducting a survey within two days of the announcement and after two weeks inviting employee feedback through response cards provided in pay envelopes.

Action Objectives

The ultimate objectives for most public relations activities should focus on bottom-line issues for an organization, primarily the action sought from the key publics. In this evaluation phase

Phase Four

STEP
9

of the planning process, careful consideration should be given to ways to measure these action objectives. Three approaches to action-focused evaluation research involve audience participation, direct observation and relative media effectiveness.

AUDIENCE PARTICIPATION

Figures on the number of people who actively responded to the message generally are easy to obtain. Attendance figures are effective measures when attendance itself is the desired objective, as may be the case with concerts and exhibitions, athletic competitions, benefit fundraising events, and the like. Implicit in these attendance figures also is a measure of the effectiveness of publicity and promotion that preceded the events.

However, attendance figures can be misused if the presumption is made that attendance at some information-sharing session necessarily equates with action impact. For example, attendance at an event in which a political candidate gives a major speech can't be used as a reliable indicator of either audience acceptance or eventual action in the voting booth. People heard the speech and the message was presented, but desired action is not guaranteed. Therefore, be careful how attendance figures are interpreted and what value is placed on them.

DIRECT OBSERVATION

Sometimes the simplest way to measure the effectiveness of action objectives is to look around. It's called **direct observation**. Let's say the objective sought an outcome of enough voter support to win an election. If your candidate won, your objective was achieved. If you sought financial contributions of $2.2 million, count the total of donations and pledges; anything above the target amount means you were that much more successful than planned. Some other easy-to-quantify objectives deal with capacity attendance for sporting and artistic events, sales figures, academic scores and membership expectations.

In some instances, the action objective deals with the general outcome rather than with any quantification. For example, passage (or defeat) of a particular piece of legislation may fully satisfy an action objective. Some evaluation research calls for strategic and creative thinking.

Individual behavior that may not be easily observable is more difficult to measure than the preceding examples. Here is an example of how to deal with a difficult-to-evaluate action objective: to increase the use of seat belts. One possible way to evaluate this objective would be to place observers in highway tollbooths and have them record the number of drivers and driver-side passengers wearing seat belts as they pass through the booths.

Or consider this objective: to have elementary, secondary and college teachers become more active in lobbying state government for increased support of education. An evaluation plan might include a tactic that encourages the sending of e-mail letters to state officials, with instructions for sending a copy to your organization. A simple count of the number of copies received would yield data to evaluate this objective. To take it to a higher level of sophistication, an organization might work with several sympathetic state legislators and compare the number of e-mail messages sent to their office with the number of copies the organization received. From the difference, the organization could extrapolate the number of messages sent by teachers to all legislators.

Some of the benchmark techniques for evaluating acceptance objectives, noted earlier, can be equally useful for evaluating action objectives.

Phase Four

HOW TO MEASURE PUBLICITY EFFECTS

Measuring the effects of media relations takes a bit of creativity, but it's not impossible. Consider the following possibilities:

1. *Set clear objectives* in advance and establish the criteria that will form the basis for success.
2. *Do a pretest* such as an awareness survey to identify the beginning point.
3. *Do a post-test* to measure changes in awareness in comparison with results of the pretest.
4. *Use a focus group* to probe the relationships among awareness, acceptance and action.
5. *Track media placement* with clippings and logs. Evaluate these not only in terms of distribution, use and other measures of audience exposure but also conduct some form of content analysis to evaluate the effectiveness of the message itself.
6. *Measure action* in some way, such as by noting changes in attendance, traffic, purchase or other behaviors associated with the campaign.

RELATIVE MEDIA EFFECTIVENESS

A final method of evaluating action objectives deals with the behavior generated by a particular medium compared to others. For example, did people vote for a candidate because of television coverage of a live debate or because of the candidate's Internet advertising? Often it is difficult to sort out the impact of a specific medium or tactic. But here's an example of how one organization managed to make the comparison.

In 2007, SeaWorld San Antonio introduced a new roller-coaster ride, Journey to Atlantis. The theme park invited members of the media to try out the new ride. The park's public relations–marketing team decided to include social media in the mix. Twenty-two blogs and media forums were identified for their focus on roller coasters and invited to write about the new ride. Eventually 12 did so. The result was that SeaWorld San Antonio received 50 links from coaster-oriented websites. Media posted on YouTube, Flickr and other social media sites generated hundreds of thousands of downloads, along with many positive comments.

Over two weekends two months later, a standard exit interview for SeaWorld visitors asked a typical question: Where did you hear about Journey to Atlantis? Forty-seven percent of respondents indicated social media as a source of their information. The research team looked at the various media used to promote the new ride (television commercial, newspaper ad, social media, radio spot, billboard, and so on) and concluded that the cost per impression for social media was 22 cents, compared with $1 for each television impression.

Data Analysis and Reports

Having gathered the data through a variety of means, it is now time to analyze it carefully. Match the observed and reported results with the expectations outlined in your statement of

Phase Four

STEP
9

objectives. If the program failed to meet its objectives, do some further analysis. Try to learn if the shortfall was because of a flawed strategy that undergirded the program or because the tactics were not implemented as effectively as they might have been. Consider also if there might be a flaw in the evaluation techniques used to gather the data.

If evaluation of the program is particularly important, ask an outside auditor to review the data. For some formal presentations of research findings, in order to enhance credibility, an organization may ask an outside expert or a panel of stakeholders to attest to the validity of the tools used in the evaluation research.

MEASURING THE IMPACT OF SOCIAL MEDIA

As public relations practitioners increasingly use social media as part of their media mix, the question eventually turns to matters of methodology and metrics: How can we evaluate the impact of social media? It isn't easy, but it is necessary to measure its effectiveness. One approach focuses on the engagement that web users display.

At her blog The Measurement Standard and her website (measuresofsuccess.com), Katie Delahaye Paine suggests that *engagement* is a synonym for *relationship*. It's something public relations practitioners are continually trying to nurture, though less often attempting to measure.

Likewise, blogging expert Robert Scoble suggests that engagement is an appropriate measurement of the effectiveness of blogging. To what extent does the reader become engaged in the piece? To what extent is dialogue taking place among readers who add comments? For example, Scoble suggests that people engaged in a corporate blog are likely eventually to buy the product (Scoble, 2006). For more information, see his blog, scobelizer.com and @Scobelizer on Twitter.

Meanwhile, Eric Peterson defines engagement as "an estimate of the degree and depth of visitor interaction on the site against a clearly defined set of goals" (2007). He has developed a matrix for calculating visitor engagement at websites, which he outlines at his blog, WebAnalytics Demystified.com. His approach uses concepts such as click-depth, recency, duration, brand, feedback, interaction, loyalty and subscription. The matrix counts, for example, the percentage of visitors who give their e-mail addresses, the number of sessions that include visits to more than five pages, the number of visitors who return more than five times, and so on.

Here are several no-cost or low-cost steps that an organization can take to measure the effectiveness of its website and other social media:

- Use Google Analytics or another visitor-tracking device.
- Have visitors register for full access to the site.
- Connect a blog through your website and collect the names and e-mail contact of those who leave comments.
- Post a poll at your website and see how many readers respond.
- Review the ratings and comments of your posts on sites such as YouTube and or Flickr.
- Write an e-book, report or other information source and make it available for free upon request.
- See how many people have joined sites such as Facebook. Post a question there and count replies.

Phase Four

After the evaluation is completed and the information gathered and analyzed, make sure it is presented in a form that is understandable and accessible to decision makers within the organization. They usually are busy executives and managers with global but not necessarily specific understandings of the issue. They may not have a high level of insight or information about the program, so be careful not to obscure evaluation findings in the final report. Instead, be very clear, draw obvious conclusions, and highlight the most important data.

If the decision makers have been involved in establishing the objectives of the program, they probably will be disposed to using the evaluation findings. Another way to increase the likelihood that the evaluation will be used is to concentrate on elements that can be changed in subsequent programs.

There is much variety within evaluation reports, which can be of several types. These may be presented separately or merged into a single report. The report itself can take the form of a formal document, an oral presentation or a meeting agenda item. Whether written or verbal, evaluation reports should be carefully crafted to clearly link the expectations outlined in the objectives with the outcomes.

When writing a report, note how the outcomes were measured, discuss the degree to which they achieved the objectives, and note the significance of this achievement (or lack of it). Finally, make clear recommendations closely linked with the data. For reports of major significance, visual elements such as photographs, tables and charts can enhance the understanding of readers and listeners.

Evaluation reports sometimes become the basis of a news release or even a news conference if the topic under review is one that is particularly newsworthy. For example, the final evaluation of public relations programs on popular and highly visible social issues such as campaigns to reduce drug abuse or bullying may warrant a news report.

Any evaluation report longer than five pages should be preceded by an **executive summary** that provides an overview of the findings and a simplified set of recommendations. An executive summary serves the needs of those decision makers—sometimes the most important ones—who may not have the time to digest the longer document.

Ultimate Evaluation: Value-Added Public Relations

Most evaluation of public relations and other strategic communication programs focus on objectives and tactics: What did we do? What did we accomplish by doing it? How effectively did this achieve what we set out to do? These questions are very important. But there is another equally important question to be answered: What did public relations do for the organization as a whole?

Once again, a reminder: The premise underlying *Strategic Planning for Public Relations* is that strategic communication is about more than mere tactics and activities.

Rather, it deals with the overall planned program of both proactive and reactive communication that enhances the relationship between an organization and its various publics, a relationship that needs to be linked to the bottom-line concerns of the organization. You might call it value-added public relations, the notion that public relations offers value and benefit to the organization as a whole.

Sometimes public relations practitioners are challenged to calculate the **return on investment** (ROI) for their client or boss as a way to justify the cost of public relations activities. ROI is the ratio of money gained or lost relative to the cost of a program or product. In some ways, this is an unfair expectation, because ROI is a financial metric measuring dollars spent vis-à-vis dollars saved or earned or offset by other revenue. Rather than return on investment, public relations practitioners prefer to deal in value that their activities add to an organization.

Based on qualitative interview research with both public relations practitioners and their CEOs, Linda Childers Hon (1997) has reported six such values that effective public relations bring to organizations or to the clients of a consultant or agency. Keep these in mind as you complete your evaluation and present it to your client or organization:

1. Effective public relations helps organizations *survive* by reversing negative opinions, by promoting awareness of organizational benefits to the community and by effecting balanced media coverage.
2. Effective public relations helps organizations *make money* by generating publicity about products and services as well as the organization's plans and accomplishments; by attracting new customers, volunteers, donors and stockholders; and by improving employee performance and productivity.
3. Effective public relations helps other organizational functions *make money* by creating an environment of understanding and goodwill, by influencing supportive legislation, and by enhancing fundraising efforts.
4. Effective public relations helps organizations *save money* by inducing favorable legislation, by retaining members and by minimizing negative publicity during crisis incidents.
5. Effective public relations helps organizations *weaken opposition* by generating favorable public opinion and by obtaining cooperation from governmental and other organizations.
6. Effective public relations helps organizations *save lives* through social goals such as advancing highway safety, medical care and research, and the like.

Public Relations Metrics

We noted earlier in this chapter that metrics are standards of measurement used to quantify performance outcomes and to measure the level to which objectives are met. Don Bartholomew of Ketchum Public Relations has introduced a hierarchy for public relations metrics:

*   **exposure metric**: how publics have been exposed to a message;
*   **engagement metric**: how publics interact with the organization and with each other vis-à-vis the message;
*   **influence metric**: the degree to which message exposure and engagement impact on the publics' perceptions and attitudes;
*   **action metric**: how the public acts on the message.

Bartholomew believes his model applies to both traditional and emerging media, though he developed it mainly with social media in mind. (For more information, see Bartholomew's MetricsMan blog at wordpress.com.)

Applied to social media, metrics for exposure might include the number of hits to a website, the number of unique visitors, search-engine ranking, and objective analysis of online comments or discussion. Engagement metrics could be repeat visitors, likes and recommendations,

Phase Four

message recall measures, and RSS subscriptions. Examples of metrics for the influence category include measured change in awareness or attitudes, brand association and purchase considerations. Action metrics might be store visits, event attendance or the logical close-the-loop action such as purchases, votes, memberships, and so on.

Game Changer for Public Relations Evaluation

Public relations practitioners from around the world met in Spain in 2010. Their mission was to articulate standards and common approaches for measuring and evaluating public relations. The Barcelona Declaration of Measurement Principles emerging from these discussions includes seven principles. For a download, search "barcelona" at instituteforpr.org.

GOALS

It is important to set and manage goal setting and measurement in a process that is quantitative and holistic.

QUANTITY AND QUALITY

Rather than measuring media placement, evaluation should consider the quality of media coverage including tone, credibility, relevance, message delivery, spokespersons and prominence in the medium.

ADVERTISING EQUIVALENCY

This approach measures the cost of media space and is rejected as a concept to place a value on public relations. Likewise, multipliers intended to present a formula for media cost as a factor of public relations value should not be applied.

SOCIAL MEDIA

There is no single metric for measuring social media, but an evaluation program should be developed for organizational use of social media.

OUTCOMES

It is more important to measure the effect on outcomes (including awareness, comprehension, attitude and behavior) rather than outputs. Measurement requires quantity and quality.

RESULTS

Measurement should be focused on business/organizational results and the impact of public relations activity on the bottom line.

RELIABILITY

Measurement methods should be both transparent and repeatable.

Some observers are calling the Barcelona Declaration a game changer for public relations. They predict that the new principles will sound a death knell to AVEs and multipliers that try to fix a dollar value on public relations by falsely comparing it to advertising. They are excited to envision the use of well-planned evaluation programs in every strategic communication plan.

CASE IN POINT   Southwest Airlines

Southwest Airlines engaged in a series of evaluation tools as part of its media relations strategy, specifically its plan to link public relations with sales (Watson and Noble, 2007). Here's the company's five-point program:

1. Southwest conducted keyword research to learn how people search online. For example, research into 1.3 million searches during one month revealed 1.3 million searches for "Southwest Airlines" but only 400,000 for "Southwest."
2. With this information, the company edited its news releases to include the full "Southwest Airlines" search term, making it more likely that online readers would find the company's postings.
3. Because research also showed that many online news readers do not scroll to the bottom of the release for links to additional information, Southwest imbedded links within its online news releases. Thus a release about a particular offer included a link to a web page where the visitor could purchase it and where the company could track it.
4. Southwest distributed its new releases through wire services that are "crawled" by Google, Yahoo and AOL News, increasing the likelihood that online searchers would find the company information.
5. The airline evaluated three news releases to link publicity with sales. It found evidence that one release about a new route resulted in $80,000 in ticket sales, a Spanish-language online release led to $38,000 in sales, and the third release with a hyperlink in the first paragraph resulted in more than $1 million in ticket sales.

Additionally, the supporters expect organizational executives and CEOs to embrace these principles, especially as they lead to more accountability for public relations and more integration with the organization's bottom line.

What's Next?

This ends the nine steps of strategic planning. In that sense, nothing is left to do. You've learned all the elements that go into an effective and efficient campaign for public relations or marketing communication.

In a very real sense, though, you've only just begun. Take the knowledge you've gained from this text and the practical experiences you have in working through the various activities you have encountered and run with them.

Phase Four

STEP
9

PLANNING EXAMPLE 9 Evaluating the Strategic Plan

Upstate College will evaluate its Initiative on Transfer Students according to the following five-part plan:

1. placement report tracking distribution and media use of news releases and other materials disseminated by its public relations department;
2. telephone survey among people who applied to UC two, three and four years ago but did not attend; the purpose of this survey will be to assess awareness about the expansion and attitudes toward it;
3. focus group of new applicants to UC, discussing the source of their information about the expansion and their reasons for applying;
4. content analysis of newspaper articles, radio and television news reports, and newspaper letters to the editor and editorials, studying the positive/negative nature of the reports about UC's expansion;
5. brief survey as part of the application process, asking applicants the source of their information about the UC expansion.

The evaluation report will be provided to the college president and provost, who prefer a well-documented and candid report. This report will become the basis for future recruitment and development activities.

(Note: You will develop similar evaluation plans for the other initiatives.)

Tiny Tykes Toys will evaluate the employee-oriented phase of its public relations program according to the following plan:

- *Before-and-After Survey*. Develop surveys of both employees and employees' family members, dealing with employee morale, job satisfaction, pride in company, and knowledge of recall, safety and quality issues. The results of these surveys will be compared to ascertain any change in knowledge, attitudes and behavior associated with the public relations program.
- *Employee-Initiated Feedback*. Review copies of comments and suggestions in the suggestion box, notes to company managers, letters to the editor of the company newsletter or other publications, and other print and/or e-mail messages regarding the reintroduction program. These messages will be summarized and analyzed.
- *Analysis of Media Coverage*. Track placement, measure employee awareness of coverage, and do a simply content analysis on articles and news reports as to their positive or negative reflection of Tiny Tykes employees.

A written final evaluation will be presented to company managers and then will be shared with employees.

☑ *Checklist 9* **Evaluation Plan**

Basic Questions

1. How will you measure awareness objectives?
2. How will you measure acceptance objectives?
3. How will you measure action objectives?

Expanded Questions

A. METHODOLOGY

1. How and when can this information be obtained: via after-only study or before-and-after study?
2. Which research methodologies would be most effective?

   - Judgmental assessment: personal experience or outside experts.
   - Interviews with key people. Which people?
   - Focus groups with representative publics. Which publics?
   - Survey of representative publics. Which publics? Control group?
   - Content analysis of representative artifacts. Which artifacts?
   - Readership study
   - Media tracking

B. EVALUATION CATEGORIES

1. Indicate how each of the methodologies below might be used to evaluate each individual tactic.
2. What standards of accuracy and reliability are needed for the evaluation?
3. Who can provide information for evaluation?

Evaluation of Outputs
- Message production
- Message dissemination
- Message cost analysis
- Advertising equivalency

Evaluation of Awareness Objectives
- Message exposure
- Message content analysis
- Readability measures
- Message recall

Evaluation of Acceptance Objectives
- Audience feedback
- Benchmark (baseline) study

Phase Four

Evaluation of Action Objectives

- Audience participation
- Direct observation of results

C. AUDIENCE

1. Who will receive the final evaluation?
2. How will it be used?
3. What level of candor are decision makers willing to receive?

D. EVALUATION SCHEDULE

1. Timeline for implementation report.
2. Timeline for progress report.
3. Timeline for final evaluation.

E. EVALUATION PROGRAM CHECKLIST

For this evaluation program:

- Is it useful to the organization?
- Is it clearly linked to established objectives?
- Is it appropriate as to cost?
- Is it appropriate as to time?
- Is it appropriate as to other resources?
- Is it ethical and socially responsible?
- Is it credible, with accurate data?
- Is it doable?

APPENDIXES

APPENDIX A

Applied Research

Academic Research and Applied Research

As a student, you probably are already familiar with academic research from journals and textbooks. **Academic research** generates theory, explores new interests and focuses on universal knowledge. This is knowledge for its own sake. Academic research also is called **theoretical research**, **basic research** and **pure research**.

In your professional life beyond the classroom, however, you are more likely to deal in **applied research** (sometimes called **market research** or **administrative research**). This type of research delves into the practical problems faced by an organization and guides effective resolution of those problems. Your bosses and clients will ask you to get information as quickly and inexpensively as possible to help solve their very real problems. Your applied research may contribute to the theory base of your profession, but that is a side benefit. Its primary role is to deal with practical matters for your client.

This appendix focuses on applied research. It will give you a how-to guide to several techniques for doing applied research. In addition to discussing the ethics of research, we'll also look at sampling techniques, secondary research, interviews, focus groups, case studies, surveys and content analysis.

Each **research** technique in this section takes you through a four-phase process of (1) defining the research problem; (2) designing a way to obtain information; (3) actually gathering the information; and (4) analyzing your findings and applying them. Specifically, this appendix has the following categories:

- research topics
- research ethics
- sampling
- secondary research
- interview
- focus group
- case study
- survey research
- content analysis.

ACADEMIC VERSUS APPLIED RESEARCH TOPICS

Most of the studies published in the *Journal of Public Relations Research* deal with academic research, which by its nature is public and meant to be shared, challenged and continuously developed.

Here are some topics from the last few years: attribution theory and crisis communication, contingency theory of accommodation, race/ethnicity, the Internet and litigation, ethics, the rhetorical-organizational approach to organizational identity, social media, knowledge predictors, integrated symmetrical model of crisis communication, self-efficacy theory, blog-mediated crisis communication, image and symbolic leadership, news credibility, and information processing and situational theory. Several other journals also publish academic research focused on public relations.

Applied research more often than not remains unpublished because it is proprietary, meaning that it is conducted for and owned by a particular client.

A review of the websites of several major public relations agencies indicates they have conducted the following research topics for specific clients and companies: media content analysis, a survey of residents to identify a location for a chemical plant, monitoring legislation and conducting legislative research, corporate reputation, the impact of public relations and advertising programs, Internet monitoring, audience surveys, surveys of the impact of congressional hearings, and audience analysis of sports organizations to increase both fan and corporate support.

Research Topics

Applied research is especially important when program planning brings together a specialist (you) working for an expert (your boss or client), because the research can help prevent problems by putting both the specialists and the experts more in touch with their publics.

Take, for example, the experience of a senior campaigns class in which university students developed a comprehensive public relations and advertising program for a new space exhibit at a science museum. The museum had a wealth of marketing research, but as part of the course assignment the four student teams tried out several different strategic concepts on a sampling of their target public: schoolchildren and their parents. This research paid off.

One team considered three different themes: a digitized close-up of a man in a spacesuit with the slogan "Put Your Face in Space"; a rocket being fired from its launch pad with the slogan "Blast Off! Explore the Infinite Possibilities"; and a close-up of a footprint on the moon with the slogan "Space. Touch it!" When they presented the three possible approaches to the museum CEO and his marketing and public relations directors, the clients were enthusiastic and unanimous. They really liked the footprint, because it so poignantly reflected the Apollo 11 lunar landing. But the students cautioned, "Don't jump to conclusions. Our research supports the second option; it shows that the children you want to attract like the action of the space launch much more. For them and their parents, the footprint from the first moon landing in 1969 is part of history, not something that excites their imagination." Applied research prevented a false start with a misguided theme.

Do-It-Yourself Research

Many research experts offer a simple warning: Don't try this at home! Research methodologies can be incredibly complex, and many pitfalls exist for the novice who plunges headlong into research using inappropriate techniques that result in inaccurate data and unwarranted conclusions.

Clearly some issues are so critical and the needed research so important that you really should get professional research assistance. Nevertheless, the research techniques explained here are not impossible for the do-it-yourselfer. The key is knowing when you should do it yourself and when to call in an expert. So the advice here is: Learn how to do it, then try to do it yourself. Even if you have to turn to a research specialist, this appendix will help you manage the project.

Consider the following generalization: you might do your own research if your project meets all or most of the following criteria:

- You need objective data.
- You have the time, interest, patience, ability and self-confidence to conduct your own study.
- Your organization, boss or client have enough confidence in you to respect and use your findings.
- You can be objective in your study even though it involves your own organization.
- You don't need highly accurate statistics and other data.
- The decisions riding on the study are relatively minor in terms of your organization's overall mission.
- Your budget is such that the choice is between doing your own research or doing none at all.

Research Ethics

Ethics deals with the rightness or wrongness of behavior, especially professional or organizational behavior (as compared with personal morality). Social science research involves several areas that can pose ethical risks and temptations.

The Principles of Disclosure of the National Council on Public Polls (ncpp.org) pledges the commitment of member organizations "to standards of disclosure designed to insure that consumers of survey results that enter the public domain have an adequate basis for judging the reliability and validity of the results reported."

Most colleges and universities have clearly defined policies related to research ethics. So do many companies and public relations counseling agencies. Specific standards may vary, but some common ground can be found in many ethical guidelines. Broadly speaking, the areas of common ground deal with the treatment of the people involved in the research study and the use of information.

Ethical Treatment of People

Below are eight guidelines for dealing ethically with people involved in research programs or projects. These principles apply to the kind of applied research that is common in public relations and marketing research, such as interviews, focus groups and surveys. The principles do not apply to content analysis, because no active participants are involved in that kind of research.

DIGNITY

Respect the dignity of participants in every study. This is the umbrella that covers all the other principles. It is rooted in common sense and decent interaction with people. Most colleges and universities, as well as other research organizations, have formal requirements for research involving human subjects, so make sure your research is in compliance with these regulations.

PRIVACY

Respect the privacy of participants. Abide fully by any privacy commitments that are made. Note the difference between anonymity and confidentiality. **Anonymity** means the participant's identity will not be known to anybody, including the researcher, and thus cannot be linked to a particular response. **Confidentiality** means the researcher will not disclose the participant's identity nor allow it to be linked to a particular response.

Anonymity is difficult for most public relations research. Interviews and focus groups obviously can't be anonymous, and it is difficult to maintain anonymity for surveys that require more than one mailing. Confidentiality is the more likely protection for participants.

Remember that any privacy guarantees extend beyond the time of the research study. Questionnaires and notes should be stored in a nonpublic place and should be discarded when they are no longer needed.

VOLUNTEER PARTICIPATION

Seek only voluntary participation by respondents. Would-be participants in interviews, focus groups, and surveys should be told explicitly that they may choose not to participate. They must be allowed to decline at the beginning of the research activity or to end their participation at any point. The voluntariness of participation is less of an issue with mail or phone surveys, where respondents can easily ignore the questionnaire or hang up on the researcher.

CONSENT

Obtain informed consent. Participants should be told enough about the research project so they clearly know what they are being asked to do. When a person agrees to participate in an interview, survey or focus group, informed consent can logically be presumed, and asking participants to sign consent statements could negate a guarantee of anonymity that might be part of the project.

Increasingly, however, researchers are asking participants in studies involving sensitive matters to sign a consent form; the confidentiality issue can be handled by having the consent form separate from any questionnaire that is part of the research tool. Consent forms are generally used for experiments, and they are becoming more common with other types of public relations or marketing research. Informed consent extends to practical matters, such as telling respondents how much time will be expected for their participation.

PURPOSE

Disclose the purpose of the research to the participants. In some cases, the researcher does not want to indicate the full purpose of the study up front, because this might contaminate the results by causing the respondents to provide less-than-truthful information. Even if the respondents try to be truthful, knowing too much about the project could bias their responses. However, respondents or participants have the right to know at least the general purpose of the study. Participants usually can be told the purpose of the research when their role is ended.

RESEARCHER IDENTITY

Disclose the identity of the researcher. Active participants should know who you are and that you are conducting research. This often can enhance the credibility of the study.

SPONSOR IDENTITY

Disclose the identity of the research sponsor. Would-be respondents and other participants have the right to know the name of the organization sponsoring and benefiting from the research. As with the item above about the purpose of the research, the identity of the research sponsor may be withheld until the conclusion of the study, so participants can act and provide information without bias.

RESULTS

Inform participants of the research results. By debriefing participants, the researcher can explain the study and allow participants to see themselves in relation to the total sample. Especially if the researcher concealed information about the purpose or sponsor to ensure candid responses by participants, explaining to them afterward can make up for the deception.

ETHICAL USE OF RESEARCH DATA

Three ethical considerations are paramount related to the use of research data for public relations and marketing research of the kind considered in this book. Different ethical principles would apply to more experimental or laboratory-based social research.

Here are the three ethical considerations:

- *Develop a fair research process*. Draw samples with care so that they are likely to represent the target population, and don't yield to the temptation to obtain simply an easy or quick sample. In reporting your research, explain the methodology you used in drawing the sample, and acknowledge any shortcoming in the sampling process.
- *Develop fair measurement tools*. Questions and response items should be designed to elicit honest responses, and research participants should not be tricked into giving information they don't believe in. Manipulation and coercion have no place in research.
- *Analyze and report data ethically*. Treat each piece of data with great respect; never fudge or falsify any data. Discard any data that is unclear, indecipherable or otherwise contaminated. In analyzing the data, draw only those conclusions justified by the information obtained; never discount or misinterpret data in favor of your own bias or your client's wishes. Fully report the circumstances of the research project: its geography and time frame, sampling techniques and methodology. Include copies of questionnaires and other data-gathering tools.

Sampling

The purpose of research is to describe various characteristics (such as the level of information, the existence of attitudes or opinions, or the extent of certain behaviors) of a **population**, which is a large group of subjects that are of interest to the researcher. For example, depending on the interests of the researcher, the residents of Kansas could be a population; so too Hispanic athletes at all Kansas colleges and universities, or restaurants with vegetarian menus in the Sunflower State.

The individual **element** of the population (also called the **unit of analysis**) usually is a person. However, elements could be organizations, products, media artifacts such as news reports or editorials, public relations artifacts such as news releases or brochures, or advertising artifacts such as television commercials or print ads. Each research activity also has a particular time period (usually defined in weeks, months or years) and an extent (a geographic location such as a region, state or neighborhood).

Sometimes we conduct a **census**, which is a comprehensive study that includes every member of the population in our study. An example of a census is a poll that a small business might conduct with every employee about an issue of companywide interest.

Other times, however, it is impractical to survey every member of a very large or scattered population. In such cases, a good alternative is **sampling**, the identification of a subset of the population of individuals (or objects) who reflect and represent the larger body. This subset is known as a **sample**. The value of sampling is that it saves time and money, allowing researchers to study a small group and then use those findings to make predictions for a much larger population, a process called **extrapolation**.

Depending on how a sample is pulled together, it may or may not be based on the concept of **probability**, which means that every element in the population has an equal chance of being selected for the sample. To help you understand sampling, consider the analogy of cooking stew. A cook mixes a variety of vegetables and herbs in a pot, then stirs—that's the key. Presumably, the stirring has mixed all the ingredients evenly. The cook then dips the ladle and takes a taste. No need to eat the entire pot to determine if more seasoning is needed; one ladle from a well-stirred pot provides a true sampling of the entire stew.

Over the years, the accuracy of polling has improved tremendously. Consider three national presidential polls. In 1936 the influential *Literary Digest* forecast that Alf Landon would beat Franklin Roosevelt 57 to 43 percent. Instead, Roosevelt easily won re-election with a landslide 61 percent of the vote. In 1948, the Roper Poll predicted that Thomas Dewey would beat Harry Truman by a 5-point margin in the presidential election. Instead, Truman won by 5 points.

In contrast, in the 2010 midterm election, most major poll predictions were accurate within a 2 percent margin of error.

The evolution of polling accuracy lies in the improved sampling techniques. *Literary Digest* polled 2 million people using a volunteer sampling frame including telephone listings (in 1936, phones were for the well-to-do) and country club memberships, favoring the wealthy and excluding the poor. The 1948 poll was a cluster sample of 20,000, weighted toward rural Republican voters rather than urban Democratic voters.

Now, sampling is down to an average size of about 1,000 respondents for the estimated 200 million voting-age Americans. These respondents are scientifically selected on age, income, ethnicity, location, occupation, religion, education and many other factors that, taken

PROBABILITY AND NONPROBABILITY SAMPLING

Probability sampling involves the selection of a sample in a manner through which every member of the population has an equal chance statistically of being selected for the sample.

- simple random sampling
- systematic sampling
- stratified sampling
- cluster sampling.

Nonprobability sampling involves the selection of a sample in a manner through which each member of the population has an unequal chance statistically of being selected.

- convenience sampling
- volunteer sampling
- purposive sampling
- snowball sampling
- quota sampling.

together, present an accurate picture of the American electorate. Progressively smaller but more representative samples have yielded greater accuracy.

Polling has become refined as it focuses on "likely voters," particularly for surveys that take place within a few days prior to an election. Surveys earlier in the election cycle often still rely on registered voters who are uncommitted at that stage. The increasing incidence of Internet polling is hampered by greater likelihood of error than more traditional polling techniques.

Another area of concern for pollsters is the prevalence of cell phones, which generally are off the radar for telephone polls. An estimated one-fourth of the American population use cell phones primarily. This subpopulation includes more political independents and Democrats than Republicans, another challenge for generating accurate samples.

Sampling can be largely divided into nonprobability and probability techniques. Let's look at each type.

Nonprobability Sampling

A variety of techniques are identified as nonprobability sampling because every person or artifact in the population does not have an equal chance of being selected for the study. These techniques offer both advantages and disadvantages. On the plus side, nonprobability samples can be chosen simply, quickly and inexpensively. This technique allows subjects to be selected even if they cannot be identified ahead of time. On the minus side, because subjects are chosen with no great care as to their makeup, nonprobability sampling has limited credibility.

Here are five types of nonprobability samples: *convenience*, *volunteer*, *purposive*, *snowball* and *quota*.

CONVENIENCE SAMPLING

A frequently used technique is **convenience sampling**, which draws subjects because they are readily available to the researcher, such as people walking through a shopping mall, students enrolled in a particular college course, or participants in so-called (but not really) random street-corner interviews by reporters. This type of sampling is haphazard but not random. It generally is an unreliable indicator of a larger population, unless that population is, for example, shoppers at a particular mall.

VOLUNTEER SAMPLING

Another sampling technique, **volunteer sampling**, uses subjects who ask to be included in the research study. One example of self-selected samples is magazines or websites that invite readers to respond to a printed questionnaire; another is talk show hosts who invite their radio listeners to phone in with comments.

The problem with volunteer sampling is that it sometimes is interpreted as being representative when it really isn't. What should we think about the situation in which the talk show's callers overwhelmingly support a political candidate who nevertheless is soundly defeated at the polls? We should remember that such programs attract people with certain preconceptions and biases. Thus the callers are not representative of the voters, perhaps not even of all the program's listeners. They merely are those listeners who felt strongly enough about the issue and took the time to express their opinion.

PURPOSIVE SAMPLING

A technique in which research subjects are chosen because they have certain demographic characteristics is called **purposive sampling** (also known as **judgment sampling**). For example, they may be people who were patients in a particular hospital, or they may be individuals who drive a particular brand of automobile. They are chosen on purpose for a study merely because they fit that single criterion. But remember that they are not representative of the entire population of hospital patients or motorists.

SNOWBALL SAMPLING

The technique of **snowball sampling** (also called **sociosampling**) begins with a small group of individuals with a certain characteristic who are asked to identify others to participate in the research. This technique often is used for populations where member lists do not exist and whose members are hard to identify, at least by outsiders.

QUOTA SAMPLING

A sampling technique that attempts to be more representative of the population is **quota sampling**. This involves the selection of subjects to fit a predetermined percentage. For example, if 40 percent of a company's employees have college degrees, a quota sample would include college graduates as 40 percent of the sample. Appropriate quota categories include age, gender, ethnicity, religion, occupation, geography and other demographic factors. But like the purposive sampling, quota sampling is haphazard because it is not representative of the entire population under study; instead it reflects only one characteristic (or a couple of characteristics) that the researcher considers most important.

The disadvantage of nonprobability sampling is that it gives no reasonable certainty that findings will be representative of the larger population. To be useful, most sampling research must be applicable to the entire population rather than to only the relatively few people sampled.

Still, nonprobability sampling is not without its good side, and these techniques have a legitimate role for public relations and marketing research. Consider using nonprobability sampling in the following situations:

- when the purpose of the study is to gain general, nonspecific insight into a particular group;
- when a high margin of error is not a major concern;
- when the budget does not allow for more costly probability sampling;
- when the schedule does not allow for more time-consuming probability sampling.

Remember: Avoid using a nonprobability sample when you want to be able to project the findings of your research onto a larger population.

Probability Sampling

The other category of sampling techniques is probability sampling. This approach follows the guidelines of mathematical probability, generally earning higher respect among researchers.

When the research study seeks to learn the attitudes, opinions or behaviors of a large number of people, probability sampling ensures that every element within the population has an equal and known chance of being selected. Thus, some researchers refer to probability sampling technique known as an **EPSEM sampling** (equal probability of selection method). By using probability sampling, the researcher can legitimately calculate how accurately the sampled findings reflect the entire population.

Probability sampling requires that the researcher is able to identify every **sampling unit**, which is the individual element to be analyzed. Sampling units reflect the range noted earlier for population elements. For surveys, they usually are people in the various categories needed. But sampling units also may be organizations or products. In content analysis, the sampling unit would be media artifacts such as news releases, newspapers, magazine, advertisements, and so on.

The actual listing of sampling units is called the **sampling frame**. Often these are membership rosters or other comprehensive directories.

Some random samples have been based on telephone directories, though phone books generally are bad choices for general populations because they screen out people without landline phone service and those with unlisted numbers. This is an example of **sampling bias**, when the sampling technique itself introduces an element of weakness into the process.

Sampling bias also may be related to the timing of the data gathering. Consider, for example, a restaurant that has a busy professional lunch crowd, an early-bird dinner special that caters to college students and senior citizens, a formal and relatively upscale dinner crowd, and a trendy after-theater clientele. A study that draws its sample from only the early-bird group would yield significantly different results than one drawing from each of the four customer groups.

Following are four types of probability sampling: *simple random*, *systematic*, *stratified* and *cluster*.

SIMPLE RANDOM SAMPLING

The basic type of probability sampling is **simple random sampling**. Think of a lottery-style drawing such as pulling names from a hat. Anybody who has ever played Bingo or a state lotto knows the pure randomness of such sampling.

Researchers often use a table of random numbers to select the subjects for their study. For example, if you are researching the behavior of 5,000 college students, you might work with a list from the registrar's office and assign every student a number, 0001 through 5000. Let's say you decide to have 250 respondents. Simply generate a list of random four-digit numbers, select the first 250 that match them up to the numbered names and interview the students.

The major advantage of **random sampling** is that it produces a sampling in which everyone in the population has an equal chance of being selected. This provides a generally unbiased group of respondents, which in turn is good for a research study seeking to project findings for the entire group. Random sampling is particularly good when a population is homogeneous, with no significant divisions within it.

However, simple random sampling has two major disadvantages. First, it requires a sampling frame, which may not be available for all target populations. Second, while random sampling gives every element within the population an equal chance of being selected, it does not necessarily produce a representative sampling if significant subsets exist within the population. For example, a sample of 250 students identified randomly out of a population of 5,000 could produce no students majoring in a foreign language. That could be a limitation, especially if the study dealt with something like international exchange programs, language requirements for graduation or student fees for language labs.

SYSTEMATIC SAMPLING

Another common technique is **systematic sampling** (also called **systematic interval sampling**). This involves the selection of subjects spaced at equal intervals, such as every twentieth name on a membership roster.

Let's stay with the example of the survey of college students. If you do the simple math and divide 5,000 by 250, then you would select every twentieth name from your sampling frame. To make the systematic sampling truly unbiased, use a systematic sampling with a random start. This involves a random selection of the starting number (in this case, a number from 1 to 20).

Don't use systematic sampling if a particular order or recurring pattern exists within the ranking. For example, if a listing of sororities always begins with the names of officers, then a systematic sampling of every fifteenth name with a starting number of 2 would result in a sampling top-heavy with sorority vice presidents—not very random after all.

Again, the inherent disadvantage of systematic sampling is that it doesn't account for specific groups within the population (such as the language issue noted above). The next technique can address this challenge.

STRATIFIED SAMPLING

A modification of random and systematic techniques is **stratified sampling**. This technique involves a ranking of elements on a list, such as four subset lists (freshmen, sophomores, juniors and seniors) for your study of college students. Other relevant demographic categories for research might include age, gender, income, religion, media use, academic major and product use—and in the case of the language issue, language proficiency and international experience.

By stratifying a sampling frame by important characteristics, the researcher is able to ensure a greater likelihood that the sample will be representative of the population. One problem with stratified sampling is that the subsets may indicate more than they appear to. For example, subsets related to residency in different parts of a city may reflect not only geography but also different ethnic, occupational or socioeconomic patterns.

Stratified sampling may be proportionate, with research sizes based on their proportion in the population, such as a research project with a sample of 45 percent men and 55 percent women used for a college with a student population of the same gender proportions. Or it may be **disproportionate** (also called **weighted sampling**) if particular attention is given to underrepresented members of a population.

Using the college language scenario, if the student population is 4 percent international and foreign language majors also account for 3 percent of the student population, the researcher may want to have a sample of more than those percentages to provide a stronger representation among the respondents than might be expected with a random 3 or 4 percent. The researcher may weight the samples, perhaps replicating by five the responses of both groups.

CLUSTER SAMPLING

A technique known as **cluster sampling** (also called **multistage sampling**) is used when the researcher can't readily generate a sampling frame listing the entire population but can obtain listings of particular groups within the population.

For example, if your research population was all college and university students within your state, you would have a difficult time putting together a complete sampling frame listing every student in the state from which to draw a random, systematic or stratified sample. But using the cluster sampling technique, you first would identify several schools (either randomly or through a stratified technique based on criteria such as size or location). Then you would select individual students (randomly, systematically or through stratified techniques) using separate sampling frames, such as enrollment lists obtained from each school identified in the first stage.

Sampling Error and Size

In textbooks dedicated to research methodologies, you can find sophisticated information about research statistics. To simplify things here, let's consider a few key terms that deal with the inevitable limitations of sampling.

The **sampling error** (sometimes called the **margin of error**) is the extent to which the sample does not perfectly correspond with the target population. Sampling error is usually reported as a percentage. For example, a finding of 62 percent with a sampling error of 3 percent indicates that the finding actually could fall between 59 percent and 65 percent. The statistic used to describe sampling error is called the *standard error* (more correctly, the **standard error of the mean**). Since sampling is an imperfect reflection of the population, researchers always expect some potential sampling error.

What is the ideal number of subjects for a research study? There is no single answer to this question, because so much depends upon what the researcher needs to accomplish. Focus groups use only a few people, generally 5 to 12 for each session. Surveys for pretest studies may use a sample of 15 to 30 subjects.

Two concepts about sample size often are difficult for nonresearchers to grasp. First, a bigger sample doesn't necessarily mean better results. Second, the appropriate size of the sample is not based in any way on a percentage or fraction of the population. In general, samples of 200 to 400 are commonplace.

Roger Wimmer and Joseph Dominick (2010) note that researchers often use a sample of 100 subjects for each relevant demographic group likely to have distinctive characteristics (for example, 100 men and 100 women; or 100 each of undergraduates, graduate students and alumni). Here are commonly used guidelines for samples with a 5 percent margin of error: 217 for a population or demographic breakout group of 500; 278 for 1,000; 322 for 2,000; 357 for 5,000; 370 for 10,000; 381 for 50,000, and 384 for an infinite number. Fewer could be used if you can tolerate a higher margin of error; more if you need a lower margin.

One thing is certain: More doesn't necessarily mean better. Very good research can be based on modest sample sizes. The idea underlying sampling is to use the smallest number of research subjects that can accurately predict characteristics of the population. A small appropriate sample is better than a larger haphazard one. Remember also that the smaller the sample size, the less expensive the study will be; the less time it will take; and the easier it will be to calculate, analyze and report.

A common way of determining sample size is first to decide what margin of error you can tolerate in your sample. If the answer is zero, you are headed for a census of the entire population rather than a sampling. But think again, because research seldom requires perfect data. Even if your client or boss wants that, there probably isn't enough money in the budget to achieve it, unless the target population is very small.

Do a simple online search for "margin of error calculator" and you'll find several easy-to-use Internet sites for your research.

Secondary Research

One of the first steps in conducting research is to conduct **secondary research**. That is research conducted to find out what information already is available through existing sources. It is distinguished from **primary research**, which generates new data collected specifically for this investigation.

Why use existing information? Because it's there. And because it is less expensive to analyze existing data than if you gather new data. Secondary research also helps refine the research topic, build files of previous findings and keep current with new developments in the field. It also provides a launch point for your own additional research.

When using secondary information, evaluate it carefully. Consider the circumstances surrounding the data, such as when and how it was gathered, for what purpose, by what researcher and with what sample. Most especially, consider the objectivity and professionalism with which it was gathered. All these factors can affect the usefulness of the information to your situation.

Even if you have to purchase the data from a commercial information service, it still may be more cost effective than mounting your own primary research activity. Remember that even though you are interested in applied research for a particular client, you still can learn a lot from academic research. Because it is seeking insights into topics more than solutions to specific problems, academic research can provide valuable background information.

Types of Secondary Information

Secondary information is available in many different sources, including organizational files, trade and professional associations, public and academic libraries, government records, commercial information companies, and computer-assisted or online research sources. Let's look briefly at each.

ORGANIZATIONAL FILES

Information in the organizational files of your employer or client can provide a wealth of information for researchers and practitioners. Many public relations offices include extensive files of news releases, brochures, annual reports and internal documents, as well as information files about relevant issues. Some organizations also have extensive archives with historical data and artifacts.

TRADE AND PROFESSIONAL ASSOCIATIONS

Industry groups may offer much useful information for public relations and marketing researchers. For example, the Public Relations Society of America (PRSA) has extensive files about various aspects of public relations that it makes available to members. The *Encyclopedia of Associations* lists thousands of professional groups that can be very helpful in obtaining information about a specific industry.

PUBLIC AND ACADEMIC LIBRARIES

Public libraries in towns and cities as well as academic libraries on college and university campuses provide an accessible source of information. Information also may be available in specialized libraries such as those operated by companies, museums, industries, hospitals, professional organizations, and so on. Materials available in libraries can be categorized as a one-step resource that provides information directly (such as encyclopedias and textbooks) or as a two-step resource that directs the researcher to information in other sources (such as indexes and directories).

GOVERNMENT RECORDS

Information gathered by governmental agencies is available both in public and academic libraries and directly from the agencies themselves. Vast amounts of information are generated by the U.S. Census Bureau, which actually produces 11 different censuses (population, governments, agriculture, housing, transportation, manufacturing, mineral industries, selected construction industries, selected service industries, retail trade and wholesale trade). Other information is available from individual federal agencies dealing with commerce, education, labor, justice, and the like.

A useful guide to information available through the federal government is the monthly *American Statistics Index* compiled by the Congressional Information Service or the annual *Statistical Abstract of the United States*; both publications are available in most libraries.

luch information is available from state, county and local governments. Additionally, ual foreign nations have information available to varying degrees, and the United s provides information about countries and about various global issues.

IERCIAL INFORMATION SERVICES

Commercial sources of information include polling firms such as the Gallup Organization, Harris Polls and Zogby International. Other polling centers are associated with higher education, such as the National Opinion Research Center at the University of Chicago or the

---

RESEARCH WEBSITES

Research Companies

- Arbitron Company—arbitron.com
- Claritas/PRIZM—claritas.com
- Gallup Organization—gallup.com
- Harris Poll—harrisinteractive.com
- A. C. Nielsen Corporation—acnielsen.com
- Pew Research Center—people-press.org
- Princeton Survey Research Associates—psra.com
- Public Agenda—publicagenda.org
- Survey USA—surveyuse.com
- Yankelovich Partners—yankelovich.com
- Zogby International—Zogby.com

Media-Related Polling Organizations

- ABC News Polling Unit—abcnews.go.com
- CBS News Poll—cbsnews.com
- FOX News Poll—foxnews.com
- NBC News Poll—msn.com
- New York Times Poll—nytimes.com
- Los Angeles Times Poll—latimes.com
- Washington Post—washingtonpost.com

University-Related Polling Organizations

- Marist College, Marist Institute for Public Polling—maristpoll.marist.edu
- Quinnipiac University, Polling Institute—quinnipiac.edu/institutes-and-centers/polling-institute
- Rutgers University, Eagleton Poll—eagletonpoll.rutgers.edu
- University of Chicago, National Opinion Research Center—norc.uchicago.edu
- University of Connecticut, Roper Center for Public Opinion Research—ropercenter.uconn.edu
- University of Pennsylvania, Annenburg Public Policy Center—annenburg publicpolicycenter.org

Quinnipiac University Polling Institute. Meanwhile, the Roper Center for Public Opinion Research at the University of Connecticut conducts no research of its own but instead serves as an archive (updated daily) for research from more than 125 research organizations.

Trade and professional associations also are sources of syndicated data. Media-ratings companies such as Arbitron and A. C. Nielsen also have useful demographic data. Stanford Research Institute pioneered the VALS (values and lifestyles) system of **psychographics**, which combines demographic and lifestyle data.

Other companies have begun offering census-based marketing services using a technique called **geodemography**, which combines census and other demographic information with zip codes, census tracts, and other data to describe the characteristics of particular neighborhoods and the people who live in them. Geodemography has proved very useful for marketing and fund-raising purposes. Sources of this information include PRIZM (Potential Rating Index Zip Markets), created by the Claritas Corporation, Strategic Mapping's ClusterPLUS, Equifax's MicroVision and ACORN (A Classification of Residential Neighborhoods) by CACI.

ONLINE RESEARCH

Information searches conducted via computer are becoming increasingly common. CD-ROM and online sources can provide data direct from sources such as the Census Bureau or through commercial databases. Sources for online information can be identified through directories such as the *Directory of Online, Portable and Internet Databases* published by Gale Research. The Cambridge Information Group publishes *FINDEX: The Worldwide Directory of Market Research Reports, Studies, and Surveys*, and the British Overseas Trade Board prepares *Marketsearch: International Directory of Published Market Research.* Some online resources helpful to public relations and marketing practitioners include AMI (*Advertising and Marketing Intelligence*), *LexisNexis*, the *Foundation Directory*, the *National Newspapers Index*, the *Wilson Index* and the *Dow Jones News/Retrieval*, as well as *Psychological Abstracts* and *Sociological Abstracts*.

With its ability to connect you directly with the home pages of many businesses, nonprofit organizations and other organizations, the Internet is a powerful research tool. However, there is also plenty of garbage and gossip on the Web. In judging the quality of information you find on the Internet, ask yourself the following questions:

- Is the source or sponsor of the information indicated?
- Is the information source respected?
- Is the information source knowledgeable about the subject?
- Is the information source free from bias on the subject?
- Is the information presented in an objective manner?
- Is the information documented and verifiable?
- Is the information current?
- Is the information consistent with information from other sources?
- Does the website present links to other sources of unbiased information?

If you can answer "yes" to the above questions, it is probably safe to assume that the information is trustworthy and accurate. However, let common sense prevail. Trust your instincts, which may suggest that some information may not be fully reliable. And remember always to attribute the source of information obtained from the Internet, just as you would any other information obtained from books, periodicals or other sources.

HOW TO SPEAK BOOLEAN

Many computer-assisted information searches use the principles of **Boolean logic**, named for the nineteenth-century British mathematics teacher George Boole. This simply is a method of describing the relationship among several items. The basic Boolean operators are AND, OR and NOT. Your search for citations will be more effective if you communicate with the computer in terms it understands.

   Use common terms. Remember that computers are very literally minded. You may think college means about the same as university, but the computer doesn't know this. Be prepared to modify your searches using different variations of your topic. Here are the common Boolean operators used in searches:

1. OR statements yield citations that include either term within a text. For example, "research OR survey" will give you a long list of items that include either but not necessarily both terms. Thus, OR is the operator that yields the largest number of citations. Another use for the Boolean OR is when words have more than one spelling, such as "online OR on-line OR on line," or when a term has synonyms, such as "survey OR poll."
2. AND statements yield citations that include both terms. "Research AND survey" will give you a shorter list of items that feature both terms together.
3. NOT statements will yield citations that include the first terms but exclude the second. "Research NOT survey" will give a list of items about research that do not mention surveys.
4. NEAR statements are available with some search engines. They are like AND but more restrictive. NEAR locates items that appear within a certain proximity, but this varies up to about 20 words apart. With some search engines, you can indicate the distance between the two words. For example, "research NEAR survey" would locate phrases such as "survey research," "research using telephone surveys," and "survey techniques for professional research projects."
5. Most search engines have a way to keep two or more words together, such as "public relations" or "Edward Bernays." For some, single or double quotation marks or parentheses around the terms will keep them together. For most search engines, Boolean AND is a default so you don't need any special notations.
6. You can combine the various features in Boolean searches. "Research AND survey AND sampling" will generate citations that feature all three terms but not those with only one or two of them.
7. You can force the order of a search by using parentheses around items you want cited before another operation occurs. The process is called **nesting**. Example: "(Public relations OR marketing) NOT advertising" will yield all citations dealing with either public relations or marketing but excluding anything dealing with advertising. The parentheses force the computer to generate the OR list first, then to extract from it any citations mentioning advertising. "Public relations OR (marketing NOT advertising)" would generate marketing listings, extract advertising mentions from this, then add all public relations listings, even those that mention advertising.
8. Some search programs allow you to seek a root word and various endings, called a **wildcard**. For example, "alum?" or "alum*" or "alum$"—the feature differs among search engines—might generate the various forms of alumnus, alumni, alumna and alumnae. But it also would give you unrelated words such as aluminum and alumroot, so you'd be better off using the root *alum* in your search.

Interview

Whatever you need to know, someone probably already knows it. As public relations and marketing research needs move beyond the information available through secondary research, interviews become a commonly used research tool. Researchers can obtain information by phone, e-mail, Internet chat or voice protocol such as Skype. In-person interviews generally are the best, however. They have the added benefit of allowing the interviewer to "read" the body language of the person providing the information.

All interviews have a common purpose: to obtain information. Some are general and open-ended, allowing the interview to unfold according to the interaction of the participants and as the information rolls out. Others are more focused and in-depth, with the interviewer sticking to a prepared list of questions. The latter approach is especially good for comparative studies when you ask each interviewee more or less the same set of questions.

Interview Questions

Interviews are a good way to get a lot of information quickly and easily. Good interviews require competence and cooperation by both parties. The quality of the information they yield can be limited by several factors, including poor rapport between the interviewer and the interviewee; an interviewer who does not understand the significance of the information; or an interviewee who is unable, unwilling or uncomfortable about providing information. Still, when interviews are done professionally, they can be excellent research tools. Here are several suggestions for effective interviewing:

1. *Plan the interview.* Identify the topic of your research, noting specifically what information you need to obtain and where you might obtain it.
2. *Decide whom to interview.* Ask yourself who is likely to have the information you need. Perhaps people within your own or your client's organization would be good information sources. Librarians, government or industry officials, regulators and professionals in the field also may have the information you need. Consider reporters or other public relations practitioners familiar with your topic of interest. Witnesses to events can be particularly helpful.
3. *Build on what you already know.* Make notes on the information already available to you about the subject. If you cannot identify specific sources of information, try to identify knowledgeable people who could refer you to these information sources.
4. *Learn as much as you can beforehand.* Prior to the actual interview, study the topic by doing secondary research.
5. *Write out questions.* Before the interview, prepare a set of questions. Make sure they cover all the areas in which you need information. Be prepared to use these questions as a guide, but remain flexible to allow the discussion to move along its own natural course.
6. *Take good notes.* For lengthy interviews, consider tape-recording the information, so you are freer to interact with the interviewee. Make certain the interviewee knows you are recording the conversation and has no objections to this.
7. *Build rapport.* At the beginning of the interview, try to create a bond with the interviewee. Show an interest in this person and the topic under discussion. Note

what you might have in common with the interviewee. Explain the purpose of your interview and briefly summarize the background information you have already obtained.

8. *Build on existing information.* Instead of asking vaguely, "What do you think about the location for the zoo?" show that you have done your homework by saying, for example, "The planning commission is expected to recommend moving the zoo to the waterfront redevelopment area. What do you think of such a move?"

9. *If the interviewee closes a door, look for a window.* For example, if the head coach of a professional football team refuses to tell you why the contract has not been renewed for an assistant coach, ask what qualities the coach is looking for in a replacement. That might give you some insight into the firing.

10. *Distinguish between knowledge and opinion questions.* You will need some facts. You might ask for explanations: "What happened?" "How does this work?" "What do you know about X?" Ask for examples or anecdotes to clarify abstract points: "Can you give me an example of . . .?" "Can you tell me about a specific case in which . . .?" But go beyond the basics and probe for additional information by asking opinion questions that take you beyond the facts. "Why did this happen?" "How is this useful?"

11. *Consider attitudinal questions.* More than simple opinion items, affective or feeling questions seek to elicit how someone responds emotionally. "How does this make you feel?" may yield a different response than "What do you think about this?"

12. *Distinguish between experience-based and hypothetical questions.* It may be important to know both what an interview subject did in a certain situation and what he or she might do in a speculative setting.

13. *Don't rush into sensitive areas.* Tread gently if you wish to guide the interview into topics dealing with touchy areas, especially if they may be illegal, immoral or otherwise antisocial, or if they could impact negatively on the interviewee. Unless the interviewee clearly wishes to discuss such topics, build up to them gradually. When you have established a level of trust, such issues will be easier to discuss. One technique is to frame a question as a hypothetical: "If someone you trust asked how to buy some cocaine, what would you tell her?"

14. *Don't argue with your interviewee.* Ask for clarification of anything you don't understand, and point it out if what you are hearing seems to run counter to other information you have.

15. *Remain neutral.* Your role as an interviewer is somewhat akin to that of a psychologist. Try to be nonjudgmental about the information you receive. If the interviewee says something offensive or outrageous, don't yell, "You did *what*?" or "Are you *insane*? I can't report that!" Refrain from commenting on what your interviewee says to you. Even positive feedback can be a problem. "That's good" or "I like what you are saying" could prompt the interviewee to focus on certain topics and avoid others.

16. *Nudge additional information.* Use probing or follow-up questions to elicit additional information from your subject. For example, use questions such as "Who else was involved?" "How did that come about?" and "What else was happening?" Use sentences such as "Tell me more about that" and "Give me an example."

17. *Invite additional information.* Conclude by asking the interviewee to provide any additional information that seems relevant to the topic. Ask if there is anything

important that you didn't discuss. Review your notes and verify dates, spellings and other important details. Try to arrange a time when you can contact the interviewee to clear up any questions that may arise later.

Listening During an Interview

Good interviewing requires good listening skills. Consider the difference between merely hearing and actually listening. **Hearing** is the physiological process of sound waves making the eardrums vibrate, which in turn stimulate nerve impulses to the brain. Hearing is the result of something that happens to us. **Listening**, on the other hand, is something we *choose* to do. Listening is an interpersonal process in which you not only hear words but also interpret them, attempting to obtain essentially the same meaning in the words as the sender intended.

As the questioner during an interview, focus on what is being said. Avoid distractions, whether they are worries about your recording equipment or plans for your next question. Effective listening also involves understanding the speaker; try to achieve this, to the extent that one person can appreciate the background and experiences of another. As listening involves the interpretation of messages, try to obtain information with your senses beyond hearing. For example, listen with your eyes by observing the interviewee's body language and perhaps the surroundings as well.

Effective listening involves more than concentration. A person may pay close attention when someone speaks in a foreign language she has studied, though she still may not be able to understand the speaker very well.

Communicators talk about active listening or strategic listening, which goes beyond simply paying attention. Raymond Zeuschner (2002) identifies four steps for active listening:

1. Get physically and mentally prepared to listen.
2. Stay involved physically and mentally with the communication.
3. Keep an open mind while listening.
4. Review and evaluate the information after it has been received.

In addition to one-on-one interviews, researchers sometimes obtain information from an **intensive interview** (also called an **in-depth interview**). This involves a lengthy and detailed interview on a particular topic that can be conducted individually with several respondents. Intensive interviewers often present a set of carefully designed parallel questions for each respondent, so that information more easily can be compared or blended together.

Use this type of research technique when it is important both to give the research subject the opportunity to provide personal opinion and insight, and also to keep the subject on a narrow course. Another benefit of intensive interviews is that they reduce variation among different interviewers, since each is working from the same set of questions. Follow-up questions probe more deeply along the prearranged line of questioning.

Focus Group

A particular type of small-group discussion is a **focus group** (or less formally, a **group interview**), in which a researcher guides a conversation about an issue under study and, in doing so, enables group members to stimulate each other with their comments. The result is a more interactive and complete discussion than would be possible through individual interviews. These controlled group discussions are recorded and later analyzed by the researcher.

Focus groups generate ideas, comments and anecdotes. These can help you gain insight into and understanding about an issue. Focus groups are good techniques for clients who want to know "why?" "how?" and "what if?" Specifically, they are used by public relations and marketing practitioners to test concepts, copy and campaigns, or to evaluate potential logo designs and advertisements or even program and product names.

Focus groups are inappropriate if you need statistical data. If your client wants to know "how much?" or "how many?" conduct a survey instead. Remember also that focus groups are not decision-making or problem-solving sessions; don't expect the group participants to resolve the issue you are researching.

In some cases, focus groups are the primary research technique used. Other times, researchers use them to complement surveys, either as preliminary tools to gain a better understanding of the issue to be surveyed, or as follow-ups to shed light on the survey findings.

PRO AND CON

Focus groups have the advantage of being quick, inexpensive, flexible and very practical. On the other hand, they can become expensive and more complex if the client requires videotaping and a special viewing room with one-way mirrors. Such a video setup is particularly associated with marketing research, which has been criticized as being somewhat of a show for clients who, unseen behind their mirrors, believe that they are privy to consumer revelations. Still, it can be a useful tool in the right research situation.

Focus Group Process

Here's how to create an effective focus group. Assemble a small group of people who, as closely as possible, reflect your target population or a specific segment within the population. The group typically consists of between 8 and 12 people, though some researchers find they get better interaction from groups as small as 5.

The **moderator** (sometimes called a **facilitator**) generally introduces the topic, explains a few ground rules, then invites comments on the topic, often with an icebreaking question. For example, in a focus group with college-bound high school students, the moderator might begin by asking each participant his name, areas of academic interest and future career plans. After the introductions, the real research begins—gently, often wandering through the discussion topic. The session generally lasts 60 to 90 minutes.

Focus groups are meant to be flexible. The moderator has an agenda of topics and themes to present to the group, though not necessarily a specific list of questions. A good moderator is agile, allowing the discussion to flow gracefully through group interaction and keeping obvious control of the discussion to a minimum. In some focus sessions, the moderator will give a high degree of direction; in others, the moderator will manage the group with so much flexibility that it does not feel manipulated.

Consider the following real-life situation: a researcher conducted a pair of focus groups for post–master's degree students (all of them midcareer educational professionals), discussing the ideal learning environment as part of a study commissioned by a university vice president for renovating classrooms.

When the findings were shared with participants in a follow-up session, several said they were pleased to have felt unrestrained in their discussions. They confided that they had expected the focus groups merely to seek justification for foregone conclusions by the university. A few apologized for wandering away from the topic.

They were even more surprised when the researcher showed them a discussion outline, which included nearly every topic they had discussed. Instead of keeping a tight rein on their interaction, the moderator had allowed the discussion to meander through various aspects of the topic so gently that they felt they were involved more in a casual conversation than a research study. The research goals were accomplished without a feeling of manipulation or control. Mission accomplished.

WHO'S WHO IN A FOCUS GROUP?

The technique of a focus group involves a team of people to make it effective. Here is an overview of the various players on the field: *research leader*, *moderator*, *assistant moderator*, *host*, *recorder* and *technician*.

The **research leader** is the person who articulates the topic, conducts appropriate secondary research, selects the participants, and—most important—develops the discussion guide with its questions and agenda topics. After the session, the research leader prepares the formal written report.

The **moderator**, who often is also the research leader, is responsible for the flow of the discussion, especially keeping it on point. The moderator will use open-ended questions such as "What do you think about . . . ?" "Tell me more about . . ." and "Let's now talk about . . ." The moderator encourages discussion by reserved participants and tempers the involvement of those who may be overly talkative or aggressive. The moderator must be emotionally detached from the issue under study; don't ask the public relations director to moderate a group about the effectiveness of the newsletter or her own staff's edits.

The **assistant moderator** or **host** greets and seats participants, offers refreshments if these are available, prepares nametags if this is appropriate and escorts any latecomers to their seats. The host is a liaison between the moderator and any viewers who might be present, sometimes delivering to the moderator questions that a viewer-client might wish to have discussed.

The **recorder** takes notes throughout the discussion, producing a log of the discussion and making it easier to obtain quotes from the transcript later on. Special sheets can be prepared for recording key words and phrases of participants; who said what; significant nonverbal activity such as body language, excitement, nods, and so on; and personal observations or insights. The recorder also prepares the typed transcript that the researcher will use in preparing a final report. In some situations, the recorder may be out of view, but in most focus group settings the participants easily ignore a recorder sitting off to the side. Two recorders may be used, perhaps alternating between discussion topics, or perhaps with one recording comments and the other noting nonverbals.

The **technician** is in charge of audio- or videotaping. This person should be as unobtrusive as possible.

It is possible to combine these roles. Many setups involve two people: a research leader/moderator and an assistant moderator/recorder/technician. For very simple situations, the research leader might handle all the roles.

Conducting a Focus Group

Various researchers may have slightly different approaches for preparing and conducting a focus group. Edmunds (2000), for example, identifies several variations on the standard focus group. These include a **telefocus group** conducted via a telephone conference call, a **minifocus group** with only five or six participants, a **triad** with only three participants, an **online focus group** facilitated with software such as Skype, and a **video focus group** conducted via teleconference.

Regardless of the variations, most researchers would find their personal techniques reflected in the following 12-step outline for conducting focus groups:

1. Identify the research topic.
2. Select the moderator.
3. Select the sample.
4. Determine the number of groups needed.
5. Select the participants.
6. Select the site.
7. Arrange to record the session.
8. Prepare the discussion guide.
9. Conduct the focus group.
10. Review and analyze the information obtained from the focus group.
11. Report the data.
12. Make recommendations based on the data analysis.

RESEARCH TOPIC

Do enough secondary research to gain a good understanding of the topic. Redefine or narrow the topic if you are not convinced the information generated by the focus group will have practical significance for your organization or client, or try a different research technique.

MODERATOR

Professional focus group moderators are available through marketing research firms and some public relations agencies, as well as through some colleges and universities. Look for someone who is unbiased about the issue under study, who has good communication skills (both listening and speaking), a strong ability to probe and analyze, a good memory and an engaging personality. The moderator must also be able to quickly learn new concepts.

Usually a professional moderator can handle almost any topic, but in some sensitive areas, consider carefully who should be selected as moderator. For example, female participants in a focus group dealing with reconstructive surgery following breast cancer may be more comfortable with a moderator of their own gender, as might a group of men discussing products such as condoms.

Should you facilitate your own focus group? It can save time and money, and you probably have more knowledge of the issue than an outside moderator. But the problem of bias, even an unconscious bias, can be difficult to overcome. Internal moderators may be tempted to explain and defend rather than merely elicit comments from participants. Meanwhile, participants may be less than candid with a focus group moderator who is professionally involved with the topic under discussion.

SAMPLE

Remember that the small size of focus groups makes a truly representative sample unlikely. A focus group studying attitudes toward a proposed new chain of coffee bars might include veteran coffee drinkers, young professionals and retired persons. Some researchers find it useful to separate participants by age, gender or other important characteristics, especially if such homogeneity would enhance interaction within the group. To obtain a group that is as unbiased as possible, avoid populating it with friends, colleagues or people associated with the client, such as donors, employees, customers, and so on.

NUMBER OF GROUPS

Determine how many focus groups you will need to obtain an adequate range of opinions. Because focus groups are so easily swayed by intragroup dynamics, it is wise to plan for at least a couple of groups; some researchers prefer as many as five similar groups for a true reading.

PARTICIPANTS

Identify the number of participants you will need. Perhaps add a few extra to compensate for the inevitable no-shows. Some researchers recruit 20 percent more than they actually need. When the research is done for commercial marketing purposes, it is customary to pay participants a participation fee. The rate varies, but currently $25 to $50 is common, with more for doctors, lawyers and others with professional degrees.

SITE

Focus groups sometimes are held in special research labs equipped with video cameras, built-in microphones and a viewing room behind a one-way mirror. A cost-effective alternative is a professionally furnished conference room with a circular or rectangular table and comfortable chairs. Focus groups also can be conducted in classrooms or in a living room or around a kitchen table. Make sure the site is conveniently accessible to your participants and that it is comfortable for them.

RECORDING

Decide whether audio-only is appropriate or whether you will need full videotaping. Though marketing-oriented focus groups often are videotaped, some researchers find the practice intrusive and instead prefer audiotaping.

The primary reason for taping focus groups is to generate a written transcript of the discussion, which means videotaping probably isn't necessary. Some focus group work done for public relations purposes can be accomplished with audiotaping; an omnidirectional zone-type microphone can be set inconspicuously in the middle of a conference table, and a recorder on a side table will scarcely be noticed by participants. It is a good idea to make a back-up recording or at least to have a microcassette recorder available.

Videotaping allows a more careful review of body language and other nonverbal cues. It also allows researchers to edit the tape for presentations to clients, which can be more powerful than transcripts or quotes presented in a written report. On the negative side, videotaping can be intrusive for the dynamics of interaction among the focus group participants.

Meanwhile, having clients observe a focus group through a one-way mirror sometimes offers more of a show for clients than a process for gathering useful and actionable information.

DISCUSSION GUIDE

Prepare an outline of the questions that the moderator will use in leading the focus group. Organize any participant materials such as samples, brochures, photographs, advertising sketches, slides, and the like.

EXAMPLE: FOCUS GROUP DISCUSSION GUIDE

Client: Central University Enrollment Management Office

Purpose: To guide marketing decisions for recruiting program

Participants: 8–10 high school honor students (seniors)

1. **Introduction**
   a. Identify moderator and assistant moderator.
   b. Explain purpose of focus group.
   c. Note ground rules (confidentiality, candor, mutual respect, equal participation).

2. **Perceptions of Central University**
   a. What would your family/friends say if you decided to attend Central University?
   b. What do you know about Central University? How much?
   c. From what you do know, what does Central University do well?
   d. From what you do know, what does Central University not do well?

3. **College/University Selection**
   a. What are students looking for in a college/university? (prompt re: location, cost, courses, reputation, jobs, parties)
   b. What do your parents ask you to consider in choosing a college?
   c. What role do guidebooks and websites play in your college/university choice?

4. **Comparisons**
   a. What colleges/universities are you seriously considering attending? Why?
   b. How does Central University compare to these colleges/universities? (Prompt re: pros, cons.)
   c. In one sentence, what is your impression of Central University?

5. **Marketing Critique**
   a. Discuss samples of logos.
   b. Discuss samples of newspaper/magazine ads.
   c. Discuss samples of billboard ads.
   d. Discuss messages.

CONDUCTING THE FOCUS GROUP

Note the various distinct roles for the research team conducting the session. Make sure that the research process includes appropriate training for the moderator, assistant moderator, recorder and technician. If this will be the first time this team has conducted a focus group, the research leader should arrange for a mock run-through so that every person on the research team feels confident about how the session should unfold.

ANALYSIS

Immediately after the session, review the tape. If any parts of it were not recorded properly, write down everything you can remember. Even if the tape is complete, listen to it and review your notes. Add any additional observations or insights that you didn't have time to note during the session. Transcribe the tape.

Then begin to analyze the information obtained through the focus group. Unlike many other research methodologies, focus groups do not generate usable data in the form of numbers or percentages. There simply are not enough participate in a focus group to calculate percentages. Rather, focus groups provide comments that can be more meaningful than numbers and percentages.

The comment section of the focus group report includes both direct quotes and paraphrases drawn from the discussion, often divided into subtopics. Researchers usually highlight comments and themes that were echoed by several participants. For example, the research report may separate comments that enjoyed general endorsement from those that were mentioned by only one or two persons.

FOCUS GROUP REPORT

The report to the boss or client generally is prepared by the moderator. It should include a statement of the purpose of the research, an overview of the selection process for participants and a copy of the discussion guide.

The body of the report generally includes both selected comments made by the participants and perhaps recommendations gleaned by the researcher.

RECOMMENDATIONS

Some focus group reports conclude with specific recommendations that the researcher feels flow from the comments and observations. The decision about including recommendations is based on the expectations and needs of the client, as well as the agreed-upon role of the researcher.

Case Study

A type of research useful for public relations and marketing communication is the **case study** (sometimes called a **case history** or more generally, **field research**). A case study investigates a single event, product or situation, looking at how an organization has handled it. The purpose of this investigation is to understand and learn from a real-life example.

The underlying idea is a simple one: Let's see what we can learn from someone who has been there. A public relations director in Virginia might contact a colleague in Iowa about a crisis situation she had successfully managed a year or so earlier. That is a case study, learning from someone else's success.

Case studies don't necessarily have to present successful cases. Sisters Hospital in Buffalo, New York, faced so much community opposition that it had to cancel its plan to open a methadone clinic in a residential neighborhood. Instead, the clinic was located within the hospital. The failure became a good case study for other hospitals around the country planning to open similar off-site drug-treatment centers. Public relations practitioners could learn what not to do as well as what to do to avoid such community opposition.

Case studies often are labeled as qualitative research, meaning that they rely more on the researcher's insight than on hard facts. However, Robert Yin (2008) notes that both contemporary and historical case studies can rely on quantitative evidence.

PRO AND CON

Like any other research technique, case studies feature both advantages and disadvantages. On the plus side, they can suggest why something happened and can deal with a wide spectrum of evidence, such as documents, interviews, even surveys (Babbie, 2010). On the other hand, case studies can't easily be generalized, making it risky to presume that what happened in the observed case will necessarily predict what could happen in other situations.

Though case studies have some limitations, they nevertheless can be very useful. Many university professors have found that both graduate and undergraduate students appreciate the practical value of case studies.

Practitioners and students alike can learn a lot about crisis communication by looking at the classic cases: Three Mile Island and the Nestlé boycott in the late 1970s, Tylenol and Exxon in the 1980s, Dow Corning's breast-implant imbroglio, and TWA's downed Flight 800 in the 1990s. The twenty-first century added Olympic drug scandals and the Ford/Firestone crisis in the first decade. For the current decade, think Deepwater Horizon and Penn State athletics. That's in addition to a variety of other crisis cases dealing with embezzlement (United Way of America), scandal (Covenant House), consumer fraud (Sears Auto Centers), product

---

BASIC SKILLS FOR A CASE STUDY RESEARCHER

Here are five basic research skills necessary for people involved in preparing case studies. The case study preparer should:

1. Be able to ask good questions, and to interpret the answers.
2. Be a good listener and not be trapped by his own ideologies or preconceptions.
3. Be adaptive and flexible, so that newly encountered situations can be seen as opportunities, not threats.
4. Have a firm grasp on the issues being studied, whether this is a theoretical or policy orientation, even if in an exploratory mode. such a grasp focuses the relevant events and information to be sought to manageable proportions.
5. Be unbiased by preconceived notions, including those derived from theory. Thus, a person should be sensitive and responsive to contradictory evidence.

Source: Yin (2008)

tampering (the Pepsi syringe hoax), product credibility (Intel Pentium), customer injury (McDonald's), and employee behavior (U.S. Navy "Tailhook"). That's just a few cases dealing with crises. We can learn from thousands more dealing with employee communication, community relations, investor relations, and so on.

Conducting a Case Study

As a research method, case studies offer much flexibility to the researcher. However, some common approaches are helpful. Here are 11 steps for conducting a case study, following by a closer look at each:

1. Identify the research situation.
2. Select a relevant case to investigate.
3. Identify the information you need.
4. Identify the data sources.
5. Articulate questions.
6. Develop a study protocol.
7. Conduct a pilot study.
8. Gather the information.
9. Analyze the information.
10. Make recommendations.
11. Report the information.

RESEARCH SITUATION

Identify the problem within your organization that generates your research. Make sure the problem is one that can be addressed by making a comparison to another organization.

RELEVANT CASE

Identify a suitable case to investigate. Make sure the organization associated with the case is at least somewhat comparable to your own or your client's organization, so that the comparison is a meaningful one.

INFORMATION NEEDS

Identify the information you will need to address the research situation. A case study can yield a wide range of information, but you can make your study more efficient by first noting the parameters of what you need to find out. Remember that you are not seeking merely a journalistic report of events but an insightful analysis of causes and effects, strategies and tactics.

INFORMATION SOURCE

Identify an organization that is likely to have experienced a situation from which you can learn for your own organization or client. Then locate the information sources, which generally are personal observation, interviews or documentation such as news releases, press clippings and other published information, as well as internal documents such as letters, organizational files, agendas, reports and surveys. Often the best information source may the public relations person associated with the organization you are investigating.

RESEARCH QUESTIONS

Articulate the questions and topics that you will use with the data sources to obtain the information you seek.

STUDY PROTOCOL

Develop a plan of action for formal case studies to be reported in writing (optional). Create a document that identifies the study's purpose and procedures, definitions, data sources, questions, and plan for analysis and reporting.

PILOT STUDY

Conduct a preliminary study to pretest and perhaps refine the questions for the eventual investigation.

GATHERING INFORMATION

Use your skills as both an interviewer and a secondary researcher to gather the information you think is needed to shed some light on your research situation. Do your homework first, reviewing both published and online sources. Then conduct an in-person, telephone or online interview with the information source you identified.

INFORMATION ANALYSIS

Look not only at the individual facts but also at their relationship and potential interaction. Apply the information to your own organization.

RECOMMENDATIONS

If the information obtained through the case study is useful, it may offer some suggestions for your organization. Case studies often conclude with a section of recommendations that an organization might implement, based on findings (both what worked and what did not work) from the organization under review.

REPORT

Determine the best way to report the information, based on the appropriate audience (you only, professional colleagues, bosses or clients). This reporting may be verbal and informal, even conversational if you have conducted the case study for your own company, or it may be written as part of a formal series of research and recommendations for a client or as part of a major campaign.

Sampling for case studies usually involves nonprobability methods, particularly convenience, purposive and snowball sampling (discussed earlier in the section Nonprobability Sampling).

Also important to case studies are the roles of the observer and the informant. The observer is you, the person doing the research; and you are neither unobtrusive nor disinterested. Your informant, meanwhile, is the person you are interviewing to obtain information about the case. This informant also is not disinterested. Good research calls for both the observer and the informant to be objective, fair and as unbiased as possible. Questions should not be slanted to elicit hoped-for answers, and responses should tell all relevant aspects of the story as they really happened, without reinterpretation or reshaping.

Survey Research

One of the oldest and most common research techniques is the **survey**, which involves asking standard questions of many respondents and then comparing their responses.

Surveys, also known as **polls**, have many advantages. They are appropriate for description, analysis and prediction—three major research needs. They are among the least expensive and quickest types of research. They can be applied to both large and small groups of people. They can be very accurate and their findings are easy to compare. On the downside, surveys are subject to both the bias and limitations of the researcher, particularly through inadequate samples or poorly worded questions.

Surveys can be administered in a number of ways, each with certain built-in benefits and disadvantages.

TELEPHONE SURVEY

A *telephone survey* is quick to administer but limited to easy-to-understand questions. Three factors are making it increasingly difficult to conduct phone surveys: the duplicity of telemarketing posing as research; the prevalence of people with only mobile phones; and the ubiquity of caller ID, answering machines and voicemail.

MAIL SURVEY

Another common type, a *mail survey* (also called a *self-administered survey*), is convenient for respondents. However, the response rate generally is lower than for more expensive telephone surveys.

PERSONAL INTERVIEW SURVEY

A *personal interview survey* is most expensive of all because it is time-consuming. It also is subject to interpersonal variables not found in most other types of surveys.

GROUP-ADMINISTERED SURVEY

Meanwhile, a *group-administered survey* is easy to execute, but there often is a concern about the appropriateness of the group.

COMPUTER-BASED SURVEY

A newer technique, a *computer-based survey*, offers some benefits of mail surveys. But these often are focused on a volunteer sample, which may not be the most appropriate for the research needs.

Response Rate

Response rates vary considerably with surveys. Some research is reported on the basis of a response rate of 5 percent or less. Some surveys, especially those on controversial topics, have generated much publicity, despite having response rates of only 2 or 3 percent. Such low response rates raise serious doubts about findings.

Earl Babbie (2010) considers a response rate of 50 percent as adequate, 60 percent as good and 70 percent as very good. Many professional researchers also point out that a good sample is more important than a high response rate.

You'll have to decide what an acceptable rate is for your research, realizing that higher response rates generally are more reliable.

Some researchers use payments or other incentives to increase the response rate. Sometimes the payment is merely a token amount, perhaps a dollar, even a couple of pennies ("We want your two cents' worth"). Incentives may be pens, calendars, tickets or simple items associated with the sponsor. Some surveys offer a more elaborate gift through a raffle held among participants who return the questionnaires.

Better than incentives, however, is simply to develop a questionnaire that interests potential respondents, that matches their interest, and that points to some organizational decisions on topics that affect them. For example, a university conducting a survey of student interests about summer classes doesn't need to entice respondents with money or trinkets. The topic itself should lead students who might take summer classes to share their opinion and thus perhaps affect the kinds of courses, times, locations and other aspects of the summer term.

A stamped, self-addressed return envelope sometimes accompanies written questionnaires, making it easier for the respondent to return the questionnaire. Fax response may be appropriate for questionnaires sent to professionals and dealing with nonpersonal topics. Likewise, e-mail surveys are becoming increasingly popular, and they can be particularly effective when targeted to an appropriate sample.

Much depends on how carefully you select the sample and how well you groom your chosen respondents. A general rule applies: The more involved the respondents are with the sponsoring organization or the more concerned they are with the issue, the higher the response rate. Some researchers have the head of the organization send a letter to respondents asking them to complete the questionnaire they will soon receive and noting the importance of the information to the organization.

Follow-up mailings can also greatly improve the response rate. The least expensive way is to send a reminder via e-mail, postcard or letter. It is more effective, however, to send another copy of the questionnaire.

If your client or boss is serious about wanting responses, the price of second or even third mailings is money well spent. Researchers generally follow a formula that a second mailing will generate half the percentage of response as the first mailing generated, and the third mailing half that of the second. Babbie (2010) recommends two or three follow-up mailings for the best response. He cites the experience of the Survey Research Office at the University of Hawaii, which found a consistent pattern of returns. It generally obtains a 40 percent response from its initial questionnaire mailing. A second mailing two weeks later brings in another 20 percent. A third mailing yields an additional 10 percent.

Another way to ensure adequate numbers of responses is to use a larger-than-desired sample, on the notion that not everyone in the selected sample will respond. Though this adds to the mailing cost, it may be a legitimate way to obtain responses, especially if it reduces the need for follow-up mailings.

Survey Administration

Here is a simple step-by-step formula for conducting a survey. The format is general, though steps 7 through 10 deal specifically with mail surveys; modify these for surveys administered over the phone or in person. Following these general steps, we'll talk more specifically about questionnaires with a more detailed look at each.

1. Identify the topic of your research.
2. Select a sample.
3. Write the questionnaire items.
4. Print the questionnaire.
5. Test the questionnaire and, if necessary, modify it.
6. Prepare a cover letter or introduction.
7. Administer the questionnaire.
8. Monitor returns and, if necessary, send follow-up mailings.
9. Report the data.
10. Analyze the data.
11. Make recommendations.
12. Write the comprehensive report.

RESEARCH TOPIC

Identify the topic of your research. Do enough secondary research to gain a good understanding of the topic. Redefine or narrow the topic if you are not convinced the information generated by the survey will have practical significance for your organization or client. If you cannot modify it, you may need to abandon the survey and use a different research technique.

SAMPLE

Select an appropriate sample for the survey. Make sure that the sample is appropriate for your organization in terms of reliability as well as time and cost.

QUESTIONNAIRE ITEMS

Write the items to be included in the questionnaire, which is the written document that presents questions or statements to respondents. Review the wording for each item. Keep the questionnaire as brief as possible. The more concise it is, the higher response rate you can expect. (More on questionnaires in the subsequent section of this appendix.)

PRINT THE QUESTIONNAIRE

Print the questionnaire on paper with the logo of the sponsoring organization on the first page. Visually, the questionnaire should be neat and user-friendly, with clear instructions, readable type, and easy response formats. Try not to split items over pages or columns.

TEST THE QUESTIONNAIRE

Administer the questionnaire to a small group of people reflecting the characteristics of your sample. Based on what you learn in this pretest pilot, you may need to modify the questionnaire.

COVER LETTER OR INTRODUCTION

For mail and e-mail surveys, write a cover letter that introduces the survey to respondents. Identify the sponsoring organization, explain its purpose, note the level of confidentiality, and invite their participation. Include a telephone number where respondents can contact the research office with questions or simply to verify the legitimacy of the survey.

Some researchers prefer to use an advance letter in addition to the cover letter. This can be particularly useful when the questionnaires are going to people associated with the sponsoring organization, such as an advance letter from the director of a nonprofit organization announcing an upcoming questionnaire and encouraging participation.

For face-to-face administration of a survey, write a brief paragraph explaining the purpose of the survey and noting the amount of time needed from the potential respondent.

QUESTIONNAIRE ADMINISTRATION

For mail surveys, send the letter and questionnaire. Always use first-class postage. Include a return envelope with first-class postage, or use envelopes with a postage-paid business reply imprint. The latter costs more per piece when returned, but you pay for only those envelopes that are returned. On the other hand, there is a psychological advantage in using a postage stamp that respondents will know they are wasting if they don't use it in returning a completed questionnaire. Alternatively, send an e-mail with the questionnaire if you know that your intended respondents are comfortable with using e-mail.

MONITOR RETURNS

For mail and e-mail surveys, monitor the returns. Keep a daily count of the number of returns received. Be prepared to send a follow-up after about 10 days. If necessary and appropriate, send a second follow-up mailing after another two weeks. Skip this step for in-person administration of the questionnaire.

DATA REPORTING

The heart of the survey report is an item-by-item account of how the respondents replied. Report the findings for every item of the questionnaire. This reporting should include both raw numbers and percentages. Some surveys use advanced statistical analysis to report the data, though applied research for professional (non-academic) clients often rests on percentages.

DATA ANALYSIS

Equally important with data reporting is the analysis of this data. Sometimes these are two different sections of a research report. Often, however, researcher comments and observations are included within the item reporting, pointing to interesting correlations with other questions.

As online administration of surveys increases, so too does the number of survey software options—more than a hundred. Some companies offer free or low-cost basic packages with limits on the number of questions and the number of surveys that may be conducted, graduating to monthly costs for more sophisticated and larger packages. Examples of these are Survey Methods, SurveyMonkey, PollDaddy and Zoomerang. Other companies specialize in more professional, and thus more expensive, products such as SurveyGizmo, Grapevine, Moodle and Opinio.

RECOMMENDATIONS

Usually the researcher includes a set of recommendations flowing logically from the findings.

WRITTEN REPORT

Survey results usually are reported with a degree of formality because they are serious research. Generally the written report will include a statement of the purpose of the research, an outline of the methods used to obtain and contact the sample, a copy of the questionnaire, a report on the number of responses received and a notation of any limitations or weaknesses in the survey.

Questionnaire

A **questionnaire** is the tool used for surveys. It is a written document that features a series of items such as questions or statements that call for a response.

Whether the questionnaire is delivered in person, over the telephone, in print or online, the introductory statement sets the stage. This introduction should identify the researcher and the sponsoring organization, indicate the topic, explain why the respondent was selected, guarantee confidentiality and note the approximate time required of the respondent.

Don't *ask* the respondent to participate, because this provides an opportunity for the respondent to decline. Instead provide the preliminary information and get right to the first question.

TIMING AND WORDING AFFECT POLL RESULTS

The timing of polls and the way questions are worded can have a big impact on how people answer them. Here is an example related by Adam Clymer (2001), a columnist with the *New York Times*, who reflected on the fact that several conflicting surveys were being reported about supposed public support for federal funding of human embryonic stem cell research.

As the issue was heating up, an NBC News/Wall Street Journal poll said that 69 percent of Americans favored the research. A Gallup Poll for CNN and USA Today reported 54 percent in favor. A poll by ABC News and Beliefnet (a religious website) found 58 percent in favor. These three news-related polls had significant differences.

Meanwhile, two less-than-disinterested parties had reported even more disparate results. A poll by the Juvenile Diabetes Foundation, which favored stem cell research, said 70 percent of Americans favor the research. But the Conference of Catholic Bishops, which opposed the research on human embryos, reported a survey that said only 24 percent of Americans approve.

Clymer noted that some of the variations in the polling could be traced to how the questions were phrased. The NBC/Journal poll used the phrase "potentially viable human embryos," while the bishops' poll said "the live embryos would be destroyed in their first week of development." The bishop's poll also referred to "experiments," while the others alluded to the goals of the research.

Perhaps more important, the polls were so dissimilar because many respondents were unfamiliar with the topic. Each poll asked long and involved questions. Only the Gallup Poll allowed respondents to answer that they did not know enough about the issue to have an opinion, and 57 percent chose that response category.

Clymer quoted research experts that the polls were measuring "nonattitudes." One survey expert focused on the newness and complexity of the issue: "Americans are acquiescent so they'll give you an answer. [But] the mere fact that you've got to offer a lengthy summary implies that it's too early to sort it out."

The insightful columnist concluded with a warning for all of us: "Sometimes, the pollsters are measuring phantoms, and the politicians are calling on them for support."

Data in questionnaires fits into several categories. The main content items generally follow the same hierarchy as do public relations objectives: awareness (knowledge, understanding or retention of information); acceptance (interest or attitude); and action (opinion or behavior). Additionally, demographic items deal with the respondent's background or environment, which is useful information for analyzing the data gathered.

GENERAL TIPS FOR QUESTIONNAIRES

Asking the right questions in the right way is basic to conducting a good survey. Following are some general tips for questionnaire items, whether they are framed as statements or questions:

- *Keep items short.* Using several short, specific items is better than using fewer items that are complex and confusing.
- *Use clear and simple language.* Make sure the words and phrases are familiar to the respondents. Avoid jargon unless the respondents share the language. Avoid all but the most commonly used abbreviations.
- *Be specific.* Avoid ambiguous words and phrases. For example, the seemingly simple question "Where do you live?" could actually generate a range of responses. Is the desired answer "United States"? Or perhaps "Cleveland," "23 Oriole Road," "In an apartment building" or "With my parents." Likewise, a question such as "What do you think about the mayor's tax proposal?" is unclear. One respondent may focus on the timing, another on the amount of money to be collected, still another on the method of collection or the eventual use of the money raised.
- *Ask relevant questions.* Don't let your curiosity run amok. Use only those items that are relevant to the research topic.
- *Place items in a logical order.* Usually this means easy to difficult. Group items that deal with a similar topic together. Demographic items about the respondents should be kept together. Mail and e-mail surveys often place these items at the end, while telephone surveys may lead with these because they are easy for respondents to answer.
- *Use positive constructions.* Arrange sentences to avoid negative phrasing. For example, ask "Do you participate in group exercise or fitness programs?" instead of the more negative "Do you avoid group exercise or fitness programs?" Especially avoid double negatives, such as the awkward "Do you disagree that lack of exercise is unhealthful?" (Presuming you have an opinion on the issue, try figuring out how to respond to that question.)
- *Use words with clear meanings.* Every respondent must understand and interpret the questionnaire items exactly the same way. For example, "Have you ever considered having an affair?" begs the question of what "consider" means in this context. And what is an "affair"? Instead, try asking: "While you were married, did you ever engage in sexual activity with another person other than your spouse?"
- *Avoid "double-barreled" items.* These are items that include two different thoughts. For example, the question "Do you think Portland is a friendly and progressive community?" is difficult for respondents to answer if they think Portland is friendly but not very progressive. The relationship between the two modifiers is unclear; they don't belong in the same question.

WRITING IMPARTIALLY

In general, researchers want questionnaires to be unbiased. Following are a few pointers in writing impartial questions.

- *Keep your wording neutral.* Avoid leading items that indicate to the respondent what the researcher apparently sees as the "correct" answer. Example: "Do you agree with most Americans that more violent criminals should receive the death penalty?" Telling the respondent that most Americans agree with this statement is biasing the response.
- *Don't signal your own bias.* Make sure the wording doesn't suggest that you as the researcher might think is the appropriate response such as, "Do you prefer reading good literature or just popular novels?" Good literature? Just novels? No doubt about the preferred answer here.
- *Take care with socially or politically charged words.* Kenneth Rasinski (1989) analyzed the wording in several national surveys. He found, for example, that 63 percent of respondents said too little money was being spent on "assistance to the poor," but only 23 percent said too little was being spent on "welfare." The difference is all in the wording.
- *Realize that words have different meanings.* This may be especially true with commonly used social and political terms. It's the old issue of connotation and denotation. Example: "Are you pro-abortion?" Respondents may consider themselves pro-choice but not pro-abortion, or they might be disinclined to answer such a complex question with a simple "yes" or "no." Whenever respondents feel a need to explain their interpretation of a questionnaire item, it is poorly worded.
- *Avoid a prestige bias.* Don't make associations with respected authorities or well-known figures. Example: "Do you agree with the mayor that property taxes are too high?" The same is true with disrespected figures. If the mayor has just been indicted for embezzlement and tax fraud, respondents may hedge on stating any agreement with a disgraced public official.
- *Use leading questions only in special situations.* Use them if you are dealing with a potentially embarrassing or controversial issue or if you feel a need to "give permission" to respondents to be truthful. For example: "Recently, several political leaders have admitted to adultery . . ."

INFORMATION ITEMS

Items dealing with the respondent's level of information may offer a particular challenge to questionnaire writers.

- *Set the stage.* If necessary, include a brief definition of key terms.
- *Write for your intended respondents.* Make sure the topic is within their competence and comprehension. For example, don't ask a sample of people without a strong scientific background if fusion or fission is a better process for nuclear energy. Any response would be little more than an uninformed guess.
- *Carefully explain when you are testing the knowledge of respondents.* Example: "A main purpose of this survey is to find out how much residents know about the bridge proposal. The following six items present multiple-choice items about the proposal. Circle the answers you think are correct."

OPINION ITEMS

Some special guidelines apply to questionnaire items that seek to elicit the respondent's opinion or attitude.

- *Don't ask for opinions on questions that are matters of fact.* For example, don't ask "Do boys get higher grades in mathematics than girls do?" because that question doesn't call for an opinion. You can easily research the facts on math grades. But a legitimate opinion question might be "Why do you think boys get higher grades in mathematics than girls do?" especially if your questionnaire is being answered by teachers, parents, psychologists or others whose opinions might be relevant.
- *Avoid speculative or hypothetical questions.* Example: "Would you prefer to move to a colony under the sea or in outer space?" An exception to this is if the item deals with a potential activity of the sponsoring organization. Example: "Given the opportunity, would you consider purchasing a vacuum cleaner that also served as an air purifier?"
- *Avoid terms that call for subjective judgment.* This can vary from person to person. Example: "Is the current tax structure reasonable?" The word "reasonable" may be interpreted differently by various respondents. Instead ask more specifically, "Is the current tax structure affordable?" (or "equitable" or whatever else you really want to know).
- *Be careful about mixing fact and opinion.* If a national magazine has just ranked Austin as one of the top 10 progressive cities in the US, don't ask, "Is Austin a progressive city?" It's unclear if you are asking about the respondent's awareness or opinion. Instead ask, "Do you agree with a magazine ranking that Austin is progressive?"

ACTION ITEMS

Items dealing with actions and behaviors, whether current or past, also can be particularly difficult for the questionnaire writer.

- *Ask for relevant behaviors.* Example: "Do you ever shop at GreenGrocers?" *Ever?*
- *Make sure the questions can reasonably be answered.* Avoid asking for highly detailed information, such as, "In the last six months, how many hours of television have you watched?" Instead, use a time frame easier for the respondent, such as, "On an average weekday, how many hours of television do you usually watch?" or, "On an average weekend, how many hours of television do you usually watch?" Then you do the math.
- *Make sure the topic is within the respondent's relevant experience.* Asking women about how frequently they practice self-examination techniques for testicular cancer isn't a useful question. Either limit it to male respondents or replace it with a question dealing with the frequency of self-examination techniques in general, such as for two easily detectable cancers (breast cancer or testicular cancer).
- *Don't word the questions so that they presume a particular answer.* This is especially important with sensitive issues. Example: "How often do you smoke marijuana?" This wording presumes that one smokes it at least sometimes. This might be better handled with a primary and a contingency question, "Do you smoke marijuana?" and then the contingency, "If yes, how often?"

- *Be careful with intrusive or potentially embarrassing questions*, especially those that deal with legal, social or moral transgressions. "Are you always truthful on your income tax returns?" may result in a less-than-truthful answer, in part because the respondent may be concerned about the confidentiality of the study, and in part because the respondent may simply be unwilling to confess a crime, even to himself.

DEMOGRAPHIC ITEMS

Asking for age, educational level and other types of demographic information also requires careful attention by the questionnaire writer.

- *Use ranges.* Rather than ask a respondent's age or income, group such sensitive questions into ranges. Example: "Which of the following best describes your family income last year? Less than $40,000; $40,001 to $80,000; more than $80,000."
- *Tailor response categories to your target population.* For example, fit educational levels to your research purpose, and consider asking for the highest grade or degree completed. Example: "How much education have you completed? Less than high school; high school; some college but no degree; associate's degree; bachelor's degree; graduate degree." If this was directed to academic professionals, the response choices might be "Bachelor's degree; academic master's degree; terminal master's degree (MFA, MSW); academic doctorate (PhD); professional doctorate (JD, MD, DDS); postdoctoral study."
- *Take care with racial or ethnic background.* When asking for such information, make sure all options are included. Also consider the wording of the question. The US Census Bureau asks people to indicate the race they consider themselves to be, a subtle difference over the strictly matter-of-fact question, "What is your race?" Rather than a narrow black/white/other configuration, try to provide options for people to indicate their specific racial/ethnic identity. For example, though Arab and Hispanic are not racial categories, many members of those backgrounds choose "other" rather than "white." Similarly, people of Caribbean background often do not identify immediately with "black." Understand who may be asked to respond to the questionnaire and adjust the demographic options to reflect this. Also, because a growing number of people identify themselves as biracial or multiracial, consider allowing respondents to indicate more than one category, which will yield more information than a single "mixed" category.
- *Tailor the demographic information to the research needs.* For example, for surveys conducted near the northern U.S. border, demographic items might include the name of the specific province for someone who indicates a Canadian background. Likewise, in the Southwest, items might include the names of specific Central or Latin American countries or perhaps Mexican states, if that information is relevant to the researcher.

Types of Responses

Questionnaire design must give attention to the response categories for the various items. First of all, make the options visually simple and consistent. Use checkmarks, circles, boxes or other simple marks. One of the first considerations is the type of response categories. **Open-ended items** allow respondents to answer in their own words; **closed-ended items** provide for check-offs to predetermined response categories.

GUIDELINES FOR OPEN-ENDED VERSUS CLOSED-ENDED ITEMS

Here are some guidelines for when to use open-ended questions and when closed-ended questions are more appropriate. Remember that both can be used within the same questionnaire.

Use closed-ended items if you:

- prefer that respondents use predetermined choice;
- want to make it easier for respondents by using predetermined choices;
- can anticipate the range of response choices;
- want to directly compare and correlate responses.

Use open-ended items if you:

- prefer that respondents answer in their own words;
- want to make it easier for respondents by answering in their own words;
- don't know the range of response choices;
- are willing to consider dissimilar comments from respondents.

Researchers have devised several different types of items that can be used for responses in questionnaires. Some of the more common types are multiple-choice items, checklist items, forced-choice items and rating scales. A questionnaire may include more than one type of item, though it's generally a good idea to group similar items.

MULTIPLE CHOICE

Questions or statements with a limited number of responses are called **multiple-choice items**. These allow respondents to choose from a predetermined set of choices. For example: "Indicate your favorite major television news network: ABC, CBS, CNN, FOX, MSNBC, NBC." Often multiple-choice items include an "other" category. Note that the responses are arranged alphabetically.

Response categories for choice items must be both comprehensive and mutually exclusive.

- A comprehensive set of responses ensures that each response category provides a full range of potential responses so there is an appropriate response category for every respondent.
- Mutually exclusive responses ensure that there is only one possible response for each respondent.

For example, on a demographic question asking the income of respondents, the response categories might be "$20,000 or less"; "$20,000 to $60,000"; "$60,000 to $100,000"; and

"$100,000 or more." The categories are comprehensive, covering all the bases. But they are not mutually exclusive because they overlap—both the second and third choices are appropriate for someone earning $60,000 a year. A better way to write response categories might be "less than $20,000"; "$20,000 to $59,999"; "$60,000 to $99,999"; and "$100,000 or more."

CHECKLIST

Sometimes it is more effective to allow respondents to indicate more than one response through a **checklist**. Example: "What kind of country music do you listen to most often? Check all that apply: classic country, new country, alternative country, honky-tonk, bluegrass, nugrass, rockabilly, gothabilly, cowboy, cowpunk, country rock, country pop, western swing, outlaw country, progressive country, soul country, Christian country."

FORCED CHOICE

Another type of response category is **forced-choice items** that feature two or more statements, with directions for respondents to select the one that most closely reflects their opinion. Example: "Of the following statements, select the one that comes closer to your own belief: Voting is a privilege and thus should be optional. Voting is a responsibility and thus should be required. Voting is a useless activity with no real consequences."

RATING SCALE

Some items have the advantage of focusing on the intensity of the respondent's feelings rather than eliciting a simple yes or no response. These are **rating scales**, in which respondents are asked to rate the degree of their feeling or certainty about an item. Some rating scales are bipolar instruments because they move in both directions from a neutral center point to either positive or negative points. Others are unipolar instruments that range from low to high points.

The popular **Likert scale** (pronounced LICK-ert) is a bipolar scale that asks the intensity of respondents' agreement to a statement along a range of negative and positive response categories, such as strongly disagree, disagree, agree and strongly agree. The wording for the Likert scale can be modified, such as by asking approval, belief, interest, and so forth instead of agreement.

In some versions, the Likert scale includes a central or neutral option ("neither agree nor disagree"), and sometimes a "no opinion" item. For some issues, researchers use the neutral option; for others they would rather eliminate the midpoint and force the respondent to indicate a preference one way or the other.

When using rating scales, define response options carefully. Rating scales sometimes offer choices such as excellent, very good, average, fair, poor, and so on. A problem with such scales is that too many response categories can leave respondents confused about the differences among the categories—for example, between average and fair or between excellent and very good.

To avoid this ambiguity, some rating scales are presented numerically, as in the following example: "Indicate your preference for various flavors of ice cream (1 being dislike, 5 being like): Vanilla 1–2–3–4–5. Chocolate 1–2–3–4–5. Strawberry 1–2–3–4–5" (and so on). When rating scales are used numerically, it is logical to arrange them so that a low or negative response translates into low numbers. Example: "Rate the following on a scale of 1 to 5 (1 being low priority, 5 being high priority)." Reversing this, to rank low priority items with a five and high priority items with a one, would be confusing to respondents.

Appendixes

HOW AM I DOING?

The customer satisfaction survey is commonplace in helping managers understand how their customers feel about their products and services. Such surveys are used by manufacturers and retailers as well as by nonprofit organizations such as hospitals, colleges, cultural organizations and service agencies. They also are commonly used to measure employee satisfaction.

With any survey, especially one that seeks to gauge the level of satisfaction by customers, readers, employees and other key publics, it is important to ask the right question. Most **customer satisfaction surveys** ask variations on "How am I doing?" Here are examples of some different scales that address this question (listed alphabetically):

- *Acceptability*: not at all acceptable, slightly acceptable, moderately acceptable, very acceptable, completely acceptable.
- *Appropriateness*: absolutely inappropriate, inappropriate, slightly inappropriate, slightly appropriate, appropriate, absolutely appropriate.
- *Awareness*: not at all aware, slightly aware, moderately aware, very aware, extremely aware.
- *Beliefs*: not at all of what I believe, slightly true of what I believe, moderately true . . ., very true . . ., completely true . . .
- *Expectation*: much less than expected, less than expected, as much as expected, more than expected, much more than expected.
- *Performance*: poor, fair, good, excellent, superior.
- *Requirement Frequency*: never meets requirements, rarely meets requirements, occasionally meets requirements, usually meets requirements, always meets requirements.
- *Requirement*: did not meet requirements, nearly met requirements, met requirements, exceeded my requirements.
- *Satisfaction*: very dissatisfied, dissatisfied, neither satisfied nor dissatisfied, satisfied, very satisfied.

Professional researcher Howard Waddel observes that each of these scales share a weakness: They potentially point to problems but don't indicate to management how to act on these indications of customer satisfaction. Waddell, president of Decision Resource of Miami, suggests a better approach focusing on corrective action (1995).

The improvement scale presumes there generally is room for better performance, and it makes this the central point of the research. This scale can be used to guide management decisions about a variety of product and service factors. Using this approach, researchers ask customers to indicate how much improvement, if any, they feel is needed by the company. Only three response choices are offered: no improvement needed, some improvement needed, and considerable improvement needed.

This **improvement scale** offers several advantages over the other types noted above. It is unambiguous and thus simple for customers to understand. It evokes candor by not inviting charitable responses. And it fits all kinds of product and service attributes.

Rating scales can even be presented visually, such as with smiley face caricatures for children's surveys, ranging from very sad through very happy. Writing about questionnaires in a series of books on survey research, Arlene Fink (2002a) recommends five types of response options for rating scales (presented here in lowest-to-highest logical order):

- *Endorsement*: definitely false, false, don't know, true, definitely true.
- *Frequency*: never, almost never, sometimes, fairly often, very often, always.
- *Comparison*: much less than others, somewhat less than others, about the same as others, somewhat more than others, much more than others.
- *Influence*: no problem, very small problem, small problem, moderate problem, big problem.
- *Intensity*: none, very mild, mild, moderate, severe.

Note that the first four items are bipolar, with negative and positive ends of the scale. The last two examples are unipolar, moving from a zero point.

The **semantic differential scale** asks respondents to select a point on a continuum between two opposing positions. The scale generally uses opposing adjectives, usually with a five-point or seven-point scale. Example: "What are your perceptions about professional football? Interesting/uninteresting. Enjoyable/unenjoyable." This scale also can be presented numerically. For example:

| Uninteresting | 1 | 2 | 3 | 4 | 5 | Interesting |
| Unenjoyable | 1 | 2 | 3 | 4 | 5 | Enjoyable |

Content Analysis

Some problems are inherent in focus groups and surveys. When you directly ask people their opinion, their response may not be genuine. It may be shaped by the fact that you asked in the first place, or it may be colored by their desire to give you what they think is an acceptable answer.

For example, ask an acquaintance if he likes you and the answer may be "Yes, of course." But is he saying that just because you asked; because he'd be embarrassed to answer "not really"; or because he doesn't want to hurt your feelings? Instead of asking outright, you could observe what he says and does without being asked. List all the significant interactions the two of you have had in the last several weeks—conversations, shared experiences, and so on. Then evaluate each activity as being either unfriendly or friendly (or perhaps more elaborately: very unfriendly, unfriendly, neutral, friendly, very friendly—essentially a 5-point rating scale).

If the friendly activities far outweigh the unfriendly ones, you can conclude that he likes you. If the negative interactions predominate, he doesn't act as though he likes you, no matter what he might say.

That's the idea behind the research methodology known as **content analysis**. This is the objective, systematic and quantitative investigation of something that has been written down (or at least something that can be written down for research purposes). Content analysis implements the maxim that actions speak louder than words. As a formal research methodology, content analysis has been used for years to study mass media. This research technique can be used to shed light on the messages of communication, assess the image of a group or organization, and make comparisons between media and reality.

Using Content Analysis

Researchers involved in public relations and marketing communication have found that content analysis can be useful in several different ways. Here are a couple of examples of how content analysis can be used to study various practical issues that could be important to your organization or client.

Let's say your client, an insurance agency, has a new policy covering sports cars. You want to reach your public—sports car drivers—on radio, using both public relations and advertising techniques. As you plan your campaign, you determine that you need to identify the most popular radio stations among people who drive sports cars. You could survey the drivers, but that might be unwieldy, because obtaining a sampling frame would be difficult. You could ask the radio stations about audience demographics, but they probably don't know the kind of cars their listeners drive.

Instead, you might take a different tack. Ask mechanics at several maintenance and repair shops specializing in sports cars to keep a list of which stations the radios are tuned to when the cars are brought in. That's content analysis.

Here's another example. Perhaps you are researching consumer issues for your company, a garment manufacturer. Specifically, you want to know what people think about the new line of lightweight, high-insulating winter coats. You could conduct a survey or a focus group if you had the time. Instead, you might check the letters and phone calls received by the consumer affairs department and compare these with customer comments about other products. This, too, is an example of content analysis.

Remember that the various research methods we're dealing with in this appendix don't have to stand alone. Content analysis can be used to complement other types of research. Researchers in public relations and marketing communication sometimes compare the results of their content analysis with the information they are able to obtain from surveys or focus groups.

For instance, if you are evaluating the effectiveness of your internal newsletter as part of an overall program review of your employee relations program, you might begin with a content analysis of the last three years' issues to identify topics that have been covered. Then you could conduct a focus group or readership survey to find out what topics your employees want to read about. Finally, you might compare the results of the content analysis with the results of your questioning, and from that comparison create a more popular employee publication.

Let's look at one final example. Let's say you are a media relations manager for a large public utility. You know that many of your news releases have been ignored by the newspapers and broadcast media in your service area. At a "meet the editors" forum sponsored by the local PRSA chapter, you hear from editors and news directors that they prefer stories with a strong local flavor. You realize you should evaluate the content of your releases as they focus on information of apparent significance to each locality within your service area. So you decide to do a content analysis of your releases of the last two years.

Specifically, you evaluate four aspects of each release: the extent of the local significance of the issue or activity (1) as you know it to be; (2) as evident in the body of the release; (3) as identified in the lead sentence or paragraph; and (4) as specifically featured in the headline or title on the release. By combining the information you received from the media gatekeepers and your own analysis of local content, you can gain some helpful insight for both topics and effective writing techniques for your future releases.

Pro and Con

Content analysis has several advantages, including a low investment of time and money. It can be done by a person working alone with little equipment beyond a simple calculator or a computer with standard software. Content analysis is unobtrusive research done "after the fact," without any effect on the people or issues being studied. It also has the advantage of allowing you to look at the facts without being caught up by the heat of the moment, free of the passion and enthusiasm that often surrounds surveys or focus groups.

Content analysis also has the advantage of allowing you to go back in time to examine past messages. It can be used to compare an organization with industry norms or with wider trends. Finally, it helps the researcher separate the routine from the unusual.

Among the disadvantages of content analysis are its limitation to recorded (or recordable) information and its susceptibility to coder influence and bias, in part because content analysis deals with what researchers call manifest content, the obvious and apparent meanings and interpretations that, unfortunately, are not always equally obvious and apparent to everyone. Also, while content analysis can point to coincidences and concurrences, it doesn't establish cause-and-effect relationships.

Another aspect of content analysis—not necessarily a negative, but certainly a concern— is the notion of *intercoder reliability*. This is the degree to which several coders agree on how to label the content being studied. The more consistency that exists among various coders, the stronger the reliability of the study.

Doing Content Analysis

Following is a step-by-step explanation of how to conduct a research study via content analysis.

1. Select an appropriate topic.
2. Identify the population, and select a sample.
3. Identify the units of analysis for the study.
4. Develop the mechanics for the study.
5. Report the data.
6. Analyze the data.
7. Make recommendations.

Let's look at each step in depth. The following explanations are framed around a running example of how a health-care company might use content analysis.

APPROPRIATE TOPIC

Begin by selecting a topic appropriate to this type of research. Content analysis has many applications for all the social sciences. For academic research, it has been used in studies dealing with media content such as sex and violence. As a tool of applied research in public relations and marketing communication, content analysis can be used by planners who want to know what people are saying about their organizations, or how what they are saying coincides with the way they are acting. Consider the following possibilities for public relations/marketing applications of content analysis:

- news coverage (topics, balance, frequency);
- media artifacts (video news releases, radio actualities, blog posts, photographs);
- organizational reputation among various media or particular public;
- letters to the editor (opinions, topics);
- customer comments (e-mails, letters, telephone calls);
- competitors (claims, offerings, positioning, advertising themes);
- trends in graphic design or publishing techniques;
- effectiveness of various persuasive appeals;
- public issues affecting an organization;
- preferences of various media (story type, political bias, editorial coverage).

Topics appropriate for your organization are those that deal with the content of artifacts that have already been written (reports, releases, publications, scripts, etc.) or that can be put into writing for research purposes (lists of characteristics, conversations, speeches, etc.). The text may originate within your organization, or it may be rooted in the communication or activity of one of your significant publics. Ask yourself how accessible the texts will be for you. Also consider how the information will be useful to your organization, especially because content analysis can help you learn facts about the content but not reasons behind those facts.

POPULATION AND SAMPLE

Select an appropriate population to study. This may be people such as all your employees or just the employees with less than two years' experience on the job. Or the population may center on artifacts such as news releases, company publications, advertisements, and the like. After you identify the population, decide on a census or a representative sample.

UNIT OF ANALYSIS

Next, determine the appropriate unit of analysis for this research. Carefully define the terms related to what you want to study. For purposes of public relations and marketing communication, the unit of analysis may relate to one of the following aspects of communication. Many research studies would involve several of the following approaches mixed together to provide a general view of the whole issue:

- subject: sorted by themes and topics;
- communication element: headline, lead, news article, photo caption, letter to the editor, advertising illustration, and the like;
- incoming communication: sorted by various channels, such as newspapers, magazines, television, radio, direct mail, telephone calls, letters, coupons and e-mail;
- outgoing communication: sorted by various tactics such as newsletter, e-mail, brochure, advertising spot and webpage;
- source of communication: sorted broadly by various publics or more narrowly by specific individuals or organizations or by subdivisions such as department, work site, and so on;
- destination: sorted broadly or narrowly; the same as for the source of communication (above);
- results: sorted by outcome, effect and consequence.

Develop categories for coding your tallies of these units of analysis. These categories must meet the same two major criteria as response categories for surveys—that is, they need to be comprehensive (by including all the possible responses) and mutually exclusive (by not duplicating other possible responses).

Incoming telephone calls, for example, may be categorized as being positive, negative, neutral or other. Too many responses in the "other" category indicate faulty categories. Newspaper articles may be studied to count the number of references to your organization, by both name and implication, and then to assess these references as to how positive they are or how accurately they portray your organization and its products or services. It might also record the message source and the paragraph number in which the source was first identified.

MECHANICS OF STUDY

Develop the mechanics of the study; that is, the way in which you will implement it. This is a simple follow-up step to the previous one. Create a standardized coding form that allows you to record the numbers in each category. Usually this involves simple forms with space for tally marks (卌).

You may have other people work on this project with you. Using multiple coders is a good idea to minimize **coder bias**, which is the potential bias or differing judgments of individual coders doing content analysis. With multiple coders comes the need to train these coders so they are applying consistent and uniform standards. Essentially this means writing out and explaining all your definitions so each coder approaches the item in the same way. Because some of the category selection is subjective, there may be some differences here: a positive reference to one person may be neutral to another. That's one of the shortcomings of content analysis. One way around this is to have three coders do each item and then record the majority response.

At this stage you also should pretest the coding instrument before actually doing the research. Go through a dozen or so items and see if the coding instrument works well. If not, go back and rethink your categories. When all of these tasks are completed, you are ready to actually measure the information and record it for later analysis.

DATA REPORTING

Indicate the data found through the content analysis. For every unit of analysis, report the findings as both raw numbers and the percentages. Keep the data reporting simple so you can more easily draw insight from it.

As you might guess, researchers have developed some sophisticated statistical techniques for use with content analysis. If you want intricate statistics, contact a professional researcher or refer to a statistics textbook. But you don't have to deal heavily with statistics. Many excellent content analyses rely on simple percentages.

DATA ANALYSIS

Once the data is reported, the researcher analyses it. This analysis may generate formal reports to your client organization or employer, or it simply may remain as scribbling on your notepad for your own perusal and pondering.

The stage of data analysis calls for the researcher to use knowledge of the issue and the client organization as the basis for making informed and insightful observations. It calls for

Appendixes

the ability to make connections among disjointed bits of data. As with the data reporting stage, analysis also calls for clear and simple presentation of data.

Note, for example, what was said above that percentages are more useful than raw numbers. You don't know much, for example, if you are told that 25 employees have made money-saving suggestions via the company suggestion box. Is that 25 out of 50 workers? Out of 5,000? But if you are told that those 25 employees represent one-third of the night shift, and that 75 percent of them work in the computer department, you have learned something very interesting and potentially very useful about the quality of ideas originating with night-time computer workers.

RECOMMENDATIONS

Many reports conclude with recommendations based on the findings and insights. Some researchers provide these at the request of the client. In other situations, clients may prefer to have the data, from which to draw their own conclusions and recommendations.

If you choose to prepare a formal report of the content analysis, include an explanation of the reason for your research, information about your sample and a copy of the coding form. Report the results in raw numbers, percentages or—usually—both. Discuss generalities and insights that you glean from those findings.

EXAMPLE: CONTENT ANALYSIS

Here is an example of a content analysis plan for a hypothetical organization, MetroHealth, a large statewide health maintenance organization.

Appropriate Topic. You are public education manager for MetroHealth. One of your job responsibilities is to promote a series of patient workshops on topics such as weight loss, nutrition, exercise and general fitness. You want to get an accurate picture of how the largest daily newspapers in the state deal with these issues. Your purpose for gaining this information is to arm yourself for an eventual public-education campaign that will look to the newspapers for support.

Before asking for this support, you decide that it will be helpful to know something about the newspapers' current and recent coverage of these topics.

Population and Sample. You identify the six largest newspapers in your state as the population for your study. Let's say you decide to limit your study to their news sections (local and national/international), as well as to relevant specialized sections such as lifestyle and science/health. Because it would be impractical to study every newspaper for every day over the last few years, you select a sample of publications.

This sample includes each of the six newspapers for the following varied schedule throughout the last 12 months; one daily edition each month according to this schedule: Monday, first week of January; Tuesday, second week of February; Wednesday, third week of March; Thursday, fourth week of April; Friday, first week of May; Saturday, second week of June; Monday, third week of July; Tuesday, fourth week of August; and so on. It also includes seven to nine Sunday editions, every sixth week following the beginning week, indicated by a throw of a dice.

Unit of Analysis. You will search each sampled newspaper, and count the number of articles and news briefs that deal with one of the topics of your interest (weight loss, nutrition, exercise, general fitness, and so on), as you have defined them. These numbers will be compared to the total number of articles and briefs in the publication. You then analyze each mention of these topics according to the following criteria:

- *Type of Article*: Code each published story as an article or a news brief. Define these terms clearly. For example, you might define the difference in terms of length—a brief is up to three paragraphs and an article is longer, or a brief is fewer than 150 words while an article is longer.

- *Attitude*: Each article related to fitness will be coded as "positive," "negative," or "neutral," depending on how its tone relates to MetroHealth's message of encouraging fitness.

- *Accuracy*: Each article will be coded as "very accurate," "moderately accurate," or "inaccurate," based on how well it presents information that is currently accepted by medical and fitness professionals. Or you might count the number of factual inaccuracies and unwarranted conclusions within the brief or article.

- *Prominence*: Each article will be rated for a "prominent position" (any location on Page One of a section, or top-of-page placement on an inside page) or "nonprominent position" (placement elsewhere on a page).

- *Demographics*: Each article will be coded as to its evident appeal based on gender (men, women, or both) and age (young, middle, older readers or all ages). This may be determined through criteria such as placement in a particular section (such as women's page, youth tab, etc.) or by the people shown in accompanying photographs or cited as examples within the article.

Mechanics of Study. You will work with a team of four coders. After training to ensure that coders are consistent in how they code the units of analysis, you will do a pilot test. This may lead you to rework the definitions for the coding.

Once you are confident that your coders are on track to generate consistent data, you will conduct the content analysis of each sample newspapers. You will have three coders review each unit of analysis and average their responses.

Data Reporting. Let's say that in coding your categories you arrive at the following results for three different newspapers, A, B and C:

News Articles

Newspaper	Total Articles	Fitness Topic (#)	Fitness Topic (%)
A	1,000	60	6
B	940	54	5.7
C	1,060	25	2.4

News Briefs

Newspaper	Total Articles	Fitness Topic (#)	Fitness Topic (%)
A	400	40	10
B	640	50	7.8
C	800	0	8.8

Articles and News Briefs re: Fitness

Newspaper	Positive (%)	Negative
A	80	20
B	82	18
C	53	47

Articles and News Briefs re: Fitness

Newspaper	Accurate (%)	Inaccurate (%)
A	95	5
B	88	12
C	62	38

(Additional data would follow re: prominence and demographics.)

Data Analysis. The research shows that Newspapers A and B provide similar amounts of coverage to fitness-related information, both as news stories and as news briefs.

Newspaper C offers significantly less coverage to fitness information in the form of news articles, though it devotes slightly more space than the other newspapers do to fitness-related news briefs. Newspaper C also has a higher number of negative articles and briefs, as this relates to MetroHealth's conclusion about how the articles are likely to promote an appreciation for fitness. This newspaper also has a higher percentage of inaccurate articles and briefs, based on MetroHealth's understanding of up-to-date reliable information.

(Other findings would reflect additional data.)

Recommendations. Based on the data from this content analysis, we will consider the following recommendations:

1. *Review of public relations materials.* Based on what was learned about Newspaper C, we should review our public relations procedures. For example, perhaps news releases and other media materials should be reviewed to make sure that they clearly articulate the benefits for readers of the newspaper.

2. *Contact with Newspaper C.* We should contact the editorial staff of Newspaper C and arrange a meeting between you as MetroHealth public education manager and editors of the various news, health and lifestyle sections. The purpose of such a meeting would be to learn what the reporters and/or editors might find useful in information emanating from your organization. At this meeting, we will noncritically present your findings that indicate the newspaper's relative disinterest in fitness-related articles. Admitting that you are an advocate for fitness information, you might point to surveys indicating a growing interest within the general population (and thus newspaper readers), offering possible ways in which your organization could assist the newspaper in increasing its coverage of this topic. Perhaps you will learn that you could foster more articles by suggesting strong local angles to general fitness information or by offering experts from your organization as interview subjects.

3. *Contact with Newspapers A and B.* We also should contact Newspapers A and B and share your findings concerning their performance, encouraging their continued attention to fitness matters. For future research you might conduct a similar study in one or two years to note any changes in the media trends.

Appendixes

APPENDIX B

Ethical Standards

Public Relations Society of America (PRSA)

Member Code of Ethics

Approved by the PRSA Assembly (October, 2000)
Reprinted with permission of the Public Relations Society of America (prsa.org)

PREAMBLE

- Professional Values
- Principles of Conduct
- Commitment and Compliance.

This Code applies to Public Relations Society of America (PRSA) members. The Code is designed to be a useful guide for PRSA members as they carry out their ethical responsibilities. This document is designed to anticipate and accommodate, by precedent, ethical challenges that may arise. The scenarios outlined in the Code provision are actual examples of misconduct. More will be added as experience with the Code occurs.

The Public Relations Society of America is committed to ethical practices. The level of public trust PRSA members seek, as we serve the public good, means we have taken on a special obligation to operate ethically.

The value of member reputation depends upon the ethical conduct of everyone affiliated with the Public Relations Society of America. Each of us sets an example for each other—as well as other professionals—by our pursuit of excellence with powerful standards of performance, professionalism, and ethical conduct.

Emphasis on enforcement of the Code has been eliminated. But, the PRSA Board of Directors retains the right to bar from membership or expel from the Society any individual who has been or is sanctioned by a government agency or convicted in a court of law of an action that is in violation of this Code.

Ethical practice is the most important obligation of a PRSA member. We view the Member Code of Ethics as a model for other professions, organizations, and professionals.

PRSA Member Statement of Professional Values

This statement presents the core values of PRSA members and, more broadly, of the public relations profession. These values provide the foundation for the Member Code of Ethics and set the industry standard for the professional practice of public relations. These values are the fundamental beliefs that guide our behaviors and decision-making process. We believe our professional values are vital to the integrity of the profession as a whole.

ADVOCACY

* We serve the public interest by acting as responsible advocates for those we represent.
* We provide a voice in the marketplace of ideas, facts, and viewpoints to aid informed public debate.

HONESTY

* We adhere to the highest standards of accuracy and truth in advancing the interests of those we represent and in communicating with the public.

EXPERTISE

* We acquire and responsibly use specialized knowledge and experience.
* We advance the profession through continued professional development, research and education.
* We build mutual understanding, credibility, and relationships among a wide array of institutions and audiences.

INDEPENDENCE

* We provide objective counsel to those we represent.
* We are accountable for our actions.

LOYALTY

* We are faithful to those we represent, while honoring our obligation to serve the public interest.

FAIRNESS

* We deal fairly with clients, employers, competitors, peers, vendors, the media, and the general public.
* We respect all opinions and support the right of free expression.

PRSA Code Provisions

FREE FLOW OF INFORMATION

Core Principle: Protecting and advancing the free flow of accurate and truthful information is essential to serving the public interest and contributing to informed decision making in a democratic society.

Intent:

- To maintain the integrity of relationships with the media, government officials, and the public.
- To aid informed decision making.

Guidelines: A member shall:

- preserve the integrity of the process of communication;
- be honest and accurate in all communications;
- act promptly to correct erroneous communications for which the practitioner is responsible;
- preserve the free flow of unprejudiced information when giving or receiving gifts by ensuring that gifts are nominal, legal, and infrequent.

Examples of Improper Conduct under This Provision:

- A member representing a ski manufacturer gives a pair of expensive racing skis to a sports magazine columnist, to influence the columnist to write favorable articles about the product.
- A member entertains a government official beyond legal limits and/or in violation of government reporting requirements.

COMPETITION

Core Principle: Promoting healthy and fair competition among professionals preserves an ethical climate while fostering a robust business environment.

Intent:

- To promote respect and fair competition among public relations professionals.
- To serve the public interest by providing the widest choice of practitioner options.

Guidelines: A member shall:

- follow ethical hiring practices designed to respect free and open competition without deliberately undermining a competitor;
- preserve intellectual property rights in the marketplace.

Examples of Improper Conduct under This Provision:

- A member employed by a "client organization" shares helpful information with a counseling firm that is competing with others for the organization's business.
- A member spreads malicious and unfounded rumors about a competitor in order to alienate the competitor's clients and employees in a ploy to recruit people and business.

DISCLOSURE OF INFORMATION

Core Principle: Open communication fosters informed decision making in a democratic society.

Intent:

- To build trust with the public by revealing all information needed for responsible decision making.

Guidelines: A member shall:

- be honest and accurate in all communications;
- act promptly to correct erroneous communications for which the member is responsible;
- investigate the truthfulness and accuracy of information released on behalf of those represented;
- reveal the sponsors for causes and interests represented;
- disclose financial interest (such as stock ownership) in a client's organization;
- avoid deceptive practices.

Examples of Improper Conduct under This Provision:

- Front groups: A member implements "grass roots" campaigns or letter-writing campaigns to legislators on behalf of undisclosed interest groups.
- Lying by omission: A practitioner for a corporation knowingly fails to release financial information, giving a misleading impression of the corporation's performance.
- A member discovers inaccurate information disseminated via a website or media kit and does not correct the information.
- A member deceives the public by employing people to pose as volunteers to speak at public hearings and participate in "grass roots" campaigns.

SAFEGUARDING CONFIDENCES

Core Principle: Client trust requires appropriate protection of confidential and private information.

Intent:

- To protect the privacy rights of clients, organizations, and individuals by safeguarding confidential information.

Guidelines: A member shall:

- safeguard the confidences and privacy rights of present, former, and prospective clients and employees;
- protect privileged, confidential, or insider information gained from a client or organization;
- immediately advise an appropriate authority if a member discovers that confidential information is being divulged by an employee of a client company or organization.

Examples of Improper Conduct under This Provision:

- A member changes jobs, takes confidential information, and uses that information in the new position to the detriment of the former employer.
- A member intentionally leaks proprietary information to the detriment of some other party.

CONFLICTS OF INTEREST

Core Principle: Avoiding real, potential or perceived conflicts of interest builds the trust of clients, employers, and the publics.

Intent:

- To earn trust and mutual respect with clients or employers.
- To build trust with the public by avoiding or ending situations that put one's personal or professional interests in conflict with society's interests.

Guidelines: A member shall:

- act in the best interests of the client or employer, even subordinating the member's personal interests;
- avoid actions and circumstances that may appear to compromise good business judgment or create a conflict between personal and professional interests;
- disclose promptly any existing or potential conflict of interest to affected clients or organizations;
- encourage clients and customers to determine if a conflict exists after notifying all affected parties.

Examples of Improper Conduct under This Provision:

- The member fails to disclose that he or she has a strong financial interest in a client's chief competitor.
- The member represents a "competitor company" or a "conflicting interest" without informing a prospective client.

ENHANCING THE PROCESSION

Core Principle: Public relations professionals work constantly to strengthen the public's trust in the profession.

Intent:

- To build respect and credibility with the public for the profession of public relations.
- To improve, adapt and expand professional practices.

Guidelines: A member shall:

- acknowledge that there is an obligation to protect and enhance the profession;
- keep informed and educated about practices in the profession to ensure ethical conduct;

- actively pursue personal professional development;
- decline representation of clients or organizations that urge or require actions contrary to this code;
- accurately define what public relations activities can accomplish;
- counsel subordinates in proper ethical decision making;
- require that subordinates adhere to the ethical requirements of the code;
- report ethical violations, whether committed by PRSA members or not, to the appropriate authority.

Examples of Improper Conduct under This Provision:

- A PRSA member declares publicly that a product the client sells is safe, without disclosing evidence to the contrary.
- A member initially assigns some questionable client work to a non-member practitioner to avoid the ethical obligation of PRSA membership.

PRSA Member Code of Ethics Pledge

I pledge:

- to conduct myself professionally, with truth, accuracy, fairness, and responsibility to the public;
- to improve my individual competence and advance the knowledge and proficiency of the profession through continuing research and education;
- and to adhere to the articles of the Member Code of Ethics 2000 for the practice of public relations as adopted by the governing Assembly of the Public Relations Society of America.

I understand and accept that there is a consequence for misconduct, up to and including membership revocation.

And, I understand that those who have been or are sanctioned by a government agency or convicted in a court of law of an action that is in violation of this Code may be barred from membership or expelled from the Society.

Canadian Public Relations Society

Declaration of Principles

Reprinted with permission of the Canadian Public Relations Society (cprs.ca)

Members of the Canadian Public Relations Society are pledged to maintain the spirit and ideals of the following stated principles of conduct, and to consider these essential to the practice of public relations.

1. *A member shall practice public relations according to the highest professional standards*. Members shall conduct their professional lives in a manner that does not conflict with the public interest and the dignity of the individual, with respect for the rights of the public as contained in the Constitution of Canada and the Charter of Rights and Freedoms.

2. *A member shall deal fairly and honestly with the communications media and the public.* Members shall neither propose nor act to improperly influence the communications media, government bodies or the legislative process. Improper influence may include conferring gifts, privileges or benefits to influence decisions.

3. *A member shall practice the highest standards of honesty, accuracy, integrity and truth, and shall not knowingly disseminate false or misleading information.* Members shall not make extravagant claims or unfair comparisons, nor assume credit for ideas and words not their own. Members shall not engage in professional or personal conduct that will bring discredit to themselves, the Society or the practice of public relations.

4. *A member shall deal fairly with past or present employers/clients, fellow practitioners and members of other professions.* Members shall not intentionally damage another practitioner's practice or professional reputation. Members shall understand, respect and abide by the ethical codes of other professions with whose members they may work from time to time.

5. *Members shall be prepared to disclose the names of their employers or clients for whom public communications are made and refrain from associating themselves with anyone who would not respect such policy.* Members shall be prepared to disclose publicly the names of their employers or clients on whose behalf public communications are made. Members shall not associate themselves with anyone claiming to represent one interest, or professing to be independent or unbiased, but who actually serves another or an undisclosed interest.

6. *A member shall protect the confidences of present, former and prospective employers/clients.* Members shall not use or disclose confidential information obtained from past or present employers/clients without the expressed permission of the employers/clients or an order of a court of law.

7. *A member shall not represent conflicting or competing interests without the expressed consent of those concerned, given after a full disclosure of the facts.* Members shall not permit personal or other professional interests to conflict with those of an employer/client without fully disclosing such interests to everyone involved.

8. *A member shall not guarantee specified results beyond the member's capacity to achieve.*

9. *Members shall personally accept no fees, commissions, gifts, or any other considerations for professional services from anyone except employers or clients for whom the services were specifically performed.*

International Public Relations Association

IPRA Code of Conduct

Adopted in 2011, the IPRA Code of Conduct is an affirmation of professional and ethical conduct by members of the International Public Relations Association and recommended to public relations practitioners worldwide. The Code consolidates the 1961 Code of Venice, the 1965 Code of Athens and the 2007 Code of Brussels.

Reprinted with permission of the International Public Relations Association (ipra.org)

1. RECALLING the Charter of the United Nations which determines "to reaffirm faith in fundamental human rights, and in the dignity and worth of the human person";
2. RECALLING the 1948 "Universal Declaration of Human Rights" and especially recalling Article 19;
3. RECALLING that public relations, by fostering the free flow of information, contributes to the interests of all stakeholders;
4. RECALLING that the conduct of public relations and public affairs provides essential democratic representation to public authorities;
5. RECALLING that public relations practitioners through their wide-reaching communication skills possess a means of influence that should be restrained by the observance of a code of professional and ethical conduct;
6. RECALLING that channels of communication, such as the Internet and other digital media, are channels where erroneous or misleading information may be widely disseminated and remain unchallenged, and therefore demand special attention from public relations practitioners to maintain trust and credibility;
7. RECALLING that the Internet and other digital media demand special care with respect to the personal privacy of individuals, clients, employers and colleagues;

In the conduct of public affairs, practitioners shall:

1. *Observance*. Observe the principles of the UN Charter and the Universal Declaration of Human Rights;
2. *Integrity*. Act with honesty and integrity at all times so as to secure the confidence of those with whom the practitioner comes into contact;
3. *Dialogue*. Seek to establish the moral, cultural and intellectual conditions for dialogue, and recognise the rights of all parties involved to state their case and express their views;
4. *Transparency*. Be open and transparent in declaring their name, organisation and the interest they represent;
5. *Conflict*. Avoid any professional conflicts of interest and to disclose such conflicts to affected parties when they occur;
6. *Confidentiality*. Honour confidential information provided to them;
7. *Accuracy*. Take all reasonable steps to ensure the truth and accuracy of all information provided to public authorities;
8. *Falsehood*. Not intentionally disseminate false or misleading information, and shall exercise proper care to avoid doing so unintentionally and correct any such act promptly;
9. *Deception*. Not obtain information from public authorities by deceptive or dishonest means;
10. *Disclosure*. Not create or use any organization to serve an announced cause but which actually serves an undisclosed interest;
11. *Profit*. Not sell for profit to third parties copies of documents obtained from public authorities;
12. *Remuneration*. While providing professional services, not accept any form of payment in connection with those services from anyone other than the principal;

13. *Inducement.* Neither directly nor indirectly offer nor give any financial or other inducement to members of public authorities or public representatives;

14. *Influence.* Neither propose nor undertake any action which would constitute an improper influence on public authorities;

15. *Competitors.* Not intentionally injure the professional reputation of another practitioner;

16. *Poaching.* Not seek to secure another practitioner's client by deceptive means;

17. *Employment.* Only employ personnel from public authorities subject to the rules and confidentiality requirements of those authorities;

18. *Colleagues.* Observe this Code with respect to fellow IPRA members and public relations practitioners worldwide.

IPRA members shall, in upholding this Code, and agree to abide by and help enforce the disciplinary procedures of the International Public Relations Association in regard to any breaching of this Code.

American Marketing Association

Statement of Ethics

(Adopted 2008)

Reprinted with permission of the American Marketing Association (MarketingPower.com)

PREAMBLE

The American Marketing Association commits itself to promoting the highest standard of professional ethical norms and values for its members (practitioners, academics and students). Norms are established standards of conduct that are expected and maintained by society and/or professional organizations. Values represent the collective conception of what communities find desirable, important and morally proper. Values also serve as the criteria for evaluating our own personal actions and the actions of others. As marketers, we recognize that we not only serve our organizations but also act as stewards of society in creating, facilitating and executing the transactions that are part of the greater economy. In this role, marketers are expected to embrace the highest professional ethical norms and the ethical values implied by our responsibility toward multiple stakeholders (e.g., customers, employees, investors, peers, channel members, regulators and the host community).

Ethical Norms

As Marketers, we must:

1. *Do no harm.* This means consciously avoiding harmful actions or omissions by embodying high ethical standards and adhering to all applicable laws and regulations in the choices we make.

2. *Foster trust in the marketing system.* This means striving for good faith and fair dealing so as to contribute toward the efficacy of the exchange process as well as avoiding deception in product design, pricing, communication, and delivery of distribution.

3. *Embrace ethical values.* This means building relationships and enhancing consumer confidence in the integrity of marketing by affirming these core values: honesty, responsibility, fairness, respect, transparency and citizenship.

Ethical Values

Honesty—to be forthright in dealings with customers and stakeholders. To this end, we will:

- Strive to be truthful in all situations and at all times.
- Offer products of value that do what we claim in our communications.
- Stand behind our products if they fail to deliver their claimed benefits.
- Honor our explicit and implicit commitments and promises.

Responsibility—to accept the consequences of our marketing decisions and strategies. To this end, we will:

- Strive to serve the needs of customers.
- Avoid using coercion with all stakeholders.
- Acknowledge the social obligations to stakeholders that come with increased marketing and economic power.
- Recognize our special commitments to vulnerable market segments such as children, seniors, the economically impoverished, market illiterates, and others who may be substantially disadvantaged.
- Consider environmental stewardship in our decision-making.

Fairness—to balance justly the needs of the buyer with the interests of the seller. To this end, we will:

- Represent products in a clear way in selling, advertising and other forms of communication; this includes the avoidance of false, misleading and deceptive promotion.
- Reject manipulations and sales tactics that harm customer trust.
- Refuse to engage in price fixing, predatory pricing, price gouging or "bait-and-switch" tactics.
- Avoid knowing participation in conflicts of interest.
- Seek to protect the private information of customers, employees and partners.

Respect—to acknowledge the basic human dignity of all stakeholders. To this end, we will:

- Value individual differences and avoid stereotyping customers or depicting demographic groups (e.g., gender, race, sexual orientation) in a negative or dehumanizing way.
- Listen to the needs of customers and make all reasonable efforts to monitor and improve their satisfaction on an ongoing basis.
- Make every effort to understand and respectfully treat buyers, suppliers, intermediaries and distributors from all cultures.

- Acknowledge the contributions of others, such as consultants, employees and coworkers, to marketing endeavors.
- Treat everyone, including our competitors, as we would wish to be treated.

Transparency—to create a spirit of openness in marketing operations. To this end, we will:

- Strive to communicate clearly with all constituencies.
- Accept constructive criticism from customers and other stakeholders.
- Explain and take appropriate action regarding significant product or service risks, component substitutions or other foreseeable eventualities that could affect customers or their perception of the purchase decision.
- Disclose list prices and terms of financing as well as available price deals and adjustments.

Citizenship—to fulfill the economic, legal, philanthropic and societal responsibilities that serve stakeholders. To this end, we will:

- Strive to protect the ecological environment in the execution of marketing campaigns.
- Give back to the community through volunteerism and charitable donations.
- Contribute to the overall betterment of marketing and its reputation.
- Urge supply chain members to ensure that trade is fair for all participants, including producers in developing countries.

Implementation

We expect AMA members to be courageous and proactive in leading and/or aiding their organizations in the fulfillment of the explicit and implicit promises made to those stakeholders. We recognize that every industry sector and marketing sub-discipline (e.g., marketing research, e-commerce, Internet selling, direct marketing, and advertising) has its own specific ethical issues that require policies and commentary. An array of such codes can be accessed through links on the AMA Web site. Consistent with the principle of subsidiarity (solving issues at the level where the expertise resides), we encourage all such groups to develop and/or refine their industry and discipline-specific codes of ethics to supplement these guiding ethical norms and values.

APPENDIX C

Sample Campaigns

Following are examples of public relations and integrated marketing campaigns, accompanied by the author's comments about the lessons that public relations students might learn by becoming familiar with each.

These campaigns include a public education program by Johnson & Johnson, a reputation building campaign by DeVry University, an Army recruiting program, a Coca-Cola social-media project for reputation enhancement and a project relaunch by Philips Norelco. Each campaign has an interesting twist. Johnson & Johnson works with "mommy bloggers," DeVry deals with a negative environment, the Army campaign has a multicultural dimension, Coke is an international project and Norelco deals somewhat humorously with body grooming for men.

All the campaigns showcased here won a Silver Anvil award from the Public Relations Society of America. As presented here, each example is not the fully articulated campaign but rather the summary and overview provided for the awards competition, presented in the following categories as outlined for Silver Anvil entries:

- *Situation Analysis or Overview*: Optional category; set the stage; provide an introduction to the campaign presentation that follows.
- *Research*: Public relations situation; quality of original or secondary research used to identify the problem or opportunity and the approaches likely to be successful; relevance of the research in shaping the planning process; assessment of how the research helped define the situation or the publics.
- *Planning*: Correlation of the plan to research findings; objectives; overall strategy; originality and judgment in selecting strategy and techniques; publics; accuracy of budget; difficulties encountered.
- *Execution*: Implementation and outcome of the plan; key tactics; materials used; in-progress adjustments to the plan; techniques in winning management's support; other techniques; difficulties encountered; involvement of other organizations; effectiveness of the program's employment dollar, personnel and other resources.
- *Evaluation*: Methods of evaluation; efforts made to identify, analyze and quantify results; degree to which the program met its objectives.

CHARACTERISTICS OF WINNING CAMPAIGNS

A study of recent recipients of Silver Anvil awards noted some characteristics of award winners. The study was conducted by Catherine Ayles and Courtney Bosworth (2002), both of Florida International University.

A key factor to excellent campaigns is that they begin with solid research. The most common research techniques were interviews with key contacts within a public (65 percent), telephone interviews (57 percent), focus groups (38 percent) and mail surveys (12 percent).

Secondary research consisted of literature searches (44 percent), comparative analysis (42 percent), archival research (25 percent), media audits (22 percent) and sales and market-share data (22 percent). General online research was used in 19 percent of campaigns. In terms of experimental research, 37 percent tested messages and 18 percent tested specific communication tactics.

Ayles and Bosworth found that only 45 percent benchmarked awareness prior to the campaign. They find this surprising, because 79 percent set awareness objectives. Silver Anvil judges told the researchers that objectives are the most important aspect of an effective campaign. However, only 43 percent indicated a time frame in the objectives, and only 35 percent indicated the amount of change desired. That, in turn, led to weak evaluations.

Common evaluation techniques included message exposure via media placement (73 percent), audience participation (52 percent) and positive message content (50 percent), leading one judge to caution against "thinly veiled attempts" to equate campaign success with mere news clips.

Additionally, 87 percent of winning campaigns documented behavior change. But only 18 percent of winning campaigns cited opinion change and 24 percent noted attitude change, suggesting a need for greater attention to evaluating awareness and acceptance objectives that, by necessity, must precede action objectives.

So what indicates a great campaign? Creative execution and measured results, one judge told Ayles and Bosworth. A strategic campaign with clear objectives, targeted messages and obvious results, said another. Still another said the key to success is careful application of the four-phase process.

Check out the PRSA Silver Anvil website (prsa.org/awards) for outlines on all the competition winners since 1968. The annual Silver Anvil competition represents the best of the best, at least as represented by the entries in the national contest.

The following examples from the many recent Silver Anvil winners have been selected to give you a model of a particularly effective use of at least one aspect of the planning process. They are presented here for your consideration and discussion. With each case, the author draws your attention to some of the lessons the campaign exemplifies.

Notice, however, that even the best are sometimes inexact in how they use some of the elements of a good campaign that have been presented in this textbook. For example, some Silver Anvil winners have fuzzy approaches to goals and objectives, others mislabel or blend strategy and tactics, and some use inappropriate evaluation criteria such as advertising equivalency.

When you review the Silver Anvil winners, take each one with a grain of salt. Determine for yourself what particular elements of the campaign are good models for you to follow.

Text4Baby: Going Mobile with Pregnancy Education

Silver Anvil Award of Excellence (2011)

Organization: Johnson & Johnson. Agency: Hill & Knowlton
Category: Public Service; Consumer Marketing; Partnerships
Outcome: Raising awareness

Build a Coalition

This campaign rests solely on public relations, with no advertising support. As you read through this case, look for three lessons from how Johnson & Johnson handled the campaign:

- using research to clarify the message and identify likely channels of communication;
- blending established media with emerging digital and social media (both traditional health reporters and "mommy bloggers" who can leverage other social media);
- building coalitions (from a handful of initial partners to more than 500).

PROJECT OVERVIEW

Each year, 500,000 American babies are born prematurely and 28,000 die before their first birthday. Medical experts can't fully explain the cause, but they do know that awareness of proper prenatal care, including nutrition, avoiding cigarettes and alcohol, and regular prenatal doctor visits can help a mother deliver a healthy baby. Text4Baby makes receiving this information easy by delivering it directly to mobile devices where it's more likely to be read given that 90 percent of Americans have a mobile phone.

Recognizing both the scope of this public health problem and a potential solution, Johnson & Johnson teamed with the Healthy Mothers Healthy Babies Coalition, Voxiva and CTIA–The Wireless Foundation to create Text4Baby, and recruited Hill & Knowlton to promote this valuable resource. Text4Baby is the first free service to use weekly text messages to alert young women to ways to protect their babies' health. The public relations program to date has helped build a network of 134,000+ subscribers and helped recruit 500+ partners to spread the word. But we didn't do this without overcoming significant challenges.

RESEARCH

We conducted focus groups in seven key markets to test health messages sent via text. While these groups looked at a number of factors, the tone of the messages was seen as critical. These mothers wanted messages to sound as if they were coming from a trusted friend, not something they were told to do. And they wanted messages to be action oriented and informative but also balanced with messages about the joys of motherhood.

Next, we researched possible celebrity spokespersons to serve as a credible voice with our primary audience. Among the factors we looked at were age, ethnicity, tone, accessibility and relevance, meaning could the target audience relate to this person and see her as credible.

We researched potential media partners to extend our reach. Among those we looked at were American Urban Radio Networks and BET given their appeal to young, African Americans and both broadcast nationwide. We researched opportunities at MTV because of its appeal to the younger demographic, it's popular among a variety of platforms, including MTV.com, and airs programming popular among young women.

PLANNING

We edited messages based on the focus group feedback and developed talking points and materials accordingly. Our spokesperson research led us to Sherri Shepherd of *The View*. Ms. Shepherd was ideal because she appeals to a younger, African-American audience, and her son had prematurity-related health problems.

MTV was our top choice for media partner, as the network is heavily watched by our target demographic and has programming possibilities in reality shows that focus on teen mothers. We approached MTV about a multi-tiered partnership.

With the help of the White House Office of Science and Technology Policy (OSTP) and the US Department of Health and Human Services (HHS), which joined as early partners, we secured space in the White House for a meeting to attract and inform new partners before the launch. This meeting and other initial outreach positioned us well for the launch, with 17 initial partners, including a number of state health agencies, plus 18 wireless carriers. We planned a media launch with HHS Secretary Sebelius.

Objectives. Increase awareness of Text4Baby and gain subscribers. Gain trust of users and third parties as a credible source of critical health information. Create a broad coalition of partners to educate pregnant women and new moms about Text4Baby. Convince government and lawmakers to support and promote Text4Baby.

Target Audience Analysis. Young pregnant women and new mothers from various backgrounds were our primary audience. According to the Centers for Disease Control and Prevention (CDC), the infant mortality rate among African-American women is 2.4 times the rate for non-Hispanic white women. Young African-American women at lower income levels from Southern states were a particularly important audience as they have the highest infant mortality rates and receive the least prenatal care. To reach these young women with our limited budget, we knew we would need to reach partners at the national, state and community levels—those who work directly with mothers and families. Traditional health reporters and mommy bloggers were targeted as well, as they influence potential third-party supporters ranging from non-governmental organizations and health plans to the federal government, including the White House, HHS, and members of Congress.

Strategy. Given challenges that included a very limited budget ($150,000) and no advertising support, as well as the scope of the task at hand, the strategy relied on creativity, creating partnerships, and then leveraging those partnerships and resources to promote Text4Baby through earned media coverage.

The strategy relied on: (1) creating buzz about Text4Baby at launch; (2) generating free coverage with a local radio PSA campaign featuring pro-bono celebrity spokesperson, Sherri Shepherd; and (3) securing a media partnership while building national and local partners.

A fourth key element of the strategy was to provide tools—such as event ideas and press material templates—that partners could use to promote the program independently. And while Text4Baby is a texting service, we believed an integrated social media campaign would increase awareness. We engaged "mommy bloggers" to secure stories on popular sites like BabyCenter.com, MomsLikeMe.com and MochaMoms.org, and used social networks like Facebook.

EXECUTION

Challenges arose quickly: our announcement event was canceled close to launch day so we moved to plan B—to launch quickly without an official event. We offered the story as an exclusive to the Associated Press, followed by a next-day announcement by US Chief Technology Officer Aneesh Chopra at a key health conference. OSTP issued a release and Chopra wrote a post on the White House blog, providing an opportunity to highlight administration support. We issued a bilingual news release, and worked with 20 partner organizations to issue the release themselves and tweet the news. We promoted the launch with national TV networks, which provided B-roll to affiliates. Next, we distributed the Shepherd PSA to 1,000 radio stations nationwide, with an emphasis on those skewing younger. MTV highlighted Text4Baby in the finale special, "Teen Mom with Dr. Drew." Dr. Drew directed listeners to sign up for Text4Baby, resulting in nearly 1,500 new Text4Baby subscribers. MTV also featured a bonus clip of "16 and Pregnant," in which one mother shared important health messages she received through Text4Baby. Coverage of the launch resulted in more than 500+ new partnerships, which drove additional media coverage using materials provided in the tool kit.

EVALUATION

Objective 1: Increase awareness of Text4Baby; gain subscribers. Result: 650+ placements and 75 million impressions were created, driving 134,000+ subscribers. PSAs received 15,750 broadcasts, reaching 32 million. The Text4Baby Facebook page has more than 2,000 friends and growing.

Objective 2: Secure the trust of users, third parties so Text4Baby is viewed as trusted information source. Result: 96 percent of enrollees reported they would recommend Text4Baby to a friend. Text4Baby is regularly asked to speak on panels, and cited as an innovative program.

Objective 3: Create coalition of public, private-sector partners to educate pregnant women/new moms. Result: From a handful of initial founding partners, recruited 500+ government agencies, hospitals, corporations, academic institutions, professional associations and non-profit organizations.

Objective 4: Convince government to support, promote Text4Baby. Result: Secured support of HHS, OSTP, DoD, 22+ state agencies, including New York City which advertises the program via distribution of birth certificates; Honored by Secretary Sebelius with prestigious HHSinnovates award, given to innovations that have improved HHS service. Text4Baby hosted a congressional briefing, and secured a recommendation letter from Representative Lois Capps, encouraging members of Congress to promote the service, which they did; Women, Infants, Children (WIC) program disseminates info to its offices across the country.

DeVry University: Getting an Education on Reputation Building

Silver Anvil Award (2011)

Organization: DeVry University. Agency: MSLGROUP
Categories: Reputation Management; Media Relations
Outcome: Reputation Management

Be Proactive

Read through this case, and consider several lessons exemplified in the successful campaign by DeVry University:

- communicating proactively in the face of a growing negative environment;
- creating a benchmark by doing content analysis of current media coverage;
- developing a particular outreach to a major group within the key public (women);
- preparing a remedy for potential controversy (a playbook to quickly and proactively address "negative noise");
- helping the organization separate itself from others in its sector.

SITUATION ANALYSIS

"Battle lines drawn over for-profit colleges"

"The predatory nature of some for-profit colleges"

"High costs, loan defaults expose for-profit colleges"

These are a handful of the headlines that appeared in top-tier media outlets in 2010 as for-profit universities faced growing scrutiny from law makers, activists and regulators regarding their integrity and value as educational institutions. As influencer dialogue about the value of traditional vs. non-traditional higher education grew more heated, the negative news stories on for-profit universities grew more widespread and more accusatory. It was quickly becoming clear that if nothing changed, current students and prospective students would soon have little more than "negative" sector media coverage to reference as they considered their educational options. The communications team at DeVry University recognized the need to insulate the brand from the onslaught of negative sector media coverage and correct misinformation about the University.

The DeVry University team turned to MSLGROUP to develop a proactive public relations program that would achieve two key communications goals: 1) protect *and* 2) enhance DeVry University's reputation as the true champion of those seeking to enhance their careers.

To achieve the program's goals, MSLGROUP created a tactical plan based on three strategic pillars:

1. *Proactive outreach* focused on positioning the University as a resource for actionable, career-focused advice.
2. Media-worthy *events* that promoted DeVry University's substantive involvement in key career issues and topics.

3. An issue and crisis preparedness *plan* that would help correct misinformation about the University by managing messaging in the face of sector controversy.

Objectives of the 6-month campaign (July to December, 2010) were specifically to grow volume /share of coverage (vs. competitors) and increase positive tonality of media coverage for DeVry University. As a result of this campaign, DeVry University jumped above competitors to lead the category in overall volume of media coverage and to dominate positive coverage in the sector.

RESEARCH

Defining the Target and How to Reach It. DeVry University has a diverse student population with 72 percent of the student body at 25 years of age and more than 10,000 students between ages 40 and 49. Approximately 60 percent of the students come from a multi-cultural background with 28 percent being African American and 14 percent being Hispanic. MSLGROUP worked with the national DeVry University team and integrated marketing partners to conduct extensive research on the "student journey" to pinpoint how and when students evaluate universities and choose to go to school.

DeVry University prospective student was described as "the stalled dreamer," or someone with career aspirations who has been unable to pursue these aspirations for one reason or another. These prospective students do not take the traditional route to school and are likely to be the first in their family to attend a university. Career stability is their core motivation for going back to school. This made it clear to MSLGROUP that we needed to reach out to these students and prospects leveraging a career-focused platform in channels that reached them where they live their day-to-day lives—local traditional outlets and online properties that spoke to their local focus and their-career focused interests.

Measuring Results. Research from Cision, a third-party data collection agency, allowed the team to track total volume and tonality of media coverage across the competitive set of schools. Prior to the campaign, sentiment for the category was 36 percent positive and 25 percent negative. DeVry University's tonality was 39 percent positive and 34 percent negative, while share of voice was 53 percent. These statistics were used as a benchmark to track results.

PLANNING

With more than 90 campuses across the nation and a significant online enrollment, the team needed to develop a coherent and consistent brand-elevating narrative that would reach key audiences through a range of channels. MSLGROUP's over-arching strategy was to demonstrate the value and opportunity a DeVry University degree brings to non-traditional students by offering actionable career advice and leveraging the credibility of third parties to demonstrate that DeVry University offers educational options that lead to multiple career paths. When discussing careers, DeVry University chose to focus on the fastest growing careers in the US—where the University offered degrees on a majority of its campuses and online.

Three *core strategies* were identified:

- *Conduct proactive outreach focused on actionable, career-focused advice.* Story development and placement was generated through a News Bureau that functioned based on a "conversation calendar." A core initiative, "Career Conversations," enlisted independent career experts as DeVry University spokespeople to drive sustained conversation around timely career topics while feature stories/pitches and ongoing support of local market activities were plotted on the calendar to maintain ongoing outreach and focused "bursts" of activity that presented a coherent narrative across traditional and social media.

- *Develop media-worthy events that elevate and promote DeVry University's substantive involvement in key career issues and topics.* Individual DeVry University campuses have a long history of reaching out to female high school students to demonstrate career opportunities in STEM in a program known as HerWorld, but little was done to tie the initiatives together or package them for national media interest. MSLGROUP created a single national, attention-getting, celebrity-driven event that drew attention to the depth and breadth of these programs and leveraged the event across DeVry University communications channels. Additionally, the agency created a new initiative, the "Career Blogger Conference," specifically focused on developing relationships with "career conversation drivers" online, to make certain the University was front and center in the blogosphere.

- *Create an issues and crisis preparedness plan that would credibly address misinformation and credibly manage reputation in the face of controversy.* With a lot of negative noise about the sector, and the tendency of media to lump together all for-profit educational institutions, DeVry University needed to be ready to respond to negative conversations on line and in negative media coverage. The playbook offered a step-by-step process and an outline of responsibilities for internal audiences at DeVry University to mobilize and share facts and perspective externally, while the President's Blog served as tool to converse with audiences without filters.

EXECUTION

The following activities were implemented to protect and enhance DeVry University's reputation and reach key audiences with a cohesive and elevating brand narrative:

News Bureau. The team identified third-party spokespeople (Kimberly Bishop and Dan Schawbel) for Internet media tours, satellite media tours, twitter chats, and media interviews to share advice on timely job search topics while positioning DeVry University as a leader in career-focused education. Regional campuses were directed to submit potential news content to the PR team through online forms which were carefully evaluated for newsworthiness to streamline the communications process. The team created its first ever national database of faculty spokespeople to provide resources for comment on newsworthy stories in media outreach. While emphasis was placed on supporting national initiatives in priority markets (national open house and career skills workshops), the team also promoted newsworthy local initiatives such as campus grand openings, unique senior projects and local community-oriented activities to increase positive media tonality.

President's Blog. The team developed a blog on behalf of the president of DeVry University that was integrated into devry.edu in just six short weeks. The blog enabled the president to share his point-of-view externally without filters to provide transparency and authenticity and opened a conversation with prospective students and influencers while serving as a tool to share student and alumni success stories, offer advice, and to demonstrate legitimacy and ongoing successes.

HerWorld. MSLGROUP created a national initiative around DeVry University's HerWorld program by enlisting actress, best-selling author, and mathematician Danica McKellar to promote national HerWorld month and bring widespread attention to the importance of STEM fields. Nearly 7,200 high school girls across the country participated in more than 50 HerWorld events nationwide. The team facilitated media outreach in priority and select regional markets to garner local awareness and coverage and executed a national event in New York City with McKellar that generated "Today Show" attention and a NY1 feature story that had national impact. The team also produced an SMT with McKellar to further enforce HerWorld messaging across regional and local markets.

*Blogger Conference on In-Demand Careers***.** MSLGROUP executed a first-of-its-kind career conference hosted by career expert and author Alexandra Levit where influential bloggers who write about careers convened to discuss the future job market and develop actionable advice for job-seekers. Levit delivered credible third-party endorsements, and blogs and Twitter feeds from guest bloggers were posted. Video of the conference was edited and distributed online. Levit participated in a satellite and Internet media tour to share the actionable advice developed at the DeVry University sponsored conference across regional markets.

*Issues Management Playbook***.** MSLGROUP developed a refined process and extensive messaging and responses to potential questions to address the negative coverage and online conversations that attached the University. The playbook was put into action to quickly address questions and concerns generated from a *Frontline* and *Nightline* segments that focused on sector schools, without targeting DeVry University. Questions about DeVry University from various audiences were answered immediately and conversation included the DeVry University point of view.

EVALUATION

Results that demonstrate MSLGROUP protected and enhanced DeVry University's reputation by meeting the two goals:

Increasing Coverage and Conversation. During the course of our program, DeVry University New Bureau activities generated 22 percent more editorial placements than the rest of the category combined: DeVry University: 8,492 vs. Category: 6,934. Overall, DeVry University increased its share of voice from 53 percent to 55 percent.

- The Blogger Career Conference resulted in 348 tweets tagged #DeVryCareers and 196,000+ followers reached. An SEO optimized news release was posted to 227 online outlets including *USA Today* and the *New York Times*, was #1 in Google news searches for "DeVry careers" and #5 in Google news searches for "In-Demand Careers." One blogger at the event, Harriette Cole from Sense and Sensitivity.com said, "My perception of DeVry pre and post event is dramatically different I am very impressed".

The live twitter chat with Dan Schawbel received 329 Tweets, 87 @ DeVry mentions and 2,713,058 approximate impressions.

- The President's Blog has received nearly 18,000 visits in six months and has received dozens of legitimate comments.
- HerWorld garnered more than 20 million impressions including *Today Show* coverage and a feature on NY1 and 1,268 total placements across national and local media.
- The regional campuses submitted several article topics to the national office for media pitching and communications planning. The team has secured 594 stories as a result and 27,331,886 impressions.

Increase Positive Tonality. Overall positive sentiment for DeVry University increased by 33 percent during the course of the program (from 39 percent positive to 72 percent positive), while negative tonality decreased from 34 percent to 6 percent. Meanwhile, aside from DeVry, all other schools in this category combined experienced a 28 percent increase in negative coverage.

Connecting Army and America

Silver Anvil Award of Excellence (2011)

Organization: U.S. Army. Agency: Weber Shandwick
Categories: Reputation Management; Integrated Communications; Public Affairs-Government Relations; Social Media
Tactics: New Communications Media (RSS, Blogs, Podcasting)
Outcome: Building Trust; Reputation Management; Employee Recruitment

Use High Credibility Participants

As you read through this case, look for some key points in the successful Army campaign:

- *addressing the middle element of the hierarchy of public relations objectives (awareness, acceptance and action). Visibility was high, but research showed low understanding and appreciation, resulting in low levels of desired action;*
- *using high-credibility message sources (actual participants in the program; that is, soldiers themselves);*
- *focusing on the role of opinion leaders in various sectors (education, community and social media);*
- *using digital and social media tactics that research showed to be particularly relevant to the key publics.*

SITUATION ANALYSIS

Creating a deeper understanding of the value of Army service and what it means to be a soldier is at the core of what Weber Shandwick does to help U.S. Army Accessions Command—the division responsible for recruiting an all-volunteer force to meet the Army's manpower requirements.

After several years of declining enlistments, the "Army Strong" campaign was launched in 2006 to combat negative perceptions of the Army and stem the recruiting decline. Weber Shandwick has managed all public relations-related portions of the campaign's integrated communications including:

- proactive media relations to tell the Army story through soldiers' voices;
- community/grassroots organizing to build advocacy for Army service and create a nation of advocates willing to help improve the local recruiting environment;
- social media engagement to create opportunities for potential recruits to connect directly with soldiers in transparent, authentic conversations;
- multicultural marketing to deepen the Army's connection in African-American, Hispanic markets;
- events support to amplify the Army's sponsorship investments;
- strategic counsel to Army senior leadership.

The result: The Army has met its recruiting mission every year since 2006 and generated more than 1.3 billion total media impressions in FY 2010.

RESEARCH

The Army's annual marketing plan is deeply rooted in research conducted by the Army and the agency, as well as the Department of Defense, on behalf of all the Armed Forces. That research demonstrates that while overall awareness of the Army as a brand is high, under-standing and appreciation for what it means to be a soldier and the value of Army service is low.

Research provided insights into the lagging awareness among prospective recruits of the Army's true opportunities (i.e. benefits, ways to serve) and with those who influence prospects' decisions to enlist. In addition, the research indicated that the more influencers and educators knew about Army opportunities, the more likely they were to support a prospect's decision. Agency research conducted following outreach efforts clearly demonstrated improved perceptions about the Army and Army service

To demonstrate a successful ROI, Weber Shandwick researched and developed core metrics to track success, including: quality media score; quality media impressions; cost per quality media impression; social media contagion score; influencer engagement score; and cost per quality engagement.

PLANNING

From the research, a strategic approach was developed with the following objectives:

1. Tell the Army story through the voice of soldiers to help build understanding of Army service and connect directly with potential recruits and those who influence them.
2. Build a nation of advocates to create deeper understanding and advocacy for Army service.
3. Create opportunities to engage soldiers and build understanding of the benefits of Army service by amplifying the Army's investment in key events and sponsorships.
4. Increase the Army's digital and social media engagement by humanizing the Army, building trust, and fostering two-way communication between the Army and its online

recruiting audiences. Engage audiences on social networks including Facebook and Twitter.

Measurable objectives were established as follows:

1. Generate 400 million quality media impressions; 750 million total impressions. Secure key placements in five top-tier targeted media outlets for digital storytelling.
2. Increase blogger base (recruit an additional 40 soldier bloggers) and increase site traffic by 30 percent.
3. Reach 10 social media influencers in the U.S. by inviting them to experience career and educational opportunities within the Army and share those experiences with their followers.

Target audiences:

- media
- community influencers/leaders
- education influencers (administrators, teachers, counselors, coaches)
- high school students/ethnic students
- social media influencers.

EXECUTION

Strategy 1: Tell the Army story through the voice of soldiers to help build understanding of Army service and connect directly with potential recruits and those who influence them.

- secured coverage through traditional media relations;
- engaged prospects, and those who influence them, through social media opportunities.

Strategy 2: Build a nation of advocates to create deeper understanding and advocacy for Army service:

- used grassroots engagement to establish community advisory boards in select priority markets;
- engaged key education influencers (administrators, teachers, counselors, coaches) and national organizations to drive knowledge of the Army's commitment to education and create awareness for Army training;
- introduced advocate philosophy and tools to allow local recruiting units and Army advocates to drive the program;
- increased the number of grassroots advisory boards from five markets to nearly 40;
- launched the Strengthening America's Youth (SAY) with national leadership representing community organizations to help establish goals and identify specific outreach efforts that will shape the success of our nation's youth;
- developed Project Partnership for All Students' Success (Project PASS) along with the National Association of State Boards of Education to engage students in middle and high school in an effort to improve graduation rates/reduce dropout rates.

Strategy 3: Create opportunities to engage soldiers and build understanding of the benefits of Army service by amplifying the Army's investment in key events and sponsorships:

- engaged high school students through an interactive "Planning for Life" workshop designed to teach them important lessons about remaining in school, staying in shape and setting goals;
- used multicultural partnerships to reach ethnic audiences and build understanding about the Army;
- leveraged Army sponsorships around key events (U.S. Army All American Bowl, NASCAR, NHRA) to drive media coverage and highlight soldiers.

Strategy 4: Increase the Army's digital and social media engagement by humanizing the Army, building trust and fostering two-way communication between the Army and its online recruiting audiences.

- developed an award-winning soldier-driven blog, ArmyStrongStories, featuring more than 600 soldiers sharing their authentic Army experiences;
- elevated Army service as a respected option via a highly integrated education community outreach effort;
- built a resilient network of supportive influencers;
- created a system that can respond quickly and effectively to negative events and positive opportunities;
- launched a database of more than 20,000 advocates to help build for the future of recruiting.

EVALUATION

Objective 1: Generate 400 million media impressions through traditional media; 750 million total impressions. Result: Generated 716 million quality media impressions; 1.3 billion total media impressions.

Objective 2: Secure key placements in five top-tier targeted media outlets for digital storytelling. Result: Secured six key media placements: PR Week, Technorati, Harvard Business Review, Financial Times, Forbes.com and NBC News.

Objective 3: Increase blogger base (recruit an additional 40 soldier bloggers) and increase site traffic by 30 percent. Result: Enlisted 251 new soldier bloggers and posted more than 415 written and video stories. Increased site visits by more than 1 million.

Objective 4: Reach 10 social media influencers in the US by inviting them to experience career and educational opportunities within the Army and share those experiences with their followers. Result: Successfully coordinated 10 blogger engagement activations resulting in positive blogs. Reached more than 550,000 fans and followers with the Army story.

Overall, the US Army's public relations efforts generated more than 1.3 billion media impressions across all programs in FY2010.

Appendixes

Coca-Cola's Expedition 206: 365 Days, 206 countries, 1 Mission

Silver Anvil Award of Excellence (2011)

Organization: Coca-Cola Company. Agency: Fast Horse
Categories: Reputation Management; Global Communications; Media Relations
Tactics: New Communications Media: RSS, Blogs, Podcasting
Outcome: Reputation Management

Bring Power to Special Events

This case offers several imitation-worthy elements for an international campaign:

- reviewing research that links customer loyalty with online engagement;
- linking products with issues of a significant personal interest (in this case, research into the concept of happiness and factors leading to it);
- creating special events to present opportunities for publics to interact with each other and with organizational spokespersons;
- using intensive digital and social media may be appropriate for a key public (teens and 20-somethings, in this case).

SITUATION ANALYSIS

As a brand that's blogged, tweeted, YouTubed and Flickr'd thousands of times each day, Coca-Cola has an opportunity to harness the power of the digital culture and engage a worldwide audience of teens and 20-somethings. But how could we create compelling content for the online venues where these young people are active while driving word-of-mouth buzz and positive media coverage? The answer came in the form of another question: What if we sent a team of young people on an unprecedented journey to 206 countries where Coca-Cola does business in just 365 days? While on the road, we'd ask them to seek out and document what makes people happy, a quest consistent with the brand's Open Happiness campaign. Armed with laptops, cameras and mobile phones, these "happiness ambassadors" would interview the people they meet, tell interesting stories and document it all in real-time—leveraging every facet of social media. With that, Expedition 206 was born.

RESEARCH

Coca-Cola's ongoing consumer loyalty studies show that people who are actively engaged in Coca-Cola's online programs demonstrate higher brand love scores; they are 31 percent more likely to "like" Coke, 43 percent more likely to "love" Coke and 68 percent more likely to "exclusively love" Coke. This knowledge fueled the desire to create an innovative program that engages global consumers online in an entirely new way. Review of a report from the Pew Internet & American Life Project showed, "The use of social media—from blogging to online social networking to creation of all kinds of digital material—is central to many teenagers' lives." The study found 39 percent of "online teens" share their own artistic creations online, such as artwork, photos, stories or videos and an overwhelming majority of these creators report their content "often starts a virtual conversation." These conversation starters are exactly the audience for whom Expedition 206 was built.

In 2008, the Coca-Cola Happiness Institute published a study that included 3,000 interviews, close work with psychologists and deep secondary research on the factors that lead to happiness. While the research certainly didn't pinpoint a single cause of happiness, it did shine light on the connection between happiness and "the smaller things in life." This knowledge helped define the mission of Expedition 206, focused much more on simple interactions and everyday people than celebrities and high-profile events. Fast Horse solicited feedback on the expedition from targeted media, bloggers and online influencers to determine the kinds of content and updates they would be interested in receiving throughout the year. Finally, success of the communications efforts would rely heavily on Coca-Cola's marketing teams in each of the 206 markets, so they were brought into the conversation early. Their insights into local publicity opportunities helped shape the route and timing of visits.

PLANNING

Communication objectives:

1. Create compelling content for and increase engagement with a worldwide audience of teens and 20-somethings;
2. Secure positive global blog and media coverage for a program that can be activated in each of the countries in which Coca-Cola is sold; and
3. Increase brand affinity and brand love among teens and 20-somethings.

Target audiences:

1. teens and 20-somethings who are active in social media;
2. residents of the countries and cities Coke's team of "happiness ambassadors" would visit.

Strategies:

1. Launch the program with a bang and quickly put Expedition 206 on the map;
2. Engage consumers before the journey begins;
3. Showcase personalities of the happiness ambassadors;
4. Create relevant opportunities to tell the story to multiple audiences, including media and bloggers covering youth culture, pop culture, travel, technology, social media, marketing and business; and
5. Leverage Coca-Cola's global marketing and communication teams, on whom the program's successful local activation would depend.

Giving consumers a sense of ownership and engaging them throughout the expedition would be essential to the success of the campaign. The decision was made to involve them from the beginning with a worldwide vote to select the lucky happiness ambassadors. After a targeted search for candidates, an eclectic group was chosen not only for their personal traits but also to reflect the diversity of Coke's global audience. The voting process would allow fans to become invested early in the people they'd be following throughout the year and also would serve as a unique news hook for the program's launch.

Extensive media and blogger lists were compiled across multiple categories in preparation for the launch, and we identified the influencers most likely to generate excitement and help spread word of the expedition quickly. Most significant was an advance story pitch planned for the Associated Press, which would bring immediate worldwide attention. Before the winning team was selected, plans were already in place to introduce them to the world with a special event in Coke's hometown, and an outreach toolkit was developed to help drive buzz throughout 2010.

EXECUTION

Phase 1: Program launch and voting kick-off. Plans were previewed for Coke's marketing teams around the world to ensure a thorough understanding of the program's goals and strategies. Fast Horse then built a global activation toolkit to empower local outreach, which included template media materials, social media outreach guidelines, sample media pitches, key messages, suggestions for local activation, photos, video clips, and more. On Oct. 21, 2009, Expedition 206 was unveiled and the global vote to choose the team of three happiness ambassadors began. A press kit in Coke's online newsroom accompanied the news release and served as a useful tool for distributing photos and videos to outreach partners and media. That morning, the AP story hit the wire and appeared in news outlets worldwide. Aggressive follow-up to media and bloggers built on the initial buzz, and the nine finalists served as compelling spokespeople as they campaigned for votes from around the globe.

Phase 2: Announcement of winners. After the "happiness ambassadors" were selected, we needed to continue building momentum prior to the team hitting the road on January 1, 2010. The ambassadors were extensively trained for the media onslaught they were about to encounter. They were revealed to the world during "Happiness Ambassador Training Camp" at the World of Coca-Cola museum in Atlanta. On Nov. 16, 2009, Tony Martin, Kelly Ferris and Antonio Santiago participated in activities designed to create interesting online content and compelling visuals for media. Activities included preparing their palates with an array of exotic foods and tackling a travel-themed obstacle course. Key bloggers and media—including teen-focused pop-culture site JSYK.com and the world's most popular technology blog, Mashable.com—attended the event, took photos and taped video interviews with the team.

The event was strategically staged in conjunction with a global Coca-Cola investor event, increasing media exposure to the high-profile business and marketing reporters in attendance. The training camp event also provided an opportunity for an updated global activation toolkit, complete with event photos and B-roll footage, to accompany traditional and social media outreach. The buzz continued the next morning, when the ambassadors conducted a booked-solid, five-hour satellite media tour, appearing on morning shows from New York to Ottawa to Mexico City—including Univision, Telemundo, and other Hispanic outlets—followed by interviews with print and online media around the world via phone, Twitter and Skype. The attention continued in the following weeks, particularly when the winners returned home with near-celebrity status.

Phase 3: Expedition begins. The expedition kicked off on Jan. 1, 2010, in Madrid, Spain, home to the Coca-Cola Happiness Institute, which the team visited after a traditional Spanish New Year's Eve celebration. An extensive activation toolkit gave local markets ideas and resources to bring Expedition 206 to life before, during and after the team's visit, including ongoing programs, event suggestions, and template media materials. Activation ideas include the selection of local "happiness hosts" to serve as guides and the presentation of one-of-a-kind Coke bottles specially decorated to depict simple moments of happiness from country. The toolkit is routinely updated to share best practices as the journey progresses. Fast Horse and Coca-Cola maintain the @x206hq Twitter account and frequently update an online press center, which serve as a "news bureau" to aid in media and blogger outreach. The traveling team maintains the main @x206 Twitter account, sharing updates on their whereabouts and the people they meet. The team members also write blog posts, publish photos to Flickr, post videos to YouTube, and share updates on Facebook. Fast Horse also manages Coca-Cola's use of Promoted Tweets (Twitter ads) designed to increase engagement with the @x206 Twitter account. The conclusion of the expedition generated another wave of global coverage, and a live webcast Q&A with the happiness ambassadors gave fans and media from around the world a chance to hear from and interact with the team as they shared some of their findings about the roots of happiness.

EVALUATION

Objective 1: Create compelling content for and increase engagement with teens and 20-somethings worldwide. Expedition 206 has been the subject of more than 900 blog posts and online news stories, and Web analytics data shows the excitement around the program is truly global: During the voting period, 75 percent of voters were from outside the US, as was 76 percent of the total traffic to expedition206.com. The website has served nearly 900,000 page views since the program's launch, and visitors spent an astounding average of more than 6.5 minutes on the site per visit. The seven Promoted Tweets sent from the @x206 Twitter account were viewed a total of 124,105 times by twitterers from around the world, resulting in a total of more than 4,300 clicks, retweets and replies. Response rates varied from 2.5 percent to nearly 9 percent—unusually high for online advertising—all for a cost per engagement of just 24 cents and cost per impression of less than 1 cent.

As an example of local-market activation, a partnership with QQ.com, China's largest social networking site, led to the creation of an Expedition 206-themed "virtual stamp" program in which users collect and trade badges that adorn their online profiles. One billion users collected and exchanged more than 10 billion Expedition 206 stamps—a record-breaking campaign for QQ. In New Zealand, Expedition 206 offered the local Coke marketing team a significant platform for content creation and community engagement; the local Coke Facebook page nearly doubled its fan base—to 10,020 fans from 5,440—during the month surrounding the team's visit.

When fans were presented with an opportunity to participate in a live Q&A webcast with the Expedition 206 team, 3,000 people from 112 countries tuned in to the live event, asking questions of the ambassadors and chatting with other fans. A recording of that Q&A is available, and the webcast has been watched more than 21,000 times by people from 130 countries.

Objective 2: Secure positive global blog and media coverage for a program that can be activated in each country. Expedition 206 was covered in more than 400 media outlets before the team even hit the road, including the Associated Press, BBC, Mashable, Fox Business News, LA Times, Telemundo, Univision, CNBC and AOL's JSYK.com. As the team's journey nears its completion, the program has received widespread media coverage in each region they've visited, resulting in more than 4,300 media stories. Global media and online outreach has resulted in 775 million media impressions.

Objective 3: Increase brand affinity and brand love among teens and 20-somethings. The program has been received very positively, helping Coca-Cola stand out as an innovator and build a new crop of global brand ambassadors. In addition to increasing engagement on the brand's Facebook page, 3,500 visitors to the program's website logged in to expedition206.com via their Facebook, Twitter, MySpace or Yahoo accounts to post chat comments, share the site with friends, and interact with our happiness ambassadors. Coca-Cola's brand love research demonstrates that increased engagement translates into increased sales, and as one of Coca-Cola's most visible non-advertising programs, Expedition 206 contributed to driving growth in case sales worldwide. In the fourth quarter of 2009, which included the program's initial announcement and the introduction of the winning team of happiness ambassadors, sales rose 4 percent. In the first, second and third quarters of 2010, as Expedition 206 roamed the earth, sales increased by 3 percent, 5 percent, and 4 percent, respectively. In each instance, Coke's official earnings report for the quarter attributes the growth, at least in part, to the brand's broad "Open Happiness" marketing campaign, of which Expedition 206 is a major part. Further, select regional sales growth coincides with Expedition 206 events in those regions. China, a major market for Expedition 206, saw 6 percent growth in the second quarter of 2010, which included the team's visit to the World Expo in Shanghai.

The expedition earned the "Innovator of the Year" award from TravelCom, and the program was named "Campaign of the Month" by *PRWeek* in January 2010. Additionally, the following are samples of what other influencers are saying:

> "Throughout the entire trip, fans have been invited to interact with the team, offering or recommending places to stay, not-to-miss attractions, amazing places to eat, and more. The whole concept is pretty creative inviting consumers not just to think about the product but the message of unity that Coca-Cola can bring to the world. That's a difficult message to convey with traditional advertising."—*Mashable.com*

> "Good for Coke, they totally get it! Building a brand is all about connecting with people's feelings and associating the product with the right image that resonates with their audience."—*Commenter on Mashable.com*

> "Coca-Cola is using social media to make the brand not only about consumers but extremely accessible to them, as well."—*Student-run Emerging Media & The Market blog*

> "A truly big idea from Coke that celebrates their brand essence of 'happiness' in a culturally relevant and interesting way for global youth. . . .'Happiness' as a territory has been done to death by many brands, but only Coke can truly take a leadership position on it and their product genuinely delivers on it."—*Branding/marketing blogger Dan Pankraz*

Philips Norelco: Deforest Yourself, Reforest the World

Silver Anvil Award (2011)

Organization: Philips Norelco. Agency: OneVoice
Categories: Special Events-Observances; Marketing; Green Marketing; Sustainability; Social Responsibility; Launch/Relaunch; Integrated Communications
Tactics: New Communications Media: RSS, Blogs, Podcasting
Outcome: Increasing Sales

Stick with a Winning Strategy

This case represents the relaunch of a product for which Norelco earned a Silver Anvil award in 2007 (interestingly, with a different agency). Here are some lessons offered by this campaign:

- building a comprehensive campaign through research;
- maintaining and building on a strategy that effectively launched the product four years earlier (the product launch featured innuendo humor, social media and an interactive website);
- playing the role of a good corporate citizen by linking to a social issue relatable in theme to the product's benefit, thus linking a socially desirable issue (environment) with a socially undesirable trait (excess body hair).

SITUATION ANALYSIS

To connect with young men and appeal to their natural interests, Philips Norelco turned a grooming product launch into an environmental action campaign. Norelco Bodygroomers had been established as a necessary tool for manscaping, largely due to the iconic website shaveeverywhere.com. However, for the launch of their new Bodygroom Pro 2040 in April 2010, Norelco needed a new story to tell, so a new crop of consumers would shave their bodies, and choose the BG 2040.

OneVoice developed the campaign: Philips Norelco: "Deforest Yourself, Reforest the World." The brand tamed two hairy issues at once: under-groomed men and over-groomed forests. By vowing to plant a tree for every Bodygroom sold, Norelco donated $75,000— 75,000 trees—to the Arbor Day Foundation and galvanized men because by deforesting themselves, they helped reforest the world.

The campaign began on Arbor Day in New York City's Madison Square Park, where a call for hairy men to be groomed by Carmen Electra turned out the media. To engage consumers and address these overgrown issues, an integrated program bloomed, offering advice on "bodily deforestation" and info about environmental deforestation. The idea motivated men to buy the BG 2040 as product sales grew by 18 percent at launch.

OBJECTIVES

Our challenge was: How do we introduce the new BG 2040 with the same tongue-and-cheek tone the brand was known for, but leverage something fresh and relevant to this young male audience to spark awareness, conversation and sales in April 2010?

Business Goals—Drive Sales at Launch: Boost sales of the BG 2040, specifically timed around launch, April 2010.

Target Relevance and Engagement—Entertain and Inspire Men:

1. Generate traffic to shaveeverywhere.com to re-build awareness in Norelco Bodygroomers and create an understanding of the benefits of purchasing a BG 2040: by grooming yourself, you can also impact the environment;
2. Ensure target-right spokesperson is mentioned in at least 30 percent of the coverage;
3. Spark conversations among men online with at least 100 posts on Carmen Electra's Facebook or Twitter accounts.

Media Goals—Efficiently Reach Men:

1. Generate 80 million impressions;
2. Obtain at least half (50 percent) of 50–100 total placements in "Tier A" outlets (national and/or male-targeted);
3. Deliver key branded messages: "Philips Norelco" or "Norelco" in 100 percent of coverage; mention of an additional campaign message in 50 percent of coverage;
4. Ensure majority of coverage is positive or neutral in tonality;
5. Achieve a CPM of $5.00 or less.

AUDIENCE ANALYSIS

Philips Norelco aims to reach men aged 25–50. These men had been introduced to the concept of manscaping, but not all of them have adopted body grooming habits or purchased a Bodygroom. For the BG 2040 introduction, we were charged with targeting the younger half of this audience, men 25–35, or even younger, because gaining young customers is a more valuable proposition for the brand over time. We learned through global research men groom to please the ladies and they can view being too hairy as "socially unacceptable,"so teasing the idea of approval from the opposite sex would work to motivate them to groom. To understand what drives guys to buy one product over another, we dug into Millennial lifestyle trends and cause interests. We found a strong tie to the environment, and specifically to programs that offer instant gratification. We also saw from Philips reports that young men like to experiment, stand out, so we deduced that bold messages and new ideas would not only continue the brand image established years ago with shaveeverywhere.com, but a provocative campaign could really resonate with and attract this younger target to participate with our campaign, and buy our product.

RESEARCH

To ensure authenticity for the target and the brand, we unearthed the most credible partners.

Cause: Research showed 87 percent of men 20–49 say preserving the environment is important to them (MRI 2009) and 64 percent of Millennials would be willing to pay more for a product if they knew some of their investment was going to an environmental cause. April 30th, Arbor Day, became launch day and "deforestation" was the cause to tame. As the largest U.S. non-profit dedicated to the planting of trees, the Arbor Day Foundation (ADF) became a natural fit. We defined the commitment of $75,000, or 75,000 trees.

Spokesperson: We researched a spokesperson to appeal to men. We chose Carmen Electra because E-Poll Market Research showed 80 percent name recognition among men 25–54. Additionally, 76 percent of all survey respondents "like" her. Among men, that stat increases to 85 percent.

Integration: The integrated plan included an event and media tour, a robust presence online with a micro site, social media activity, sweepstakes, banner ads and a radio spot. We worked with agency partners to create key performance indicators (KPI's) to be our minimum quantitative and qualitative results to measure success.

STRATEGY

In order to drive awareness, conversation and sales we needed to give men a new and compelling reason to learn about grooming, talk about it and be inspired to buy.

Seeding the Concept: Associate the BG 2040 with a captivating and motivating cause and one that would prompt men to reconsider body grooming and buy the new Norelco product.

Planting a Stake in the Ground: Reframe body grooming as "deforesting your body" to make the link between the two hairy issues Philips Norelco is committed to tame: one that is socially unacceptable and considered unattractive (body hair and the need to remove it) with one that is socially acceptable and a passion point for men (deforestation and the resolution to re-plant trees).

Branching Out: Leverage the most credible partners and make an offer guys can't refuse: create immediate call-to-action with credible environmental charity. Time the launch at Arbor Day to connect with a natural time to talk about the environment. Offer incentive to purchase the BG 2040 by planting a tree for every Bodygroom sold. Leverage a compelling spokesperson to attract the attention of men and use innuendo and humor to seed and spread the story.

EXECUTION

We embarked on a fully integrated program.

Arbor Day Launch Event: Announced campaign by inviting hairy men to be deforested by Carmen Electra. Hundreds showed up to be shaved and media covered the photo op. Produced and distributed 200 coupons for the new product.

Online Engagement: Created www.shaveeverywhere.com/deforestation with tips about how to keep men's personal forests under control, info about world deforestation. Developed sweeps for men to win an eco-adventure. Purchased banners for site traffic and linked to ADF site.

Spokespeople: Worked with Carmen Electra, event host and designated groomer; Brad Brandt, Reforestation Manager at ADF and Jacopo D'Alessandris, VP of Marketing, Philips. Focused on Carmen for national entertainment media, local TV and print, celebrity sites, grooming blogs and national radio. Used Brad and Jacopo for trade, business and cause-related media.

Media Outreach: Employed a "multiple exclusive" strategy; pitched *The New York Times* for a national print exclusive, and influential outlets (SportsIllustrated.com) to offer a spot at event for one reader to be deforested by Carmen. Released multiple Tweets, Facebook posts to engage Carmen's 500,709 mostly male followers, invite them to the event, introduce the BG 2040 and promote the cause.

EVALUATION

Drive Sales at Launch: During the week of April 26th, sales of the BG 2040 rose 18 percent from the week prior on Amazon.com (Norelco s largest online retailer). On April 30th, Norelco sold 51 units, compared to 80 units the prior week. The BG 2040 broke into the Top 100 SKUs on Amazon.com on launch day, jumping to #90 from its previous place: #1565. At launch, the BG 2040 ranked #3 as Amazon.com s "Movers and Shakers," measuring the biggest gainers in sales over 24 hours.

Engage Men:

1. The campaign drove more than 364,000 unique visitors to www.shaveeverwhere.com; 40 percent credited PR activity leading them there.
2. Carmen Electra was mentioned in 94 percent of coverage, exceeding goal by 68 percent.
3. There were 700 comments on Facebook, 700 additional "likes" to Carmen's posts and at least 1.8 million Twitter impressions.

Efficiently Reach Men via Media:

1. We generated 138 million impressions in 144 placements, exceeding goal by 72 percent.
2. 66 percent of 144 placements were in "Tier A" outlets.
3. The brand name was included in 100 percent of coverage, and 94 percent included an additional mention of the campaign or product.
4. Coverage was 100 percent positive or neutral.
5. The CPM achieved: $2.96.

APPENDIX D

Effective Media Engagement

Media engagement deals with the various philosophical and practical ways an organization interacts with the news media. Sometimes this is called **media training** or **interview training**. However, "engagement" suggests much more than merely practicing certain techniques. Media engagement involves a mindset through which an organization effectively and energetically interacts with the media as part of its overall efforts toward advancing its mission and promoting its bottom-line goals.

Some people talk about the elevator pitch, a brief (and usually rehearsed) explanation of the benefit of a product or the key element of a concept. Grant Common of Network PR in Australia and New Zealand approaches media training as more than interview techniques. He asks a simple question of corporate CEOs: "Tell me, Sir, what exactly does your company do?" The result often is either numbing detail or marketing hype. But effective media training is really about messaging.

What follows is an approach drawn from various actual media-interview training programs and crisis-communication consultations developed by the author, who has provided such training in both corporate and nonprofit settings. The principles themselves are straightforward and are drawn from standard approaches toward effective engagement with the media.

This appendix is arranged in three sections:

- Reputation and Media Relations
- Credibility
- Crisis Communication.

REPUTATION

The first aspect of effective media engagement calls for a focus on reputation. This is presented as a discussion-starter with the participation of both top- and mid-level management of organizations as well as their senior support staff. It is important, for example, not only to help a program director or corporate vice president be effective in communicating on behalf of the organization but for administrative assistance to help create an environment that gives priority to opportunities presented through the media.

This section seeks to provide insight into the role of the news media in molding the organization's reputation with various important constituent groups. Its aim is to help organizational leaders better understand both the benefits that a healthy relationship with the news media offers and the role these leaders can play in enhancing that relationship.

CREDIBILITY

The second section is presented as a hands-on coaching of individuals likely to find themselves in front of cameras and microphones. It flows from three professional observations:

1. The media will report on an organization in good times and bad, with or without organizational involvement. The organization can impact that reporting positively or negatively.
2. By becoming more competent in communicating through the news media, spokespersons can extend the organization's message and foster public support for its mission.
3. Every interview offers the organization an opportunity to increase its credibility and enhance its reputation.

CRISIS

The third section of this appendix deals with crisis communication. Effective media engagement reaches its advanced stage with concepts for organizational administrators who need to communicate in times of crisis. The premise is that, while a certain amount of crisis is inevitable within any organizations, their consequences can be controlled. Indeed, organizations can turn a crisis into an opportunity to enhance its credibility and its position vis-à-vis its many publics.

The objectives of this section on crisis communication are directed toward public relations managers and other organizational executives:

- to increase awareness and understanding of both the complexity of crises as well as the opportunities for successfully managing them;
- to increase confidence that they can effectively manage crisis situations;
- to enhance their crises management skills.

Review Step 1 in the strategic planning process for additional information on **crisis management**.

Reputation and Media Relations

The dictionary defines **reputation** as "honor, credit, recognition, or esteem given to a person or organization." Reputation lies at the heart of strategic communication. Effective engagement of news media requires a solid appreciation of the role that reputation plays in the life of an organization.

Structurally, this section presents a series of professional observations, followed by points for discussion. It should be used in a group setting, with a public relations professional guiding organizational executives through an active discussion of how reputation affects their organization and how they might impact that process.

Reputation and Performance

Reputation involves perception. The reputation of an organization is the estimation by which it is commonly held, whether favorable or unfavorable. Reputation is based both on what people know about us and what they feel about us based on that knowledge.

Reputation should reflect performance. Ideally, what people think of the organization's performance will mirror its actual performance. More often, however, there is a distortion between our performance (what we do and how well we do it) and their perception (what people know and think about what we do).

> **DISCUSSION POINTS**
> • How important is your organization's reputation to your job?
> • Is your job unaffected by your organization's reputation?

Reputation as a Strategic Tool

A good reputation has practical value. In general, a positive reputation can give an organization a competitive advantage that others cannot easily match. What is your organization's reputation? Answer this carefully, based not on wishful thinking but on an honest assessment of how others perceive you.

A good reputation is an insurance policy. Especially in times of trouble, your organization's good reputation can maintain credibility and goodwill. These, in turn, give supporters reasons to continue their trust, defer criticism, balance the picture, and generally maintain their support.

> **DISCUSSION POINTS**
> • Does your organization have the ability to shape its reputation?
> • To what extent is this possible?

Reputation Management

Every organization can enhance its reputation. Reputation is manageable. It can be molded and developed by the way we actively and strategically interact with important groups of stakeholders. Reputation management involves research, strategic planning, deliberate implementation of that plan, and continual monitoring and evaluation.

Every organization can also jeopardize its reputation. Reputation will suffer if, through misjudgment or neglect, an organization fails to remain credible or responsive with important groups or if it does not communicate accurate and positive information about ourselves.

> **DISCUSSION POINT**
> • How important do you think the news media are in developing your organization's reputation?

Reputation and News Media

The news media help shape an organization's reputation. Newspapers, radio and television offer opportunities for organizations to proactively present messages that strengthen their reputation and promote their mission. The media also provide opportunities to respond to media inquiries, present positive messages and minimize negative impressions.

> **DISCUSSION POINT**
> • What offices or entities within your organization should try to influence the organization's reputation?

Organizations risk their good reputation by not responding to media inquiries. The media *will* report on your organization when they choose to. The issue is *to what extent* the organization will effectively and positively impact such reporting. If your voice is absent from the media, you give up the opportunity to talk with your publics, allowing others to interpret you to the community.

<table>
<tr><td>

DISCUSSION POINT
• How have recent events that have been reported in the news media affected your organization's reputation?

</td><td>

Reputation as a Participant Activity

Your reputation is everybody's business. Public relations and similar offices may manage publicity and promotional activities that affect the organization's reputation. But ultimately, everyone associated with your organization can help or hurt its reputation. Consciously or not, an organization's reputation is impacted by everything said and done by management, employees, volunteers, even customers.

</td></tr>
</table>

Your reputation is fragile. Like an old-growth forest ravaged by fire, a reputation can be destroyed in minutes. All associated with an organization must be continuously aware that what they do and say affect the reputation. Poor delivery of services and negative publicity easily lead to dissatisfied and angry consumers, the ultimate threat to reputation.

<table>
<tr><td>

DISCUSSION POINTS
Consider each of the headlines on the right from three different perspectives:

1. As the parent of a high school student considering attending this university, how does the headline affect your thoughts about the university? What is the likelihood that you and your child will want to be associated with this institution?

2. As a student or faculty member here, how does the headline affect your pride in being associated with this university? Do you have any concerns about what others think of you and your colleagues?

3. As director of public relations for the university, what alternative headline would you have preferred in this situation? What could your institution have done to warrant your preferred headline?

</td><td>

Headlines and Bottom Lines

News coverage can affect many different publics of an organization, often in unanticipated ways. This exercise uses the examples of a nonprofit organization (a university), but the principles can apply to any other nonprofit, as well as a corporation, membership organization or government agency. Consider each of the following headlines.

Headline:
"Low, Delayed Graduation Rates at Local University Cited in Report"

Headline:
"Coed Nabbed for Prostitution; Blames Snafu in Financial-Aid Office"

Headline:
"Local Student Charged with Arson, Attempted Murder for Firebombing Car of Fellow Student"

Headline:
"Local University Drops in Rankings of Top Colleges, Universities"

Headline:
"Local Professor Accused of Anti-Gay Harassment"

Headline:
"Dorm Fire Leaves 300 Homeless After Explosion by Student Cooking Drugs."

</td></tr>
</table>

Media Relations

Media relations is the subset of public relations and marketing communication dealing with an organization's ongoing involvement with news media for the purpose of enhancing its reputation and promoting its mission.

Media Relations . . . from the Media Side

Reporters want news. News is information that is timely, accurate and of significance to a particular audience. It may show subjects in a positive or negative light. In gathering news, reporters try to talk with many news sources: insiders, experts and other people involved in the issue. They expect access to public institutions such as the university. They try to report all sides without taking sides.

> **DISCUSSION POINTS**
> • What does your organization expect from reporters?
> • What does your organization want from reporters?

Reporters are skeptical. They see it as their mission to probe beneath the surface, to not take things at face value and to seek out hidden agendas. They consider nothing to be none of their business. And if they catch someone doing something wrong and expose that, they see this as the rendering of public service.

Not all reporters are alike. Each medium of public communication has its own style of operating, and reporters have differing practices for interviewing:

- Newspaper reporters often work over the telephone. Their interviews may be either brief or in-depth. They may ask questions on side issues as well as the main topic, and they may quote extensively.
- Radio reporters usually do interviews in person, though they sometimes do brief telephone interviews to get a "sound bite."
- Television reporters interview their news sources on camera. A television reporter may talk with a news source on camera for five minutes or more and then use only one or two sentences during a newscast.
- Television reporters are interested in photogenic situations that are colorful, active and interesting.
- Bloggers or Internet journalists often are independent agents who value their autonomy and often are advocates of a particular social or partisan perspective.

Media Relations . . . from the Organization Side

Your organization wants fair treatment. As the subject of a news report, it wants, needs and deserves reporting that is fair and professional. This means expecting reporters to treat the organization with objectivity and neutrality. The organization also wants to be recognized as a contributing and respected member of its industry or profession and of its community.

> **DISCUSSION POINT**
> • How can your organization use the news media to its advantage?

Your organization benefits from a healthy relationship with the media. With fair and accurate reporting, your organization benefits by having a strong and respected voice in its industry or profession. Healthy media relations enables the organization to be recognized as a course of commentary about matters of interest to the community. It also gives the organization the opportunity to balance criticism. In short, healthy media relations can allow the organization to maximize "good news" and minimize "bad news."

Media Relations . . . from Both Sides

DISCUSSION POINTS • In what ways has your organization communicated with the media, both proactively and reactively? • What sources of information have the media used in reporting on your organization?

Your organization communicates in two ways: proactively and reactively. Proactively, the organization provides story ideas and offers of interviews to reporters. It also disseminates news releases and fact sheets, and it presents speeches and news conferences. Reactively, the organization responds to reporters' questions and allegations.

Reporters have many news sources. In gathering information for their stories, reporters contact many different organizations and individuals. They check the validity of their information and question the motivations of their sources. Here are some of the ways they might obtain information:

- official sources such as the public relations office and organizational spokespersons, through information vehicles such as news releases and interviews;
- publications such as an employee newsletter, member magazine, mailings and other semipublic publications, as well as information at your organization's website;
- public records such as documents and statements involving regulatory agencies, as well as police and legal records;
- unofficial sources such as employees, customers and other persons willing to speak about (but not necessarily on behalf of) your organization. This includes people who may be misinformed or disgruntled;
- Buzz and the word on the street, rumor and scuttlebutt, hearsay and gossip.

Reputational Bumps and Bruises

Which puts the bigger dent in your organization's reputation? Consider the following:

- inadequacy or arrogance?
- bad judgment or dishonesty?
- negative reports or poor performance?
- unpopular decisions or unexplained actions?
- being scrutinized or being found unresponsive?

Twelve Principles of Effective Media Relations

1. A relationship is both inevitable and necessary between your organization and the media. The behavior of the organization will determine if this relationship is good or bad.
2. The organization should publicly speak with one voice in any situation, by designating and preparing a single spokesperson authorized to speak in the name of the organization.

3. The person closest to the situation should be the designated spokesperson, or at least should be in close communication with the spokesperson.
4. "No comment" is never an option. Every bona fide question should be answered.
5. The organization should look upon reporters as allies rather than as intruders or enemies.
6. The organization should consider itself accountable to its various publics: employees, volunteers, customers, donors, supporters and the community. Further, it should view the news media as one of the vehicles available for communicating with these constituencies.
7. The organization should not expect to control the media's agenda or their assessment of what is newsworthy. But you can help add issues to that agenda.
8. Public relations professionals should always be "in the loop" in all newsworthy situations, especially those with negative potential.
9. Reporters should be accommodated with professional assistance such as parking permits and a functioning media room.
10. The organization should expect that it occasionally will "take a hit" in the media. The response should be to accept this, try to understand it and get over it as quickly as possible. Lingering hostility to reporters never serves the organization's interests.
11. Media skepticism and scrutiny can be more bearable when the organization interacts with reporters in a timely manner and with openness, accuracy and candor.
12. Media coverage is considerably more credible than either advertising or the use of internal media such as brochures, publications and websites. Effective use of the news media gives the organization a believable voice in the community.

Points for Consideration

TRUE OR FALSE?

I shouldn't waste time talking with reporters who are already biased against my organization.

Consider this: If you want people to support you, first they have to understand you. Much of their impression about your organization comes through the media. Your time spent with reporters is not doing the reporter a favor; rather it is setting up a means of communication with your publics.

TRUE OR FALSE?

Reporters don't understand what I'm doing and they always get it wrong, so I should avoid them.

Consider this: You can direct the tone of an interview. Invest whatever time it takes to educate reporters about what you are doing. Prepare for the interview, perhaps by providing a glossary and background sheet if necessary. Explain the significance of your actions and opinions.

TRUE OR FALSE?

If I don't talk to reporters, I won't get into trouble.

Consider this: If you don't talk to reporters, people won't know how honest, competent and effective you are.

TRUE OR FALSE?

It's a real compliment to hear that our organization is one of the best-kept secrets in our area or within our industry or profession.

Consider this: Being called a best-kept secret is an insult to everyone associated with your organization. It means that neither you nor your colleagues are doing enough to share information about your organization's achievements and boast about its successes.

Credibility

Effective media engagement involves an applied set of skills and practices to help organizational spokespeople. This section offers tips and techniques on various aspects of interviewing, from the standpoint of the person being interviewed.

Interview Setting

There are at least nine different ways that an organizational spokesperson or executive might be interviewed by the news media:

1. *Individual news interview.* This is the most common interview situation you are likely to face. You are being interviewed by a single reporter for print, radio or television. The interview may take place in your office, in a studio or in a remote location. Unless it is an ambush situation, you will have time to prepare for the news interview. Maintain eye contact and respond directly to the reporter. Ignore microphones and/or camera operators.
2. *Straight-to-the-camera interview.* You are being interviewed by a single television reporter who is doubling as the camera operator. Look directly at the camera, but visualize an individual member of your audience and speak to him.
3. *Telephone interview.* You are being interviewed over the telephone by a reporter. This is most commonly used by print reporters, who will either record your voice or simply take notes. It is used sometimes by radio reporters and only infrequently by television reporters. Maintain a professional demeanor and posture even though you cannot be seen. Maintain a professional control of your voice. Handle this interview as carefully as you would a face-to-face encounter. Always presume you are being taped throughout the entire telephone interview.
4. *News conference interview.* News conferences have three parts: you present a brief statement or announcement; you then distribute prepared printed materials to a gathering of reporters from various media; this is followed by a question-answer session with these reporters. News conferences generally are videotaped; on rare occasions, they may be broadcast live.
5. *Panel interview or debate.* You are one of two or more interviewees being questioned by reporters from various media. Panels and debates often are held before an audience and many are broadcast live. They often involve questions from a panel of interviewers and/or from members of the audience. Before the interview, investigate the position of your co-panelists, and then frame your message with their positions in mind. Be prepared to fight for a fair share of time to present your message. Avoid shouting matches, but do not hesitate to differentiate your position from that of others.

6. *Call-in radio interview.* This is an increasingly popular format for live radio. You are interviewed in a radio studio by a host, and at some point during the interview you will respond to phone-in callers. Listen carefully to questions and respond as personally as possible to each individual caller.

7. *Call-in television interview.* This is similar to the call-in format for live radio, except that you are being televised as you interact with the on-camera host and the phone-in callers.

8. *Videoconference interview.* This is a live format similar to a call-in interview, except that your audience can see you on a video monitor. Usually the audience gathers at remote sites, where they can telephone questions to you. As with a simple call-in interview, listen carefully to questions and respond in a personal tone.

9. *E-mail interview.* Sometimes distance prevents one of the above real-time interview formats, so reporters occasionally resort to providing a set of questions via e-mail. This gives the news source time to carefully weigh the message, but make sure you don't become long-winded in responding to such questions.

If You Are Asked for an Interview

1. Make sure you understand the topic to be discussed.

2. Decide if you can do the interview. Do you have the basic information? Being available to reporters is more important than having every last detail on an issue, which would be more than you'd need anyhow. Being unavailable breeds suspicion among the organization's publics. It also ignores an opportunity to present your message, which will be accepted by somebody else, often a person with lesser qualifications to speak authoritatively.

3. Are you the appropriate person to speak on behalf of your organization? If not, try to suggest another news source. Don't put reporters off without good cause. But if you must decline the interview opportunity, tell them why.

4. Ask the reporter to identify the source of the information on which the interview will be based. If it is information with which you are unfamiliar, try to get a copy of the source material; usually the reporter will provide you with a copy or direct you to the source.

5. Ask about the nature, length and eventual use of the interview. Find out if the interview will be taped or live.

Dress for Interview Success

Organizational spokespeople appearing on television need to dress appropriately. Generally this means wearing conservative professional attire that you would normally wear at work, avoiding fashion fads that might distract some viewers and detract from your effectiveness as a credible representative of your organization. Here are some reminders:

1. Keep the look simple. Avoid busy patterns such as narrow stripes, small checks, plaids, herringbone and other clothing with tight repeating patterns. These can cause video pictures to flutter.

2. Avoid large and flashy items of jewelry, especially necklaces, earrings and tie pins. Avoid clothing with large, shiny buttons.

3. Seek moderation. Avoid extremes of black and white. Instead prefer medium and dark colors in place of black. Prefer light pastels in place of white. Ideal professional and television-friendly attire is a conservatively cut suit of gray or navy, with a shirt or blouse of pale blue, pink or beige, and a scarf or tie of a strong but not garish accent color.

4. Use medium colors. If you have light or medium skin tones, prefer medium and dark colors. People with darker skin tones may use medium or light colors. In any case, avoid strong or loud colors, especially bright reds, oranges and purples except as accents (such as ties and scarves).

5. If the interview is to be conducted while you are seated, wear clothing that does not constrict your neck. Avoid clothing that bulks up around your chest and shoulders.

6. Just before the interview, make a final check for gaping buttons and mussed hair. Men should check for socks that are too short.

7. Don't worry about eyeglasses. If you normally wear glasses, wear them for the interview; not to wear them will probably make you uncomfortable and you will look unnatural to others. Let camera operators and lighting crews worry about eliminating any glare. Avoid wearing lenses that darken under bright lights.

8. Consider wearing distinctive professional clothing if you are to be interviewed in your work setting. A lab coat, for example, would be very appropriate for an on-site interview. Generally it is not a good idea to wear such clothing in a studio setting.

Interview Posture

Your posture will go a long way in helping you present a positive image during televised interviews. Here are a few reminders.

1. Sit with your back straight, knees together, both feet on the floor. Avoid twitching or moving your legs and feet.

2. Don't slouch into a comfortable position; on television, casual looks sloppy. Even in a radio or print interview, your posture will spill over into your voice.

3. If you feel a need to reposition yourself, lean in toward the interviewer and/or camera. Never lean away.

4. Place your hands in your lap or in the arms of the chair.

5. Use your hands naturally, but avoid nervous movements. Don't drum your fingers.

6. Maintain eye contact with the interviewer.

Interview Planning

Here is a threefold approach to interview planning. In the first part, consider the following points of planning, which relate specifically to the organization.

1. *What*: State the issue clearly and concisely.

2. *Significance*: Note the importance of the issue and its potential impact on your organization.

3. *Who*: List individuals and groups involved.
4. *When*: Indicate any relevant time factors (future focus is preferred).
5. *Where*: Note any relevant locations or boundaries (try to focus on local situations).
6. *Communication history*: Consider the nature and extent of your previous communication on this issue.
7. *Credibility*: Consider how people perceive your organization's credibility on this issue.
8. *Organizational expectations*: Note what your organization wants from you regarding this situation.
9. *Motivation*: Summarize your motivation for being involved in this issue.

In the second part of your planning, consider the following points as they relate to the media audience and the organization's publics.

10. *Key publics*: List those groups most notably affected on this issue.
11. *Understanding the publics*: Note the wants, interests, needs and expectations of the key publics you have identified.
12. *Benefits*: Summarize the benefits and advantages your organization offers each key public.
13. *Media interest*: Indicate why the media are (or could become) interested in this issue.
14. *Media expectations*: Note if the media want to or might interview you.
15. *Opponents*: List any groups or individuals who are likely to oppose you on this issue.
16. *Balance*: Indicate the nature and credibility of opposing perspectives.

Finally, conclude the planning by considering objectives and strategy.

17. *Awareness objectives*: Indicate the impact you hope to make about the publics' knowledge and understanding on this issue.
18. *Acceptance objectives*: Indicate the impact you hope to make about the publics' interest and attitudes on this issue.
19. *Action objectives*: Indicate the impact you hope to make about the publics' opinions and behavior around this issue.
20. *Tone of message*: Note appeals to authority, fear or guilt, or appeals for confidence, responsibility, calm, caution, and the like.
21. *Visuals*: Try to incorporate visual elements and interesting locations into your interview.
22. *Power words*: Identify any particularly powerful and memorable words or phrases that you might incorporate into your message.

Preparing for the Interview

1. Never try to "play it by ear."
2. Know yourself. Rely on your own expertise.
3. Know your audience.
4. Know what you want to say.
5. Know what impact you hope to make.
6. Anticipate questions a reporter may ask.

7. Think of an anecdote or example that can enhance your key message.
8. Rehearse out loud.
9. Practice with a tape recorder.
10. Immediately before the interview, take a few moments to focus yourself.
11. Relax, but not too much. A little anxiety can give you an energetic edge.

Be-Attitudes for Interview Success

1. *Be accurate.* There is almost nothing worse than making an error of fact.
2. *Be honest.* The one thing worse than an error of fact is a deliberate error of fact. Remember that the long-term credibility of both you and your organization is at stake.
3. *Be brief.* Use short words and simple sentences. Think in terms of two or three sentences to present your message, or just enough time for a quick answer to a few questions. For most questions, you should be able to give one-sentence responses. Practice these.
4. *Be interesting.* Use colorful and pithy language. Give brief anecdotes and easy-to-understand analogies so your audience can grasp your message.
5. *Be enthusiastic.* Even be passionate. State your case and give your opinions with excitement. Show you care about the issue.
6. *Be clear.* Avoid technical or scientific language that you might use around your colleagues. Remember that your audience probably doesn't understand your professional jargon.
7. *Be positive.* Instead of dwelling on accusations, tell your side of the story.

Interview Attitude

1. *Remain confident.* You are the expert the reporter has sought out. You represent your client or organization in public.
2. *Remember your conviction.* Let your audience know that you believe in your message. If you appear to be unsure or unconvinced, you aren't likely to persuade others. Let your enthusiasm show on your face and in your speech.
3. *Try to be credible.* Persuasive message sources are those who are perceived as being both expert and sincere, in touch with their audiences, and friendly and/or worthy of respect.
4. *Display your motivation.* The impression you leave with the audience will linger far after it has forgotten your words.
5. *Speak clearly.* Speak distinctly in your normal voice. If you are a fast talker, try to slow down a bit.
6. *Smile naturally.* Don't overdo this, especially if smiling doesn't come naturally. There are fine lines distinguishing a smile, a smirk, and a pretentious display of teeth.
7. *Keep your cool.* Don't shout; don't swear; don't attack the questioner (even if you are asked a truly malicious question). Never show anger, no matter how angry you may feel.
8. *Don't be intimidated.* You are not on trial, nor are you obliged to "air dirty laundry" in public. In an interview, you have rights. One of them is the right to discontinue a line of questioning if the reporter persists in trying to draw you where you don't wish to go.

9. *Remember that an interview has mutual benefits.* It can help both you and the reporter. You are helping the reporter do a job; the reporter is helping you communicate with your audience toward achieving your strategic objectives.

Communicating during the Interview

1. *Note your common bond with the audience.* Show that you share their concerns and clearly explain the direct benefit for them.
2. *Propose convenient action* (if any) for the audience.
3. *Develop a sound bite*—a meaningful, succinct and easy-to-recall message that you want your audiences to remember. Aim for 15–20 seconds.
4. *Stick to your key message.* Don't ramble, and don't allow yourself to be sidetracked. The more you talk, the more opportunity you give a reporter to use peripheral comments instead of central information. State the key message in different ways; keep coming back to the main topic.
5. *Don't comment if you can't.* "Off the record" is not an option. If you cannot answer a question publicly, don't try to answer at all. Don't put reporters in the awkward position of knowing information they cannot use.
6. *Give a reason for not commenting.* If for good reason you cannot comment, tell the reporter (and the audience) that reason. Don't say "No comment" if you mean "I don't know" or "I can't/won't talk about it now." Realize that most people interpret "No comment" as meaning that you have something to hide.
7. *Don't address the reporter by name.* Instead, speak to the audience. Imagine one individual (not the reporter) who is representative of your target public and address your comments to that person.
8. *Let the reporter worry about dead air.* Take a few seconds to think before you respond to the question. Rephrase the question while you're thinking of the best answer.
9. *Don't guess.* Say "I don't know" or "I'll find out for you." (But try not to appear ill-prepared or uninformed.)
10. *Signal your message.* "The most important thing about this is . . ." or "Three things stand out here. One . . . Two . . . And finally . . ."
11. *Humanize statistics.* Say "two out of three people" rather than "65% of the population." Avoid using numbers as much as possible.
12. *Pay attention to body language and facial expressions.* Your nonverbal actions should complement your words.
13. *Don't be drawn into criticism.* Don't comment about what your opponent may do or say unless you strategically decide to do so.
14. *Don't volunteer information* unless it is something you really want to say.
15. *Have notes with you as you wish.* Glance at them, but don't read from them.

Problem Interviews

Most reporters you deal with will be professional. Expect this, and treat all reporters as professionals unless they prove otherwise. A professional, competent interviewer (1) has prepared and is familiar with the issue; (2) has a no-nonsense approach; and (3) is friendly without being overly familiar. Appreciate this, and be professional in return.

Occasionally you may get a dud. If you encounter problem interviews, consider the following responses.

- A *misinterpreter* draws an unwarranted conclusion.
  Your response: Refute the incorrect statement.

- A *paraphraser* puts words into your mouth.
  Your response: Restate your response slowly, word for word.

- A *mind reader* presumes to know your thoughts before you speak.
  Your response: Dispute the unwarranted insinuation and state your message clearly.

- An *unprepared reporter* did not adequately get ready for this interview.
  Your response: Suggest questions to support your message. This opportunity in disguise lets you give basic information. Keep things simple.

- A *bully* attacks with charges and allegations.
  Your response: Refute the charges as you are able, but do not repeat the accusations.

- A *machine-gunner* strafes you with nonstop questions.
  Your response: Pick the one you prefer to answer and ignore the others.

- An *interrupter* cuts you off before you have finished responding.
  Your response: Make sure you are being concise. If so, ignore the interruption and continue your previous response. Stick to your own agenda.

- An *extremist* frames the issue only in polarized terms.
  Your response: Point out the middle ground, and speak from that perspective.

- A *speculator* asks you why so-and-so said such-and-such.
  Your response: Avoid the temptation to guess. Don't try to explain the motives of another.

- A *false starter* frames questions on a false foundation.
  Your response: Clarify and restate the question. Then answer it.

- A *flatterer* puts you off guard with compliments.
  Your response: Repeat your main message. Don't be lulled into a false sense of security. A tough question may be lurking.

- A *trapper* tries to pit your personal opinion against organizational policy.
  Your response: Say what you can, but never speak "off the record." A news interview probably is not the best place for loyal dissent.

After the Interview

1. Review your performance. Note any misstatements and assess what you learned from the interview.
2. Take note of how the reporter handles the information, but don't second-guess the writing or reporting. You may have told the story differently, but that wasn't your role.

3. Put it behind you. You can't take back anything you said, and it's unlikely you can add anything useful to what you did say.
4. If you truly have been misquoted and your organization misrepresented in a way that will have long-term negative consequences, speak first with your media relations person. If there is consensus to seek redress, contact the reporter and, if necessary, the editor or news director. Ask for a follow-up interview; settle for a clarification (but don't expect most audiences to read it).

Crisis Communication

This is the advanced stage of effective media engagement. It involves both strategy and technique, building on two assertions: (1) that crises are inevitable within any organization and (2) that it is within an organization's ability to influence the direction of media coverage and thus the consequences of a crisis.

First, a definition. The dictionary defines crisis as "a turning point for better or worse; a decisive moment." It is interesting to note that the Chinese/Japanese character for crisis combines two concepts: "danger" and "opportunity." This is particularly fitting for public relations professionals seeking to guide their organization through times of crisis.

It is important to understand that a crisis is not a mere problem for an organization. Problems are irritating annoyances commonplace in business and organizational life. Problems often focus on individuals and on interpersonal conflict. They can be serious—such as the need to fire an employee or to report low sales to stockholders—but they seldom rise to the level of a crisis, based on the following definition.

But a crisis is much more. It is a major, unfortunate, sudden and unpredicted event. A crisis . . .

- can interfere with and seriously disrupt an organization's activity;
- is likely to have a negative impact on the organization's "bottom line" or mission;
- threatens the reputation and other assets of the organization;
- demands quick reaction by the organization;
- generally escalates in intensity;
- occurs in a public environment, so that even private businesses and nonprofit organizations cannot shield themselves from the expectation of being held accountable;
- invites outside scrutiny that can jeopardize the organization's reputation.

If handled properly, a crisis presents the organization with an opportunity to create a positive impression on its key publics. A crisis shows what an organization is made of, by making visible under adverse situations its values, priorities and commitments. A crisis brings out the best or the worst.

Types of Crises

The Institute for Crisis Management (crisisexperts.com) defines **crisis** as "a significant business disruption that stimulates extensive news media coverage. The resulting public scrutiny will affect the organization's normal operations and also could have a political, legal, financial, and governmental impact on its business."

Not surprisingly, not all crises are the same. Here are ten types of crises, four of them in the violent category, six nonviolent:

1. *Disaster (violent)*: A natural occurrence such as earthquake, flood, and the like with immediate damage. Example: a school destroyed by fire.
2. *Disaster (nonviolent)*: A natural occurrence such as drought, epidemic, and the like with delayed damage. Example: farm crops destroyed by an early frost.
3. *Accident (violent)*: A mishap involving people or equipment, with immediate injury or death. Example: an accident caused by a company truck in which a pedestrian is killed.
4. *Accident (nonviolent)*: A mishap involving people or equipment, with immediate damage. Example: an accident caused by company truck in which parked cars are damaged.
5. *Crime (violent)*: A personal action violating legal standards causing injury or death. Example: a pharmaceutical employee sabotaging medicine with a poisonous substance.
6. *Crime (nonviolent)*: A personal action violating legal standards, with delayed damage. Example: a company executive stealing money from an employee pension fund.
7. *Ethical/moral failing (nonviolent)*: A personal action violating ethical or moral standards (though not necessarily legal standards), with either immediate or delayed damage. Example: a public relations practitioner intentionally lying in a news release about a company product, with resulting media coverage of the lie.
8. *Mismanagement (nonviolent)*: Bad professional judgment impacting an organization's operations and procedures, with either immediate or delayed damage. Example: a financial planner losing hundreds of thousands of dollars for clients because of poor investments.
9. *Opposition (violent)*: Negative impact by external or internal forces, including product tampering, terrorism, and the like, with immediate damage. Example: rioting, with injuries occurring, at a political rally.
10. *Opposition (nonviolent)*: Negative impact by external or internal forces, including competition, protests, recalls, lawsuits etc., with delayed or damage. Example: heckling at a political rally by supporters of the opposition candidate.

The institute reported in 2008 the following categories of organizational crises, noting that most crises are not the result of natural disaster or employee error but instead are caused by management decisions, action or inaction:

19%	White-collar crime
15%	Workplace violence
11%	Mismanagement
9%	Class-action lawsuits
9%	Labor disputes
7%	Catastrophes
7%	Casualty accidents
5%	Consumer activism
5%	Defects and recalls

4%	Financial damages
3%	Discrimination
2%	Environmental
1%	Sexual harassment
1%	Executive dismissal
1%	Whistleblowers

Over the past 10 years, ICM concludes that management has been responsible for 52 percent of all organizational crises, employees for 29 percent, and other factors for the remaining 19 percent.

The institute also distinguishes between a **sudden crisis** (a disruption of business that occurs without warning, with the likelihood of generating negative news coverage) and a **smoldering crisis** (a business problem not generally recognized that may generate negative news coverage if and when it goes public). ICM says a smoldering crisis begins as a small problem that someone in the organization should have recognized as a potential trouble spot and could have fixed it before it became a public issue.

Important in this and other schemes of categorizing crises is the observation that few crises are unpredictable. They may be unpredicted, but it often is human error that caused a problem or early warning to be overlooked, mushrooming into a full crisis.

Sudden crises resulting from fires, floods and other natural occurrences are unusual. Even some of these are somewhat predictable, such as a school or manufacturing company built in a flood zone or a high-rise office tower built in an area prone to earthquakes.

Most crises, however, are of the smoldering type. Smoldering crises thus are the result of management error of some sort: safety checks improperly made, inadequate supervision of employees or others, deficient background checks on employees working with children or the infirm, unsatisfactory handling of consumer complaints, failure to apply laws dealing with discrimination or harassment—all management failings that could have been avoided.

The 2008 ICM report indicated that 65 percent of all organizational crises were of the smoldering type, while only 35 percent were sudden.

Six Principles for Crisis Communication

Crises are inevitable within every organization. You can minimize their occurrence but you can't prevent them entirely. Rather, your aim should be to exercise control in the way you manage the crisis, impacting on whether the outcome is positive or negative. Here are several principles for crisis communication:

Principle of existing relationships. In crisis situations, communicate with employees, volunteers, stockholders, donors and other constituent groups, as well as with colleagues. Minimally, keep these publics informed, because their continued support will be important in your rebuilding process following the crisis. Ideally, enlist their assistance during the crisis to communicate credibly and effectively.

Principle of quick response. Become accessible to your publics as quickly as possible. The one-hour rule applies here; within one hour of learning about a crisis, the organization should have its first message available to its publics, particularly the media, which generally are the most significant public in the early stages of a crisis.

Principle of full disclosure. Silence is not an acceptable response during a crisis. Without admitting fault, the organization should provide as much information as possible. The presumption should be that everything the organization knows should be made available, subject to specific justification for not releasing certain information.

Principle of one voice. A single spokesperson should represent the organization. If multiple spokespersons are needed, each should be aware of what the others are saying, and all should work from the same set of facts and the same coordinated message.

Principle of media-as-ally. In crisis situations, organizations are best advised to treat the news media as allies that provide opportunities for the organization to communicate with its key publics and constituents. In situations in which the media are intrusive and/or hostile to the organization, this often is because the organization has not been forthcoming in providing legitimate information to the media and its other publics. A good existing program of media relations can minimize media hostility.

Principle of recovery. The most pressing need in a crisis situation is for the organization to put the issue behind it and initiate a recovery program. Focus on repairing any damage to the organization's reputation and its relationship with important publics.

Crisis Strategy

During a crisis, every organization has a range of strategic responses available to it. Here is an overview of eight strategic responses to crisis. These strategies exist on a continuum between full responsibility and full blame. Note that some of the strategies may be used in combination. For a fuller treatment of these strategic options, review Step 5 of the planning process outlined in this book.

1. *Attack.* The organization confronts the person or group who claims that a crisis exists or who the organization accuses of causing the crisis, and threatens to use force or pressure against the person or group. Do not use this strategy to blame the messengers reporting the crisis. Use this strategy only when a strong case can be made that accusers have grossly overstated the organization's involvement in the crisis.
2. *Denial.* The organization states that no crisis exists and explains why there is no crisis. Or the organization denies that any culpability in a crisis that does exist. Use this strategy only when the organization can present a strong case that it did not cause the crisis.
3. *Excuse.* The organization tries to minimize responsibility for the crisis such as by denying any intention to do harm or claiming that it had no control over events that led to the crisis. Use this strategy, perhaps in conjunction with compassion, when a strong case can be made that the organization did not intentionally cause any harm.
4. *Justification.* The organization tries to minimize the perceived damage associated with the crisis or claims that it had no control over events that led to the crisis. Use this strategy, perhaps in conjunction with compassion, when a strong case can be made that the organization is not to blame.
5. *Ingratiation.* The organization takes action to cause its publics to like and side with the organization. Use this strategy when the crisis has been a nonviolent one and when the organization has not been culpable in the crisis.

6. *Corrective action.* The organization takes steps to contain the crisis, repair the damage and/or prevent a recurrence. Use this strategy if the organization was in any way unprepared or negligent in preventing the crisis in the first place.

7. *Compassion.* The organization expresses regret, remorse and/or concern without admitting guilt. Use this strategy when injury, death or serious damage has occurred to express the humanity of the organization.

8. *Apology.* The organization takes full responsibility, asks forgiveness and makes compensation or restitution. Use this strategy when the organization is at fault and when long-term rebuilding of relationships is more important than short-term stalling.

An organization's choice among various crisis strategies depends on several interdependent factors, including the following:

- *Severity of the crisis.* The more serious the crisis, the less likely that excuses or denials will be accepted without strong and compelling evidence. Also, the more severe the crisis, the harsher the public verdict will be against the organization.
- *Culpability of the organization.* If the organization is fully or even partly responsible for the crisis, this inevitably will be revealed. Crisis managers must be aware of the role the organization played in the evolution of the crisis.
- *Preventability of the crisis.* Crisis managers must be aware of the extent to which the crisis could have been prevented. Culpability can be mitigated if the organization tried to prevent or minimize the crisis before it struck.
- *Organizational reputation.* As in every aspect of public relations, the reputation of the organization prior to the crisis will play a major role in how the organization manages the crisis and recovers from it. The goodwill of the public is invaluable to an organization.

Crisis Messaging

An organization's friends and supporters can tolerate error, but they will not tolerate lies or arrogance. Crisis communication must show that the organization values their support and that it will communicate honestly and respectfully. In addition to specific facts and attention to legal concerns, keep the following messages in mind:

1. Reassure publics about key points, including safety and security, as well as likelihood of recurrence.
2. Don't attempt to shift blame.
3. Show concern and compassion for injury, death and other loss.
4. Stick to the facts.
5. Avoid speculation. In particular, don't speculate as to the cause or fault for the crisis, nor the financial or other costs involved. While the crisis is going on, it is too early to accurately assess either cause or consequences, and particularly when life and safety are at stake, it is unseemly to speculate about cost.
6. Be candid and honest.
7. "No comment" isn't an option. It implies guilt or cover-up.

8. If you can't comment, indicate why silence is necessary at this time and when you expect to have a comment.
9. Don't minimize the situation. Never characterize a real emergency as a minor incident, and don't point out that other situations may have been worse.
10. Balance the data content of your message with the symbolism and emotion it carries.
11. Try to prevent any unauthorized statements from organizational personnel.
12. Provide timely updates.
13. Communicate with all publics, not only with the media.
14. Try to time your communication program. Giving comment too early means you may not have adequate facts and could appear to be uninformed. Offering comment too late means that the media will release the facts first and you will appear to be hiding information.

Preparing for Crisis

Because crisis is an inevitable fact of life for every organization, preparedness is essential. Here are several aspects of preparing for crisis:

1. *Establish a crisis management team.* Provide training for its members, establish organizational policy for use during a crisis and conduct regular drills.
2. *Develop a crisis management plan.* Include a series of "to do" lists. Also include an outline of both the chain of command and the chair of communication. To implement these procedures, develop information materials such as telephone and e-mail contact lists, media lists, fact sheets and related information.
3. *Conduct regular crisis research.* Identify emerging issues with the potential for crisis. Investigate these issues and respond to them before they reach crisis stage. Even if they do emerge as crises, you will gain the support of your publics by showing that you tried to prevent or minimize them.
4. *Pay attention to rumors.* Listen to "the word on the street," which can serve as part of the early-warning system within the organization.
5. *Be prepared to communicate.* Create a plan for prompt communication with important publics and key constituents.
6. Try to avoid mistakes that lead to crises.

Flow of Information during a Crisis

Consider how each key public receives information during a crisis:

News media

- public relations representative of the organization
- organizational spokesperson or other official
- police, fire or other emergency scanners
- unauthorized "leaks"
- rumor
- eyewitnesses or bystanders with knowledge

- bystanders with hearsay information
- outside "experts"
- organizational and other websites.

Employees, volunteers, clients, students, patients

- direct knowledge
- other employees, volunteers, clients, etc.
- news reports
- organizational and other websites
- e-mail and text messaging
- managers
- rumor.

Supporters, donors, stockholders

- news reports
- e-mail
- letters
- organizational and other websites
- telephone contact
- newsletters
- rumor.

Community residents, public officials

- news reports
- organizational newsletters
- organizational and other websites
- rumor.

Glossary

Number in parenthesis indicates the section in this textbook where the primary reference is located: 0 indicates Introduction, 1–9 indicate steps, letters indicate appendices

academic research (1, A) type of research that generates theory, explores new interests and focuses on universal knowledge (also called **theoretical research**, **basic research** and **pure research**)

acceptance objective (4) second level of objectives, the affective or feeling component, dealing with levels of interest or attitude (compare with **awareness objective** and **action objective**)

accident (5) (*see* **excuse**)

accounts (5) theory that identifies various communication responses to manage relationship in the wake of rebuke or criticism

action metric (9) measure of how a public acts on a message

action objective (4) third and final level of objectives, the conative or behavioral component, dealing with opinion (verbal action) or behavior (physical action)

action strategy (4) category of proactive public relations that involves organizational performance, audience participation, special events, alliances, and coalitions, sponsorships, and strategic philanthropy

active public (3) stage of development in which a public recognizes that it shares an issue with an organization, perceives consequences as being relevant, and is organized to discuss or act

activism (5) confrontational proactive public relations strategy focused mainly on persuasive communication and the advocacy model of public relations

activist (2) type of opponent, similar to an **advocate**, but seeking change rather than focusing on discussion

actuality (7) voice accompanying a news release and providing actual quotes or sound bites; may be cassette or digitized computer download

adaptation (5) willingness and ability of an organization to make changes necessary to create harmony between itself and key publics

administrative research (A) (*see* **applied research**)

advertising (0) persuasive communication through purchased media to promote a product, service or idea on behalf of an identified organization or sponsor

advertising and promotional media (7) category of communication tactics using controlled and paid media

advertising value equivalency (9) type of outputs evaluation focusing on the relative costs that a particular public relations message would carry if instead it had been an advertising message

advertising inserts (7) magazine inserts such as coupons or postcards

advertisorial (7) type of print advertisement that features a series of consecutive pages dealing with a single theme or product/service line

advocate (2) type of opponent that uses mainly vocal tactics against an organization because the advocate supports something else and because the organization appears to stand in the way of the advocate's goal

aerial advertising (7) category of advertising associated with airplanes, including blimps, skywriting and airplane tows

affective component (4) emotional aspect of a public relations objective (see **acceptance objective**)

after-only study (9) type of research design that reviews a situation after a communication project has been implemented (compare with **before-after study**)

agenda-setting theory (5) theory that identifies the relationship between the **media agenda** and **public agenda**, observing that, by reporting an event or focusing on an issue, the media signal to audiences the importance of the event or issue

aggregate (3) non-homogeneous assortment of individuals with little in common (see **audience**)

all-you-can-afford budgeting (8) provides for public relations funding when the organization's financial condition is sound, but limits funding during lean times (compare with **unit-of-sales budgeting** and **percentage-of-sales budgeting**)

alliance (5) informal, loosely structured and often small working relationship among organizations (compare with **coalition**)

analogy (6) persuasion technique and type of verbal evidence using familiar situations and allusions to help an audience understand new ideas

announcement release (7) type of news release, generally dealing with events, personnel, progress, bad news, programs or products (compare with **response releases** and **hometowner releases**)

annual report (7) category of organizational media; type of progress report required by the Securities and Exchange Commission of American companies that issue stock

anonymity (A) research term indicating that a respondent's identity project will not be known by anybody, including the researcher (compare with **confidentiality**)

ANR (7) (*see* **audio news release**)

anti (2) type of opponent that acts as a dissident on a global scale, being against seemingly everything associated with an organization

apathetic public (3) stage of development in which a public is aware of an issue involving an organization but is nevertheless unconcerned about this issue or its potential consequences

apologetics (6) systematic attempt to explain the reasonableness of religious faith and to refute opposing arguments (see **homiletics**)

apologia (5) formal defense that offers a compelling case for an organization's opinions, positions or actions

apology (5) vocal commiseration strategy in which an organization admits sorrow and accepts blame

applied research (A) type of research that deals with practical problems faced by organizations and guides effective resolution of such problems (also called **market research** or **administrative research**)

arena poster (7) billboard-like advertisements on walls and fences of sports arenas, entertainment centers or similar facilities

assistant moderator (A) person in focus group who greets participants and serves as liaison between moderator and client (also called **host**)

association (5) (*see* **excuse**)

Astroturf (6) group that pretends to be grass roots but actually is organized by a corporation with a vested interest in the issue

attack (5) offensive response strategy of claiming that an accusation of wrongdoing is an attempt to impugn the organization's reputation by an accuser who is negligent or malicious

attractiveness (6) aspect of persuasion that focuses on the message source's physical looks, demeanor, poise and presence

audience (3) people who pay attention to a particular medium of communication (compare with **aggregate**)

audience feedback (9) type of acceptance evaluation based on the voluntary reaction of an audience

audio news release (7) news release written and produced specifically for radio stations, presented as an edited story package (abbreviated **ANR**)

authority (6) aspect of persuasion that focuses on an audience's acceptance of a message source's right to rule over or direct its actions

AVE (9) (*see* **advertising value equivalency**)

average (6) term for usual or ordinary instance; statistically this can be a **mean**, **median** or **mode**

aware public (3) stage of development in which a public recognizes that it shares an issue with an organization and perceives consequences as being relevant, but is not yet organized to discuss or act on the issue

awareness evaluation (9) research focusing on the content of a message. Evaluation includes message exposure, message content, readability measures and message recall

awareness objective (4) first level of objectives, the cognitive or thinking component, dealing with levels of information, understanding and retention (compare with **acceptance objective** and **action objective**)

B-roll (7) (*see* **video B-roll**)

backgrounder (7) narrative article providing objective information on an issue

balance theory (6) theory that identifies the tension caused by inconsistent information baseline study (*see* **benchmarking**)

baseline study (9) (*see* **benchmark**)

basic research (A) (*see* **academic research**)

before-and-after study (9) type of research design that reviews a situation before a communication project has been implemented, then investigates the situation after the project is completed (also called **pretest/post-test**; compare with **after-only study**)

benchmark study (1, 9) a specific and measurable standard, against which an organization can compare its own products and services, with an eye toward improving these (also called **baseline study**)

benefit statement (3) part of planning process that articulates a benefit or advantage that a product or service offers a public

best practice (1) method of documenting and analyzing the behavior of an acknowledged leader in the field; involves continuous and systematic research process of measuring an organization and its products or services against the best practices of strong competitors and recognized industry leaders, in order to improve the organization's performance

billboard (7) stationary outdoor advertising sign with changeable messages

biography (7) type of feature release focusing on the background of a person

blame shifting (5) (*see* **denial**)

bleed ad (7) type of print advertisement that eliminates page borders and carries the image to the edge of the paper

blog (7) short for web log—an open-to-all website—usually maintained by an individual

blogger relations (7) subcategory of media relations focusing on journalistic blogs

Boolean logic (A) method of describing the relationship among several items for computer-assisted searches

bottom line (3) term that identifies an organization's mission or fundamental goal

brainstorming (6) group-creativity technique consisting of two steps (*see* **divergence** and **convergence**)

branded clothing (7) promotional items such as T-shirts and hard

branded entertainment (7) (*see* **product integration**)

branding (6) creation of a clear and consistent message for an organization

break-even point (7) level of success required to offset the cost of the development and implementation of a strategic plan; the point beyond which profit begins accruing

breakout ad (7) targeted approach to advertising in national publications, in which an advertiser buys space for copies distributed in a narrow geographic area or to a particular demographic group of subscribers

brochure (7) category of organizational media; stand-alone publication dealing with a particular topic or issue and used for recruiting, product/service lines, membership and other purposes

Glossary

Glossary

budget (8) outline of financial and other resources within a strategic plan, including personnel, material, media costs, equipment and facilities, and administrative costs

bulletin (7) type of organizational publication featuring only headlines and short body text

bursting (8) (*see* **flighting**)

bus sign (7) advertising located on busses, including street-side, curbside, front and back

cable crawl (7) message scrolled across the bottom of a TV screen, often associated with news/weather announcements, sports scores, election returns, and so on

cable television (7) system of TV programming via coaxial or fiber-optic cables

campaign (0) systematic set of public relations activities, each with a specific and finite purpose, sustained over a length of time and dealing with objectives associated with a particular issue (compare with **project** and **program**)

campaign plan book (8) formal written presentation of research findings and program recommendations for strategy, tactics and evaluation

car card (7) advertising placed above windows inside trains and busses

case history (A) (*see* **case study**)

case study (A) qualitative research technique based on the investigation of a single event, product or situation and looking at how an organization has handled it, undertaken for the purpose of understanding and learning from a real-life situation (also called **case history** or **field research**)

casual research (1, A) gathering of information haphazardly and informally

census (A) research study involving every element within a population (compare with **sample**)

center spread (7) type of print advertisement that features two facing pages

charisma (6) aspect of persuasion that focuses on the magnetic appeal or personal charm of a message source (associated with **familiarity**, **likability**, **similarity** and **attractiveness**)

checklist (A) response type allowing respondents to indicate more than one response

citizen journalism (7) (*see* **participatory journalism**)

civil disobedience (5) type of activism that involves nonviolent, nonlegal activities, generally with a strong visual component

claim (6) (*see* **proposition**)

clarity (6) aspect of verbal communication dealing with the ease with which a message can be understood

classified ad (7) type of advertisement common in newspapers featuring brief all-text messages

clipping service (9) company that tracks publications and/or broadcasts and provides evidence that a public relations message has been used

closed-ended item (A) format for survey questionnaire that provides for check-offs to predetermined response categories (compare with **open-ended item**)

cluster sampling (A) probability sampling technique that first subdivides a large and heterogeneous population, breaking into smaller sections before drawing the final sampling; also called **multistage sampling**

coalition (5) formal, structured relationship among organizations (compare with **alliance**)

coder bias (A) potential bias or differing judgments of individual coders in content analysis

cognitive component (4) informational aspect of a public relations objective (*see* **awareness objective**)

cognitive dissonance theory (6) theory that explores the role of psychological discomfort rooted in information that contradicts beliefs, values or attitudes

commercial speech (0) legal term denoting advertising messages

communication manager (0) organizational decision maker, either a **tactical manager** or a **strategic manager**

communication output (9) tactic implemented during a communication campaign, such as fact sheets distributed or news conferences held

communication strategy (5) part of an organization's inventory of proactive strategies focusing on publicity, newsworthy information and transparent communication

communication tactic (7) menu of vehicle that an organization can use to present messages; four categories include **interpersonal communication**, **organizational media**, **news media** and **advertising and promotional media**

communication technician (0) organizational specialist in public relations and marketing communication who performs tasks directed by others

community calendar (7) (*see* **event listing**)

comparison (6) persuasion technique and type of verbal evidence highlighting the characteristics or value related to an issue

competence (6) aspect of persuasion that focuses on the ability of a message source to remain calm under pressure and to be clear and dynamic in presenting the message

competitive parity (8) approach to budgeting based on the cost of similar activity by major competitors

competitor (2) public that is doing the same thing as an organization in the same area, thus competing head-to-head for the same resources

conative component (4) behavioral aspect of a public relations objective (*see* **action objective**)

concern (5) vocal commiseration strategy in which an organization expresses that it is not indifferent to a problem, without admitting guilt

concession (5) diversionary response strategy by which an organization tries to rebuild its relationship with its publics by giving the public something it wants

condolence (5) vocal commiseration strategy in which an organization expresses grief over someone's loss or misfortune, without admitting guilt

confidentiality (A) research term indicating that the identity of a participant in a research project, though known to the researcher, will not be disclosed or linked to a particular response (compare with **anonymity**)

conflict resolution (6) process of dialogue that involves making peace and restoring harmony, with communication as the primary tool

congruity theory (6) theory that adds the aspect of measuring attitudes to consistency theories

conjecture proposition (6) type of proposition stating that something probably exists, based on reasoned conclusion drawn from physical evidence

consensus building (6) process of dialogue that identifies and then prevents or overcomes barriers between people and/or organizations

consistency theory (6) family of theories dealing with the existence or lack of consistent information and the effect of this on message receivers

consumer kit (7) (*see* **user kit**)

consumer magazine (7) type of magazine commonly found at newsstands or obtained through subscriptions

content analysis (A) quantitative research technique based on the unobtrusive and after-the-fact analysis of a set of media artifacts such as a news cast, editorials or articles on a particular topic

context (5) (*see* **justification**)

contingency statement (7) type of public relations writing in which an organization prepares written comment for various potential outcomes of a situation, releasing only that version appropriate to the outcome (also called **standby statement**)

continuity (8) approach to scheduling that presents a message at a consistent level throughout a time period

control (6) aspect of persuasion that focuses on a message source's command over an audience and on the perceived willingness to exercise that power

controlled before-and-after study (9) more sophisticated than **before-and-after study** as takes outside factors into consideration and involves two sample groups drawn from the same key public. One sample is the group to receive the message; the other is a control group that does not receive the message

controlled media (7) media that allow the organization to determine various attributes (compare with **uncontrolled media**)

convenience sampling (A) nonprobability sampling technique that draws subjects because they are readily available to a researcher

convergence (6) part of brainstorming technique for creative problem solving in which a group pares down a list of possible solutions/questions

corporate video (7) (see **nonbroadcast video**)

corrective action (5) rectifying behavior strategy in which an organization takes steps to contain a problem, repair the damage and/or prevent its recurrence

cost per thousand (9) standard measurement for expense of reaching media audiences, calculated not individually but rather as thousands (abbreviated **CPM**)

cost-benefit analysis (8) identifies the cost of implementing a tactic, then compares this cost to the estimated value of the expected results

CPM (9) (*see* **cost per thousand**)

credibility (6, D) aspect of persuasion that focuses on the power to inspire belief, demonstrated through expertise, status, competence and honesty

crisis (D) significant business disruption that stimulates extensive news media coverage, resulting in public scrutiny that affects an organization's normal operations

crisis management (1, D) process by which an organization plans for, deals with and tries to overcome out-of-control issues

customer (3) type of public that receives the product or services of an organization, such as consumers, clients, patients, fans, parishioners, members, etc.

customer satisfaction survey (A) research to help managers understand how customers feel about products and services

cybernetic model of communication (6, 9) theory that identifies a model for two-way communication, moving from sender to receiver and returning via feedback

daypart (7) time period reflecting different audience demographics and usage patterns for television or radio, such as prime time and morning drive time

defamation (6) legal situation in which language (1) is false; (2) is published or communicated to a third party; (3) identifies a person; (4) holds that person up to public hatred, contempt or ridicule; and (5) involves some measure of negligence and/or malice on the part of the communicator

demographic noise (6) communication disruption caused by differences between message sender and receiver based on ethnicity, age, social status, and so on (*see* **noise**)

demographics (3) audience characteristics based on measurable physical criteria such as age, income, education, gender, geography, and so on (compare with **psychographics**)

denial (5) defensive response strategy in which an organization refuses to accept blame by claiming innocence or mistaken identity or by shifting blame

deontological ethics (1) approach to decision making rooted in a standard or moral code, suggesting that certain actions are, in and of themselves, good (compare with **teleological ethics** and **ethical relativism**)

dialogue model (6) conceptual approach to communication that focuses on conscious interaction of two parties in communication for the purpose of mutual understanding

diffusion of innovations theory (3) theory that identifies the role of opinion leaders as models in the process of mass adoption of news products or ideas

digital billboard (7) electronic advertising for advertising and public service purposes

digital media (7) category of organizational media focusing on computer-based electronic media vehicles, such as e-mail, websites, Intranets, etc.

digital radio (7) radio transmitted via satellite, therefore covering far larger areas than conventional terrestrial broadcasting (also called **subscription radio**)

diorama (7) (*see* **station poster**)

direct information subsidy (5, 7) category of news media including information presented to the media in ready-to-use format, such as news releases or feature releases

direct mail (7) category of organizational print media featuring written messages disseminated to individual recipients

direct observation (9) type of action evaluation based on proof of audience activity, such as voting outcome, attendance, sales, and so on

disassociation (5) diversionary response strategy that attempts to distance an organization from wrongdoing associated with it

display ad (7) type of advertisement common in newspapers and magazines, featuring headlines, illustrations and copy blocks

disproportionate sampling (A) approach to stratified sampling in which each demographic group is sized not according to its proportion in the population in order to compensate for its being a small proportion (also called **weighted sampling**)

dissident (2) type of opponent that combats an organization because of positions or actions taken by the organization

divergence (6) part of brainstorming technique for creative problem solving in which a group surfaces a large number of ideas on how to solve a problem or answer a question

doublespeak (6) words and phrases that are deliberately misleading and thus both dishonest and unethical attempts to obscure meaning, violating ethical standards (compare with **pretentious language**)

drawing conclusions (6) presenting the evidence and then explicitly telling the audience how to interpret it

drive-motive theory (3) (see **hierarchy of needs**)

e-mail (7) type of organizational media using computers to transmit memos and letters

editorial conference (7) formal meeting between news sources or organizational representatives with editors and editorial boards of newspapers in order to increase understanding between reporters and organizations and to elicit media support for the organization's agenda

electronic media (7) media delivered primarily through electronic vehicles (compare with **print media**)

element (A) (*see* **unit of analysis**)

embarrassment (5) offensive response strategy of trying to lessen an opponent's influence by using shame or humiliation

enabler (3) type of public that serves as a regulator by setting the norms or standards for an organization, opinion leader, allies or media

endorsement (6) persuasion technique and type of verbal evidence using comments by people who espouse an organization's ideas

engagement metric (9) measure of how publics interact with an organization and each other vis-à-vis an organizational message

environmental scanning (1) process of seeking information in an organization's external environment to help managers chart the organization's future course of action

EPSEM sampling (A) equal probability of sampling methods (see **probability sampling**)

ethical relativism (1) approach to decision making suggesting that actions are ethical to the extent that they reflect particular social norms (compare with **deontological ethics** and **teleological ethics**)

ethos (6) principle identified with Aristotle that focuses on the communication effectiveness based on the character of a speaker and on the common ground shared by speakers and audiences

event listing (7) simple newspaper notice announcing upcoming events (also called **community calendar**)

example (6) persuasion technique and type of verbal evidence providing conclusions drawn from related instances

excuse (5) defensive response strategy in which an organization tries to minimize its responsibility for harm or wrongdoing by citing provocation, lack of control, victimization or mere association

executive summary (9) one- or two-page synopsis of a strategic plan or other report intended as an overview for executives and others who need general information but not details

existing relationships (1) strategic principle of crisis management that an organization should communicate with employees, volunteers, stockholders, community leaders, customers and other groups with which it has an existing relationship in order to strengthen existing support

expertise (6) aspect of persuasion that focuses on the degree to which a message source knows what he or she is talking about (compare with **competence**)

exposure metric (9) measure of how publics have been exposed to a message

external impediment (2) social, political or economic factor outside an organization that might limit the effectiveness of a public relations program (compare with **internal impediment**)

external media (7) media that exist outside of an organization (compare with **internal media**)

extra (7) name for additional feature within a spectacular billboard (*see* **spectacular**)

facilitator (A) (*see* **moderator**)

fact sheet (7) category of organizational media that presents information in bullet form

factual proposition (6) type of proposition stating that something exists, based on provable evidence

false assumption (6) error in logic featuring a conclusion that an audience may not accept

familiarity (6) aspect of persuasion that focuses on the extent to which an audience already knows the message source

fanatic (3) type of zealot opponent without social stabilizers

FAQ (7) presentation of frequently asked questions about a particular issue or organization (*see also* **fact sheet**)

Glossary

fear appeal (6) persuasion technique and type of negative appeal based on anxiety and worry

feature release (7) media release focusing on background info (categories include **history**, **biography**, **backgrounder**, **Q&A**, **service article**)

field research (A) (*see* **case study**)

final report (9) (*see* **summative report**)

fixed fee (8) (*see* **project fee**)

flier (7) category of organizational media; stand-alone publication meant to be read as a single unit

flighting (8) approach to scheduling that presents a message in waves over a period of time (also called **bursting**)

focus group (A) qualitative research technique involving conversation among several participants, guided by a monitor and recorded for later analysis (also called **group interview**)

Fog Index (6, 9) formula to calculate the level of reading difficulty for any piece of writing (also called **Gunning Readability Formula**)

forced-choice item (A) response type allowing respondents to indicate only one response

formal opinion leader (3) opinion leader whose influence is based on structured authority role (compare with **informal opinion leader**)

formative research (1) first phase of strategic planning process, dealing with gathering and analyzing information about the public relations situation, the organization and its publics (also called **situation analysis**)

framing (5) manner in which the media provide a perspective or frame of reference that influences public discourse on a topic

front organization (6) group set up to appear to operate independently, but actually controlled by another organization that wants to remain anonymous in the relationship

full disclosure (1) strategic principle of crisis management that an organization should provide as much information as possible, without admitting fault or speculating about facts not yet known

full-cost budget (8) inclusion within budgets of the value of all items, not only those to be purchased but also those inherent within an organization (such as personnel and overhead) and generated income (such as contributed goods or services, donations, grants and fees)

Gantt chart (8) common type of flow chart listing tactics and associated tasks, with indication of the time needed for each task

gatekeeper (5) media person (such as editor, producer or webmaster) who controls the flow of information in publications, newscasts, and so on

general-interest newspaper (7) publication appealing to diverse interests of wide spectrum of readers

geodemography (A) research technique combining elements of demographics and census data

ghost blogging (7) authoring a blog in someone else's name

goal (4) part of organizational strategy; statement rooted in organization's mission or vision, acknowledging an issue and sketching out how the organization hopes to see it settled

good intention (5) (*see* **justification**)

grabbers (6) (*see* **power words**)

grassroots journalism (7) (*see* **participatory journalism**)

group interview (A) (*see* **focus group**)

guerrilla theater (5) (*see* **street theater**)

guest editorial (7) enhanced letter to the editor, often commissioned by a publication (also called **op-ed piece**)

guilt appeal (6) persuasion technique and type of negative appeal based on shame

Gunning Readability Formula (6) (*see* **Fog Index**)

halo effect (6) phenomenon in which a message is likely to be believed mainly because the source is perceived as credible, charismatic and/or in a position of control over an audience

Hawthorne effect (9) (*see* **placebo effect**)

hearing (A) physical process of sound waves making the eardrums vibrate, stimulating nerve impulses in the brain (compare with **listening**)

hierarchy of needs (3) theory of human motivation that identifies structured levels of human needs, with one needing to be met before another becomes relevant

history (7) type of feature release focusing on the background or history of an organization

hometowner (7) type of news release focusing on announcements about people and disseminated to their home towns

homiletics (6) application of effective communication for preaching (*see* **apologetics**)

honesty (6) aspect of persuasion that focuses on the willingness and ability of a message source to provide full and accurate information, operating without bias

horns effect (6) opposite of **halo effect**

host (A) (*see* **assistant moderator**)

hourly rate plus expenses (8) fee structure for public relations agencies, charging actual time spent plus cost of materials, production and media

house ad (7) type of advertisement placed in performance programs and other publications associated with special events, often focusing simply on corporate identity

house organ (7) (*see* **organizational newspaper**)

how-to piece (7) (*see* **service article**)

human motivation (3) (*see* **hierarchy of needs**)

humor appeal (6) persuasion technique and type of positive emotional appeal based on comedy and amusement

idealism (5) (*see* **justification**)

image restoration (5) theory based on the presumption that, in the face of criticism, both people and organizations seek to maintain or rebuild a positive reputation

implementation report (9) (research report documenting how program tactics are carried out

improvement scale (A) type of research to guide management decisions toward better performance

in-depth interview (A) (*see* **intensive interview**)

inactive public (3) (*see* **latent public**)

indirect information subsidy (7) category of news media including information presented for media guidance but not meant to be published or aired, such as media advisories and announcements of news conferences

inflatable (7) category of advertising using giant outdoor balloons or air-filled promotional items

influence metric (9) measure of the degree to which message exposure and engagement impact on the public's perceptions and attitudes

infomercial (7) program-length television advertisement often packaged as an interview, game show or educational program

informal opinion leader (3) opinion leader whose influence is based on force of personality and circumstance (compare with **formal opinion leader**)

information exchange (7) category of interpersonal communication tactics centering on opportunities for organizations and publics to meet face to face

information model (6) conceptual approach to communication that focuses on the content and channels of communication

information subsidy (7) information from public relations sources that editors use to help underwrite the cost of reporting news

information-seeking publics (7) people who have gone somewhat out of their way to interact with the organization

ingratiation (5) diversionary response strategy in which an organization tries to charm its publics or gives them something of little significance to the organization in an attempt to turn the spotlight away from criticism

innocence (5) (*see* **denial**)

inoculation theory (6) theory that explores the role that persuasive information has on previously unchallenged beliefs and attitudes

integrated communication (0, 7) blending of communication functions within an organization designed to make all aspects of communication work together toward common goals, increasing impact at minimal cost; combination of the concepts and tools of both **public relations** and **marketing communication**

intensive interview (A) qualitative research technique involving lengthy, detailed and systematic interview conducted with several respondents (also called **in-depth interview**)

interactive media (7) communication tactics that allow organizations to send message to an audience and to generate feedback

intercession (3) process of using an influential go-between to link an organization and its public

intercessory public (3) transitional public that serves as a bridge between an organization and other publics

internal impediment (2) obstacles within an organization that might limit the effectiveness of a public relations program (compare with **external impediment**)

internal media (7) media that exist within an organization (compare with **external media**)

internal video (7) (*see* **nonbroadcast video**)

Internet (7) vast computer network linking smaller computer networks worldwide

Internet radio (7) (*see* **online radio**)

interpersonal communication (7) category of communication tactics offering face-to-face opportunities for personal involvement and interaction

interstitial ad (7) computer advertising that insinuates itself on computer users without invitation; also called **pop-up ad** (compare with **superstitial ad**)

interview notes (7) verbatim transcripts presented in a question-and-answer format, based on an interview that a public relations writer has done with an organizational news source

interview training (D) (*see* **media training**)

investigation (5) rectifying behavior strategy in which an organization promises to examine a situation and then to act as the facts warrant

issue (1) situation that presents a matter of concern to an organization; trend, event, development or matter in dispute that may affect an organization

issues management (1) process of monitoring and evaluating information by which an organization tries to anticipate emerging issues and respond to them before they get out of hand

judgment sampling (9) (*see* **purposive sampling**)

judgmental assessment (9) evaluation methodology based on hunches and personal experience

justification (5) defensive response strategy in which an organization admits doing wrong but claims it was for a good reason, citing good intention, context, idealism or mitigation

key public (3) (*see* **strategic public**)

lack of control (5) (*see* **excuse**)

latent public (3) stage of development in which a public shares an issue with an organization but is not yet aware of this fact

lead time (7) amount of time it takes reporters and other media professions to gather and present stories

libel (6) written or broadcast **defamation**

likability (6) aspect of persuasion that focuses on the extent to which an audience admires what it knows about a message source or what it sees and hears when the source begins to communicate

Likert scale (A) popular bipolar scale used in questionnaires to elicit response in categories such as "strongly agree," "agree," "disagree" and "strongly disagree"

limiter (3) type of public that reduces or undermines the success of an organization, including competitors, opponents and hostile forces

linkage (3) patterns of relationships that exist between an organization and its various publics

listening (A) interpersonal process in which a person not only head words but also interprets them, attempting to obtain essentially the same meaning as the sender intended (compare with **hearing**)

listservs (7) electronic mailing lists

logo (6) type of nonverbal communication in which an image identifies an organization

logos (6) principle identified with Aristotle that focuses on communication effectiveness based on rational appeal of messages

long-form television and radio (7) advertising longer than two minutes

love appeal (6) persuasion technique and type of positive emotional appeal based on aspects of love such as family, nostalgia, compassion, sympathy, etc.

magazine (7) category of news media; periodic publication featuring news, commentary and feature information

management by objectives (4) process by which organizations plan their activities based on prior objectives rather than present opportunities (abbreviated **MBO**)

manager (0) (*see* **communication manager**)

margin of error (A) (*see* **sampling error**)

market (3) segment of a population including people with characteristics (age, income, lifestyle, and so on) that can help an organization achieve its consumer-oriented goals

market research (A) (*see* **applied research**)

marketing communication (0) management function that focuses on products and services that respond to the wants and needs of consumers, fostering an economic exchange between the organization and its consumers (compare with **public relations**)

mass media (7) media that are accessible to most people and thus enjoy vast audiences (compare with **targeted media**)

massing (8) bunching of various presentations of a message into a short period of time

mathematical theory of communication (6) theory that identifies a model for one-way communication, moving from sender to receiver

MBO (4) (*see* **management by objective**)

mean (6) type of statistical average calculated by dividing a total by the number of elements (compare with **median** and **mode**)

media advisory (7) type of indirect news material providing media gatekeepers with information about upcoming news opportunities (also called **media alert**)

media agenda (5) topics the media report on (compare with **public agenda**)

media alert (7) (*see* **media advisory**)

media directory (7) books and online resources providing information on media outlets, such as advertising rates, names of editors and publication information

media engagement (D) philosophical and practical ways an organization interacts with news media

media impressions (9) potential total audience of people who could have been exposed to a message presented in a particular medium

media kit (7) collection of materials for reporters attending news conferences and other news-oriented events; includes news releases, biographies, photos, backgrounders, fact sheets, etc. (less accurately called **press kit**)

media relations rating points (9) Canadian standard for evaluating and reporting editorial media coverage

media training (D) type of preparation for organizational spokespersons who will interact with journalists and other publics (also called **interview training**)

media-as-ally (1) strategic principle of crisis management that an organization should treat news media as an ally offering an opportunity to communicate with the organization's publics

median (6) type of statistical average calculated from the middle number on a list (compare with **mean** and **mode**)

memo (7) category of organizational media; brief written message, usually internal to an organization

message cost (9) type of outputs evaluation focusing on the expense associated with the production of a particular message

message distribution (9) type of outputs evaluation focusing on the frequency and manner of message dissemination

message exposure (9) type of awareness evaluation based on the number of people in key purpose who were exposed to a message

message frequency (8) number and pattern of messages presented to a particular public in a given period of time (compare with **message reach**)

message production (9) type of outputs evaluation focusing on the number of messages written or produced

message reach (8) number of different people who are exposed to a single message (compare with **message frequency**)

message recall (9) type of awareness evaluation based on how frequently and accurately audiences remembered a previous advertising or public relations message

minifocus group (A) focus group research with only five or six participants

missionary (2) self-righteous type of activist in support of a cause, often operating under the presumption of moral imperative

mistaken identity (5) (*see* **denial**)

mitigation (5) (*see* **justification**)

mobile billboard (7) painted side of tractor-trailer or delivery trucks, often leased for advertising purposes

mode (6) type of statistical average calculated as the most frequently occurring number (compare with **mean** and **median**)

moderator (A) person who leads a focus group; also called facilitator

MP3 blog (7) type of music blog

MRP (9) (*see* **media relations rating points**)

multiple-choice items (A) questionnaire items with a limited number of responses

multiplier (9) dubious method of calculating the value of publicity as if it were advertising (*see also* **advertising equivalency**)

multistage sampling (A) (*see* **cluster sampling**)

nesting (A) process of forcing search order using Boolean logic for computer-assisted information gathering

network placement (7) use of television advertising at the network level, with distribution through all stations affiliated with the network (compare with **spot advertising**)

network radio (7) same as network placement in reference to radio advertising

networking (3) (*see* **intercession**)

news (5) information that offers an audience a new idea or the latest development; information that involves action, adventure, change, conflict, consequence, contest, controversy, drama, effect, fame, importance, interest, personality, prominence, proximity (*see also* **SiLoBaTi+UnFa**)

news brief (7) type of news releases presenting two or three paragraphs of information

news conference (7) hybrid of speech and group interview used to announce important news to reporters

news fact sheet (7) bulleted presentation of newsworthy information (compare with news release)

news interviews (7) sessions in which journalists ask questions and public relations practitioners or organizational spokespersons respond

news media (7) category of communication tactics using journalistic media

news peg (5) topic that media are already reporting on that also touches on an organization

news release (7) news-type article written by a public relations practitioner and presented to a newspaper or other publication or media outlet; meant to be used either verbatim or as background information (compare with **news fact sheet**)

newsletter (7) category of organizational media; organizational publication combining the informative approach of newspapers with relationship-building features of mail

newspaper (7) category of news media; periodic publication featuring objective news and information; various types include general-interest, trade, special-interest, special-audience and organizational newspapers

niche (2) aspect of an organization's internal environment focusing on the specialty or the unique function or role that makes the organization different from others

noise (6) concept identifying potential interferences with message communication; may be **physical**, **psychological**, **semantic** or **demographic**

nonapology (5) an insincere or halfhearted apology

nonbroadcast video (7) category of organizational media using television technology for internal distribution (also called **corporate video** and **internal video**; compare with **web video**)

nonprobability sampling (A) a series of techniques for selecting samples of a population not based on the principle of probability (categories include **convenience**, **volunteer**, **purposive** and **snowball sampling**)

nonpublic (3) group that does not share any issues with an organization

nonpublic media (7) media that are restricted in their coverage and their availability (compare with **public media**)

nonverbal communication (6) communication occurring through actions and cues other than words (compare with **verbal communication**)

objective (4) part of organizational strategy; statement emerging from an organization's goal, presented in clear and measurable terms, pointing toward particular levels of awareness, acceptance or action (compare with **goal**)

objective-based budgeting (8) approach to budgeting based on established goals and objectives

obstacle (1) public relations situation limiting the organization in realizing its mission (compare with **opportunity**)

one voice (1) strategic principle of crisis management that a single, trained spokesperson or coordinated team of spokespersons should represent the organization by presenting a coordinated message

one-way media (7) communication tactics that allow organizations to send message to an audience without feedback

online focus group (A) focus group research facilitated with software such as Skype

online radio (7) type of radio carrying web-based stations and radio-like music collections (also called **Internet radio** and **streaming radio**)

op-ed piece (7) (*see* **guest editorial**)

open-ended item (A) format for survey questionnaire that allows respondents to answer in their own words (compare with **closed-ended item**)

opinion leader (3) individual with a particular influence on an organization's publics; opinion leaders may be **formal** or **informal**

opponent (2) public that is against an organization

opportunity (1) public relations situation offering a potential advantage to the organization or its publics (compare with **obstacle**)

order of presentation (6) refers to how an argument unfolds; that is, the result of a strategic decision to offer certain bits of information before others

organizational media (7) category of communication tactics using media that are published or produced by organizations, which control the message content as well as its timing, packaging and distribution

organizational newspaper (7) type of newspaper published by an organization or business (also called **house organ**)

out-of-home advertising (7) advertising venues designed to reach people in locations other than home or offices, including billboards, transit and aerial advertising

out-of-home video (7) category of advertising featuring video in public locations such as sports arenas and concert halls

out-take (9) something a public takes away following a public relations engagement

outcome (9) accomplishment of objectives through a public relations engagement

output (9) work done in a public relations activity

outputs evaluation (9) evaluation methodology focusing on communication outputs

over-the-air television (7) (see **terrestrial television**)

paint (7) stationary outdoor advertising sign, also called painted bulletin, with relatively permanent message

participatory journalism (7) category of news reporting associated with bloggers (also called **citizen journalism** and **grassroots journalism**)

pathos (6) principle identified with Aristotle that focuses on communication effectiveness based on emotional appeal of messages

pci (7) (*see* **per column inch**)

per column inch (7) basic unit of measure for print advertising; abbreviated **pci**

per-capita cost (8) association of budgetary expenses with the number of people needed to cover the cost

percentage-of-sales budgeting (8) drawn from the field of marketing, where some companies base their advertising budget on the previous year's profits

performance (2, 5) aspect of an organization's internal environment focusing on the quality of the goods and services provided by the organization, as well as the viability of the causes and ideas it espouses

performance fee (8) fee structure for public relations or advertising agency tying compensation to the achievement of stated objectives

personal involvement (7) action of an organization involving its publics and creating an environment rooted in two-way communication

persuasion model (6) conceptual approach to communication that focuses on ethical attempts to influence people

PERT chart (8) common type of flow chart using circles and arrows to visually display tasks associated with a strategic plan

photo op (5) publicity stunt with visual appeal, designed to attract media coverage in newspapers and magazine, television and online video and photographic venues

physical noise (6) communication disruption caused by use of inefficient communication channels

placebo effect (9) research phenomenon in which change is noted but attributed not to the content of the campaign but rather to the mere fact that participants knew that a campaign was in progress and/or that they were being observed (also called **Hawthorne effect**)

podcasts (7) Internet-based audio feeds that allow users to listen to postings

policy proposition (6) type of proposition identifying a new course of action and encouraging its adoption

polls (A) (*see* **survey**)

pop-up (7) (*see* **interstitial ad**)

popular magazine (7) (*see* **consumer magazine**)

popular media (7) media that focus on information of interest to people in their personal lives (compare with **trade media**)

population (A) research term indicating a large group of subjects that are of interest to a researcher

position paragraph (7) shorter version of a position statement

position statement (4, 7) type of opinion material used by organizations to analyze issues and present formal opinions on issues of public policy (also called **white paper**; compare with **position paragraph**)

positioning (4) process of managing how an organization distinguishes itself with a unique meaning in the mind of its publics

poster (7) generic name for several kinds of outdoor stationary advertisements, including billboards, paints and spectaculars

power (6) aspect of persuasion that focuses on the raw and recognized ability of a message source to dominate and to reward or punish

power words (6) aspect of verbal communication dealing with strong and evocative language (also called **grabber**)

prebuttal (5) term linked to the notion of pre-emptive strike when bad news is inevitable, referring to the practice of an organization announcing its own bad news

prepotency (3) ordered internal relationship among needs by which more basic needs must be addressed first (*see* **hierarchy of needs**)

press packet (7) (*see* **media kit**)

pretentious language (6) words and phrases that imply more than is warranted, thus risking misleading audiences and raising ethical issues (compare with **doublespeak**)

pretest/post-test study (9) (*see* **before-after study**)

primary research (1, A) generation and analysis of new information to address a research question or problem (compare with **secondary research**)

priming (5) manner in which the media set the stage to provide a context for public discourse on a topic

print media (7) media delivered primarily through print vehicles (compare with **electronic media**)

privacy (6) legal right to be left alone

proactive strategy (5) approach to organizational strategy that enables an organization to launch a communication program under the conditions and according to the timeline that seems to best fit the organization's interests (compare with **reactive strategy**)

probability (A) the notion that every element in a population has an equal chance of being selected for a sample

probability sampling (A) series of techniques for selecting samples of a population based on the principle of probability; categories include **simple random**, **systematic**, **stratified** and **cluster sampling** (also called **EPSEM sampling**)

producer (3) type of public that provides input to an organization, including employees, volunteers, suppliers and financial backers

product integration (7) company pays for a commercial product to be woven into a TV or movie storyline (*see* **branded entertainment**)

product name (6) title strategically designed to associate a product with characteristics that are thought to be desirable in the mind of the key public (compare with **program name**)

product placement (7) (*see* **stealth advertising**)

program (0) ongoing public relations activity dealing with several objectives associated with a goal; part of a continuing mission within the organization and focused on its relationship with a particular public (compare with **project** and **campaign**)

program name (6) parallel of a product name for services of both nonprofit organizations and businesses

progress report (9) research report monitoring program tactics at various key points during implementation period

project (0) single and usually short-lived public relations activity designed to meet an objective (compare with **campaign** and **program**)

project fee (8) fee structure for public relations or advertising agency featuring costs associated with specific tasks

propaganda (6) debasement of persuasive communication associated with half-truths and hidden agendas

proportionate sampling (A) approach to stratified sampling in which each demographic group is sized according to its proportion in the population

proposition (6) primary idea in a speech, editorial, advertisement, television program or other communication vehicle; may be a **factual proposition**, **conjecture proposition**, **value proposition** or **policy proposition** (also called **claim**)

provocation (5) (*see* **excuse**)

pseudo-event (5) (*see* **staged activity**)

psychographics (A) audience characteristics based on lifestyle characteristics and interests (compare with **demographics**)

psychological noise (6) communication disruption caused by emotional distractions by the receiver

psychological type (6) concept observing that people have different natural preferences in gathering and processing information, making decisions and acting on those decisions (compare with **temperament**)

public (3) group of people that shares a common interest vis-à-vis an organization, recognizes its significance and sets out to do something about it

public agenda (5) topics the citizenry or media audiences are interested in (compare with **media agenda**)

public media (7) media that are generally accessible by everybody (compare with **nonpublic media**)

public relations (0) strategic communication process that builds mutually beneficial relationships between organizations and their publics; it is part of the management of an organization and includes research, planning, implementation and evaluation (compare with **marketing communication** and **integrated communication**)

public relations audit (2) analysis of the strengths and weaknesses of the public relations concerns of an organization or client

public relations situation (1) set of circumstances facing an organization, whether an **opportunity** or an **obstacle**

publicity (5) aspect of communication strategy that involves the attention given by the news media to an organization

publicity stunt (5) gimmick planned by an organization mainly to gain publicity, having little value beyond attention (compare with **staged activity**)

pulsing (8) approach to scheduling that combines **continuity** and **flighting** approaches, resulting in a continuous base of messages augmented with intermittent bursts of greater communication activity

purdah (5) (*see* **strategic silence**)

pure research (A) (*see* **academic research**)

purposive sampling (A) nonprobability sampling technique that includes subjects simply because they have a particular demographic characteristic (also called **judgment sampling**)

Q&A (7) (*see* **question-and-answer piece**)

qualitative research (9) type of research based on informal methodologies not capable of generating number-based information and conclusions

quantitative research (9) type of research based on formal methodologies, generating number-based information and conclusions

quarterly report (7) category of organizational media published voluntarily to keep stockholders and others informed about an organization's progress

query letter (7) type of indirect news material inquiring whether editors or news directors would be interested in a particular article, particularly one contemplated by a freelance writer or producer

question-and-answer piece (7) type of feature release written in question-and-answer format (also called **Q&A**)

questionnaire (A) instrument used in survey research that presents a series of questions/items and response choices

quick response (1) strategic principle of crisis management that an organization should be as accessible to its publics as possible, aiming to end the crisis as soon as possible

Glossary

quota sampling (A) nonprobability sampling technique that begins with a selection of subjects based on demographic criteria, then continues with other nonprobability techniques

random sampling (A) (*see* **simple random sampling**)

rating scale (A) response technique used in survey questionnaires calling for respondents to rate the degree of their feeling or certainty about an item

reactive strategy (5) approach to organizational strategy in which an organization responds to influences and opportunities from its environment (compare with **proactive strategy**)

readability (6) level of reading difficulty that can be calculated for any piece of writing, allowing the writer to tailor the writing to the abilities of the intended audience

recorder (A) person in a focus group responsible for taking notes

regret (5) vocal commiseration strategy in which an organization admits sorrow and remorse for a situation, without directly admitting fault

reiteration (6) internal repetition of main ideas within a persuasive message

relabeling (5) diversionary response strategy that tries to distance an organization from criticism by offering an agreeable name to replace a negative label applied by others

relationship management goal (4) type of goal focusing on how an organization connects with its publics

repentance (5) rectifying behavior in which an organization demonstrates a change of heart and change in action, signaling full atonement and becoming an advocate for a new way of thinking and acting

reputation (2, D) aspect of an organization's external environment dealing with how people evaluate the information they have about an organization

reputational management goal (4) type of goal dealing with an organization's identity and perception

reputational priorities (1) strategic principle of crisis management that an organization should set objectives to maintain and/or restore credibility, using a crisis as an opportunity to enhance its reputation

research (9) formal program of information gathering (*see* **academic research** and **applied research**)

research design (A) plan for program evaluation that outlines criteria for determination of what to evaluate, based on particular criteria related to objectives

research leader (A) person for articulates the topic, conducts secondary research, selects participants and develops discussion guide for focus group research

response release (7) type of news release that deals with new or updated information, comments, public interest tie-ins and speeches

response strategies (5) category of reactive public relations

restitution (5) rectifying behavior strategy in which an organization makes amends by compensating victims or restoring a situation to its earlier condition

retainer fee (8) structure for public relations or advertising agency featuring fixed monthly rates paid in advance for a predetermined level of agency availability

return on investment (9) ratio of money gained or lost relative to the cost (abbreviated **ROI**)

rhetoric (6) art of using words effectively in speaking and writing for the purpose of influencing, persuading or entertaining

risk management (1) process of identifying, controlling and minimizing the impact of uncertain events on an organization

ROB (7) (*see* **run of book**)

robocall (7) automated telephone call from robots

ROI (9) (*see* **return on investment**)

ROP (7) (*see* **run of press**)

ROS (7) (*see* **run of station**)

rotary paint (7) type of outdoor advertising sign that can be moved from place to place

run of book (7) indication that an advertisement can be placed anywhere within a magazine, compared to special placement (abbreviated **ROB**)

run of press (7) indication that an advertisement can be placed anywhere within a newspaper, compared to special placement (abbreviated **ROP**)

run of station (7) indication that an advertisement can be placed anywhere with a daily cycle for radio advertising, compared with placement on a particular program (abbreviated **ROS**)

salience (4, 6) degree to which information is perceived as being applicable or useful to an audience

same-as-before budgeting (8) looking at how much an organization spent on a similar recent project and allowing the same budget for the new project

sample (A) subset of a population to be studied

sampling (A) research practice of first identifying a subset of a population that reflects and represents the larger body, then using this sample as the basis of study)

sampling bias (A) element within the sampling process that leads to an incomplete or insufficient sample

sampling error (A) extent to which a research sample does not perfectly correspond with its population (also called **margin of error**)

sampling frame (A) actual listing of sampling units

sampling unit (A) conceptualization of individual element within a sample

satellite media tour (7) type of news interview featuring a news source at one location and reporters linked via satellite television from various locations (abbreviated **SMT**)

satellite television (7) system of providing TV signal on TV sets or computers

scrutiny (6) aspect of persuasion that focuses on the ability of a message source to examine or investigate an audience and thus to pronounce blame, proclaim innocence or grant forgiveness

seat-of-the-pants evaluation (9) (*see* **judgmental assessment**)

secondary customer (3) subgroup of customer public that uses the services of the organization's primary customers, such as graduate schools or businesses that receive a college's graduates

secondary research (1, A) re-analyzing existing information obtained by previous researcher for a new and specific purpose (compare with **primary research**)

semantic differential scale (A) type of rating scale asking respondents to select a point on a continuum between two opposing positions

semantic noise (6) communication disruption caused by use of language not understood or appropriately interpreted by the receiver

service article (7) type of feature release providing step-by-step directions and practical information (also called **how-to piece**)

service mark (6) words or phrases developed to be closely associated with specific organizations and protected by law for the use of those organizations

sex appeal (6) persuasion technique and type of positive emotional appeal based on gender, nudity and sexuality

shadow constituency (3) subgroup of customer public involving people who, though they do not have a direct link to the organization's products or services, can affect a public's perception of an organization

shelter poster (7) advertising panels located in or on bus shelters

shock (5) offensive response strategy of deliberately agitating the mind or emotions of publics through the use of surprise, disgust or other strong and unexpected stimulus

shovelware (7) term for the posting of already-published articles from newspapers and magazines in their original print version

signage (7) generic name for range of stationary outdoor signs promoting an organization and its facilities

SiLoBaTi+UnFa (5) acronym identifying the major elements of newsworthy information: significance, local, balance, timely, plus unusual and famous

similarity (6) aspect of persuasion that focuses on the extent to which a message source resembles the audience

simple random sampling (A) probability sampling technique exemplified by a lottery-type drawing

single-issue public (3) may be active on all of the issues important to an organization, active only on some popular issues or active on single and often controversial issues (see **active public**)

situation (1, 2) (see **public relations situation**)

situation analysis (1) (see **formative research**)

situational ethics (1) see **ethical relativism**)

slander (6) spoken **defamation**

slogan (6) catchphrase developed as part of a communication program or campaign (also called **tagline** or **verbal logo**)

smoldering crisis (D) disruption of business that is not generally recognized as potentially generating negative news coverage

SMR (7) (*see* **social media release**)

SMT (7) (*see* **satellite media tour**)

snipe (7) billboard overlay that can update existing poster messages without the need to change the poster completely

snowball sampling (A) nonprobability sampling technique that begins with a small group of individuals with certain demographic characteristics and continues with similar individuals they recommend (also called **sociosampling**)

social judgment theory (6) theory that observes that individuals accept or reject messages to the extent that they perceive the message as corresponding to their beliefs and attitudes

social media release (7) type of news release intended for online use (*see* **blogs** and **websites**)

social networking (7) online service aimed to building and reflecting a relationship among people who share common interests

sociosampling (A) (*see* **snowball sampling**)

sound bite (7) (*see* **actuality**)

speaker's bureau (7) organizational program to promote availability of knowledgeable and trained employees or volunteers to give presentations

special event (5, 7) category of interpersonal communication tactics centering on planned activities created by an organization for the purpose of interacting with its publics

special-audience newspaper (7) type of newspaper focusing particular audience

special-interest newspaper (7) type of newspaper focusing on particular theme or market

spectacular (7) type of billboard featuring an element beyond the standard rectangular surface, sometimes 3-D add-ons, use of lighting with a billboard or other feature

sponsored news (7) organizations use their expertise to present objective and credible information to their publics

sponsorship (5) proactive strategy of offering or supporting programs oriented toward community relations

spot advertising (7) use of television advertising at the local level (compare with **network placement**)

spot radio (7) same as spot advertising in reference to radio

stage-of-life-cycle budgeting (8) examination of the phases of development, knowing that start-up programs generally require more financial resources than maintenance programs (compare with **zero-based budgeting**)

staged activity (5) activity developed or orchestrated by an organization to provide an opportunity to gain attention and acceptance of key publics; also called **pseudo-event** (compare with **publicity stunt**)

stakeholder (3) person or group that relates to an organization through its potential impact on the organization's mission and objectives

standard error of the mean (A) statistic used to describe **sampling error**

standby statement (7) (*see* **contingency statement**)

station poster (7) advertising panels located in subway, train and bus stations and in airport terminals (also called **diorama**)

statistics (6) persuasion technique and type of verbal evidence providing clear and hard-to-dispute facts to make a case

status (6) aspect of persuasion that focuses on the social position or prestige of a message source

stealth ad (7) type of advertising now readily apparent to audiences (see **product placement**)

stereotype (3) oversimplified shortcut to describe groups of people, based on common and repeated perceptions of who people are, how they act and what they think and value

story idea memo (7) type of indirect news material proving media gatekeepers with tips and ideas for feature articles (also called **tip sheet**)

strategic ambiguity (5) refusal to be pinned down to a particular response, often by artfully dodging a question

strategic communication (0) planned communication campaigns associated with public relations or marketing communication, undertaken by an organization, usually for information or persuasive purposes

strategic inaction (6) public relations response strategy of making no statement and taking no overt action, allowing a situation to fade

strategic manager (0) organizational manager who makes decisions concerned with management, trends, issues, policies and corporate structure (compare with **tactical manager**)

strategic news (5) information involving an organization that is of interest to both the news media and the key public

strategic philanthropy (5) proactive strategy in which businesses fund or otherwise support community relations gestures with an eye toward employees and customers

strategic public (3) public with which an organization chooses to engage in communication and relationship (compare with **target public**)

strategic research (1) systematic gathering of information about issues and publics that affect

strategic silence (5) by not responding to criticism an organization may be able to shorten the life span of a crisis situation (also called **purdah**)

strategy (4, 5) organization's overall plan, determining what it wants to achieve and how it wants to achieve it, offering direction in both proactive and reactive organizational activity and messages: theme, source, content and tone (compare with **tactic**)

stratified sampling (A) probability sampling technique that first ranks elements according to demographic factors, then draws elements from each factor using **random** or **systematic sampling** techniques

streaming radio (7) (*see* **online radio**)

streaming video (7) (*see* **nonbroadcast video**)

street theater (5) type of activism that focuses on dramatization in public places (also called **guerrilla theater**)

Streisand effect (5) unintended consequence of creating further publicity for negative information in an attempt to censor it

structure (2) the role public relations plays within the organization's administration

studio interview (7) hybrid of interview and news conference, featuring a media interviewer or host questioning one or more guests or spokespersons

subscription radio (7) (*see* **digital radio**)

sudden crisis (D) disruption of business that occurs without warning (compare with **smoldering crisis**)

summative report (9) research report at conclusion of strategic program, reviewing the impact and outcome of the complete program (also called **final report**)

superstitial ad (7) computer advertising that insinuates itself onto computer screens to fill in time between moves from one site to another (compare with **interstitial ad**)

supporter (2) public that currently or potentially can help an organization achieve its objectives

survey (A) quantitative research technique based on a standard series of questions and yielding statistical results and conclusions (also called **poll**; compare with **questionnaire**)

SWOT analysis (2) strategic planning tool analyzing an organization's strengths, weaknesses, opportunities and threats

symbol (6) type of nonverbal communication in which visual representations point to realities beyond themselves

symbolic consensus (6) tagline that acts as a rallying cry for supporters

symmetry theory (6) theory that extends consistency theory to groups

systematic sampling (A) probability sampling technique involving the selection of subjects spaced at equal intervals (also called **systematic interval sampling**)

tactic (7) visible element of a strategic plan; a specific vehicle of communication

tactical manager (0) organizational manager who makes day-to-day decisions on practical and specific issues (compare with **strategic manager**)

tactical research (1) gathering of information to guide the production and dissemination of messages (compare with **strategic research**)

tagline (6) (*see* **slogan**)

target public (3) term sometimes used as synonymous with strategic public but carrying the connotation that the public is an object of action by an organization rather than a partner in a relationship (compare with **strategic public**)

targeted media (7) media that have narrow and homogeneous audiences (compare with **mass media**)

Glossary

task management goal (4) type of goal concerned with getting certain things accomplished

technician (A) person in focus group responsible for audio- or videotaping

teleconference (7) (*see* **videoconference**)

telefocus group (A) focus group research conducted via telephone conference call

teleological ethics (1) approach to decision making focused on the impact that actions have on people, rooted in the notion that good results come from good actions (compare with **deontological ethics** and **ethical relativism**)

temperament (6) concept observing that people have different approaches and predispositions (compare with **psychological type**)

terrestrial radio (7) AM and FM formats with signals sent via transmitters

terrestrial television (7) TV signal transmitted by radio waves (also called **over-the-air television**)

testimonial (6) persuasion technique and type of verbal evidence using comments by witnesses and by people who have used an organization's products or services

theoretical research (A) (*see* **academic research**)

theory of accounts (5) (*see* **accounts**)

theory of image restoration (5) (*see* **image restoration**)

third-party endorsement (5) concept referring to the added credibility that comes with the endorsement of an outside and unbiased agent, such as a reporter or editor

threat (5) offensive response strategy involving the promise of harm toward an accuser

timeline (8) implementation schedule for strategic plan

tip sheet (7) (*see* **story idea memo**)

trade media (7) media that focus on information of interest to people in their professional lives (compare with **popular media**)

trade newspaper (7) category of newspapers with focus on particular industry or profession

transit advertising (7) category of advertising on vehicles, including bus signs and mobile billboards

transparent communication (5) concept of proactive public relations strategy referring to open and observable activity by an organization that helps publics understand the organization and support its actions

triad (A) focus group with only three participants

triggering event (5) activity that generates action among key publics

two-step flow of communication theory (3) theory that identifies opinion leaders as a key link in the process of organizational communication with publics

uncontrolled media (7) media that limit or eliminate an organization's ability to determine various attributes (compare with **controlled media**)

unique selling proposition (6) niche statement about a produce, service or organization that distinguishes it from competitors (abbreviated **USP**)

unit of analysis (A) individual element of a population being studied

unit-of-sales budgeting (8) based not on dollars but on prior outcomes

unobtrusive research (9) where the subjects in a study do not know they are being observed

unwarranted conclusion (6) error in logic based on a deduction not supported by evidence

user kit (7) organizational print material providing background and how-to information for consumers

USP (6) (*see* **unique selling proposition**)

value proposition (6) aspect of logical persuasive appeal arguing the virtue or merits of something

verbal communication (6) communication occurring through written and spoken words (compare with **nonverbal communication**)

verbal evidence (6) type of proof claim in a discussion or argument based not on physical evidence but rather on words and ideas

verbal logo (6) (*see* **slogan**)

victimization (5) (*see* **excuse**)

video B-roll (7) sound bites and raw, unedited footage provided to television stations to use in news reports

video focus group (A) focus group research conducted via teleconference

video news release (7) news release written and produced specifically for television stations, presented as an edited story package (abbreviated **VNR**)

video wall (7) out-of-home advertising venue with ever-moving series of computer-generated images

videoconference (7) television technology used to produce live informational or educational programs for remote audiences; also called **teleconference**

viral philanthropy (7) type of fundraising in which many people are asked to donate and encourage their friends to do likewise

virtual ads (7) advertising that is digitally inserted for the TV audiences, such as product billboards that appear in the background during a televised sporting event

virtue appeal (6) persuasion technique and type of positive emotional appeal based on values that individuals and society hold in esteem

visibility (2) aspect of an organization's external environment focusing on the degree to which its publics know about the organization and the accuracy of that information

vlog (7) blog that primarily consists of video

VNR (7) (*see* **video news release**)

vocal activist (3) type of opinion leader who is linked with a particular issue and/or who acts as an advocate for a cause

vocal commiseration (5) response strategy of expressing concern, condolence, regret or apology

volunteer sampling (A) nonprobability sampling technique that draws subjects who willingly offer themselves to be part of a study

Glossary

wall mural (7) type of outdoor advertising featuring the painted exterior of a building leased for advertising purposes (also called **wallscape**)

web 1.0 (7) one-way use of Internet technology to post commercial or promotional information

web 2.0 (7) interactive use of Internet technology to allow users to share postings and generate content for a website

web video (7) (*see* **nonbroadcast video**)

web-only commercials (7) video advertisements produced for and used only on the Internet

website (7) set of interconnected web pages, usually prepared and maintained as a collection of information by a person, group or organization

weighted sampling (A) (*see* **disproportionate sampling**)

what-if-not-funded analysis (8) approach to budget that examines consequences of inaction and their effect on the organization's mission

white paper ((7) (*see* **position statement**)

wiki (7) collaborative website where all users can edit and update content

wildcard (A) character used in Boolean search to identify root words and various endings

word-of-mouth support (3) effective type of communication relying on opinion leaders

zealot (2) single-issue activist acting with missionary fervor

zero-based budgeting (8) approach to budgeting based on current needs rather than past expenditures

Citations and
Recommended Readings

Introduction

Austin, E. W. and Pinkleton, B. E. (2006). *Strategic public relations management: Planning and managing effective communication programs* (2nd ed.). Mahwah, NJ: Erlbaum.

Blakeman, R. (2007). *Integrated marketing communication: Creative strategy from idea to implementation*. Lanham, MD: Rowman & Littlefield.

Botan, C. H. (1997). Ethics in strategic communication campaigns: The case for a new approach to public relations. *Journal of Business Communication*, 34(2), 188–202.

Botan, C. H. and Soto, F. (1998). A semiotic approach to the internal functioning of publics: Implications for strategic communication and public relations. *Public Relations Review*, 24(1), 21–44.

Burnett, J. and Moriarty, S. (1998). *Introduction to marketing communications: An integrated approach*. Upper Saddle River, NJ: Prentice Hall.

Caywood, C. L. (1995). *International handbook of public relations and corporate communications*. Hillsdale, NJ: Erlbaum.

Caywood, C. L. (1997). *The handbook of strategic public relations and integrated communications*. New York: McGraw-Hill.

Clow, K. E. and Baack, D. E. (2006*). Integrated advertising, promotion and marketing communications* (3rd ed.). Upper Saddle River, NJ: Prentice Hall.

Crifasi, S. C. (September 2000). Everything's coming up Rosie. *Public Relations Tactics*, 7(9).

Cutlip, S. M., Center, A. H. and Broom, G. M. (2012). Effective public relations (11th ed.). Upper Saddle River, NJ: Prentice Hall.

Goldman, J. (1984). *Public relations in the marketing mix: Introducing vulnerability relations*. Lincolnwood, IL: NTC Business.

Gray, R. (1998, June 11). PR does the business. *Marketing*, 24–26.

Gronstedt, A. (2000). *The customer century: Lessons from world class companies in integrated marketing and communications*. New York: Routledge.

Grunig, J. E. (Ed.) (1992). *Excellence in public relations and communication management*. Hillsdale, NJ: Erlbaum.

Grunig, J. E. and Hunt, T. (1984). *Managing public relations*. New York: Holt, Rinehart, & Winston.

Harris, T. L. (2000). *Value added public relations: The secret weapon of integrated marketing*. Chicago, IL: NTC Business.

Harris, T. L. and Whalen, P. T. (2006). *The marketer's guide to public relations in the 21st century*. Mason, OH: Thomson/South-Western Educational.

Hendrix, J. and Hayes, D. C. (2009). *Public relations cases* (8th ed.). Belmont, CA: Wadsworth.

Hiebert, R. W. (2000, Fall). The customer century: Lessons from world class companies in integrated marketing and communications. *Public Relations Review*, 26(3), 381.

Holmes, P. (1998, September 28). With Bell's appointed, Y&R's commitment to integration now goes beyond lip service. *Inside PR*, 5(9), 2, 10.

Italian American stereotypes in U.S. advertising (Summer 2003). Washington, DC: Order of Sons of Italy in America.

Kelly, K. S. (2001). Stewardship: The fifth step in the public relations process. In R. I. Heath and G. M. Vasquez (Eds.), *Handbook of public relations* (pp. 279–290). Thousand Oaks, CA: Sage.

Kendall, R. (1997). *Public relations campaign strategies: Planning for implementation* (2nd ed.). New York: Addison-Wesley.

Kitchen, P. J. and Schultz, D. E. (1999). A multi-country comparison of the drive for IMC. *Journal of Advertising Research*, 39(7), 21–38.

Kotler, P., Roberto, N. and Lee, N. (2002). *Social marketing: Improving the quality of life* (2nd ed.). Thousand Oaks, CA: Sage.

Ledingham, J. A. and Bruning, S. D. (2001). Community relations. In R. L. Heath (Ed.), *Handbook of Public Relations* (527–534). Thousand Oaks, CA: Sage.

Marston, J. E. (1963). *The nature of public relations*. New York: McGraw-Hill.

McElreath, M. (1997). *Managing systematic and ethical public relations campaigns* (2nd ed.). Madison, WI: Brown & Benchmark.

Nemec, R. (1999). PR or advertising: Who's on top? *Communication World*, 16(3), 25–28.

Newsom, D., VanSlyke Turk, J. and Kruckeberg, D. (2006). *This is PR: The realities of public relations* (9th ed.). Belmont, CA: Wadsworth.

Ostrowski, H. (1999). Moving the measurement needle. *Public Relations Strategist*, 5(2), 37–39.

Parkinson, M. and Ekachai, D. G. (2005). *International and intercultural public relations: A campaign case approach*. Boston: Allyn and Bacon.

PRSA (2006). State of the PR Profession Opinion Survey. www.prsa.org/SearchResults/view/2D-0008/0/2006_State_of_the_PR_Profession_Opinion_Survey.

PRSA (2011a). State of the Society. Retrieved August 27, 2012 from www.prsa.org/AboutPRSA/StateOfTheSociety.

PRSA (2011b) Business Leaders Survey. Retrieved August 27, 2012 from www.prsa.org/Intelligence/BusinessCase/MBAInitiative/PRSA%20Business%20Leaders%20Survey.

Ries, A. and Ries, G. (2002). *The fall of advertising and the rise of PR*. New York: HarperCollins.

Ross, B. I. and Richards, J. I. (Eds.) (2008). *Where shall I go to study advertising and public relations? Advertising and public relations programs in the United States colleges and universities*. Lubbock, TX: Advertising Education Publications.

Scheufele, D. A. (1999) Framing as a Theory of Media Effects. *Journal of Communication*, 49(4), 103–122.

Schultz, B., Caskey, P. and Esherick, C. (2009). *Media relations in sport* (3rd ed.). Morgantown, WV: Fitness Information Technology.

Schultz, D. E., Tannenbaum, S. I. and Lauterborn, R. F. (1993). *Integrated marketing communications: Pulling it together and making it work*. Lincolnwood, IL: NTC Business.

Seitel, F. P. (2006). *The practice of public relations* (10th ed.). Upper Saddle River, NJ: Prentice Hall.

Sirgy, M. J. (2004). *Integrated marketing communications: A systems approach*. Upper Saddle River, NJ: Pewarson.

Wilcox, D. L., Ault, P. H., Agee, W. K. and Cameron, G. T. (2005). *Public relations: Strategies and tactics* (8th ed.). New York: Longman.

Wilson, L. (2000). *Strategic program planning for effective public relations campaigns* (3rd ed.). Dubuque, IA: Kendall-Hunt.

Zappala, J. and Carden, A. R. (2004). *Public relations worktext: A writing and planning resource.* Mahwah, NJ: Erlbaum.

Phase One

Aguilar, F. J. (1967). *Scanning the business environment.* New York: Macmillan.

Bakhsheshy, A. (2003). Chapter 5. Retrieved from www.business.utah.edu~mgtab.

Boe, A. R. (1979). Fitting the corporation to the future. *Public Relations Quarterly*, 24, 4–6.

Chang, Mitchell. (2010) The State of Asian American, Native Hawaiian and Pacific Islander Education in California. University of California, Asian American and Pacific Islander Policy Multicampus Research Program.

Chase, W. H. (1977). Public issue management: The new science. *Public Relations Journal*, 33(10), 25–26.

Cuddeford-Jones, M. (2002, March). Brand redemption and risk management: Morag Cuddeford-Jones asks if it is possible for brands to redeem themselves after a PR disaster. *Brand Strategy*, p. 10.

Dearing, J. W. and Rogers, E. M. (1996). *Communication concepts 6: Agenda-setting.* Thousand Oaks, CA: Sage.

Dewey, J. (1927). *The public and its problems.* Chicago, IL: Swallow.

Esman, M. J. (1972). The elements of institution building. In J. W. Eaton (Ed.), *Institution building and development* (pp. 78–90). Beverly Hills, CA: Sage.

Evan,W. H. (1976). *Interorganizational relations.* New York: Penguin.

Ewing, R. P. (1997). Issues management: Managing trends through the issues life cycle. In C. C. Caywood (Ed.), *The handbook of strategic public relations and integrated communications* (pp. 173–188). New York: McGraw-Hill.

Finn, D. (1998). How ethical can we be? Retrieved from www.ruderfinn.com/persp/how_ethical.html

Grunig, J. E. and Hunt, T. (1984). *Managing public relations.* New York: Holt, Rinehart & Winston.

Hart, R. (2006, April). Measuring success: How to "sell" a communications audit to internal audiences. *Public Relations Tactics*, 13(4).

Hedrick, T. E., Bickman, L. and Rog, D. J. (1993). *Applied social research methods; Vol. 32, Applied research design: A practical guide.* Newbury Park, CA: Sage.

Italian American stereotypes in U.S. advertising (Summer 2003). Washington, DC: Order of Sons of Italy in America.

Jackson, P. (Ed.) (1994). *Practical, actionable research for public relations purposes.* Exeter, NH: PR Publishing.

Jones, B. L. and Chase, W. H. (1979). Managing public policy issues. *Public Relations Review*, 5, 2–23.

Klein, P. (1999). Measure what matters. *Communication World*, 16(9), 32.

Lauzen, M. (1997). Understanding the relation between public relations and issues management. *Journal of Public Relations Research*, 9(1), 65–82.

Lazarsfeld, P. F., Berelson, B. and Gaudet, H. (1944). *The people's choice.* New York: Columbia University Press.

Ledingham, J. A. and Bruning, S. D. (2000). *Public Relations as relationship management: A relationship approach to the study and practice of public relations.* Mahwah NJ: Erlbaum.

Lippmann, W. (1922). *Public opinion.* New York: Macmillan.

Readings

Lukaszewski, J. E. (1997). Establishing individual and corporate crisis communication standards: The principles and protocols. *Public Relations Quarterly*, 42, 7–14.

Martin J. (2008, June 1). Miss Manners. Syndicated column. *Washington Post*.

Maslow, A. (1987). *Motivation and personality* (3rd ed.). Boston, MA: Addison-Wesley.

Matera, F. R. and Artigue, R. J. (2000). *Public relations campaign and techniques: Building bridges into the 21st century*. Boston: Allyn & Bacon.

Mau, R. R. and Dennis, L. B. (1994). Companies ignore shadow constituencies at their peril. *Public Relations Journal*, 50(5), 10–11.

Morton, L. P. (2002a). Targeting Native Americans. *Public Relations Quarterly*, 47(1), 37.

Morton, L. P. (2002b). Targeting Generation Y. *Public Relations Quarterly*, 47(2), 46.

Nisbet, M. C. and Kotcher, J. E. (March 2009). A two-step flow of Influence? Opinion-leader campaigns on climate change. *Science Communication*, 30(3), 329–354.

Opinion leaders. New study outlines how to reach them. (1992, October 5). *PR Reporter*, 35(38), 1–3.

Packard, V. (1964). *The hidden persuaders*. New York: Pocket Books.

Rawlins, B. L. (2006). *Prioritizing stakeholders for public relations*. New York: Institute for Public Relations Research.

Regester, M. and Larkin, J. (2005). *Risk issues and crisis management* (3rd ed.). London: Kogan Page.

Rogers, E. (2003). *The diffusion of innovations* (5th ed.). New York: Free Press.

Salmon, R. and De Linares, Y. (1999). *Competitive intelligence: Scanning the global environment*. Bucharest, Romania: Economica.

Sandman, P. (2003). Stakeholders. Retrieved August 27, 2012 from www.petersandman.com/col/stakeh.htm

Schwartz, P. and Gibb, B. (1999). *When good companies do bad things: Responsibility and risk in an age of globalization*. New York: Wiley.

Tsai, M., Veziroglu, A, Warren, S. and Que, Y. (2006) New energy opinion leaders' lifestyles and media usage. Proceedings of the International Conference on Emerging Nuclear Energy Systems.

Zaharna, R.S., Hammad, A.I. and Masri, J (2009) Palestinian public relations: Inside and out, in K. Sriramesh and D. Vercic (Eds.). *The handbook of global public relations theory, research, and practice. Vol. 2*. London: Routledge, 220–242.

Phase Two

Barlow, W. G. (1995). *Establishing public relations objectives and assessing public relations results*. Gainesville, FL: Institute for Public Relations Research.

Barnhurst, K. G. and Mutz, D. (1997). American journalism and the decline in event-centered reporting. *Journal of Communication*, 47(4), 27–53.

Benjamin, J. (1997). *Principles, elements, and types of persuasion*. Fort Worth, TX: Harcourt Brace.

Benoit, W. L. (1995). *Accounts, excuses, and apologies: A theory of image restoration strategies*. SUNY Series in Speech Communication. Albany, NY: State University of New York Press.

Berlo, D. (1960). *The process of communication: An introduction to theory and practice*. San Francisco, CA: Rinehart.

Botan, C. (1997). Ethics in strategic communication campaigns: The case for a new approach to public relations. *Journal of Business Communication*, 34(2), 188–202.

Bouchez, Colette. (n.d.) Hollywood takes action on health. Retrieved August 27, 2012 from http://men.webmd.com/features/hollywood-takes-action-on-health.

Buber, M. (1947). *Between man and man*. London: Routledge & Kegan Paul. Reprinted in F. W. Matson and A. Montagu (Eds.). (1967). *The human dialogue: Perspectives on communication*. New York: Free Press.

Christians, C. G., Fackler, M., Richardson, K. B. and Rotzoll, K. B. (2011). *Media ethics: Cases and moral reasoning* (9th ed.). New York: Longman.

Cody, M. J. and McLaughlin, M. L. (1985). Models for the sequential construction of accounting episodes: Situational and interactional constraints on message selection and evaluation. In R. L. Street and L. Capella (Eds.), *Sequence and pattern in communication behavior* (pp. 50–69). London: Edward Arnold.

Cody, M. J. and McLaughlin, M. L. (1990). Interpersonal accounting. In H. Giles and W. P. Robinson (Eds.), *Handbook of language and social psychology* (pp. 227–255). Chichester, England: Wiley.

Commentary: It's time to put the *Valdez* behind us (1999, March 29). *Business Week*.

Delwiche, A. (n.d.) *Fear*. Retrieved August 27, 2012 from propagandacritic.com/articles/ct.sa.fear.html.

Edelman Change and Employee Engagement, in partnership with PeopleMetrics. (2006). New frontiers in employee communications. Retrieved August 27, 2012 from www.edelman.com/news/story crafter/uploads/NewFrontiers2006_Finalpaper.pdf.

Fearn-Banks, K. (2007). *Crisis communications: A casebook approach* (3rd ed.). Mahwah, NJ: Erlbaum.

Festinger, L. (1957). *A theory of cognitive dissonance*. Stanford, CA: Stanford University Press.

Fitzpatrick, K. R. and Rubin, M. S. (1995). Public relations vs. legal strategies in organizational crisis decisions. *Public Relations Review*, 21(1), 21–33.

Goffman, E. (1974). *Frame analysis: An essay on the organization of experience*. London: Harper & Row.

Gottschalk, J. A. (Ed.) (1993). *Crisis response: Inside stories in managing image under siege*. Detroit, MI: Gale Research.

Hammad, A.I. (2005). Theory and practice of public relations in the governmental organizations of Palestine: The fashioning of the national image in a non-sovereign state. (Unpublished dissertation, Aristotle University, Thessaloniki, Greece).

Hearit, K. M. (1994). Apologies and public relations crises at Chrysler, Toshiba, and Volvo. *Public Relations Review*, 20(2), 113–125.

Heath, R. L. (1997). *Strategic issues management: Organizations and public policy challenges*. Thousand Oaks, CA: Sage.

Heider, F. (1946). Attitudes and cognitive organization. *Psychological Review*, 51, 358–374.

Heider, F. (1958). *The psychology of interpersonal relations*. New York: Wiley.

Hon, L. C. (1998). Demonstrating effectiveness in public relations: Goals, objectives, and evaluation. *Journal of Public Relations Research*, 10(2), 103–135.

Infante, D., Rancer, A., & Avtgis, T. (2009). *Contemporary communication theory*. Dubuque, IA: Kendall-Hunt.

Infante, D. A., Rancer, A. S. and Womack, D. F. (2003). *Building communication theory* (4th ed.). Prospect Heights, IL: Waveland.

Iyengar, S. and Kinder, D. R. (1987). *News that Matters: Television and American opinion*. American Politics and Political Economy. Chicago, IL: University of Chicago Press.

Jackson, P. (Ed.) (1997). Items of importance to practitioners. *PR Reporter*, 40(46), 3.

Jenkins, P. (2003). *The new anti-Catholicism: The last acceptable prejudice*. New York: Oxford University Press.

Johnston, D. D. (1994). *The art and science of persuasion*. Boston: McGraw-Hill.

Juice-Poisoning Case Brings Guilty Plea and a Huge Fine. (1998, July 24). *New York Times*.

Readings

Keirsey, D. (1998). *Please understand me II: Temperament, character, intelligence.* Del Mar, CA: Prometheus Nemesis.

Kelly, J. A., St. Lawrence, J. S., Diaz, Y. E., Stevenson, L. Y., Hauth, A. C., Brasfield, T. L., et al. (1991). HIV risk behavior reduction following intervention with key opinion leaders of a population: An experimental community-level analysis. *American Journal of Public Health*, 81, 168–171.

Kelly, J. A., St. Lawrence, J. S., Stevenson, L. Y., Hauth, A. C., Kalichman, S. C., Diaz, Y. E., et al. (1992). Community AIDS/HIV risk reduction: The effects of endorsement by popular people in three cities. *American Journal of Public Health*, 82, 1483–1489.

Kotler, P., Roberto, N. and Lee, N. (2007). *Social marketing: Influencing behaviors for good* (3rd ed.). Thousand Oaks, CA: Sage.

Kowalski, R. M. and Erickson, J. R. (1997). Complaints and complaining: Functions, antecedents and consequences. *Psychological Bulletin*, 119(2), 179–196.

Larson, C. U. (2000). *Persuasion: Reception and responsibility* (9th ed.). Belmont, CA: Wadsworth.

Larson, R. J., Woloshin, S., Schwartz, L. M. and Welch, H. G. (2005, May 4). Celebrity Endorsements of Cancer Screening. *Journal of the National Cancer Institute*, 97(9), 693–695.

Lasswell, H. D. (1948). The structure and function of communication in society. In L. Bryson (Ed.), *The communication of ideas* (p. 34). New York: Harper.

Lee, F., Peterson, C. and Tiedens, L. (2004). Mea culpa: Predicting stock prices from organizational attributions. *Personality and Social Psychology Bulletin*, 30(12), 1636–1649.

Leiserowitz, A., Smith, N. and Marlon, J.R. (2010). *Yale Project on Climate Change Communication: Americans' knowledge of climate change.* New Haven, CT: Yale University. Retrieved August 27, 2012 from http://environment.yale.edu/climate/files/ClimateChangeKnowledge2010.pdf.

Lipstein, B. (1985). An historical retrospective of copy research. *Journal of Advertising Research*, 24(6), 11–14.

The Lives We Touch. (1992). In J. A. Hendrix, *Public relations cases* (2nd ed.). Belmont, CA: Wadsworth.

Macdaid, G. P., McCaulley, M. H. and Kainz, R. I. (1986). *MBTI Atlas of Type Tables* (2 vols.). Gainesville, FL: Center for Applications in Psychological Type.

Marconi, J. (1996). *Image marketing: Using public perceptions to attain business objectives.* Lincolnwood, IL: NTC/Business.

Martin, J. (1999, May 10). Miss Manners. Syndicated column.

Martinelli, K. A. and Briggs, W. (1998, Winter). Integrating public relations and legal responses during a crisis: The case of Odwalla, Inc. *Public Relations Review*, 20, 443–460.

Martosko, D. (2005). *Holy cows: How PETA twists religion to push "animal rights."* Washington, DC: Center for Consumer Freedom.

McCombs, M. E. and Shaw, D. L. (1972). The agenda-setting function of mass media. *Public Opinion Quarterly*, 36, 176–187.

McGuire, W. J. and Papageorgis, D. (1961). The relative efficacy of various types of prior belief defense in producing immunity against persuasion. *Journal of Abnormal and Social Psychology*, 62, 327–337.

Miciak, A. R. and Shanklin, W. L. (1994). Choosing celebrity endorsers: The risks are real, but sports and entertainment spokespersons still burnish corporate images and sell brands. *Advertising Management*, 3(3), 51.

Minogue, S. (2003, June 30). How can you get the most marketing value out of CSR? *Strategy*, 18.

Myers, I. B. (1987). *Introduction to type.* (Rev. A. L. Hammer.) Gainesville, FL: Center for Applications of Psychological Type.

Myers, I. B. and Myers, P. B. (1980). *Gifts differing: Understanding personality type*. Palo Alto, CA: Consulting Psychologists Press.

Nager, N. R. and Allen, T. H. (1984). *Public relations management by objectives*. Lanham, MD: University Press of America.

Newcomb, T.M. (1953). An approach to the study of communicative acts. *Psychological Review*, 60, 393–404.

Nyer, P. U. (1999). Cathartic complaining as a means of reducing consumer dissatisfaction. *Journal of Consumer Satisfaction, Dissatisfaction and Complaining Behavior*, 12, 15–25.

Nyer, P. U. (2000). An investigation into whether complaining can cause increased consumer satisfaction. *Journal of Consumer Marketing*, 17(1), 9–19.

Osgood, C. E. and Tannenbaum, P. H. (1955). The principle of congruity in the prediction of attitude change. *Psychological Review*, 62, 42–55.

Pfau, M. and Parrott, R. (2001). *Persuasive communication campaigns*. Boston, MA: Pearson.

Pharma Opinion Leaders. (2003, November 11). *PR Newswire*.

Rank, H. (1976). Teaching about public persuasion. In D. Dieterich (Ed.), *Teaching and doublespeak* (pp. 3–19). Urbana, IL: NCTE.

Ray, M. (1973). Marketing communication and the hierarchy of effects. In P. Clarke (Ed.), *New models for communication research* (pp. 147–176). Newbury Park, CA: Sage.

Ries, A. and Trout, J. (2001). *Positioning: The battle for your mind*. New York: McGraw-Hill.

Rogers, E. (2003). *The diffusion of innovations* (5th ed.). New York: Free Press.

Roser, C. and Thompson, M. (1995). Fear appeals and the formation of active publics. *Journal of Communication*, 45(1), 103–119.

Ross, R. S. (1994). *Understanding persuasion* (4th ed.). Englewood Cliffs, NJ: Prentice Hall.

Scheufele, D. (1999). Framing as a theory of media effects. *Journal of Communication*, 49(1), pp. 103–122.

Schramm, W. (1971). The nature of communication between humans. In W. Schramm and D. F. Roberts (Eds.), *The process and effects of mass communication*. Urbana, IL: University of Illinois Press.

Schreiber, A. L. (1994). *Lifestyle and event marketing: Building the new customer partnership*. New York: McGraw-Hill.

Seideman, T. (1997, May/June). Nonprofit prophets. *Reputation Management*, 46–53.

Shannon, C. E. and Weaver, W. (1949). *The mathematical theory of communication*. Urbana, IL: University of Illinois Press.

Sherif, M. and Hovland, C. I. (1961). *Social judgment*. New Haven, CT: Yale University Press.

Sieberg, E. (1976). Confirming and disconfirming organizational communication. In J. L. Owen, P. A. Page and G. I. Zimmerman (Eds.), *Communication in organizations*. St. Paul, MN: West.

Simons, H. W., Morreale, J. and Gronbeck, B. (2001). *Persuasion in society*. Thousand Oaks, CA: Sage.

Smith, R. D. (1993). Psychological type and public relations: Theory, research, and applications. *Journal of Public Relations Research*, 5(3), 177–199.

Smith, R. D. (2012). *Becoming a Public Relations Writer: A Writing Workbook for Emerging and Established Media* (4th ed.). New York: Routledge.

Sperry, R. W. (1985). Consciousness, personal identity and the divided brain. In D. F. Benson and E. Zaidel (Eds.), *The dual brain: Hemispheric specialization in humans*. UCLA Forum in Medical Sciences, No. 26. New York: Guilford Press.

Stewart, C. J., Smith, C. A. and Denton, R. E. (2001). *Persuasion and social movements* (4th ed.). Prospect Heights, IL: Waveland.

Readings

Sugimoto, N. (1997). A Japan-U.S. comparison of apology styles. *Communication Research*, 24(4), 349–370.

Wiener, N. (1954). *The human use of human beings: Cybernetics and society* (2nd ed.). Boston, MA: Houghton Mifflin.

Wild, C. (1993). *Corporate volunteer programs: Benefits to businesses. Report 1029.* New York: Conference Board.

Young, D. (1996). *Building your company's good name: How to create and protect the reputation your organization wants and deserves.* New York: American Management Association.

Zaharia, R.S., Hammad, A.I. and Masri, J. (2009) Palestinian public relations: Inside and out. In Sriramesh, K. and Vercic, D. (Eds.), *The global public relations handbook: Theory, research, and practice.* New York: Routledge.

Phase Three

Amos, J. S. (1995). *Fundraising ideas: Over 225 money making events for community groups, with a resource directory.* Jefferson, NC: McFarland.

Armstrong, J.J. (2007, October). Don't touch that dial! Using long-form TV and radio programs to send health messages. In *Public Relations Tactics*, 14 (10), 15.

Brogan, K. S. (Ed.) (2007). *2008 writer's market.* Cincinnati, OH: Writer's Digest Books.

Brown, M. S. (Ed.) (2008). *Giving USA, 2008* (53rd ed.). Glenview, IL: Giving USA Foundation.

Bulldog Reporter and TEKgroup International (2010, October). *2007 journalist survey on media relations practices.* Pompano Beach, FL: Bulldog Reporter/TEKgroup International.

Cameron, G. T. (1994). Does publicity outperform advertising? An experimental test of the third-party endorsement. *Journal of Public Relations Research*, 6 (3), 185–207.

Corder L., Deasy, M. and Thompson, J. (1999a, Spring). *PR is to experience what marketing is to expectations.* Public Relations Quarterly, 44 (1), 23–26.

Corder L., Deasy, M. and Thompson, J. (1999b, May). Answering the age-old marketing question: What have you done for me lately? *Public Relations Tactics*, 12.

Curtain, P. A. (1999). Reevaluating public relations information subsidies: Market-driven journalism and agenda-building theory and practice. *Journal of Public Relations Research*, 11 (1), 53–90.

Edelman Change and Employee Engagement, in partnership with PeopleMetrics (2006). New frontiers in employee communications. Retrieved from www.edelman.com/news/storycrafter/uploads/NewFrontiers2006_Finalpaper.pdf.

Gale Research (2005). *Newsletters in print* (19th ed.). Detroit, MI: Gale.

Gillin, P. (2007). New media, new influencers and implications for the public relations profession. Retrieved August 27, 2012 from http://sncr.org/node/370.

Giving USA Foundation (2011). Giving USA 2011: The annual report on philanthropy for the year 2010. Chicago, IL: The Giving Institute.

Glass, S.A. (2001). *Approaching fundraising: Suggestions and insights for fundraising; No. 28, Summer 2000: New directions for philanthropic fundraising, sponsored by the Center on Philanthropy at Indiana University.* San Francisco, CA: Jossey-Bass.

Harris Interactive (2005, November). *Executive, congressional and consumer attitudes toward media, marketing and the public relations profession.* Rochester, NY: Harris Interactive.

Harris Poll (2001, May 18). *Presenting: The class of 2001: Millennium's first college grads are "connected, career-minded and confident"—way!* Rochester, NY: Harris Interactive.

Hunt-Lowrance, K. (Ed.) (2007). *Gale directory of publications and broadcast media* (142nd ed.). Detroit, MI: Gale Research.

Kim, J. B. (1995). The cassette is in the mail. *Advertising Age*, 68, 51.

Krugman, H. E. (1972). Why three exposures may be enough. *Journal of Advertising Research*, 12, 11–28.

Lang, K. and Lang, G. E. (1983). *The battle for public opinion: The president, the press, and the polls during Watergate*. New York: Columbia University Press.

Lippy, C. H. (Ed.) (1986). *Religious periodicals of the United States: Academic and scholarly journals*. New York: Greenwood.

Maddux, D. (Ed.) (2008). *International yearbook 2008* (88th ed.). New York: Editor & Publisher.

McManus, J. (1994). *Market-driven journalism: Let the citizen beware?* Thousand Oaks, CA: Sage.

Middleberg, D. and Ross, S. S. (2001). *The Middleberg/Ross survey of media in the wired world, 2000*. New York: Middleberg Euro.

Moriarty, S., Mitchell, N. and Wells, W. D. (2007). *Advertising: Principles and practices* (8th ed.). Upper Saddle River, NJ: Prentice Hall.

Newport, F. and Saad, L. (1998). A matter of trust: News sources Americans prefer. *American Journalism Review*, 20 (6), 30–33.

Pew Research Center for the People and the Press (2008, January 11). *Social networking and online videos take off; Internet's Broader Role in Campaign 2008: A survey conducted in association with the Pew Internet and American Life Project*. Washington, DC: Pew Research Center for the People and the Press.

Piirto, R. (1994). Why radio thrives. *American Demographics*, 16 (5), 40ff.

Project for Excellence in Journalism (2011). State of the News Media 2011. Retrieved August 27, 2012 from www.stateofthemedia.org/2011.

Rules of engagement: Six tips for pitching the blogosphere—and finding the right blog for your client (2005, April). *Ragan's Media Relations Report*.

Smith, R. D. (2012). *Becoming a Public Relations Writer: A Writing Workbook for Emerging and Established Media* (4th ed.). New York: Routledge.

Stenson, P. (1993). How (and why) corporate communicators use video. *Communication World*, 10 (10), 14–15.

Survey shows radio use patterns. (1996). *PR News*, 52 (15).

Tyson, C. B. and Snyder, L. B. (1999). The impact of direct mail video. *Public Relations Quarterly*, 44 (1), 28–32.

Vanden Bergh, B. G. and Katz, H. E. (1999). *Advertising principles: Choice, challenge, change*. Lincolnwood, IL: NTC Business.

West Glen Communications. (2002, April). West Glen Communications releases new PSA survey. New York: West Glen Communications.

Wigley, S. and Fontenot, M. (2010). Where media turn during crises: A look at information subsidies and the Virginia Tech shootings. Paper presented at the annual meeting of the Association for Education in Journalism and Mass Communication, Chicago. Online pdf Retrieved August 30, 2012 from www.allacademic.com/meta/p272080_index.html.

Wilcox, D. L. and Cameron, G. T. (2011). *Public relations: Strategies and Tactics* (10th ed.). Boston, MA: Allyn & Bacon.

Wilcox, D. L., Cameron, G. T., Ault, P. H. and Agee, W. K. (2005). *Public relations: Strategies and tactics* (8th ed.). Boston, MA: Allyn & Bacon.

Williams. W. (1994). *User friendly fund raising: A step-by-step guide to profitable special events*. Alexander, NC: WorldComm.

Readings

Phase Four

Bissland, J. H. (1990). Accountability gap: Evaluation practices show improvement. *Public Relations Review*, 16 (2), 25–35.

Broom, G. and Dozier, D. (1990). *Using research in public relations: Applications to program management*. Englewood Cliffs, NJ: Prentice Hall.

Corder L., Deasy, M. and Thompson, J. (1999, May). Answering the age-old marketing question: What have you done for me lately? *Public Relations Tactics*.

Delahaye Paine, K., (2011*). Measure what matters: Online tools for understanding customers, social media, engagement, and key relationships*. New York: Wiley.

Dozier, D. M. (1984). Program evaluation and the roles of practitioners. *Public Relations Review*, 10 (2), 13–21.

Edelman Public Relations, Opinion Research Corporation and Northwestern University. (1997, Aug. 25). Planning, goals and measurement (Corporate Communications Benchmark 1997, Section III). Cited in Written PR plans now common—but many not integrated. *PR Reporter,* 3–4.

Evaluation research on the rise, study finds. (1994). In P. Jackson (Ed.), *Practical, actionable research for public relations purposes*. Exeter, NH: PR Publishing.

Fischer, R. (1995). Control construct design in evaluating campaigns. *Public Relations Review*, 21 (1), 45–58.

Gofton, K. (1999, April 12). The measure of PR: Measurement and evaluation of public relations campaigns. *Campaign*, S13 (1).

Hon, L. C. (1997). What have you done for me lately? Exploring effectiveness in public relations. *Journal of Public Relations Research*, 9 (1), 1–30.

Hon, L. C. (1998). Demonstrating effectiveness in public relations: Goals, objectives, and evaluation. *Journal of Public Relations Research*, 10 (2), 103–135.

Lindenmann, W.K. (2006). Public relations research for planning and evaluation. Retrieved August 27, 2012 from www.instituteforpr.org/topics/pr-research-for-planning-and-evaluation/.

Peterson, Eric. (2007). How to measure visitor engagement-redux. Retrieved August 27, 2012 from http://blog.webanalyticsdemystified.com/weblog/2007/10/how-to-measure-visitor-engagement-redux.html.

Rice, R. and Atkin, C. (2002). Communication campaigns: Theory, design, implementation, and evaluation, in J. Bryant and D. Zillmann (Eds.), *Media effects: Advances in theory and research*. (pp. 427–452). Hillsdale, NJ: Lawrence Erlbaum.

Rossi, P. H., Lipsey, M. W. and Freeman, H. E. (2003). *Evaluation: A systematic approach* (7th ed.). Newbury Park, CA: Sage.

Scoble, R. (2006). New audience metric needed: Engagement. Retrieved 27 August 2012 from http://scobleizer.com/2006/10/25/new-audience-metric-needed-engagement/.

Tellis, G. J. and Ambler, T. (1998). *The Sage handbook of advertising*. Reading MA: Addison-Wesley.

Watson, T. and Noble, P. (2007). *Evaluating public relations: A best practice guide to public relations planning, research and evaluation*. Philadelphia, PA: Kogan Page.

Weiner, M. (1995, March). Put client "values" ahead of newsclips when measuring PR. *PR Services*, 48.

Wiener, N. (1954). *The human use of human beings: Cybernetics and society* (2nd ed.). Boston, MA: Houghton Mifflin.

Xavier, R., Johnston, K., Petel, A., Watson, T., Simmons, P. (2005, September). Using evaluative techniques and performance claims to demonstrate public relations impact: An Australian Perspective. *Public Relations Review*, 31 (3) pp. 417–424.

Appendixes

Ayles, C. B. and Bosworth, C. C. (2002, Summer). Campaign excellence: A survey of Silver Anvil award winners compares current PR practice with planning, campaign theory. *Public Relations Strategist.*

Babbie, E. (2010). *The practice of social research* (5th ed.). Belmont, CA: Wadsworth.

Clymer, A. (2001, July 22). The nation: Wrong number; the unbearable lightness of public opinion polls. *New York Times.*

Edmunds, H. (2000). *The focus group research handbook.* Lincolnwood, IL: NTC Business.

Fink, A. (2002a). *The survey kit: 2. How to ask survey questions.* (2nd ed.). Thousand Oaks, CA: Sage.

Fink, A. (2002b). *The survey kit: 6. How to sample in surveys.* (2nd ed.). Thousand Oaks, CA: Sage.

Fletcher, A. D. and Bowers, T. A. (1991). *Fundamentals of advertising research* (4th ed.). Belmont, CA: Wadsworth.

Haskins, J. and Kendrick, A. (1993). *Successful advertising research methods.* Lincolnwood, IL: NTC Business.

Lindenmann, W. K. (1977). Opinion research: How it works, how to use it. *Public Relations Journal,* 1, 13.

Mangione, T. W. (1995). *Mail surveys: Improving the quality.* Applied Social Research Methods Series No. 40. Thousand Oaks, CA: Sage.

Merton, R. K. (1987). The focused interview and focus groups: Continuities and discontinuities. *Public Opinion Quarterly,* 51, 550–566.

Morgan, D. L. (1997). *Focus groups as qualitative research* (2nd ed.). Qualitative Research Methods Series Vol. 16. Thousand Oaks, CA: Sage.

Rasinski, K. A. (1989). The effect of question wording on public support for government spending. *Public Opinion Quarterly,* 53, 388–396.

Rubenstein, S. M. (1995). *Surveying public opinion.* Belmont, CA: Wadsworth.

Seitel, F. P. (2006). *The practice of public relations* (10th ed.). Upper Saddle River, NJ: Prentice Hall.

Singletary, M. (1994). *Mass communication research.* White Plains, NY: Longman.

Waddell, H. (1995). Getting a straight answer: CSM scales all ask the wrong question: "How am I doing?" *Marketing Research,* 7 (3), 5–8.

Wimmer, R. G. and Dominick, J. R. (2010). *Mass media research: An introduction* (9th ed.). Belmont, CA:Wadsworth.

Yin, R. K. (2008). *Case study research: Design and methods* (4th ed.). Applied Social Research Methods Series No. 5. Thousand Oaks, CA: Sage.

Zeuschner, R. (2002). *Communicating today: The essentials.* Boston, MA: Allyn & Bacon.

Readings

Index

The index does not list the Cases and Examples which are contained in a separate index beginning on page xxii.

Note: page numbers in *italic type* refer to Exhibits.

3Cs of communicators 178–182, *179*

A. C. Nielsen 375
abortion: rhetorical warfare 206; and statistics 194–195
academic research 361–362
acceptance objectives 103, 104, 105, 108, 232–233; evaluation of 333, 346–348, 357; and successful campaigns 422, *see also* objectives
accessibility, of publics 61
accident 151
accountability 11
Accounts, Excuses, and Apologies (Benoit) 144–145
ACORN (A Classification of Residential Neighborhoods) 375
acronyms 208
action items, questionnaires 396–397
action metric 353
action objectives 103, 104, 106, 108; evaluation of 333, 348–350, 358; and successful campaigns 422, *see also* objectives
action strategies *14*, 16; proactive 113–144, 168–171; reactive 113, 144–166, 168–171
active listening 379
active publics *75*, 76, 90
activism 114, 128–130, 169
activists 48, 66
actuality 278–279
adaptation 114
addresses (speeches) 236
administration, budget item 318
administrative research *see* applied research

advertising 6, 7; advertising and promotional media tactics 229, *231*, 289–303, 308; AIDA pattern (attention, interest, desire, and action) 104; and commercial speech 10; and integrated communication 12–13; measurement 335; newspaper revenues form 267
advertising agencies, costs of 317
advertising inserts 291
advertising value equivalency (AVE) 342–343; Barcelona Declaration of Measurement Principles 354
advertisorial 291
advocacy 173; model of public relations 2, 9–10, 172
advocates 48, 128
aerial advertising 290, 300
affective changes 104, 105
affective displays 212
Africa, storytelling tradition 178
after-only studies 336
Agenda Setting (Dearing and Rogers) 25
agenda-setting theory 142
aggregates 58
Aguilar, F.J. 26
AIDA pattern (attention, interest, desire, and action) 104
Alciun 177
all-you-can-afford budgeting 319–320
Allen, T. Harrell 97
alliance strategy 114, 120–121, 169
alliteration 206
Allstate Insurance Companies 27
ambiguity, strategic 145, 165, 170
American Indian Science and Engineering Society 80

American Indians 209; stereotyping 79–81
American Marketing Association, code of ethics 418–420
American Society of Magazine Editors 270–271
American Statistics Index 373
AMI (Advertising and Market Intelligence) 375
analogy 192
announcement releases 278
annual reports 248
annual stockholder meetings 235
anonymity; research ethics 364
ANRs (audio news releases) 279
anti-science stance 192
antis 48
apathetic publics 75–76, *75*, 90
apologetics 177
apologia 144–145
apology strategy 145, 157–161, 170, 461
appeal letters 250
applied research 361–362; case studies 385–388; content analysis 401–409; do-it-yourself research 363; focus groups 379–385; interview 377–379; research ethics 363–365; research topics 362; sampling 366–372; secondary research 372–376; survey research 389–401
Applied Research Design (Hedrick, Bickman, and Rog) 24
apps 254
Aquinas, Thomas 177
Arab Americans, and stereotyping 82–83
Arab countries, face-saving 85
Arbitron 375
arena posters 290, 299

Aristotle 177, 178
Armstrong, James 297
Artigue, Ray 19
artistic events 232, 239
Asia, face-saving 85, 86
Asian Americans, and stereotyping 81
Asian Nation 81
Assembly of First Nations 80
assistant moderator (focus group role) 381
Associated Press (AP), style guidelines 266
Association for Education in Journalism and Mass Communication 9
Astroturf organizations 209
attack strategy 145, 147–148, 167, 170, 460
attitude change, and successful campaigns 422
attractiveness, of communicator *179*, 182
audience 58, 60, 172, 358; message exposure 345
audience confusion 313
audience engagement strategy 114, 115–117, 169
audience exposure 335
audience feedback 347
audience interaction, media type 228
audience participation 349; and successful campaigns 422
audience profile, newspapers 267
audience reach, and persuasive impact *231*
audience size: media type 228; news media 264
audience type, media type 228
audience-site involvement 232, 234
audio feeds, information source for journalists 285
audio media 246, 251–252, 263
audio news releases (ANRs) 279
Augustine of Hippo 177
authority, of communicator *179*, 183
AVE *see* advertising value equivalency
average, in statistics 194
aware publics *75*, 76, 90
awareness objectives 103, 104–105, 108; evaluation of 332, 333,

343–346, 357; and successful campaigns 422, *see also* objectives
Ayles, Catherine 422

Babbie, Earl 389, 390
baby boomers 59
backgrounders 278, 282
Bacon, Francis 177
Bacon's Information 7
Bakhsheshy, Abe 25
balance theory 175
Barcelona Declaration of Measurement Principles 354–355
Barnhurst, Kevin 131
Bartholomew, Don 353
baseline studies *see* benchmarking
Basic Books Inc. v. Kinko's Graphics Corp case 228
before-and-after studies 336–337; controlled 337–338
behavior: evaluation research 334; observation of 349; research 349, 350
behavior change, and successful campaigns 422
behavior objectives 104
belief objectives 104
Bell Telephone Laboratories 173
benchmarking 26, 43; evaluation research 337, 347–348, 349; and successful campaigns 422
benefit statements 87, 88, 89, 92
Benoit, William 144–145
BEP (break-even point) 325, 326
Berlo, David 173
Bernays, Edward 105, 207
best practice approach 26
bias, in sampling 369
Bickman, Leonard 24
bill inserts 250
billboards 296, 298
biographies 278
Bissland, James 344
black people, diversity among 87
blame shifting 150
bleed ads 291
blogs 230, 246, 257–259; corporate 281; evaluation 350, 351; information source for journalists 285
body language *see* nonverbal communication
Boe, Archie 27

booklets 247
Boolean logic 376
Bosworth, Courtney 422
Botan, Carl 176
boycotts 235
brain, left brain/right brain differences 197
brand consciousness 59
branded clothing 300
branded entertainment 295
branding 219–220; brainstorming for 222; language of 220–221; lessons about 221, 223; naming rights 210
break-even point (BEP) 325, 326
breakout ads 291
Briggs, Catherine 197
Briggs, William 158
British Overseas Trade Board 375
Broadcast mainland 348
brochures 247; cost per thousand (CPM) 342; sample budget 321–323, *322*, *323*
Broom, Glen 3
Bruning, Stephen 3
Buber, Martin 175
Buddhism, and rhetoric 178
budgeting 225, 315–316, 328; approaches to 318–321; budget items 316–318; budget management 321–323, *322*, *323*; campaign plan book 310; full-cost 324–325; message cost 341
Building Your Company's Good Name (Young) 114
bulletin boards 249
bulletins 247
Burke, Kenneth 177
Burson-Marsteller 46
bursting (message repetition) 313
bus signs 300
business cards 250
business letters 250

cable crawls 295
cable television advertising 273, 290, 295; cost per thousand 341
CACI 375
Cambodian population 81
Cambridge Information Group 375
campaign budget 315–326
campaign, definition 15
campaign plan book 310–311

campaign scheduling 310, 312–315
Canada: Assembly of First Nations 80; television stations 273
Canadian Public Relations Society 212; codes of ethics 415–416; media relations rating points (MRP) 342
canvassing 234
Caplan, Arthur 185
car cards 300
carnivals 236
case studies: as a research tool 385–388; successful campaigns 421–442
casual research 20
catalogs 246, 251; electronic 296
CCN (Crisis Communications Network) 32
celebrity endorsement 132, 193
celebrity spokespersons 183–187
census, in sampling 366
Center, Allen 3
center spreads 291
CEOs, as company spokespeople 187
charisma, of communicators 178, *179*, 181–182, 190
Chase, W. Howard 26
checklists, questionnaire responses 399
China, face-saving 85
chronemics 214
Cicero, Marcus Tullius 177
circulars 247
circulation of newspapers 267
citizen journalism 258
civic events 232, 236
civil disobedience 128
claims 191
Claritas Corporation 375
clarity, of messages 206–207, 218
classified ads 292
Cleveland 123
climate change, anti-science stance 192
clipping services 345
closed-ended responses 397, 398
clothing: branded 300; dressing for interviews 451–452; symbolic 216
Cloze Procedure readability formula 346
cluster sampling 371
ClusterPLUS system 375
Clymer, Adam 393

coalition strategy 114, 120–121, 136
Cobb, Michael 184
codes of ethics 11; American Marketing Association 418–420; Canadian Public Relations Society 415–416; International Public Relations Association 416–418; PRSA (Public Relations Society of America) 36, 212, 257, 411–415
Cody, Michael J. 159
cognitive changes 104
cognitive dissonance theory 175
colloquiums 234
color, symbolic 217
commercial speech 10
commiseration strategy 145, 156–161, 170, 461
community calendars 276
Common, Grant 443
communication: barriers to *174*, 206; open 11; proactive strategies 114, 130–144, 170; and publics 78, 91; transparent 114, 140–142, *see also* integrated communication; marketing communication; proactive communication; strategic communication
communication managers 1–2
communication process 172–176
communication tactics 227; advertising and promotional media tactics 229, 230, *231*, 289–303, 308; checklists 243–244, 262–263, 288–289, 302–303; conventional 227–229; interpersonal communication techniques 229, 230–244, *231*, 308; news media tactics 229, *231*, 264–289, 308; organizational media tactics 229, *231*, 245–263, 308; packaging of 304–309; planning examples 242–243, 261–262, 287–288, 301–302; Step 7 of strategic public relations planning model *14*, 16; strategic 229–230
communication technicians 1–2
communication theory, two-step flow of 65–66
communicators, characteristics of 178–182, *179*
company spokespeople 187–188

comparison 192
competence, of message source *179*, 180
competition, checklist 54–55
competitive environment 11
competitive parity budgeting 319
competitors *44*, 47–48
complaints, soliciting 116
comprehension *see* readability measures
computer-based surveys 389
Communication World 46
conative (behavioural) changes 104, 106
concern strategy 145, 156, 170, 461
concession 145, 153–154, 170
conclusions, drawing 205
condolence 170
condolence strategy 145, 156, 461
conferences 234, 235
confidentiality, research ethics 364
conflict resolution 175, 176
conflicts of interest, PRSA (Public Relations Society of America) code 414
Confucius 178
Congressional Information Service 373
congruity theory 175
conjecture propositions 191
consensus 24–25; building 175, 176; symbolic consensus 21
consent, research ethics 364
consumer kits 246, 249
consumers, understanding of 9
content analysis 401–409
content of messages 206–212
contests 237
context 151–152
contingency statements 283
continuity (message repetition) 313
control, of communicators 178, *179*, 182–183, 190
controlled before-and-after studies 337–338
controlled media 227
convenience sampling 368
conventions 234, 235
convergence, in brainstorming 222
cooperation 11
copyright law 228
Corax of Syracuse 176–177, 192
corporate social responsibility (CSR) 124
corporate videos 253

corrective action strategy 145, 162, 170, 461
cost-benefit analysis 320
cost per thousand (CPM) 341
costs: advertising and promotional media tactics 290; and interpersonal communication tactics 232
costumes 300
councils (educational gatherings) 234
Countrywide Porter Novelli 7
creativity 225; effective 17; evaluation research 334; and implementation 305–306; and structure 18
credibility 444, 450–457; of communicators 178–181, *179*, 190, 200; news media 264; and news sources 230
Crifasi, Sheila 13
crisis management 30, 32–35, 47, 153–154, 158, 444, 457; crisis messaging 461–462; information flow 462; preparation 462; six principles for crisis communication 459–460; strategic principles for 31; strategy 460; Toyota 99–100; types of crises 457–459, *see also* reactive strategies
Crisis Response: Inside Stories in Managing Under Siege (Gottschalk) 153–154
CSR (corporate social responsibility) 124
Cuddeford-Jones, Morag 32
cultural context 84–86
cultural differences, nonverbal communication 213–214
customer satisfaction surveys 400
customer–driven response 11
customers 61–62, *62*, 64; checklist 72
Cutlip, Scott 3
Cutting Edge Information 121
cybernetic model of communication 173, 338

daily rates, public relations agencies 317
Dale-Chall readability formula 346
data analysis and reports 350–352
dayparts 293, 294
Dearing, John 25

debates 236
decision-making process, and strategic communication 11
decoding, of information *174*
defamation 211
defensive response 145, 150–153, 170
deliberate inaction 145, 164–166, 170
Delwiche, Aaron 200
demographic items, questionnaires 397
demographic noise 206
demographics: of American Indians 79; of Arab Americans 82; data 375; of Muslims 82–83; of publics 78, 88, 91
demonstrations, public 235
denial strategy 145, 150, 170, 460
deontological ethics 36
departments, packaging tactics by 308
design, of research 332, 336–338
Dewey, John 57
dialogue model of communication 172, 173, 175–176, 233
dialogue/relationship-building model of public relations 3, 9–10, 12, 172
diffusion of innovation theory 66, 121, 305
digital billboards 298–299
digital media 229, 246, 253–255, 263; ads 290, 296; radio 272; television 273
dignity, research ethics 364
dinners 238
dioramas 300
diplomacy 5
direct information subsidy 276–281
direct mail 246, 250–251, 262–263; promotional items 301; videos 253, *see also* mail surveys
direct observation 349
directory advertising 290, 292
Directory of Online, Portable and Internet Databases 375
disassociation 145, 154–155, 170
disclosure, in crisis management 31
disclosure of information, PRSA (Public Relations Society of America) code 413
discussion guides, focus groups 384
display ads 292
Disraeli, Benjamin 194

dissidents 48
distinctiveness 96
distinguishability, of publics 60
divergence, in brainstorming 222
diversionary response 145, 153–154, 170
diversity, among black people 87
do-it-yourself research 363
dominant coalition 26
Dominick, Joseph 372
donors, and ethics 239, 240
doublespeak 156, 211
Dow Jones News/Retrieval 375
drawing conclusions 205
DVDs 253

e-zines 271
Easy Listening Formula (Fang) 346
Editor & Publisher International Year Book 267, 269
editorial conference 287
Edmunds, H. 382
education: American Indians 80; Asian Americans 81; Muslims 83; for public relations 9
educational gatherings 232, 234
Effective Public Relations (Cutlip, Center, and Broom) 3
electronic catalogs 296
electronic media 229, 246, 251–253, 263; advertising 290, 292–298, 302
electronic publishing 246, 253
element, in sampling 366
elevator pitch 443
e-mail 253–254; e-mail releases 280
embarrassment 145, 148, 170
emblems 212–213
emergencies, and social media 256
emotional appeals 201–202, 203–204; negative 199–201; positive 196–199
enablers *62*, 63, 64; checklist 72
encoding, of information *174*
Encyclopedia of Associations 373
endorsement 193; celebrities 132; third-party endorsement 130
engagement metric 353
entertainment media, taglines 221
environmental scanning 26
EPSEM sample 369
Equifax 375
equipment, budget item 318
Erasmus, Desiderius 177

Ernst & Young 46
errors of logic 193
esteem needs 77
ethical relativism *see* situational
    ethics
ethical standards 11
ethics: and activists 129; and
    dialogue 176; and fundraising
    239, 240; and language 211,
    219; and naming 208; and
    philanthropy 239, 240; of
    positioning 97; and public
    relations 36–37, *44*, 45; of
    publicity stunts 119; of research
    363–365; and social events 239;
    and spokespeople 188; and
    sponsored public affairs
    programming 296–297; and
    strategic responses 166
ethnic background information,
    questionnaires 397
ethos, message strategies 178–190
evaluation criteria 332–333, 335
evaluation techniques, and
    successful campaigns 422
evaluative research *14*, 17,
    329–330; checklist 357–358;
    data analysis and reports
    350–352; evaluation plan,
    campaign plan book 310;
    methodology 339–350; planning
    examples 356; reasons for not
    doing 329–330; value-added
    public relations 352–355; what
    to evaluate 331–335, 347; when
    to evaluate 335–338
events listings 276
events-management companies
    241
evidence: verbal 192–193; visual
    193
Ewing, Raymond 26
example 192
*Excellence in Public Relations and
    Communication Management*
    (Grunig) 3
excuse strategy 145, 151, 170, 460
executive summaries, and
    evaluation reports 352
expertise, of message source
    179–180, *179*
exposure metric 353
external environment *44*, 47–49,
    54–56
external impediments *44*, 49, 55

external media 228
external publics 63, 120, 232
eye behavior (occulesics) 213

face-saving 85–86, 159
facilitator (focus group role) 380
facilities, budget item 318
fact sheets 228
factual propositions 191
fairs 236
*Fall of Advertising and the Rise of
    PR, The* (Ries and Ries) 13
false assumptions 193
familiarity, of communicator *179*,
    182
fanatics 49
Fang, Irving 346
FAQs 228
fear appeals 199–200, 203
feature releases 278
fee structures, public relations
    agencies 317
feedback, audience 116, 347
Festinger, Leon 175
festivals 236
field research *see* case studies
final word 205
financial media 270
*FINDEX: The Worldwide Directory
    of Market Research reports,
    Studies, and Surveys* 375
Fink, Arlene 401
Finn, David 37
Fitzpatrick, Kathy 158
fixed fees, public relations agencies
    317
Flesch, Rudolf 346
Flesch-Kinkaid readability grade
    level 346
fliers 247
flighting (message repetition) 313
flow charts 314–315, *315*, *316*
focus groups 379–385, 422
Fog Index (Gunning Readability
    Formula) 207, 346
folders 247
Fontenot, Maria 275
forced choice, questionnaire
    responses 399
formative research phase of
    strategic public relations
    planning *14*, 15–16; overview of
    19–20
forums 236
Foundation Directory 375

framing theory 144
frequency, of tactics 312–313
front organizations 209
Front Row Analytics 140
Fry, Edward 346
fundraising events 232, 239
fundraising, and social networking
    260

Gale Directory of Publications and
    Broadcast Media 269
Gale Research 375
Gallup Organization 374
Gantt charts 314–315, *315*
gatekeepers 130–131
Gay Games IX 123
gender roles 84
general-interest newspapers 267
generating news 133–136
Generation X 59
Generation Y, as a public 59
geodemography 375
ghost blogging 258
Gibb, Blair 26
goals *14*, 16, 95, 97–100; Barcelona
    Declaration of Measurement
    Principles 354; checklist 111;
    definition 95; packaging tactics
    by 307; planning example 110
Goffman, Erving 144
Gofton, Ken 335
good intention 151
Google Analytics 351
government organizations 41
government records, secondary
    research 373
grabbers (power words) 207–208
grassroots journalism 258
Greece, classical 176–177
group interviews *see* focus groups
group-administered surveys 389
Grunig, James 2, 3, 9, 10, 74, 172
guerrilla theater 128
guest editorials 283
guilt appeal 183, 201, 204
Gunning Readability Formula (Fog
    Index) 207, 346

halo effect 181–182
Hammad, Ahmed Ibrahim 85
haptics 213
harmony, and public relations 25
Harris Polls 374
Harris, Thomas L. 9
Hart & Partners 42–43

Index

Hart, Rebecca 42
Hawthorne effect 338
Hayes, Darrell 13
hearing 379
Hearit, Keith Michael 144
Hedrick, Terry 24
Heider, Fritz 175
Hendrix, Jerry 13
hierarchy of needs (Maslow) 76, 77
historic commemorations 238
histories 278
Hmong population 81
Hobbes, Thomas 177
holiday events 232, 237–238
home accessories 301
Homer 176
hometowner releases 278
homiletics 177
homilies 236
homogeneity, of publics 60
Hon, Linda Childers 353
honesty, of message source *179*, 180
horns effect 181–182
host (focus group role) 381
hourly rates, public relations agencies 317
house advertising 290, 292
house organs 269, 270
Hovland, Carl 175
how-to pieces 278
humor: humor appeal 198, 203; and taglines 221
Hunt, Todd 2, 3, 9, 74, 172

idealism 152
Iliad 176
illness, and celebrities 118, 132
Image Index 47, 53
impartiality, in surveys 395
impediments: external *44*, 49, 55; internal *44*, 45, 52, *see also* obstacles
implementation reports 335
implementation schedules (timelines) 314–315, *315*
implementation of strategic plan *14*, 17, 304; campaign budget 315–326; campaign schedule 312–315; checklists 309, 328; packaging communication tactics 304–309; planning examples 308–309, 326–327
importance, of publics 60
in-depth interviews 379

inaction, strategic 145, 165–166, 170
inactive publics *see* latent publics
indirect information subsidy 281–282
inflatables 290, 300
influence metric 353
infomercials 293, 298
information: newsworthy 114, 137–140, *139*, 170; salience of 115
information exchange 232, 234–236, 244
information items, questionnaires 395
information model of communication 172, 173, *174*, 176
information needs, of media 274–276
information-seeking publics 233, 245
information services, commercial 374
information sources: abortion statistics 194; for a public relations audit 46; for publics 66
information subsidy 274, 275; direct 276–281; indirect 281–282
ingratiation strategy 154, 170, 460
innocence 150
innovation, diffusion of innovation theory 66, 121, 305
inoculation theory 175
Institute for Crisis Management 32, 43, 457–459
Institute for Public Relations 32; and advertising value equivalency (AVE) 343; evaluation research 335; and outcomes 344
integrated communication 6–7, 9–10, 12, 225; and advertising 12–13
intensive interviews 379
Interactive Advertising Bureau 345
interactive media 228; engagement 283–287
intercessory publics 65
intercoder reliability 403
internal audiences, distribution of news releases to 248
internal environment 43–46, *44*, 51–52

internal impediments *44*, 45, 52
internal media 228
internal publics 63, 120, 232
internal videos 253
International Public Relations Association, codes of ethics 416–418
international relations 5
Internet: and Generation Y 59; radio 272; as a research resource 375–376; resource for journalists 285; web-only commercials 296, *see also* websites
interpersonal communication techniques 229, 230–244, *231*, 308
interstitial ads 296
interviews 283–284, 377–379; behavior afterwards 456–457; communication during 455; dressing for 451–452; interview notes 271; personal interview surveys 389; planning for 452–453; posture 452; preparation for 453–454; problem 455–456; settings 450; successful attitudes for 454–455; and successful campaigns 422; training for 180, 283, 286, 443
investigation 145, 162, 170
invitations 246, 251
issues management 25–27
Italian Americans, and stereotyping 81
Iyengar, Shanto 143

Jackson, Pat 140
Japan: and apologies 159; face-saving 85, 86; national anthem 215; newspaper circulation 267
journalists, media relations practices 285
judgment sampling 368
Jung, Carl 197
al Jurjani, Abd 177
justification strategy 145, 151–152, 170, 460

Keirsey, David 197
Kelly, Kathleen 13
Kendall, Robert 13
Ketchum Public Relations 348, 353
key performance indicators (KPIs) 102

Index

key publics 67, 69, 74–76, 78, 88–92, 313
Kinder, Donald 143
kinesics 212–213
Klein, Pamela 46
knowledge objectives 104
Kotcher, John 66
Kotler, Philip 13, 104
KPIs (key performance indicators) 102
Krugman, Herbert 312

lack of control 151
Landsberger, Henry 338
language 84, 87, 215–216; American Indians 79; of branding 220–221; and clarity 206–207; and ethics 188, 211, 219; legal 211–212; paralanguage 213; sign language 212–213; wording of surveys 393, 395
Laotian population 81
Larking, Judy 27
Lasswell, Harold 173, 344
latent publics 75, *75*, 90
Lauzen, Martha 27
lawsuits, and apologies 161
Lazarsfeld, Paul 65–66
lead times 269
leaflets 247
lean resources 11
lectures 236
Lee, Fiona 161
Lee, Nancy 13, 104
left brain/right brain differences 197
legal language 211–212
Leo, John 208
letters 246, 250; to the editor 283
LEXIS/NEXIS 375
libel 211
libraries, secondary research 373
lifestyle data 375
likeability, of communicator *179*, 182
Likert scale 399
limiters *62*, 63, 64, 72–73
Lindenmann, Walter K. 335, 344
linkage 61
Lippman, Walter 78
listening, in interviews 379
logic, errors of 193
logos 214–215, 305; on clothing 300; verbal 220

logos (appealing to reason) 191–196, 201, 202–203
Lonergan, Bernard 178
long-form television and radio 296–298
love appeal 196, 198, 203
love needs 77
Lukaszewski, James 30, 31, 153–154
luncheons 238

McCombs, Maxwell 142
McGuire, William 175
McLaughlin, Margaret L. 159
McLuhan, Marshall 178
magazines 270–271; advertising 290; cost per thousand (CPM) 341; lead times 269
mail surveys 389, 422, *see also* direct mail
mailing lists 247
management by objectives *see* MBO
management role, of strategic communication 11
Managing Public Relations (Grunig and Hunt) 2
manuals 249
marathons 237
marches 235
margin of error 371
market research *see* applied research
market segments 58, 60
marketing communication 5, 6
markets 58
Marketsearch: International Directory of Published market Research 375
Marshall, Alice 259
Marston, John 13
Martimelli, Kathleen 158
mascots 184, 216
Maslow, Abraham 76, 77
mass media 11, 228
massing (message repetition) 313
Matera, Fran 19
materials, budget item 316–317
mathematical theory of communication 173
Maximizing Corporate Reputations (Burson-Marsteller) 46
MBO (management by objectives) 97, 100–101

Measures That Matter (Ernst & Young) 46
media: American Indians 80; attacking 146–147; categories of 227–229; changes in 11; and crisis management 31, 33; gatekeepers 130–131; information needs 274–276; as intercessory public 65
media advisory 281–282
media alerts 281
media categories, packaging tactics by 306–307
media cost, budget item 317
media directories 265–266
media effectiveness, relative 350
media engagement, effective 443; credibility 450–457; crisis management 457–463; media relations 447–450; reputation 443–444, 444–450
media kits 280
Media Matters 208
media ownership, media type 229
media placement, and successful campaigns 422
media production, media type 229
media relations 447–450; practices 285; and reputation 444–450
media relations rating points (MRP), Canadian Public Relations Society 342
media theory 142–144
media training 180, 283, 286, 443; Chilean mine rescue case 33
media-ratings companies 375
meetings 232, 235
membership organizations 41; and sponsorship 122–123
memos 250
mere association 151
message appeals: emotional 106–202, 203–204; rational 191–196, 202, 203–204
message content 206–212, 345
message cost 341
message distribution 341
message exposure 344–345, 422
message frequency 312
message production 341
message reach 312

message recall 346
message sources 178–190
message strategies *14*, 16, 172;
    branding the message 219–223;
    checklists 190, 202–204,
    218–219; communication
    process 172–176; ethos
    (message sources) 178–190;
    logos (appealing to reason)
    191–196, 201, 202–203;
    nonverbal communication
    212–214, 217, 218;
    organizational spokespeople
    183–188; pathos (appealing to
    sentiment) 196–202, 203–204;
    planning examples 189,
    201–202, 217–218; rhetorical
    tradition 176–178; verbal
    communication 204–212,
    217–218, 218–219; visual
    communication 214–217
message structure, verbal
    communication 204–206,
    218–219
metrics 102, 332; choice of 347;
    public relations 353–354
Miciak, Alan 187
Microsoft Word, readability score
    346
MicroVision 375
Middle East, face-saving 85
Milton, John 177
minifocus groups 382
mission statements 41, 42
missionaries 49
mistaken identity 150
mitigation 152
mobile billboards 300
mobile devices 254
mobile technology 230
moblogs 257
models of public relations, Grunig
    and Hunt 2–3, 9–10
moderator (focus group role) 380,
    381, 382
Morton, Linda P. 59
movie theaters, advertising 300
movies, taglines 221
MP3 blogs 257
MRP (media relations rating
    points), Canadian Public
    Relations Society 342
multiple tools 11
multiple-choice responses
    398–399

multipliers: advertising value
    equivalency (AVE) 343;
    Barcelona Declaration of
    Measurement Principles 354
multistage sampling 371
multistep flow theory 65–66
music 215, 271
Muslim Americans: and Ground
    Zero mosque 134–136; and
    stereotyping 82–83
Mutz, Diana 131
Myers, Isabel 197
Myers-Briggs personality types
    197

Nager, Norman 97
names, of products/programs
    208–210, *see also* relabeling
national anthems 215
National Council on Public Polls,
    Principles of Disclosure 363
national elections, fundraising
    events 239
National Native American Law
    Students Association 80
National Newspapers Index 375
National Opinion Research Center,
    University of Chicago 374
National Public Radio (NPR) 271;
    credibility of 277
national symbols 214
Native Americans 209; stereotyping
    79–81; storytelling tradition 178
Nature of Public Relations, The
    (Marston) 13
needs, Maslow's hierarchy of 76,
    77
negative publicity 131, 133, 149
network placement 293
network radio 295
networking 65
Newcomb, Theodore 175
newsletters, online 254
news: credibility 181, 264, 266,
    277; generation 133–136;
    newsworthy information 114,
    137–140, *139*, 170;
    sources of 230, 264, 275–276, 277,
    see also information subsidy
news briefs 278
news conferences 284–285; and
    evaluation reports 352
news fact sheets 276
news media tactics 229, *231*,
    264–289, 308

news releases 277–278; AP style
    guide 266; distribution to
    internal audiences 248; and
    evaluation reports 352
newsletters 245–247
Newspaper Association of America
    267
newspapers 265, 266–270;
    advertising 290, 291–292; cost
    per thousand (CPM) 341, 342;
    information needs 274, 275; lead
    times 269
NGOs (non-governmental
    organizations) 41
niche 44, *44*
niche marketing 123
Nisbet, Matthew 66
"no comment" responses 165, 449,
    455
noise, in communication systems
    174, 206
non-governmental organizations *see*
    NGOs
non-official technology sources 275
nonapology 159
nonattitudes 393
nonbroadcast video 253
noncommercial enterprises 41;
    branding 220, *see also* nonprofit
    organizations
nonprobability sampling 367–369
nonprofit organizations 41; annual
    reports 248–249; branding 220,
    221, 223; fundraising events
    239; and integrated
    communication 13; and
    philanthropy 124; program
    names 208, 210; social media
    256, 261; television advertising
    294, *see also* noncommercial
    enterprises
nonpublic media 229
nonpublics 74–75, *75*
nonverbal communication 212–214,
    217, 218
NPR *see* National Public Radio

objectives *14*, 16, 100–101;
    checklist 111, 112; definition 95;
    elements of 101–103; examples
    of 103; hierarchy of 104–106;
    objective-based budgeting 321;
    packaging tactics by 307;
    planning example 110–111;
    poorly-worded 109; and

successful campaigns 422;
writing 107–109
obstacles 21–22, 24, 45, *see also*
impediments
occulesics 213
Odyssey 176
offensive response 145, 147–150,
170
office accessories 301
one voice principle, in crisis
management 31
one-sided argument 204
one-way media 228
online focus groups 382
online newsrooms 281
online polling 46
online publication 254
online radio 272
online research 375–376, 422
op-ed pieces 283
open communication 11
open house events 311
open-ended responses 397, 398
opinion change, and successful
campaigns 422
opinion items, questionnaires 396
opinion leaders 65–67, 121
opinion polls 366, *see also* survey
research
opinion subsidy 282–283
opponents *44*, 48–49, 128
opportunities 21–22, 24
opposition, checklist 55
orations 236
order of presentation 205
organization analysis 41–43;
checklists 51–56; external
environment *44*, 47–49, 54–56;
internal environment 43–46, *44*,
51–52; planning example 48–50;
public perception *44*, 45–47,
53–54; publics 78; Step 2 of
strategic public relations
planning model *14*, 15
organizational control, media type
227–228
organizational files, secondary
research 373, 375
organizational media tactics 229,
231, 245–263, 308
organizational newspapers 269
organizational performance strategy
114–115, 169
organizational process, public
relations as 2–3

organizational site involvement
232, 233–234, 311
organizational spokespeople
183–188
organizational tie, media type 228
Osgood, Charles 175
out-of-home: advertising 290,
298–300, 302–303; video 290,
299–300
out-takes 335, 344
outcomes 344; Barcelona
Declaration of Measurement
Principles 354
outdoor posters 290, 298–299
outputs 344; evaluation 342–343,
357
over-the-air television 273

packaging communication tactics
304–309
Paine, Katie Delahaye 331, 351
painted bulletin 298
Palestine, public relations 85
Palser, Barb 230
pamphlets 247
panels 236
Papageorgis, Demetrios 175
parades 235, 236
paralanguage 213
participants, focus groups 383
participation, of audience 115–116
participatory journalism 258
pathos (appealing to sentiment)
196–202, 203–204
pay stuffers 250
PBS (Public Broadcasting Service)
277
people: ethical treatment in research
363–365; as symbols 216
per-capita cost 325–326
percentage-of-sales budgeting 319
Perelman, Chaim 178
performance 43, *44*; checklist 51;
and reputation 445
performance fees, public relations
agencies 317
performance measurement: KPIs
(key performance indicators)
102; of objectives 102, 108
personal interview surveys 389
personal involvement 232,
233–234, 243
personality preferences, of publics
78, 86
personality types 197

personnel; budget item 316
persuasion: model of
communication 172, 173, 176,
233; research into 175, 199;
three stages of 104, *see also*
rhetoric
persuasion/advocacy model of
public relations 2, 9–10, 12, 172
persuasive impact, and audience
reach *231*
PERT charts 314, 315, *316*
Petersen, Christopher 161
Peterson, Eric 351
petition drives 234
Pew Research Center for the People
and the Press 230, 264
philanthropy: and ethics 239, 240;
strategic 114, 123–127; viral 260
photo ops 117, 119
physical artifacts 216
physical noise 206
physical stature 180
physiological needs 77
pickets 235
pie throwing 129–130
placebo effect 338
Plato 177
podcasts 252
policy propositions 191
Polish Americans 152–153
political correctness 208
politicians, use of social networking
260
polling organizations 374
polls *see* opinion polls; survey
research
pop-up ads 296
popular media 228
population: research 404, 405; in
sampling 366
position statements 95, 96, 282
positioning 95–97, 110, 112
*Positioning: The Battle for Your
Mind* (Ries and Trout) 97
postcards 246, 251
posters 249; outdoor 290, 298–299
Potential Rating Index Zip Markets
(PRIZM) 375
power, of communicator *179*, 183
power words 207–208, 211, 219
PR Reporter 140
pre-emptive action 145–147, 170
prebuttal 145–147, 170
presentation, order of 205
presentation software 253

Index

presidential campaigns, use of music in 215
press agentry model of public relations 2, 9, 172
press packets 280
Presto Vivace Communications 259
pretentious language 211
pretest/post-test studies 336
primary publics 63
primary research 20, 373
priming theory 143
print advertising 290, 291–292, 302
print media 229, *see also* newspapers
priority publics 68, 70
privacy 211; research ethics 364
PRIZM (Potential Rating Index Zip Markets) 375
proactive communication 11
proactive strategies: action 113–130; checklist 169–170; communication 114, 130–144; planning example 168–169; typology 114
probability sampling 366, 367, 369–371
producers *62*, 63, 64, 72
product exhibitions 232, 234–235
product integration 295
product names 208–210
product placement 294–295
professional associations, secondary research 373, 375
program, definition 15
program names 208–210
progress reports 246, 248–249, 335–336
progress-oriented events 238
project, definition 15
Project for Excellence in Journalism 265
project fees, public relations agencies 317
promotional items 290, 300–301, 303
promotional media tactics 229, 230, *231*, 289–303, 308
propaganda 173, 200
propositions 191
protests, public 235
provocation 151
proxemics 213
PRSA (Public Relations Society of America) 7, 9; and American Indians 80; code of ethics 36,

212, 257, 411–415; competition 412; conflicts of interest 414; definition of public relations 3–4, 58; disclosure of information 413; enhancing the profession 414–415; free flow of information 411–412; Health Academy 47; member pledge 415; safeguarding confidences 413–414; Silver Anvil awards 329; statement of professional values 411
pseudo-apologies 147
pseudo-events 117
psychographics 375
Psychological Abstracts 375
psychological noise 206
psychological types 197
Ptah-Hotep 176
Public Broadcasting Service (PBS) 277
public information model of public relations 2, 9, 172
public interest public relations 8
Public and Its Problems, The (Dewey) 57
public media 229
public perception *44*, 45–47, 53–54
public relations: definition of 3–4, 58; as a management function 4; and marketing 6–7, 9–10, 11, 12; and media theory 142–144; metrics 353–354; and the public interest 8; strategic 13–17; value of to organizations 353
public relations audits 42–43, *44*; sources of information 46
Public Relations Campaign Strategies (Kendall) 13
Public Relations Cases (Hendrix and Hayes) 13
public relations directors, as company spokespeople 187–188
Public Relations Management 97
Public Relations Management by Objectives (Nager and Allen) 97
public relations practitioners, two categories of 1
Public Relations Quarterly 59
public relations situation 21–25, 77
Public Relations Society of America *see* PRSA
Public Relations Tactics 42, 269
public speaking, coaching for 180
publications 245–250, 262

publicity 114, 130–133, 170; events 239, 241; stunts 117, 119
publicity value, measurement 342
publics 9, 172; active publics *75*, 76, 90; analysis of 57–58, 60; apathetic publics 75–76, *75*, 90; aware publics *75*, 76, 90; benefit statement 87; categories 61–63, *62*, 64, 65; characteristics 60–61, 76–78; checklist 72–73, 89–92; cultural context 84–86; definition 57; Generation Y 59; identifying *60*, 69, 71; intercessory public 65; internal and external 63, 120; key public 67, 69, 74–76, 78, 88–92; latent publics 75, *75*, 90; nonpublics 74–75, *75*; opinion leaders 65–67; packaging tactics by 307; primary and secondary 63; planning example 69, *70*, 71, 88–89; priorities worksheets 68, 70; rethinking 86–87; single-issue publics 76; special 63; stages of development 74–76, *75*; Step 3 of strategic public relations planning model *14*, 15–16; stereotypes of 78–84; typology of 64
pulsing (message repetition) 313
purdah 164
purpose, research ethics 364–365
purposive sampling 368

Q&As 278
qualitative research 340, 386
quality 114
quality performance 11
quantitative research 340, 386
quarterly reports 248
query letters 282
question-and-answer pieces 278
questionnaires 391, 392, 393–401
questions, in interview 377–379
quick response, in crisis management 31
Quinnipiac University Polling Institute 375
Quintillianus, Marcus Fabius 177
quota sampling 368–369
quotes, strong 210

RACE (research, action, communication, evaluation) acronym 13 racial background information, questionnaires 397

radio 271–272; commercials 290, 295; cost per thousand (CPM) 341; dayparts 293, 294, 295; information needs 274–275; lead times 269

RAISE (research, adaptation, implementation strategy, evaluation) acronym 13

rallies 232, 235

random sampling 370

Rasinski, Kenneth 395

rating scales, questionnaire responses 399, 401

reactive strategies 144–145; checklist 170; defensive response 145, 150–153; deliberate inaction 145, 164–166; diversionary response 145, 153–154; offensive response 145, 147–150; planning example 168–169; pre-emptive action 145–147; rectifying behavior 145, 162–164; typology 145; vocal commiseration 145, 156–161, *see also* crisis management

readability measures 345–346

Readability Score (Flesch) 346

reason, appealing to (logos) 191–196, 201, 202–203

recall 346

reception 238

recognition programs 250

recorder (focus group role) 381

recording, focus groups 381, 383

rectifying behavior 145, 162–164

Regester, Michael 27

regret 145, 156–157, 170

reiteration 205–206

relabeling 145, 155–156, 170, *see also* names, of products/programs

relationship marketing 11

relationship-building model of public relations 3, 9–10, 172

relationships: and crisis management 31, 159; relationship management goals 98; and strategic communication 11

reliability, Barcelona Declaration of Measurement Principles 354

religion: American Indians 80; Arab Americans 82; Muslims 83; and rhetoric 177; and shock 149–150; speeches 236; symbols 214

religious organizations, fundraising events 239

Religious Periodicals of the United States: Academic and Scholarly Journals 271

repentance 145, 162–164, 170

repetition, of message 312–313

reports, surveys 392

reprints 228

reputation *44*, 45–47, 114, 144, 443–444; checklist 53; of communicators 178; and crisis management 31; and media relations 444–450; reputation management goals 98; and strategic communication 11

research: case studies 385–388; content analysis 401–409; and creativity 17; do-it-yourself research 363; ethics 363–365; evaluative research phase of strategic public relations planning *14* 17, 329–330; focus groups 379–385; formative research phase of strategic public relations planning *14*, 15–16; interview 377–379; online 375–376; research based objectives 102; research topics 362, 382, 403–404, 406; sampling 366–372; secondary research 372–376; and successful campaigns 422; survey research 389–401; websites 374

research leader (focus group role) 381

research methodology 339; acceptance objectives 346–348; action objectives 348–350; awareness objectives 343–346; communication outputs 340–343; data analysis and reports 350–352; design 332, 336–338; judgmental assessment 339–340; qualitative research 340; quantitative research 340

research reports 246, 249; case studies 388; focus groups 385

research results, and ethics 365

researcher identity, research ethics 365

response rates 389–390; direct mail 250

response releases 278

response strategies *14*, 16; proactive 113–144, 168–171; reactive 113, 144–166, 168–171

responses, types of in survey research 397–401

restitution 145, 162, 170

results, Barcelona Declaration of Measurement Principles 354

retainer fees, public relations agencies 317

return on investment (ROI) 352–353

reversal 145, 152–153

rhetoric 176–178, 191; rhetorical warfare 206, *see also* persuasion

Richardson, Jason 121

Ries, Al 13, 97

Ries, Lorna 13

right brain/left brain differences 197

risk management 27–29

Roberto, Ned 13, 104

robocalls 252

Rog, Debra 24

Rogers, Everett 25, 66, 121

ROI (return on investment) 352–353

Rome, classical 177

ROPE (research, objectives, programming, evaluation) acronym 13

Roper Center for Public Opinion Research, University of Connecticut 375

ROPES (research, objectives, program, evaluation, stewardship) acronym 13

Roser, Connie 200

ROSIE (research, objectives, strategy, implementation, evaluation) acronym 13

rotary paints 298

Rubin, Maureen 158

run of book (ROB) advertising 291

run of press (ROP) advertising 292

run of station (ROS) placement 295

safety needs 77

salience 115, 207

same-as-before budgeting 319

sample campaigns 421–442
sampling 366–367, 406; bias 369;
    case studies 388; focus groups
    383; nonprobability sampling
    367–369; probability sampling
    367, 369–371; research 334;
    sample error 371; sample size
    372; surveys 391
sampling frames 369
sampling units 369
satellite media tours (SMT) 287
satellite radio 272
satellite telecommunications 230
satellite television 273
saving face 85–86, 159
scheduling 225; campaign 310,
    312–315, 328
Scheufele, Dietram 144
Schramm, Wilbur 173
Schwartz, Peter 26
Scoble, Robert 351
scrutiny, of communicator *179*, 183
seat-of-the-pants evaluation 339
secondary customers 62, *62*, 64
secondary publics 64
secondary research 20, 372–376,
    422
Securities and Exchange
    Commission (SEC) 248
selective exposure 175
self-actualization needs 77
self-administered surveys 389
semantic differential scales 401
semantic noise 206
seminars 234
sentiment, appealing to (pathos)
    196–202, 203–204
serial publications 245–247
sermons 236
service articles 278
service marks 221, 223
settings, symbolic 217
sex appeal 199, 203
sexual abuse, statistics 196
shadow constituencies 62, *62*, 64
Shanklin, William 187
Shannon, Claude 173
Shaw, Donald 142
shelter posters 300
Sherif, Muzafer 175
shock 145, 148–150, 170, 199
sidewalk chalk 299
Sieberg, Evelyn 175
sign language 212–213
signage 290, 299

silence, strategic 145, 164–165, 170
SiLoBaTi + UnFa 137
Silver Anvil awards, PRSA (Public
    Relations Society of America)
    329
similarity, of communicator *179*,
    182
simple random sampling 370
single-issue publics 76
site, focus groups 383
situation analysis 21; campaign
    plan book 310; checklist 38–40;
    crisis management 30–35; issues
    management 25–27; planning
    example 38; public relations and
    ethics 36–37; public relations
    situation 21–25; risk
    management 27–29; Step 1 of
    strategic public relations
    planning model *14*, 15
situational ethics 36
size: of publics 60–61; sample size
    372
slander 211
slogans 220
snowball sampling 368
social benefit organizations *see*
    noncommercial enterprises
social capital 46
social events 232, 238–239
social judgment theory 175
social marketing campaigns 13,
    104
social media 6, 230, 246, 255–261,
    263; Barcelona Declaration of
    Measurement Principles 354;
    evaluation 350, 351, 353–354;
    as a news information source
    275–276; releases (SMRs) 280
social networking 246, 259–261
social norms 84
Sociological Abstracts 375
sociosampling 368
Socrates 177
Sorry Works Coalition 161
sound bites 279
South Korea, face-saving 86
space, social (proxemics) 213
speaker's bureau 236
special events 114, 115–119, 232,
    236–242, 244
special publics 63
special-audience newspapers
    269
special-interest newspapers 268

spectaculars 299
speeches 228, 232, 235–236
Sperry, Roger 197
spirituality, and public relations 25
spokes-characters 184
spokespeople 183–189; in crisis
    management 31
sponsor identity, research ethics
    365
sponsorship 114, 121–123, 169;
    and clothing 300; sponsored
    news 296; sponsored public
    affairs programming 296–297
sporting events 232, 237
sports venues, branding rights
    210
spot advertising 293
spot radio 295
stage presence 180
stage-of-lifecycle budgeting 320
staged activities 117
stakeholders 58
stand-alone publications 246,
    247–248
standard error (sampling) 371
standby statements 283
Stanford Research Institute 375
Starch Readership Reports 346
station posters 300
*Statistical Abstract of the United
    States* 373
statistics 193, 194–196
status, of message source *179*,
    180
stealth ads 294–295
stereotyping 78–81, 84, 211
story idea memos 282
strategic ambiguity 145, 165, 170
strategic communication 5–6, 11
strategic inaction 145, 165–166
strategic listening 379
strategic managers 1
Strategic Mapping 375
strategic philanthropy 114, 123–127
strategic plan: evaluation of, Step 9
    of strategic public relations
    planning model *14*, 17;
    implementation of, Step 8 of
    strategic public relations
    planning model *14*, 17
strategic planning, four-step model
    of 14, *14*, 15–17
strategic public relations 13; nine-
    step model 14, *14*, 15–17;
    terminology of 15

strategic publics *see* key publics

strategic research 19, 20

strategic silence 145, 164–165, 170

strategy phase of strategic public relations planning *14*, 16; overview 93–94

stratified sampling 370–371

streaming radio 272

streaming videos 253

street theater 128

Streisand effect 167

strong quotes 210

structure 44–45, *44*; checklist 51; and creativity 18

studio interviews 286–287

subscription radio 272

suggestion boxes 249

Sugimoto, Naomi 159

summative reports 336

supporters *44*, 47

survey research 389; administration 390–392; questionnaires 393–401; response rates 389–390, *see also* opinion polls

Swann, Patricia 97

SWOT analysis 43

symbolic consensus 21

symbolism 214, 216; value of 129

symmetry theory 175

symposiums 234

systematic sampling 370

tablets, electronic 254

tactical managers 1

tactical research 19, 20

tactics phase of strategic public relations planning *14*, 16–17; overview 225–226

taglines 220–221, 223

talks 236

Tannenbaum, Percy 175

target publics *see* key publics

targeted media 228

task management goals 98

Tchividjian, Emmanuel 37

technician (focus group role) 381

technology, and communication tactics 230

Tekakwitha Conference 80

teleconferences 253, 382

telefocus groups 382

telemarketing 251–252

teleological ethics 36

telephone interviews, and successful campaigns 422

telephone media 251–252

telephone surveys 389

television 272–274; advertising 290, 293–295; dayparts 293, 294; information needs 274–275; lead times 269; use of VNRs 279

temperament 197

terrestrial radio 272

terrestrial television 273

testimonial 193

theory of accounts 144

theory of image restoration 145

third-party endorsement 130, 264

Thompson, Margaret 200

threat 145, 150, 167, 170

three-exposure formula (message frequency) 213

Tiedens, Larissa 161

timelines 314–315, *315*

timing, of surveys 393

tip sheets 282

topics, for research 362, 382, 403–404, 406

touching 213

tournaments 237

town meetings 236

tracts 247

trade associations, secondary research 373

trade media 228; newspapers 268

trade shows 234–235

tragedy 117, 118

training sessions 234

transit advertising 290, 300; cost per thousand (CPM) 341

transparent communication 114, 140–142

triads 382

triathlons 237

triggering events 116–117

Trout, Jack 97

two-sided argument 204–205

two-step flow of communication theory 65–66

two-way public relations 26, 338

UAE (United Arab Emirates) 115

uncontrolled media 228, 264

uniforms 300

unit of analysis 366, 404, 407

unit-of-sales budgeting 319

unobtrusive research 338

unwarranted conclusions 193

Upshaw, Jim 295

U.S. Census Bureau 378

U.S., television stations 273

user kits 246, 249

USP (unique selling proposition) 207

VALS (values and lifestyles) system 375

value propositions 191

value, of public relations to organizations 353

values statements 42

vehicles, promotional 305

verbal communication 204–212, 217–218, 218–219

verbal evidence 192–193

victimization 151

video: media 246, 253; video B-rolls 279; video feeds, information source for journalists 285; video focus groups 382; video news releases (VNRs) 279–280; video walls 299; videoconferences 253; viral 261

viral philanthropy 260

viral video 261

virtual ads 296

virtue appeal 198, 203

visibility *44*, 45, 47

vision statements 41, 42

visual appeal 128, 133

visual communication 214–217

visual supporting evidence 193

vlogs 257

vocabulary: and clarity 206; and ethics 188

vocal commiseration 145, 156–161, 170

vocal quality 180

vocalics 213

volunteer participation, research ethics 364

volunteer sampling 368

volunteering 126–127

Waddel, Howard 400

wall murals/wallscapes 299

Weaver, Richard 178

Weaver, Warren 173

web videos 253

web-only commercials 296

Index

websites 254–255; evaluation of 333; information source for journalists 285; as news source 275; research 374, *see also* Internet
weighted samples 371
what-if-not-funded analysis 320
white papers 282
Wiener, Norbert 173, 338
Wigley, Shelley 275
wikis 246, 256–257
Wilson Index 375

Wimmer, Roger 372
window displays 249
women, symbolic clothing 216
word-of-mouth support 66, *see also* opinion leaders
wording, of surveys 393
workshops 234
Writer's Market 270
writing: Associated Press style guidelines 266; for public relations 206–207; survey impartiality 395

Yin, Robert 386
Young, Davis 114
young people, access to news 266

zealots 49, 66
zen of public relations 25
zero-based budgeting 320–321
Zeuscher, Raymond 379
Zogby International 374
zoos, and sponsorship 122–123